# DIETRICH BONHOEFFER WORKS, VOLUME 11

*Ecumenical, Academic, and Pastoral Work: 1931–1932*

This series is a translation of
DIETRICH BONHOEFFER WERKE
Edited by
Eberhard Bethge†, Ernst Feil,
Christian Gremmels, Wolfgang Huber,
Hans Pfeifer†, Albrecht Schönherr†,
Heinz Eduard Tödt†, Ilse Tödt

IN MEMORIAM

Hans Pfeifer
1930–2011

This volume has been made possible through the generous support of the Lilly Endowment, Inc.; the Thrivent Financial Foundation for Lutherans; the New England Synod, ELCA; the Bowen H. and Janice Arthur McCoy Charitable Foundation; the Lutheran Theological Seminary at Philadelphia; the German Lutheran Church of Washington, D.C.; and the gifts of numerous members and friends of the International Bonhoeffer Society.

DIETRICH BONHOEFFER WORKS

General Editors
Victoria J. Barnett
Barbara Wojhoski

DIETRICH BONHOEFFER WORKS, VOLUME 11

# DIETRICH BONHOEFFER

# *Ecumenical, Academic, and Pastoral Work: 1931–1932*

*Translated from the German Edition*
*Edited by*
EBERHARD AMELUNG AND CHRISTOPH STROHM

*English Edition*
*Edited by*
VICTORIA J. BARNETT, MARK S. BROCKER, AND MICHAEL B. LUKENS

*Translated by*
ANNE SCHMIDT-LANGE, WITH ISABEL BEST, NICOLAS HUMPHREY, AND MARION PAUCK

*Supplementary Material Translated by*
DOUGLAS W. STOTT

FORTRESS PRESS MINNEAPOLIS

DIETRICH BONHOEFFER WORKS, Volume 11

Originally published in German as *Dietrich Bonhoeffer Werke*, edited by Eberhard Bethge et al., by Chr. Kaiser Verlag / Gütersloher Verlagshaus, Gütersloh, in 1998; Band 11, *Ökumene, Universität, Pfarramt: 1931–1932*, edited by Eberhard Amelung and Christoph Strohm. First English-language edition of *Dietrich Bonhoeffer Works*, Volume 11, published by Fortress Press in 2012.



The translation of this work was subsidized in part by a grant from the Goethe-Institut Inter Nationes, Munich.

Jacket design: Cheryl Watson
Cover photo: Dietrich Bonhoeffer, 1931. © Chr. Kaiser/Gütersloher Verlagshaus, Gütersloh, Germany, a division of Random House
Book design: HK Scriptorium, Inc.
Typesetting: Ann Delgehausen, Trio Bookworks

The paper used in this publication meets the minimum requirements for American National Standard for Information Sciences—Permanence of Paper for Printed Library Materials, ANSI Z329.48–1984.

Manufactured in the U.S.A.
16 15 14 13 12 1 2 3 4 5 6 7 8 9 10

# CONTENTS

## Part 3
## Sermons and Meditations

# General Editor's Foreword to Dietrich Bonhoeffer Works

The German theologian and pastor Dietrich Bonhoeffer has become one of the most influential Christian thinkers of all time. Barely twenty-seven years of age when the Nazi regime came to power in Germany, Bonhoeffer emerged immediately as a radical Protestant voice against the ideological co-optation of his church. He was one of the earliest critics of the Nazi regime and an outspoken opponent of the pro-Nazi "German Christians." From 1933 to 1935, he served as pastor of two German-speaking congregations in England, leading them to join the Confessing Church—the faction within the German Protestant Church that opposed the nazification of the Christian faith. He returned to Germany to become director of a small Confessing Church seminary and, after the Gestapo closed it, continued to work illegally to educate Confessing clergy. Throughout the 1930s, he attended ecumenical meetings, effectively becoming the voice of the Confessing Church throughout the European and American ecumenical world. In 1939, his ecumenical friends urged him to accept a position in New York. Rejecting the security of a life in exile, Bonhoeffer chose instead to join the ranks of the German conspiracy to overthrow the regime, like his brother Klaus and his brothers-in-law Hans von Dohnanyi and Rüdiger Schleicher. He was arrested and imprisoned in April 1943 and executed in the Flossenbürg concentration camp in April 1945.

In a eulogy published shortly after Bonhoeffer's death, his former professor and friend Reinhold Niebuhr wrote that Bonhoeffer's story "is worth recording. It belongs to the modern acts of the apostles. . . . Not only his martyr's death, but also his actions and precepts contain within them the hope of a revitalised Protestant faith in Germany. It will be a faith, religiously more profound than that of many of its critics; but it will have learned to overcome the one fateful error of German Protestantism, the complete dichotomy between faith and political life."[1]

In the ensuing decades, Niebuhr's prescient insight that Bonhoeffer's life and work offered lasting insights for modern Christian experience and witness has been more than fulfilled. Bonhoeffer wrote hundreds of letters, sermons, and biblical reflections in addition to his published theological works. After 1945, Bonhoeffer's former student and close friend Eberhard Bethge worked with publishers to reissue and translate the books Bonhoeffer had published in his lifetime. In translation, these works—*Discipleship, Ethics,* and *Letters and Papers from Prison*—became classics, finding a wide readership among Christians throughout the world.

Yet there was a growing sense that these works should not stand alone—a realization of the significance of the biographical and historical context of his thought. Bonhoeffer's papers also included lecture notes that had been made by his students, documents from the German Church Struggle and ecumenical meetings, circular letters that were sent to his seminarians, sermons, extensive correspondence with theologians and religious leaders in Europe and the United States, and prison writings. Bethge published several early compilations of some of these documents (*Gesammelte Schriften* and *Mündige Welt*) and incorporated additional material into his magisterial biography of Bonhoeffer, which first appeared in English in 1970 and then, in a revised and unabridged edition, in 2000.

Bethge and leading Bonhoeffer scholars in Germany decided to publish new annotated editions of Bonhoeffer's complete theological works, together with most of the documents from the literary estate, including historical documents and correspondence to Bonhoeffer. The *Dietrich Bonhoeffer Werke* series was published by Chr. Kaiser Verlag, now part of Gütersloher Verlagshaus. The first German volume, a new edition of Bonhoeffer's dissertation, *Sanctorum Communio,* appeared in 1986; the final volume, Bonhoeffer's complete prison writings, appeared in April 1998. A seventeenth volume, an index for the entire series, appeared in 1999; this volume also included documents discovered after their respective volumes had been published. Whenever possible these documents have been included in the appropriate volumes of the English edition; documents that continue to be discovered are published in the *Dietrich Bonhoeffer Jahrbuch,* a series published by Gütersloher Verlagshaus.

---

[1.] Reinhold Niebuhr, "The Death of a Martyr," *Christianity and Crisis* 5, no. 11 (1945): 6–7.

Discussion about an English translation of the entire series began as soon as the first German volumes appeared. In 1990, the International Bonhoeffer Society, English Language Section, in agreement with the German Bonhoeffer Society and Fortress Press, undertook the English translation of the German *Dietrich Bonhoeffer Werke.* The project began with an initial grant from the National Endowment for the Humanities with Robin Lovin serving as project director, assisted by Mark Brocker. An editorial board was formed for the Dietrich Bonhoeffer Works, English Edition, staffed by Wayne Whitson Floyd Jr. as general editor, and Clifford J. Green of Hartford Seminary as executive director. Wayne Whitson Floyd Jr., at that time director of the Dietrich Bonhoeffer Center at the Lutheran Theological Seminary in Philadelphia, served as general editor from 1993 to 2004, overseeing publication of the first seven volumes as well as volume 9. Victoria J. Barnett, director of church relations at the U.S. Holocaust Memorial Museum, joined the project as associate general editor in 2002 and became general editor in 2004, joined by Barbara Wojhoski, a professional editor who prepared the manuscripts of the final volumes for publication.

The *Dietrich Bonhoeffer Works, English Edition* (*DBWE*) is the definitive English translation of Bonhoeffer's theological and other writings. It includes a great deal of material that appears for the first time in English, as well as documents discovered only after the publication of the original German volumes. *DBWE* is a significant contribution to twentieth-century theological literature, church history, and the history of the Nazi era. Particularly in their portrayal of the daily implications of the Protestant Church Struggle in Nazi Germany and the response of Christians outside Germany, these volumes offer a detailed and unique glimpse of Bonhoeffer's historical context and its great challenges for the churches and for all people of conscience.

The translators of the *DBWE* volumes have attempted throughout to render an accurate and readable translation of Bonhoeffer's writings for contemporary audiences, while remaining true to Bonhoeffer's thought and style. Particular attention has been paid to the translation of important theological, historical, and philosophical terms. Bonhoeffer's language and style are often reflective of his age, particularly with regard to gendered language, and this is reflected in the historical and church documents. Nonetheless, in the translations of the early volumes of his theological writings (*DBWE* volumes 1–7), the decision was made to use gender-inclusive language, insofar as this was deemed possible without distorting Bonhoeffer's meaning or unjustifiably dissociating him from his own time.

Each volume includes an introduction written by the *DBWE* volume editor(s), footnotes provided by Bonhoeffer, editorial notes added by the

German and English editors, and the original afterword written by the editor(s) of the German edition. Additions to or revisions of the German editors' notes are enclosed within square brackets and initialed by the editor of the respective volume. When any previously translated material is quoted within an editorial note in altered form—indicated by the notation [trans. altered]—such changes should be assumed to be the responsibility of the translator(s). Where available, existing English translations of books and articles in German and other languages are cited in the notes.

Bonhoeffer's own footnotes—which are indicated in the body of the text by plain, superscripted numbers—are reproduced in precisely the same numerical sequence as they appear in the German critical edition, complete with his idiosyncrasies of documentation. In these, as in the accompanying editorial notes, the edition of a work that was consulted by Bonhoeffer himself can be determined by consulting the bibliography at the end of each volume.

Each volume also contains a list of abbreviations frequently used in the editorial notes, as well as a bibliography of archival sources, sources used by Bonhoeffer, literature consulted by the editors, and other works relevant to that respective volume. Each volume also includes a chronology of important dates relevant to that volume, an index of scriptural references, an index of persons with relevant biographical information, and an index of subjects. Bibliographies at the end of each volume provide the complete information for each written source that Bonhoeffer or the various editors have mentioned in the current volume.

Bonhoeffer's literary estate—the notes, sermons, and other writings, as well as correspondence, and the personal library of materials that belonged to him and survived the war—was cataloged by Dietrich Meyer and Eberhard Bethge; this catalog has been published as the *Nachlaß Dietrich Bonhoeffer.* Most of the documents cited in the *Nachlaß* are collected in the Berlin Staatsbibliothek, although some documents remain in other archives. All documents listed in the *Nachlaß*, however, have been copied on microfiches that are now at the Staatsbibliothek in Berlin and in the Bonhoeffer collection at Burke Library, Union Theological Seminary, New York. References to any of these documents are indicated within the *DBWE* by the abbreviation *NL*, followed by the corresponding catalog number. Books in the bibliography from Bonhoeffer's own library are indicated by the abbreviation *NL-Bibl.*

Volumes 1–7 of the English edition, which contain only Bonhoeffer's own writings, retain his original organization of the material, either as chapters or as sections or unnumbered manuscripts. Volumes 8–16 contain collected writings from a particular period of Bonhoeffer's life, including correspondence from others and historical documents. With the exception of volume 8, these final volumes are divided into three sections, with the documents in each section arranged chronologically: (1) Letters, Journals, Documents; (2) Essays, Seminar Papers, Papers, Lectures, Compositions; (3) Sermons, Meditations, Catechetical Writings, Exegetical Writings. Documents are numbered consecutively within the respective sections. In editorial notes these items are labeled by the *DBWE* volume number, followed by the section number, document number, and finally the page number; for example, *DBWE* 10, 1/109, p. 209, ed. note 1, would refer to the English edition, volume 10, section 1, document 109, page 209, editorial note 1.

The *DBWE* also reproduces Bonhoeffer's original paragraphing (exceptions are noted by a ¶ symbol to indicate any paragraph break added by the editors of the English edition or by conventions explained in the introductions written by the editor[s] of specific volumes). The pagination of the *DBW* German critical edition is indicated in the outer margins of the pages of the translated text. Where it is important to give readers a word or phrase in its original language, a translated passage is followed by the original, set within square brackets. All biblical citations come from the New Revised Standard Version (NRSV) unless otherwise noted. Where versification of the Bible used by Bonhoeffer differs from the NRSV, the verse number in the latter is noted in the text in square brackets.

The publication of the *Dietrich Bonhoeffer Works, English Edition* would not have been possible without the generous support of numerous individuals and institutions. The verso of the half-title page of each volume provides a list of supporters of that particular volume. The series as a whole is indebted to many individual members and friends of the International Bonhoeffer Society, and to family foundations, congregations, synods, seminaries, and universities. Special thanks are due to the following foundations and donors for major grants: the National Endowment for the Humanities; the Lilly Endowment, Inc.; the Thrivent Financial for Lutherans Foundation; the Aid Association for Lutherans; the Stiftung Bonhoeffer Lehrstuhl; the Bowen H. and Janice Arthur McCoy Charitable Foundation; and Dr. John Young and Mrs. Cleo Young. The Lutheran Theological Seminary at Philadelphia and its former auxiliary have provided space and ongoing support. We have been extraordinarily fortunate to work with Augsburg Fortress Publishers as the publisher of *DBWE*, and particular gratitude goes to Will Bergkamp, publisher and managing director, as well as to his predecessors, editorial directors Michael West and Marshall Johnson.

The existence of this series in English and other languages is testimony to the international community of those who have found Dietrich Bonhoeffer to be a profoundly important companion in their own journey. That community would not exist without the wisdom, generosity, and dedication of Eberhard Bethge (1909–2000) and his wife, Renate. Bethge was himself a pastor in the Confessing Church. After 1945, he was convinced that the future of a living church in Germany depended on its addressing its failures under Nazism and on a new understanding of Bonhoeffer's lasting question, Who is Christ for us today?

The editors of this English edition are particularly grateful to the original editorial board of the German edition—composed of Eberhard Bethge†, Ernst Feil, Christian Gremmels, Wolfgang Huber, Hans Pfeifer†, Albrecht Schönherr†, Heinz Eduard Tödt†, and Ilse Tödt. As liaison between the German and English editorial boards, Hans Pfeifer offered steadfast and congenial support to his colleagues on both sides of the Atlantic. The editors of the individual German volumes have been generous with their time and expertise. As work on *DBWE* has proceeded, a new generation of Bonhoeffer scholars in Germany has assisted us as well: Christine Kasch, Andreas Pangritz, Holger Roggelin, Christiane Tietz, and Ralf Wuestenberg.

We remain grateful to those whose original translations of Bonhoeffer's words introduced most of us to his work. It is only fitting, however, that this English edition be dedicated, finally, to the remarkable group of scholars who over the years have devoted their time, their insights, and their generous spirit to the translation, editing, and publication of these volumes. That dedication should begin with a special acknowledgment of the capable editorial leadership of Wayne Whitson Floyd Jr., who brought eight volumes to publication, and to Clifford J. Green, whose steady hand has guided the project throughout its existence and ensured the financial foundation for its completion.

The translators who have brought Bonhoeffer's words to new life in these volumes are Victoria Barnett, Douglas Bax, Claudia Bergmann, Isabel Best, Daniel W. Bloesch, James H. Burtness†, Lisa Dahill, Peter Frick, Barbara Green, David Higgins, Nick Humphrey, Reinhard Krauss, Peter Krey, Nancy Lukens, Scott Moore, Mary Nebelsick, Marion Pauck, Barbara Rumscheidt†, Martin Rumscheidt, Anne Schmidt-Lange, Douglas W. Stott, and Charles West.

The following individuals serve on the editorial board of the *Dietrich Bonhoeffer Works, English Edition*: H. Gaylon Barker, Victoria Barnett, Mark Brocker, Keith Clements, Peter Frick, Clifford J. Green, John W. de Gruchy, Barry Harvey, Reinhard Krauss, Michael Lukens, Larry Rasmussen, and Barbara Wojhoski. In addition, James H. Burtness†, Wayne Whitson Floyd Jr., Barbara Green, James Patrick Kelley, Geffrey B. Kelly, Robin W. Lovin, Nancy Lukens, Paul Matheny, Mary Nebelsick, F. Burton Nelson†, and

H. Martin Rumscheidt all previously served on the board, and many of them continue to serve the project through its advisory committee.

In September 1943, Dietrich Bonhoeffer wrote his parents from prison: "In normal life one is often not at all aware that we always receive infinitely more than we give, and that gratitude is what enriches life. One easily overestimates the importance of one's own acts and deeds, compared with what we become only through other people."[2] Everyone who has worked on this project will, I believe, find meaning in those words and feel gratitude for Bonhoeffer's life and witness. It is a privilege to have been part of this long, deep, and rich conversation with Bonhoeffer's thought, and to extend that conversation to the readers of these volumes.

Victoria J. Barnett

[2.] Letter of September 13, 1943, *DBWE* 8, 2/57, p. 154.

# Abbreviations

| | |
|---|---|
| BA | Bundesarchiv |
| *DB-ER* | *Dietrich Bonhoeffer: A Biography* (Fortress Press, rev. ed., 2000) |
| *DBW* | *Dietrich Bonhoeffer Werke*, German edition |
| *DBWE* | *Dietrich Bonhoeffer Works*, English edition |
| EKD | Evangelische Kirche in Deutschland |
| EZA | Evangelisches Zentralarchiv |
| *GS* | *Gesammelte Schriften* |
| Lic. | Licentiate |
| LKA | Landeskirchliches Archiv |
| *LW* | *Luther's Works*, American edition |
| *NL* | *Nachlaß Dietrich Bonhoeffer* |
| *NL-Bibl.* | Restbibliothek Bonhoeffers in *Nachlaß Dietrich Bonhoeffer* (supplement to the literary estate of Dietrich Bonhoeffer) |
| NRSV | New Revised Standard Version |
| NSDAP | Nationalsozialistische Deutsche Arbeiterpartei; the Nazi Party |
| NT | New Testament |
| OT | Old Testament |
| *PAM* | *Predigten—Auslegungen—Meditationen* (Chr. Kaiser, 1984–85) |
| *RGG* | *Religion in Geschichte und Gegenwart* |
| RM | reichsmarks |
| SA | Sturmabteilung (Nazi storm troopers) |
| SS | Schutzstaffel |
| *WA* | Weimarer Ausgabe (Weimar edition), Martin Luther |

| | |
|---|---|
| *WA.Tr* | Weimarer Ausgabe, *Tischreden* |
| WCC | World Council of Churches |
| WDZ | Wolf-Dieter Zimmermann |
| YMCA | Young Men's Christian Association |

Michael B. Lukens, with
Victoria J. Barnett and Mark S. Brocker

# Editors' Introduction to the English Edition

This volume covers the period from June 1931, when twenty-five-year-old Dietrich Bonhoeffer returned from his year of study at Union Theological Seminary in New York, to the turbulent weeks of the waning Weimar Republic in October 1932. The shift from student life to the beginning of a professional career is a significant transition in any life, but as Eberhard Bethge later wrote, for Bonhoeffer it marked a major caesura:

> Bonhoeffer's return to Germany in 1931 represented a break in his development that was certainly sharper than the momentous and ecclesiastical upheaval that followed two years later. The second major phase of his career began now, not in 1933.
>
> The period of learning and roaming had come to an end. He now began to teach on a faculty whose theology he did not share, and to preach in a church whose self-confidence he regarded as unfounded. More aware than before, he now became part of a society that was moving toward political, social, and economic chaos.[1]

This new phase of Bonhoeffer's life coincided with the growing political and social turmoil that was beginning to permeate every sphere of German life,

[1.] *DB-ER*, 173.

including the churches. By 1932 German unemployment had risen to 30 percent. The governing coalition parties in the Weimar Republic were openly feuding, and the extreme parties—the Communists and the National Socialist German Workers' Party—were gaining new public support. The German parliamentary crisis in the early summer of 1932 culminated in a runoff election for the Reichstag in which the Nazi party received 37.3 percent of the popular vote. Although nationally prominent Field Marshall Paul von Hindenburg won that election, it had made Adolf Hitler a rising star in Germany, particularly after his "Führer over Germany" campaign, in which he chartered an airplane and campaigned in towns around the country. During the final months of 1932, Hitler's refusal to join a coalition government and the fragmentation within the other political parties paved the way for his appointment as chancellor, by Hindenburg, on January 30, 1933.

These political events had already led to troubling developments in some sectors of the German Evangelical Church. The "German Christian" movement (*Deutsche Christen*), which subsequently promoted the nazification of the German Evangelical Church and sparked the Church Struggle, was founded in May 1932; its early leaders were part of the Berlin church and ecumenical circles in which Bonhoeffer began to move during this period.[2]

During the sixteen months covered by this volume, Bonhoeffer was pursuing a dual career track. By now he had completed his theological examinations and ordination requirements. He was ordained by Ernst Vits in November 1931. His first assignment was as an assistant pastor at the Zion Church in Berlin, where he began to teach confirmation classes and to preach.[3] Yet he was still considering an academic career, and in November he began teaching as a lecturer (*Privatdozent*) at the University of Berlin (Friedrich Wilhelm University).[4]

A third realm of work engaged his interest and would profoundly influence his life after 1933: the international ecumenical movement. In September 1931, Bonhoeffer attended the World Alliance Conference in Cambridge, England, and was appointed one of three youth secretaries; in November he was appointed secretary to the German Provisional Bureau for Ecumenical Work.[5]

[2.] In this volume see especially the "Primary Report on the Conference of the Provisional Bureau" (2/13) for a detailed account of one such meeting.

[3.] See 1/2.

[4.] See documents 2/3–2/10.

[5.] See 1/19.

The ecumenical movement in Europe was also undergoing great changes in 1931 and 1932. In its early days in the 1920s, it had been infused with an "idealistic internationalism,"[6] but this idealism was disappearing under the weight of the world economic crisis and the rise of nationalism and fascism in Europe. As Dutch ecumenical leader Willem Visser 't Hooft wrote in September 1932, "The forces at work in the world did not work towards peace but towards war."[7]

Bonhoeffer encountered these forces directly in 1932. The rise of the German Christian movement reflected a growing ethnic nationalism in German theological circles, promoted by leading scholars such as Paul Althaus, Emanuel Hirsch, and Wilhelm Stapel.[8] This volume documents this development and depicts Bonhoeffer's role in the theological debates that emerged.[9] In fact, this volume includes some of the most explicit and prescient statements Bonhoeffer ever made about political issues.[10] As he wrote Erwin Sutz in May 1932: "The situation here really looks desperate. One lives from one day to the next; simply no one can see further ahead. It may be that the day after tomorrow everything turns to chaos, and not because something great and new appears on the horizon, but simply because something rotten breaks down completely."[11]

Dietrich Bonhoeffer was a dialectical thinker, and particularly in the debates with Protestant nationalists who were already in the process of creating an "Aryan" theology he began to articulate the theological counterargument, notably in the debates about the so-called orders of creation theology.[12] But some of his other lectures also include commentaries on the political developments in Germany,[13] and his warnings about *völkisch* ideology even appear in the catechism that he wrote with Franz Hildebrandt:

---

[6.] Visser 't Hooft, *Memoirs*, 33.

[7.] Ibid.

[8.] Stapel's 1932 book *Der christliche Staatsmann: Eine Theologie des Nationalismus* (The Christian statesman: A theology of nationalism) was a key example; Bonhoeffer described it as "a dangerous book" to his students in 1933 (cf. *DBWE* 12:206–9). On Althaus and Hirsch, see Ericksen, *Theologians under Hitler.*

[9.] See esp. 2/16. Other documents that include commentary on the German political situation or criticism of the emerging German Christian theology include 2/7 (esp. p. 262–63), 2/8, and 2/9. Even three of the sermons in this volume (3/2, 3/11, and 3/13) include direct criticism of the theological implications of the new racist ideology and nationalism.

[10.] See esp. his letters to Erwin Sutz (1/59) and to Paul Lehmann (1/68a).

[11.] 1/59.

[12.] See 2/13.

[13.] See especially "The Right to Self-Assertion" (2/5).

> A defiant ethnic pride [ein völkisches Trotzen] in flesh and blood is a sin against the Holy Spirit. Zeal that only blindly asserts itself is brought under control by the state. God has established the state for the service of God, so that we might serve God as Christians.
>
> How then should the Christian behave politically?
>
> As much as the Christian would like to remain distant from political struggle, nonetheless even here the commandment of love urges the Christian to stand up for his neighbor. His faith and love must know whether the dictates of the state may lead him against his conscience. In every such decision, he experiences the irreconcilable conflict between the peace of Christ and the hate of the world.[14]

Here we already find the language and thinking that later emerge in Bonhoeffer's critiques of both the Nazi state and his church, for example, in his 1933 essay "The Church and the Jewish Question," his 1934 peace address at Fanø, and of course during the resistance period, in sections of *Ethics* and the *Letters and Papers from Prison.*[15]

Theologically, then, this volume portrays a young man already coming into his own. It also documents one of the most significant theological events in Bonhoeffer's life: his encounter with Karl Barth in July 1931. Bonhoeffer realized the significance of this encounter immediately and wrote Paul Lehmann that same day.[16] Days later, he wrote his friend Erwin Sutz:

> Now everything is very much or completely different when it comes to Karl Barth himself. You can breathe freely. You are no longer afraid you will die for lack of oxygen in the rarefied atmosphere. I have, I believe, seldom regretted not having done something in my theological past as much as I now regret that I did not go to hear Barth sooner. . . . There is an openness, a willingness to listen to a critical comment directed to the topic at hand, and with this such concentration and with a vehement insistence on the topic at hand, for the sake of which he can speak proudly or humbly, dogmatically or with utter uncertainty, in a way that is certainly not intended primarily to advance his own theology. It is becoming easier and easier for me to understand why it is unbelievably difficult to grasp Barth through the literature. I am impressed by his discussion even more than by

[14.] 2/7.

[15.] Cf. *DBWE* 12, 2/6 and 2/13; *DBWE* 13, 2/3; *DBWE* 8, 3/145 (esp. p. 389) and the prologue "After Ten Years" (*DBWE* 8:37–52).

[16.] 1/2a.

his writing and lectures. He is really fully present. I have never seen anything like it nor thought it possible.[17]

It was the beginning of a long and rich conversation with Barth that would continue in the crucial months after January 1933 and end only with Bonhoeffer's execution in April 1945. In fact, much of the present volume should be read in the context of the larger church, political, and theological conversations that precede and follow the period documented here. While the period from June 1931 to October 1932 was a transitional one for Dietrich Bonhoeffer, the contents of this volume are very much a part of the larger story told by the preceding volume (*DBWE* 10, *Barcelona, Berlin, New York: 1928–1931*) and the subsequent one (*DBWE* 12, *Berlin: 1932–1933*). As Christoph Strohm, coeditor of *DBW* 11, wrote in the afterword to the volume, "the texts from the years 1931–32 assembled in the present volume document fundamental theological decisions that occupy a significant place in Bonhoeffer's work and life path. The disputes, decisions, and positions taken at the beginning of the 1930s were not merely preliminary skirmishes of the coming struggle; instead, they set a course that would have considerable consequences that to a large degree remained decisive even beyond the more acute stages of the Church Struggle."

### Organization and Content of *DBWE* 11

As in the other *DBWE* volumes, the contents of this volume have been organized into three parts: Bonhoeffer's correspondence, his lectures and notes, and his sermons. Within each section the material is organized chronologically. New archival material discovered since the publication of the German *DBW* 11 volume (notably the correspondence with Paul Lehmann: 2a; 8a; 16a; 37a; 59a; 68a; 93a) has also been included. Two additional new documents—a book inscription (9a) discovered in 2009 in Burke Library by Clifford Green and Bonhoeffer's notes from his assistantship at the University of Berlin (27a)—are also included. With the exception of the book inscription, all these documents were first published in *DBW* 17 (the book inscription was first published in the Bonhoeffer *Jahrbuch*). Appendix 2 is a list of documents from Bonhoeffer's literary estate that have not been included in this volume.

Despite the extensive material in the Bonhoeffer literary estate, there are certain areas of Bonhoeffer's work during this period for which little or

[17.] Letter of July 24 to Erwin Sutz (1/6).

no documentation exists. As editor Eberhard Amelung noted in his introduction to the German volume, there are virtually no documents from his confirmation classes and student retreats, and many of his lecture manuscripts have been lost or exist only in fragmentary form.[18] The documentation for his major university lecture courses here (2/3 and 2/9) has been reconstructed from student notes, and in some places where there were gaps in the notes Professor Amelung added and sometimes revised the text for clarification. These additions are always bracketed within the text.

## Part 1: Bonhoeffer's Correspondence

The correspondence related to Bonhoeffer in this period can be divided generally into four categories: notes and letters to his family; documents related to ecclesial standing and professional responsibilities; the ecumenical efforts; and his personal letters, primarily with his closest friends. This correspondence expands our information about Bonhoeffer's activities and work, but their deeper importance may be in the less formal information that it renders about the nature of his activities as well as his own insights on the various tasks in which he was engaged. As such, they are invaluable as a reflection of several significant developments in his views of theology, church, and the political situation in Germany, providing valuable correlations with his writings in parts 2 and 3.

*Family*: Since Bonhoeffer was once again living at the home of his parents in Berlin and in close proximity to siblings as well, the relatively few family letters are mostly descriptions of his excursions and travels. Yet even these few give us a continuing portrait of close and caring relationships and offer glimpses into this more private dimension of Bonhoeffer's life. He writes of his visit with his brother Karl-Friedrich and his wife, Grete, in Frankfurt to celebrate the birth of their newborn son and then a return to Bonn (his continuing visit with Karl Barth) by Rhine steamship, which he describes as "cheerful."[19] There are notes related to the occasion of the ninetieth birthday of his beloved grandmother, Julie (Tafel) Bonhoeffer, with its brief discussion of his gift to her of a work by Thomas à Kempis, probably the *Imitatio Christi*.[20] His letter of birthday greetings to his father in March 1932, from the family retreat in Friedrichsbrunn in the Harz Mountains, reminds us of how much he loved hiking in those woods and meadows.[21]

[18.] See the editor's introduction to the German volume, *DBW* 11:6 and 8–9.
[19.] 1/1 and 1/3.
[20.] 1/78.
[21.] 1/48.

He was there with members of his confirmation class, and he conveys the importance of such an experience for them with implied gratitude to his father for supporting the excursion. We see such gratitude as well in a brief remark of satisfaction for the stable quietness of being at home with them in the midst of his turbulent schedule.[22] These are modest documents, but they reflect a balancing dimension to Bonhoeffer's strenuous work and are a reminder of the enriching family background that framed his life.

*Professional Correspondence*: Bonhoeffer returned to Berlin in the late summer of 1931 primed for the pastoral ministry and teaching at the Friedrich Wilhelm University in Berlin. The ministry assignment had been arranged while he was still in America. In June, just before Bonhoeffer's departure from New York, he was given the assignment to serve as an "assistant pastor in the city" (*Stadtvikar*), a vicariate position within the synod that meant special duties supervised by the general superintendent, Emil Karow.[23] This new pastoral work was to begin on August 1, the date his leave of absence concluded. In April, while still at Union Seminary, Bonhoeffer requested that his leave of absence, due to expire on July 31, be extended to October 1, to provide additional time for writing about the American experience and to prepare for both his new pastoral work and the expected university courses.[24] Max Diestel, his immediate superintendent and mentor, had initiated Bonhoeffer's new pastoral assignment and notified him at the end of May that this extension request had been denied, even though he had strongly supported it.[25] Nonetheless, it seems that Diestel succeeded informally, since he informed Bonhoeffer that Karow, his new superior, was willing to grant Bonhoeffer the necessary time as "vacation," both to participate in a major ecumenical conference in September in Cambridge and to work further on reflections about the American experience.[26] It is also apparent that in this same period Diestel assigned him a new ecumenical role; it was to be a fateful initiative.

The central pastoral focus of Bonhoeffer's assignment was a chaplaincy to students at the Technical College in Charlottenburg. While such a position had long existed at the university, Karow's suggestion that Bonhoeffer might work in a parallel way with the pastor there proved ineffective.[27] This was a new effort at the Technical College, a very different environment

[22.] Ibid.

[23.] Assignment as Assistant Pastor in the City, Berlin, June 12, 1931 (1/0).

[24.] *DBWE* 10:296–97.

[25.] *DBWE* 12:303, ed. note 2.

[26.] 1/2.

[27.] Ibid.

from the university, and Bonhoeffer rarely refers to it in his letters. Bonhoeffer tried a number of innovative strategies, but over the next year he came to regard it as an unsatisfying and unproductive experience.[28] Nonetheless, this chaplaincy qualified for the obligatory service of newly ordained ministers in the provincial church and was in effect renewed a year later, in August 1932.[29]

Bonhoeffer's ordination authorization is documented here;[30] the ordination took place on Sunday, November 15, 1931, at St. Matthew's Church in Berlin.[31] It is curious that there is no other extant correspondence about this event, either in connection with the family's response or Bonhoeffer's understanding of its meaning for him.[32] The surviving records are exclusively bureaucratic.

At the same time, Bonhoeffer began teaching lecture courses and seminars as an adjunct lecturer at the university, on a recommendation from Reinhold Seeberg and subsequent appointment by Professor Wilhelm Lütgert in 1929, and in concert with the publication of his doctoral dissertation (*Sanctorum Communio*) and the acceptance of his postdoctoral thesis (*Act and Being*).[33] Upon his return, he once again assumed his duties as a teaching assistant to the chair of the systematic theology department (Wilhelm Lütgert, who had succeeded Seeberg), a position that he had held before his year in America. This assistantship included a variety of mundane duties assigned by the chair of the department, such as managing the department library and preparing bibliographies.[34] Lütgert requested that this be a paid position for Bonhoeffer in May 1930 (he had previously served as an unpaid "volunteer"), but there was no official confirmation until November 1931, when the previous assistant, Arnold Stolzenburg, become a full professor. Bonhoeffer's status was then made retroactive from August 1931.[35] Bonhoeffer's teaching became a much more intense focus, rivaled only by his pastoral duties. The letters, especially those to Erwin

[28.] 1/34; 1/91 and 92. See also *DB-ER*, 222–26. Bonhoeffer continued his student chaplaincy work in late 1932 and early 1933; see *DBWE* 12.

[29.] 1/78a.

[30.] 1/17.

[31.] 1/17, p. 64.

[32.] See *DB-ER*, 221–22.

[33.] Published in this series as *DBWE* 1 and 2. The publication of *Act and Being* much concerned Bonhoeffer in this period, even though he indicated reservations about it. See 1/3; 1/9; 1/39.

[34.] See 1/27 (Bonhoeffer's letter to Erwin Sutz) and 1/27a ("Notes from the Time as Assistant, 1931–1932").

[35.] *DBWE* 10:215, ed. note 2.

Sutz and Paul Lehmann, demonstrate the extraordinary seriousness and demanding nature of the university's expectations.[36]

*Ecumenical Engagement*: The largest group in this collection of letters, more than a third,[37] relates to Bonhoeffer's ecumenical work, particularly his work within the World Alliance for Promoting International Friendship among the Churches and a number of youth conferences that were sponsored by the World Alliance. Bonhoeffer had moved quickly to significant participation and leadership within the German ecumenical scene after his return from America in July 1931. Starting with the Cambridge conference in September, he became thoroughly immersed in ecumenical matters at the national level, including the deep conflicts over ecumenical involvement within German Protestantism.[38] This new venture for Bonhoeffer had been initiated by Diestel, an ecumenical leader in Germany and a major figure within the German section of the World Alliance.[39] He had Bonhoeffer in mind for a youth leadership role a year or so earlier and used his influence to champion him with his ecumenical colleagues.[40] In his view, Bonhoeffer was an ideal person for such a role because of his theological prowess, academic accomplishments, and his international experience, especially his fluency in English and the recent experience in America. Through Diestel's efforts, Bonhoeffer attended the Cambridge conference and returned as one of three international youth secretaries for the work of the World Alliance in Europe. In this position, Bonhoeffer became a member of the Provisional Bureau for Ecumenical Youth Work, a coordinating body in Germany for the various Protestant groups committed to ecumenical work. Much of the correspondence in this section reflects his work in the Provisional Bureau and his collaboration with its leadership, principally August Schreiber and Wilhelm Stählin and the Church Federation Office.[41] Diestel also brought Bonhoeffer into the central governance

[36.] See, for example, 1/11, 1/16a, 1/27.

[37.] A key reason for this substantial number of documents is that many were retained as part of the bureaucratic records of the various ecumenical organizations.

[38.] See 2/1.

[39.] See Bethge's description of the most important figures on the German ecumenical scene in *DB-ER*, 190–93.

[40.] See Diestel's letter of May 29, 1931, to Bonhoeffer, when he was still at Union Seminary, concerning arrangements already made for his participation in the international conference of the World Alliance in Cambridge in September 1931 (*DBWE* 10, 1/177). It is interesting that he did this apparently without any consultation with Bonhoeffer and signed that letter "your Ephorus," referring in Latin to a figure with overseer authority. See also Diestel's earlier letters of strong recommendation for Bonhoeffer (*DBWE* 10, 1/102, 1/126, as well as *DBWE* 10, 1/114, ed. note 11).

[41.] 1/10, 1/13, 1/16, 1/19, 1/44, 1/45, 1/46, 1/84, and 1/85.

of the German Section of the World Alliance, its management committee, as a "specialist in youth work."[42]

As the World Alliance youth secretary for central Europe and Scandinavia, Bonhoeffer was principally involved in planning international conferences and shaping the organization's educational and theological program, working primarily through the Provisional Bureau. His duties were both pedestrian and grand. The letters frequently suggest the managerial nature of his office, the enlistment of delegates, the publication of reports and papers, and the continual struggle for financial support. He also had to deal with significant political resistance to ecumenical participation within the church, due to the widespread political resistance in Germany to any kind of international involvement, especially with churches in England, France, and the United States, signatory nations of the despised Treaty of Versailles. These countries, and by association their churches, were seen as exploitative and inimical to German interests. The ultranationalist movements in Germany pressured the churches to isolate themselves from such engagement. This nationalist opposition would become for Bonhoeffer a matter of increasing attention, in both his ecumenical work and his teaching.

The planning and implementation of a series of youth conferences dominated Bonhoeffer's ecumenical work from the fall of 1931 through 1932.[43] His work was both organizational and theological. The letters reflect ordinary concerns about budgets, programs, and conference leadership and later publication of papers in the influential ecumenical journal *Die Eiche*. Yet there were certainly weightier dimensions, clearly relished by Bonhoeffer. In the four major conferences in 1932—the Theological Conference in Berlin (April 29–30), the Westerburg Conference (July 12–14), the meeting at Ciernohorské Kúpele (July 20–30), and the Gland Conference (August 25–31)—Bonhoeffer either was central in setting the program agenda or played a critical role in the conference's theological leadership, often both.[44] Although the planning letters indicate only indirectly the theological significance of this work, his formal reports to the Central Office and the World Alliance, which appear in part 2 of this volume,[45] indicate the central issues as well as his assessment of distinctive

[42.] 1/38.

[43.] 1/16.

[44.] Bonhoeffer attended the Epsom Conference in April 1932 but this was a French-English conference in which he had no direct role. He did not participate in planning the Czech conference at Ciernohorské Kúpele, but his address there was a highly significant one (2/14 and 2/15).

[45.] 2/1, 2/2, 2/11, 2/12, 2/13, 2/18, 2/19.

perspectives and difficulties that were encountered.[46] In these reports, Bonhoeffer elaborated on his abbreviated comments in the letters about the prevailing poverty of theological foundations for ecumenical work; the tendency of the churches to make grandiose yet ultimately anemic resolutions about the kingdom of God and peace in place of hard, realistic, ethical proposals that would address the real problems of the time; and the serious threat of ultranationalism that comes dressed as confessional and biblical theology. Although the letters mostly show the planning and programmatic development of the conferences, his reports and addresses convey the fuller themes and critique in this ecumenical work and demonstrate important developments in Bonhoeffer's theology in this period.

*Letters to Friends*: The year in America had been for Bonhoeffer an extremely full and provocative year. In spite of a generally negative view of American theological education and church life,[47] there is considerable evidence, even if Bonhoeffer was unaware at the time, that this was indeed a vitally shaping experience.[48] During this critical time, several new friendships at Union developed, each of which became deeply influential for Bonhoeffer.

There were four particularly influential friendships from his year at Union: Jean Lasserre, a French participant with Bonhoeffer in Union's Visiting Fellows Program; Frank Fisher, one of the first African American students at Union; Paul Lehmann, an American; and Erwin Sutz from Switzerland. Only the latter two are correspondents in this volume. While Jean Lasserre is generally credited with playing a very significant role in the development of Bonhoeffer's interest in pacifism, there is little evidence of correspondence in the period covered by the present volume or, of course, during the war years.[49] During a visit to Switzerland primarily to see Sutz, he visited the Lasserre family with great pleasure for two days at their vacation home near

[46.] See esp. 2/11, 2/18, 2/19.

[47.] See his report on that year to the German Church Federation Office, *DBWE* 10:305–22.

[48.] There is an increasing perspective in Bonhoeffer studies that this experience is to be seen within a larger theological and spiritual "turn" in the years 1930–32, in which Bonhoeffer's academic and abstract theology became integrated with pastoral sensitivity and social activism toward a view of Christian life as discipleship, justice, and service. This understanding was initially signaled by Bethge (*DB-ER*, 173, 202–6). See also the editor's introduction to *DBWE* 10:35–43; and Pfeifer, "Learning Faith and Ethical Commitment."

[49.] Lasserre and Bonhoeffer did connect again through the ecumenical movement in 1934, however, notably at the Fanø meeting in August and at a special gathering in Bruay, France, the following month, where Bonhoeffer also visited Lasserre's parish (cf. *DBWE* 13, 1/145 and 2/3a, as well as *DB-ER*, 389).

Chamonix.[50] With Frank Fisher, there is no documented contact at all. Even though Fisher was pivotally important for Bonhoeffer's introduction to Harlem's Abyssinian Church and for insights into the discrimination and stress afflicting African American communities, correspondence between Fisher and Bonhoeffer lapsed. Bonhoeffer was clearly displeased with this lapse, implying that he had tried to communicate with Fisher, although we have no documentation of this. In a letter to Lehmann, he mentioned this regret in a casual way but also with a rare snide tone.[51]

The correspondence with Sutz and Lehmann, on the other hand, reflects a continuing and substantial relationship. Paul Lehmann became Bonhoeffer's most important American contact and friend. Lehmann was a doctoral student at Union during Bonhoeffer's time there, with similar interests in both Barth and Emil Brunner. Their correspondence continued in these first years after Bonhoeffer's return to Germany and then resumed following Bonhoeffer's decision to return to Union Seminary in the summer of 1939.[52]

Together with Sutz, Lehmann was one of Bonhoeffer's strongest compatriots in things Barthian during the year at Union Seminary, and Bonhoeffer was eager to share with him his continuing enthusiasm, as, for example, in his letter to Lehmann on the day of his first visit with Barth in Bonn.[53] His later letters continued this high valuation of Barth's work and also descriptions of the woeful conditions in Germany.[54] He advised Lehmann and his wife as they prepared to come to Europe in order to study with Brunner in Zürich.[55] Later, Bonhoeffer convinced Lehmann to help him by writing a draft of the history of the social gospel movement in America, which he acknowledged as "a brazen request."[56] It is a mark of their friendship that Bonhoeffer could admit that he was overwhelmed by his commitments and felt free to turn to Lehmann in such an open and trusting way:

> Now, I am very much at a loss because the simple fact is that I actually do not know enough about the material and am coming to you, hoping confidently that you will help me. . . . It can't be that much trouble

[50.] 1/76.

[51.] 1/37a.

[52.] See *DBWE* 15.

[53.] 1/2a.

[54.] 1/68a.

[55.] Bonhoeffer made a vigorous attempt to convince Lehmann to drop the plan to study with Brunner and to turn more fully to Barth. See 1/59a and 1/68a.

[56.] 1/93a.

> for you, of course, and you would be doing me a really great favor. After that, you can ask of me what you will—up to half a kingdom—and I will do it for you; only please help me quickly in this difficulty. I actually have so ridiculously much to do with the university and the ministry and innumerable lectures that I just could not work my way into it from the beginning. So please be so kind and help me![57]

The paper, "The Social Gospel," based on Lehmann's draft, was circulated within the German branch of the World Alliance in December 1932.[58]

It is the correspondence with Erwin Sutz, however, that clearly includes Bonhoeffer's most intense theological interests and his pastoral concerns. These letters are also the most frankly personal. As in the case of Lehmann, Bonhoeffer's friendship with Sutz began at Union Seminary in 1930, grounded in a common commitment to Barth's theological work and a strong mutual bond. Barth was the primary mentor for them both. It was Sutz who wrote on Bonhoeffer's behalf for the visit with Barth in Bonn in July 1931, and Sutz was thus the obvious person to hear his fullest reactions.

There are three important dimensions to the correspondence with Sutz: (1) the dialogue between them about Barth, with its opportunity to test ideas with a trusted friend who shared a common theological enthusiasm, especially in areas where Bonhoeffer was developing critical disagreements with Barth; (2) reflections on Bonhoeffer's growing commitment to the ministry, with its deepening sense of compassion for the wretched social conditions that gave him such serious foreboding (evident also in his sermons from this period); and (3) several rare self-reflective admissions.

Bonhoeffer's initial letters to Sutz are full of gratitude and enthusiasm.[59] He was eager to discuss not only his very positive impressions of Barth but also the genesis of some disagreements, particularly about ethics. This discussion was refined as the correspondence continued into the next year. In April 1932, a lecture by Barth in Berlin occasioned a letter to Sutz with personal impressions about the theological atmosphere in Berlin but was mainly a return to the discussion of ethics in Barth and Brunner, a topic that was, as he put it, "becoming more and more acutely and unbearably critical."[60] The centrality of this preoccupation with ethics emerged even more clearly in his letter to Sutz in August, where he reflected on his experience

[57.] Ibid.

[58.] *DBWE* 12:236–43.

[59.] 1/4 and 1/6.

[60.] 1/59.

at the ecumenical conference at Ciernohorské Kúpele (Czechoslovakia).[61] He had given a lecture on the theological foundations for ecumenical work that, even though it was well received, he himself found unsatisfying:

> There are still very many question marks that have to be brought up there. Basically, it all depends on the problem of ethics, that is, actually on the question of whether it is possible for the concrete commandment to be proclaimed through the church. . . . It is simply not enough and therefore false to say that the principle of concretion could only be the Holy Spirit himself. . . . The concrete form of the proclamation of grace is, after all, the sacrament. But what is the sacrament of the ethical, of the commandment? We must talk about that when we see each other.[62]

It is highly likely that this matter was a central focus when they were together at Sutz's home in Switzerland the following October.

Some of the most striking reflections in this correspondence with Sutz relate to Bonhoeffer's experience with the Zion Church confirmation class in the north of Berlin (Prenzlauer Berg). In his February 1932, letter to Sutz, he gave the single most extensive description of his confirmands, their marginal social setting, and his strategies for dealing with numerous difficulties.[63] In a 1931 Christmas Day letter, he had previously written about his relief that he had such pastoral work, amid a generally boring teaching enterprise.[64] As he had done in earlier letters, Bonhoeffer reiterated the desperate social situation in Germany. Although this deep social concern is present in his more formal writings, particularly in the ethical challenges expressed in his ecumenical papers, his assessment of the deprivations of unemployment and hunger is striking and immediate in these letters to Sutz.[65] In his letter just one day before the concluding examination of the confirmation class (February 29), he wrote with enthusiasm and a sense

[61.] 1/72. Bonhoeffer's summary reflection here is quite striking: "I have just come back from a very mediocre conference in Czechoslovakia that once again made me have doubts about the value of all this ecumenical work." See also 1/66.

[62.] Ibid.

[63.] 1/39.

[64.] 1/27. Bonhoeffer did not find his lecture course in the winter semester of 1931–32 (see 2/3) satisfying, but the seminars were evaluated highly, because of "an elite of interested and in part amazingly clever and intelligent people." He also mentioned the awkwardness and tension in his reception at the university. At the end of that semester, in his February letter (1/39), he termed the lecture course "boring."

[65.] 1/11 and 1/27.

of achievement about the experience, including that of living in the same neighborhood as his confirmands. Yet in his comments about their situation and the challenges of teaching in that situation, one senses not only his strong commitment to such work but also his cautious assessment of the viability of this work. He shared his uncertainty about the effectiveness of the church in a social setting of deprivation, tension, and tenuous morality: "Maybe it really is the end of our kind of Christianity. . . . We have learned to preach again, at least a very little bit, but pastoral care?"[66]

It is often noted that Bonhoeffer was a most reserved person and did not often or easily share his inner life and self-assessments. One of the aspects of his friendship with Sutz was a trust sufficient for him to feel that he could share such thoughts—even though he still maintained a formal correctness and distance in his use of the formal *Sie* rather than the informal *du*. These are rare moments, which make such expressions particularly valuable. He registered his growing sense of frustration with ecumenical work in his letter of May 1932, written just after the Epsom conference in England, which he termed "a very superfluous conference."[67] To this, he added a sense of frustration about his teaching, about his continuing struggle with the issues of concretion and certainty in ethics, the desperation and seeming hopelessness in German society, and the absence of truly creative theological discussion; there is a sense of discouragement and foreboding in the letter. Even more striking is his revealing admission of almost overwhelming expectations upon his return to Germany in 1931, when he faced so many new commitments:

> Now I am sitting here preparing for my lecture course, and for the work as pastor for the students and would sometimes be happy if I could be in the country somewhere for a while, to get away from everything everyone wants from and expects of me. It's not that I'm afraid of disappointing—at least I hope not primarily—but that sometimes I simply cannot see how I will be able to do all these things right. The cheap consolation that one just does what one can, and that there are others who would do it even worse, isn't always enough. It is certainly not right for me to come into such things so soon—and also on the basis of what qualifications? Now and then I would like to laugh grimly about all of that.[68]

[66.] 1/39.
[67.] 1/59.
[68.] 1/11.

The importance of this relationship became especially evident to him in his visit with Sutz and his family in Switzerland in September 1932. A month later, he wrote Sutz expressing his deep gratitude for that visit and their friendship. He was struck by their similarities and common commitments despite different backgrounds and made it very clear that, although they were in a sense in different worlds, the continuation of this friendship was important to him: "I hope that now we do not lose track of each other, after we have had this time together. (Sometimes I think with a shudder that we are perhaps alike because we are both leading existences somehow at the edge of our church—both in very different locations.) I am eager to know about the paths in your life; they are much less predictable than mine. And that is what is bad about my situation, yet nice as far as yours is concerned. But please help see to it that we keep an eye on each other."[69]

The themes found in these letters commonly reflect Bonhoeffer's central interests in this period, foreshadowing the more thorough treatments of them in his theological writings in part 2. In addition to the major areas cited above, this collection also contains some interesting hints at profound themes and controversies on the horizon. Two can be readily discerned: Bonhoeffer's leadership in the effort to gather support within the theological community for the defense of Günther Dehn, the socialist-pacifist professor who had come under attack from ultranationalists and the National Socialists;[70] and his role in the Working Group of Theologians and Economists, in which he clashed with Pastor Friedrich Peter over the issues of "orders of creation" and the *völkisch* theology of the fervent nationalists.[71] These documents presage Bonhoeffer's fateful conflict with the Nazis, which was only months away. As a whole, the letters and documents in the first section of the volume clarify his work and activities in this period, offering a broader view of Bonhoeffer's life and work during a time of strenuous demands and challenges.

---

[69.] 1/89.

[70.] 1/40. See also the sermon on Matt. 24:6–14 (3/5) in this volume and the comments in the German editor's afterword on the Dehn case, as well as *DBWE* 12:107 and 262, and *DB-ER*, 177 and 235–36.

[71.] Peter, a member of the Nazi Party and later the German Christian bishop of Magdeburg, espoused a theology of a special divinely ordered destiny for the German people. Letters 1/18, 1/28, 1/36, 1/49 concern this group. For the theses of Bonhoeffer's lecture to the group in January 1932, see "The Discernible Nature of the Order of Creation" (2/8).

## Part 2: Reports, Theological Studies, and Texts from the University Period

The themes that emerge from the letters are further developed in the theological and ecumenical writings in part 2. When Bonhoeffer returned to Berlin, he immediately resumed his work at the Friedrich Wilhelm University. Prior to his time in America, he had served as an academic assistant to the theological faculty, specifically to the chair of the faculty. His mentor, Reinhold Seeberg, had recommended him to Wilhelm Lütgert, Seeberg's successor, and Bonhoeffer began that work in 1930. Even during his time in New York in 1930–31, he had anticipated further university service, both in administrative duties and in teaching.

In addition to assisting Lütgert with bibliographical work and departmental library supervision,[72] Bonhoeffer had permission to teach. This allowed him to offer lecture and seminar courses on his own interests; these lectures shed light on the development of his theology.[73]

Bonhoeffer's entry into teaching came at a time of substantial expansion of interest in theology, and it is estimated that more than a thousand students were enrolled in the university's theology department.[74] Bonhoeffer had no difficulty attracting students; word seems to have spread that, in addition to offering intellectual rigor, he represented a refreshing and challenging new voice in the political and theological context of the times.[75] In his critique of traditional theology and the new nationalism, he pressed the kind of foundational questions that students felt necessary. Bethge has described the circle of students coalescing around Bonhoeffer in this period as connected by ideals of theology, spirituality, and social activism that needed yet to be integrated.[76] Bonhoeffer's probing, listening, and patient encouragement made him all the more attractive as a teacher. He also communicated an impatience with traditional theological education—an attitude that he realized set him apart.[77] Both his commitment

---

[72.] For an example of this work, see 1/27a.

[73.] Although this teaching arrangement did not carry an established salary, Bonhoeffer was paid a stipend for his departmental assistance. The contract for departmental assistantship was not completed until January 1932 but was applied retroactively. See 1/24. This income was later used for the cabin that he built in Biesenthal. See 1/30 and *DB-ER*, 207.

[74.] See *DB-ER*, 207; 1/27.

[75.] See, for example, the reflections of Zimmerman, *I Knew Dietrich Bonhoeffer*, 59–67.

[76.] *DB-ER*, 207–8.

[77.] See 1/27. This is also reflected in his understanding of the integral connection between theology and pastoral care. See his letter of February 28, 1932, to Sutz (1/39).

to Barth's thought and his developing differences with Barth supported this independence.

Part 2 also includes the course work of the 1932–33 winter semester and the 1932 summer semester. In both semesters, Bonhoeffer offered a lecture course and a seminar. In the winter semester, he held a lecture course titled "The History of Twentieth-Century Systematic Theology" (2/3) and a seminar titled "The Idea of Philosophy and Protestant Theology in the Twentieth Century." (There are no extant notes from the latter; however, "Thesis Fragment about M. Heidegger and E. Grisebach" [2/4] was probably used for that seminar.) In the summer semester, his lecture course was "The Nature of the Church" (2/9) and the seminar was "Is There a Christian Ethic?" (2/10).

There is no evidence that any of the manuscripts for Bonhoeffer's courses in these years survived.[78] Some student notes are available for the lecture courses, and these have become the basis for reconstructing those texts in this volume. No student notes from the seminars, however, seem to exist. The only seminar material is the fragments of Bonhoeffer's notes on Heidegger and Grisebach (2/4) and excerpts, actually a brief outline, from the summer seminar on Christian ethics (2/10). The lack of material from the seminars may reflect the contrast between formal lecturing that encourages note-taking and the informal and less directed nature of the university seminar.

Obviously, the dependence of the German editors on student notes has the inevitable consequence of imprecision about Bonhoeffer's actual presentation and thinking. Nonetheless, the notes provide a clear outline of topics, dominant themes, and interpretive orientation. In this volume, the German editors reconstructed the course manuscripts by determining a primary set of notes from a small pool of extant student notes, with variant contributions from other note sets offered in footnotes when the meaning is differentiated or an alternative record of an expression changes the point being made. The particular note sets that have been used are cited in the opening footnote to each document.

Thus, although we have very little textual material from the seminars, we have extensive notes on the lectures.[79] His first lecture course, on the

[78.] An exception is the text for his course the following year, "Creation and Sin," from the winter semester of 1932–33, due to its later publication. See *Creation and Fall* (*DBWE* 3).

[79.] Bonhoeffer, however, valued his seminar work much more than the lectures that he gave. It is clear that he preferred seminar teaching and that this was his major focus. See his letter of February 28, 1932, to Sutz (1/39).

history of recent systematic theology, reflects Bonhoeffer's own theological development and cultural background as a backdrop for his foundational reorientation, his major "turn" (*Wende*), on the basis of the theology of Karl Barth. The lectures began with a general intellectual history before focusing quickly on a review of the dominant perspectives in his own theological training. Bonhoeffer surveyed the concept of religion in the nineteenth century, in the development of liberal theology, and with respect to major philosophical systems in this period, before turning to an extensive treatment of various understandings of the "essence" of Christianity. The work of Schleiermacher, the neo-Kantians, Friedrich Nietzsche, Rudolf Otto, Adolf von Harnack, Karl Holl, Wilhelm Herrmann, Franz Overbeck, and Reinhold Seeberg were engaged, as one would expect.[80] What is quite striking, however, is the prominence and influence of Ernst Troeltsch and Friedrich Naumann in an assessment of the enhanced importance of a synthesis of theology and ethics.[81] All were preparation for Bonhoeffer's emphasis on the turning point in the theology of Karl Barth, for in Barth the theological enterprise had shifted dramatically, "spelling God" in a new way. It was both a radical critique of religion and a reorientation of the starting point for Christianity:

> Barth opposes religion in the name of God. . . . [Religion is] always [in] danger of thinking it has God, knows about God, even humbly and modestly. Religion then becomes one area among others. . . . With this as starting point, the central issue becomes that of religion and culture. . . . Instead of beginning with religion, theology should begin by speaking from the word of God. . . . We should begin with God's own beginning set for us. Nobody knows that in advance, we must each receive it as told to us; God's word [is] the absolute petitio principii. Deus dixit—to accept this is the beginning of all genuine theological thinking, to allow space for the freedom of the living God.[82]

Bonhoeffer then moved to the Barthian accents on the centrality of Scripture, the location of theology within the church as the servant of the church, and the critical importance of preaching. He expounded on the

[80.] The absence of an extensive discussion of Heidegger and Bultmann is perhaps explained by Bonhoeffer's concurrent seminar focus on the relation of philosophy and Protestant theology.

[81.] Troeltsch and Naumann are also central in the summer-semester seminar on ethics.

[82.] 2/3, pp. 230–31.

dialectical nature of this orientation grounded in God's freedom and its consequences for more-traditional theological concerns, such as justification and sanctification. At the end of the lecture course, he returned to a related interest that was becoming more central: the "problem of ethics and obedience." One can clearly see through these notes the dramatic sense of divergence that Bonhoeffer represented, in both the turn to Barth and his own growing sense of differentiation from Barth.

In the summer semester, Bonhoeffer moved to his primary interests in ecclesiology and ethics, with lectures on the nature of the church and his seminar on the distinctive nature of a Christian ethic, both of which are completely consistent with his refined theological focus.

In his lectures on the church, there is evidence of continuity with his dissertation, *Sanctorum Communio* (*DBWE* 1), with its foundational assumptions of the church as the presence of Christ and its reality as a social community. In the early part of the course, he analyzed the problems of a "need" for the church and its place in the world. In seeking a preferred place, the church had lost its real place as the "place of God himself," as the place of the present Christ in the world.[83] But since this belied any particular place, the church had found itself to be peripheral in relation to the critical center of its world, and it is to this center, where the word is believed and obeyed, that God wills the true place of the church. In this first part of the course, Bonhoeffer also explored the most effective theological schema for an understanding of the church, in dogmatic theology and within theological systems, including contrasting Catholic and Protestant views, especially where the church is simultaneously presupposition and object of theology. Again, Barth's influence is pervasive, yet Bonhoeffer vigorously objected to an individualizing element in Barth (and in Tillich) that needs to be offset by the communal nature of the church (Luther's conception of the church-community).

The second part of this lecture course was preoccupied with the christological nature of the church. Bonhoeffer centered this understanding in the presupposition of the church as the form (*Gestalt*) of God's revelation, as the revelation of the wholeness of God, as opposed to the individually willed religious community. His explication first revolved around an extensive discussion of Adam and Christ, heavily reflective of material from *Sanctorum Communio*,[84] in the struggle between "humanity-in-Adam" as reflecting the alienated individual (all humanity falls in Adam [*Allein-Adam*]) and the new humanity of the church. The resurrection and

[83.] 2/9, p. 278.
[84.] *DBWE* 1:107–18.

salvific nature of Christ speaks to the church as community: "The new, whole humanity is set in Christ. Christ as new humanity, as church: the church is with Christ on the cross and resurrected with him."[85] The whole of humanity is here encompassed and so too the church as a community. Here, too, is Bonhoeffer's reintroduction of the concept of "vicarious representative action" (*Stellvertretung*), well known from *Sanctorum Communio,* as a central christological concept that grounds his theological anthropology in both the distinctive atoning work of Christ and the unifying nature of such action with the other. Hence, he strongly emphasized the communal sense that is integral to the nature of Christ. This incisive christological concept of "vicarious representative action" paved the way for a central affirmation in these lectures: "The church of today is the presence of Christ on earth,"[86] from which the church's foundation reflects three essential characteristics: "(1) Christ is himself the church-community; (2) Christ is [the] Lord of the church-community; (3) Christ is [the] brother in the church-community."[87]

In the lectures that followed, Bonhoeffer elaborated on several consequences and distinctions that follow from this ecclesiology, including its actualization through the Holy Spirit; the distinction between this concept of the church and religious community; the relation of Scripture, preaching, and confession within a notion of church-community; and the role of theology. He understood the relation of members within the church-community as a community of love that entails an interrelated "being-with-each-other" and "being-for-each-other."[88] Finally, he explored the "worldliness" of the church-community and its boundaries, with a concern to distinguish the church from the kingdom of God and especially from the state. In this last lecture, there is a clear reflection of the most difficult situation of the church in the midst of the Weimar crisis and the impending threat from the fascist right:

> Obedience to [the] state exists only when [the] state does not threaten the word. [The] battle about the boundary must then be fought out! The decision will be difficult in the development of our future state.

[85.] 2/9, p. 295.

[86.] 2/9, p. 304.

[87.] 2/9, p. 305.

[88.] 2/9, p. 319. Cf. Bonhoeffer's discussion of the structure and nature of the church in *Sanctorum Communio*: "(1) *Church-community and church member being structurally 'with-each-other' [Miteinander] as appointed by God* and (2) *the members' active 'being-for-each-other' [Füreinander] and the principle of vicarious representative action [Stellvertretung]*" (*DBWE* 1:178).

> [The] office of the state is neither Christian nor godless; the office must be carried out in a responsible and objective way. [The] existence as church depends upon whether its criticism can come from listening to the gospel alone. Criticism of the state [is] demanded where [it] threatens [the] word. The church can come [through] difficulties only when it sees to it that it stands or falls with the word of *Christus praesens* as its Lord alone.[89]

It was a prescient remark, expressing a conviction that would become central in the Church Struggle after 1933.

In these lectures, perhaps in the whole of Bonhoeffer's academic work in this period, there is not only continuity with his earlier writings but also clear reflections of his concurrent pastoral and ecumenical efforts. His entire theology in this period speaks to his concern for a church that is effectively engaged in the social and international issues that so permeated the time. The ethics seminar, to the degree that its content can be deciphered, indicates this strong correlation between Bonhoeffer's theological critique, reflected in the concurrent lectures on the nature of the church and the practical issues related to his work within the ecumenical movement and other discussions of this period, for example, those within the Working Group of Theologians and Economists.[90] Thus the document that has survived from the summer-semester ethics seminar should be understood within the context of such controversies as well as the urgencies of the international efforts toward peace and disarmament—as well as in the context of Bonhoeffer's frustration over the poverty of the church's relevance within such broad social crises.

The document related to the summer 1932 ethics seminar (2/10) has severe limitations but nonetheless a certain value. Only one set of student notes from this seminar is extant, and it is far from comprehensive. The German editors have rendered only a portion of those notes; their fragmentary nature means that it is not possible to represent it as a reconstruction of Bonhoeffer's comments and interpretations. Its value lies in the listing of basic ideas, definitions of key problems, and an indication of the seminar's plan.[91]

The first part of the seminar seems to have been a review of the most important ethical literature and took up the first half of the semester. Bon-

[89.] 2/9, p. 332.

[90.] See 1/28 and 1/33.

[91.] See 2/10, ed. note 1. The German editors have indicated that the actual course of the seminar differed from the noted plan. See 2/10, ed. note 23.

hoeffer's attention focused on the ethical imperative in God's will, in an examination of its principal sources and the distinctions that should be made between law and commandment. This first part concluded in a discussion of the relation of ethics and the gospel, eventually isolating three streams in Karl Barth, Paul Althaus, and Friedrich Gogarten, but on the whole its seems to have included a wide range of prominent theological voices.[92]

The second part of the seminar dealt with "the New Ethics on the basis of the gospel," focusing on three possible relationships of law and gospel. Not surprisingly, it was the interpretation centered in Barth that seems to have garnered the most attention, a view that starts not with an independent category of law but rather with revelation. This moved the discussion toward the imperative will of God in the context of preaching, in the proclamation of forgiveness and judgment, and the "promise of the Gospel . . . in a concrete situation."[93] The concrete nature of the gospel was, it seems, a highly developed end theme in the seminar. There is also an appended fragment (2/10.2) from a different set of notes, a single page apparently from the concluding session of the seminar, dealing with the matter of ethical certainty. Six avenues were explored, including the orders of creation and the Sermon on the Mount as law—all were discounted. In this apparently final discussion, Bonhoeffer critiqued the orders of creation with his countertheme of the "orders of preservation directed toward Christ."[94] The inherently christological nature of ethics reemerges, as the final sentence in the student notation states: "The present Christ is the place from which our action is always determined anew."[95]

### Part 3: The Sermons

By the time Bonhoeffer was ordained, he had some experience of preaching regularly in the Barcelona parish.[96] It was characteristic of Bonhoeffer, however, that he agonized over the writing and preaching of a good sermon and gave much thought to the challenge of making God's word

[92.] The seminar apparently had a rigorous reading list. It is apparent that Troeltsch and Naumann were once again prominent in this discussion; perhaps Bonhoeffer was building on conclusions evident in his winter-semester course on systematic theology. Karl Barth was central. The notes indicate that Otto Piper, Reinhold Seeberg, Albrecht Ritschl, and Luther were discussed in addition to Althaus and Gogarten.

[93.] 2/10.1, p. 339.

[94.] P. 341.

[95.] P. 341.

[96.] See *DBWE* 10, part 3.

concrete in a way that his congregation would understand: "How should I preach such things to these people? Who still believes that anymore? Invisibility is ruining us. . . . This madness of being constantly thrown back to the invisible God himself—no one can stand that anymore."[97]

He answered his own question at the beginning of his sermon on Luke 16:19–31: "One cannot understand and preach the gospel concretely [handgreiflich] enough. A real evangelical sermon must be like holding a pretty red apple in front of a child or a glass of cool water in front of a thirsty person and then asking: do you want it? We should be able to talk about matters of our faith in such a way that the hands reach out for it faster than we can fill them."[98] In sermon after sermon contained in *DBWE* 11 and subsequent volumes, Bonhoeffer sought to preach the gospel as concretely as possible. Later in the sermon on Luke 16 he asked: "Where do we get the incredible presumption to spiritualize these things that Christ saw and did very concretely?"[99]

For Bonhoeffer, concrete reality includes both the reality of God and the reality of the world. To ignore either the reality of God or the reality of the world leads to abstraction. Concrete reality is embodied in Jesus Christ, in his life, death, and resurrection. Certainly the Lutheran theology of the cross shaped his preaching. But for Bonhoeffer evangelical preaching was also shaped fully by the incarnation and the resurrection.

For Bonhoeffer, then, evangelical preaching was a descriptive task. The preacher seeks to describe the truth and the reality of God, and the reality of the world and our relationships to God and the world. Two of the sermons in this volume (3/7 and 3/13) focus on John 8:32: "The truth shall set you free." As he says in his sermon at the Technical College in summer 1932, "religion is primarily interested in only one thing, namely, to be true."[100] In the final sermon of this volume, a baptismal sermon, he expresses this in a different way: "To be awake means to be realistic, to live not in dreams and wishes but in the bright light of reality."[101]

The text for sermons 11 and 12 is Colossians 3:1–4. For Bonhoeffer, so much depended on our faith that we "have been raised with Christ" (Col. 3:1). He affirmed that God comes to the people of God in the world of the Bible, the world of Christ. The challenge for the preacher is to articulate how God came to the people of God in biblical times and then to articulate

[97.] Letter of October 18, 1931, to Helmut Rössler (1/14).

[98.] 3/10, p. 443.

[99.] 3/10, p. 446.

[100.] 3/7, p. 434.

[101.] 3/14, p. 474.

how that same God comes to us in our current situation in the world. In every sermon he sought to discern and describe as concretely as possible how God was coming to the community of faith before him. Discerning and describing God's coming to us in as concrete a way as possible is complicated by the reality that "our life is hidden with Christ in God" (Col. 3:3).

Bonhoeffer was also radically incarnational in his understanding of God's presence in our neighbor. For example, in his sermon on Psalm 63:4, he wrote: "If you want my loving kindness to stay with you, serve your neighbor, for in him God himself meets you."[102] In his sermon on Genesis 32:25–32, he explained that when dawn came, Jacob saw "the face of his brother not as an enemy, but 'like seeing the face of God.' He [saw] in his brother God himself and his love."[103]

Sermon 12 contains the famous quotation: "If that really is the way it must be, we should not be surprised if for our church, too, times will come again when the blood of the martyrs will be required. But this blood, if we really still have the courage and honor and faithfulness to shed it, will not be as innocent and untarnished as that of the first witnesses. On our blood would lie great guilt of our own: the guilt of the worthless slave, who is thrown into the outer darkness."[104] Bonhoeffer's preaching is prophetic not just because of the way it can challenge us but also because of the way he "saw" things before others did and was not afraid to articulate them.

As challenging as Bonhoeffer's preaching could be and as truthful as he could be about humankind's sin, he powerfully affirmed God's mercy and grace—an aspect of his preaching that is abundantly evident throughout the sermons in this volume. That mercy and grace would sustain Bonhoeffer in the years to come as he faced the challenges of life and ministry in Nazi Germany.

### Acknowledgments

This volume is dedicated to the memory of Hans Pfeifer, a pastor, teacher, and member of the editorial board of the German edition. In that capacity he served as the appointed liaison between the German and English editorial boards, and from the beginning was a thoughtful and astute consultant for our translations, including the present volume. He was a treasured colleague who will be deeply missed.

[102.] 3/1, p. 405.
[103.] 3/6, p. 432.
[104.] 3/12, p. 458.

We also wish to acknowledge the contributions of a number of colleagues and advisers, beginning with the gifted and patient translators who worked on it: Isabel Best, Nicolas Humphrey, Marion Pauck, and Anne Schmidt-Lange. Particular thanks here should go to Anne Schmidt-Lange for her extensive work on the translation of parts 1 and 3. The German editor of *DBW* 11, Eberhard Amelung, helped with early reviews of the manuscript and offered insightful advice. His unexpected death was a real loss, and we are grateful to his colleagues on the German DBW board, particularly Hans Pfeifer and Christiane Tietz, for stepping in to assist with the review of the remaining translations in parts 2 and 3. The complexity of the theological texts in part 2 required particular knowledge of Bonhoeffer's early works, *Sanctorum Communio* and *Act and Being*. Clifford Green was generous here with his time and expertise; and Michael DeJonge, author of the forthcoming *Bonhoeffer's Theological Formation: Berlin, Barth, and Protestant Theology*, served as a consultant for "The History of Twentieth-Century Systematic Theology" (2/3).

The editors also thank Ruth Tonkiss Cameron, archivist for Union Theological Seminary, New York, and the Burke Library Collections; Connie J. Meulemans, director of Interlibrary Loan Services, the Miriam and James Mulva Library, St. Norbert College; and Jutta Weber, deputy director of the Handschriftenabteilung at the Staatsbibliothek, Berlin, for their assistance with interlibrary loans and prompt and helpful replies about archival queries.

So much of the theological material in this volume is significant, in terms of both Bonhoeffer's own thought and the Church Struggle that would soon divide his church: the turning point marked by his encounter with Barth, the ecumenical material, the lectures that build on *Sanctorum Communio* and *Act and Being*, and the sermons. Yet, as in all the *DBWE* volumes, the present volume traces these theological developments hand in hand with the biographical story of this remarkable individual. In the afterword that concludes this volume, the German editor notes that "if a more profound turn in [Bonhoeffer's] life in the larger sense can be discerned, it took place during these years. . . . When in 1933 the National Socialist seduction and threat coerced many people into passive conformity, Bonhoeffer had already dealt with the enormous tensions within himself such that he was now able . . . to take the difficult path of the minority who rejected the National Socialist regime not just occasionally but fundamentally."

Michael B. Lukens, with Victoria J. Barnett and Mark S. Brocker
September 2011

# PART 1
# Letters and Documents

## 0. Assignment as Assistant Pastor in the City [Stadtvikar][1] 17:89

June 12, 1931

In accordance with § 1 of the Church Law of March 4, 1930, Concerning the Assignment of Candidates for the Ministry to Work as Assistant Pastors in the Church—K.G. u. V. Bl.[2] 1930, p. 113f.—your year of work as an assistant pastor begins on August 1, 1931.

We assign you, effective beginning on that date until further notice, to work as *assistant pastor in the city* [Stadtvikar] in Berlin[3] for the time being, doing whatever work is possible without ordination.

Please see General Superintendent Dr. Karow[4] in Berlin-Charlottenburg well before that date; he will decide about your further work as an assistant pastor in the church and give you the necessary instructions for your work.[5]

Also, please introduce yourself to the superintendent and the pastor to whose church district and congregation, respectively, you will be assigned and request the necessary instructions for your work.

A separate order will be issued concerning your ordination.

From the aforementioned date onward, your compensation will be 183.68 17:90
reichsmarks per month, in accordance with Number 13 of the Instructions for Implementation of the Church Law of May 10, 1930, concerning the Assignment of Candidates for the Ministry to Work as Assistant Pastors in the Church—as cited above, p. 115ff.—in conjunction with the Decree of December 1, 1930, of the Reich president concerning the safeguarding of the economy and finances. The congregation will also provide you with a place to live free of charge. In case we should determine that this is not possible, you will receive a cash grant for housing costs at the level set for Prussian civil servants of salary grade V according to the local classification for your official place of residence for this work,

[1.] *NL*, D 11(69), Personnel File of the Consistory; typewritten on official stationery with printed letterhead: "Evangelical Consistory of the Mark Brandenburg, Berlin Division, Berlin SW 68, Lindenstrasse 14"; file number: K. II No. 3707. Previously published in *DBW* 17:89–90 and *GS* 6:211–12. [A *Stadtvikar* (literally, "city vicar") would imply an urban ministry for the whole city, but in Bonhoeffer's case this was a misnomer for his actual position, which was *Stadtsynodalvikar*, i.e., vicar assigned to the city synod. He was assigned not only directly to an urban parish, but also to the larger Berlin city synod on special assignment, supervised by the superintendent. See below 1/2, ed. note 5—MBL.]

[2.] [*Kirchliches Gesetz- und Verordnungsblatt* (Gazette of church laws and regulations). —MBL]

[3.] Handwritten underlining, probably made at a later time.

[4.] Emil Karow.

[5.] Vertical line marking the section "further work as an assistant pastor . . . instructions for your work" and handwritten in the margin: "Have already spoken with Dr. Karow. D[iestel]."

namely, 72 reichsmarks per month (special category). Salary and, if applicable, cash housing grant will be paid by the congregation monthly in advance, with a receipt given.

We are to be informed immediately of the day on which you begin your work as assistant pastor.

For the office

Wolff[6]

13 **1. From Karl-Friedrich Bonhoeffer**[1]

June 25, 1931

Dear Dietrich,

When you arrive home, you should at least find a greeting from us waiting for you. It's really too bad that we won't be there when you get there. There's so much I would like to ask you about America, and I would really like to know what impressions you have brought back with you. Once you've told all about it and talked it all out, you won't feel like repeating it, so we can't hope to hear it all later.

But we really are counting on your coming to see us for a short visit before you go to Bonn.[2] It's really hardly out of your way,[3] as you yourself have to admit now, compared to the distances in America. So come, have a look at the boy,[4] who it seems to me looks a little like you sometimes. Probably that was the reason he pleased you in the photograph. And have a look at where we are living and what our life is like. If you have a little time, you also have to see the

[6.] Handwritten signature (Consistory Councillor Wolff); under this, stamped imprint: "Superintendent's Office Kölln-Land I, Telephone: Lichterfelde 476, Dahlemerstrasse 87, Berlin-Lichterfelde, *June 15, 1931*, Daily Log Number 2555 Diestel" (italicized portions entered by hand). At the bottom of the page, typed: "To the Candidate for Ministry Licentiate Dr. Bonhoeffer, currently in U.S.A."; added by hand: "Grunewald, Wangenheimstr. 20."

[1.] *NL*, C 3; handwritten.

[2.] On July 10, Bonhoeffer went to Bonn for three weeks to sit in on the lectures of Karl Barth and "to get in on as much as possible of the end of the semester at Bonn" (*DB-ER*, 175–76). [The summer semester at German universities usually runs from April to July.—MBL]

[3.] Karl-Friedrich Bonhoeffer was a professor of physical chemistry in Frankfurt.

[4.] Karl Walter Paul Bonhoeffer, born January 10, 1931; Bonhoeffer was supposed to baptize him in the summer after his return from America (see Bonhoeffer's letter of April 12, 1931, to Karl-Friedrich and Grete Bonhoeffer, *DBWE* 10:293), but since Bonhoeffer was not yet ordained at the time, this plan did not work out.

institute, which I've built up myself in the meantime. So it will be worth your while, even if it's only for twenty-four hours. But of course, the longer the better. I won't tell you much now about things here, simply because you should see everything. Besides, we'll call tomorrow night and hope to speak to you on the telephone then. We three are all doing fine (and I mean that).

Many greetings to the whole family gathered around you from your
Karl Friedrich

## 2. From Emil A. O. Karow[1] 14

Seefeld i. T.,[2] July 10, 1931

Dear Mr. Bonhoeffer:

I have just received your letter of the seventh of this month.[3] If I am not mistaken, the consistory has assigned you to me[4] from August 1 on as an assistant pastor in the city [Stadtvikar].[5] Your official duties will consist of providing pastoral care for the students at the Technical College.[6] It is a field where no work has been done up to now and to which you will devote your energy. It is my wish that you work in cooperation with Pastor Bronisch-Holtze,[7] whose main assignment is to work with students at the university. Yours will be a different kind of work than his. One reason is that your colleague is a parish pastor as well, has a regular preaching position, and has rooms in his parsonage and parish

[1.] *NL*, A 30,1 (10); handwritten; letterhead: "Dr. Karow—Generalsuperintendent—, Charlottenburg, Marchstrasse 4–5 II." Previously published with stylistic corrections in *GS* 6:212–13.

[2.] [Seefeld im Tirol, in the Tyrolean Alps on the German-Austrian border near Kufstein; Karow may have been on vacation there.—MBL]

[3.] Not extant.

[4.] Karow refers here to the Evangelical Consistory order of June 12, 1931 (see *NL*, D 11,69; previously published in *GS* 6:211; see also letter 1/0 above). The Evangelical Consistory was the highest administrative body of the provincial churches.

[5.] [The correct designation was "assistant pastor in the city synod" (*Stadtsynodalvikar*). This indicates that Bonhoeffer was assigned to a larger group of congregations that had joined together to form a city synod.—MBL]

[6.] [The Technical College (in the Charlottenburg section of Berlin) emphasized engineering and practical and applied sciences, whereas the university in Berlin (in Bonhoeffer's time the Friedrich Wilhelm University, renamed after the Second World War as the Alexander von Humboldt University) focused on academic programs oriented to the humanities, the arts, and social and natural science research.—MBL]

[7.] Ernst Oskar Paul Bronisch-Holtze had been pastor of the Church of the Trinity (Dreifaltigkeitskirche) since 1927 and at the same time student chaplain at the University (*DB-ER*, 223–25).

house that he can use. He has had experience in this field of work. I would like you to contact him and, when I am back in Berlin again, present a plan to me showing how you expect to approach your work.

Your work here will not actually begin until after the months of August and September.[8] I will be glad to give you vacation for these months.

With best wishes I remain yours truly
Karow

17:90 **2a. To Paul Lehmann**[1]

Bonn, July 10, [19]31.

My dear Paul,

this morning at 7 o'clock for the first time I heard K[arl] Barth. I could not help thinking all the time very strongly of you.[2] How much would you have enjoyed this lecture! But as a weak consolation: Barth is not giving
17:91 the lecture on:[3] Why does one study theology? Only "Prolegomena" and two Schleiermacher seminars. How nice it would be if you were here! I am completely alone. So—next year for sure! In the meantime live ἐν ἐλπίδι.[4] New York is nice, too, at least it was last year. I will send books from Berlin. Enjoy your vacation a lot! You both need it. Soon again and more. Kindest regards to you and your wife

Yours faithfully,
Dietrich Bonhoeffer

[8.] [The winter semester traditionally began in October and continued until February.—MBL]

[1.] Paul Lehmann Collection, Special Collections, Princeton Theological Seminary Library; handwritten picture postcard from Bonn (with a picture of the Drachenfels, a scene on the Rhine River); address: "Mr. Paul Lehmann c/o Pres[ident]. Lehmann, Elmhurst-Chicago, College of the Evang[elical] Synod, U.S.A."; postmark: "Bonn [illegible] July 1931." Originally published in *DBW* 17:90–91; Bonhoeffer began the letter in English [unedited here] but then changed to German.

[2.] On the friendship with Paul Lehmann, see *DB-ER*, 155–56.

[3.] [After this point, the letter continues in German.—MBL]

[4.] "In hope."

### 3. To His Parents[1] 15

My dear Parents,

Yesterday I came back by steamboat on the Rhine from Frankfurt, where I had visited Karl-Friedrich and Grete[2] for two days.

I have now met Barth[3] and got to know him quite well at a discussion evening at his house. I like him very much indeed and am also very impressed by his lectures. Everything is so well worked out and has not yet become mechanical to him. I think I shall gain a great deal from the time spent here.

The proofs[4] arrived. I've already sent them back.

I believe I had forgotten to tell you, from the evening at Siegmund-Schulze's,[5] that I'm supposed to travel to England as soon as August 14, which I want to do.[6] There's a kind of retreat there for students and academics 16

---

[1.] *NL*, A 28, 1(1); handwritten postcard from Bonn to Berlin, postmarked July 14, 1931. Partially reproduced in *GS* 6:203–4.

[2.] Margarete Bonhoeffer, née von Dohnanyi.

[3.] In the fall of 1930, Karl Barth had gone from Münster to Bonn, where he had been called to succeed Otto Ritschl in the Chair for Systematic Theology. In his lectures he covered the contents of the first volume of his *Church Dogmatics*; the title of the seminar was "Introduction to Schleiermacher's Doctrine of Faith [*Glaubenslehre*]"; [at the same time] the seminar discussion group was working through Schleiermacher's *Brief Outline on Theology as a Field of Study* (information from Dr. Klara Stoevesandt, Karl-Barth-Archiv, Basel, May 5, 1988). "A new feature of this series of lectures was that Barth opened each of them with a short devotion in which he read aloud the passage for the day from the Community of Brethren Bible readings* and led the students in a chorale." *"(The Herrnhut [Moravian] brethren publish annually a book of texts [*Losungen*] with Old and New Testament sayings for each day of the year, which then, as now, was widely used by individuals and in churches)" (cited from Busch, *Karl Barth*, 214).

[4.] Refers to the proofs of Bonhoeffer's postdoctoral dissertation, *Act and Being* (*DBWE* 2). The [original edition of the] book appeared in print in September 1931, published by Bertelsmann Verlag, Gütersloh; see *DB-ER*, 136. [At German universities it is necessary to write a second, postdoctoral thesis (*Habilitationsschrift*) and discuss it publicly in order to become a university lecturer (*Privatdozent*).—MBL]

[5.] Correction: "Siegmund-Schultze." Friedrich Siegmund-Schultze, one of the earliest proponents of the ecumenical idea and cofounder of the International Fellowship of Reconciliation, was International Secretary of the World Alliance for Promoting International Friendship through the Churches and served in this capacity as one of the main organizers of the conferences in Cambridge.

[6.] The reference here is to the following conferences: 1. The student conferences in St. Leonards and Westcliff on Sea, England, August 14–27, 1931; 2. the Youth Conference of the International Section of the World Alliance for Promoting International Friendship through the Churches, August 29–31, 1931, in Cambridge [England]; and 3. the main conference of the World Alliance for Promoting International Friendship through

of all nationalities, and those who are taking part at Cambridge[7] can participate in the retreat for five m[arks] a day. Could you please be so good as to telephone Diestel[8] and ask him how I can register there. Could you do that for me then? The sixty m[arks] must, I believe, be sent at the same time and the registration should be sent in as soon as possible.

Many thanks! Many greetings from your grateful

Dietrich

Karl Friedrich and Grete were very cheerful. So was the Rhine.

### 4. To Erwin Sutz[1]

Dear Mr. Sutz,

I'm sitting here in the park in front of the university. Barth lectured at seven this morning. I spoke with him briefly. Tonight there is an evening of discussion at his house with people from Maria Laach.[2] I'm looking forward
17 to that very much. In spite of the extensive preparation you gave me, some things in the lecture course still surprised me. By the way, he looks frightfully unwell. Does he always look that way? He is *unfortunately* not lecturing

---

the Churches, September 1–5, 1931, in Cambridge. The latter gave Bonhoeffer the decisive impetus toward ecumenical work (*DB-ER*, 189–94).

[7.] Concerning the conference of the International Section of the World Alliance for Promoting International Friendship through the Churches in Cambridge, September 1–5, 1931, see 2/1 below.

[8.] Max Diestel, superintendent of the church district Kölln 1 [in Berlin], to which the Bonhoeffer family belonged, mentored Bonhoeffer on his way into the church and introduced him to ecumenical work (see *DB-ER*, 91, and 1/10 below). In 1931, as chairman of the German Section of the World Alliance for Promoting International Friendship through the Churches, he helped put together the German delegation for the conferences mentioned above. Concerning the difficulties Diestel had in getting permission from the Church Federation Office for Bonhoeffer to take part in the conference, see *DBWE* 10:303–4, especially ed. note 2.

[1.] *NL*, A 29,4(2) (a); handwritten picture postcard from Bonn, postmarked July 15, 1931; see also *NL*, 29,4(2) (b); later typewritten transcription by Eberhard Bethge. Partially reproduced in *GS* 1:17–18. Bonhoeffer had gotten to know Erwin Sutz in 1930–31 at Union Theological Seminary in New York (see *DBWE* 10:256–57 and *DB-ER*, 152–53). In 1931–32, Sutz was doing his pastoral internship in Pratteln near Zürich. He had arranged for Bonhoeffer to become personally acquainted with Karl Barth and Emil Brunner and later, during the war, became an important contact for Bonhoeffer.

[2.] The reference is to Maria Laach, an abbey on the Laacher See, founded in 1093 by Heinrich II, Count Palatine of Rhenish Franconia, and since 1892 an abbey of the Benedictines, with whom Barth had a good relationship.

on the encyclopedia![3] I am completely alone here and am killing time for the rest of the day quite unproductively. Too bad you are not here anymore. At least [it was] good that you were in New York. I thank you for the card.[4] I would like to come and visit you. But on August 15 I will be sent to England for three weeks to the Cambridge conference.[5] After our time in America, what should we relate about the friendship work done by the churches? At least maybe not nonsense like what Hirsch [wrote] recently in *Theologische Blätter.*[6] Let me hear from you.

Sincere greetings from
Your Dietrich Bonhoeffer

**5. To Erwin Sutz**[1]

July 24, 1931

Dear Mr. Sutz,

This is the precursor of a letter that I intend to put on paper for you during the next two hours. This one will go along with your faithful Hans 18
Fischer,[2] with whom, after Barth's lecture course, I have just taken a long

[3.] Barth had indeed intended to lecture on a theological "encyclopedia" in the summer semester of 1931. He became ill with diphtheria of the ear, however, in February 1931, and this illness lasted for weeks, which kept him from carrying out this plan (information from Eberhard Busch, Göttingen, May 9, 1988; see also Busch, *Karl Barth*, 209).

[4.] Not extant.

[5.] Annual Conference of the World Alliance for Promoting International Friendship through the Churches, September 1–5, 1931.

[6.] In May [1931], Paul Althaus and Emanuel Hirsch had sent a "statement" on the topic of "The Protestant Church and International Understanding [*Völkerverständigung*]" to selected journals. This statement appeared in *Theologische Blätter*, among other publications. To this statement Karl Ludwig Schmidt, editor of *Theologische Blätter*, wrote: "Its content can be summarized in the sentence: 'German theologians, when they speak responsibly to theologians of the nations [*Völker*] who are our enemies, must under all circumstances and as a *conditio sine qua non* [absolutely essential condition] of all further understanding and cooperation, bring into the discussion a condemnation of the anti-German politics practiced by these nations since 1914'" (*Theologische Blätter* 10 [1931]:178–79). The statement set off a bitter discussion (see *DB-ER*, 195). Althaus, coauthor of the statement, is conspicuously not mentioned in Bonhoeffer's postcard.

[1.] *NL*, A 29,4(3); handwritten postcard from Bonn, postmarked July 27, 1931. Partially reproduced in *GS* 1:18.

[2.] Hans Fischer, student of theology and in 1931 a student of Karl Barth in Bonn.

theological morning walk along the Rhine. We both, I believe, enjoyed it very much.

Sincere greetings from

Your
Dietrich Bonhoeffer[3]

**6. To Erwin Sutz**[1]

July 24, 1931, Bonn

Dear Mr. Sutz,

Hans Fischer has just left. I have just read again the last two pages of Barth's *Ethics II*[2] from a notebook, and now I want to write. The letter you told me you were sending me about your trip has not reached me yet. When I found your other letter at home—when I came back from a trip to Maria Laach—I was so happy that I would have liked to have answered it immediately, but I wanted to wait for the one you had sent before it. Now it is not here yet, and I will write anyway. You yourself can imagine that I have often wished you were here, sometimes especially strongly, so that in some situations within the circle of the initiated disciples, I, as one yet uninitiated, could have a good laugh. I don't dare do that here really, just a little shy laugh (that sounds unlikely, doesn't it?), but I, with my theological *bas-*
19 *tard origins,*[3] have little reason to laugh, as I note again here very clearly. Here they have a very finely honed sense for recognizing thoroughbreds. No *Negro* can pass "for white."[4] His fingernails and the soles of his feet

[3.] Also on the postcard is the following greeting from Hans Fischer to Sutz: "Erwin, I have said yes to the decision, which has been 'stalking through our house,' and I am happy that I am here. This noon I'll be with Barth—the walk was good! It would be excellent if you were still here. You would meet the American from Marburg here." The "American from Marburg" could not be identified.

[1.] *NL,* A 29, 4(4) (a); handwritten; *NL,* A 29, 4(4) (b); later typewritten transcription by Eberhard Bethge; the postscript of this letter was accidentally listed as a separate document under the same file number: *NL,* A 29, 4(4). Partially reproduced in *GS* 1:18–22.

[2.] Karl Barth had held this lecture in Münster in the winter semester 1928–29 and repeated it in the winter semester 1930–31 in Bonn (see Karl Barth, *Ethik II,* VII).

[3.] Bonhoeffer is referring here to his studies in the Department of Theology in Berlin, in which liberal theology and its methodology played a dominant role.

[4.] ["For white" in English.—MBL]

are inspected.[5] I am still being shown the hospitality due the unknown foreigner.

Now everything is very much or completely different when it comes to *Karl Barth* himself. You can breathe freely. You are no longer afraid you will die for lack of oxygen in the rarefied atmosphere. I have, I believe, seldom regretted not having done something in my theological past as much as I now regret that I did not go to hear Barth sooner. Now it is only three weeks that I can be here, lectures—Oh, excuse me. I just remembered that it is so hard for you to read my German script handwriting. But I don't want to write all of that again—otherwise I won't write it—so, I hope it will be better now.

The seminar, the Societät,[6] an open-house evening, and now yesterday a couple of hours for lunch at Barth's. There you can really hear and see something. There's no point in my writing to you about something that you have seen much better for yourself. But it is important and surprising in the nicest way to see how Barth still stands beyond his books. There is an openness, a willingness to listen to a critical comment directed to the topic at hand, and with this such concentration and with a vehement insistence on the topic at hand, for the sake of which he can speak proudly or humbly, dogmatically or with utter uncertainty, in a way that is certainly not intended primarily to advance his own theology. It is becoming easier and easier for me to understand why it is unbelievably difficult to grasp Barth through the literature. I am impressed by his discussion even more than by his writing and lectures. He is really fully present. I have never seen anything like it nor thought it possible.

My visit at his home yesterday, about which I was really somewhat hesi- 20
tant, especially because I knew how busy he is at the moment, was like you had told me when you described such occasions. At first we spoke—of course—about you. Barth, while speaking very warmly of you, said he had

[5.] On Bonhoeffer's participation in Karl Barth's seminar, see Maechler, *Ein Christ in den Wirren des 20. Jahrhunderts*, 24. "I first met him at an open house evening at Karl Barth's. We had been discussing the content of each of his [Barth's] lectures on dogmatics. A blond, Germanic-looking man stood up and said, 'There is a saying from Luther: For God the curse of a godless man can be more pleasing than the Hallelujah of the pious!' Barth jumped up from his chair: 'That's great! Where is that quotation and who in the world are you?'" [See also *DB-ER*, 176 and 961, ed. note 10.]

[6.] [The *Societät* was a separate small discussion group for advanced undergraduates, graduate students, and doctoral candidates. Often it centered on a topic independent of the lecture series and traditionally had a more intense and specialized thematic or textual focus.—MBL]

always thought you were a somewhat unreliable character,[7] that after having looked at things long enough from the inside out, you were tempted to suddenly look at them again from the vantage point of Mount Zürich.[8] Now you're familiar with this criticism yourself, and that's exactly it, of course. I'm only writing to you about it because Barth probably expects that I will, and it may possibly be of interest to you again—as a "review."

We got to the ethical problem then very quickly and had a long discussion. He did not want to concede to me what I had expected he would have to. He said there were, besides the one great light in the night, many other little lights, so-called relative ethical criteria, although he could not make their meaning, justification [Recht], and nature understandable to me. There was only the simple referral to the Bible. At the end, he said he thought I was making grace into a principle and was bludgeoning everything else to death with it. Naturally, I disagree with him on the first point and would like to know why all the rest should *not* be bludgeoned to death. If you had been there, we would have had a third battlefront, and maybe some things would have become even clearer. But I was very happy to be able to hear Barth's opinion in detail. We then talked about many other things. He urged me to write the little paper I probably already told you about on the differentiation from Catholicism in contemporary theology.[9] Many a delightful and funny bon mot came out in the course of the conversation, but it would be too stupid to repeat them here. Finally, I made the hard decision to leave, and I went home. This is really someone from whom one could learn something, and there one sits in poor, desolate Berlin and
21 is discouraged because there is no one there from whom one can learn theology and some other useful things along with it. But it is true that, ultimately, that's not really what makes the most difference, and one shouldn't ask for too much. Tonight I've been invited to join a group of Barth's closest

[7.] [This is wordplay on the phrase *unsicherer Kantonist*, literally meaning "unreliable character" and often in Germany referring to people whose attitudes and ideas may be inconsistent, but here referring to Sutz's origin in Switzerland as a resident of a *Kanton* ("canton," or Swiss province).—MBL]

[8.] This is a reference to Sutz's orientation toward Emil Brunner, who taught in Zürich. Brunner was a professor of systematics and practical theology there from 1924 to 1953. [There were times of gracious but nonetheless intense controversy and competition between Barth and Brunner.—MBL]

[9.] As far as we know, this paper was never written, but see Bonhoeffer's doctoral examination paper in the field of dogmatics, written in answer to the question: "To what extent is the question of certainty of personal salvation the decisive difference between Catholicism and Protestantism?" See *DBWE* 9:441–44, and Bonhoeffer's paper on "The Catholic Church" for the "Thursday Circle" (*DBWE* 9:525–29).

students for the evening, and after that is the small discussion group [Societät].[10] It's all over next Tuesday. I won't want to go home. This morning after the lecture course, I was speaking with Elmer Arndt[11]—who has been here for a week and leaves again tomorrow and naturally has not understood very much—when suddenly your friend Fischer came up to me and said hello. Right then we took a very nice walk together. He really understands a lot and is very Barthian. In any case, we will be seeing each other again soon in Berlin. This noon he is at Barth's. Barth had kindly told me he was here and also told him I was here.

In the course of the day (it is already noon now), your letter[12] finally did arrive after all. By mistake it had been left lying at my home. Thank you very much. I am amazed that you could decide to fly home despite your hay fever. Was it at least nice? And I find it right and understandable that you didn't want to leave right away on another trip, since you also have to give your mother support and can take sunbaths in the meadow with Brunner and *filiis*,[13] and since, after all, any trip with a firm destination usually turns out differently than you think beforehand. I would have liked to have come to Zürich, or even to your mountains, but the Emergency Decree concerning Foreign Travel[14] makes it not only financially impossible but also makes one a little hesitant about activities of that sort. Why don't you come to Berlin? There are no emergency decrees yet in your country! I have probably already written that I am supposed to go to Cambridge. But I hope I can take a pass on having to talk about things I know nothing about.

By the way, at the moment I am studying up energetically on economics
—you are partly responsible for that—and am reading several really inter- 22
esting and simple books about it.

The church has given me two more months of vacation. On October 1, I will be the pastor for the students at the Technical College.[15]

Now I must close. I must go to meet the students. Take care. I have understood a lot about you better since I have gotten to know Barth. Enjoy your mountains and the solitude that is not allowed me—I beg you, that

[10.] [See ed. note 6 above.—MBL]

[11.] Elmer Jakob Frederick Arndt was a "resident fellow" [and associate of Bonhoeffer] at Union Theological Seminary in New York in 1930–31.

[12.] Not extant.

[13.] "With Brunner and sons."

[14.] The Emergency Decree concerning Foreign Travel of July 18, 1931, referred to here, required a payment of one hundred reichsmarks for trips to foreign countries.

[15.] Berlin/Charlottenburg.

is nothing to be envied—neither is the other, especially the dullness, and that least of all.

Sincere greetings from your faithful
Dietrich Bonhoeffer

In reading over this letter again now, I have some doubts about whether I may possibly not have given a really fair portrayal of Barth's students. After all, they are at least people who are really interested and who have some understanding and try to conceal their "pride of knowledge." I have spent some pleasant hours with them. Yesterday, at the last open-house evening, they put on a play that Barth had written at the age of fifteen in the style of Schiller.[16]

### 7. To His Parents[1]

July 27, 1931, Bonn

My dear Parents,

Since Barth finishes his lectures tomorrow, I want to come home on Wednes-
23 day. I don't know the exact train yet [ . . . ][2] toward evening in any case. Yesterday I came back from Düsseldorf,[3] where it was very nice. I have to go to the seminar. That's why this is so brief. I'll see you day after tomorrow.

Many greetings from your
Dietrich

The proofs[4] came and have been sent on.

[16.] This was a play titled *Leonardo Montenuova oder Freiheit und Liebe* (Leonardo Montenuova or freedom and love), which Barth had written in 1901. Helmut Gollwitzer was responsible for this performance of the play. (See Busch, *Karl Barth*, 28.)

[1.] *NL*, Anh. A 14(10); handwritten transcription by Karl-Friedrich Bonhoeffer of a postcard. Original formerly owned by the Leichtle family in Germany, now in the possession of Colin Fraser, Ontario, Canada. See also *NL*, A 28,1(2); typewritten transcription. Partially reproduced in *GS* 6:204.

[2.] Illegible.

[3.] Gertrud Wedell, Bonhoeffer's cousin, lived in Düsseldorf.

[4.] The proofs of Bonhoeffer's postdoctoral dissertation, *Act and Being* (*DBWE* 2).

## 8. From the Evangelical Consistory of the Mark Brandenburg[1]

Berlin SW 68, August 17, 1931

Reminder

The order of June 12, 1931—K. II No. 3707—regarding the beginning of work as an assistant pastor,[2] requires a response by September 1, 1931.

If this deadline cannot be met, the reasons must be given.

On behalf of the consistory:
Schlabritzky

## 8a. To Paul Lehmann[1] 17:91

August 23, [19]31

My dear Paul,[2]

Many thanks for your kind letter. After so many weeks, I was very glad to hear from you and your wife. I hope, too, that both of you have recovered from your attacks of toothache and can really take advantage of the last weeks of your vacation to get a lot of extra sleep and be lazy in preparation for the coming strenuous winter. I will soon be leaving now for Cambridge[3] and have been loaded down with so much work up to now. I wrote a catechism together with a friend.[4] When it is printed, you will get it.[5]—

---

[1.] *NL*, A 30,1(9); typewritten document.

[2.] See the order of June 12, 1931, from the superintendent's office regarding Bonhoeffer's assignment as assistant pastor in the city: *NL*, A 30,1(7) and *NL*, D 11,69. See letter 1/0 above.

[1.] Paul Lehmann Collection, Special Collections, Princeton Theological Seminary Library; handwritten letter, from Berlin. Previously published in *Evangelische Theologie* 56 (1996): 466–68, and in *DBW* 17:91–94. The editorial notes here were written by Hans Pfeifer.

[2.] [The salutation is in English; Bonhoeffer alternates between English and German in the original. Most of the letter, including irregularities and errors, is in Bonhoeffer's original English.—MBL]

[3.] To attend the conference of the Youth Commission of the International Section of the World Alliance for Promoting International Friendship through the Churches (August 29–31, 1931) and, immediately following, the Conference of the World Alliance for Promoting International Friendship through the Churches (September 1–5, 1931) in Cambridge, England. See 2/1 and p. 494.

[4.] The friend is Franz Hildebrandt. The catechism is titled "Glaubst du, so hast du" (As you believe, so you receive). See 2/7. [Bonhoeffer and Hildebrandt used the German title, "Glaubst du, so hast du," in reference to a renowned passage on the priority of faith alone in Luther's treatise "On the Freedom of the Christian" (*LW* 31:348–49).—MBL]

[5.] [The letter continues here in English.—MBL]

The time at Bonn[6] was marvellous not only from the theological point of
17:92 view but also or perhaps even more by the fact that I learned to know Barth personally. He really is a theologian at home as well as in the classroom. His whole thinking swings around one point, and whosoever is willing to keep his eyes straight on this point is considered by Barth a good theologian no matter how ever he tries to formulate his ideas and views. I do not have to tell you that this point is the cross and the resurrection of Christ, truly a strange thing for a modern and intelligent man to concentrate his thoughts and his whole life to. But when you see Barth you know at once—even if [you] come entirely from outside—that there is something worthwhile to risk one's life for. He is personally very modest, he knows how to listen to other people and he has a splendid humor. I had some long discussions with him concerning the ethical problem—which we were discussing for so many times with Sutz at Union[7] and Elmhurst![8]—and I learned to admire his tremendous power of concentration to the one main thing in theology. He is not wordcatcher [*sic*] and there is no strife about words, he does not care very much for his own formulation, but what he wants solely is never to loose [*sic*] the only possible and real ground of theology. He is himself not yet quite clear about many important ethical problems and he confesses that frankly. It certainly was a pity that you were not there at that time. I thought of you many a time. But since the main lecture was not given you can be consoled.[9]—At the time I was [at] Bonn, the situation in Germany became more and more endangered,[10] as you know very well. For some days we did not believe anymore that it would be possible to keep down the fascists and communists; there were many revolts in the cities and as a matter of fact it is almost a miracle that in those days Germany did not turn [into] a battlefield. Now after the election[11] the whole mood is a little

---

[6.] See the postcard of July 10, 1931. See 1/2a, and *DB-ER*, 175–76.

[7.] Union Theological Seminary, New York.

[8.] The friends had stopped over in Elmhurst [Illinois, accompanied to that point by Paul Lehman, whose parents lived in Elmhurst—MBL] on a trip to Mexico. See *DB-ER*, 152.

[9.] [See 1/4, ed. note 3.—MBL]

[10.] The world economic crisis that began on "Black Friday," October 25, 1929, was now affecting Germany as well. The respected Darmstädter and Nationalbank closed its customer windows on July 13, 1931. Following this, there was a general bank crash in Germany.

[11.] This may refer to a referendum on August 9, 1931, on dissolving the Prussian [regional] parliament. It did not receive a majority of votes.

more quiet than before, but probably only for a short time. The prospects for the winter are perfectly horrible, we count on more than 7 millions [*sic*] 17:93 unemployed people! The taxes are raised from month to month, the misery is frightful; and the most terrible thing of all is the hopelessness of this situation. The Hoover plan was "a drop in the bucket."[12] And at the same time Germany is near the complete breakdown[13] our Western neighbour is prospering and his policy remains selfish and brutal.[14] You certainly know about the new idea of Danubian monarchy[15]—against Germany. It is hardly credible that only anxiety causes such procedure.[16] We know how much we would need the church, especially during the next winter, but what is its message and who will listen to it? It is awful to be almost damned to inactivity!

Now about your books. I can get Ritschl: Rechtfertigung . . . 3rd edition[17] for thirty-nine marks, maybe even less. Do you want it? Barth's Römerbrief[18] will be sent to you as a gift from me, Wort Gottes und Theologie[19] as well. Dogmatik[20] costs 14. Do you want it? "Zwischen den Zeiten"[21] fifteen a year. I'll be getting other copies of Ritschl offered to me. Just write me approximately how much you want to spend. I'll send it then right away. The prices at the bookstore[22] are too high! Now one

---

[12.] On July 6, 1931, the so-called Hoover moratorium was passed. In it, the United States convinced France in particular, despite strong opposition, to agree to suspension of payment of German war reparations to the Allies for one year. [The phrase in the original letter is in German: "drop on a hot stone" (*ein Tropfen auf den heissen Stein*).—MBL]

[13.] There were continuing raises in bank rates by up to 15 percent, closing of trading on the stock market, and so on.

[14.] Regarding the anxiety and anger over France's policies, see the comments by Ernst Jansen in 1931 and Johannes Schattenmann in 1932, in Alston and Welker, "Dietrich Bonhoeffer," 467–68n5.

[15.] In the fall of 1931 and spring of 1932, French prime minister Tardieu pursued a plan toward the political and economic unification of the Danube region under French leadership.

[16.] Here the original letter continues in German.

[17.] The reference is to Ritschl, *Christian Doctrine of Justification and Reconciliation.*

[18.] Barth, *Epistle to the Romans.* [The reference is to the 2nd edition from 1922. —MBL]

[19.] Barth, *Word of God and the Word of Man.*

[20.] *Die Lehre vom Wort Gottes: Prolegomena zur christlichen Dogmatik.*

[21.] The journal *Zwischen den Zeiten* (Between the times), published by Karl Barth, Friedrich Gogarten, and Eduard Thurneysen from 1923 to 1933.

[22.] [The original text has "bookstore" in English, probably referring to the bookstore at Union Theological Seminary, New York.—MBL]

more request. Could you send me a commemorative stamp[23] for seven,
17:94 nine, eleven, thirteen cents (unused). I will then deduct that amount from what you owe for the books. It is for a friend of mine. If you could take a few regular American stamps (used!) from your letters and send them to me, for a little cousin[24] of mine, I would be grateful. Now enough for today.[25]

Give my greetings to your wife. I am thinking often of both of you and of the great time I could have with you in your New York home.[26] Let me thank you therefore once more.

I remain as ever Yours very affectionately
Dietrich Bonhoeffer

**9. To Paul Althaus**[1]

Berlin-Grunewald, September 16, 1931

Dear Professor Althaus:[2]

I take the liberty of sending you by the same mail a copy of the book that has just been published and which was published due in large part to your
24 kind recommendations.[3] I would like to send you my sincere thanks again today for your help and for the great kindness with which you showed support for me last winter. In the current situation, we younger ones are almost entirely dependent on such help and are deeply grateful when it is offered to us.

[23.] In original text "commemorative stamp" in English. This is a reference to stamps in the "American Presidents" series: seven cents, McKinley; nine cents, Jefferson; eleven cents, Rutherford Hayes; and thirteen cents, Harrison. These were not newly issued but were "reprints" (information from Clifford Green).

[24.] Walter von Hase, a considerably younger brother of Hans Christoph von Hase. He was killed in the war.

[25.] [Here the original text continues in English.—MBL]

[26.] See the letter of November 5, 1931, 1/16a.

[1.] *NL*, Anh. A 10, 2 (a); photocopy of the handwritten letter. Some missing parts along the right margin had to be added. See also *NL*, Anh. A 10, 2 (b); later typewritten transcription.

[2.] [Bonhoeffer uses the formal mode of address: "Highly esteemed Professor" (*Hochverehrter Herr Professor*).—MBL]

[3.] The reference is to Bonhoeffer's postdoctoral dissertation, *Act and Being* (*DBWE* 2). In a very favorable review, Paul Althaus had recommended publication of the book in the series Beiträge zur Förderung christlicher Theologie (Contributions to the advancement of Christian theology). See *DB-ER*, 136.

I also take the liberty of enclosing the book *Sanctorum Communio*, which was submitted in 1927 as the dissertation for the Licentiate but did not appear in print until 1930.[4] Its characteristics as the work of a novice are obvious to me today, but I am sending it along anyway. For me there is a connection between the essence and the factual content of the two works, which are both basically about nothing other than the church.

In sincere admiration and gratitude I remain yours respectfully
Dietrich Bonhoeffer

### 9a. Bonhoeffer Inscription at Union Theological Seminary[1] Dietrich Bonhoeffer to Franz Hildebrandt,[2] in *Act and Being*, Berlin, after mid-September 1931[3]

"And now a catechism is supposed to come out of this?!"[4]

---

[4.] [*Sanctorum Communio: A Theological Study of the Sociology of the Church* (*DBWE* 1), which was Bonhoeffer's doctoral dissertation.—MBL]

[1.] Edited by Clifford Green. First published in *Dietrich Bonhoeffer Jahrbuch* 4:15. See also the article in the same volume, "Commentary: Three Bonhoeffer Inscriptions at Union Theological Seminary Library."

[2.] Inscription in ink written at the top of the front cover of the 1st edition of *Akt und Sein*. The Burke Library Archive at Union Theological Seminary, New York, purchased the volume in 2008 from the daughter of Franz Hildebrandt, Esther Shreeve.

[3.] *Akt und Sein* was published by Bertelsmann-Verlag, Gütersloh, in September 1931. On September 16, Bonhoeffer mailed a copy to Paul Althaus, who had recommended the volume to Adolf Schlatter and Wilhelm Lütgert, general editors of the series Beiträge zur Förderung christlicher Theologie. See the cover letter (1/9) in this volume. As Holger Roggelin discovered in 2005, Lütgert had written the report recommending to the faculty the acceptance of the *Habilitationsschrift* (cf. *DBWE* 10:210–14). (In the same package Bonhoeffer also included a copy of *Sanctorum Communio*, which had been published in 1930.)

[4.] [The German inscription reads: "Und daraus soll nun ein Katechismus werden?!"—VB] After his return from the year at Union Theological Seminary, Bonhoeffer had written a catechism together with Franz Hildebrandt in the summer of 1931; see document 2/7 in this volume. For a similar sentiment about *Akt und Sein*, see Bonhoeffer's letter of February 28, 1932, to Erwin Sutz, his Swiss friend from Union Seminary days (1/39).

## 10. From Wilhelm Stählin to the German Section of the World Alliance for Promoting International Friendship through the Churches[1]

Münster i[n] W[estphalia], September 19, 1931

Dear Mr. Petrick,[2]

In Cambridge[3] we did not have time to talk about the meeting that is planned for the Provisional Bureau[4] for Ecumenical Youth Work. I am confident in the hope that a way can be found to continue the work of this administrative office, which is not very extensive, together with an office of the German Section of the World Alliance for Promoting International Friendship through the Churches,[5] even after the office you have headed on Georgenstrasse is closed on October 1 as a result of the difficulties in the Inner Mission and the difficult situation in these times in general.[6] I have already spoken with Superintendent

[1.] LKA Nuremberg, XVIII: Nachlaß Stählin; carbon copy; one carbon copy, which has not been preserved, went to Bonhoeffer.

[2.] Herbert Petrick held a full-time position as secretary of the Administrative Office of the German Section of the World Alliance for Promoting International Friendship through the Churches until September 30, 1931, and was Bonhoeffer's predecessor as secretary of the Provisional Bureau for Ecumenical Youth Work (*DB-ER*, 192–93 and 239). In October 1931, he was relieved of his position due to the financial difficulties of the German Section of the World Alliance for Promoting International Friendship through the Churches. See the letter of November 5, 1931, from Schreiber to Schönfeld, EZA 623/77.

[3.] Wilhelm Stählin had been in Cambridge as the representative of the International Committee of the International Section and of the Council of the German Section of the World Alliance for Promoting International Friendship through the Churches, with Herbert Petrick as a representative of the Youth Delegation of the German Section of the World Alliance for Promoting International Friendship through the Churches (see the list of participants in *Handbook of the Eighth International Conference*, 19 and 21).

[4.] The Provisional Bureau for Ecumenical Youth Work (Mittelstelle für ökumenische Jugendarbeit) was founded at Stählin's initiative on April 24, 1931. It served as an informal office coordinating the youth work of church organizations and the youth organizations of the German Reich (see the organizational diagram, appendix 4, p. 505). In September 1931, Bonhoeffer took over from Petrick the work as secretary of the Provisional Bureau. Bonhoeffer was supposed to intensify contacts with the Church Federation Office and the Administrative Office of the German Section of the World Alliance for Promoting International Friendship in Berlin. [Cf. also *DBWE* 12:56, ed. note 1.—MBL]

[5.] The reference here is to the World Alliance for Promoting International Friendship through the Churches, which was founded in 1914 and had set itself the task of working through the churches, independent of any denominational questions, toward the goal of maintaining world peace. See the organizational diagrams in appendix 4.

[6.] Because of financial difficulties, the German Section of the World Alliance for Promoting International Friendship through the Churches had closed its office at

Diestel[7] in Cambridge about steps that should be taken. Also, the German youth representative elected in Cambridge, Licentiate Bonhoeffer, has kindly agreed to help Superintendent Diestel with the work for the Provisional Bureau for Ecumenical Youth Work. So I am confident in the hope that the concerns you mentioned in Cambridge, that this work might have to stop when the administrative office is closed, are unfounded.

You will probably be continuing as the head of the administrative office on Georgenstrasse until the first of October, and so I assume that you will still be doing the planning for the conference of the Provisional Bureau scheduled for October. But just in case, I am sending a copy of this letter to Licentiate Bonhoeffer and would ask you two to work it out with each other. It is very important to me that under all circumstances the continuation of this work is assured. That is why I think it is important that Mr. Bonhoeffer should be informed about the discussions that have taken place up to now.

The result of the discussions with Dr. Stange[8] is that Tuesday, October 20, is a possible date for the conference of the Provisional Bureau.[9] We will need 26
to meet longer this time, if we want to cover everything that is planned for this meeting. For this reason, I suggest that we meet at ten o'clock in the morning and plan to meet, with a short break, until about five or six p.m. Please inquire at the Church Federation Office whether we can have the conference room in the Church Federation Office for that day. If that request meets with any difficulties, we could, as Dr. Stange has suggested, go to the YMCA House, Wilhelmstrasse 34. The house is, admittedly, not very nice at all, but it would have the advantage that some of the dignitaries who will be attending have meetings on the same day, as far as I know in the same building, and might be better able to participate in our meeting at least for a short time.

---

Fruchtstrasse 64, Berlin O 17 [postal code], as of September 30, 1931, and let the secretary, Herbert Petrick, go. The office of Superintendent Diestel, Dahlemerstrasse 87, had taken over the work of the secretariat (see the letter from Schreiber to Schönfeld, EZA 623/77).

[7.] In 1927 Superintendent Max Diestel had been entrusted by General Superintendent Otto Dibelius with the development of ecumenical youth work. Since 1931 he had been executive chairman of the German Section of the World Alliance for Promoting International Friendship through the Churches (*DB-ER*, 141 and 192).

[8.] Erich Stange, national leader of the German Protestant Young Men's Association (Ev. Jungmännerwerk Deutschlands) and from 1921 to 1927 secretary of Life and Work.

[9.] The meeting of the Provisional Bureau mentioned above took place on October 20, 1931, in the Church Federation Office, Berlin.

As an agenda I suggest:

1. Discussion of our experiences at this year's ecumenical youth conferences, especially Cleveland and Cambridge.[10]
2. Plan for the work of the Provisional Bureau:
   Newsletter
   Preparation of a card file[11] (The questionnaire for which I gave you suggestions would have to be ready for this meeting.); suggestions for the promotion of ecumenical ideas in church youth work, especially in religion classes.[12]
3. Preliminary planning for a theological conference to discuss ecumenical questions in the spring of next year. Preparation of a draft of the guidelines for this larger conference.

The invitations to the meeting on October 20 would have to be sent out as soon as possible to all groups and organizations affiliated with the Provisional Bureau. I would ask you to state specifically in the invitation the wish that was strongly expressed at the meeting on April 24[13] that as far as at all possible the same representatives who already participated in the earlier meetings should be sent. One question that does not seem to me to be completely settled yet is the question of whether the groups that belong to the committee of the German Protestant Youth Associations should only be sent invitations through this committee, that is, through Dr. Stange, or whether they should be sent invitations directly. I consider the latter to be better and more proper; it should just be handled in such a way that the same procedure is followed for all the groups that come into question.

27 Finally, I ask that, before the administrative office of which you are the head is closed, you request reimbursement from the Church Federation Office for the expenses to date. May I remind you as well that I have not yet been reimbursed for my expenses from April, in the sum of fifteen marks.

Sincerely,
Yours [W. Stählin]

[10.] The twentieth world conference of the YMCA took place August 4–9, 1931, in Cleveland. At this conference, a resolution on the question of responsibility for the First World War was passed, which contained a refusal to assign sole responsibility to one nation or group.

[11.] See 1/12.

[12.] [I.e., in the public schools.—VB]

[13.] See the minutes of this meeting, LKA Nuremberg, XVIII: Nachlaß Stählin.

**11. To Erwin Sutz**[1]

Berlin-Grunewald, October 8, 1931

Dear Mr. Sutz,

Since you are in favor of efficiency, you are receiving a typewritten letter, which you will also appreciate for other reasons.[2] A sense of pity has moved me to buy a typewriter, and I have a strong feeling that in doing this I have really entered the age of technology—even if it is only in an imperfect way.

First, I must thank you for two very kind letters,[3] in return for which my sending my book[4] was too simple a response. The same goes for the pictures,[5] which really pleased me very much. Thank you very much for remembering me in such a nice way. The last picture attracted a great deal of attention here, naturally.[6] Since I heard Gogarten yesterday—by the way, after the picture, his appearance was somewhat of a disappointment—only Thurneysen is still missing in the list of Olympians.[7]

Gogarten gave a lecture on ethics[8] that included a couple of very good formulations but was received with anger and disdain on the part of the people here—they were education majors. With a break of ten minutes, he had
talked for three hours! It was again surprising to me to see how great the 28
difference is from Barth in purely human aspects. I wouldn't feel at all especially attracted to Breslau, while I would go to Bonn again in a minute.[9] That was really an unusual time there.

I was very happy to see from your letter how much you like being in Pratteln.[10] If only once in my life I had been able to meet and work together

---

[1.] *NL*, A 29, 4(5) (a); typewritten with handwritten greeting; cf. *NL*, A 29, 4(5) (b); later typewritten copy by Eberhard Bethge. Partially reproduced in *GS* 1:22–24.

[2.] [This is probably a reference to the difficulty of reading Bonhoeffer's handwriting. See an indirect confirmation of Sutz's earlier complaint in 1/6.—MBL]

[3.] Not extant.

[4.] Bonhoeffer's postdoctoral thesis, *Act and Being* (*DBWE* 2).

[5.] See the photos from the time they were both in America, in Bethge and Gremmels, *Life in Pictures*, centenary ed., 46–49. [The comment that follows (referring to Gogarten and Thurneysen), indicates that at least one photo included Gogarten. There is no such photo in the *Life in Pictures* volume.—VB]

[6.] [The reference is uncertain.—MBL]

[7.] That is, of the leading theologians of so-called dialectic theology.

[8.] The lecture given in Berlin on October 7, 1931, by Friedrich Gogarten, professor of systematic theology in Breslau, was published as "Das Problem der Ethik und die Erziehung" (The problem of ethics and education).

[9.] Barth was teaching in Bonn, Gogarten in Breslau.

[10.] Erwin Sutz was an intern pastor (vicar) in Pratteln, under the guidance of Lukas Christ.

with an older man who could have really been a teacher for me—I don't know why that was never granted me. Would I possibly not have been able to take it? In any case, you have it good. It must give you an unbelievable sense of security.

Now I am sitting here preparing for my lecture course, and for the work as pastor for the students, and would sometimes be happy if I could be in the country somewhere for a while, to get away from everything everyone wants from and expects of me. It's not that I'm afraid of disappointing—at least I hope not primarily—but that sometimes I simply cannot see how I will be able to do all these things right. The cheap consolation that one just does what one can, and that there are others who would do it even worse, isn't always enough. It is certainly not right for me to come into such things so soon—and also on the basis of what qualifications? Now and then I would like to laugh grimly about all of that.

At the present time, I am especially conscious of these things in the unprecedented situation of our public life here in Germany. It really looks unbelievably serious. There apparently is really no one in Germany who has even the slightest overview of things. But in general everyone has a strong feeling that very great changes in the course of world history are before us. Whether it will lead to Bolshevism or to a wider general understanding—who knows? And who even knows, in the long run, what is better? But the coming winter in Germany will probably leave no one in Germany unaffected. Seven million unemployed, that means fifteen or twenty million
29 people hungry. I don't know how Germany and how each individual can live through that. Intelligent people in the field of economics have told me that things look as if we are being pushed at an enormous speed toward a destination that no one knows or could prevent. But will our church survive *another* catastrophe?[11] Will it not reach the end of its existence then, if we do not change immediately, speak and live completely differently? But how? Next Wednesday is a meeting of all Berlin pastors to discuss the winter problems; let's see what kind of problems there are! I fear bad things from this meeting. But no one knows how to do it better. And in times like these! What good is a person's theology? In a couple of weeks the work will start. The *omina*[12] are strange.

[11.] Perhaps Bonhoeffer considers the separation of church and state in the Weimar Republic to be a result of the First World War and fears now that the worsening economic crisis might have similar consequences for the church.

[12.] "The omens."

Take care! I'm always very happy when I receive a letter from you. Write soon. Excuse a letter like this, but I really could not have written much differently, try as I would. Soon again and more.

Sincere greetings from
Your Dietrich Bonhoeffer

## 12. Circular Letter of the Provisional Bureau for Ecumenical Youth Work[1]

Münster in Westphalia, October 15, 1931

Questionnaire for a Catalog

As an important part of its work, the newly founded Provisional Bureau for Ecumenical Youth Work plans to prepare a list of all young people who might come into question as participants in international meetings of Protestant youth. The necessity of such a list is obvious. Sending representatives to international meetings is a special responsibility for us Germans. Participation will be left to 30
chance unless one central location keeps an overview of which young people from the different associations would come into question for the different tasks. For this reason, the Provisional Bureau requests that all organizations, groups, and individuals associated with it answer the following questions by . . . . . . . and send the lists to [. . . . . . ].[2]

If this card index is to be of use, all the questions on the enclosed sheet must be answered exactly for each individually named young person, and the organizations should make it a point to correct and add to this information each year by the . . . . . . . Otherwise, such a listing quickly becomes outdated because of the rapid changes in all youth groups.

It is specifically requested that not only the members of individual associations and organizations be named but also young people who are not members of organizations but who have shown their ability in the youth activities of a congregation or possibly in student life.

[signed] Dr. Stählin

[1.] LKA Nuremberg, XVIII: Nachlaß Stählin; carbon copy. At this time Bonhoeffer was already taking part in the work of organizing the Provisional Bureau for Ecumenical Youth Work. Bonhoeffer sent out the questionnaire again in 1932 (see 1/31).

[2.] [Presumably dates and addresses were entered into specific letters by hand.—MBL]

Model Questionnaire

Which young people (in general ages 18–25 years) in your organization—field of work—are suited for participation in international (ecumenical) conferences?

Name

Year of Birth

Education

Profession

Organizational Membership

Which international conferences attended up to now?

To what extent was this participation successful?

Especially familiar with which questions of theology, church work, youth work, Germans living outside Germany, minorities, question of responsibility for the war, other international political questions?

31 Which languages does he understand and which does he speak?

Able to take time off to attend such conferences?

**13. To Wilhelm Stählin**[1]

Berlin-Grunewald, October 17, 1931

Dear Professor Stählin:[2]

Finally, I was able to speak directly with Dr. Schreiber[3] about the date of the meeting for the Provisional Bureau.[4] There is some dissatisfaction at the Church Federation Office, because the Provisional Bureau has sup-

[1.] LKA Nuremberg, XVIII: Nachlaß Stählin; handwritten manuscript.

[2.] [Bonhoeffer uses the formal term *hochverehrt* (esteemed) in the salutation.—MBL]

[3.] August W. Schreiber, High Consistory Councillor in the Church Federation Office, had hosted regular ecumenical evening gatherings at his home, out of which the Provisional Bureau had developed (see *DB-ER*, 192). [The titular address refers to an honorary doctorate.—MBL]

[4.] [The Provisional Bureau for Ecumenical Youth Work.—VB]

posedly upstaged the ecumenical working group[5] that Hosemann inaugurated. In order to secure further support of the Church Federation Office for our work now, Schreiber thinks it would be good to ask the Church Federation Office whether this time our meeting might be held on the same day as the meeting of the ecumenical working group, since actually almost all those attending would be there anyway. (Apparently it also seems that there is some danger that the people would otherwise not come to the "ecumenical working group.") That meeting is on the eighth of December.[6] Now the gentlemen know, however, that this date is not good for you, but they are requesting very strongly that you somehow find a way to make it possible to come, nonetheless. Dr. Zoellner[7] would be there anyway.

I doubt that the continuation of the discussion in April[8] can really just 32
be taken up again today. Shouldn't we just start over again? May I ask that you let me or Dr. Schreiber know soon? What I said above about the Church Federation Office I naturally request you to treat as confidential.

In sincere admiration I remain yours most respectfully
Dietrich Bonhoeffer

---

[5.] The German ecumenical working group, founded by Johannes Hosemann, was an informal gathering of the ecumenical groups in Germany. The German subcommittees of Life and Work, Faith and Order, and the World Alliance for Promoting International Friendship through the Churches (*DB-ER*, 241–42), among others, met here. That meant that some of the groups organized there were also represented in the Provisional Bureau for Ecumenical Youth Work. See the organizational diagram in appendix 4.

[6.] As far as one can tell from Stählin's literary estate, a meeting did not take place on December 8, 1931. The meeting announced here was probably postponed until April 29, 1932.

[7.] Wilhelm Zoellner was the general superintendent of the Westphalian church. He retired in 1931 but continued to be active in ecumenical work. Zoellner had organized a working group of younger pastors, which primarily discussed problems of "Faith and Order" (see *DB-ER*, 239).

[8.] On April 24, 1931, the constituting meeting of the Provisional Bureau for Ecumenical Youth Work had taken place in the Church Federation Office (see the minutes of the meeting, LKA Nuremberg, XVIII: Nachlaß Stählin).

**14. To Helmut Rößler**[1]

Berlin-Grunewald, October 18, 1931

Dear Friend,

I can hardly believe that I am doing today what I have wanted to do since the last day of December, when I received your letter,[2] which riveted my attention and occupied me like almost nothing else. When you wrote me then, what you said about your work stayed with me for a long time. I wanted very much to send you a long and detailed answer. Then Christmas came, it became later and later, and finally I could not decide to do it anymore. At that time I did something that I must also confess to you. Namely, I read your letter aloud to a group of American friends, to give them a firsthand impression of the work and the opinions of a young German pastor—if that is not all right with you, please excuse me for it. In any case, it seemed to
33 me to be a very welcome opportunity for once to let a completely different voice be heard in that ridiculously Europeanized world, and that was also felt very much. My stay in America[3] and recently also in England[4] has made one thing clear to me: the absolute necessity of cooperation and at the same time the inexplicable divisions that seem to make such a coming together simply impossible. Seen from over there, our situation and theology seem so local, and one just can't imagine that in all the world it should be Germany, and there only a few men, who should have understood what the gospel is. But then I don't see a gospel message from anywhere else. The huge project of American mission is hollow on the inside. The mother

[1.] *NL*, A 20,4(7); photomechanical reproduction from Bonhoeffer, *Einführung in seine Botschaft*, 60ff.; the original manuscript was not accessible. Edited version published in *GS* 1:60–62. Helmut Rößler was a friend of Bonhoeffer's from his days as a student in Berlin (see *DB-ER*, 82 and 96).

[2.] Not extant.

[3.] On Bonhoeffer's time as a student in New York, see *DBWE* 10 [and *DB-ER*, 147–66—MBL].

[4.] Bonhoeffer is referring to the conference in Cambridge (see 2/1 below).

church itself is dying. And yet it is certain that our current understanding of the gospel simply cannot be heard over there. There is an unparalleled gap between us. One large country I would still like to see, if perhaps the great solution will come from there—India.[5] For otherwise it seems to be over; the great dying out of Christianity seems to be here. Is our time over? Has the gospel been given to another people, perhaps proclaimed with *completely* different words and actions? How do you see the eternal nature of Christianity in light of the world situation and our own way of living? It is becoming less and less understandable that for the sake of *one* just man "the city should be spared."[6] I am presently the pastor for the students at the Technical College. How should I preach such things to these people? Who still believes that anymore? Invisibility is ruining us. If we cannot see in our personal life that Christ has been here, then we want at least to see it in India, but this madness of being constantly thrown back to the invisible God himself—no one can stand that anymore.[7] I had hoped very much to be able to see you sometime and to speak with you. One actually has the feeling that any minute something very big must be about to happen, but we are told just to wait. Will the winter bring the great change for things?
I hope and yet fear—not. Take care—give my kindest regards to your wife 34
and your little boy, whom I don't know yet. He must make you see many things differently. The perspective on the future must be a completely different one. Let me hear from you!

In sincere friendship
Yours faithfully, Dietrich Bonhoeffer

[5.] On Bonhoeffer's plans to get to know India, see 2/5 below and *DB-ER*, 105, 147–48, 165, 233–34.

[6.] See Gen. 18:22–33.

[7.] [Bonhoeffer may be referring here to an exclusively abstract theology in the face of the need for practical realization of gospel values, attained in concrete ethical actions.—MBL]

**15. To Paul Sandegren**[1]

Berlin-Grunewald, October 24, 1931

Dear Pastor Sandegren:

The Youth Commission[2] that was newly constituted in Cambridge has planned an international youth conference[3] for next summer. At this conference, young people are to be made acquainted with the international problem of unemployment, not in order to publish any kind of resolutions, but simply to study the problem seriously and from a Christian point of view. In order to make this possible, we would like to have very extensive informative material available. I now have the task of asking you to send me some material about the conditions in your country. The request is not for details but only for a short report (possibly with some figures) about the factual situation and a few remarks about the attempts to overcome the difficulties (insurance, financial aid, etc.) and finally for a short presentation of the moral and religious effects. A second topic of the conference will treat the question of why people show so little interest in general in the church today. If I could also hear something from you on this point, I would be extraordinarily grateful. If you should have an expert on these questions in your organization,[4] someone like that could probably answer the questions without much trouble.

---

[1.] Sandegren Collection, Church of Sweden Archives, Uppsala, Sweden; typewritten with handwritten signature; letterhead: "Licentiate of Theology Dietrich Bonhoeffer, Lecturer at the University of Berlin, Berlin-Grunewald, Wangenheimstrasse 14, October 24, 1931, International Youth Secretary of the World Alliance for Promoting International Friendship through the Churches." Previously published in *Mündige Welt*, 5:52–53. Paul Sandegren was at that time pastor of the Marienkirche in Stockholm and general secretary of the Swedish Section of the World Alliance for Promoting International Friendship through the Churches.

[2.] In Cambridge Tom Craske, Pierre C. Toureille, and Bonhoeffer were named voluntary youth secretaries of the International Section of the World Alliance for Promoting International Friendship through the Churches. Edward A. Burroughs was chairman of the Youth Commission. Henry-Louis Henriod was his vice chairman (see World Alliance for International Friendship through the Churches, *Annual Report and Handbook 1932*, 108).

[3.] The Youth Conference of the World Alliance for Promoting International Friendship through the Churches and of the Universal Christian Council for Life and Work in Gland [Switzerland], August 24–31, 1932. The topic of this conference, "The Call of Christianity in the Present Crisis," was broader than the originally planned "Question of Unemployment." This topic was included under the broader theme (see below 1/16 and *DB-ER*, 250).

[4.] Referring to the Swedish Section of the World Alliance for Promoting International Friendship through the Churches.

With sincere thanks for all your efforts and most respectful greetings I remain yours in fellowship

Dietrich Bonhoeffer

### 16. Circular Letter from Henry-Louis Henriod to the Youth Secretaries of the World Alliance for Promoting International Friendship through the Churches[1]

October 28, 1931

To the Secretaries
Of the Youth Commission, World Alliance
For Promoting International Friendship through the Churches

Dear Friends,

Important decisions were taken at Cambridge concerning the carrying on of
the work of the Youth Commission. But uncertainty as to reorganisation of
the Secretariat of the Alliance and as to financial resources available for Youth
Work have delayed somewhat this letter. I feel nevertheless that we should not 36
wait any longer for taking some of the steps decided and for consultation with
one another and the division of work as suggested at Cambridge. It is of course
a great decision that three secretaries have been appointed for initiating and
coordinating Youth Work and that they have been coopted by the Management
Committee at the meeting of the latter on September 4th at Cambridge. The
report of our Chairman[2] was circulated. I made also an oral statement, and
both seem to have met with the full approval of the Committee although no time
was allowed for questions or discussions. The points stressed can be summed
up as follows:

---

[1.] Literary estate of Eberhard Bethge, Staatsbibliothek Berlin; carbon copy. Above the letterhead is the following original typewritten notation: "Lecturer Dietrich *Bonhoeffer*, Berlin-Grunewald, Wangenheimstr[asse]. 14. / Rev. F. W. T. *Craske*, 35 Brookland Hill, London N.W. 11. / Past[or]. Pierre *Toureille*, Congénies, Gard. / *The Lord Bishop of Ripon* (for his information) / Also to M. le Pasteur Jézéquel (a copy)." [The letter is in the original, unaltered English.—MBL] The initials at the end of the letter "HLH/CP" indicate that H.-L. Henriod is the writer of the letter. Concerning the question of the sender of the letter, see Dickinson's discussion of the Conference in Paris in World Alliance for International Friendship through the Churches, *Reports 1931*, pt. 1, 8. According to this source, Mr. Fox, M. Henriod, and M. Jézéquel and Lord Dickinson were in Paris. According to *DB-ER*, 240n197, Henriod was the author of the letter.

[2.] The chairman of the Youth Commission was the Lord Bishop of Ripon, the Right Reverend Edward Arthur Burroughs. The Bethge papers contain a carbon copy of the September 4, 1931, report to which Henriod refers ("Report of the Youth Commission").

(1) The Youth Commission should be active and effective to the maximum with a minimum of means.

(2) Its officers are to be: the Lord Bishop of Ripon, Chairman;[3] H.-L. Henriod, Vice-Chairman; Secretaries—Privatdozent Dietrich Bonhoeffer, Berlin; Rev. F. W. T. Craske, London; Past. F. Toureille, France.

(3) The list of former members of the Youth Commission should be reviewed and all those who can effectively continue their cooperation, used as advisors. Advantage should be taken of those present at meetings of the Management and of the International Committees. The proposed addition of Dr. Bacon, Chairman of the Youth Conference at Cambridge, was postponed after consultation with the British Council of the World Alliance.

(4) It is desirable that each National Council appoints a corresponding member for work among youth so as to insure the closest possible cooperation between the Youth Commission and the National Alliances.

(5) Proposed Activities:

(a) Maintain, develop or create effective cooperation with Christian youth movements in existence;

(b) encourage any effort done by National Alliances among youth;

(c) promote the following conferences:

The Commission wants to use the opportunity of the next meeting of the Management Committee which is likely to be held in Geneva, August 1932,[4] for holding in the neighbourhood of Geneva a small but representative *International Conference* of some 40 to 60 young people. Accommodation should be very
37 simple: camp life if possible. The Conference to last 5 to 6 days. The Secretaries of the Youth Commission should undertake preparatory work for this Conference along three lines in their respective areas:

First, Unemployment among youth

Second, Attitude of youth towards the Church

Third, Where to look for making international peace a reality.

Delegates to the Conference should include young people from the working class, among them unemployed; from the business class as well as from among intelligentzia [*sic*].

Three *Regional* Conferences have been asked for:

i. An *Anglo-French Conference*,[5] to follow up the contacts established at the Cambridge Conference; plans and details to be arranged in consultation with

---

[3.] Edward Arthur Burroughs had been Lord Bishop of Ripon since 1926.

[4.] See 2/18 and 2/19.

[5.] The regional conference took place in Epsom near London, April 5–9, 1932 (see Henriod, *Bericht über die Tatigkeit des Weltbundes*, 5).

the French and British Alliances by Tourville [*sic*][6] and Craske. Not more than 20 people.
ii. A *Franco-German Conference*. Bonhoeffer to take initiative in consultation with Toureille and the two National Alliances.[7]
iii. A *Balkan Conference for Youth*.[8] This was proposed by Professor Alivisatos[9] and met with a hearty approval of representatives of the other Orthodox Church leaders from the Balkan countries present at Cambridge. This Conference should bring together some 40 delegates: youth representatives from Bulgaria, Greece, Roumania [*sic*], Yougoslavia [*sic*] and Turkey (30); 5 to 6 senior leaders and 4 to 5 visitors from the West.

Finances:
It is uncertain yet whether the Youth Commission will have the financial resources required for our plans. I am to meet in Paris with Lord Dickinson[10] and other leaders of the Alliance on November 26th and 27th on the occasion of an important conference on disarmament, and hope to obtain definite assurances as to financial support.

This should not delay any action by the Secretaries in establishing contact 38
with their respective areas. With very limited grants from the World Alliance it should be possible, with the help of the National Alliances concerned, to prepare and held [*sic*] the first two regional conferences. Correspondence should also be established soon with friends in the areas allotted to the Secretaries so that we can bring forward to the Executive Committee of the Alliance concrete proposals based on definite reaction from the field. May I remind you that we agreed at Cambridge on a rough division of responsibilities as to our correspondence:

*Craske*—British Empire, U.S.A., Far East.

*Bonhoeffer*—Germany, northern and central Europe, including Hungary and Austria.

*Toureille:* France, Latin Europe, Balkans, Poland, Czechoslovakia.

---

[6.] Correct: "Toureille."

[7.] German-French regional conference at the Westerburg, July 12–14, 1932.

[8.] The Youth Conference for the Balkan states, which had been planned for 1932 and was very carefully prepared, had to be "postponed until May 1933 due to financial difficulties, the chaotic political situation, and the illness of one of the secretaries of the World Alliance" (World Alliance for International Friendship through the Churches, *Annual Report 1932–33*, 32).

[9.] Hamilcar Alivisatos was secretary of the Orthodox group of the Universal Christian Council for Life and Work in 1931.

[10.] Dickinson, Lord Willoughby of Painswick, was president of the International Section of the World Alliance for Promoting International Friendship through the Churches from 1931 to 1935.

Also that a round letter[11] was to be launched among the Secretaries for further suggestions on the proposed programme of the International Conference to be held next summer,[12] and if I am not mistaken that Craske was to begin it. May this be done without delay, if it has not been started yet.

Could the Secretaries secure also from some of the Alliances at least the name of the person who can act as corresponding member for work among youth.

Until we know exactly on which budget we can count for our work I suggest that each of the Secretaries secures the authorisation and help of the Secretaries of the Alliances in London, Berlin and Paris respectively for any postage, stationery and other petty expenses which may be required for the first steps necessary to fulfill our programme.

I would appreciate it very much if I could receive a word from each of you not later than November 20th,[13] with indications of any important steps you have taken so that I can report to the leaders of the Alliance when I meet them a few days later in Paris.

It will be necessary for our group to meet for a full day session, as you may remember the date of March 31st was suggested as being possible for the Bishop of Ripon, our Chairman.[14] As soon as I have assurance that the travelling expenses involved can be covered and that the date is suitable to all of you, we
39 shall make it definite. I shall write again after I have met in Paris Lord Dickinson and the other leaders of the Alliance.

Yours very sincerely,
[H.-L. Henriod]

P.S. This letter is being sent to:
The Lord Bishop of Ripon (Palace, Ripon, England)
Privatdozent Dietrich Bonhoeffer (Berlin-Grunewald,
Wangenheimstr. 14, Germany)
Rev. F. W. T. Craske (35 Brookland Hill, London N.W. 11, England)
Past. Pierre Toureille (Congénies, Gard, France)

[11.] Not extant.

[12.] Reference is to the conference in Gland near Geneva.

[13.] Bonhoeffer's reply has not yet been found.

[14.] Edward Arthur Burroughs was chairman of the Youth Commission of the World Alliance (see World Alliance for International Friendship through the Churches, *Annual Report and Handbook 1932*, 108).

**16a. To Paul Lehmann**[1] 17:94

November 5, [19]31

Dear Paul,

Thank you very much for your letter. It awakened many nice memories for me. At this time a year ago, the first phase of adjusting to the new place[2] was over and together with you and Sutz the first protests began to make themselves heard. I think the seminar gave the impetus for that.[3] But at the same time it was the beginning of the phase when I started to understand English without too much difficulty, and the time when after lunch, at your tempting suggestion, I took a little detour to your apartment to bring lunch to a dignified close with a cigarette (or several) and a chat.—Those days are now long past and yet they are present for me as if they were yesterday. 17:95

¶Now I am in the midst of the semester's work again and am enjoying the work with the seminar[4] especially. It's a small circle of really interested people; a couple of them studied for some time with Barth and were recommended to me by him or his students. That's why I'm hoping that we will be able to work together quite productively, especially since I have a topic that I myself am not actually able to solve. It is the idea of philosophy and systematic theology. How nice it would be if you were there; we[5] could have a great time. I suppose you are working very hard on your thesis. What has come out as the final formulation of the topic?[6]

---

[1.] Paul Lehmann Collection, Special Collections, Princeton Theological Seminary Library; typewritten with handwritten closing, from Berlin, on stationery with the printed address: "Licentiate in Theology Dietrich Bonhoeffer, Lecturer at the University of Berlin, Berlin-Grunewald, Wangenheimstrasse 14." Previously published in Alston and Welker, "Dietrich Bonhoeffer," 468–70, and *DBW* 17:94–96. Editorial notation by Hans Pfeifer. [Bonhoeffer alternates between German and English in the original.—VB]

[2.] See *DB-ER*, 156–58, and the letter to Deißmann in *DBWE* 10, 1/135a [Deißmann wrote a letter of reference for Bonhoeffer in September 1930 to Henry Sloane Coffin, the president of Union Seminary from 1926 to 1945—MBL].

[3.] Bonhoeffer is probably referring to Professor Baillie's "Seminar in Philosophical Theology," which he had taken in the winter semester 1930–31; see *DBWE* 10:643–45.

[4.] See 1/27.

[5.] [Here Bonhoeffer continues in English.—MBL]

[6.] The topic of Lehmann's doctoral dissertation at Union Seminary in 1936 was "A Critical Comparison of the Doctrine of Justification in the Theologies of Albrecht Ritschl and Karl Barth." The dissertation was published under the title *Forgiveness: Decisive Issue in Protestant Thought.* See Lehmann's letter of August 4, 1941, to Erwin Sutz (*DBWE* 16:201).

¶I[7] notice that typing English goes much more slowly than typing German; since I don't have much more time today—I absolutely must do some work on my lecture—I will continue writing in German and hope you won't hold it against me. Unfortunately, at the present time the type of students studying theology is quite disappointing. All other professions are more than full and this leads many to theology today who should not touch it. The bad thing is that then these people, with no selection process at all if they have passed their examination, are turned loose on the people, and it is completely unavoidable that they cause so much damage to the church's reputation that even a Barthian theology will not help anymore.

¶Last Sunday I was installed in the church where I am to preach from now on.[8] I think I wrote you already that it is the church attended by Hindenburg (once a month on average).[9] So I met him personally last Sunday. He seems very discouraged—no wonder, considering the state of things. Actually I don't much like having this very highly visible place to preach. All
17:96 the ceremonial atmosphere that comes as well from the tradition of Schleiermacher, who preached here, is not really my style. But my main work will be in the office hours anyway.

¶The political situation hasn't changed since I last wrote.[10] But it really will probably not be long until the National Socialists (Hitler) go on the offensive [losschlagen]. If it happens by means of violence, it's all over for us because then at the same moment the communists will rise up and we will have civil war in the country. A prelude to what can be expected from the National Socialists at the university is taking place right now in Halle, where the students are refusing to continue studying (not only the theology students) if a recently called pacifist professor of theology, who is an extraordinarily capable man, is not fired immediately.[11] The kind of intel-

[7.] [Here Bonhoeffer resumes in German.—MBL]

[8.] Dreifaltigkeitskirche (Church of the Trinity) in Berlin.

[9.] [Paul von Hindenburg was the widely respected commander of the German army in World War I and president of the republic from 1925 until his death in 1934.—MBL]

[10.] See letter 1/8a (August 23, 1931). Since October 16, 1931, the Reich president had been governing with presidential cabinets and Heinrich Brüning was chancellor.

[11.] Günther Dehn. On this matter, see Bonhoeffer's draft petition on the Dehn case to the Department of Theology in Halle, March 1932, 1/40. See also Karl Barth, "Der Fall Dehn und die 'dialektische Theologie'" (1932) and "Warum führt man den Kampf nicht, wie es sich gehört, auf der ganzen Linie?" (1932) in Bizer, "Der 'Fall Dehn.'" [The "Dehn affair" had a substantial impact on Bonhoeffer and his colleagues. Günther Dehn, a pastor, socialist, and radical pacifist (and subsequently a member of the Confessing Church), was dismissed from his professorship in Halle and blocked from a professorship in Heidelberg for his pacifist views. Much of the opposition against him was organized by students and faculty sympathetic to National Socialism. See Bonhoeffer's statement

lectual level that is coming into the universities now is simply dreadful. Union[12] looks good in comparison! By the way, neither Baillie nor Lyman have replied to me about the book.[13] Why is that? Niebuhr wrote recently very kindly.[14]

¶Now good-bye; give my kindest regards to your wife. I[15] think often of you all! Give my regards to the friends at the seminary,[16] also Prof. White when you see him, King Gordon[17] as well, when you write.

I am very happy to hear from you again. The books will be sent to you the day after tomorrow. A bill will follow. Can you send the money by registered mail in dollars?

Sincere greetings and good wishes for your work—

Yours faithfully, Dietrich Bonhoeffer

### 17. Order of the Evangelical Consistory of the Mark Brandenburg[1]

Berlin SW 68, November 11, 1931

To fulfill the requirement for auxiliary service as an assistant pastor[2] you have been assigned to our provincial church. Your ordination is to take place on Sunday,

---

on the affair in this volume (1/40) and the German editor's afterword to this volume, pp. 482–83; *DB-ER*, 177, 235–36; *DBWE* 12:103, 493; and the editor's introduction to this volume. See also Schwab, "Günther Dehn."—MBL]

[12.] Union Theological Seminary, New York.

[13.] *Act and Being* (*DBWE* 2). John Baillie taught systematic theology at Union Theological Seminary from 1930 [until 1934]. It was through the philosopher of religion Eugene W. Lyman that Bonhoeffer encountered the philosophy of William James. [Lyman was professor of philosophy of religion at Union from 1918 to 1940.—MBL]

[14.] [Reinhold Niebuhr was professor of applied Christianity at Union from 1928 to 1960.—MBL]

[15.] Handwritten from this point onward.

[16.] This probably refers to Union Theological Seminary.

[17.] [A reference to Professor Gaylord White and J. King Gordon, a fellow student from Bonhoeffer's time at Union.—MBL]

[1.] *NL*, A 30, 1(11); typewritten order with handwritten notes bottom left: "Sincerely wishing you blessings! Diestel"; below this a stamped imprint: "Superintendent's Office Kölln-Land I / Telephone: Lichterfelde 476, Dahlemerstrasse 87 / Berlin-Lichterfelde, November 12, 1931, daily log number 4306."

[2.] This obligatory service in the church (*kirchliche Hilfsdienstpflicht*) refers to the time after a pastor's ordination during which the pastor could not yet apply for a pastoral position of his own and was assigned by the consistory to a pastor or institution to serve as assistant pastor (letter to the German *DBW* editor from Bishop Albrecht Schönherr, May 15, 1991). [Albrecht Schönherr was a student and close friend of Bonhoeffer from the Confessing Church seminary time at Finkenwalde.—MBL]

the fifteenth of November 1931, at ten o'clock in the morning, by General Superintendent Dr. Vits in the St. Matthew's Church in Berlin. The service of confession and Holy Communion, which your family may also attend, will take place after the ordination.

To discuss further details, please meet with General Superintendent Dr. Vits on November 14 of this year, at five o'clock in the afternoon at his residence, Berlin W 10, Matthäikirchstrasse 22, and with the head of the department, Consistory Councillor Coulon, on Saturday at ten o'clock in the morning in our office building.

Before the ordination a fee of 5 RM is to be paid to the custodian to cover the costs of the ordination (payment for the church employees, etc.).

For the department
[. . .][3]

17:97 **17a. Ordination**[1]

I. Instructions concerning Ordination

Berlin, *November 11, 1931*[2]

[*To*[3] *fulfill the requirement for auxiliary service as an assistant pastor*] you have been assigned [*to our provincial church*].[4] [. . .] Your ordination is to take place on Sunday, the *fifteenth of November 1931*, at ten o'clock in the morning, by General Superintendent Dr. *Vits* in the *St. Matthew's* Church in Berlin. The service of

[3.] Illegible.

[1.] *NL*, D 11, 71, personnel file of the consistory; typewritten form, 2 pages, with handwritten entries (here indicated with italics); letterhead: "Evangelisches Konsistorium der Mark Brandenburg"; file number K. VII No. 4848. Abbreviations in the form have been written out in full in most cases; alternatives and crossed-out instructions in the form are indicated by square brackets [. . . ]; excerpt given immediately above (1/17). [This is the consistory office form of the ordination instructions, i.e., essentially the same as the document just above (1/17). It is the office copy that preceded the official notice to Bonhoeffer, cited above. The form was filled out by hand in the allotted blank spaces with specific details of the ordination, date, place, address, etc., and an extra note to the officiant.—MBL]

[2.] Handwritten addition, underlined: "Immediately [s*ofort*]!" From here on the form has two columns. The left contains official instructions and notations, which will be reproduced here in the footnotes; "/" indicates the end of a line in the original.

[3.] Beginning of the right column.

[4.] The printed text "You are . . . as pastor" has been replaced; square brackets ([ ]) are handwritten in the form.

confession and Holy Communion, which your family may also attend, will take place after the ordination.[5]

To discuss further details, please meet with General Superintendent Dr. *Vits* on *November 14 of this year, at five* o'clock *in the afternoon* at his residence, *Berlin W 10, Matthäikirchstrasse 22*, and with the head of the department, Consistory Councillor *Coulon*, on Saturday at ten o'clock in the morning in our office building.[6]

Before the ordination a fee of 5 RM is to be paid to the *custodian*[7] to cover the costs of the ordination (payment for the church employees, etc.).[8] [. . .]

We[9] respectfully request that the Very Reverend [General Superintendent 17:98
Dr. Vits] be so good as to ordain the candidate for ministry *Licentiate Dietrich Bonhoeffer*, assigned [as shown on preceding page],[10] on *November 15, 1931*.[11]

2. Certificate of Ordination[12]

The candidate for ministry *Mr. Dietrich Bonhoeffer, who has been assigned to our provincial church to fulfill the requirement for service as an assistant pastor,* was ordained by us today here in the *St. Matthew's Church*, pursuant to the order of the Evangelical Consistory of the Mark Brandenburg of *November 11, 1931, K. VII. 4848.*

[5.] Next to this in the left column: "1.) to the candidate for pastoral ministry *Licentiate Dietrich Bonhoeffer* in *Berlin-Grunewald Wangenheimstrasse 14* in care of the superintendent of the church district *Kölln-Land I / Prepared for 1 and 2 and sent N. 11*). / Remarks of the head of the department: "The aforementioned *Bonhoeffer*—born on *February 4*, 19*06*, has completed the twenty-fifth year of life (canonical age) [. . .]."

[6.] Left column: "3.) Immediately after this is sent out (a) to be shown to Consistory Councillor Wolff *seen Wolff thirteenth of November* (b) to be noted in the ordination list (with the personnel files): *v Cua* [signature illegible] *sixteenth of November* [. . .])."

[7.] Replaces "the general superintendent."

[8.] Left column: "4.) *Waived by special order.* At the end of the first page: "No. 66"; "Personnel Files *Bo-67*."

[9.] Beginning of the second page.

[10.] The words "as shown on the preceding page" are set in square brackets, referring to the first sentence, "To fulfill the requirement . . ."

[11.] Left column: "2.) to the Very Reverend General Superintendent Dr. *Vits*, here. (First and last names)." Below the text to the right the signatures: "*For the Department. Verified by Karow. Luberg [illegible] 9/XI (November 9) / C[oulon] 7/11 / Cua* [illegible, same as on first page left column under "3.). . . (b)"] *6/11*."

[12.] *NL*, A 6 (9); official form with handwritten entries (here in italics).

This is herewith certified for him with the most sincere wishes for blessings for his work.

Berlin, *November 15, 1931*

The Evangelical General Superintendent: Assisting Clergy
*Dr. Vits* *Dr. A. W. Schreiber, High Consistory Councillor*
*Damerow, Pastor*[13]

Ordination Certificate[14]

40 **18. To Reinhold Krause**[1]

November 13, 1931

Dear Dr. Krause,

I have just received your circular letter. As I see, the meetings will usually be taking place on Monday.[2] I had already told you at the last meeting

---

[13.] General Superintendent Ernst Vits; High Consistory Councillor August Wilhelm Schreiber; Damerow: Pastor of the St. Matthew's Church.

[14.] Above this is a seal with the following text printed around the circumference: "General Superintendent of the Neumark and Niederlausitz." In the personnel file, in addition to the two papers printed above concerning the ordination, there is also an official "order" concerning the completed ordination, *NL*, D 11 (72).

[1.] Archiv des Diakonischen Werkes, Berlin, KSB 410; typewritten with handwritten signature and handwritten illegible notation, possibly by Krause.

[2.] The reference is to the meetings of the Working Group of Theologians and Economists (Arbeitsgemeinschaft der Theologen und Nationalökonomen), which met every two weeks. The organization of the working group was under the auspices of the Church-Social Federation (Kirchlich-sozialer Bund). The independent Conference of Church and Society (Freie Kirchlich-soziale Konferenz), which carried the name Church-Social Federation after 1918 (Kupisch, "Kirchlich-sozial," 1622) had been founded by Adolf Stoecker in 1899, one year after he withdrew from the Protestant Social Congress (Evangelisch-sozialer Kongress). The Conference of Church and Society was more practically oriented and influenced by the church's right wing and the Inner Mission [the latter group oversaw church-sponsored social-service organizations such as soup kitchens and institutions for the disabled—MBL]. The founding of the Conference of Church and Society was an expression of protest against the influence of liberal theology within the Protestant Social Congress, which the Conference of Church and Society countered with the ideals of Wichern and the fellowship movement (*Gemeinschaftsbewegung* [a pietist movement within German Protestantism—VB]) (Schneemelcher, "Kirchlich-sozial," 1496). [The Inner Mission encompassed a broad range of voluntary religious, charitable, and social projects that were organized by churches but operated outside their traditional parish activities. It was an urban evangelistic effort to serve and reclaim those who had lost connection with the church, rooted in nineteenth-century renewal and reform efforts, organized by J. H. Wichern in Hamburg in the 1840s, and continuing into Bonhoeffer's

that this time on Monday is hardly possible for me because of a seminar.[3] Apparently it was not possible to agree on another time.[4] Unfortunately, the last time I could only attend for a very short time, too. Naturally, I will try now to get free at least for a short time for the meeting. I will probably only rarely be able to attend the whole meeting. If instead of me you would like to have a member of the working group who can participate somewhat more fully, I would of course understand that completely.

Unfortunately, even apart from the aforementioned reasons, it will not be possible for me to present the lecture, which I see you have now announced I will be delivering, before December 14.[5] Since I did not hear any more 41
from you after that Monday, November 2, I assumed you had found someone and have now had to accept several other lecture engagements for the beginning of December,[6] so that it is simply not possible for me to give thorough preparation to a presentation on this topic. Aside from that, I would of course probably not be able to be there for the discussion anyway.

With best wishes I remain
Very respectfully yours, Bonhoeffer

### 18a. Assignment to the Position of Assistant[1] 17:99

November 21, 1931

In accordance with the application of November 19, 1931, I appoint to the position of adjunct [außerplanmäßig] assistant, which became available at the end of

time. After World War II, it became a part of the *Hilfswerk*. See *The Oxford Dictionary of the Christian Church*, 833 and 1739.—MBL] The goal of the Church-Social Federation was, among other things, to bring together the "non-Marxist groups in the workers' movement" and to strengthen the Christian workers' movement (Jagow, "Die soziale Arbeit der Kirche," 363).

[3.] This is a reference to Bonhoeffer's seminar "The Idea of Philosophy and Protestant Theology in the Twentieth Century" (see 2/4, ed. note 1).

[4.] Beginning January 19, 1932, the meetings were moved to Tuesday afternoon at five o'clock (see 2/28).

[5.] This is a reference to Bonhoeffer's lecture "The Discernible Nature of the Order of Creation," which he held on January 19, 1932 (see 2/8).

[6.] Nothing is known of such lectures. Possibly Bonhoeffer means his lecture series at the Technical College [in Berlin] (see 2/5, ed. note 1).

[1.] *NL*, Anh. A 32 (1); typewritten, from Berlin; letterhead: "Director of Administration of the Friedrich Wilhelm University" (the director of administration was Dr. Karl Büchsel); file number: "III 4080/31 19.11"; address: "To the Head of the Division of Systematics of the Department of Theology, Berlin" (Professor Wilhelm Lütgert). Previously published in *Mündige Welt*, 5:31; excerpt previously published in *GS* 6:221.

April due to the departure of Prof. Dr. *Stolzenburg*, Licentiate Dietrich *Bonhoeffer*, effective August 1, 1931, until June 30, 1933, for a compensation of (285.––5% –2.50 =)

273.25 reichsmarks

per month.

Beginning on October 1, 1931, Licentiate *Bonhoeffer* will receive compensation of 235 RM[2] per month, after deduction of the reductions required by the emergency decrees that have been issued up to this time.

I request that Licentiate *Bonhoeffer* be asked to come to my office on December 7, 1931,[3] at 1:00 p.m. to sign the contract and to bring a stamp for 1.50 RM with him.

signed Dr. Bü[chsel][4]

### 19. From Wilhelm Stählin to the Protestant Church Federation Office[1]

Münster i[n] W[estphalia], November 25, 1931

To the Protestant Church Federation Office

Enclosed I am sending you the report on the meeting of the Provisional Bureau for Ecumenical Youth Work.[2] I would be very grateful if the Church Federation Office would, as for the first meeting,[3] again this time make copies of this report and send them to the affiliated organizations. At the same time, I believe it would be a good idea to make this first report about a longer meeting of the Provisional Bureau available to the Ecumenical Working Group[4] and its members as well, since in our meeting a plan (for the theological conference)[5]

[2.] On October 1, 1931, additional salary reductions required by emergency decrees went into effect.

[3.] Concerning this date, see also Bonhoeffer's letter of December 4, 1931, to Büchsel (1/22).

[4.] Handwritten signature, underlined.

[1.] LKA Nuremberg, XVIII: Nachlaß Stählin; carbon copy; a further carbon copy, which has not been preserved, went to Bonhoeffer.

[2.] The reference here is probably to the "Report of the Meeting of the Provisional Bureau of Ecumenical Youth Work," regarding the meeting held on October 20, 1931 (see 2/2).

[3.] The first, constituting meeting of the Provisional Bureau had taken place on April 24, 1931.

[4.] See Bonhoeffer's letter to Stählin, 1/13.

[5.] The theological conference of the Provisional Bureau took place April 29–30, 1932, in the Church Federation Office [see 2/13—MBL].

was discussed, which can and should only be carried out together with the Ecumenical Working Group.

At the same time, may I inform you that Licentiate Dr. Bonhoeffer, Berlin-Grunewald, Wangenheimstrasse 14, has kindly agreed to assist me as secretary of the Provisional Bureau. The fact that Mr. Bonhoeffer is a pastor for students in Berlin and that he, as its newly elected youth secretary, is a member of the Management Committee of the World Alliance for Promoting International Friendship through the Churches, ensures the personal connection on several sides that we desired. Mr. Bonhoeffer will also keep up the close contact with 42
Superintendent Diestel, as vice chairman of the German Section (of the World Alliance), in whose office their business office is located at the present time.[6]

Most respectfully
[W. Stählin]

### 20. From Wilhelm Stählin to August W. Schreiber[1]

Münster i[n] W[estphalia], November 25, 1931

Dear High Consistory Councillor Schreiber:

In accordance with your request, as given to Licentiate Bonhoeffer, I signed the report on the meeting of the Provisional Bureau[2] and sent it to the Church Federation Office with an accompanying letter.[3] I would not like to neglect to thank you once again most sincerely for the warm support you are giving to our work and for the trouble you have taken again now in preparing this report.

At the same time, I would like to take the liberty of asking whether any further steps have been undertaken in preparation for our theological conference,[4] such as whether by now a final decision has been made about the location. If I

[6.] Due to financial difficulties, the secretariat of the World Alliance for Promoting International Friendship through the Churches in Berlin O 17, Fruchtstrasse 64, had been closed at the end of September 1931, and its work moved into the office of Superintendent Max Diestel (Berlin-Lichterfelde, Dahlemerstrasse 87); see 1/10, ed. note 2.

[1.] LKA Nuremberg, XVIII: Nachlaß Stählin; carbon copy. Another carbon copy, which has not been preserved, went to Bonhoeffer.

[2.] See the report on the meeting of the Provisional Bureau for Ecumenical Youth Work on October 20, 1931, in 2/2.

[3.] See 1/19.

[4.] That is, the "Theological Conference of the Provisional Bureau." [The report of the meeting of the Provisional Bureau proposed an international "theological conference for the discussion of ecumenical questions" to be held in March 1932 (see the report, 2/2). The conference actually took place on April 29–30, 1932, in Berlin (see 2/13).—MBL]

recall correctly, concerning these practical matters, first the gentlemen in Berlin wanted to check on the financial aspects and then choose the location. It would perhaps be a good idea, then, to contact the gentlemen whose participation we had in mind as soon as possible. Naturally, I am willing to work in this matter, or better stated, I feel it is my responsibility to do so. I would simply not like to have two people working from two different sides on the same task at the same time. So I would be grateful if you could, perhaps through Mr. Bonhoeffer, keep me informed about progress on the project. A copy of this letter goes to Mr. Bonhoeffer.

In sincere admiration yours respectfully
[W. Stählin]

43 **21. To Mr. Pauli**[1]

Grunewald, the—

Esteemed Sir:[2]

Professor Dr. Karl Barth in Bonn has asked me personally to allow his student Mrs. Gertrud Staewen[3] to attend my lecture class "The History of Twentieth-Century Systematic Theology," Mondays and Thursdays from three to four o'clock. Since the lady is unable to pay the tuition fees, the administrative office of the Department of Theology had issued her a form permitting her to attend. Now this has been taken away from her, and I was told that I should contact you with the request that an attendance permission form be issued to her. May I ask you to issue such a form to me, which I can then give to the lady?

With the greatest respect, very sincerely yours
D. B.

[1.] *NL*, A 29, 1(9): handwritten draft, undated; Mr. Pauli was the head of the university administrative office of the Friedrich Wilhelm University in Berlin. The lecture "The History of Twentieth-Century Systematic Theology" (2/3) was held in the winter semester 1931–32, so the letter can probably be dated to the winter of 1931.

[2.] "Pauli" is crossed out.

[3.] Karl Barth's followers met at the home of Gertrud Staewen, a trained social worker, in Berlin. [Staewen, who had loose connections to the Confessing Church, became a member of the Kaufmann resistance circle in Berlin during the war. She remained close to Barth, who secretly aided her resistance activities from Switzerland. See Barnett, *For the Soul of the People*, esp. 21–22 and 150–51.—VB]

### 22. To Karl Büchsel[1]

Berlin-Grunewald, December 4, 1931

Dear Administrative Director:[2]

The funeral for the late Pastor Müller[3] will take place on Monday, December 7, at 1:30 at Zion Church. Since I have acted as a substitute teacher for him in his confirmation class for the last several weeks, I must attend the 44 funeral with his confirmands. That will conflict with the appointment you have given me for the signing of the contract for my assistantship.[4] Under these circumstances, may I ask you to give me another appointment? If I do not receive an answer, may I count on your approval?

With the greatest respect I remain
Very sincerely yours, Bonhoeffer

### 23. To Paul Althaus[1]

[1.] *NL*, Anh. A 32,2; typewritten with handwritten signature. Previously published in *Mündige Welt*, 5:31. Dr. Karl Büchsel was the administrative director of the Friedrich Wilhelm University in Berlin.

[2.] [The German salutation is very formal (*Hochverehrter Herr Verwaltungsdirektor!*).—MBL]

[3.] Johannes Franz Max Müller (who used the first name Max) was the third pastor of Zion Church (Zionskirche) [in the Mitte section of Berlin—MBL].

[4.] Upon application by Wilhelm Lütgert and after his return from America, Bonhoeffer had been given a temporary adjunct assistantship in systematics in the Department of Theology. The contract was signed January 14, 1932, but backdated to August 1, 1931. Bonhoeffer was paid the salary due him for the earlier months (see *DB-ER*, 207, and *NL*, A 6,11: contract for Bonhoeffer's assistantship). [See also 1/18a.—MBL]

[1.] [Because of a correction to the date, this letter, originally included as letter 23 in *DBW* 11, has been published in *DBWE* 12 as letter 13a.—VB]

### 24. From Karl Büchsel[1]

Berlin, December 9, 1931

(1) To the adjunct assistant Licentiate Bonhoeffer, in care of the head[2] of the department of systematics in the Department of Theology, Berlin.

Re: Letter of the fourth of this month.

I request you kindly to come to my office January 14 at three o'clock to sign the contract and to bring a 1.50 RM stamp with you.

(2) Add to appointment calendar (installation)[3]

(3) After this, into the file

Bü[chsel]

### 25. To Richard Ern[1]

December 13, 1931

Dear Richard,

Although you, too, haven't heard much from me in the last few weeks—there is just too much to do—Christmas should not come without my send-
46 ing especially sincere greetings to you and your dear parents. I have also thought a lot about all of you in the last few weeks and about the nice hours at your house and the walks in the woods. How I would like to drop by your home again and see you all. You will certainly have grown quite a bit again, and I hope the piano and the flute are making good progress. In the meantime, you are, of course, a year older! I am wondering how all of you

[1.] *NL*, Anh. A 32,3; typewritten order of the Friedrich Wilhelm University with handwritten signature; as an extraordinary assistant, Bonhoeffer was originally supposed to receive an honorarium of 276 RM, but this was reduced by 41 reichsmarks to 235 RM due to reductions required by the Emergency Decrees (see *NL*, Anh. A 32[1]) [see 1/18a—MBL]. According to the assistantship contract signed on January 14 (*NL*, A 6,11), Bonhoeffer received only 214 RM; this probably refers only to base salary, in addition to which, according to a notice from the university treasury of March 1932, he received a supplementary payment of 40 percent (*NL*, A 30[15]) [see also 1/28a—MBL].

[2.] The head of the systematics department in the Department of Theology was Wilhelm Lütgert.

[3.] [That is, the swearing-in, or installation, of Bonhoeffer in his new position.—VB]

[1.] *NL*, Anh. A 33,15; typed with handwritten signature. Bonhoeffer had come to know Richard Ern on board the ship Columbus on the crossing to America and kept up contact with the Ern family during his stay in America. See *DBWE* 10, 1/136, ed. note 2.

are, and especially how your little sister is doing. Did you bring her over for Christmas, or will you have to wait until Easter? When are you all coming to Germany again? I'm looking forward to seeing you again; for me to come to America again so soon is, unfortunately, for the time being completely out of the question.

In addition to my work teaching at the university and working as a pastor for students, I am now doing something else, which takes up all my time and attention; that is teaching a confirmation class for fifty boys in the northern part of Berlin. Most are children of unemployed fathers.[2] There you see so much suffering and can only help a little. The boys don't get anything from home for Christmas, naturally, so I have to try, with the help of some friends, to give them something little that will make them happy. Often they don't have the most necessary things, shoes, trousers, etc. So that I can help out here, this time all my other friends to whom I would have liked very 47
much to give Christmas gifts will have to forgo their gifts in favor of these boys. And I think that you, too, will understand that this time one of these boys will receive the gift that I otherwise would have sent to you. Once you have seen these people, you don't want anything else for yourself. You see then how well we are still doing, that we still have food, and clothes to wear, and coal for heating. These boys often don't have all of that. And it is unfair to talk to them all the time about love of your neighbor and do nothing. So this year you will have to make do with sincere greetings from me and think about one of the poor boys being very happy. Considering this terrible situation for so many people, it is not easy for me to celebrate Christmas, and

[2.] On this topic, see the reminiscences of Pastor W. Engler, formerly of the Zion Church in Berlin, quoted by Fritz Figur: "Dietrich Bonhoeffer was living at that time in a house in the Oderbergerstrasse 61, corner of Chorinerstrasse, on the fourth floor [in a room] at Mrs. Heide's. . . . In 1931–32 our Zion Church had two deaths which were particularly painful for the congregation. On December 3, Pastor Max Müller died after twenty-seven years at Zion, and on October 1, 1932, Pastor Dr. Ewald passed away after thirty years at Zion. Both had been ill for some time. In this time of need in the congregation, Lecturer-Licentiate Bonhoeffer was sent to Zion as an assistant pastor of the synod (probably assistant pastor of the city synod)—and took over Pastor Müller's boys confirmation class (probably while Pastor Müller was still alive, since he couldn't really cope with the boys) and on March 6, 1932, confirmed them in our Zion Church, according to the information in our confirmation records. . . . In addition, Dietrich Bonhoeffer held worship services with sermons and baptisms (documented in the baptism records)." Fritz Figur, "An der Zionskirche," in Zimmermann, *Begegnungen*, 47. [In the English translation of Zimmermann's book, *I Knew Dietrich Bonhoeffer*, Figur's recollections are titled "At Zion Church," 55–56. The English translation does not include the entire passage cited here and gives a different street address (Oderbergerstrasse 58). See also Wilfried Schulz, "Bonhoeffers Konfirmanden kamen nicht aus dem Stadtteil Wedding."—MBL] one can celebrate Christmas best this year by giving as much as one possibly can.

Over there where you all are, it certainly also doesn't look so good. But you just cannot imagine the dire need of the unemployed and completely discouraged workers here unless you have seen it.

I want to close now; I must get back to work. But I will think often of you and your parents in the next few days, and I will not forget that you all made my stay in America[3] especially good. Thanks again and again to your parents for that. Now good-bye! Have a nice Christmas celebration and go into the New Year in good health and come to visit me soon. Give my kindest regards to your parents and do not completely forget your faithful

Dietrich Bonhoeffer

### 48 **26. To Sabine and Gerhard Leibholz**[1]

Berlin, December 23, 1931

Dear Sabine and Gert,

A Christmas letter really shows you clearly the limitations of a typewriter. But since it can only be short anyway, it will do for this time. It's really too bad that you're not coming! We were all looking forward to it, and I had even made a bet that you could be swayed from your decision not to come. Unfortunately I seem to have lost that bet now for good. Too bad! This way we will be completely without children and it won't sound very convincing tomorrow when the family choir, ages twenty-five to eighty-nine, sings "Ihr Kinderlein kommet."[2]

I wish you an especially nice Christmas celebration in your small family circle. How do you do it at your house, or will you have to create your family Christmas tradition this year for the first time? Up to now you were probably still always here? We're having real winter weather, which, considering the fact that tomorrow is Christmas, will probably have changed to the opposite

[3.] Among other things, the Ern family allowed Bonhoeffer to use their car for his trip to Mexico (see *DBWE* 10:299–300).

[1.] Reprinted from Leibholz-Bonhoeffer, *Weihnachten im Hause Bonhoeffer*, 48–49. Original in the possession of the Leibholz family. Partially reproduced in *GS* 6:222.

[2.] That is, in addition to Bonhoeffer, Julie Bonhoeffer celebrated Christmas 1931 at Karl and Paula Bonhoeffer's home on Wangenheimstrasse. [The reference is to the German Christmas hymn "O Come, Little Children."—VB]

by then. A year ago I was sitting in incredibly hot weather in Cuba.[3] Those were different times!—A couple of days ago, I was on a two-day excursion in the snow with some of my confirmands. I learned a lot and they probably did, too. My interest at Christmas this year is concentrated strongly on these confirmands, and wrapping Christmas gift packages alongside my preparations for the lecture course is a thoroughly enjoyable change and seems to 49
me no less important.

Tomorrow I'll be thinking of you over there as you will probably be thinking of us. Maybe we'll talk by telephone. Say a special hello to my godchild.[4] She will not be getting a gift from me this time (that sounds as if she had always gotten something, which I hardly believe was the case), but I'll hide again this time behind the Christ child,[5] who conceals the identity of the givers. The real reason is simply that in the last few days I haven't been able to think enough about Christmas and to make my preparations. So good-bye, have a nice Christmas celebration, and come into the New Year well and without too many worries; they don't help much after all.

Affectionate greetings to you and the children
Your Dietrich

**27. To Erwin Sutz**[1]

December 25, 1931

Dear Mr. Sutz,

Since I didn't even manage to write you for Christmas, I will have to at least take one day of the Christmas holiday to try to convince you of the seriousness of my intention to write. It will surprise you that the typewriter has the honor of being allowed to write you a Christmas letter, and it will not be hard for you, by an old habit, to come back at me with one of the comments

[3.] In 1930 Katharina (called Käthe) Horn had invited Bonhoeffer and Erwin Sutz for Christmas. At that time she was the principal of the German school in Havana (Leibholz-Bonhoeffer, *Weihnachten im Hause Bonhoeffer*, 46). She had been Sabine's and Dietrich's teacher; her sister, Maria, had been the governess for the twins (*DB-ER*, 151–52, 24, and 35). On Bonhoeffer's stay in Cuba, see *DBWE* 10:265ff.

[4.] Marianne Leibholz.

[5.] [A reference to a German tradition that it is the Christ child who brings Christmas gifts to children.—MBL]

[1.] *NL*, A 29,4(6); typewritten, with handwritten addition in the margins of the second page: "informed that . . . Dietrich Bonhoeffer." Partially reproduced in *GS* 1:24–26.

I made myself during our time in America when you received typed letters from Barth. But why should you not have *that* pleasure and why should I take longer to write this letter for that reason; that is, you see that I don't say (also from old habit) don't laugh!, but: go ahead and laugh! This introduction is rather idiotic, as I just noticed, since the transition to the topic is in no way prepared, but rather the opposite, it is made very difficult. But since I don't want to continue by wishing you, like that well-meaning boy with no sense of time, "happy holidays after the fact," I probably will just have to move on to wishing you a good New Year. The fact that I am doing this in this form, because of the condition of my head from the holiday celebrations, does not diminish my sincerity. This closes the first part (which means that two more must follow).

The first half of the semester is now happily finished; at least I am happy about it. You always have something to do, and it always seems so unnecessary. Only the seminar is really enjoyable. I think I really have an elite of interested and in part amazingly clever and intelligent people. My theological origin is gradually becoming suspect here, and they seem to have somewhat the feeling that they have been nurturing a viper in their bosom.[2] I almost never see any of the professors, not to my inconsolable regret. Since I came back from Bonn, things here seem even more desolate. Recently on two days, one after the other, I invited first the lecturers and then my students here to the house, and I must say that the students were considerably more interested in theology than the lecturers. Luckily I have the practical work; at this time that's not so much the Technical College, but that of course, too. But what keeps me busier at the moment is the confirmation class that I am teaching for fifty boys in the north of Berlin. That is about the toughest neighborhood of Berlin, with the most difficult socioeconomic and political conditions. At the beginning the boys were acting wild, so for the first time I really had discipline problems. But here too one thing helped, namely, just simply telling the boys Bible stories in massive quantity, and especially eschatological passages. By the way, in doing this I also made use of the Negroes.[3] Now it is absolutely quiet, and the boys see to that

[2.] Within the theology department in Berlin, which was predominantly oriented toward liberal theology, Bonhoeffer's orientation toward Karl Barth apparently attracted negative attention.

[3.] [During his studies from 1930 to 1931 at Union Seminary in New York, Bonhoeffer attended Abyssinian Baptist Church in Harlem regularly and learned a great deal from the African American church. He drew upon those experiences when he returned to Germany, particularly in his later work with his seminarians; he had also brought back with him recordings of Negro spirituals. See *DBWE* 10:29–32.—VB]

themselves, so that I no longer have to fear the same fate as my predecessor, whom they rather literally aggravated to death.[4] Recently I took several of 51
them out of the city for two days; tomorrow it's another group's turn. This time together was very enjoyable for us. Since I will be keeping the boys until confirmation, I'll have to visit all fifty parents, and for this purpose I will move to that area for two months.[5] I'm looking forward to this time very much. It's really work. Most of the home conditions are indescribable, poverty, disorder, immorality. Yet the children are still open. I am often speechless at how it is possible that a boy is not completely ruined under these conditions, and, of course, you ask yourself at the same time how you would react to an environment like that. These people must have a very strong capacity for resilience—probably morally as well.

Barth's book on Anselm[6] is a great joy to me. In your leisure hours you must read it, too. He shows the innumerable scholarly cripples thoroughly for once that he knows far more precisely how one interprets and yet remains sovereign. With regard to content, nothing has become less unquestionable.

Recently Dibelius[7] informed us in a lecture[8] that the church has 2,500 too many theology students and that because of this (!) theology students should face particularly strict requirements, the first of which would

[4.] [See 1/25, ed. note 2.—MBL]

[5.] On this experience, see also the report of Fritz Figur, former pastor of the Church of the Benediction (Segenskirche) in Berlin: "One day the master baker Mr. H. from the Oderbergerstrasse came to me. He had a furnished room to rent, and now someone had been to see him about it, a *Stadtsynodalvikar* ["assistant pastor within the city synod," i.e., a minister on special assignment in the city—MBL] Bonhoeffer. Was that "a Catholic"? I could reassure him that Bonhoeffer was not at all "a Catholic," and so Bonhoeffer moved into the Oderbergerstrasse 58 in Berlin North, between Alexander Platz and the old 'Exer,' so not at all in Moabit as is sometimes claimed. At that time he held the significant position of Assistant Pastor in the City Synod, that is an assistant pastor at the Zion Church, with a monthly salary of 420.00 marks. But he had not found a place to stay in his own district. Since in Berlin the streets run through from one parish into the next, his residency requirement was considered to be met even though he lived 400 meters across the boundary, inside the district of the neighboring parish of the Church of the Benediction, in my pastoral district" (Fritz Figur, "At Zion Church," in Zimmermann, *I Knew Dietrich Bonhoeffer*, 55). [See also Schulz, "Bonhoeffers Konfirmanden kamen nicht aus dem Stadtteil Wedding."—MBL]

[6.] Barth, *Fides quaerens intellectum.*

[7.] Otto Dibelius had been general superintendent of the Kurmark since 1925. [The Kurmark denotes the provincial area of the Mark Brandenburg, which encompasses Berlin.—MBL]

[8.] Published as *Was erwartet die Kirche von der jungen Theologen-Generation?*

be a willingness to accept martyrdom (in a battle in which religious and
52 political ideals would be linked!)—the situation being that the younger ones would find this idea difficult, but the older ones would have been well acquainted (!) with it for a long time (!). The auditorium trampled like mad.[9] Long live the "purple church."[10]

With that I will close for today. Many thanks for your letter[11] and write again soon! Once again, many good wishes for the coming year!

Sincere greetings from your
Dietrich Bonhoeffer

17:99 **27a. Notes from the Time as Assistant**[1]

1. Departmental Rules[2]

(1) Only members of one of the combined departments have access. Special permission required for exceptions.

17:100 (2) All the rooms of the department are open to every member. For this a book inspection station at the entrance to the whole department is neces-

[9.] [Traditionally in Germany, student approval in a lecture is evidenced by vigorous stomping of the feet on the floor or rapping of knuckles on desk tops, instead of clapping.—MBL]

[10.] The "purple church" [*violette Kirche*] is an allusion to Dibelius's understanding of the official church, which he describes in his book *Das Jahrhundert der Kirche,* which was bound in purple cloth. In it, Dibelius specifically welcomes the opportunities that had developed for the church through the separation of church and state in 1919.

[11.] Not extant.

[1.] *NL,* A 31,6. Published in *DBW* 17:99–100. In the Nachlaß catalog the following three notes are dated to the time 1931–33. The topics are not related; they might possibly only be related in time. If the retirement of Professor Arthur Titius in 1931 is assumed to have already taken place, as can be deduced from Bonhoeffer's draft of the department rules, the winter semester 1931–32 could be considered as a possible date.

[2.] *NL,* A 31,6 (II); handwritten, probably prepared by Bonhoeffer at the request of Professor Lütgert. This list of rules for the department may have been one of the first

sary[3] (by the doorman or by students?). The charge applies to all departments and will be assigned according to the number of users. (Amount of this?)

(3) The libraries of the systematics departments should be combined. The Seminar I library should be integrated into the Seminar II library (Titius). What should be done with the duplicate copies? Should the New Testament and the History of Doctrine literature from all combined departments be collected in one place? Where should help be found for this work?

(4) A combined catalog for all departments should be prepared.

In agreement[4]

The questions in (3) require more consideration. Duplicate copies, if the books are not heavily used, could be traded in with the help of a used-book dealer (Gsellius).[5]

The second question is made more difficult by the fact that the New Testament department remains in the university. So we probably will have to keep the New Testament literature.

Lütgert

---

assignments given to Bonhoeffer as an assistant. On March 25, 1931, Erich Seeberg, as dean, had written to the minister for science, art, and public education (*Minister für Wissenschaft, Kunst und Volksbildung*), among other things: "Now that the three main divisions of the Department of Theology along with the Departments of Postbiblical Judaism and Early Christian Archaeology and Christian Art have been located together in the department building at Dorotheenstrasse 3, the preparation of a complete catalog of all the books available in this building is absolutely necessary" (Archiv der Humboldt-Universität, Theologische Facultät, Bd. 46, "Verschiedenes, 1929–1944," Bl. 46).

[3.] Bonhoeffer knew this procedure from the library of Union Theological Seminary, New York.

[4.] Beginning of Professor Lütgert handwritten comments.

[5.] Illegible.

17:101 2. Literature List for Arnold Stolzenburg[6]

{Augustine}[7]
{Luther, Sermons, vols. 1. 2. 4}[8]
{Calvin}[9]
Theologia Deutsch[10]
Spener, Pia Desideria[11]
{Kant, only "Anthropologie"[12] present}
Hamann,[13]—
{Schopenhauer, Welt als Wille . . .}[14]
{Nietzsche, only "Genealogie der Moral"[15] present}

[6.] *NL*, A 31,6 (III); handwritten. This list does not reflect in any way the literature used by Stolzenburg in his publications during these years (only Frank, Luther, Ritschl appear there as well). There is also no discernible reason for him to have asked to have a list of these titles compiled. It is more probable that Bonhoeffer put together this list from available holdings for his own teaching, that Stolzenburg showed an interest in the list prepared by Bonhoeffer as a person familiar with libraries (see "Department Rules" above), and that Stolzenburg received a marked list. The marked titles (enclosed in curly braces [{. . .}] here) and unmarked titles reflect Bonhoeffer's theological thinking and his work during this time. The titles named were definitely available in the department library during Bonhoeffer's time there. Titles that can no longer be documented there are indicated by a dash enclosed in parentheses, (–). [In *DBW* 17 publishing information was included in the notes; in this volume it is included in the bibliography. Stolzenburg became the successor to Professor Titius in systematic theology in 1933.—MBL]

[7.] Available works of Augustine: Aurelius Augustinus, *Ausgewählte Schriften*; idem, *Opera omnia*.

[8.] Probably refers to the following volumes in the series Quellenschriften zur Geschichte des Protestantismus: no. 1: *Die ältesten ethischen Disputationen Luthers* (1904); no. 2: *Die Wittenberger Artikel von 1536* (1905); no. 4: *Luthers sermo de poenitentia* (1906) (vol. 3 contains the Heidelberg Catechism).

[9.] J. Calvinus, *Opera quae supersunt omnia*; idem, *Opera selecta*, vols. 1, 3–5.

[10.] *Theologia deutsch* (1908). [This refers to Luther's edition (published partially in 1516 and completely in 1518) of an anonymous medieval mystical text from a German cleric, originally titled the *Theologia Germanica*.—MBL]

[11.] Philipp Jakob Spener, *Pia Desideria*.

[12.] Immanuel Kant, *Anthropologie in pragmatischer Hinsicht*.

[13.] Possibly deleted; available in the department was the several-volume work [edited by C. H. Gildemeister], *Johann Georg Hamann's des Magus im Norden, Leben und Schriften* [Hamann was an important religious voice in eighteenth-century Germany, asserting spiritual individualism and opposing excesses in Enlightenment rationalism. —MBL]

[14.] (–) Arthur Schopenhauer, *Die Welt als Wille und Vorstellung*.

[15.] Friedrich Nietzsche, *Zur Genealogie der Moral*.

{Feuerbach, Wesen der Religion}[16]

Löhe, Drei Bücher von der Kirche[17]

Kliefoth, 8 Bücher von der Kirche[18] 17:102

{Kierkegaard, only "Einübung im Christentum"[19] present}

{Frank, Theologie der Konkordienformel}[20]

{A. Ritschl, Unterricht in der christlichen Religion. Metaphysik und Theologie, christliche Vollkommenheit}[21]

v. Hofmann, {Schriftbeweis};[22] Weissagung und Erfüllung[23]

{W. Hermann, Dogmatik}[24]

{J. Müller, Lehre von der Sünde}[25]

{Müller, reformierte Bekenntnisschriften}[26]

Culmann, Ethik[27]

{Scholz, Religionsphilosophie}[28]

{Tillich,—}[29] [. . .]

Grisebach, Gegenwart; Grenzen des Erziehers[30]

Heidegger, Sein und Zeit[31]

{Husserl, Logische Untersuchungen}[32]

Przywara, Ringen der Gegenwart, 2 volumes, Religionsphilosophie katholischer Theologie[33]

---

[16.] (–) Ludwig Feuerbach, *Das Wesen der Religion.*

[17.] (–) Wilhelm Löhe, *Drei Bücher von der Kirche.*

[18.] Theodor Kliefoth, *Acht Bücher von der Kirche.*

[19.] Søren Kierkegaard, *Einübung im Christentum.*

[20.] Franz Hermann Reinhold von Frank, *Die Theologie der Concordienformel.*

[21.] Albrecht Ritschl, *Unterricht in der christlichen Religion, Die christliche Vollkommenheit,* (and in the same volume) *Theologie und Metaphysik.*

[22.] (–) J. Chr. K. von Hofmann, *Der Schriftbeweis.*

[23.] (–) J. Chr. K. von Hofmann, *Weissagung und Erfüllung im Alten und Neuen Testamente.*

[24.] Wilhelm Herrmann, "Christlich-protestantische Dogmatik."

[25.] (–) Julius Müller, *Die christliche Lehre von der Sünde.*

[26.] Title here is incorrect; it should be Johannes T. Müller, *Die symbolischen Bücher der evangelisch-lutherischen Kirche.*

[27.] Philipp Theodor Culmann, *Die christliche Ethik,* vol. 1.

[28.] Heinrich Scholz, *Religionsphilosophie.*

[29.] Probably P[aul] Tillich, *Die religiöse Lage der Gegenwart.*

[30.] Ebèrhard Grisebach, *Gegenwart* und *Die Grenzen des Erziehers und seine Verantwortung.*

[31.] Martin Heidegger, *Sein und Zeit.*

[32.] Edmund Husserl, *Logische Untersuchungen.*

[33.] Erich Przywara, *Ringen der Gegenwart*; idem, *Religionsphilosophie katholischer Theologie.*

{Heiler, Katholizismus}[34]
17:103 {Bartmann, Dogmatik}[35]
Fendt, religiöse Grundkräfte des katholischen Dogmas[36]
Missale Romanum,[37]
Brevierbuch[38] Breviarum romanum 4 volumes available[39]
Corpus iuris canonici[40]
With kindest regards

Bonhoeffer

For Professor Stolzenburg

3. Topics for Seminar Papers[41]

| | | |
|---|---|---|
| Zimmer | 1st Commandment | Geislautern[42] Saargebiet |
| Paeplow | Romans 9–11. L[uther][43] | Pankow Maximilianstr[asse] |
| Brauer | 1st Commandment | Spandau Neuendorfer [Strasse] 75 |
| Bronisch | Predestination | Züllichau–Kirchplatz in Aug[ustine][44] |
| Andrich | Romans 9–11. Barth[45] | |

[34.] Friedrich Heiler, *Der Katholizismus.*

[35.] Bernhard Bartmann, *Lehrbuch der Dogmatik.*

[36.] Leonhard Fendt, *Die religiösen Kräfte des katholischen Dogmas.*

[37.] *Missale Romanum ex decreto sacrosancti Concilii Tridentini restitutum.*

[38.] *Breviarium romanum ex decreto SS. Concilii Tridentini restitutum.*

[39.] "Breviarum . . . available" added in another hand.

[40.] *Corpus iuris canonici.*

[41.] *NL*, A 31,6 (I); handwritten. The list with names and topics might be associated with the seminar "The Idea of Philosophy and Protestant Theology [in the Twentieth Century]" ("Die Idee der Philosophie und die protestantische Theologie"), winter semester 1931–32 [see Chronology, p. 495]. On this topic, see also the letters to Sutz (1/27) and to Lehmann on November 5, 1931 (1/16a). The list might also refer to the seminar on the topic "Is There a Christian Ethic?" from the summer semester 1932; see 2/10.

[42.] Near Völklingen.

[43.] See Luther, *Vorlesungen über den Römerbrief, 1515–1516* (vol. 2: *Capitulum nonum bis Capitulum undecimum*). Bonhoeffer used this edition; the lectures had not yet been published in the Weimarer Ausgabe (*WA*) in 1931.

[44.] See Augustine, *De praedestinatione sanctorum.*

[45.] See Barth, *Epistle to the Romans.* Further down the page, there is a notation in Eberhard Bethge's handwriting: "probably Lütgert seminar."

## 28. Circular Letter of the Working Group of Theologians and Economists[1]

December 28, 1931

Re: Working Group of Theologians and Economists

In response to several requests we have decided to change the meeting time for the last three gatherings of the Working Group of Theologians and National Economists for this semester to Tuesday afternoon.[2] At our next meeting, which will take place on

*Tuesday, January 19, at five o'clock in the afternoon*

Lecturer Licentiate Bonhoeffer will give an introductory talk on the question of the *"Discernible Nature of the Order of Creation."*[3]

In the following meeting, which will take place on 53

*Tuesday, February 2, at five o'clock in the afternoon*

Pastor Peter will address the topic *"People and State as Order of Creation."* For this topic we ask that the members of the working group familiarize themselves with the content of the book by P[astor] Peter, *Wenn die Würfel fallen* (Verlag des Ostdeutschen Jünglingsbundes, [Berlin] N54, Sophienstrasse 19. Price 1.50 reichsmarks).[4]

In our last meeting, for which the date has not yet been set, we will in all likelihood have a discussion on the question of "The Nature of Work."

For the next time a different room at the theological department will probably be made available to us. For this reason we request that those attending ask the doorman, who will give information about the location.

With greetings from the association,
signed Licentiate Sasse

---

[1.] Archiv des Diakonischen Werkes, Berlin, KSB 410; typewritten; letterhead left: "Church Social Federation / Regional Group for Greater Berlin [Kirchlich-sozialer Bund / Landesgruppe Groß-Berlin], right: "President: Administrative Director/ Dr. Büchsel / Business Office: Berlin-Spandau / Johannesstift / Telephone: C7 Spandau 2425 / Postal Bank Account: Berlin No. 1112 / Berlin-Spandau." Hermann Sasse had apparently written the circular letter at the request of Reinhold Krause, since the top of the document shows Krause as the sender, but it was signed by Sasse.

[2.] The original meeting time of Monday afternoon conflicted with Bonhoeffer's seminar "The Idea of Philosophy and Protestant Theology [in the Twentieth Century]" (see 1/18).

[3.] [See 2/8.—MBL]

[4.] This is a publication of the speaker, Friedrich Peter, *Wenn die Würfel fallen* (1931).

17:104 **28a. Assistantship Contract**[1]

A stamp of 1.50 reichsmarks value must be submitted for the original document.

Today [. . .] the following contract has been agreed upon between the director of administration at the Friedrich Wilhelm University and *Licentiate Dietrich Bonhoeffer*:

§ 1

From *August 1, 1931, until June 30, 1933, Licentiate Bonhoeffer* will be assigned to fill a position as an adjunct assistant in the *Department of Systematics in the Department of Theology* of the University in Berlin.

§ 2

*At the current time, Licentiate Bonhoeffer* will receive for his work at the above-named institution a salary of *214* RM[2] (in words: *two hundred and fourteen* reichsmarks—pfennig) [. . .] *to be paid on the fifteenth of each month for that month by the university financial office.*

§ 3

This contract can be ended by *Licentiate Bonhoeffer* any time at the end of a month with six weeks' notice, by the institution only at the end of a quarter.

§ 4

In accepting a position as an adjunct assistant *Licentiate Bonhoeffer* does not receive the status of a tenured civil servant nor the right to be appointed to a position as an assistant with full salary.

Berlin, *January 14, 1932*

The Director of Administration at the
Friedrich Wilhelm University
Licentiate Dietrich Bonhoeffer Dr. Büchsel

Contract (employment of an *extra*-ordinary[3] [*außer*planmäßig] assistant).

[1.] *NL*, A 6 (11); form (typewritten) with typed entries (indicated here with italics) for information concerning the special contract with Bonhoeffer; items crossed out on the form shown by "[. . .]"; both signatures handwritten; unpublished.

[2.] Note the decrease in salary compared to the original contract for the position of assistant of November 21, 1931. See 1/18a.

[3.] The word *außer* is italicized in the original [meaning outside the regular operation and budget; elsewhere in these documents it is translated as "adjunct," which comes closest to the U.S. equivalent of Bonhoeffer's status there.—MBL]

## 29. From Johannes Hosemann to the Members of the Provisional Bureau[1]

Berlin-Charlottenburg 2, January 19, 1932

To the members of the Provisional Bureau for Ecumenical Youth Work

I am sending for your information, at the request of the director,[2] Professor Stählin in Münster,[3] a copy of the report on the meeting of the Provisional Bureau for Ecumenical Youth Work that took place in Berlin on October 20, 1931.

Concerning the free copies of the Universal Christian Council for Life and Work[4] publication *Mitteilungen*,[5] which High Consistory Councillor Dr. 54
Schreiber mentions under topic no. II 1), we have had word from Geneva[6] that they are willing to make the *Mitteilungen* available to the German Ecumenical Working group.[7] A list from the Provisional Bureau has been sent to Geneva, so that the *Mitteilungen* can be sent to those who do not already receive it.

---

[1.] LKA Nuremberg, XVIII: Nachlaß Stählin; carbon copy with original greeting and official notarization; letterhead: "The President / of the German Protestant Church Commission / (Church Federation Office)" [Der Präsident / des / Deutschen Evangelischen Kirchenausschusses / (Kirchenbundesamt)] / K.A. III 762."

[2.] [The director of the Provisional Bureau.—VB]

[3.] [The reference is to Wilhelm Stählin, professor of practical theology, Münster. —MBL]

[4.] The movement for "Practical Christianity" ("Life and Work") emerged from the 1919 meeting in Oud Wassenaar, Holland, where the World Alliance for Promoting International Friendship through the Churches was founded. In 1925 at the "General Conference of the Church of Christ for Practical Christianity" ("Allgemeine Konferenz der Kirche Christi für Praktisches Christentum") in Stockholm, the Universal Christian Council for Life and Work (Ökumenischer Rat für Praktisches Christentum) was created to continue this work; it was this council that subsequently established ecumenical offices in Geneva and eventually merged (in 1938) with the Faith and Order movement, setting the foundation for the creation of the World Council of Churches in 1948.

[5.] *Mitteilungen* was a quarterly ecumenical publication, published in Geneva in German, English, and French, that conveyed information about the activities of Life and Work and the International Institute of Social Sciences (Internationales Sozialwissenschaftliches Institut) of Life and Work, Geneva. [The English version was titled *Life and Work: Bulletin of the Internationalen Sozialwissenschaftlichen Instituts der Weltkirchenkonferenz für Praktisches Christentum*. The quarterly appeared in the years following the 1925 Stockholm conference; after 1931 it was published as *Die Kirchen am Werk: Mitteilungen*.—VB]

[6.] The secretariat of the Universal Christian Council for Life and Work was located there.

[7.] The "German ecumenical working group," founded by August W. Schreiber and supported by the Church Federation Office, brought together the Protestant youth organizations, the World Alliance for Promoting International Friendship through the Churches, the Faith and Order movement, and the Life and Work movement (see the organizational chart in appendix 4, p. 505).

Professor Stählin lets us know that Licentiate Dr. Bonhoeffer, Berlin Grunewald, Wangenheimstr. 14, has agreed to assist him as the secretary of the Provisional Bureau. Licentiate Bonhoeffer was an assistant pastor in Barcelona, then an exchange student in New York, and is now pastor for the students at the Technical College in Berlin-Charlottenburg. In Cambridge he was elected youth secretary of the Management Committee of the World Alliance for Promoting International Friendship through the Churches and is in close contact with Superintendent Diestel, Berlin-Lichterfelde, the vice chairman of the German Section of the World Alliance, in whose office their administrative office is currently located.

I would like to note respectfully that at the request of Professor Stählin, especially because of the theological conference suggested by the Provisional Bureau for Ecumenical Youth Work, the report has also been sent to the other members of the German Ecumenical Working Group.[8]

For the office
signed Dr. Hosemann
Notarized
Schater
Financial Manager of the Consistory Office

### 55 **30. From the Executive Committee of the City Synod in Berlin**[1]

Charlottenburg 2, January 25, 1932

Regarding the letter of December 31, 1931
Re: Increase of income tax for January 1932

As requested in your letter of November 30, 1931, we sent you the *first* income tax card, which was in our office, to be presented to the tax office. On December 31, 1931, you sent back to us the *second* income tax card for 1931. We had to assume that you would wish to have the same assignment of the income tax cards for 1932 as well. For that reason it was necessary for us in calculating your income tax for January 1932 to withhold income tax from your entire salary, on the assumption that the monthly amount of 100 RM deductible from income

[8.] The German Ecumenical Working Group was a subcommittee of the German Protestant Church Council, on which the World Alliance for Promoting International Friendship through the Churches and most of the organizations working with the Provisional Bureau [for Ecumenical Youth Work] were represented (see 1/45).

[1.] *NL*, A 30, 1(16); typewritten.

tax would be deducted by *the* office to which you—as on December 12, 1931—sent[2] your *first* income tax card for 1932.

But now you have sent your first income tax card for 1932 to *us*.[3] Unless you exchange this first card for the second card immediately, we will give you a credit for the excess tax withheld for January 1932 when calculating income tax withholding for February 1932.

For the office
signed Niedlich
Prepared by:
Senior Secretary

### 31. Circular Letter of the Provisional Bureau[1] 56

Berlin-Grunewald, January 27, 1932

I am enclosing, at the request of Professor Dr. Stählin–Münster[2] in accordance with the motion passed by the Provisional Bureau for Ecumenical Youth Work on October 20, 1931,[3] the circular letter of October 15, 1931, with several copies of the questionnaire for the card file,[4] which should

[2.] Crossed out: "sent back."

[3.] After being asked by the administrative director of the Friedrich Wilhelm University to sign the contract as an assistant (see above, 1/24), Bonhoeffer had submitted his first income tax card to the university, to use the income tax deduction for his assistant's salary. As an adjunct assistant, he received 214 RM beginning August 1, 1931; as an assistant pastor in the City Synod, Bonhoeffer earned an additional 184 RM, plus a housing allowance of 72 RM beginning in August (*NL*, A 30,1[7]). It was necessary to change the income tax cards again because when Bonhoeffer was appointed assistant pastor in the City Synod at Zion Church, his salary was raised to 420 RM. With an annual income of ca. 7,000 RM, Bonhoeffer fell into only the fourth of ten possible income brackets, but as far as the distribution of taxable income among the number of wage earners was concerned, in 1928 about 16 million were in the first income bracket (up to 1,200 RM) and about 11 million in the second (up to 3,000 RM). At that time fewer than 500,000 wage earners were included in the income brackets five through ten (*Statistisches Jahrbuch für das Deutsche Reich 1941/42*, 606, as cited in Petzina et al., *Sozialgeschichtliches Arbeitsbuch*, 3:105.

[1.] LKA Nuremberg, XVIII: Nachlaß Stählin; carbon copy.

[2.] [Münster was where Stählin taught.—VB]

[3.] See the questionnaire and the accompanying letter of October 15, 1931, in 1/12.

[4.] Wilhelm Stählin had already sent the questionnaire to the members of the Provisional Bureau in October 1931 (see LKA Nuremberg, XVIII: Nachlaß Stählin).

facilitate acquiring an overview of those young people who seem suited for international conferences. I request that the completed forms be sent back to me by April 1.

(signed) Licentiate Dietrich Bonhoeffer

### 32. From Erich Stange to Wilhelm Stählin[1]

Kassel-Wilhelmshöhe, January 28, 1932

Dear Professor Stählin:

I acknowledge with many thanks the receipt of the report on the meeting of the Provisional Bureau on October 20 of last year, which was sent to me by the Church Federation Office.

Especially because I was unable to attend the meeting, I followed the discussion as reported in the minutes with great interest and took the liberty of giving a copy of the minutes to Ministerial Director von Kameke,[2] since he will probably, at least when I myself am unable to attend, continue to represent us at the Provisional Bureau.

57 My particular interest, naturally, is in the progress of the preparations for the theological conference,[3] which we talked about briefly at lunch earlier.

As far as the topics are concerned, I would suggest formulating them somewhat more pointedly, to ensure a certain level of relevance to the current situation right from the beginning.

---

[1.] LKA Nuremberg, XVIII: Nachlaß Stählin; typewritten with handwritten signature; letterhead: "The National President of the German Protestant Young Men's Association / Dr. Erich Stange"; a carbon copy, which has not been preserved, went to Bonhoeffer.

[2.] Karl Otto von Kameke, who had been a senior director ["ministerial director" indicates a high-ranking civil servant of the rank of agency director—MBL] at the Ministry of the Interior since 1927; as the representative of the National Federation of Protestant Young Men's Associations [Reichsverband der ev. Jungmännerbünde], he attended the meetings of the Provisional Bureau.

[3.] Theological Conference of the Provisional Bureau, April 29–30, 1932, in the Church Federation Office. [See 2/13.—MBL]

There is some question whether we can stay with the date (March 6–12), since by now it is getting very close to the time. But perhaps you have made more preparations in the meantime?

Finally, as far as the card file is concerned, I see certain difficulties in fulfilling your wishes, both on principle and also with respect to the size of our national organization, which makes such a survey extremely difficult if it is to be even somewhat reliable. It is not necessary to go into that, though, since in the meantime the executive committee of our organization, following a statement that I had already given to the general secretary of our world organization, has made the following decision:

"After serious critical discussion among its own members, the German Protestant Young Men's Association had decided to send representatives to the World Conferences in the summer of 1931 in North America because of the difficult decisions that were expected to be made there, despite the fact that the situation in Germany hardly seemed as if that could be managed, and it also would be unavoidable for this to be misunderstood by those outside our group. In the meantime, the situation of our nation has worsened so much in every respect that our group *cannot even consider* sending representatives to international meetings of youth or leaders like the one the world organization is planning for 1932. Even if financing could be made available for such trips, and the German organization has no funds at all available for this, one cannot expect that a people [Volk] that is fighting for its existence has time for and interest in such conferences. I ask you, therefore, not to count on participants from Germany at these conferences and meetings.

"For those within our world organization who are interested in solidarity and internal fellowship with us, there is a way to do that without these camps and conferences. In the coming weeks, as decisions are made that will determine the fate of our people, we will listen eagerly to see if anywhere in the world, from the groups in the national organizations affiliated with us, a voice of protest
arises against injustice and exploitation. A single clear statement of this sort will 58
mean more for understanding within the Christian community than many international camps and conferences."

Even if this primarily concerns a certain type of retreat-like meetings within our Young Men's Associations, it would of course also apply to our group's participation in similar meetings of other ecumenical groups. That does not prevent our considering each such invitation on a case-by-case basis, but it makes such a general survey like the one for the establishment of a card file unnecessary.

I have had a copy of this letter sent to Licentiate Bonhoeffer for his information and remain with best wishes

Most respectfully yours,
Dr. Stange

## 33. Circular Letter of the Working Group of Theologians and Economists[1]

January 28, 1932

Re: Working Group of Theologians and Economists

The talk by Lecturer Licentiate Bonhoeffer on the topic "The Discernible Nature of the Order of Creation"[2] led to a lively discussion that summarized the results of the previous meetings and could not be finished. Participants have expressed their wish to continue the discussion. At the same time, several gentlemen have called our attention to the fact that February 2, the planned date of our next meeting, is a date for which many other events are scheduled. So, with the consent of Pastor Peter, our next scheduled speaker, we have decided to call the next meeting for *February 9*, at which the discussion on the Bonhoeffer paper will be continued and brought to a conclusion.[3] The talk by Pastor Peter, "The People [Volk] and the State," will take place, then, on March 1, again at the
59 theological department, Dorotheenstrasse 3. The doorman can be asked for the exact room number.

Greetings in the spirit of our church-social group,
signed Licentiate Sasse signed Dr. Krause

## 34. To the Wingolf Fraternity, Charlottenburg[1]

To the Wartburg Fraternity "Lietzenburg"
Charlottenburg
Wingolf Fraternity at the Technical College

Dear Senior,[2]

Before the Christmas vacation I had sent you a letter[3] with the question and request that you would kindly let me know if the idea of introducing morning devotions at the Technical College finds approval in your frater-

[1.] Archiv des Diakonischen Werkes, Berlin, KSB 410; typewritten; letterhead as above in 1/28 [see ed. note 1—MBL] with typewritten notation top left: "Please note the changes / From: Dr. Krause."

[2.] [See 2/8.—MBL]

[3.] On the planning for the working group preceding this date, see 1/28.

[1.] *NL*, A 29,1(2) (a); handwritten draft. Cf. *NL*, A 29,1(2) (b); later typewritten transcription by Eberhard Bethge. Previously published in *GS* 6:213–14. The letter was probably sent at the end of January before the devotional services began or at the beginning of February 1932, shortly after they started. The Charlottenburg chapter of the

nity and to what degree you would be willing to support carrying out this plan. Since to date I have not received an answer, I am afraid there may have been some misunderstanding. If possible, I would like to start with these devotions next week and would like to know approximately how many I can count on to attend.

With best regards, most respectfully yours,
D. B.

### 35. To Henry-Louis Henriod[1] 60

February 14, 1932

Dear Mr. Henriod,

Many thanks for your letter, which I had already been expecting. I wrote to Toureille[2] immediately. You have obviously been wrongly informed about *the date* of the German-French conference.[3] At that time we had been

Wingolf fraternity (Charlottenburger Wingolf) was founded in 1897 because the Berlin chapter of Wingolf, which since 1848 had been a fraternity whose members wore sashes and insignia in the fraternity colors, refused to accept the students from the Technical College (Gladen, *Geschichte der studentischen Korporationsverbände*, 2:131–32). This fraternity tried to compensate for its shorter history by using the name "Lietzenburg," the earlier name of Charlottenburg, and by referring specifically to old traditions of the traditional German fraternities.

[2.] [The title of the head of the local fraternity chapter—MBL]

[3.] Letter not extant.

[1.] *NL*, A 28,3(1); typewritten with handwritten signature; letterhead: "Lic. Bonhoeffer / Berlin-Grunewald / Wangenheimstr. 14." Previously published in *GS* 6:238–39. Henry-Louis Henriod had been general secretary of the World Alliance for Promoting International Friendship through the Churches and the Universal Christian Council on Life and Work since 1931. After the conference in Cambridge [Cambridge, England, September 1931—MBL], he also took on the office of secretary of the Youth Commission, for which Bonhoeffer was one of three youth secretaries (see *DB-ER*, 200).

[2.] At the Youth Conference of the World Alliance in Cambridge, September 5–9, 1931, Pastor Pierre C. Toureille was appointed to be one of the three voluntary international youth secretaries who, with the financial assistance of the World Alliance, were to travel and coordinate [programs on behalf of the youth efforts of the World Alliance —MBL]. All three youth secretaries were, at the same time, appointed members of the Management Committee and of the International Council of the International Section of the World Alliance for Promoting International Friendship through the Churches (see 1/16 and *DB-ER*, 200) [see also appendix 4, p. 504.—MBL]

[3.] The German-French Regional Conference of the World Alliance for Promoting International Friendship through the Churches took place July 12–14, 1932, at the Westerburg [in Germany—MBL].

considering April 15–17, since most of us cannot leave our congregations at Easter.

The increase in the *budget* is, of course, extremely good news, since at the present time we cannot expect any German participant to be in a position to pay anything himself.

*Paris* was, as I thought at the time, considered as the location for the meeting of the Youth Commission because of a meeting of the Management Committee at the same time there. But I believe I can say today, although I must wait for the reply from church headquarters to a request in this matter, that I could just as well be in England[4] April 3–4.

I would just be grateful for definitive information soon.

With kindest regards, I am most respectfully yours,
Bonhoeffer

61 **36. To Reinhold Krause**[1]

February 17, 1932

Dear Dr. Krause:

I am enclosing to you the theses in brief form.[2] I apologize for the delay. But I did not get to it until now.

With best regards. Most respectfully yours,
Bonhoeffer

[4.] The conference of the International Youth Secretariat took place April 4, 1932, in Epsom, near London.

[1.] Archiv des Diakonischen Werkes, Berlin, KSB 410; handwritten with illegible handwritten notations, which may be by Krause.

[2.] See 2/8. At the beginning of November, Krause had asked Bonhoeffer to give a lecture at a meeting of the Working Group of Theologians and Economists (see 1/18). Then, on January 19, 1932, he held a lecture on "The Discernible Nature of the Order of Creation" (2/8), which was followed by lively discussions in the subsequent meetings (see 1/33). The copies of these theses probably served as a basis to work from [in the meetings—MBL] (see also 1/49).

**37. From August W. Schreiber**[1]

Berlin-Charlottenburg, February 18, 1932

Dear Lecturer Bonhoeffer,

Following our telephone conversation, I would like to ask you to tell Professor Stählin in Münster that the information I gave you is of a completely personal nature. The official handling of this makes it necessary to ask Professor Stählin to give the Church Federation Office more detailed information about the conference we intend to hold.

The discussions you have had with me and with Professor Stählin as well as Professor Stählin's discussions[2] with General Superintendent Dr. Zoellner,[3] Professor Althaus, and Bishop Dr. Rendtorff,[4] have already resulted in the conclusion that the conference[5] cannot take place before the end of April, we hope with the participation of Dr. Zoellner and Dr. Rendtorff.

I would be grateful if, in his letter to the Church Federation Office, Professor 62
Stählin could first request that the next meeting of the Provisional Bureau for Ecumenical Youth Work might be set for the same time as a general meeting of the German Ecumenical Working Group; further, that the Church Federation Office give its approval to the planned theologians' conference, since then the request could be added that the Church Federation Office might kindly make a meeting room available and would also approve the use of funds to cover the travel costs for the speakers, if necessary.

Sincerely yours,
Dr. Schreiber

[1.] LKA Nuremberg, XVIII: Nachlaß Stählin; typewritten, with handwritten signature.

[2.] See Wilhelm Stählin's invitations to the gentlemen mentioned above in LKA Nuremberg, XVIII: Nachlaß Stählin.

[3.] Wilhelm Zoellner was the general superintendent of Westphalia until 1931 and was a member of the German committee of Faith and Order.

[4.] Heinrich Rendtorff, regional bishop of Mecklenburg-Schwerin since 1930 and honorary professor at Rostock.

[5.] Theological Conference of the Provisional Bureau [for Ecumenical Youth Work] in the Church Federation Office [Berlin], April 29–30, 1932. [See 2/13.—MBL]

17:105 **37a. To Paul Lehmann**[1]

February 19, 1932

Dear Paul,

Today only a very short letter with a question. Actually, I intended to write long ago, but you have not written for longer than I. That is really a shame! Because I am always looking forward very much to hearing from you. Are you still suffering from the shock of Niebuhr's wedding,[2] which I heard about through the *Bulletin* today? I would rather have him this way than the other—you understand, don't you?

At the moment I have incredibly much to do. I am living here in the north of Berlin[3] where I am teaching,[4] and every day I see the most dreadful living conditions. With my very limited means, I am almost unable to help at all. And now to preach the gospel under these circumstances! In confirmation class things sometimes go amazingly well. They really listen, with their mouths open. Then sometimes they are really bratty again.[5] But now to the questions. Because it is late at night and I still have to work on a sermon for Memorial Day[6]—probably the worst day there is on which to preach![7]

---

[1.] Paul Lehmann Collection, Special Collections, Princeton Theological Seminary Library; typewritten with handwritten signature, from Berlin. Previously published in *Evangelische Theologie* (1996): 470–71, and *DBW* 17:105–6. Editorial notes by Hans Pfeifer.

[2.] During 1930–31, the year they were studying together at Union, the three friends, Bonhoeffer, Sutz, and Lehmann, had learned about the difficulties for Niebuhr in his upcoming wedding. It all stemmed from his separation from his mother; see Fox, *Reinhold Niebuhr: A Biography*, 126–28 and 131: "He [i.e., Niebuhr] was not just leaving his childhood home; for Lydia [Niebuhr's mother] at least it was abandonment, if not desertion, divorce, and remarriage." Sutz and Bonhoeffer had also told Niebuhr of their concern. Lehmann was probably more discouraged by the fact that Ursula Niebuhr was (Anglo-) Catholic. [Ursula (Keppel-Compton) Niebuhr came to Union in 1930 from Oxford, where she had been a superior student in both history and theology. She and Reinhold Niebuhr were married in Winchester Cathedral in England on December 22, 1931. She was deeply committed to the Anglican Church, especially its liturgy and traditions, which presented some difficulties for Niebuhr's family and tension even among his friends and associates. See Sifton, *Serenity Prayer*, 134–37, for the daughter's reflections on this tension and on the relationship with Bonhoeffer and Barth.—MBL]

[3.] Berlin, Oderbergerstrasse; see *DB-ER*, 226–27.

[4.] [The reference is to the Zion Church confirmation classes in Berlin-Mitte.—MBL]

[5.] See *DB-ER*, 226–29 and the letter of December 25, 1931, to Sutz (1/27).

[6.] [*Volkstrauertag*; a traditional national day in memory of those who died in the First World War.—MBL]

[7.] See 3/5.

First, I would like to know what actually became of my article in the *Journal of Religion.*[8] It was supposed to be published in October. Second, concerning Ritschl and the other books. Ritschl is presently not available in a cheap edition. You will have to pay about fifty marks. Do you want it? Further: Did the book dealer back then enclose a bill? If not, please be so good as to send the ten dollars to my address. I paid that to the book dealer. 17:106

Do write soon. I am completely without news. Fisher[9] has never written at all. Soon I'll begin to hold that against him. He doesn't have that much to do. He can give up one evening for his "boyfriend" instead of his "lady friend."[10]

Give my kind regards to your wife. The time when we will see each other is coming closer!

So long! Sincerely yours,
Dietrich Bonhoeffer

**38. From Max Diestel**[1]

Dear Licentiate Bonhoeffer:

In its last meeting on February 12, the German Section of the World Alliance elected you as a member of the German Management Committee and appointed you to be the specialist for youth work. We welcome you very sincerely to our group and would like to request that from now on whenever your schedule makes it at all possible, you attend the meetings of the Management Committee. From now on, you will be sent minutes of these meetings[2] regularly. Should

[8.] The article ("Concerning the Christian Idea of God," by Dietrich Bonhoeffer, University of Berlin) appeared in April 1932 in *Journal of Religion* 12, no. 2 (1932): 177–85; it is reprinted in *DBWE* 10:451–61.

[9.] Bonhoeffer's student friend Frank Fisher helped him in his efforts to get to know the "Negro centers of life and culture," as they were called then, in Harlem and to gain entry to the churches and groups there; see *DB-ER*, 150–52.

[10.] [Bonhoeffer uses the English words "boyfriend" and "lady friend," clearly meaning himself as a male friend.—MBL]

[1.] Literary estate of Jürgen Winterhager; transcription of the typewritten letter with handwritten signature of February 20, 1932, from Diestel's files on the World Alliance for Promoting International Friendship through the Churches, file: Management Committee [Arbeitsausschuß]. Max Diestel was chair of the German Section of the World Alliance for Promoting International Friendship through the Churches in 1931. [See appendix 4, p. 504.—MBL]

[2.] The minutes of the meetings of the German Section of the World Alliance for Promoting International Friendship through the Churches have not been found to date.

you have any corrections to these, we request that you let us know orally or in writing before the next meeting.

We would also be very grateful to you if you would occasionally take the floor at these meetings to talk about the ecumenical Provisional Bureau for Youth Work or another topic that is of interest to us in our work with the World Alliance [for Promoting International Friendship through the Churches] and is important for us to know.

Sincerely,
Diestel

63 **39. To Erwin Sutz**[1]

Berlin, February 28, 1932

Dear Mr. Sutz,

The semester is over. The lecture class[2] is finished; it was boring enough, too—at least for me. But the seminar[3] was really nice and interesting. I had a couple of really lively fellows from Barth and Gogarten in it.[4] Do you know Stadelmann?[5] He is a very unusual man.

For weeks my conscience has been bothering me because I didn't answer your letter[6] right away. It had pleased me so much at the time. It was the first serious answer about my book,[7] for which I am so grateful to you, even if you are much too kind about the thing. In the meantime, I don't like that product much anymore. Soon I'll bother you with something completely different and ask for your critique of it.

It is a very brief draft of a catechism that I wrote with a friend[8] last summer and which is being published[9] now. I will send it in the next few days. Recently, in the middle of all my work that was piling up, I had a very nice

[1.] *NL*, A 29,4(7); typewritten with handwritten addition: "Do you ever see Barth . . . Bonhoeffer"; on the left margin some words had to be filled in. Partially reproduced in *GS* 1:26–29.

[2.] Winter semester 1931–32: "History of Twentieth-Century Systematic Theology." See 2/3.

[3.] Winter semester 1931–32 seminar: "The Idea of Philosophy and Protestant Theology [in the Twentieth Century]." [See 2/4.—MBL]

[4.] [I.e., students who had attended one of Barth's or Gogarten's seminars.—VB]

[5.] Probably Walter Stadelmann.

[6.] Not extant.

[7.] *Act and Being* (1931) (*DBWE* 2); see above, 1/11.

[8.] Franz Hildebrandt, who had been a close friend of Bonhoeffer's since 1929 (*DB-ER*, 138).

[9.] Published in *Monatsschrift für Pastoraltheologie* 28 (1932): 167–72 (see 2/7).

evening with Hans Fischer, which was especially good because at the end Fischer read aloud your sermon on "Legion."[10] If you would just finally understand that you should now start writing, then I could very quickly pack up and quit and would be delighted to do it. The sermon pleased me unbelievably and made me feel inadequate at the same time. But now, please, send me one, too! Why don't you do that?

Tomorrow is the examination for the confirmands. Confirmation then 64
in two weeks. I have given almost all of the second half of the semester for the confirmands. Since New Year's, I've been living here in the north,[11] so that I can have the boys here every evening, naturally not all at the same time. We eat dinner together; afterward we play something—I have taught them chess and now they're playing it with great enthusiasm. In general, any of them can also come without an appointment. And they all like to come. So the criticism doesn't go that far.[12] At the close of each evening, I read something from the Bible, and following that we have a little catechetics, which is often very serious. The class instruction itself was such that I can hardly bear to leave it. Naturally, the boys were still often dumb and didn't concentrate, but I actually liked that sometimes. Because, on the other hand, it was really possible to talk to them about central and profound things, and they listened, often with their jaws fairly dropping. It is simply new to them to have anything other than learning the catechism. I structured the entire class around the concept of church-community, and the boys, who hear daily from political party organizations, notice very well here what it's all about. But they also see the boundaries unbelievably clearly, so that again and again, whenever we talked about the Holy Spirit in the life of the church-community, the objection came up: but in reality it's all completely different, for indeed the parish comes far behind any political youth organization or sports club. In the club we feel at home, but in the church?—And then, again and again, the discussion found its way from belief in the communion of saints to the forgiveness of sins, and I believe that now they have understood something of it. Nothing happened

---

[10.] According to information from Mrs. Dora Sutz (letter of December 8, 1988), the sermon has not been preserved.

[11.] Berlin N58, Oderbergerstrasse 61 (Franz Figur, "At Zion Church," in Zimmermann, *I Knew Dietrich Bonhoeffer*, 55–56). [See also Schulz, "Bonhoeffers Konfirmanden kamen nicht aus dem Stadtteil Wedding."—MBL]

[12.] [The German here is "Soweit geht die Verhetzung also nicht." *Verhetzung* means to stir up trouble against someone; the implication here is that the antichurch polemics in that part of Berlin weren't so extreme that they prevented the youth from attending.—VB] On the political orientation of the confirmands and their parents, see 1/59, ed. note 19.

suddenly, except maybe that usually they paid full attention, which the boys saw to themselves. But just possibly the groundwork has been laid for something that is slowly developing. Possibly! I also had some very serious conversations with some of the boys individually.

¶Something I almost hate to admit but which is true: I never prepared for the classes in detail. Of course, I knew the material very well, but then I just went there, talked with the boys for a couple of minutes before the class, and then just started. I didn't hesitate, quite often, just to preach[13] to the children; I believe everything else is, in the final analysis, pedagogically doctrinaire. One must simply get them to the point, through previous conversation, that they understand the sermon. But then you just have to start talking, no matter what, and then I found for myself—I myself don't know why I did it—that here the purely biblical material, and pointing to the great hope that we have, always came up together in such sermons, and that was exactly when it was most certain that the boys would pay attention, even if such a sermon lasted (more) than half an hour. But in contrast to that, I had the worst experience during my home visits. I sometimes or even usually stand there and think I really might as well have studied chemistry. Sometimes it seemed to me as if pastoral care was where our work broke down. What hours or minutes of torture often pass by when the other person or I try to have a pastoral conversation, and how hesitatingly and drearily it goes on. And in the background always the unbelievable home conditions, but about which nothing can be said. Some will tell you completely without embarrassment and naively about their very dubious lifestyle, and you have the feeling that if you said anything about it they would just not understand you. In short, that is a very sad chapter, and I often try to console myself with the fact that I think this whole kind of pastoral care is also something that didn't exist even earlier and is completely unchristian. But maybe it really is the end of our kind of Christianity [Christlichkeit] that we fail here. We have learned to preach again, at least a very little bit, but pastoral care?[14]

66 Now, time to close! I want to go to bed. I have to do the examination tomorrow, and I need a clear head. Please let me hear from you again and send me a sermon! And many thanks again for your letter and the birthday card.[15]

---

[13.] Bonhoeffer may be referring here to the homiletic theory of Karl Barth (see Barth, *Die christliche Dogmatik*, 65–67).

[14.] See the confirmation sermon, delivered on March 13, 1932 (3/6).

[15.] The letter and card have not been found to date.

Do you ever see Barth? If so, please tell him hello from me. Unfortunately, I don't know Brunner.

Take care! Most sincerely,
Your Dietrich Bonhoeffer

## 40. Draft Submission to the Department of Theology in Halle concerning the Dehn Case

### 40.1 Theses[1]

The attack on Dr. Dehn[2] confronts the church today with the question of the right of biblical proclamation. We expect a professor of Protestant theology, as a teacher of the church, to be responsible solely to biblical truth, to stand up for pure teaching of the gospel, free from any restrictions from outside the church, and from that standpoint to take a position on the questions of the present day without concern for the consequences.

It is Protestant doctrine[3] that 67

Nation and state as orders of God exist only in fallen creation. Without the justification found in the cross of Christ, they are subject to the sin of self-glorification [Selbstherrlichkeit]. That is why the proclamation of judgment and forgiveness stands above the actions of a nation and state. War, also, is sin, for in it the condition of the disturbed order of creation can be

---

[1.] *NL*, A 38,1(1) (b); typewritten version of the draft by Bonhoeffer and Hans Fischer. Previously published in *GS* 6:204–5. See also *NL*, A 38,1(1) (a); typewritten copy by Gertrud Staewen. In February, at Bonhoeffer's request, the submission drafted by Bonhoeffer and Hans Fischer was sent to a number of theologians who were close to the circle around Karl Barth and the *Neuwerk* movement with the request that they support it. [The *Neuwerk* movement, a Christian socialist group, was an offshoot of the *Jugendbewegung*; Barth, Staewen, and Paul Tillich were all involved. See Tyldesley, *No Heavenly Delusion?* 27.—VB]. But since several of those to whom it was sent refused to sign it, Barth advised "that the project be called off," if only "the little band of those on the political left" were willing to sign it (see Barth's letter of March 5, 1932, to Georg Merz; Karl Barth-Archiv, Basel). So the submission in the form edited by Barth (see ed. note 3 below) probably was never sent to the theology department in Halle. See also Bonhoeffer's letter of March 28, 1932, to his father (1/48).

[2.] Günther Dehn, pastor in Berlin until 1930. Bonhoeffer was under the impression that his call to Halle as professor of practical theology was to be prevented for political reasons.

[3.] In the final version of the submission, this paragraph was replaced by the following formulation of Barth's: "It is Protestant doctrine that nation [*Volk*] and state as orders of God exist only in fallen creation. Without the justification found in the cross of Christ, even when we human beings take seriously our responsibility to respect this order

seen fully revealed; it breaks God's commandment of peace. The Christian who obeys the commandment of creation of loyalty to his own nation and goes to war must do this in his own responsibility toward God's commandment of peace. For that reason he is dependent on God's mercy.

It is not acceptable to confuse the church's proclamation of the judgment and mercy of God over all human action with an undermining liberalistic cultural criticism.

Wherever such Protestant teaching is called into question, the church is attacked at its foundation. We consider the departments of theology to be the called and responsible representatives of the church, called to recognize the hour that threatens to endanger its existence. We reject any attempt to suppress the judging truth of this teaching by means of the unsubstantiated claim that Dr. Dehn used a supposedly pedagogically unsound style of presentation.

We demand a theological statement from a department of theology.

68 We demand a clear recognition of Dr. Dehn's teaching, which we recognize to be biblical and in the tradition of the Reformation, or a rejection based on clear reasons from Scripture.

**40.2 Cover Letter**[4]

It has come to our attention that in the matter of the Dehn conflict in Halle, a large number of theologians feel the need that an unequivocal word be spoken from the theological side about the events there. For that reason, we would like to send you the enclosed theses, which are intended as a submission to the Department of Theology in Halle, with the request that you sign this document and if possible circulate it immediately among your friends. Since, as you all know, up to now there has not been sufficient

---

we are subject to the sin of self-glorification. That is why the proclamation of judgment and forgiveness stands above the actions of a nation [*Volk*] and state. When nation and state go to war, this becomes especially clear. The Christian who obeys the commandment of creation of loyalty to his own nation [*Volk*] and goes to war must do this in his own responsibility toward God's commandment. If this Christian who obeys creation's commandment is justified in his actions, it is the mercy of God that justifies him. It is not acceptable to justify war on the grounds of human necessity. This observation has nothing to do with an undermining liberalistic cultural criticism" (see Gertrud Staewen's remark in her letter to Wilhelm Niesel of February 29, 1932, *NL*, A 38,1(4); and Barth's letter to Staewen of February 21, 1932, Karl Barth-Archiv, Basel).

[4.] *NL*, A 38,1(2); typewritten.

theological comment from the church or from the academic sphere, we ask you to support our submission.[5]

Signed: Licentiate Dr. Bonhoeffer, Lecturer at the University of Berlin
Signed: Hans Fischer, Candidate in Theology

We request that the lists be sent by February 26, 1932,[6] to:
Staewen, Berlin-Britz, Dörchläuchtingerstrasse 35

### 41. From Wilhelm Stählin[1] 69

Münster in Westphalia, March 3, 1932

Dear Colleague:

I have just received the enclosed letter from Althaus.[2] I'm sending it on to you immediately and would like to ask you to discuss it immediately with Dr. Schreiber,[3] possibly also with other gentlemen in the Church Federation Office. I

[5.] Before this submission was written, there had been a "lay protest" based on theological arguments (Gertrud Staewen is probably referring here to the submission written by twenty-seven students enrolled in Dehn's classes and submitted to the rector of the university and the university senate in Halle at the beginning of February 1932; on this, see Bizer, "Der 'Fall Dehn,'" 259). Bonhoeffer and Fischer were interested in having a theologically impeccable case, which was to be supported by as many theological professors as possible. See Gertrud Staewen's correspondence with Karl Barth and Georg Merz (February 21 and 29, 1932, Karl Barth-Archiv, Basel), as well as her letters to Wilhelm Niesel of February 20 and 29, 1932 (*NL*, A 38,1[3,4]). [See the editors' introduction to this volume, p. 16.—MBL]

[6.] Handwritten date.

[1.] LKA Nuremberg, XVIII: Nachlaß Stählin; carbon copy. In a letter of January 16, 1932, Wilhelm Stählin had asked Paul Althaus, together with Wilhelm Zoellner, to be the main speakers. It was very important to Stählin that Althaus attend the conference, which was supposed to discuss the "questions that arise from National Socialism," since Althaus had been one of the cosigners of the statement "The Protestant Church and International Understanding" (see LKA Nuremberg, XVIII: Nachlaß Stählin). [Cf. also 1/4, ed. note 6, and 2/1, ed. note 2.—VB]

[2.] The letter Althaus wrote in reply has not been preserved. See the earlier letter of January 21, 1932, from Althaus in which he writes that he could not accept an invitation for March 3 and 4, 1932, that is, for the date originally planned for the theological conference, and that he would attend a conference with "the men of the World Alliance who were being attacked" but only on the condition that he be informed of the names of the other participants in the conference and that Emanuel Hirsch and possibly others "who shared his opinions" be invited (see LKA Nuremberg, XVIII: Nachlaß Stählin).

[3.] See the letter from August W. Schreiber to Stählin (LKA Nuremberg, XVIII: Nachlaß Stählin), in which he informs Stählin that he is trying, among other things,

would not be opposed to agreeing with this request for a postponement.[4] As urgent as this issue itself is to me personally, I cannot refuse to consider the thought that the time is not right for it now.

If the Church Federation Office or, respectively, Dr. Schreiber supports the request to postpone the conference, I suggest October 1 and 2 as new dates, but October 10 and 11 would also be possible for me.

When we planned the date for April, no one could have foreseen that these days[5] would fall in such a time of high political tension.

Please clear up this question as quickly as possible. If the Church Federation Office does not think it is worthwhile to postpone the conference, the dates will
70 remain April 29–May 1 and then I will have to fill in as a substitute speaker along with Dr. Zoellner, unless a better suggestion can be made.

Sincerely yours,
[W. Stählin]

### 42. From Wilhelm Stählin[1]

Münster in Westphalia, March 18, 1932

Dear Colleague:

I'm answering immediately because I hope, if possible, still to reach you in Berlin.[2] I will naturally be very happy if the invitations[3] can go out now and just ask you to note the following items:

---

to convince Althaus to participate in the Theological Conference of the Provisional Bureau, April 29–30, 1932, in the Church Federation Office.

[4.] This concerns the date of the Theological Conference of the Provisional Bureau, which took place April 29–30, 1932. [See 2/13.—MBL]

[5.] Stählin is probably referring here to the Reich presidential elections of March 13 and April 4, 1932, which became decisively important during the period of the presidential dictatorship in Germany. [The clear winner of both elections was Field Marshal Paul von Hindenburg; "presidential dictatorship" refers to the months that followed, during which Hindenburg, often using emergency law, sought unsuccessfully to stabilize the Weimar government; this ended on January 30, 1933, when Hitler was sworn in as chancellor.—VB]

[1.] LKA Nuremberg, XVIII: Nachlaß Stählin; carbon copy.

[2.] March 19–29, 1932, Bonhoeffer was with his confirmands in Friedrichsbrunn in the eastern Harz Mountains.

[3.] See 1/45.

(1) I request that the whole event be called not a "Conference of Theologians" but a "Theological Conference." That is what we had agreed upon in order to emphasize its theological character but, on the other hand, not to shut out nontheologians.

(2) I request that it begin not at 4:00 p.m. but at 4:30 p.m. It is impossible for me to arrive earlier than 4:29 p.m. at the Zoo,[4] and I can then be at the Church Federation Office a few minutes after that.[5]

(3) Instead of *Diskussion* (discussion), please regularly use *Aussprache* (discussion).[6]

(4) In my opinion, the invitation should include a somewhat longer text. For this I suggest possibly the following formulation:

> This conference is intended to serve the purpose of clarifying the basic theological questions of ecumenical work. The enormous external and internal difficulties that confront any ecumenical work at the current time in Germany make it a special duty for us to examine the theological basis
> of ecumenical work and to share our ideas in a lively conversation about 71
> why we do ecumenical work and what purpose it can have. The two lectures are intended only to lay the groundwork for the discussion. We are most interested in a thorough discussion that includes all sides of the issues.

We request the organizations affiliated with the Provisional Bureau to send suitable representatives to this conference. Nontheologians who are interested in a theological discussion and prepared for it are specifically invited as well." (+)

I ask you to consider whether a registration card should be enclosed: "As a representative of ......................................................, ................................. will attend the theological conference on ecumenical questions." This registration card is to be sent either to you or to the Church Federation Office.

(5) "As a location for the meeting, the Church Federation Office has kindly offered to let us use its conference room (Berlin-Charlottenburg, Marchstrasse 3)."[7]

---

[4.] That is, at the Zoologischer Garten train station in Berlin.

[5.] The Church Federation Office was located at this time at Marchstrasse 2, Berlin-Charlottenburg, very close to the Zoologischer Garten train station.

[6.] [*Aussprache* (literally, "speaking out") implies a context in which participants could clearly state their views.—VB]

[7.] [Correct address: Marchstrasse 2.—MBL]

(6) I consider it absolutely necessary that, in addition to the organizations affiliated with the Provisional Bureau, a number of individual officials be invited as well. I will specifically name Dr. Althaus, Landesbischof Dr. Rendtorff, Dr. Sigmund-Schultze, Pastor Maaß-Heidelberg.[8] There are certainly a number of other names that come into consideration, and I urgently request you to telephone Dr. Schreiber and speak with him about this tomorrow. I admit I assumed that this had been done long ago. In addition, I would recommend adding a sentence to the invitation itself; at the place marked (+) above would be best: "We will gladly accept suggestions about who besides the representatives of affiliated organizations should still be personally invited."

I will send a carbon copy of this letter to Dr. Schreiber, especially in case this letter does not reach you before you leave Berlin. In any case, the invitations must go out before Easter. I will write Dr. Zoellner at the same time and let him know of the final firm date.

Sincerely yours,
[W. Stählin]

72 **43. To August W. Schreiber**[1]

March 19, 1932

Dear High Consistory Councillor:[2]

May I take the liberty of informing you briefly that today, with the permission of the general superintendent,[3] I am leaving for ten days on a retreat with my confirmands and for that reason will not be available for the planning discussions in Berlin during this time. I believe, though, that most of the preparations for the conference[4] have been made. As we agreed, I have written to Dr. Stählin,[5] have also sent him an invitation form for his signature, so that now the invitations, as soon as they come from Stählin,[6]

---

[8.] Correct: "Siegmund-Schultze" and "Hermann Maas"; both had been members of the World Alliance for Promoting International Friendship through the Churches since 1914.

[1.] *NL*, A 28,2(2); typewritten with handwritten signature. Previously published in *GS* 6:237.

[2.] [The greeting is highly formal (*Hochverehrter Herr Oberkonsistorialrat!*).—MBL]

[3.] Emil A. O. Karow was the general superintendent for the Berlin churches.

[4.] That is, the Theological Conference of the Provisional Bureau, April 29–30, 1932, in the Church Federation Office [Berlin].

[5.] Letter not extant.

[6.] See 1/45.

can be copied and will have to be sent out. In case I should be needed anyway, my address is Friedrichsbrunn/Ostharz.[7]

I wish you, highly esteemed High Consistory Councillor, a very quiet and nice Easter celebration!

In sincere admiration and gratitude I remain very respectfully yours,
Bonhoeffer

### 44. From Henry-Louis Henriod[1]

Geneva, March 23, 1932

Dear Mr. Bonhoeffer,

As my secretary[2] has written you,[3] the meeting of the Youth Committee of the Alliance will indeed take place on the fourth of April. It will be held at Epsom and you are requested to arrive the evening of the preceding day, which would 73
be the third. Mr. Craske has not yet sent me the exact address and directions to Epsom. I will ask him to send this information to you immediately. The Youth Conference of the Alliance[4] will take place April 5–8 and will end at 7:00 p.m. on the eighth. I hope indeed that you will be able to attend.

Looking forward to the pleasure of seeing you again soon, yours most sincerely,
[H.-L. Henriod]

---

[7.] The Bonhoeffer family had their vacation home here.

[1.] *NL*, A 28,3(5); carbon copy with the following address: "13 rue Salvin, Genève" and the initials at the end of the document "HLH/MT." [The original is in French. —MBL]

[2.] Ivy Marks, assistant secretary to Henry-Louis Henriod in the secretariat of the International Section of the World Alliance for Promoting International Friendship through the Churches and of the Ecumenical Council on Life and Work in Geneva.

[3.] Not extant.

[4.] On the Youth Conference of the World Alliance for Promoting International Friendship through the Churches in Epsom, see 2/11.

## 45. Invitation from the Provisional Bureau to the Theological Conference, April 29–30, 1932[1]

Provisional Bureau for Ecumenical Youth Work

Münster and Berlin, Easter 1932

The Provisional Bureau for Ecumenical Youth Work would like to invite the organizations[2] affiliated with it to a

*Theological Conference*

that will take place immediately following a meeting of the German Ecumenical Working Group

*April 29–30, 1932, in Berlin-Charlottenburg 2, Marchstrasse 2*

in the conference room of the German Protestant Church Federation Office, which has kindly been made available for this meeting.

74 *Agenda:*

Friday, April 29, 4:30: "The Unity of the Church and the Churches." Speaker: General Superintendent Dr. Zoellner–Düsseldorf.

Dinner together. Discussion

Saturday, April 30, 10:00: "The Unity of the Church and the Nations." Speaker: Professor Dr. Stählin–Münster.

Discussion

This conference, with an attendance of about fifty, is intended to serve the purpose of clarifying the basic theological questions of ecumenical work. The enormous external and internal difficulties that confront any ecumenical work at the current time in Germany make it a special duty for us to examine the theological basis of ecumenical work and to share our ideas in a lively conversation about why we do ecumenical work and what purpose it can have. The two lectures are intended only to lay the groundwork for the discussion. We are most interested in a thorough discussion that includes all sides of the issues.

[1.] LKA Nuremberg, XVIII: Nachlaß Stählin; carbon copy. Regarding the date: Easter Sunday was March 27, 1932; see Bonhoeffer's report on the theological conference (2/12 and 2/13) and Stählin's letter to Bonhoeffer concerning the invitation of Paul Althaus to this conference (1/41) as well as the letter from August Schreiber in which the negotiations that preceded this invitation are mentioned (1/37).

[2.] The invitation list for the conference is in LKA Nuremberg, XVIII: Nachlaß Stählin; see also the organizational chart, appendix 4, p. 505.

We request that the organizations affiliated with the Provisional Bureau as well as the other members of the German Ecumenical Working Group send suitable representatives to this conference. Nontheologians who are members or friends of the organizations and are prepared for this theological discussion may attend as well. Please send the names of the participants on the enclosed card to the German Section of the World Alliance for Promoting International Friendship through the Churches, Berlin-Lichterfelde, Dahlemerstrasse 87.

Please address any questions to the undersigned Licentiate Bonhoeffer, Berlin-Grunewald, Wangenheimstr. 14.

Professor Dr. Stählin
Lecturer Licentiate Bonhoeffer 75

**46. To Henry-Louis Henriod**[1]

Berlin, March 27, 1932

Dear Mr. Henriod,

Thank you very much for your letter.[2] I have not yet received any information from Mr. Craske. Please have someone let me know as soon as possible how the travel expenses to Epsom are calculated. Since I am very short on time, I will have to make my plans accordingly.

With my best thanks and greetings. Yours most respectfully,
Dietrich Bonhoeffer

**47. To Pierre C. Toureille**[1]

March 27, 1932

My dear Mr. Toureille,

Thank you very much for your letter.[2] I'm very glad that now the formalities for the conference have been taken care of.

---

[1.] *NL*, A 28,3(2); handwritten draft.

[2.] See 1/44.

[1.] *NL*, A 28,3(10) (a); handwritten draft. Cf. *NL*, A 28,3(10) (b); later typewritten transcription by Eberhard Bethge. Previously published in *GS* 6:239–40. Pierre C. Toureille was a youth secretary of the World Alliance for Promoting International Friendship through the Churches. [He was one of the three youth secretaries, along with Bonhoeffer and Craske. See 1/16 and *DB-ER*, 244–45.—MBL]

[2.] Not extant.

1. I suggest that you arrive at the Westerburg[3] on the fourteenth in the evening. We will meet you there. You can come from Bonn or Cologne. The following train connections are available: [. . .]

2. The delegates who are certain to be coming are up to now our Cam-
76 bridge friends: de Haas, Nold,[4] Söhlmann,[5] in addition to me. Two others are still uncertain. Too bad that our French friends from Cambridge,[6] whom we had been looking forward very much to seeing again, cannot come!

| | |
|---|---|
| 3. Program:[7] | Beginning Friday, April 15, 10 o'clock |
| | Two lectures (German and French) |
| | *On the Bolshevist problem* |
| | Discussion (Söhlmann and de Haas economic and cultural) |
| | Noon meal |
| | Discussion |
| | *Evening*: National Socialism in Germany |
| Saturday the 16th | Two lectures (German and French) |
| | *Nold* |
| | Same as preceding day |
| | *Evening*: National Socialism (continued) |

---

[3.] The German-French regional conference at the Westerburg in the Westerwald [in the northeast part of the Rhineland-Palatinate province—MBL] took place not on April 14–17, 1932, as originally planned, but much later, on July 12–14, 1932.

[4.] August de Haas, Reformed pastor in Dresden; Karl Nold, pastor in Nördlingen, had been a student of Karl Barth's in Göttingen. Both were members of the Youth Delegation of the German Section of the World Alliance for Promoting International Friendship through the Churches in Cambridge, 1931.

[5.] Fritz Söhlmann, theology student, journalist, and editor of the *Vormarsch*. He attended the meetings of the Provisional Bureau as a representative of the German Protestant Young Men's Association (Evangelische Jungmännerbünde Deutschlands).

[6.] Apparently more representatives of the French Section of the World Alliance for Promoting International Friendship through the Churches had been invited to the conference, possibly Pastor Jules Jézéquel and Anna Jézéquel, W. Monod, members of the French Youth Delegation (see the list of participants at Cambridge in *Handbook of the Eighth International Conference of the World Alliance for International Friendship through the Churches*, 19).

[7.] The final version of the program of the conference, its motto ("The Unity of German-French Protestantism between Catholicism and Bolshevism"), as well as the topics of the individual lectures, are in the Eberhard Bethge papers, Staatsbibliothek Berlin. Marchan's theses on "the Catholic problem" (*le problème catholique*) can also be found there.

Sunday the 17th — Unplanned, open to requests
Noon meal
Departure

I can report on the details when I see you in England,[8] but not until then.

There are no specific practical tips necessary. You will be able to travel through to the Westerburg without any difficulties and will find everything already prepared there. I'll see you in a week.

Sincerely yours,
[D. Bonhoeffer]

**48. To Karl Bonhoeffer**[1] 77

Friedrichsbrunn, March 28, 1932

Dear Papa,

This time I'm sending you birthday greetings[2] from up here. Too bad that you're[3] not here. You would have liked it, too, even though it probably would have been a little cold for Mama because it was still really winter when we got here. But the most glorious sunshine. The woods were amazingly beautiful. It turned to spring yesterday, and everything is thawing. So I can assume that it's nice and warm where you are and you can find something blooming in the woods to bring back for your birthday.

I am very happy that I can be up here with the confirmands. Even if they don't have much understanding of the woods and nature, they are enthusiastic about climbing excursions in the Bodetal and soccer in the meadow. It's sometimes not at all easy to keep these boys together, since most of them have not been raised to socialize with others, and living together in a house here and the restrictions that naturally come along with that helps a lot. I believe, too, that later you won't see any changes to the house to show that these people have been here. Except for one broken windowpane, everything is still intact. The pipe that froze at Christmas is all right again;

[8.] That is, at the conference in Epsom, April 4, 1932, and the French-British regional conference following it, to which Bonhoeffer was also invited.

[1.] *NL*, A 28,1(3); handwritten. Partially reproduced in *GS* 6:223–24.

[2.] Karl Bonhoeffer celebrated his sixty-fourth birthday on March 31.

[3.] [This is addressed to both his father and his mother.—MBL]

there's no break. Only Mrs. Sanderhoff[4] is somewhat indignant about having these proletarians[5] staying here.

Hans Christoph[6] is here, too, and is helping me a lot. But it's only possible to work in the "early" morning hours (literally 7:00–9:00 a.m.) and later in the evening, when everyone is asleep. This time will be over on Thursday. At the end of a time like this, one naturally asks oneself how worthwhile a project like this can possibly be. But in all things of this nature, one must probably learn to wait.

78 On April 3 I am supposed to be in London and will probably stay until the eighth. I can then be back again on the tenth for the election[7] and meet Barth[8] in the afternoon.

My wish for you both is that you can rest up well and will see a really beautiful spring. In the last few months, everything was somewhat turbulent because of all my activities, in the house as well, it seemed to me. Now I am looking forward very much to a quieter summer at home.

Wishing you[9] a happy birthday and a good new year,
Your grateful Dietrich

I'm sending you the Dehn material[10] and hope you won't be too angry. And along with it something else that's more positive.[11]

---

[4.] Mr. and Mrs. Sanderhoff were caretakers for the Bonhoeffers' vacation home in Friedrichsbrunn.

[5.] On the socioeconomic background of Bonhoeffer's confirmands, see 1/27 and 1/39.

[6.] Hans Christoph von Hase, Bonhoeffer's cousin, was working on his doctoral dissertation in theology at the time.

[7.] The second round of voting in the election for Reich president, in which Hindenburg was reelected, took place on April 10.

[8.] Bonhoeffer refers here to Barth's lecture "Die Theologie und die Mission in der Gegenwart" [Theology and contemporary mission], held at the Brandenburg mission conference in the auditorium of the university in Berlin on April 11, 1932. [See also Busch, *Karl Barth*, 218–19.—MBL]

[9.] [Again, addressed to both father and mother.—MBL]

[10.] See 1/40. [See also 1/16a, ed. note 11.—MBL]

[11.] Possibly the draft of the catechism (2/7).

### 49. From Hermann Sasse[1]

March 29, 1932

Dear Licentiate Bonhoeffer:

Most unfortunately, it was not possible for me to reach you before you left. At the request of Licentiate Sasse, I wanted to present a request to you. You were unfortunately not able to stay at the last meeting of our working group[2] until the end. It would have been especially valuable to us if you could have presented your criticism of Pastor Peter's comments in detail as a contrast.[3] Now it is the general wish of the participants that, first, another meeting should be devoted 79
solely to discussion of that topic,[4] on Monday, April 4, at five in the afternoon, again at the theology department,[5] and, further, they wish that you would be so kind as to read a short introductory paper. At the same time, with the request that you return it later, I am sending you Pastor Peter's book,[6] on which his lecture was based.

Unfortunately, I will be traveling due to my work during all of April. Perhaps you would be so kind, then, as to telephone Licentiate Sasse yourself. E I 1870.

Excuse me for coming to you so suddenly with this. But unfortunately I have no other opportunity, since I am leaving now myself.

With sincere greetings, most respectfully yours.

[. . .]

---

[1.] Archiv des Diakonischen Werkes, KSB 410: carbon copy, with the official notation: "Ke./Sch." [This letter was sent at Sasse's request; the author is unknown. For context, see 1/18 and 1/33.—MBL]

[2.] That is, the Working Group of Theologians and Economists.

[3.] Regarding Bonhoeffer's understanding of *Volk*, which in debate with the philosophical theories and political ideologies of his time he primarily but not exclusively defined as *Volk Gottes* [people of God], see *DBWE* 1:118–19 and his lecture in Barcelona, "Basic Questions of a Christian Ethic" (*DBWE* 10:359–78, especially 373 and 376–77). On the ambivalence of Bonhoeffer's argumentation, see H. E. Tödt, "Dietrich Bonhoeffer's Ecumenical Ethic of Peace," esp. 114–18, and K.-M. Kodalle, *Dietrich Bonhoeffer*, 37–39.

[4.] Pastor Peter had given a lecture titled "Nation [*Volk*] and State" on March 1, 1932. Since this group met every two weeks, they had already continued the discussion mentioned here at two subsequent meetings.

[5.] The meeting time, which had been changed to Tuesday afternoon during the semester at the request of Bonhoeffer and other members (see 1/28), had now been changed back to Monday.

[6.] The reference here is probably to Peter, *Wenn die Würfel fallen* (see 1/28).

### 50. Note of Excuse[1]

Since I am still suffering from the aftereffects of a case of the flu, which I had hoped would be over by today, the doctor will not allow me to go out in the evening air yet. So, to my greatest regret, I will be forced to stay away from the ecumenical training[2] evening. I ask you to be so gracious as to excuse my absence[3] and would like to take this opportunity to send you again my most humble thanks for the kind invitation.

In sincere admiration, yours,
Dietrich

### 80 51. To His Parents[1]

My dear Parents,

I have just seen this pretty picture here in the Rijksmuseum. It's a beautiful city we come from.[2] On the way,[3] I passed through it. Today I flew from England to Amsterdam and stayed there until just now, when I will be taking the night train to Berlin.

Affectionate greetings
Your Dietrich

---

[1.] *NL*, A 29,1(11); handwritten draft. The letter, which was possibly addressed to Max Diestel (see 1/38), may have been written in March 1932. On the dating, see the letter of March 22, 1932, from August W. Schreiber to Wilhelm Stählin, which also mentions Bonhoeffer having been ill with the flu at the beginning of March (LKA Nuremberg, XVIII: Nachlaß Stählin).

[2.] Illegible (*Schulungs*).

[3.] Illegible (*Abwesenheit*).

[1.] *NL*, A 28, 1(4); handwritten picture postcard from the Rijksmuseum Amsterdam with a painting of the Valkhof in Nijmegen by Jan van Goysen; postmarked April 9, 1932. Previously published in *GS* 6:235.

[2.] Bonhoeffer is referring to the fact that the Bonhoeffers immigrated to Schwäbisch-Hall [Germany] from Holland in the sixteenth century (see *DB-ER*, 9). The family lineage can be traced back into the fifteenth century, to Henrik van den Bonhoeff, a brewer from Nijmegen (see Wunder and Brandenburg, "Die Ahnenliste," 202).

[3.] That is, on the way to Epsom [England].

### 52. To the Mayor of Biesenthal[1]

Your Honor:

Please excuse me for coming to you in this way. I regret very much that even today I am not yet able to call on you in person, since I have a very painful foot injury. I will, however, not neglect to make this visit as soon as possible. I hope that by next week I will be able to come.

In the meantime, you have been told of my request and the misfortune I have had with my construction company. I wanted to give some of my needy theology students as well as some of my extremely needy confirmands, who have no opportunity to have any recreation at all, the opportunity to spend 81
a weekend now and then in fresh air and a beautiful area. For this reason, I leased the meadow from Mrs. Gröger for three years.[2] May I request that you let me know by sending me a message with the young lady who is bringing you this letter, Candidate of Theology Schulze?[3] I would be especially grateful if you would be so kind as to telephone me in case there is anything that is not clear (Pfalzbg. 2616). For me, this is about nothing else than building a small room for sleeping quarters where I can spend the night with the students and confirmands. The enclosed newly drawn draft plan is intended to serve this purpose.[4] I come to you now with the request and in hopes that you, honorable Mayor, will view my proposal with kind understanding and will not refuse to issue a building permit[5] to me.[6]

---

[1.] *NL*, A 29,2 (a); handwritten draft; letterhead: "Pastor Lic. Dietrich Bonhoeffer / Lecturer at Berlin University / Berlin-Grunewald, Wangenheimstr. 14"; cf. *NL*, A 29,2 (b); later typewritten transcription by Eberhard Bethge. Previously published in *GS* 6:206–7.

[2.] See ed. note 7; the text of the advertisement reads: "Lot near the water, ca. 600 sq. meters, near Berlin, wanted to lease for this summer" (*NL*, A 30,1[15]).

[3.] Bertha Schulze, the senior female graduate student in Adolf von Harnack's seminar, provided text citations to Bonhoeffer in 1929 for his doctoral thesis, helped him with his library work in Wilhelm Lütgert's seminar (*DB-ER*, 67–68 and 137–38), and did typing work for Bonhoeffer (see Meyer and Bethge, *Nachlaß Dietrich Bonhoeffer*, 9, 32, and 34).

[4.] Neither this draft nor the previous draft has been preserved, but see the draft of Bonhoeffer's advertisement for a building site in *NL*, A 30,1(15).

[5.] The barracks-style building was built after May 17, 1932, in Biesenthal near Berlin (see 1/59).

[6.] In the handwritten draft, the sentence "I would be especially grateful . . . (Pfalzbg. 2616)" appears both after "leased the meadow from Mrs. Gröger for three years" and here.

With sincere thanks for any kind interest and hoping soon to be able to express my thanks to you in person

I remain with the greatest respect

Yours most sincerely,
Bonhoeffer[7]

82 **53. To Mr. Decker**[1]

Dear Mr. Decker:[2]

The lecture you requested is enclosed.[3]

Concerning the book that was sent to me, I would like to inquire again about what form you are considering for a similar publication in Germany. If the purely biological aspect is to be covered as intensively as in the other[4] book, it should be written by a medical expert and I would recommend Dr. Stoevesandt[5] from Bonn for this. Then it would fall into the category of the books by Dr. Emsmann.[6] A less biological treatment of the question would allow it to be structured differently.

With best regards, yours most respectfully,
[Dietrich Bonhoeffer]

---

[7.] Crossed out: "Biesenthal was especially recommended for this purpose by my father, who is professor of medicine at the university in the Charité."

[1.] *NL*, A 29, 1(10) (a); handwritten draft; cf. *NL*, A 29, 1(10) (b); later typewritten transcription by Eberhard Bethge.

[2.] Illegible; addressee unknown.

[3.] The lecture mentioned in the text probably refers to the one Bonhoeffer delivered at the Technical College in Berlin-Charlottenburg on February 4, 1932: "The Right to Self-Assertion" (see 2/5). The publication suggested by the addressee was probably intended to treat the same topic.

[4.] Replaces "American"; uncertain reading.

[5.] Dr. Karl Stoevesandt was a physician in Bremen and taught in the Department of Teacher Training for Special Education. In his lecture "Social Welfare Work and Christian Responsibility" (*Zwischen den Zeiten* 4 [1926]), Stoevesandt speaks out against a misunderstanding of a law of heredity in Darwin, because a biologistic understanding, which assumes a biological determinism of human beings, is ruinous for the field of social welfare. According to information from Klara Stoevesandt (letter of June 6, 1991), this is Stoevesandt's only publication on this topic.

[6.] Illegible; possibly "Erdmann."

### 54. To Daniel Krencker[1]

Dear Privy Councillor Krencker:[2]

Two years ago I had the privilege[3] of meeting you at Pastor Schubert's[4] home. Now, General Superintendent Karow has advised me to come to you 83
with several questions. Since last winter the pastoral ministry for the students at the Technical College has been entrusted to me. During the first semester, it has become very clear to me how exceedingly difficult it is to get my work established at the T.C. For this reason, it would be extremely important to me to be able to discuss the whole question of pastoral ministry for the students at the T.C. with you, esteemed Privy Councillor. I would not like to bother you yet in this letter with specific questions, only to ask you to name a time when you would be able to see me.

With sincere thanks I remain in admiration very respectfully yours,
[D. Bonhoeffer]

### 55. To Henry-Louis Henriod[1]

Dear Mr. Henriod,

Many thanks for your letter. First, two items of information:

(1) Prof. Siegmund-Schultze does not think the *Baltic Conference*[2] would be suitable as an opportunity to hold a youth conference. The questions

[1.] *NL*, A 28, 3(12) (a); handwritten draft, according to Eberhard Bethge, dictated by Bonhoeffer to Bertha Schulze. Cf. *NL*, A 28, 3(12) (b); later typewritten transcription by Bethge. Previously published in *GS* 6:216–17. Daniel Krencker, honorary doctor of philosophy, doctor of engineering, and architect, was a professor at the Technical College, Berlin-Charlottenburg. ["Privy councillor" was an honorary title at the university. —VB]

[2.] [Bonhoeffer uses a highly respectful form of address (*Hochverehrter Herr Geheimrat*). —MBL]

[3.] "Privilege" replaces "honor."

[4.] Ernst August Wilhelm Schubert was pastor of the Church of the Twelve Apostles in the church district of Friedrichswerder II, Berlin, from 1928 to 1941 (see *Evangelisches Pfarrerbuch*, 1:25).

[1.] *NL*, A 28, 3(3) (a); handwritten draft, according to Eberhard Bethge, dictated by Bonhoeffer to Bertha Schulze. Cf. *NL*, A 28, 3(3) (b); later typewritten transcription by Bethge. Previously published in *GS* 6:241–42. Since Bonhoeffer refers to the originally planned date for the Baltic regional conference (the beginning of June 1932), the letter was probably written in April or at the beginning of May 1932.

[2.] The conference of the Baltic states, which was planned for 1932, had to be postponed until May 1933 due to financial difficulties, the unclear and difficult political

84 are too specific and require too much specialized knowledge. In addition, negotiations about the location for the conference are still very much in a state of uncertainty. Also, it would be impossible for him to finance another gathering of youth representatives with the money available to him for the conference.

(2) It was originally planned that Superintendent Diestel should speak at the *Czech Youth Conference.*[3] Since he is unable to come, our section[4] has asked me to travel there and give a lecture on the theological basis of the work of the World Alliance for Promoting International Friendship through the Churches.[5] Could you let me know what the relationship of this conference is to our youth secretariat?[6]

Now, to answer your letter:[7]

(1) The German-French youth conference had to be postponed at the request of our delegation for important reasons.[8] I will tell you more about it another time. We hope to hold it now at the beginning of July. So I would like to keep the five hundred francs here until then.

(2) [. . .][9] the translation of the programs[10] for the Gland conference[11] was written yesterday here at our World Alliance office.[12] It will be extremely difficult to put together the German delegation, considering the amount of money[13] made available, since, as I have already said

situation, and the illness of one of the secretaries of the World Alliance for Promoting International Friendship through the Churches (World Alliance for International Friendship through the Churches, *Annual Report*, 1932–33, 32).

[3.] International Youth Conference in Ciernohorské Kúpele, July 20–30, 1932.

[4.] The German Section of the World Alliance for Promoting International Friendship through the Churches.

[5.] Published in *Die Eiche* 20 (1932): 334–44; see 2/14.

[6.] The youth secretariat of the World Alliance for Promoting International Friendship through the Churches.

[7.] Letter not extant.

[8.] German-French youth conference at the Westerburg [in the Westerwald in the northeast part of the Rhineland-Palatinate—MBL] on July 12–14, 1932, which Bonhoeffer organized in his capacity as international youth secretary of the World Alliance for Promoting International Friendship through the Churches. This conference had been planned for April 15–17, 1932 (see 1/47).

[9.] Two illegible words.

[10.] ". . . was written . . ." replaced "The translated programs . . . will be sent to you in the next few days."

[11.] Youth Conference of the World Alliance for Promoting International Friendship through the Churches and the Universal Christian Council for Life and Work in Gland [Switzerland], August 25–31, 1932.

[12.] The secretariat of the German Section of the World Alliance for Promoting International Friendship through the Churches in Berlin.

[13.] Crossed out: "for four people, delegates."

many times, at the present time it is almost impossible to select a good and
well-qualified group of people who can pay even part of the cost of the trip
themselves. If it is considered really important that one or two unemployed
people come to the conference,[14] I see absolutely no possibility to manage 85
this with the sum of money made available. For that reason, I am very pessimistic about the outlook for our German delegation.

More soon. In friendship, yours respectfully,

[D. Bonhoeffer]

### 56. To Pierre C. Toureille[1]

Dear Friend,

Many thanks for your letter.[2] Today just briefly to let you know that[3] in the meantime two of our delegates, who are in the parish ministry, can no longer keep available the dates from the twentieth to the thirtieth. At the moment we are discussing a date at the beginning of July (ca. the eighth). I hope I will be able to tell you a final decision very soon.

By the way, soon you will be receiving a list of the theses[4] on which the German delegates intend to base their lectures, and I would appreciate it if you could announce these in the French delegation. As for our last exchange of letters,[5] perhaps it would be better if we talk about that again in person.

Most sincerely yours,
[D. Bonhoeffer]

---

[14.] For the resolutions passed by the secretariat of the World Alliance for Promoting International Friendship through the Churches, see 1/16. [These resolutions advocate conference representation from the ranks of the unemployed.—MBL]

[1.] *NL*, A 28, 3(12) (a); handwritten draft, according to Eberhard Bethge, dictated by Bonhoeffer to Bertha Schulze. Cf. *NL*, A 28, 3(12) (b); later typewritten transcription by Bethge. Previously published in *GS* 6:240. Since the final decision had not yet been made on the date for the German-French regional conference at the Westerburg [see 1/55, ed. note 8—MBL], the letter was probably written in mid-May.

[2.] Not found.

[3.] Crossed out: "I . . . the days between the twentieth and the thirtieth."

[4.] Of the theses and short lectures of both delegations, only Marchan's theses on "the Catholic problem" (*le problème catholique*) have been preserved (Eberhard Bethge papers, Staatsbibliothek Berlin).

[5.] Not found to date except for one letter (see 1/47).

86 **57. From Adolf Deißmann**[1]

May 12, 1932

To Lecturer Licentiate Bonhoeffer

Dear Colleague,

I have just read your Stockholm report[2] and found it very interesting. Although my knowledge of the individual churches is only fragmentary,[3] in general I would agree with you, also specifically concerning the Negro churches.[4] I have a more positive opinion about the current condition of the Episcopal Church[5] and the predominant Lutheran[6] churches.[7] Perhaps you had less contact with these churches.

With thanks and best wishes at Pentecost for you and your esteemed parents, I remain

Yours,
[A. Deißmann]

---

[1.] Zentral- und Landesbibliothek Berlin, Nachlaß Adolf Deißmann; typewritten carbon copy. Adolf Deißmann was professor of New Testament at the Friedrich Wilhelm University in Berlin. Bonhoeffer had attended his lectures in the winter semesters of 1924–25 and 1925–26, and a seminar in the summer semester 1926 (*DBWE* 9:584–86). As chairman of the Commission for Ecumenical Cooperation between Professors of Theology of the Universal Christian Council for Life and Work, on January 1, 1930, Deißmann had written a recommendation for Bonhoeffer for the German Academic Exchange Service (cf. *DBWE* 10:199) and asked the president of Union Seminary to support Bonhoeffer in his studies of "American Theology and Church Life" (*DBWE* 10:240).

[2.] A report by Bonhoeffer for the Universal Christian Council on Life and Work has not been preserved. It is probable, however, that in characterizing American churches or the German churches in America, Bonhoeffer drew on the first of his two reports to the Church Federation Office (see *DBWE* 10, 1/181, esp. pp. 312–17).

[3.] In 1929, Deißmann had been in the United States himself and had visited Union Theological Seminary (*DB-ER*, 156).

[4.] See *DBWE* 10:314–15.

[5.] See *DBWE* 10:313–14.

[6.] See *DBWE* 10:315–16.

[7.] In general, Bonhoeffer criticizes the American churches because, in his opinion, for them "in place of the church as the congregation of believers in Christ there stands the church as a social corporation," and Christian preaching, which attempts to be relevant to the present day, has been confused with "a political-social and apologetic sermon." The Christian gospel has been replaced by "an ethical and social idealism, borne by a faith in progress that—who knows how—claims the right to call itself 'Christian.'" What unifies the otherwise very different Christian churches is their agreement in this basic attitude. In Bonhoeffer's opinion, "some churches are basically 'charitable' churches; others have primarily a social identity" and "in both cases they have forgotten what the real point is" (*DBWE* 10:313–14).

**58. To Wilhelm Stählin**[1] 87

Esteemed Professor:

Professor Siegmund-Schulze[2] would like to have a report about our ecumenical theological conference[3] for *Die Eiche.*[4] In accordance with his request of the day before yesterday, I drafted a short note for the next issue, which goes to press today.[5] He would, however, also like to have the theses and notes from the discussion for the next issue.[6] Does this meet with your approval?

With sincere best wishes at Pentecost, I remain with admiration, yours respectfully,
[D. Bonhoeffer]

**59. To Erwin Sutz**[1]

May 17, 1932

Dear Mr. Sutz,

I believe I have never kept you waiting so long for an answer. It was last semester that I heard from you the last time[2] and didn't manage to answer. Just a few weeks ago, though, I heard from Mr. Pestalozzi[3] from Zürich

---

[1.] *NL*, A 28, 2(7) (a); handwritten draft on a calendar page for Thursday, May 12, 1932; *NL*, A 28, 2(7) (b); later typewritten transcription by Eberhard Bethge. Previously published in *GS* 6:238. Regarding the probable date, the letter was written between May 12 and May 15 (Pentecost). On the reverse side of the calendar page is the handwritten draft of Bonhoeffer's report on the English-French youth conference of the World Alliance for Promoting International Friendship through the Churches: "a meeting was held in London on April 4 . . ." up through to ". . . as at the present time in Germany" (*NL*, A 34, 3); see also *DB-ER*, 245.

[2.] Correct: "Siegmund-Schultze."

[3.] The reference here is to the Theological Conference of the Provisional Bureau, April 29–30, 1932.

[4.] [*Die Eiche* (The oak) was perhaps the most important ecumenical newspaper at this time, founded and published by Friedrich Siegmund-Schultze, who also served as international secretary of the World Alliance for Promoting International Friendship through the Churches. See Conway, "Between Pacifism and Patriotism."—MBL]

[5.] See *Die Eiche* 20 (1932): 260–61; see also 2/12.

[6.] See *Die Eiche* 20 (1932): 328–33; see 2/13.

[1.] *NL*, A 29, 4(8) (a); typed with handwritten signature; cf. *NL*, A 29, 4(8) (b); later typewritten transcription by Eberhard Bethge. Previously published in *GS* 1:30–33.

[2.] See 1/39.

[3.] Rudolf Pestalozzi, manufacturer in Zürich, friend, and supporter of Karl Barth.

about you and your work as an assistant pastor in Zürich. He had traveled
88 here with Barth to console him in the lions' den.[4] That was really necessary. Barth's confrontation with the princes of the church here was typical in every respect and discouraging as expected. There is still such an inquisitorial spirit living within these people, which satisfies itself with the symptoms without getting to the root of things—only so little incisive and so disgustingly stuffy. It was a nice choice—faculty and general superintendent had been invited to Richter's[5] the day before—when Barth, sitting like a criminal defendant on a little chair facing the great men of the church, was supposed to answer their questions and then, when the request came to start with the questions, nothing came but a long, embarrassed silence, because no one wanted to expose his ignorance first, and then, as the silence became ominous, Mr. Knaak[6] began with the question: what, in Barth's opinion, was the difference between Swiss and Prussian nationalism. This finally established the level of the questions. There were torturous hours then, from which Barth emerged fairly severely shocked, but the men of the church here went home very satisfied with what a charming person Barth was, after all. But, as I said, these hours were at least somewhat pleasant for me in that I met Mr. Pestalozzi. At first I couldn't place him at all, but then he also told me about you. Barth's lecture was received in such a way that, if I were in his position, I would actually break off any relationship with Berlin. The evening gathering afterward in a small group was too strongly marked by this feeling to have been pleasant or productive.

In the meantime, I was in England again at a very superfluous conference;[7] then the semester began. I am lecturing with great difficulty on the
89 nature of the church[8] and have a seminar on the question: is there a Chris-

[4.] On April 11, 1932, at the Brandenburg mission conference in Berlin, Barth had given a lecture on the topic "Theology and Mission in Modern Times" (see Busch, *Karl Barth*, 218–19). The day before, Bonhoeffer had met Barth at the home of Professor Julius Richter, the specialist in mission studies. Richter had invited the Berlin faculty and General Superintendent Wilhelm Karow to his home (*DB-ER*, 177 [the title of Barth's lecture in *DB-ER* is given as "Theology and Contemporary Mission"—VB]).

[5.] Julius Richter, professor of the history of missions, was a member of the German Protestant Missions Committee (Deutsche Evangelische Missionsausschuß) and of the World Alliance for Promoting International Friendship through the Churches.

[6.] Correct: Siegfried Knak, director of the Berlin Missionary Society from 1921 to 1949.

[7.] The conference of the youth secretariat of the World Alliance for Promoting International Friendship through the Churches took place in Epsom near London on April 4, 1932; immediately following this conference, the French-English regional conference took place at the same location.

[8.] [See 2/9.—MBL]

tian ethic?[9] On this topic, Brunner's book, which you had told me about some time ago, has arrived now,[10] and I jumped into it immediately. I am still pretty much at the beginning, but I can't quite get rid of the impression that here again, as earlier in the *Mediator*,[11] the work had been done somewhat too hastily. Especially in the section setting out the basic principles. I would like to start a discussion about it, because the book is indeed wonderfully clearly written and one can easily find points for discussion. But first I have to finish reading it, and I hope my concern is not justified. So please don't take this the wrong way.[12] For me the problem is becoming more and more acutely and unbearably critical. Recently, I preached on 2 Chron. 20:12.[13] In that sermon I unloaded all my desperation. But that still didn't help me any further along. So Barth himself does not agree with me on this point—that is clear to me now—but he did also recently ask me again whether my thinking is still the same[14] and said very clearly that this point is still an uncomfortable one for him, too. At present, it almost seems to me as if one would have to bring in the concept of sacrament[15] when one thinks about the degrees of certainty in proclaiming salvation and the law. The whole question of the interpretation of the *potestas clavium*[16] belongs in here. But I will not make you listen to this half-baked stuff—when will it finally be done?

With Lasserre in Mexico a year ago![17] I can hardly think of it without yearning like crazy to travel again, this time to the East.[18] I don't know yet when. But it must not be too long. There must be other people in the
world, ones who know more and can do more than we can know or do. And 90
it is simply irresponsible not to go there to learn. *In any case, the Nazis are not*

[9.] [See 2/10.—MBL]

[10.] Brunner, *Divine Imperative*.

[11.] Brunner, *The Mediator*.

[12.] Sutz had studied with Emil Brunner; he was associated with Brunner's theology and was a friend of the Brunner family (see 1/6).

[13.] See 3/8.

[14.] See Bonhoeffer's letter to Erwin Sutz (1/5), in which he reports about the discussion of this problem with Barth. "Recently" here very probably refers to Barth's visit in Berlin on April 11, 1932. [Bonhoeffer turns again to this issue in his letter to Sutz in August 1932 (see 1/72). Cf. also *DB-ER*, 183–85.—MBL]

[15.] See the lecture "The Nature of the Church" (2/9).

[16.] "Power of the key," that is, the decisive power to define correct belief.

[17.] Jean Lasserre, Bonhoeffer's friend from Union Seminary in New York; see *DB-ER*, 153–54.

[18.] On Bonhoeffer's intention to travel to India, see 2/5, p. 250, and *DB-ER*, 105, 147–48, and 233–34.

*those people and our communists, as I got to know them a little better last winter,*[19] *are not either.* The Germans are all hopelessly set in a particular direction, in which they do see and know more than the Americans, but that is not saying very much.

The situation here really looks desperate. One lives from one day to the next; simply no one can see further ahead. It may be that the day after tomorrow everything turns to chaos, and not because something great and new appears on the horizon, but simply because something rotten breaks down completely.

One thing that is always especially bad here in Berlin is that, although there are a lot of lively people here, there is almost no one with whom one can talk reasonably about theology. That was different in our time together at Union.[20] When will I ever get to see you again? August 19–31, I will be at Lake Geneva at various conferences.[21] Couldn't we do something together after that? Suggest something. We have to see each other again soon. Otherwise it's no good. When are you taking your vacation?

I have leased a piece of land, approximately seven acres,[22] outside Berlin and am having a little wooden house built on it.[23] I want to spend my weekends there with confirmands and students. Don't you want to come and visit me there sometime? You did at one time plan to come to Berlin. Do it! It's only a short trip from Bonn.[24] It would really be nice.

---

[19.] Bonhoeffer may be referring here to the home visits to the parents of his confirmands (see 1/27 and 1/39).

[20.] Union Theological Seminary, New York.

[21.] Bonhoeffer was a participant in the conference of the Management Committee of the World Alliance for Promoting International Friendship through the Churches in Geneva, August 19–22, 1932, and the youth conference that was held jointly by the World Alliance for Promoting International Friendship through the Churches and the Universal Christian Council for Life and Work, August 25–31, in Gland, Switzerland, near Geneva; see *DB-ER*, 248–49, 250–51.

[22.] [Bonhoeffer relates that the parcel size equals "9 *Morgen*." A "morgan" refers to a plot of land traditionally calculated by the area that could be plowed in a morning's work, which depended on the type of soil and, hence, varied in different areas of Germany. By the nineteenth century, a Prussian morgan became 2,553 square meters, which would have been the determination in Bonhoeffer's time. Thus, 1 morgan consisted of approximately 0.63 acres or approximately 6 acres for the whole parcel in the Brandenburg region. The editor is indebted to the staff of the Bonhoeffer Haus, Berlin, Burckhard Scheffler, director, and his associate, Knut Haemmerling, for this information.—MBL]

[23.] See 1/52.

[24.] Bonhoeffer is probably referring to Sutz's visits to Barth in Bonn.

Enough for today. Please don't return evil for evil and don't let me wait so long too!

Tell me soon about your work! What do you think of Brunner? 91

Sincere greetings as always,
Yours, Dietrich Bonhoeffer

**59a. To Paul Lehmann**[1] 17:106

May 30, 1932

My dear Paul,

Many thanks for your letter![2] So the trip is right around the corner. That's great. Of course, no one knows what times you are coming into here in Europe. At the moment it is once again looking unbelievably critical.[3] But 17:107
at least it is nice that you are coming. I think your plan to go to the south of France first is good, but only if you go to Zürich then right afterward. But on this topic, I would like to make a few critical remarks. If I remember correctly, you wanted to attend Brunner's lecture course on ethics.[4] Up to now I have been unable to find out whether he is even teaching it in the winter. Sutz will know more about it. But even if he is lecturing on it, things have changed now because his ethics volume[5] appeared in print a couple of weeks ago and you can find all the important content there. Along with that, I can't help saying that I was somewhat disappointed by this treatment of ethics. I am wondering now whether it would really be worthwhile to go to Zürich. Naturally, it would be nice to be together with Sutz and to get to know people through him. Would you not perhaps get more out of two semesters in Bonn[6] or perhaps one in Marburg?[7]—I'm not certain, but

[1.] Paul Lehmann Collection, Special Collections, Princeton Theological Seminary Library; typewritten with handwritten signature and a handwritten addition at the top of the letter, from Berlin. Previously published in *Evangelische Theologie* 56 (1996): 471–73, and *DBW* 17:106–8. Editorial notes by Hans Pfeifer.

[2.] Not extant.

[3.] Brüning had lost the confidence of Hindenburg and was dismissed the next day (May 31, 1932). With the subsequent appointment of Papen as Reich chancellor, the Weimar Republic began to come to an end.

[4.] On this, see Brunner's letter of November 2, 1930, to Lehmann, in Alston and Welker, "Dietrich Bonhoeffer," 295–96n20. Also in *Evangelische Theologie* 56 (1996): 476n13.

[5.] Brunner, *Divine Imperative.*

[6.] Karl Barth was teaching there.

[7.] Rudolf Bultmann was teaching there.

I think you should consider that, since the publication of Brunner's ethics and the discussion about it in the journals, which will no doubt start very soon, will introduce you thoroughly to the state of the current discussion on the problems. In addition, Gogarten has published his ethics,[8] and, further, a very intelligent nationalist, Stapel, has written a book about "the Christian statesman,"[9] so I assume that the next year in Germany will be very strongly oriented toward the discussion of ethical problems.

I am convinced that Barth as well will speak about this, perhaps even in the seminar, but certainly at the open-house evenings in his home, so that you might possibly hear and learn more there than from Brunner himself. In any case, I would go to Bonn first and make my further decisions depend-
17:108 ing on what happens there. Now, as far as the financial side of your stay here is concerned, I think that if you just take a room you can together get along very well in Bonn on two hundred marks a month. There's a student pub there where you can eat well for fifty pfennig. The Barthians usually had their noon meal there together. I was with them as well a couple of times. You will have to have rooms recommended to you by the student services office at the university. There you will get a lot of offers and will have to choose for yourself. About forty to forty-five reichsmarks is what I would certainly count on spending for a double room. You will see by these figures, which are from last summer and certainly have gone down somewhat since then, that you will easily get by on two hundred marks, with some entertainment included. In case you should possibly decide to study in Berlin for a semester, you would have to count on spending a little more, but not much. If I were you, I would come to Berlin for a couple of weeks at the end of the winter semester in any case. You will actually get to see in a very different way what is going on in Germany and experience it much more intensively than anywhere else. Berlin has perhaps never been so much the focal point of Germany as it is now.

Thanks very much for sending a copy of my article.[10] I[11] am very much disgusted by it. It is altogether commonplace-theology, is it not? I should be ashamed to print that stuff here; all the more it is impertinent to do it in another country. Excuse me, please, and write a better one!

---

[8.] Gogarten, *Politische Ethik.*

[9.] Wilhelm Stapel, *Der christliche Staatsmann,* Hamburg, 1932.

[10.] [The reference is to the article "Concerning the Christian Idea of God," which appeared in the April 1932 *Journal of Religion;* it is reprinted in *DBWE* 10:451–61. Cf. 1/37a, ed. note 8.—MBL]

[11.] [Bonhoeffer continues in English.—MBL]

Give[12] your wife my kind regards. If you want to know anything more, write!

Yours always,
Dietrich Bonhoeffer

Whether you are *ordained* or not is completely unimportant over here.[13]

**60. To the Office of the German Section of the World Alliance for Promoting International Friendship through the Churches**[1]

Berlin-Grunewald, June 7, 1932

To the World Alliance Office, Dahlemerstr. 87

Please inform Pastor Jordan[2] that because of my official work I will not be able to attend the meeting of the Management Committee.[3]

Bonhoeffer

[12.] [Bonhoeffer returns to German.—MBL]

[13.] Handwritten addition. According to information from Eberhard Bethge, this remark and Lehmann's question that it probably answers may refer to the fact that Bonhoeffer had difficulty holding services in the German congregation in New York because, due to his young age, he was not yet ordained. See also the reference to the so-called canonical age in the November 11, 1931, "Instructions for Ordination" (1/17a, ed. note 5: Bonhoeffer has "completed the twenty-fifth year of life [canonical age]").

[1.] *NL*, Anh. A 7,1; typewritten with handwritten signature.

[2.] Richard Theodore Jordan, pastor in Wachow since 1928, became secretary of the German Section of the World Alliance for Promoting International Friendship through the Churches after Siegmund-Schultze took over the international secretariat of that organization in 1929 (see *DB-ER*, 192–93).

[3.] That is, of the German Section of the World Alliance for Promoting International Friendship through the Churches.

**61. To Henry-Louis Henriod**[1]

Berlin, June 20, 1932

Dear Mr. Henriod,

It is unclear who in the various countries selects the delegates for Stockholm.[2] Would you be so kind as to send me information about this?

Best regards,
Bonhoeffer

92 **62. To Walter Künneth**[1]

Dear Mr. Künneth,

Just now I have heard that the next meeting[2] is to take place at your home on July 14. As glad as I am to hear the first part of this news, I am very sorry to hear the second part, since on that day I will still be at a youth conference of the World Alliance for Promoting International Friendship through the Churches in France.[3] If the date stays as planned, I ask you today to please excuse my absence.

With sincere greetings I remain yours very respectfully,
Bonhoeffer

---

[1.] WCC Archives, box 1 (World Alliance for International Friendship through the Churches—Letters from Dietrich Bonhoeffer, 1932–37); typewritten with handwritten signature; see also *NL*, A 28, 3(4). Previously published in *GS* 6:245.

[2.] "Delegates for Stockholm" refers to the delegates of Life and Work who were to take part in the conference in Gland, Switzerland. Henry-Louis Henriod was asked to decide this in his capacity as general secretary of the World Alliance for Promoting International Friendship through the Churches and of the Universal Christian Council for Life and Work.

[1.] Archiv des Diakonischen Werkes CA/AC 22, Bl. 74; handwritten postcard, postmarked June 21, 1932. Since 1927, Walter Künneth had been full-time head of the Center for Apologetics, a division of the Central Committee of the Inner Mission, founded in 1919. The offices were at first on Altensteinstrasse in Berlin-Dahlem, then from 1926 to 1932 in the Johannesstift in Spandau. [The Center for Apologetics was founded in reaction to what the church perceived as antireligious and secular movements in society; it sought to make the case for Christianity in the modern world, primarily through its publications.—VB]

[2.] The reference is to a meeting of the Working Group of Theologians and Economists (information from Walter Künneth, May 24, 1993); see 1/18, 1/28, 1/33, 1/36, and 1/49.

[3.] July 12–14, 1932, Bonhoeffer was not in France but at the German-French regional conference that took place at the Westerburg in Germany and had been organ-

**63. To August W. Schreiber**[1]

Berlin, June 23, 1932

Dear High Consistory Councillor Schreiber:

Finally I have collected the written remarks from the discussion some time ago.[2] Only Lilje has not sent me an answer.[3] From Pastor Peter so much that I had to shorten it considerably.[4] Otherwise I have reproduced almost
everything word for word as requested by the speakers. At the very end, a 93
part of the discussion is missing; I did not hear it because I was having a meeting with Lilje outside. Perhaps Dr. Heckel,[5] who led this discussion for the most part, would be so kind as to fill this in briefly. I am writing him at the same time.

Professor Siegmund-Schultze wants the lectures and discussion summaries for *Die Eiche*.[6] Dr. Zoellner and Dr. Stählin have agreed to this. For this, we will probably have to shorten even more.[7] Would the Church Federation Office be so kind as to undertake the duplication of this report?[8]

I remain, most respectfully yours, High Consistory Councillor,
Bonhoeffer

---

ized by Bonhoeffer in his capacity as youth secretary of the International Section of the World Alliance for Promoting International Friendship through the Churches.

[1.] Reprinted from Glenthøj, *Zu Dietrich Bonhoeffers Eintritt*, 25; letter with stamped reception date of the Church Federation Office and office notations; see also *NL*, A 34,4; handwritten draft of the letter.

[2.] Bonhoeffer is referring to the conference of the Provisional Bureau, April 29–30, 1932.

[3.] Johannes Lilje, general secretary of the German Christian Student Organization (DCSV) from 1927 to 1934; see *DB-ER*, 198.

[4.] The discussion remarks by Friedrich Peter, a pastor in Berlin who had belonged to the National Socialist German Workers' Party [NSDAP, or Nazi Party—MBL] since 1929, appear in *NL*, A 34,4(1,2) insofar as Bonhoeffer had included them in his handwritten draft.

[5.] Theodor Heckel, at the time high consistory councillor in the Church Federation Office in Berlin. After 1933, as bishop and as director of the Foreign Office of the German Evangelical Church, he emerged as one of Bonhoeffer's opponents in the ecumenical realm.

[6.] [See 1/58, ed. note 4.—MBL]

[7.] Handwritten notation by Schreiber: "Yes!"

[8.] Handwritten addition by Schreiber: "?"

### 64. To Theodor Heckel[1]

Dear High Consistory Councillor Heckel:

Concerning the report about the theological conference of the Provisional Bureau for Youth Work, may I come to you with the following request? At that conference, during the discussion of Stählin's lecture, I had to leave the meeting because of another meeting just as you and Dr. Stählin were in conversation and when I came in again, the discussion was almost over. I only heard something that I did not completely understand about "the question of levels." But since that obviously interested the participants very much at the time, I would like to take the liberty of asking you to put together a
94 couple of sentences about this discussion and give it to Dr. Schreiber.[2] He has the report up to that point from me. Since the report is to appear later in *Die Eiche*, we would not like to leave out an important part. Pardon me if I am bothering you very much with this!

With many sincere thanks for your kind help, I remain, honorable High Consistory Councillor,

Yours most respectfully
D. B.

### 65. From Walter Künneth[1]

Berlin-Dahlem, July 4, 1932

Dear Colleague,

It is really too bad that you cannot come to our meeting at my home on July 24.[2] As far as I'm concerned, there would be nothing to prevent changing the evening meeting. But you know yourself that it isn't easy here in Berlin to change a date once it's been agreed upon. I hope that I may welcome you here[3] another time.

Sincerely,
[Künneth]

---

[1.] *NL*, A 34,4; handwritten draft; address at top left: "Dr. Heckel (Charlottenburg) Marchstr. 2 / Church Federation Office." The letter was presumably also written on June 23, 1932 (see 1/63).

[2.] See the letter on this subject from August W. Schreiber to Theodor Heckel in Glenthøj, *Zu Dietrich Bonhoeffers Eintritt*, 25. At Heckel's request, his remarks in the discussion were not included (see 1/74).

[1.] Archiv des Diakonischen Werkes CA/AC 22, Bl. 84; carbon copy with signature.

[2.] See 1/62.

[3.] Crossed out: "in Berlin."

### 66. To Erwin Sutz[1]

Dear Mr. Sutz,

Just a brief greeting from my conference with the French,[2] which wasn't so bad. I'll very probably be free from September 1 on. A little later I'm supposed to go up to the "Bergli,"[3] at least possibly. We must certainly 95
do something together. Maybe Jean Lasserre will come! The Swiss conference[4] will certainly be very mediocre; poor topics, etc.

*Many* thanks for the sermons![5] I had a lot to do myself; that's why I didn't write until today. Soon more here, I hope.

Kindest regards,
Yours, D. B.

### 67. From Friedrich Siegmund-Schultze[1]

July 22, 1932

Dear Colleague,

General Superintendent Zoellner has just asked me what has happened with the planned publication in *Die Eiche* of the report on the discussions at the Church Federation Office.[2] You had agreed to put it together; he, Dr. Zoellner, had sent you the theses quite some time ago but had not yet heard anything more about it.

I myself am not really informed about what stage the discussions had reached at that time. Do you have a report of the discussions that is written in a way that would allow it to be used in an article in *Die Eiche*? How long is it? If we wanted

---

[1.] *NL*, Anh. A 8,2; handwritten picture postcard from Limburg on the Lahn, Germany, postmarked July 14, 1932.

[2.] German-French Regional Conference of the World Alliance for Promoting International Friendship through the Churches, July 12–14, 1932. Bonhoeffer reported on this conference in *Die Eiche* 20 (1932): 365–66 (see 2/18).

[3.] "Bergli" was the name of Rudolf Pestalozzi's summer home above Oberrieden, located above the left bank of Lake Zürich. Pestalozzi often let his friends Karl Barth and Eduard Thurneysen use it (see Busch, *Karl Barth*, 145 and 157).

[4.] Bonhoeffer is referring here to the youth conference of the World Alliance for Promoting International Friendship through the Churches and the Ecumenical Council on Life and Work in Gland, Switzerland (August 25–31, 1932).

[5.] Not extant.

[1.] EZA 51/n IV b/3, 1; carbon copy.

[2.] This refers to the theological conference of the Provisional Bureau, April 29–30, 1932, in the Church Federation Office, which Bonhoeffer and Wilhelm Stählin had organized.

to put it in the October *Eiche*,[3] it would have to be in my hands by September 15 at the latest.

With kindest regards I remain most respectfully yours,
[Siegmund-Schultze]

96 **68. To Pierre H. Steele**[1]

Berlin-Grunewald, July 31, 1932

Dear Mr. Steele:

Thank you for your letter which I received yesterday, when I came home from the Czechoslovakian conference.[2] Herewith I am sending you the names of the delegates of the countries under my care:[3]

*Germany*:

Herr Fritz Söhlmann, National Association,[4] Berlin-Eichkamp, Zikadenweg 4 bei Strecker
Herr Assessor Walter Meyer,[5] C.V.J.M.[6] Wuppertal-Barmen, Gemarker Ufer 25
Herr Pfarrer Karl Nold, Nördlingen, Bayern.

---

[3.] Bonhoeffer's short report on the conference was published in *Die Eiche* 20, no. 3 (1932): 260–61; the detailed report was published in the issue for the fourth quarter of the year 1932: no. 4:361–65 (see 2/13 and 2/18).

[1.] WCC Archives, box 1 (World Alliance for International Friendship through the Churches—Letters from Dietrich Bonhoeffer, 1932–37); typewritten with handwritten signature; see also *NL*, A 28,3(18). Previously published in *GS* 6:246–47. [Original letter is in English, reproduced here unedited.—MBL] Pierre H. Steele was the secretary of Life and Work. Bonhoeffer knew him from the conferences in Cambridge and Epsom (see *DB-ER*, 244 and 250).

[2.] International Youth Peace Conference of the World Alliance for Promoting International Friendship through the Churches in Ciernohorské Kúpele, July 20–30, 1932.

[3.] That is, the countries that lay within the area for which Bonhoeffer was responsible as international youth secretary of the World Alliance for Promoting International Friendship through the Churches.

[4.] [A reference to the National Federation of Protestant Young Men's Associations (Reichsverband der Evangelischen Jungmännerbünde).—VB]

[5.] Walter Meyer attended the meetings of the Provisional Bureau as a representative of the National Federation of Protestant Young Men's Associations.

[6.] [Christliche Verein Junger Männer: the German YMCA.—MBL]

*Denmark*:

Herr stud. mag. Hans Skovgard,[7] Gunnestrup pr. Trangbjerg St.

Herr H. Stegener Petersen,[8] C. N. Petersenvey 51, Kopenhagen F.

*Sweden*:

Herr Valter Lindström, cand phil. *Skara*, Bommagatan 12.

*Hungary*:

still questionable, perhaps Herr Bela,[9] Budapest.

*Austria*:

Fräulein Hoffer, Graz

one student whose name I do not know. Prof. Fischer,[10] Wien, has written to you already about it.

*Norway*:

no one will be able to come, since the costs for the journey are too 97
high. Would it be at all possible to exceed in this particular case the amount promised to them?

*Holland*:

No definite answer as yet.

Would you be so kind as to send any important information concerning this conference directly to the mentioned delegates?

With kindest regards Yours sincerely
D. Bonhoeffer

**68a. To Paul Lehmann**[1] 17:109

Dear Paul,

Just quickly an answer to your letter! About your eyes, I don't know, naturally, how urgent the situation is. I also cannot ask my father at the moment since he is traveling. But I can certainly say this much, that if you want to wait until you come to Berlin, my father can easily refer you to the best specialist in the

[7.] Not identified.

[8.] Not identified.

[9.] Not identified.

[10.] Dr. Franz Fischer, religion teacher, secretary of the Austrian Section of the World Alliance for Promoting International Friendship through the Churches.

[1.] Paul Lehmann Collection, Special Collections, Princeton Theological Seminary Library; typewritten with handwritten signature, on letter paper with printed address: "Lic. Dietrich Bonhoeffer, Lecturer at Berlin University, Berlin-Grunewald, [no date], Wangenheimstr. 14, H 1 Pfalzburg 2616." The letter can be dated August 1, 1932, based

country, whom we know well, and that then the price would be very moderate. A normal consultation with a professor in Berlin costs about thirty to fifty reichsmarks. But it would certainly be less expensive for you.

I can't easily give you a really good answer about your financial concerns, because the regulations are constantly changing. You can bring foreign currency into Germany, just not take it out. I think the travellerscheck[2] is still best. But the idea of leaving the money in Switzerland is not bad, either—because it's not expected that Switzerland will pass a law forbidding taking foreign currency out of the country any time soon. Maybe half and half; then you will be safe in any case.

Yesterday we had elections.[3] We're happy that the Nazis did not get a majority. But it is still bad that the parliament, which has just been elected
17:110 again, will not be able to form a government.[4] But it has not yet gone so far that one can just turn Germany over to a few adventurers—undoubtedly full of enthusiasm.

It's not possible to predict at all yet whether we will avoid violent actions on a larger scale. We first have to wait again to see how the leadership of the Nazis, that means how Hitler, reacts to the election results. I don't actually believe he will initiate something violent on his part. He has always taken a stand more on the principle of legality.[5] It's just a question of whether he can keep the masses, who are waiting finally to see some action on his part and are only running around after him for that reason, quiet any longer.[6]

---

on the reference to elections, "Yesterday we had elections" (Lehmann left the United States in mid-August, so this cannot refer to the elections on November 6, 1932). Previously published in Alston and Welker, "Dietrich Bonhoeffer"; in *Evangelische Theologie* 56 (1996): 474–75; and in *DBW* 17:109–10. Editorial notes by Hans Pfeifer.

[2.] [Original in English.]

[3.] [The national parliamentary elections on July 31, 1932.—MBL]

[4.] The National Socialists received 37.4 percent of the vote (230 seats) and together with the Communists, who received 14.6 percent of the votes (89 seats), had a "blocking minority" of more than 50 percent [i.e., no other party or combination of political parties would be able to form a new coalition government—MBL].

[5.] At a press conference with representatives of the English and American press on December 4, 1931, Hitler had insisted that he would not think of throwing the principle of legality overboard at the last minute.

[6.] A daily order from Hitler to the SA on December 2, 1931, reads: "Do not let yourselves be provoked into action and do not let your nerves get the better of you in the final hour. Power will fall into our hands all by itself." [No source is given for this citation in *DBW*, but see Orlow, *Nazi Party*, 161, for similar wording from that period.—VB]

Please write exactly when you will arrive and when you think there is the first chance for us to meet.

I wish you all the best for the last weeks over there, but especially for the voyage and the time over here. In any case, you will experience one of the most decisive times here. For that it would perhaps be better if you were in Germany, because in Switzerland one is somewhat far away from the events, but, even more, somewhat far away from the feelings and experiences of today's Germany and Europe. You will be better able to feel the pulse of the times in Germany.

Now, in the meantime, my kindest regards, to your parents, too, please. I still enjoy thinking back on the days in Elmhurst.[7]

Many greetings to your wife from me!

Yours always
Dietrich Bonhoeffer

**69. To August W. Schreiber**[1]

Berlin-Grunewald, August 1, 1932

Dear High Consistory Councillor Schreiber:

May I ask you to have the copy of the minutes of the theological conference of April 29,[2] which is at the Church Federation Office, sent to Prof. Stählin, Münster, Paulstr. 15. Siegmund-Schultze[3] is also interested in it and would like to have it immediately after Stählin[4] has read it. This is, of

[7.] On the way to Mexico (see *DBWE* 10:298). [Bonhoeffer is referring to a short stay at the Lehmann family home. Lehmann had accompanied Bonhoeffer, Jean Lasserre, and Edwin Sutz at the end of the Union Seminary term in May 1931, as far as his home in Elmhurst, Illinois, just west of Chicago, as a stop on their cross-country tour. His father, Timothy Lehmann, was president of Elmhurst College (1928–48) and a leader in the Evangelical Synod of North America (Lutheran-Reformed). See *DB-ER*, 152.—MBL]

[1.] Reprinted from Glenthøj, *Zu Dietrich Bonhoeffers Eintritt,* 26. Letterhead: "Lic. Dietrich Bonhoeffer / Lecturer at Berlin University / Berlin-Grunewald, August 1, 1932 / Wangenheimstr. 14 / H. 1 Pfalzburg 2616" [last part a telephone number—MBL].

[2.] The theological conference of the Provisional Bureau at the Church Federation Office, April 29–30, 1932, organized by Stählin and Bonhoeffer.

[3.] See 1/67.

[4.] Crossed out: "it" (*es*).

course, about publishing it in *Die Eiche.*[5] And for that, the text would have to be there as soon as possible.

I remain, highly esteemed Dr. Schreiber, most respectfully yours,
[Bonhoeffer][6]

98 **70. From Pierre H. Steele**[1]

August 3rd 1932

Dear Mr. Bonhoeffer,

Thank you for your letter of July 31st.[2] Regarding Norway, Mr. Henriod has allowed Frs. 250.—[3] for two delegates. Would you offer Frs. 200.— for one delegate? On these terms perhaps they can send one. Dr. Wissing[4] has cabled directly to us that two delegates will come from Holland. Let us hope Hungary will send one.

Yours sincerely,
[P. H. Steele]
Secretary
Youth Commission

[5.] See *Die Eiche* 20 (1932): 361–65.

[6.] Under Bonhoeffer's signature are the following official notations: "How did this matter get into the official work channel? Hosemann 3/8 / How did this personal letter get stamped officially as incoming mail? Hosemann 3/8 / Director Hosemann / The letter was apparently stamped in the usual manner with the incoming mail stamp! 3/8."

[1.] WCC Archives, box 1 (World Alliance for International Friendship through the Churches—Letters from Dietrich Bonhoeffer, 1932–37); carbon copy. [Original in English, reproduced here unaltered.—MBL]

[2.] See 1/68 and the abbreviation at the end of this letter (PHS/CB); based on this, the sender of the letter was Pierre H. Steele, secretary of Life and Work and member of its Youth Commission, which cooperated with the Youth Commission of the World Alliance for Promoting International Friendship through the Churches.

[3.] [Swiss francs.—VB]

[4.] J. C. Wissing was secretary and treasurer of the Dutch Section of the World Alliance for Promoting International Friendship through the Churches.

**71. To Werner Koch**[1]

Berlin-Grunewald, August 6, 1932

Dear Mr. Koch,

Perhaps you have heard of the conference for which I am sending you the program in this letter.[2] One of the three people in our small German delegation, Pastor Nold–Nördlingen, today cancelled his participation. I then telephoned Lilje, and he suggested that I turn to you with the request that you travel to Gland with us. I would be able to make available to you 60 RM and free room and board there. I don't know exactly what the trip 99
(holiday ticket) from Frankfurt to Geneva costs. But I could not go much higher than 60 RM. The main question is whether you have time and are interested in it. Please don't be frightened off by the program. That's just how it has to look to please the Anglo-Saxons. What we do with it is another story. The way it *is*, it is actually awful. But that's partly because of the translation. I myself am very skeptical about the conference. But that's just why it is so extremely important to me to have a good German delegation. And based on previous experience, I think it is especially important that theological concerns are expressed most forcefully by us. There's not much that can be said in advance about the topics. It all depends on a clear position being found within our delegation. May I ask you to write me immediately whether you will give us the pleasure of having you travel there with us?[3] You should not be prevented from doing this because of financial constraints. The matter is very urgent. That is why I am asking you for an answer as soon as possible.[4]

With kindest regards,
Very respectfully yours,
Dietrich Bonhoeffer

---

[1.] Papers of Werner Koch; typewritten with handwritten signature; see also *NL*, A 28, 2(6); typewritten transcription by Eberhard Bethge. Previously published in *GS* 6:247–48; facsimile reproduction in Bethge, Bethge, and Gremmels, *Dietrich Bonhoeffer: A Life in Pictures*, 94. According to Bethge, the underlining is Koch's (card of March 30, 1992). Werner Koch, who was a theology student in Berlin in 1931, was supposed to travel to Gland as a substitute for Karl Nold, who was ill.

[2.] The reference is to the youth conference of the International Section of the World Alliance for Promoting International Friendship through the Churches and the Ecumenical Council on Practical Christianity (Life and Work) in Gland, Switzerland, August 25–31, 1932. A copy of this program can be found in the Eberhard Bethge papers.

[3.] Koch's name does not appear in the list of conference participants (see WCC Archives, box 4, World Alliance for International Friendship through the Churches—Youth Commission).

[4.] Not extant.

**72. To Erwin Sutz**[1]

Berlin-Grunewald, the—

Dear Mr. Sutz,

Many thanks for your letter. It arrived just as I was writing one to you. I have just come back from a very mediocre conference in Czechoslovakia[2] that
100 once again made me have doubts about the value of all this ecumenical work.[3] But it isn't quite as stupid as Kümmel[4] seems to have described it. (In general, I'm somewhat surprised at the taste of the Zürich faculty[5]—just between us!)

¶In Czechoslovakia, I gave a lecture on the theological foundation of this work[6] and tried to ease my theological conscience with it, but there are still very many question marks that have to be brought up there. Basically, it all depends on the problem of ethics, that is, actually on the question of whether it is possible for the concrete commandment to be proclaimed through the church. And it seems to me to be a real gap in Brunner's ethics that he doesn't actually place this question at the center, but actually just poses and answers the question in passing.[7] Naturally, the question is always part of the whole and answered implicitly, but it seems to me that for theological thinking the first question and the starting point for all that follows simply lies here. That's how it happens, too, that one doesn't really feel it fully, that what Brunner really says is extraordinarily little for the church and even a real threat to the church's substance. After the whole book, it remains unclear what it means for the church that it can give a concrete

[1.] *NL*, A 29, 4(9); typewritten with handwritten addition and greeting at the end of the page: "days here . . . Bonhoeffer" [presumably referring to last line of the letter—MBL]. Written in Berlin, at the beginning of August 1932; dating notation by Eberhard Bethge. Partially reproduced in *GS* 1:33–35.

[2.] From July 24 or 25 to July 28, Bonhoeffer was at the international youth peace conference of the World Alliance for Promoting International Friendship through the Churches, which took place in Ciernohorské Kúpele, July 20–30, 1932.

[3.] [Bonhoeffer had previously mentioned this sentiment in his letter to Sutz one month earlier. See 1/66—MBL]

[4.] Werner Georg Kümmel had been adjunct professor of New Testament in Zürich since the spring of 1932. In a letter of October 10, 1964, he wrote to Adolf Mádr that he could not remember what he had said about Ciernohorské Kúpele (see Mádr, "Die Tschechoslowakische Kirche," 35).

[5.] Possibly also a pointed reference to Emil Brunner, who taught in Zürich as well.

[6.] See 2/14 and 2/15.

[7.] See 1/59.

commandment or not give it. In your sermons,[8] I was moved by the fact that it seems to be for you almost exactly as it is for me. But I just can't get past this kind of a sermon in which you try to say everything and at the end always have the terribly depressing feeling that you have talked right past the subject. It's the problem of making preaching concrete that is bothering me so much at present. It is simply not enough and therefore false to say that the principle of concretion could only be the Holy Spirit itself, as several students in my seminar[9] always insisted. The concrete form of the 101
proclamation of grace is, after all, the sacrament.[10] But what is the sacrament of the ethical, of the commandment? We must talk about that when we see each other.

¶On that, now the following plans. I will be in Geneva on August 18.[11] We have a meeting of the Management Committee of the World Alliance for Promoting International Friendship through the Churches there. Immediately following that is an international youth conference in Gland,[12] which is only partially under my leadership. At least today I don't feel responsible for running the daily events. The English have already gotten involved much too much in that. I can hardly ask you in good conscience to come have a look at the event—although perhaps in spite of everything it may be very interesting. It would be very nice, on the other hand, if Lasserre would come. Please be so good as to write him—I have actually simply lost his address and that's why I have not written for such a long time—whether he couldn't join us some way or other.[13] The conference will last until the

[8.] Not extant.

[9.] "Is There a Christian Ethic?" in the 1932 summer semester. [See 2/10.—MBL]

[10.] On this topic for Bonhoeffer in general and the relationship between this letter and the lecture "On the Theological Foundation of the Work of the World Alliance," [2/14—MBL], see Wolf, "Das Letzte und das Vorletzte," 19–20.

[11.] The meeting of the Management Committee of the World Alliance for Promoting International Friendship through the Churches in Geneva began on August 19, 1932 (see *DB-ER*, 249).

[12.] Joint youth conference of the World Alliance for Promoting International Friendship through the Churches and the Universal Christian Council for Life and Work in Gland, Switzerland, August 25–31, 1932. "Arthur Burroughs, the Bishop of Ripon, presided over the meeting, assisted by the three youth secretaries and Mr. Steele from Life and Work" (*DB-ER*, 250).

[13.] Erwin Sutz and Jean Lasserre were not on the list of participants for the aforementioned conference (see WCC Archives, box 4, World Alliance for International Friendship through the Churches—Youth Commission). For August 16–17, 1932, Bonhoeffer had been invited to the vacation home of the Lasserre family; see the entry in the Lasserre family's guest book (1/76).

thirtieth. Then I am free. Now you have to make some suggestions. I have been asked here by friends[14] of Barth and Pestalozzi to come up to the Bergli for a couple of days at the beginning of September. How does that seem to you? Honestly, I admit it seems a little pushy to me, since I actually hardly know all these people at all. But, on the other hand, I would naturally like to do it. Could you possibly come along for this? Is Brunner
102 up there? Do you think it is actually all right for me to go there? Or would one only be disturbing the people's peace and quiet during their vacation? I would like to be back in Berlin about September 9. I still have incredibly much planned during the vacation, for the winter semester and some other things.

How is your work going? Can you really expect your congregation to understand sermons like that, and aren't you sometimes afraid that you will drive people to intellectual distraction? Pardon me, that is actually directed more to myself than to you. I would like to hear you preach. Then I would also know better what is wrong with my sermons. Many thanks again for sending them to me, and don't consider my questions to be arrogance.

Take care. Write me soon with your plans. Also when I can get to see Brunner and whether he is at all willing. I'll still be here for twelve days.

Sincerely yours,
Dietrich Bonhoeffer

### 73. To Friedrich Siegmund-Schultze[1]

Berlin-Grunewald, August 8, 1932

Dear Professor Siegmund-Schultze,

Can you use another report[2] for the next edition of *Die Eiche* on this summer's youth conferences like the one enclosed? At the same time, if my

---

[14.] It could not be ascertained to whom this refers. In an earlier letter to Sutz, Bonhoeffer had mentioned this invitation, which, among others, possibly might have come from Gertrud Staewen [see 1/66—MBL]. The letter of October 1932 from Rudolf Pestalozzi to Karl Barth includes the information that Gertrud Staewen was at the "Bergli" in September (Karl Barth-Archiv).

[1.] EZA 51/P I d, 9, 1; typewritten with handwritten signature; cf. *NL*, A 34,5; handwritten draft.

[2.] Bonhoeffer had offered Siegmund-Schultze his report on the Theological Conference of the Provisional Bureau for Ecumenical Youth Work, which was then published along with Bonhoeffer's report "Ecumenical Youth Work: The English-French Youth Conference of the World Alliance for International Friendship through the Churches" in

essay[3] is not yet in print, I would like to request that it be given back to me briefly for a couple of corrections. 103

In sincere admiration I remain most respectfully yours,
Bonhoeffer

**74. From August W. Schreiber[1]**

**74.1 Letter to Dietrich Bonhoeffer**

Lecturer Licentiate Bonhoeffer

Enclosed please find a copy[2] of the letter to High Consistory Councillor Schreiber of August 1, 1932,[3] for your information.

Respectfully,
Church Federation Office
For the office

| Be[sig] | W[ahl] | Schr[eiber] |
|---|---|---|
| August 5, 32 | August 5 | August 7 |
| +He[ckel] | | |

**74.2 Enclosure: August W. Schreiber to Wilhelm Stählin**

Berlin-Charlottenburg, August 9, 1932

At the request of Lecturer Licentiate Bonhoeffer, I am sending you the report sent here dated June 23, 1932, on the theological conference of the Provisional Bureau for Ecumenical Youth Work, April 29–30, 1932, noting most respectfully that High Consistory Councillor Dr. Heckel has deleted the report on his remarks in the discussion.[4]

[August W. Schreiber]

---

*Die Eiche* 20 (1932): 260–61. [See the reports on the Youth Conferences of the World Alliance: 2/18 and also 2/19.—MBL] See the letter of May 10, 1932, from Renate Lepsius to Bonhoeffer (EZA 51/P I d, 91), in which she asks Bonhoeffer for short reports about the conferences for *Die Eiche*.

[3.] Bonhoeffer is referring here to one of the two reports mentioned above.

[1.] Reprinted from Glenthøj, *Zu Dietrich Bonhoeffers Eintritt*, 27; official notation at the bottom edge of the document: "Necessary to present again on September 1, 1932, with III 372."

[2.] August W. Schreiber is referring here to the enclosed letter to Stählin.

[3.] See 1/64.

[4.] On Theodor Heckel's remarks that were deleted, see Bonhoeffer's handwritten draft of the report in *NL*, A 34,5.

104 **75. To the Office of the World Alliance for Promoting International Friendship through the Churches**[1]

Berlin, August 12, 1932

World Alliance Office, Geneva, Miss Marks:

I will attend the meeting of the Management Committee.[2] I will arrive at the International School on August 18 in the evening.

Further, I would like to let you know that, due to the illness of Pastor Nold, Assistant Pastor Karl Gerhard Steck, Munich, NW2. Arcisstr. 13, preachers' seminary,[3] will attend the conference in Gland as a German delegate.[4] Please send the latest information to him directly as soon as possible.

Most respectfully yours,
Bonhoeffer

[1.] WCC Archives, box 1, World Alliance for International Friendship through the Churches—Letters from Dietrich Bonhoeffer, 1932–37; typewritten with handwritten signature; cf. *NL*, A 28,3(19). Miss Marks was H.-L. Henriod's assistant secretary in London until the beginning of 1932 and then in Geneva after April 1, 1932.

[2.] The meeting of the Management Committee of the International Section of the World Alliance for Promoting International Friendship through the Churches took place August 19–22 in Geneva.

[3.] [The preachers' seminary was the final phase of ministerial and pastoral training for Protestants studying for the ministry. Typically, students would live together for three to four months of intensive study and discussion. Bonhoeffer would later lead such a program in the so-called underground seminary experiences in Zingst and Finkenwalde in 1935–37 (*DB-ER*, 419–71, 561–86) and then further in the "collective pastorates" in 1938–39 (*DB-ER*, 587–96). The writings from these periods can be found in *DBWE* 14 and 15.—MBL]

[4.] Bonhoeffer had initially planned to have Werner Koch as a substitute for Karl Nold (see 1/71), but Koch had declined immediately. It is not known whether Karl Gerhard Steck attended, but he was listed as a member of the German delegation of the World Alliance for Promoting International Friendship through the Churches in the list of the conference participants (WCC Archives, box 4, World Alliance for International Friendship through the Churches—Youth Commission).

### 76. Entry in the Guest Book of the Lasserre Family[1]

August 16–17, 1932

For two beautiful and unforgettable days, which I was privileged to spend with the family of my friend Jean[2] and in which I was able to enjoy a very congenial atmosphere, here my sincere thanks

Dietrich Bonhoeffer, Berlin

### 77. To Pierre H. Steele[1] 105

Dear Mr. Steele,

Thank you for your letter.[2] I am very glad to be able to tell you that we shall have one Hungarian delegate at Gland. Mr. Sándor Kiss, Budapest VI, Muzenen körnt 37 II. m.[3] Unfortunately, the Norwegian council[4] will not be able to send anyone even on the basis of my offer of 250[5] fr. for one delegate. So you will be in the possession of the list of the delegates of all the countries under my care.

---

[1.] Handwritten; copy in the Eberhard Bethge papers, Staatsbibliothek Berlin.

[2.] Bonhoeffer was a guest at the vacation home of the Lasserre family in Le Tremble near Chamonix, France.

[1.] WCC Archives, box 1, World Alliance for International Friendship through the Churches—Letters from Dietrich Bonhoeffer, 1932–37; handwritten. [Letter is in the original English, reproduced here unaltered.—MBL] Pierre H. Steele, as secretary of the Youth Commission of the Universal Christian Council for Life and Work, shared responsibility for the organization of the conference in Gland, Switzerland, jointly held by Life and Work and the World Alliance for Promoting International Friendship through the Churches.

[2.] See 1/70.

[3.] The list of participants for the Gland conference gives a different address for Sandor Kiss: "Mr. Sandor Kiss, IX. Ulloi u. 25. I. Budapest" (WCC Archives, box 4, World Alliance for International Friendship through the Churches—Youth Commission).

[4.] That is, the council of the Norwegian Section of the World Alliance for Promoting International Friendship through the Churches.

[5.] "250" replaces "200." [See 1/70.—MBL]

Would you kindly send any further information to the delegates directly, since I am going to leave Berlin for a few days.[6]

With kindest regard Yours sincerely,
Dietrich Bonhoeffer

### 78. From Julie Bonhoeffer[1]

#### 78.1 Printed Thank-You Card

Friedrichsbrunn. August 1932

For my ninetieth birthday I received many kind congratulations, which were a great joy to me and fill me with sincere gratitude. Unfortunately I cannot answer them personally as quickly as I would like. For that reason I ask you not to hold it against a ninety-year-old if she, too, follows the new custom of sending a printed thank-you.

Julie Bonhoeffer

#### 106 78.2 Letter to Dietrich Bonhoeffer

Friedrichsbrunn. Eastern Harz Mountains[2]

Dear Dietrich,

Every day I hope to learn your address from somewhere, will send a greeting and thanks now to Wangenheimstrasse,[3] maybe something will reach you there. You gave me great pleasure with the Thomas à Kempis.[4] I like very much to read a few sections in the mornings, since I am staying in bed later and later now. Of course, I knew the little book from earlier days, but it is actually an inspiration to me every morning. Many could amply enjoy the great wealth of south German cookies, and I could send some along with the travelers for their trips. Have my sincere thanks for spiritual and physical nourishment.

---

[6.] This would indicate that the letter was written between August 3, 1932 (see 1/70) and Bonhoeffer's stay at the vacation home of the Lasserre family on August 16–17, or the beginning of the meeting of the Management Committee of the World Alliance for Promoting International Friendship through the Churches on August 19, 1932.

[1.] *NL*, C 2; handwritten on the back of a printed thank-you card; Julie Bonhoeffer, née Tafel; the card was written after Julie Bonhoeffer's birthday, August 21, 1932.

[2.] Beginning of the handwritten back side of the page.

[3.] Julie Bonhoeffer is referring to Bonhoeffer's address at Oderbergerstrasse, Berlin N 58 (see 1/27, ed. note 5). Bonhoeffer, however, intended to live there only until the confirmation of his students (March 14, 1932).

[4.] The book gift was probably the work *Imitatio Christi*.

This coming week workmen will be here. The dining room and the upstairs veranda room are to be painted, which is really not an extravagance.

If it were possible, I would say you should come out here for a bit yet, but since Käthe[5] and I have only Mrs. Sanderhof[6] to help us, it might not be very hospitable, completely so if the weather disappoints us.

Did you get my letter with the old address?[7]

With love
Grandmother

### 78a. Appointment as Assistant Pastor[1] 17:111

Berlin, *August 24, 1932* *Immediately!*[2]

We[3] appoint you *at the end of your year as assistant pastor* [. . .] beginning on *August 1, 1932,* until further notice to undertake the duties of an assistant city pastor (*Stadtvikar*) [. . .] in Berlin.[4] [. . .]

Please request [. . .] the necessary instructions for your work *from General* Superintendent *Dr. Karow* in *Berlin-Charlottenburg* [. . .].[5]

---

[5.] Possibly Katharina Horn.

[6.] Correct: Mrs. Sanderhoff; see 1/48, ed. note 4.

[7.] Not extant.

[1.] EZA; typewritten form, 2 pages, with handwritten entries (here in italics); printed letterhead with handwritten addition: "Protestant Consistory of the Mark Brandenburg, Berlin Office"; above the letterhead: "Pl. 24/8"; file number: "K. II Nr. 5713." First published in *DBW* 17:111–12. Sections that are crossed out in the form are indicated by "[. . .]." The form has two columns. The left column contains internal office instructions, which are reproduced here in footnotes; "/" indicates end of a line. Attached to the front of the letter is a sheet that documents how the item of business was handled by the office. Those involved included High Consistory Councillor Gruhl, Consistory Councillor Coulon, Administrative Councillor Berndt, General Superintendent Karow, as well as "Mr. O.-S. [perhaps the abbreviation for Obersekretär, or Senior Secretary]" Wilbert.

[2.] Addition: "*Wednesday, 24* [replaces *"23."*] *August, to be sent out.*"

[3.] Beginning of the right column.

[4.] Next to this in the left column: "(1) *To the Honorable Pastor Licentiate Dr. Bonhoeffer in Berlin Grunewald, Wangenheimer Strasse 14* in care of the Superintendent of the Church District *Kölln-Land I,* Mr. Berndt z.g. M. [*zur gefälligen Mitteilung,* or "for his information"]. *Prepared for 1–3 and sent out August 24* [. . .]."

[5.] Left column: "(b) to General Superintendent Dr. *Karow* for his information. *Seen K[aro]w August 24)* [. . .] / After it is sent out [. . .] to be noted [. . .] in the employment list for Reg[ion] VII and placed in the personnel files *(Bo–67). finished Thi*[. . .].

Please also *report each time to the Superintendent in whose church district you will be working.* [. . .]

Your salary *will be paid* from [. . .] funds of *the Financial Office of the City Synod of Berlin* [. . .].

Berlin approved. 105[6]

[. . .][7]

17:112 (Copy of 1) Copy *most respectfully submitted to Ew. pp.*[8] [. . .][9] (Copy of 1) The Administrative Committee receives a copy for its information and for payment of the *assistant pastor's salary.*[10]

### 79. To His Parents[1]

My dear Parents,

Yesterday we[2] were on the Rigi[3] after a trip across Lake Lucerne; it was
107 simply enchantingly beautiful. Today I travel home. I stayed here with my friend Sutz the whole time, and then we went together to spend some time with Barth. That was very interesting. I must get on the train!

Most respectfully, your grateful
Dietrich

[6.] Left column: "*Note: The highest salary level 200.—RM has already been approved in II 1587.* At the end of the first page on the left: "No. 68."

[7.] Page 2 begins with sections crossed out.

[8.] Abbreviation used in official German for "the aforementioned" [Latin: *perge perge*; used to stand in for official titles otherwise necessary in referring to the addressee—MBL]; in this case it stands for the "Honorable Dr. Karow."

[9.] Left column: "[. . .] *(2)* to *General* Superintendent, the Honorable Dr. *Karow* in Berlin Charlottenburg) / *(3)* to the Administrative Committee of the Berlin City Synod in Charlottenburg 2 Marchstrasse 4/5). [. . .]"

[10.] Under the text at right signatures/initials: "*B[ern]dt 19 Ke [illegible] 19/8 for Coulon Gr[uhl] 18/8. at the same time representing D. Ka. K[aro]w 24/8 Lub[er]g* [illegible, similar to the signature in the ordination instructions of November 11, 1931, in 1/17a, part 1.] *For the office 23 August (also for the president). Wilbert 18/8 by proxy.*"

[1.] *NL*, A 28,1(5); handwritten postcard from Zürich postmarked September 4, 1932; addressed to "Herrn und Frau Geheimrat [Privy Councillor—MBL] Bonhoeffer, Schönberg bei Innsbrück, Hotel Jägerwirt." Partially reproduced in *GS* 6:207.

[2.] "We" probably means Bonhoeffer and Erwin Sutz (see 1/72).

[3.] Rigi, a mountain between Lake Zug and Lake Lucerne.

## 80. From Fritz Söhlmann[1]

Berlin S 2, September 24, 1932

Dear Dietrich,

Dr. von Hovel, who works with the Christian Social Service to the People,[2] asked me some time ago for French theological books that are close to the Barth movement. Could you give me the titles of some? Journal articles might also be a possibility.

With best regards
Yours, Fritz

## 81. To the Office of the German Section of the World Alliance for Promoting International Friendship through the Churches[1]

September 25, 1932

To the World Alliance Office in Lichterfelde

I regret that, because I am attending the conference of student pastors[2] in Friedrichsrode,[3] I will be prevented from attending the meeting of the 108

[1.] *NL*, A 28,7(2); typewritten with handwritten signature, postmarked September 26, 1932. After studying theology, Fritz Söhlmann became a journalist and editor. As copublisher of the journals *Der Vormarsch* and *Junge Kirche* [*Junge Kirche* was a continuation of the journal *Der Vormarsch*—VB], he attended the meetings of the Provisional Bureau.

[2.] Dr. von Hovel, not identified to date. The Christian Service to the People (Christlicher Volksdienst) had been constituted in 1927; in 1929 it joined with the National Association of Christian Social Work (Christlich soziale Reichsvereinigung) to form the Christian Social Service to the People (Christlich soziale Volksdienst). This group disbanded in 1933.

[1.] *NL*, Anh. A 7(2); handwritten; postmarked "Berlin-Charlottenburg, September 26, 1932."

[2.] Since the 1920s, there had been student chaplains in various cities with universities and colleges (see Rohrbach, "Studentenpfarrer").

[3.] Correct: "Friedrichroda," near Gotha in the Thuringian Forest.

Management Committee[4] on the date to which it was changed. Please inform Pastor Jordan[5] of this.

D. Bonhoeffer

**82. From Renate Lepsius**[1]

October 15, 1932

Dear Licentiate Bonhoeffer:

As we discussed recently, I am sending you the material for the translation of the book by Bishop Bell,[2] and that is

1. the original of the translation;
2. a copy of pages 1–25 (new numbering 1–34), which Professor Siegmund-Schultze has already worked through once;
3. the galley proofs of the book, from which the translation was made;
4. the page proofs, which must be compared again with the translation.

I have ordered another copy of the final published book and will then send it to you. The translation was supposed to be published in 1929, so it was done based on the corrected proofs.

Along with the translation, a bibliography of the relevant literature is to be published. I will have the suggestions for this sent to you at a later time.

I would be grateful if you would briefly acknowledge that you have received the papers.[3]

With kind regards, respectfully yours,
R. L.

---

[4.] Meeting of the Management Committee of the German Section of the World Alliance for Promoting International Friendship through the Churches. On February 2, 1932, Bonhoeffer had been elected as a member of the Management Committee and appointed as a specialist for youth work (see 1/38).

[5.] Richard Theodor Jordan was the full-time secretary of the German Section of the World Alliance for Promoting International Friendship through the Churches after 1929.

[1.] EZA, 51/P III 1c; typewritten; Renate Lepsius was the secretary for Friedrich Siegmund-Schultze, publisher of the journal *Die Eiche*.

[2.] The reference is to the translation of Bell, *Brief Sketch of the Church of England*. A draft translation was edited in large part by Bonhoeffer (see *Mündige Welt*, 5:72–79). The German translation was published in 1934.

[3.] Not extant.

### 83. From Jürgen Winterhager[1] 109

October 17, 1932

Dear Licentiate Bonhoeffer:

As you will perhaps already have seen from the agenda of the upcoming meeting of the Management Committee,[2] under point 2 a report from you is planned on the ecumenical meetings you attended as well as on the work with the students this winter.[3] Would you please be so kind as to say a few words to us on these two topics at the meeting?

With kindest regards, yours very respectfully,
[J. Winterhager]

### 84. From Wilhelm Stählin[1]

Münster, October 20, 1932

Dear Colleague,

I really do not know what I could have done to arouse the anger or the fury of the Church Federation Office.[2] I consider myself to have worked together as loyally as possible with the gentlemen of the Church Federation Office and to have taken every opportunity to point out their achievement appropriately. But there are some things in church administrative offices in Berlin that I do not understand. So now a continuation of our theological discussion in conjunction

[1.] *NL*, Anh. A 7,3; carbon copy with no sender or signature shown. A notation on the document by Eberhard Bethge indicates that the letter was from Jürgen Winterhager, who had been a member of the German Section of the World Alliance for Promoting International Friendship through the Churches since 1931.

[2.] This refers to a meeting of the Management Committee of the German Section of the World Alliance for Promoting International Friendship through the Churches on October 29, 1932 (see Glenthøj, *Zu Dietrich Bonhoeffers Eintritt*, 33–34).

[3.] As recorded in the minutes of this meeting, Bonhoeffer reported on the various youth meetings of the World Alliance for Promoting International Friendship through the Churches at the Westerburg, Germany, in Ciernohorské Kúpele, Czechoslovakia, and in Gland, Switzerland. He also presented the plans for the next year, such as the planned discussion on "Brunner's Ethics of the State" at the Friedrich Wilhelm University.

[1.] LKA Nuremberg, XVIII: Nachlaß Stählin; carbon copy.

[2.] The Church Federation Office probably feared that through the activities of the Provisional Bureau, the German Ecumenical Working Group would become superfluous, since both institutions recruited most of their members from the same group of people (see 1/13); concerning the organizations and associations that participated in both institutions, see the chart in appendix 4, p. 505.

110 with the ecumenical working group is to be held, and naturally I am willing to go along with this suggestion. December 8, though, is quite difficult for me but not totally impossible. I could arrive in Berlin at 4:26 in the afternoon without difficulty. But that will probably be too late. If it is necessary, I am willing to travel through the night and be there Thursday morning. Once I'm in Berlin, naturally I will stay there Friday, so extending the theological discussion, say into Friday morning, would not cause me any difficulty.

You think we can't now simply pick up the discussion from April.[3] But what are you thinking of as a new starting point? I believe that the theses[4] from back then, which have been published in the meantime, have not at all been thoroughly discussed yet. I see two very different questions that were touched on there, which urgently require further theological clarification:

1. the theological location of the reality of "*Volk*" (possibly extended to the two sides of race and nation) and

2. the meaning of confessionalism, which is arising again today in conjunction with the ecumenical movement. In my opinion we don't need any new lectures on this, but just one or two people for each point who are willing to start the discussion about them, following the theses from last time. But we need the opportunity to really talk through these things—in two meetings of about three hours each. I ask you to be so kind as to work out these things with Dr. Schreiber and then, as soon as possible, to tell me the final plan, especially how the time will be divided.

Actually, being forced to come to Berlin unexpectedly during the semester is very welcome, because I can then visit my son, who will be studying theology in Berlin this coming winter semester.[5] By the way, on my advice, he intends to attend your classes and will come to see you right after he arrives in Berlin (he will be living at the Johanneum). He will also, moreover, be grateful if you could recommend this or that to him.

With kind regards,
Yours,
[W. Stählin]

[3.] That is, the discussion that took place on April 29 and 30, 1932, at the theological conference of the Provisional Bureau.

[4.] See Zoellner, "Die una sancta ecclesia" and "Die Einheit der christlichen Kirche."

[5.] Rudolf Stählin studied theology in Erlangen, Berlin, Basel, Münster, and later in London.

**85. To Wilhelm Stählin**[1] 111

Berlin, October 21, 1932

Dear Professor Stählin:

Many thanks for your letter. By the way, Dr. Schreiber got the date confused. It is the ninth, not the eighth, that is planned. We are very glad that you can get free, and perhaps it might be possible that you yourself do the introduction of the new discussion following the report in the next *Eiche.*[2] Unfortunately, our finances are so meager that we will not be able to have the printed copy at the meeting. For the same reason, we must ask you to adapt your travel expenses to this situation and to accept accommodation in one of our houses. Dr. Schneider[3] told me he would be especially pleased if you would stay at his home. Of course, it would also be a great pleasure for Superintendent Diestel and me to have you with us. Or, in case that all seems to you to be too far from the city center, we would try to find you a room in the city.

Dr. Schreiber thinks it would perhaps be best if you would write to the Church Federation Office yourself with the request that our meeting might be held on the ninth in the afternoon, and that the invitations to our meeting be sent out to the Church Federation Office at the same time as those for the ecumenical working group.[4] We would probably have to continue the discussion on the tenth in the morning.

I am very glad to hear that I will get to know your son during the next semester and would like to help in any way I can. 112

With respectful greetings I remain
Yours most sincerely,
Dietrich Bonhoeffer

[1.] LKA Nuremberg, XVIII: Nachlaß Stählin; typewritten with handwritten signature.

[2.] See Bonhoeffer's "Primary Report on the Conference of the Provisional Bureau," 2/13.

[3.] Probably "Dr. Schreiber." Early on, High Consistory Councillor August Wilhelm Schreiber had held ecumenical evenings in his home and was one of the initiators of the German Ecumenical Working Group (*DB-ER*, 192).

[4.] The German Ecumenical Working Group met immediately following the meeting of the Provisional Bureau in the Church Federation Office.

## 86. To Hans Brandenburg[1]

Berlin-Grunewald, October 23, 1932

Dear and esteemed Colleague:

Pardon me for bothering you at this time with a request, but I would like to take advantage of your advice and your experience in the following matter. A lady of my acquaintance intends to provide 430 RM a month over the next winter to establish a youth center for the unemployed.[2] This would mean arranging for a heated room during the day combined with something useful to do, preferably something that would serve as preparation for a job. A director and teachers would probably not be hard to find through the Student Aid Association[3] and the Academic Self-Help Organization.[4] But here as well I would ask for your advice. I would especially like to dis-
113 cuss the following questions with you. Is there a possibility that rooms from somewhere or other might be provided without charge? Does one have to apply to city offices for this—and to which ones?[5] What types of work activity would you consider especially suitable?[6] Would materials for possible

[1.] *NL*, A 28, 6(1); typewritten with handwritten signature. Previously published in *GS* 6:225–26. Hans Brandenburg was a pastor and since 1930 had been mission inspector of the City Mission in Berlin. "Bonhoeffer had met Brandenburg (in the fall of 1932) at the working group of the church-social conference, and at his request had held a Bible study on Genesis 1:1 for the young men's circle in the City Mission" (*DB-ER*, 229).

[2.] Anneliese Schnurmann, a psychoanalyst, was a friend of Susanne Dreß née Bonhoeffer. In the fall of 1932, Schnurmann established the youth center (*Jugendstube*) in Charlottenburg with Bonhoeffer and financed it. In 1933, she emigrated to England because of the onset of discussion about racial laws in Germany. [Schnurmann was considered "non-Aryan" under the Nazi racial laws.—VB]

[3.] The German Student Aid Association (Deutsches Studentenwerk) had been formed in 1929 as a product of, among other institutions, the Office for Student Loans of the German Students' Association (Darlehenskasse der Deutschen Studentenschaft), which had been founded in 1922.

[4.] The Academic Self-Help Organization (Akademische Selbsthilfe) was supported by nongovernmental welfare agencies and the Student Aid Office in Berlin. Its emergency program included job training and counseling, providing living quarters, food, and clothing for unemployed academics.

[5.] Underlined by Brandenburg: "rooms . . . provided," "to city offices . . . which ones"; note in the right margin by Brandenburg: "Winter Aid, Labor Office [illegible] / (1) State Department of Labor Office) / *Roonstr. 9* / 2) District Youth Department Office."

[6.] Marginal note by Brandenburg: "ask *Pastor Thom* craft workshops / course in cutting fabric to a pattern / mathematical calculation for sales and technical use / calligraphy-stenography."

craft workshops be contributed by some sources or other? What can even be done with 430 marks?[7] Someone suggested that the lady join with the Emergency Association for the Establishment of Housing and Food for the Unemployed.[8] What do you think of that? Since this youth center should be interdenominational and not party affiliated, joining this group is probably hardly to be recommended.[9] The lady can guarantee this sum for six months. After that, she intends to continue the project, but today it is not yet possible to make a commitment with certainty.

Pardon my coming to you so suddenly with this, but I am sure you can give me the most expert advice here. I will try to telephone you tomorrow (Monday) morning. In case I should not be able to reach you, would you please be so kind as to write me with your opinion, immediately if possible. The lady would like to leave on a trip on November 1 and would like to be able to have some overview by that time of how things are going.

With sincere thanks and best regards and hoping to see you again soon,[10] I remain very respectfully yours,

Dietrich Bonhoeffer

### 87. From Renate Lepsius[1]

October 25, 1932

Dear Licentiate Bonhoeffer:

The Leopold Klotz Publishing Company is willing to give the Church Federation Office the issue of *Die Eiche*, which includes the theses of Zoellner and Stählin and the report of the minutes,[2] at reduced prices. They would charge 1.50 marks instead of 3.00 marks per copy; for an order of one hundred copies, even down to 1.00 mark. 114

[7.] Marginal note by Brandenburg: "enough" (illegible).

[8.] [Notgemeinschaft zur Errichtung von Heimen und Küchen für Erwerbslose. —MBL]

[9.] [Many of the Depression-era emergency help groups had distinct religious or political affiliations.—MBL]

[10.] Bonhoeffer had met Brandenburg again at the Brandenburg Mission Conference in April 1932.

[1.] EZA 51/P I d/9, 1; carbon copy.

[2.] The reference here is to issue 4 of the journal *Die Eiche* 20 (1932), which included the aforementioned theses on pp. 328–33 and Bonhoeffer's report "Primary Report on the Conference of the Provisional Bureau," 2/13.

I would be grateful to you if you could possibly let me know immediately, since the issue will be printed this week. I would have to ask for a written order from Dr. Schreiber but would be grateful for a telephone message first.

Sincerely, yours respectfully,
[R. Lepsius]

### 88. From Wilhelm Stählin[1]

### 88.1 Letter to Dietrich Bonhoeffer

Münster, October 27, 1932

Dear Colleague:

I have now written the enclosed letter to the Church Federation Office. There is something that I didn't write in it, which I would like to ask you to discuss with Dr. Schreiber. From *Das Evangelische Westfalen*[2] (October 1932), I have learned of the Potsdam discussion on religion that the Christian-German–movement
115 [christlich-deutsche Bewegung] held.[3] In some respects that is actually what we had in mind, and I am now doubly sorry that it was not possible to bring Althaus and Rendtorff to our negotiating table beforehand.[4] It would be all the

[1.] LKA Nuremberg, XVIII: Nachlaß Stählin; carbon copy; a carbon copy of the enclosed letter to the Church Federation Office can also be found there.

[2.] ["Protestant Westphalia," a church publication.—VB]

[3.] The Potsdam discussion on religion was a "confidential discussion among leading theologians and other knowledgeable experts on the topic: Our Gospel Message in the Time of the German Struggle for Liberation" (see *Das Evangelische Westfalen* 9, no. 10 [1932]: 106). In 1932, the Christian-German movement was led by Regional Bishop Dr. Heinrich Rendtorff. It considered itself to be a movement for faith and mission that wanted to "call the national movement to faith and the church to service to the people [*Volk*]" and opposed the religious-political "Federation for a German Church" [Bund für deutsche Kirche], which truncated the Reformation gospel, discarded the Old Testament, and reinterpreted the gospel as a German Christianity. The publication of the Christian-German movement was the monthly journal *Glaube und Volk*, published by Paul Althaus and Emanuel Hirsch. The German *DBW* editor writes that in some National Socialist and "*völkisch*" circles, there was active resistance against the agenda of this movement (see Sasse, "Kirchliche Zeitlage," 74–76). [Not to be confused with the *Deutsche Christen* (German Christians), who gained such power after 1933, the *Christlich-deutsche Bewegung* was one of several small nationalist factions that arose in Protestant circles in the early 1930s; of course, many of its members did become part of the German Christians. See Helmreich, *German Churches under Hitler*, 78–80, for a description of this and the various other groups.—VB]

[4.] Stählin had tried in vain to have Althaus or Rendtorff as speakers for the conference of the Provisional Bureau in April 1932 (see 1/37 and 1/41, as well as Stählin's letter of February 29, 1932, to Althaus in LKA Nuremberg, XVIII: Nachlaß Stählin).

more important now to manage to have at least some of these men who have criticized the ecumenical movement take part in our discussion. And for this reason I would ask especially that Althaus and Rendtorff be invited to this conference. I am naturally willing to write to the two gentlemen but would not like to do it before I have the specific consent of Dr. Schreiber and Superintendent Diestel in the matter. Please urge Dr. Siegmund-Schultze strongly to make time in his schedule this time for our theological conference.[5] The invitations must go out as soon as possible, so that the ladies and gentlemen can really keep the dates free.

Of course, it was never my intention to burden the German Section of the World Alliance, which is struggling so hard, with the expenses of our Provisional Bureau. The work as a whole was based on the commitment of the Church Federation Office to reimburse the secretariat of the World Alliance for such expenses up to a total of five hundred marks. I must deduce from your letter that that promise either has been withdrawn somehow or is not being met. If that is the case and if then the World Alliance also has to cover the expenses for my trip from its very meager resources, I am certainly ready to take on financial sacrifices for the trip and would then only ask to have the direct travel expenses reimbursed. It is very kind that Dr. Schreiber, Superintendent Diestel, and you are making an effort to facilitate my stay in Berlin. Actually, I have a number of friends in the suburbs of Berlin with whom I could stay, so that I probably will not have to accept the hospitality you have so kindly offered. It is only a question for me whether, because of the large number of other commitments and meetings that always come up in Berlin, I may instead take a room at a hotel in the city.

If it turns out to be necessary, I would come to you well ahead of time with a request for accommodations in a private home.

Now, I have one more request that you together with Dr. Schreiber set the
exact times as soon as possible. I will have to make a large number of other 116
appointments in Berlin and need to know very soon what time I have available. Should I attend the meeting of the working group,[6] or am I not a member there?

With kind regards,
Yours,
[W. Stählin]

---

[5.] That is, the theological conference of the Provisional Bureau, which was planned for December 9 and 10, 1932, in the Church Federation Office.

[6.] The reference is to the meeting of the German Ecumenical Working Group, which took place in the Church Federation Office immediately following the conference of the Provisional Bureau.

### 88.2 Enclosure: W. Stählin to the Church Federation Office

Münster, October 27, 1932

It was the general wish of those gathered at the meeting of the Provisional Bureau for Ecumenical Youth Work, held in April of this year in the conference room of the Church Federation Office, to continue the theological discussion begun there at a time in the foreseeable future. The plan was to hold this subsequent conference at the end of October, but for various reasons this date was not possible. As I hear now from Lecturer Licentiate Bonhoeffer, the Church Federation Office intends to call the working group of ecumenical associations together for a meeting on Friday, December 9.[7] I would be very grateful if the continuation of our theological discussion could be scheduled in conjunction with this meeting. Perhaps it is not very easy for some of the participants, if they are in academic positions, to be free to come during the semester. But the meeting of the working group for ecumenical associations[8] will, in itself, bring to Berlin so many gentlemen whose participation must be important to us that I think this coordination of meeting times would be a very great advantage. I myself can get free relatively easily on this date and am available on Friday, December 9, and Saturday, December 10. So I request that the Church Federation Office invite the groups and important individuals affiliated with the Provisional Bureau for Ecumenical Youth Work to a continuation of the theological discussion in conjunction with the planned meeting of the working group of ecumenical associations. Assuming that the meeting of the working group is scheduled for the
117 morning of the ninth of December, the afternoon of December 9 would probably be available for our theological discussion. But I would assume that we will have to extend the discussion to Saturday morning as well. It would perhaps not be a good idea to include Friday evening, considering how full the schedules of the gentlemen in Berlin are, especially in the evenings.

I believe both the wishes of the group that gathered in April and the practical situation would best be served if no new lectures were held at this continuation of the theological discussion, but rather that the theses that Dr. Zoellner and I presented at that earlier date,[9] which have been published in the meantime, be

[7.] Stählin is referring to the meetings of the Provisional Bureau and the German Ecumenical Working Group.

[8.] That is, the associations organized within the German Ecumenical Working Group.

[9.] See 1/84, ed. note 4.

used as a starting point. The discussion, then, would primarily be centered on the two questions:

1. The theological place of "*Volk*."
2. The meaning of "Confession"[10] in the context of the ecumenical movement.

Lecturer Lic. Bonhoeffer will certainly be very willing to do any work necessary and possible in preparing for this new conference as well.

[W. Stählin]

**89. To Erwin Sutz**[1]

Berlin-Grunewald, October 27, 1932

Dear Mr. Sutz,

Can you imagine that a person who would have every reason to send his thanks as soon as possible should wait and drag his feet for nearly two months. I really can't believe it and am really ashamed. Forgive me! Those were days back then in September for which I will always be grateful to you.[2] For me the stay at your home was not only the *refuge* for one who was theologically homeless, for *which* I had longed for such a long time and on which I can only think back with nostalgia in the cold solitude up here—but everything was so full of new experiences and memories that those days are still very much with me today. You had to make great sacrifices of 118
time and other things, and with you, I am also very grateful to your parents and your godmother,[3] who took care of us so kindly. It was especially nice for me to be able to be with you at your home and get a glimpse of the background of your own existence in the days I was there. In many ways it is very different from mine—but we probably already knew that about each other beforehand—and yet I never felt like a stranger. There must be something there, not easy to describe, that makes it possible for two people like you and me to meet and get along together, and which cannot be traced back to an easily understandable cause. But in those days I felt strongly that that is not an illusion, and that made me especially happy. If I

[10.] [*Konfession* here meaning a distinct theological/creedal tradition that is manifest in particular denominations.—MBL]

[1.] *NL*, A 29, 4(10); handwritten. Partially reproduced in *GS* 1:35–37.

[2.] See 1/79.

[3.] Mrs. Karoline Albrecht (according to information to the German *DBW* editor from Mrs. Dora Sutz on December 18, 1988).

could show you my background here some time, that would probably lead one step further toward mutual understanding. I hope that now we do not lose track of each other, after we have had this time together. (Sometimes I think with a shudder that we are perhaps alike because we are both leading existences somehow at the edge of our church—both in very different locations.) I am eager to know about the paths in your life; they are much less predictable than mine. And that is what is bad about my situation, yet nice as far as yours is concerned. But please help see to it that we keep an eye on each other.

If I wanted to start to tell you about myself, I would write all night. Another time—when I have more energy.

Write soon! I am looking forward to it very much. Tell Brunner how grateful I am to him for the afternoon.[4]

Kind regards from your grateful
Dietrich Bonhoeffer

119 **90. To the Editors of *Die Tägliche Rundschau*[1]**

Enclosed I am sending you a brief report on the international youth conferences of the World Alliance for Promoting International Friendship through the Churches and request that you publish it in *Die Tägliche Rundschau,* if possible in the Saturday edition.[2]

Respectfully,
B.

[4.] A reference to the fact that Sutz had introduced Bonhoeffer to Emil Brunner, something Bonhoeffer in an earlier letter had asked him to do (see 1/39 and 1/72).

[1.] *NL*, A 34,7; handwritten draft. The dating of the letter to October 29, 1932, in Meyer and Bethge, *Nachlaß Dietrich Bonhoeffer*, 37, cannot be proved from the document itself.

[2.] See the report intended for *Die Tägliche Rundschau*, "Church, Youth, Peace: On the Youth Conferences of the World Alliance for Promoting International Friendship through the Churches," in 2/19. It was not possible to document the publication of this report.

**91. Circular Letter to Various Student Fraternities**[1]

[To the] Corps. . .
To the fraternity. . .
c/o the Senior

Enclosed I am sending you the semester program[2] of the student ministry and request that you post it in your fraternity house. Since to my great regret I have not yet been able to be in contact with you, I take the liberty of requesting that at your general meeting you present the question concerning your opinion on the work of a student pastor at the Technical College, discuss it, and let me know the result. Of course, nothing can be agreed on concerning the relationship each individual has to this work. But it is important to me for my work as a whole to have a clear picture of the position of the whole fraternity. From the program you will be able to see 120
fairly well what the goals of my work are. May I request that at your general meeting the introduction to the student ministry that I wrote briefly in *Die Technische Hochschule*, no. 9 (February 1932), p. 200, be read.[3]

I am interested in only voluntary, not required participation. I also prefer the opportunity of a direct, objective discussion about the burning questions of our day to beating around the bush. I am aware that with my request I am asking something unusual of you. But I am confident in the hope that you will not refuse me this help in establishing the work of the student ministry.

I would be especially grateful for any concrete suggestions concerning the organization of the work.

With kind regards. Most respectfully yours,
[Dietrich Bonhoeffer]

[1.] *NL*, A 29,1(2) (a); handwritten draft; cf. *NL*, A 29,1(2) (b); later typewritten transcription by Eberhard Bethge. Previously published in *GS* 6:217–18. According to General Superintendent Emil Karow's report about Bonhoeffer's work at the Technical College to the Consistory in Berlin (see *GS* 6:220), the letter was probably written at the beginning of the winter semester, 1932–33.

[2.] Bonhoeffer had announced discussions and working groups on the topics "The Crisis of the State and the Gospel" and "Jesus Christ" (on the attendance at these events, see the report by Karow in *GS* 6:220, mentioned above).

[3.] See 2/6.

### 92. To Two Student Fraternities[1]

To Wingolf, Lietzenburg, V. D. St.[2]

In sending you the enclosed semester program[3] with a request that you
121 post it, I remind you of my visit with you last semester[4] and take the liberty of making the following request: It would give me a much clearer picture of the nature of the work I can do at the Technical College if, at your next general meeting, you would bring up for discussion the question of your position regarding the work of a student pastor at the Technical College and then let me know the results.[5] Of course, nothing can be agreed on concerning the relationship each individual has to this work. But it is important to me for my work as a whole to have a clear picture of the position of the whole fraternity. From the program you will be able to see fairly well what the goals of my work are. May I request that at your general meeting the introduction to the student ministry that I wrote briefly in *Die Technische Hochschule*, no. 9 (February 1932), p. 200, be read.[6]

I am only interested in voluntary, not required participation. I also prefer the opportunity of a direct, objective discussion about the burning questions of our day to beating around the bush. I am aware that with my request I am asking something unusual of you. But I am confident in the hope that you will not refuse me this help in establishing the work of the student ministry.

I would be especially grateful for any concrete suggestions concerning the organization of the work.

With kind regards. Most respectfully yours,
[Dietrich Bonhoeffer]

---

[1.] *NL*, A 29,1(2) (a); handwritten draft; cf. *NL*, A 29,1(2) (b); later typewritten transcription by Eberhard Bethge. Previously published in *GS* 6:217. Bonhoeffer had written to the Wingolf fraternity at the Technical College, Berlin-Charlottenburg, early in 1932; see 1/34.

[2.] The Association of German Students (Verein Deutscher Studenten) was an organization of fraternities whose members did not wear a sash with the fraternity colors. This group was influenced by Adolf Stoecker from 1871 onward. In 1881 they joined together to form the Federation of German Student Associations (Verband der Vereine Deutscher Studenten, or VVDST; also called the Kyffhäuser-Verband). In 1933, there were forty-two fraternities in this organization.

[3.] Bonhoeffer had announced discussions and working groups on the topics "The Crisis of the State and the Gospel" and "Jesus Christ" (cf. 1/91, ed. note 2).

[4.] That is, summer semester, 1932.

[5.] Since Bonhoeffer continues exactly as in 1/91 from the line beginning "Of course, nothing can be determined . . . ," it appears that of the student fraternities to whom Bonhoeffer had written, only the two mentioned above had contacted him.

[6.] See 2/6.

## 93. To Hans Fischer[1] 122

Dear Mr. Fischer,

Do you possibly have in the C. S. V.[2] library the book by Visser 't Hooft on "The Background of the Social Gospel,"[3] and would it be possible that I could borrow the book for a couple of days? Please be so kind as to find out about it. Perhaps you would then kindly let me know.

With kind regards and thanks I remain
Yours,
Dietrich Bonhoeffer

## 93a. To Paul Lehmann[1] 17:112

October 30, 1932

Dear Paul,

You wrote me such a nice letter some time ago[2] but unfortunately forgot to put the address on the envelope, so I had a somewhat hard time with my answer. I couldn't just assume that a letter with the address Paul Lehmann, Europe, would reach you. But now I think that, in the meantime, Mr. Sutz is somewhat better oriented about where you are, or even that you may

---

[1.] In the possession of the Fischer family; handwritten. In the fall of 1932, Bonhoeffer had been asked by the Management Committee of the German Section of the World Alliance for Promoting International Friendship through the Churches to write an article about the "social gospel" (*GS* 1:528). At the beginning of December 1932, after quite a long search, Bonhoeffer had found the book [referring to the work by Visser 't Hooft—MBL] (on this, see the letter to Hans Schönfeld in *GS* 6:248–49).

[2.] This is probably a reference to the DCSV, the German Christian Student Organization (Deutsche Christliche Studentenvereinigung), one of the many associations in the communal movement (*Gemeinschaftsbewegung*). In 1895, the DCSV was constituted as an association of Christian student fraternities. It had been a member of the World Student Christian Association (Christlicher Studentenweltbund) since 1897.

[3.] See the draft of the article in *GS* 6:104–12. [Bonhoeffer's text can be found in *DBWE* 12:236–43.—VB]

[1.] Paul Lehmann Collection, Special Collections, Princeton Theological Seminary Library; typewritten with handwritten signature, on letter paper with the printed address: "Lic. Dietrich Bonhoeffer, Lecturer at the Berlin University, Berlin-Grunewald, [no date], Wangenheimstrasse 14, H 1 Pfalzburg 2616." First published in *DBW* 17:112–14. Edited by Ernst-Albert Scharffenorth.

[2.] Letter not extant.

perhaps be in Zürich[3] and see him now and then. So I am asking him to forward this letter. I am coming to you now today with a very great and urgent request, an almost brazen request. I have suddenly been asked here to write a very brief, summarizing "paper" about the social gospel[4] for our church authorities.[5] Short historical outline, the most important ideas and their development up to the present time, bibliography. Now I am very
17:113 much at a loss because the simple fact is that I actually do not know enough about the material and am coming to you, hoping confidently that you will help me. Our church administration would like to use the thing to send out throughout all of Germany as material for lectures—so the level of sophistication can be relatively modest. It should serve as information for pastors. May I just simply ask you to write a summary like that for me *as soon as possible,* which I could work over afterward? It can't be that much trouble for you, of course, and you would be doing me a really great favor. After that, you can ask of me what you will—up to half a kingdom—and I will do it for you; only please help me quickly in this difficulty. I actually have so ridiculously much to do with the university and the ministry and innumerable lectures[6] that I just could not work my way into it from the beginning. So please be so kind and help me! And another request, do let me know immediately, if possible, whether you want to do it. I must make some very necessary adjustments, since the thing is supposed to be finished to submit in three weeks. It should be about four pages long.

And now one more last request. Let me know of something I can help you with. I would be especially grateful to you for that. I am very anxious to hear how things have been going for you up to now, how you like Brunner, and how your work is coming along. Maybe now, because I am close by, I can be of help to you after all.

---

[3.] Bonhoeffer had advised Lehmann not to go to Brunner in Zürich, but rather to go to Karl Barth in Bonn and possibly to Rudolf Bultmann in Marburg. See the letter of May 30, 1932, 1/59a.

[4.] [Both "paper" and "social gospel" are in English in the original letter.—MBL]

[5.] Bonhoeffer had undertaken this assignment on October 29, 1932; see *DBWE* 12:236, ed. notes 1 and 2. Bonhoeffer's text can be found in *DBWE* 12:236–43.

[6.] On November 19, 1932, Bonhoeffer gave the lecture "Thy Kingdom Come! The Prayer of the Church-Community for God's Kingdom on Earth," which was published in 1933 (*DBWE* 12:285–97). In December, there followed (according to Winterhager's dating) the lecture "Christ and Peace" (*DBW* 17:116–20 and *DBWE* 12:258–62 [the version published in *DBWE* 12:258–62 is the text from *DBW* 17, but includes additional annotations by Ernst-Albert Scharffenorth—VB]). Bonhoeffer was probably also working on his lecture on "The Führer Principle" ("The Younger Generation's Altered View of the Concept of Führer," *DBWE* 12:266–68; see also the following lecture, "The *Führer* and the Individual in the Younger Generation," *DBWE* 12:268–82).

I have had to work very much during the last few weeks because I had to write a review of Heim's big book and that was an unbelievable amount of work.[7] I spent my free time in a little wooden house that I had built for myself near Berlin,[8] on a big meadow, with some of my unemployed confirmands. When you came to Europe, I was in Geneva and Zürich.[9] 17:114
When will we get together and discuss some theological questions? When are you coming to Berlin?[10] If only I could know that soon, first, so that I could look forward to it and, second, so that I could be certain to keep the time free. I have to travel so terribly much next spring.[11] Of course, I am so anxious to see you both again and to hear about New York.

How is your wife? How is Germany agreeing with her?

Please write soon. I will be better, too, and write more. Excuse me for springing this on you. But I hope very much that you can help me.

My sincere thanks in advance and in general.

Kindest regards to your wife and to you, yourself
Most faithfully yours,
Dietrich Bonhoeffer

---

[7.] See the essay "On Karl Heim's *Glaube und Denken*," *DBWE* 12:243–58.

[8.] The reference is to the cabin in Biesenthal near Berlin, which Bonhoeffer was able to use until the end of the summer semester, 1933. See *DB-ER*, 175, and Bethge and Gremmels, *Life in Pictures*, centenary ed., 57. After that it was taken over by the Hitler Youth (*DBWE* 12:132, ed. note 2).

[9.] Bonhoeffer was in Switzerland from the middle to the end of August 1932. In addition to attending conferences of the World Alliance for Promoting International Friendship through the Churches, Bonhoeffer apparently visited Emil Brunner in Zürich. See 1/89, ed. note 4.

[10.] See the letter of November 29, 1932, to Paul Lehmann, *DBWE* 12, 1/10b.

[11.] Only one trip can be confirmed for this time period, the one to attend the ecumenical conference in Dassel, Germany, March 6–10, 1933 (*DBWE* 12:520). [See also Bonhoeffer's paper for that conference, "The Concept of Confession from the Standpoint of the Concept of Truth," *DBWE* 12, 2/10.—VB]

# PART 2
# Reports, Theological Studies, and Texts from the University Period

# A. Reports on Ecumenical Work

## Late 1931

### 1. Report on a Conference of the World Alliance in Cambridge[1] 125

The International Conference of the World Alliance for Promoting International Friendship through the Churches in Cambridge (September 1–5, 1931)

Those who view the World Alliance with disinterest or resentment[2] should take the opportunity either to confirm their judgment based on the results of the Cambridge meeting or to revise it. The forthcoming disarmament conference in Geneva[3] and the world crisis,[4] whose problems are not insignificantly related to it, dictated the theme of the conference for the assembled representatives of the churches. In the disarmament question,

[1.] *Theologische Blätter* 10 (1931): 299–30. Previously published in *GS* 1:113–17. Cf. *NL*, A 34,2; typewritten copy.

[2.] See the anti-ecumenical statements of Paul Althaus and Emanuel Hirsch, which Bonhoeffer had also opposed on other occasions. See 1/4, ed. note 6, and 2/11, ed. note 5.

[3.] As of the mid-1920s, there was a League of Nations commission that was to prepare a disarmament conference. Germany was already bound to a comprehensive armaments restriction by the 1919 Treaty of Versailles, whereas the victorious powers, especially France, could arm themselves without restraint; this became the primary barrier to disarmament agreements. When the disarmament conference began in Geneva on February 2, 1932, the question of the equitable treatment of Germany proved to be the decisive reason for the eventual collapse of the conference (in 1933). Compromise in the early months of 1932 actually seemed near, but with the resignation of the Brüning cabinet in May 1932, chances for a settlement disappeared.

[4.] The reference is to the dramatic deterioration in the worldwide economic situation and the strong rise in unemployment in Europe and the United States, related to the spectacular collapse of the New York stock market at the end of October 1929. Further, there was the Japanese invasion of China and the unresolved tensions in Europe in the wake of the Versailles treaty. See 2/17, ed. note 7.

which was the banner under which the conference took place, the important thing for the churches was not primarily the political debate among the nations that were particularly affected by it, but rather the question
126 whether the nations[5] that are presently rearming will be resolved to stand by their given word (in Article 8 of the League of Nations covenant[6] and in the Preamble of Part V of the Versailles treaty)[7] or whether, by breaking their word,[8] the first attempt toward a moral order in international relations among nations[9] shall hopelessly collapse. At the very edge of the abyss of yet another complete moral chaos in the lives of the nations, the churches are standing firm and summon all to truthfulness and faithfulness, to respect and honor the foresworn promise. The honor of the
127 rearming nations and the justice of this cause are at stake. The English and the Americans expressed this at the conference with unparalleled clarity. Even the French presentation on the disarmament question was in agree-

[5.] The reference here is to Germany's eastern neighbors, Poland and Czechoslovakia, as well as the victorious powers—the United States, England, and France.

[6.] Article 8 of the covenant of the League of Nations, which was constituted in January 1920, reads: "The Members of the League recognise that the maintenance of peace requires the reduction of national armaments to the lowest point consistent with national safety and the enforcement by common action of international obligations. The Council, taking account of the geographical situation and circumstances of each State, shall formulate plans for such reduction for the consideration and action of the several Governments. Such plans shall be subject to reconsideration and revision at least every ten years. After these plans shall have been adopted by the several Governments, the limits of armaments therein fixed shall not be exceeded without the concurrence of the Council. The Members of the League agree that the manufacture by private enterprise of munitions and implements of war is open to grave objections. The Council shall advise how the evil effects attendant upon such manufacture can be prevented, due regard being had to the necessities of those Members of the League which are not able to manufacture the munitions and implements of war necessary for their safety. The Members of the League undertake to interchange full and frank information as to the scale of their armaments, their military, naval, and air programmes and the condition of such of their industries as are adaptable to war-like purposes" (in L. Martin, *Treaties of Peace, 1919–1923*, 13). [This and the language in the following editorial note are from the official English text of the Treaty of Versailles; there are slight differences in nuance in the official German text of that treaty in the corresponding wording in *DBW* 11:126, ed. note 6.—VB]

[7.] The Preamble to Part 5 of the Versailles peace treaty, titled "Military, Naval, and Air Clauses," reads as follows: "In order to render possible the initiation of a general limitation of the armaments of all nations, Germany undertakes strictly to observe the military, naval and air clauses which follow" (in L. Martin, *Treaties of Peace, 1919–1923*, 95).

[8.] In Bonhoeffer's opinion, the rearming nations of Europe contravened these stipulated regulations.

[9.] The founding of the League of Nations in January 1920 had as its purpose the resolution of conflicts between nations on the basis of legal and political means, rather than going to war.

ment with this thinking and, furthermore, was characterized by an extension of the concept of *securité* as a fundamental international principle, as opposed to their previously narrower version. This included a clear recognition of the justice of the German position, which means that an attempt was made to engage with deep sincerity on the level of unconditional equality of rights that serve the common cause. In this way, the conference was able to issue the proclamation unanimously to the churches of the world that, in its conviction, war as a means of settling international disputes contradicts the spirit ("mind and method"!)[10] of Christ and his church. Further, the conference called for (1) a substantial reduction in armaments of every form down to the lowest level; (2) reasonable and just relations between the armed peoples; and (3) security for all peoples against potential attacks. This message is to be advocated publicly by the churches, and the regional governments should place their full support along these lines.

It will not be possible to avoid the criticism coming from the most diverse sides that too much or too little has been said here or, on the other hand, that once again something has been merely *said*. We don't wish to minimize this criticism but would simply explain some things. The "too much" rests particularly in the theological formulations, which have been determined essentially by Anglo-Saxon theology and grasp the problematic of something like war only in the realization of an already well-established ideal, that is, conceiving the matter as a problem of action rather than as a problem of its essential nature. This is what so often gives the international church resolutions a full-bodied ring and yet to our ear a tone that is devoid of real content. The "too little" certainly lies in what was said. At the conclusion of the plenary meeting, a man from India vehemently called upon the assembly to say something more, something conclusive, that is, about what the church's actual position would be, were it to find itself again in a 128
catastrophe. This was simply the expression of the justified and yet repeatedly disappointed hope that the church would finally, finally speak out very concretely for once.[11] It is precisely at such conferences that "Christian principles"—the applied art—become most dangerous to authentic Christianity. Nonetheless, such principles must be articulated as long as one simply doesn't know what more to do, in which case it would certainly be good to admit that openly. Most circles in our countries will simply overlook the fact that the churches have once again drafted a resolution. As long as the churches do not know how to do otherwise . . . [12]

[10.] [This phrase in the original is in English.—MBL]

[11.] See 2/14, pp. 359–60.

[12.] [Ellipses in original.—MBL]

¶It is not a significant counterargument that people in England and America still believe in resolutions more than we do. And yet it will not do here to try to force more than is given us at this point. It is of more decisive importance for the meaning and progress of the work of the World Alliance that the churches give the message of the World Alliance the fullest resonance in their countries and that they provide for a hearing in the congregations as well as in the broadest public arena. Thus, in England on the day after the conference ended, the president of the English group, the Lord Bishop of Ripon,[13] Bishop Dr. Ammundsen (Hadersleben), Prof. D.[14] Dr. Martin Dibelius (Heidelberg), and others in various large churches spoke in their worship services about the message of the World Alliance. In the evening, there was also a worship service in three languages broadcast by radio, in which the retired president of the German Supreme Court, D. Dr. Walter Simons,[15] delivered the message and the bishop of Ripon in his sermon summoned the congregation to the work of Christian peace.

It is worth noting that the international youth conference affiliated with the World Alliance was unable to decide to issue a resolution. The sense was too strong that they needed first to learn to see the new circumstances in a fresh way and not immediately enter into the matter with grand pro-
129 nouncements. The major conference had other things to consider here, and we must be grateful that it brought about such a resolution, which without doubt signifies a stronger step forward than all that had been conveyed previously. Nowhere has the critique against the entire enterprise, from the most different viewpoints, been louder than in the circle of the youth conference. Incidentally, here again there has been a very pronounced intellectual [geistig] grouping of the Continental and particularly the German-French (and Danish) on the one side and the Anglo-American on the other. The young French saw many essential matters very much as we did, particularly theological matters. In these young circles, there was much thought, with great honesty, about the enormous barriers that stand in the way of total openness in our relations. Not only here, however, but essentially in the lack of a major, fundamentally theological understanding of our work (for which the hitherto almost universally accepted Anglo-Saxon foundation simply does not suffice), we saw a mutual need and a common obligation. In order to carry on the ecumenical work among young people, perceived as an urgent necessity, three international youth secretary offices have been established, for which England, France, and Germany each provide one sec-

[13.] Since 1926 this had been Edward Arthur Burroughs.

[14.] ["D." indicates an honorary doctorate.—VB]

[15.] On Walter Simons's role in ecumenical work, cf. Gründer, *Walter Simons*, 9–23.

retary.[16] For all the criticism, however, it remained evident that the work of the World Alliance is progressing slowly but surely. The urgency of its work today must fire the heart and soul of every person, but at this point we do not yet know how we could pursue it better and faster.

Despite its extremely cautious wording, the recently drafted resolution from the twentieth international YMCA (CVJM)[17] convention in Cleveland, U.S.A., opposing the idea of Germany's exclusive guilt for the war,[18]
is characteristic of a strong shift in American thinking right now—though 130
the churches didn't initiate it—especially if it is compared to the similar message of the Federal Council of Churches of Christ in America in November 1930.[19]

¶The resolution, furthermore, is clearly of very great significance for the entire work of the YMCA and will facilitate education toward Christian thinking with a broadened human vision. And yet only with difficulty will it
avoid the accusation that serious Americans leveled at the Federal Council 131
declaration at the time: once again it is ten years too late. When will the time come that Christianity speaks the right word at the right hour?

Berlin-Grunewald Dietrich Bonhoeffer

---

[16.] Pastor F. W. Tom Craske oversaw activities in the British Empire, the United States, and the Far East; Pastor P. C. Toureille was assigned to France, southern and southwestern Europe, the Balkans, Poland, and Czechoslovakia; Bonhoeffer had oversight over Germany, northern and central Europe, including Hungary and Austria.

[17.] CVJM (Christlicher Verein Junger Männer) is the German branch of the Young Men's Christian Association.

[18.] The twentieth world conference of the YMCA, which met August 4–9, 1931, in Cleveland, Ohio, passed a resolution on the controversial question of guilt for the First World War. Although the delegates announced their lack of expertise in the political implications of the issue, they expressed the need "in the spirit of that international brotherhood which the Association seeks to promote throughout the world, to dissociate themselves from the injustice of attributing to one nation or group of nations alone sole responsibility for the war" (*Federal Council Bulletin*, no. 14 [September 1931]: 19).

[19.] Bonhoeffer refers here to a resolution passed by the Executive Committee of the Federal Council of Churches of Christ in America at its annual meeting on December 2 and 3, 1930, in Washington, D.C. The wording of the resolution on the question of guilt for the First World War ran as follows: "In view of the fact that our Christian brethren in Germany feel that injustice has been done to them in the accusation of sole German responsibility for causing the Great War, and that this charge is a prolific source of international bitterness and misunderstanding, we recommend that the Federal Council assure our Christian brethren in Germany that the Federal Council of the Churches of Christ in America does not consent to the theory of Germany's exclusive responsibility for the war. We further recommend that the Commission on Relations with Churches Abroad convey to the churches of Germany the Christian greetings of the Federal council, expressing to them our confidence, our sympathy and our love" (*Federal Council Bulletin*, no. 14 [February 1931]: 18).

## 2. Report on a Meeting of the Provisional Bureau for Ecumenical Youth Work[1]

Report on the Meeting of the Provisional Bureau for Ecumenical Youth Work on October 20, 1931, from 10:00 a.m. to 3:15 p.m. in the main conference room of the Protestant High Church Council in Berlin-Charlottenburg

I.

Present:

(1) *German Protestant Church Federation Office*[2]
Senior Consistory Councillor Dr. Schreiber

II.

*Provisional Bureau for Ecumenical Youth Work*:

(1) Professor Dr. Stählin, Münster in Westphalia–Director
(2) Student Chaplain and University Lecturer Dr. Bonhoeffer, international youth secretary of the World Alliance for Promoting International Friendship through the Churches–Secretary
(3) German Association of the World Alliance for Promoting International Friendship through the Churches, Berlin-Lichterfelde, Dahlemer Str. 87
132 General Secretary of the Provisional Bureau:
Superintendent *Diestel*
(4) National Federation of Protestant Young Men's Associations and similar movements, Kassel-Wilhelmshöhe, Kirchstr. 6:
Ministerial Director von Kameke (retired)
Walter Meyer, trainee
Walter Etzien
Fritz Söhlmann and interim
Reich warden Dr.[3] E. [Erich] Stange

---

[1.] LKA Nuremberg, Personen XVIII: Nachlaß Wilhelm Stählin; typewritten. Cf. the published copy (with notes made in the margins by a staff member of the Church Federation Office) from the archives of the Church Foreign Office of the Evangelical Church of Germany, in Glenthøj, *Zu Dietrich Bonhoeffers Eintritt*, 15–19. On Bonhoeffer's activity as secretary of the Provisional Bureau for Ecumenical Youth Work, founded in 1931, see the editors' introduction to this volume, p. 10. Professor Wilhelm Stählin, director of the Provisional Bureau, was coresponsible for this report, which was sent to all the member associations. See p. 176.

[2.] [Italicized material in original text.—MBL]

[3.] [This was an honorary doctorate.—VB]

(5) Protestant National Association of Young Women
Berlin-Dahlem, Friedbergstr. 27:
Vicar Miss M. Voigt
(6) German Christian Student Organization,[4] Berlin
N.W. 87, Flensburgerstr. 9:
Theology Student Kurt Naumann
(7) National Association of Protestant Youth Offices (Youth
Chaplaincies)
Berlin N.W. 7, Georgenstr. 47: Pastor *Suderow*
(8) General Association of Protestant Societies for Working Women in
Germany: Klara *Lohmeyer,*
Representative of the National Commission of German Youth
Associations, Berlin N. E. 43, Alsenstr. 10.
(9) Protestant Press Association for Germany: Dr. Böhme
(10) League of German Bible Circles: Pastor Udo Smidt
(11) Candidate in Theology, Elisabeth Grauer, conference participant
in Cambridge.

Absent:

(1) Central Board for the Inner Missions, Berlin-Dahlem, Zietenstr. 24
(2) National Conference of Protestant Youth Pastors (Pastor Philipps),
Düsseldorf, Steinstr. 19a
(3) Conference of Protestant Student Chaplains (Pastor Kuntze)[5]
Leipzig 0 29, Preußenstr. 21 c
(4) Youth League for Decisive Christianity, Woltersdorf near Berlin.

Opening 133

Superintendent *Diestel* welcomed the participants and asked Professor *Dr. Stählin* to take over the meeting. Professor Stählin thanked the Church Federation Office and the Administrative Office of the German section of the World Alliance for Promoting International Friendship through the Churches for the assistance provided in the preparation for the meeting.

[4.] [This organization was founded in 1895 and not officially related to the German Christian movement, although after 1933 its ranks did include German Christians like Karl Fezer. The organization was banned in 1938 by the Nazi regime.—VB]

[5.] Reference is to Pastor Johann Gerhard Kunze.

### I.

### *Exchange of experiences at this year's ecumenical youth gatherings, in particular the meetings in Cambridge and Cleveland*

(1) *Dr. Stählin* gave a lengthy report about the large *Conference of the World Alliance for Promoting International Friendship through the Churches.* In accordance with the resolution passed in 1928 in Prague,[6] a youth delegation was present for the first time in Cambridge.[7] Its members had come to know each other through two youth camps arranged by Dr. Bacon (New-Castle). They were greeted warmly at the conference, even though they themselves were critical of the conference. One impediment was the separate meeting places. The youth delegation sent a resolution to the main conference. A declaration framed in general words to the youth of the world was rejected, for it was believed that nothing would be accomplished by the resolution. It is worth noting that there was a close connection here between the Germans, the Danes, and the younger French over against the Anglo-Saxons. Special meetings between the Germans and the French were proposed. Under the chairmanship of the Lord Bishop of Ripon and Mr. Henriod of Geneva, an international youth secretariat for the youth work of the World Alliance was set up with three secretaries: Pastor Craske for England, Pastor Toureille for western Europe, and Dr. Bonhoeffer for eastern Europe.[8]

*In the discussion* the grounds given for the intellectual divisions were the
134 antagonistic worldviews and the dissimilar experiences of the war. Among the Anglo-Saxons, particularly the English, self-assurance seems to begin to waver.

Dr. Bonhoeffer reported about *reservations* that were expressed in Cambridge, namely, the random nature of the composition of the youth delegation and the commissions, the absence of a meeting with Germans from outside Germany, lack of preparation of the German delegation for the conference as well as a deficiency in the theological depth of the proceedings. In response, it was acknowledged that the German delegation was indeed randomly formed, but still it had been put together well. Moreover, there had been personal contacts with Germans living outside Germany. In response to the *question* posed by Dr. Stählin, *whether alternating or permanent membership* is desirable in the delegation, the response was that, given the difficulty of ecumenical deliberations, a continuity is necessary but that does not rule out a gradual change.

---

[6.] The World Alliance conference held August 24–30, 1928, in Prague.

[7.] See 2/1.

[8.] See 2/1, ed. note 16.

(2) *The twentieth world conference of the Young Men's Christian Association in Cleveland,*[9] as Ministerial Director (retired) von Kameke reported, suffered from too many topics in which there was often a lack of appropriate expertise. On the other hand, the Oxford movement[10] seemed to stress the inner questions but in a one-sided way. In Cleveland, great care was taken to meet the demand for truthfulness, so indispensable in ecumenical gatherings, especially in the hard struggle over the war-guilt resolution.[11] Here, the relations with the French were difficult but nonetheless good.

*In the discussion,* trainee Meyer noted that the preparation for the conference had been exemplary, but that the *main issue* of all such meetings is to be the *question* about the message, *about the gospel.* Above all, young people must counteract the danger that a movement does not become an organization.[12] As Pastor Smidt commented, the tone of repentance rings within the message from Cleveland.[13] He alluded to the diversity 135
in conceptions of Christ that became evident. In reference to the ponderous theological manner of the Germans and the simpler style of the Anglo-Saxons, he emphasized the *necessity of saying complicated things simply.* Furthermore, the discussion about these difficulties has shown that one should not feel too certain even about one's own domain [Besitz]. Given the importance of working through this fundamental question, Ministerial Director von Kameke pointed out in particular the *importance of factual issues* and certainly the necessity as well that those who attend the conferences have expert knowledge and come equipped with good material. Dr. Stählin also emphasized that one should not sweep lightly past these specialized questions in social Christian enthusiasm. Indeed, a quick opinion to every particular question would fundamentally be the same as a mere Christian phraseology.

Dr. Schreiber reported, and this was confirmed by Dr. Böhme, that the *press coverage* of the German success in the question of war guilt has been noticeably sparse in the French and the English church press. Though in Germany and America, the political press has covered it well, better in this case than it did with the December 1930 announcement on the question of

[9.] See 2/1, p. 168.

[10.] This refers to the Oxford Group movement founded by Frank N. D. Buchman after his conversion to a religious revival movement. After 1938, it called itself Moral Rearmament. See *DBWE* 4:300, ed. note 43; also cited in *GS* 1:46.

[11.] See 2/1, ed. note 18.

[12.] What is actually meant is that there is a "danger that a movement would become an organization."

[13.] See 2/1, ed. note 18.

war guilt from the Federal Council of Churches of Christ.[14] He reported on measures taken for subsequently better press coverage and asked everyone to use his influence through the provincial organizations in Great Britain and France.

Dr. Stählin thanked the German representatives for creating an atmosphere of truthfulness in America.

## II.

### *Working plan of the Provisional Bureau*

#### *(1) News bulletin*

Dr. Stählin would like the publication of a short news bulletin for informational purposes, especially to provide information about the measures of
136 particular associations. Mr. Söhlmann reported on a similar bulletin that he himself had published earlier. Publication naturally requires resources, which are not, however, presently available. Therefore, for the time being, we will have to be content with the minutes, especially as Dr. Schreiber believes there is the prospect that at least sometime soon a limited number of communiqués from the ecumenical council will be freely placed at our disposal.

#### *(2) Setting up a card index*

Dr. Stählin reported on the necessity of starting a file on young persons who are suitable for participation in international meetings. The submitted questionnaire[15] was approved and should be distributed to the affiliated associations for their quick response.

## III.

### *Circulation of ecumenical ideas in church youth work, particularly in religious instruction*

Dr. Stählin emphasized that fostering ecumenical thought in *religious instruction* and among the youth who are growing up is now, because of the strong National Socialist wave, as necessary as it is difficult. The church has to stand above economic-like fluctuations in politics. What is to be done? Dr. Schreiber recalled the announcement already made at the meeting of April 24, 1931, that this task should be taken up by the "pedagogical group"

[14.] See 2/1, ed. note 19.

[15.] The printed questionnaire, which Bonhoeffer sent to the various representatives of the member organizations in the Provisional Bureau and with whose help the file would be created, may be found above, 1/12. Cf. also Glenthøj, *Zu Dietrich Bonhoeffers Eintritt,* 11.

of the German Section of the World Alliance for Promoting Friendship through the Churches (Director of Studies Dr. Heienbrock, Berlin-Steglitz, Beyme Str. 8). In issue 2, 1931, the journal *Die Evangelische Pädagogik*[16] (Teubner, Leipzig), the official publication of the Society for Pedagogy, presents the following articles: "Grundsätzliches über die Erziehung zum
ökumenischen Denken als Gegenwartsaufgabe des evangelischen Reli- 137
gionsunterrichts,"[17] "Praktische Winke für die Erziehung zum ökumenischen Denken im Religionsunterricht der Volksschule,"[18] "Ökumenische Erziehung in höheren Schulen,"[19] "Der ökumenische Gedanke in den Lehrbüchern für den Religionsunterricht."[20] Particularly suited for study circles is the work published by Furche-Verlag (Berlin) in 1931, titled *Die Einheit der Christenheit,* a biblical study of Paul's pastoral letters.[21] Mr. Söhlmann referred to the work of the Educational Commission in Cambridge, and Dr. Stählin noted the Circle of Ecumenical Educators, to which Mr. Söhlmann has been invited to participate. At the suggestion of Dr. Bonhoeffer, it was agreed that the Provisional Bureau engage a teacher of religious education on these matters.

The discussion about representation of ecumenical thought in the *student body,* which is ever more strongly dominated by National Socialism, resulted in the request to Dr. Bonhoeffer, who has been called to the position of student chaplain at the college in Berlin-Charlottenburg, to propose at the Conference of Student Pastors that this question be dealt with.

## IV.
### *Theological conference for the discussion of ecumenical questions*

Dr. Stählin stressed the necessity of a theological analysis of ecumenical problems, which is only just beginning. He proposed convening such a conference in conjunction with the next conference of the working group

[16.] ["Protestant pedagogy."—MBL]

[17.] [Principles of education in ecumenical thinking as a present task of Protestant religious instruction] written by educational consultant Dr. Otto Eberhard, Hohen-Neuendorf near Berlin, and published in *Die evangelische Pädagogik: Zeitschrift der Gesellschaft für evangelische Pädagogik* (Protestant pedagogy: Journal of the Society for Protestant Pedagogy), no. 6 (1931): 41–50.

[18.] [Practical tips for education in ecumenical thinking in elementary school religious instruction] by middle-school rector August Kain from Berlin, ibid., 50–53.

[19.] [Ecumenical education in secondary schools] by director of studies Dr. Marie Horstmeier from Berlin-Friedenau, ibid., 53–56.

[20.] [The ecumenical concept in textbooks for religious instruction] by director of studies Dr. Otto Güldenberg from Halle, ibid., 56–58.

[21.] E. Stange, *Die Einheit der Christenheit.*

of ecumenical associations that is to be called by the Church Federation Office—if possible not in Berlin.

In response to the request raised in the discussion that nontheologians
138 also be included, there was agreement that, for the present, a conference of theologians is necessary, perhaps in consultation with a few theologically trained laity. The number of *participants* should come to about *forty*. The week of March 6–12, 1932, is being considered as a prospective date.[22] The following *themes* were approved:[23]

(1) "The Unity of Christian Churches and the Churches"

(2) "The Unity of Christian Churches and the Peoples"

General Superintendent (retired) Dr. Zoellner (Düsseldorf) and Professor Dr. Althaus, Erlangen, were named as *presenters*.

The *location* for the conference remains undetermined. Further arrangements are delegated to Dr. Stählin and Dr. Bonhoeffer. They are to be in contact with the office of the Protestant Church in Germany [DEKA], since this office is authorized to call a conference of all the associations.

Signed: Bonhoeffer Signed: Dr. Stählin

[22.] The theological conference of the Provisional Bureau for Ecumenical Youth Work took place April 29–30, 1932, in Berlin (see 2/13: Bonhoeffer's report in the journal *Die Eiche*).

[23.] See 2/12.

# B. Texts from Activities in Church and University

## Winter Semester 1931–1932

### 3. Lecture Course: The History of Twentieth-Century Systematic Theology (Student Notes)[1] 139

§ 1 Society at the turn of the twentieth century

§ 2 Church and theology at the turn of the century in the context of intellectual history in general

§ 3 The concept of religion as a mediating concept
Troeltsch
The theory of religion
Neo-Kantian philosophy

---

[1.] *NL*, B 1,1; handwritten student notes by Joachim Kanitz, with additions here to the editorial notes from the student notes of Jürgen Winterhager (*NL*, B 1,2); compiled by Otto Dudzus and previously published in *GS* 5:181–227. Dudzus's interpretation has been consulted for passages difficult to understand. For Bonhoeffer's own assessment of these lectures, see 1/39. Bonhoeffer delivered these lectures during the winter semester of 1931–32 at the Friedrich Wilhelm University, Berlin, on Mondays and Thursdays from 3:00 to 4:00 p.m. Neither his manuscript nor any preparatory notes have been preserved (cf. *GS* 5:588). He began lecturing on Thursday, November 2, 1931, and presumably gave the concluding lecture on Monday, February 29, 1932. Kanitz's underlining, which, especially in §§ 6–10, emphasizes entire half pages of the manuscript, has not been replicated here. The editors unfortunately were unable to take into consideration the lecture notes of Winfried Zeller, which first came to their attention after this text had been printed. Zeller's text makes it possible to reconstruct the opening part of the lectures but is otherwise less comprehensive than that of Kanitz. Cf. Jaspert, "Dietrich Bonhoeffer's Vorlesung." [Throughout this document and other student notes, the German *DBW* editor has inserted bracketed clarifications. Where significant, the original German wording is also indicated within brackets. Parentheses in the text are those of Bonhoeffer or his students.—VB]

§ 4 Epistemology and religion
Rudolf Otto
§ 5 The essence of Christianity
§ 6 The absoluteness of Christianity
§ 7 The biblical Christ
§ 8 Justification and sanctification
Karl Holl
§ 9 The ethical problem and culture
§ 10 The turning point
§ 11 God
§ 12 The word of God and theology
§ 13 Proclamation
The problem of ethics, of obedience
§ 14 Where do we stand?

140 The History of Twentieth-Century Systematic Theology

*§ 1 Society at the turn of the twentieth century*

The Wilhemine period[2] is a period in Schleiermacher's sense, not an epoch;[3] [it is characterized by] a balance between powers and satiation. In an epoch, revolution or reformation arises, [marked by] strong one-sided exercise of power. [What are possible ways of understanding a period?] (1) Evaluating a period from within the one-sidedness of our epoch; (2) trying to reconstruct the old structure faithfully, as it truly was; both ways belong to the study of history. Most historical work only involves one of them; Paul Tillich, in *The Religious Situation,*[4] uses only the first way. The bourgeois spirit [was] understood as the "spirit of self-sufficient finitude."[5] All this

[2.] Reign of German emperor Wilhelm II, 1888–1918.

[3.] According to Friedrich Schleiermacher, a historical *period* is a time in which development is orderly, in which "events" undergo "a quiet progression." But a historical *epoch* is one dominated by "sudden new beginnings" and by "a revolutionary breakdown of previous structures." Cf. Schleiermacher, *Brief Outline of Theology as a Field of Study,* § 73, 42.

[4.] *Die religiöse Lage der Gegenwart,* 1926 [published in English as *The Religious Situation,* 1932.—MBL]

[5.] "The spirit of a finitude which lives within itself is, for our time, the spirit of capitalist society [*der bürgerlichen Gesellschaft*]. The designation itself indicates that the primary place where this spirit realizes itself is the sphere of activity. Within this sphere, however, it is economic activity which is dominant and it is its unconditioned dominance which characterizes the capitalist spirit [*den bürgerlichen Geist*] most definitely" (Tillich, *Religious Situation,* 105; cf. also 112 [with its reference to "a spirit of self-sufficient finitude"—MBL] and 125–26).

takes place in the sphere of I-It.[6] The cause is the rise of technology and politics. With Tillich the bourgeois spirit [is] already passé. 141

But the time from 1900 to 1914 [is] one of the most interesting of all. Every class was exactly balanced. Georg Simmel: *Soziologie*;[7] *das Wesen der Gesellschaft*[8] gives his sense of the society of those years. Each person had a place to do his work in peace. Each participant explored his own limited space. Behind this game of being sociable, work and struggle were carried on as seldom in any period (Van Gogh's diary).[9] Objectivity is important to people. The work ethic, especially in Max Weber.[10] Self-determination of the individual over against the society. This work ethic has been taken over by our contemporary technologists, which is why they are primarily conservatives. Grisebach's work has marks of this work ethic.[11]

[6.] According to Tillich (ibid.), bourgeois society "took its rise with the emancipation of economic activity from control by a superior social power and the development of an autonomous economic system subject only to its own laws" (105–6). This means that "the laws of such an independent economic activity . . . correspond to the rationalistic methods of natural science and lead to the same results in the relations between things and in social relations" (106). Bonhoeffer reformulated Tillich's critique of bourgeois society using Martin Buber's concepts (cf. Buber, *I and Thou*, 3–4). In contrast to the I-Thou relationship that characterizes human communication, I-It is the area of human dealings with inanimate nature, in which all relations are subject to time and space and ruled by the necessities of causality.

[7.] This refers either to Simmel's *Soziologie: Untersuchungen über die Formen der Gesellschaftung* or to his *Grundfragen der Soziologie (Individuum und Gesellschaft)*. In his edition of these lectures, Otto Dudzus (*GS* 5:183) put "1908" after the word "Soziologie" to indicate his preference for the first title. [The bibliography includes the English translations of both volumes. Bonhoeffer cited both texts in *Sanctorum Communio*. Cf. *DBWE* 1:327.—MBL]

[8.] No work by Simmel with this title was found. Possibly Kanitz understood this as a separate bibliographical reference, from Bonhoeffer's comments on Simmel, or from the subtitle of the first book mentioned in ed. note 7.

[9.] Vincent van Gogh left no diary. The reference is to his letters; see *Complete Letters of Vincent van Gogh*.

[10.] Cf. Weber's thesis of the internal affinity between certain forms of modern so-called ascetic Protestantism (Calvinism, pietism, Methodism, Baptist sects) and capitalistic culture and the work ethic that dominates them (Weber, *Protestant Ethic*).

[11.] Eberhard Grisebach developed a "critical contemporary ethic" in opposition to both the metaphysical pretensions to knowledge on the part of theology, on one hand, and to speculative philosophy, on the other, in which he concentrated on "the problem of human practical existence and the really finite events taking place in the present" (Grisebach, *Gegenwart*, 39). The ethical world to be constructed, essentially, the world of the future, is to people living in the "crisis" of the present "a serious field for their labors. . . . Every morning shows anew, by chance, how much work there is to do. This world of work comes before that of technology" (581–82). Cf. also Grisebach's "Das Arbeitsethos des künftigen Europäers," in his *Die Schicksalfrage des Abendlandes*, 299–332, esp. 299–300:

142 There was also skepticism [with regard to][12] the facade presented by the civilization of that time. It was growing to the same degree as German absolutism. It is typified by Kalckreuth's[13] paintings, especially the realism of his portraits: people trapped in finitude, fundamentally skeptical vis-à-vis[14] culture and humankind. Thus awareness of feeling inserted into time, drive of the bourgeois spirit to go beyond one's limitations. Belief in progress, pride of citizenship, etc., turned into idols (Klinger,[15] songs of choral societies, Wagner looked at in this way). Attacks on this by Nietzsche and Wilhelm Busch; N[ietzsche] in the eschatological expectation of an Overman,[16] B[usch] in the resignation and transfiguration of the least members of society.[17] Reinforced by Ibsen,[18] Strindberg, Dostoyevsky,

---

"The spiritual characteristic that epitomizes our continent [Europe] is work itself, as it developed in the course of millennia, in terms of responsibility and of objects, because we have a social conscience. . . . Work is the element through which relations among human beings can be most naturally and simply regulated and clarified."

[12.] The text has "toward."

[13.] Count Leopold von Kalckreuth was the brother of Bonhoeffer's grandmother, Klara von Hase, née Countess von Kalckreuth (cf. *DB-ER*, 4).

[14.] The text has "toward."

[15.] Around 1900, especially in secessionist circles [artists who declared independence from mainstream art], Max Klinger was considered "spiritual leader of the age." His works of art overall show a marked contrarian reaction to the societal and cultural upheavals of the nineteenth century, the contradictions of which Klinger combated through a synthesis of naturalism, symbolism, and art nouveau to give a "general expression of our worldview" ("Max Klinger," in *Lexikon der Kunst*, 3:788–89).

[16.] The "Overman" [*Übermensch*, signifying a superior human being—VB] concept belongs in the context of Nietzsche's theory of the will to power. For Nietzsche, "overmen" are strong personalities like the heroes of antiquity or Renaissance figures who fully realized their physical and mental capabilities as human beings. The concept originates in Nietzsche's *Thus Spoke Zarathustra*. To the extent that one can speak of an "eschatological expectation of an Overman" in Nietzsche [cf. "The Bestowing Virtue": "One day again you shall become my friends and children of a single hope . . . to celebrate the great noon . . . where human beings stand at the midpoint of their course between animal and Overman and celebrate their way to evening as their highest hope: for it is the way to a new morning" (*Thus Spoke Zarathustra*, 59).—MBL], this does not mean the hope for a strong personality to solve the problems of the age, but at best the hope for a time in which such overmen can better actualize themselves than, for example, in the society of the German Empire (cf. Nietzsche, *Untimely Meditations*, 193.)

[17.] The situations in the lives of ordinary people and the lower middle class were Wilhelm Busch's preferred subject. [Busch was a renowned German painter and caricaturist who specialized in illustrated stories, most famously in his early classic *Max and Moritz* (1865), often referred to as a precursor to the modern comic strip. He was also a prolific painter and sculptor.—MBL]

[18.] Cf. Bonhoeffer's 1931 book report on Ibsen for the course "Ethical Viewpoints in Modern Literature" at Union Theological Seminary in New York: "The main theme of Ibsens whole writing namely the daimoniac power of society over the individual and the

van Gogh, Wagner(?); French Impressionism [with its] rediscovery of nature; the *Rosenkavalier* of Strauss[19] [with its] exposé of society. [These are] attempts not to clarify but (to present an) objective picture. 143

The intention to be objective was expressed through subjectivity. Therefore the sciences [became] psychologized. The striving for objectivity led again to subjectivity, to the ideal of personality. The aristocratic ideal of the finest development of personality was united with an—apparent—depersonalized objectivity (making room for plebeian clichés). The will to see the whole picture and specialization exist simultaneously. Transcendence is already there, but we don't recognize it. But where one is aware of existing in the immanence, then this already goes beyond immanence, although today we speak more of transcendence.

Where the balance broke down, the question arose radically whether the bourgeois spirit was right.

Bibliography

F. H. R. von Frank: *Geschichte und Kritik der Theologie,* insbesondere der systematischen, seit Schleiermacher, 1906 von Gritzmacher.[20]

Ferdinand Kattenbusch: *Theologie von Schleiermacher bis Ritschl,* 5th ed., 1926.[21]

Troeltsch: "Zur theologischen und religiösen Lage der Gegenwart,"[22] 1902; *Gesammelte Schriften Bd.* 2, 1–21; 1st ed., similar title as Tillich's *Religious Situation.*

### *§ 2 Church and theology at the turn of the century in the context of general intellectual history*

The state regards [the church] as an organized institution, as the ecclesiastical bureaucracy (Bismarck).[23] The purpose of education [is] to guarantee 144

tragedy which society bring into the life of the individual. . . . Ibsen is enclined to the pessimistic view, society is right because society has the power" (*DBWE* 10:422 [Bonhoeffer's original, unaltered English—MBL]).

[19.] *Der Rosenkavalier,* comedy by Hugo von Hofmannsthal, opera by Richard Strauss, first performed in Dresden in 1911.

[20.] Correctly cited: Franz Hermann Reinhold von Frank, *Geschichte und Kritik der neueren Theologie, insbesondere der systematischen, seit Schleiermacher: Aus dem Nachlass des Verfassers.* [No 1906 edition has been found.]

[21.] [The reference is to *Die deutsche evangelische Theologie seit Schleiermacher: Ihre Leistungen und ihre Schäden,* the 5th ed. of *Von Schleiermacher zu Ritschl* (1892).]

[22.] [Correct title: "Die theologische und religiöse Lage der Gegenwart," in Troeltsch's *Gesammelte Schriften.*]

[23.] This refers to Bismarck's purely superficial view of the church as one of the institutions subordinate to the state.

the power of the state. Religious education is to ensure that religion must be preserved for the people, even against their will. The pastor's position with regard to party politics [is] prescribed. Whoever serves at the altar also serves the throne. Reproaches from social dem[ocracy] do not get a hearing. The case of the Catholic Church is entirely different. The Protestant Church Council [Oberkirchenrat] was tossed helplessly this way and that with regard to social issues.[24] Its hands were tied. The church belonged to the state and its economic system. This influenced the ethics of the day. The resulting tension [was] not recognized for a long time. [It was considered primarily a matter of] defense against being pestered from below. It was self-evident that the dominant system was described as orthodox.[25]

But within the offic[ial] church, there [was] already talk of breaking the tie with the state. Stoecker: abolition of the high episcopate of the princes.[26] —The court preachers[27] were seen as the moral underpinnings of society. The church's task was to educate the people as Christians whose loy-
145 alty to the state could be presumed. Preaching was centered on personal religion and morality. Christianity was understood as religion, beginning with human beings. All religion is essentially pedagogy. Religion was one respectable phenomenon among many. As one outgrows school, so one also outgrows the church.

---

[24.] According to the principle of the church's institutional autonomy in the revised Prussian constitution of 1850, the Protestant Council [Oberkirchenrat] was the highest organ of church governance in the Protestant regional church. In fact, it answered directly to the Prussian king. This dependent position was especially evident in the conduct of the Oberkirchenrat with regard to social issues: in 1890, in support of the reform policies of Wilhelm II, it urged its pastors, by decree, to become involved in social issues but had to revise this five years later when the king departed from his course of social reform (Pollmann, *Landesherrliches Regiment*, 301–2).

[25.] "Orthodox" = according to correct doctrine.

[26.] The institution of the high episcopate [Summepiskopat], which assigned the highest power in the church to the princes, was created during the Reformation as an "emergency measure," and established in the law of the state in the age of absolutism (Christian Thomasius); it was being increasingly criticized in the nineteenth century. [Thomasius was an influential German jurist and philosopher of the Enlightenment, renowned for his emphasis on natural rationalism, practical reforms, and critique of establishment theologians.—MBL] See Adolf Stoecker's objection to the state church in his *Wach' auf evangelisches Volk! Aufsätze über Kirche und Kirchenpolitik*, 11–12, 24–25, 173, 185, 278, 349, and elsewhere.

[27.] The court preachers (*Hofprediger*), the Protestant counterpart to the confessor priests at the courts of the Catholic princes, were the personal pastors and house clergy of the princes and the court churches. Depending on their personal relationships with the princes, they had great influence on church and politics; some also held responsible positions in the church bureaucracy.

Trad[itional] and dogmatic pigheadedness bound the church to the state.

Luther could never forget the real origin of the church, so he could dare to allow it to be tied [to the state]. The systematic concept Luther proposed had already broken up by the time he died. Its end [was] sealed by the beginning of the eighteenth century.[28] Schleiermacher became the builder of the temple of humanism [Humanität].[29] Individualism destroyed the Protestantism of the Reformation. In the world after Copernicus, under the influence of the English deists[30] the word *religio*[31] takes the place of "faith." It meant the final and finest possibility for human beings. Human beings were discovered to be related to God. The Reformation was seen as the discovery of humans as such beings.

Paul de Lagarde, "das Verhältnis des deutschen Staates zu Theologie, Kirche und Religion,"[32] sees the decisive antithesis between religion and Reformation faith. This assertion [is] more credible than that of [the] official theologians of the time, who were of the opinion that they were maintaining the Reformation heritage.

So the church lives first of all by the idea of "religion." It is strongly drawn 146
to immanence, to the divine background of intellectual life.

Besides this individualistic way, a third way. The object of study must be shown through evidence; metaphysics does not arise with the rise of the natural sciences.[33] That the system of categories is identical with reality

[28.] This refers to the end of Lutheran-style Reformation Protestantism; for Bonhoeffer this becomes clear in the "decay of the congregational concept" that followed Luther. Cf. also his lecture "The Nature of the Church" (2/9).

[29.] [In several places the student notes read *Humanität* (humanity), but Dudzus's notes usually render this as *Humanismus* (humanism), which would make more sense. —VB]

[30.] Deism was a philosophical religious school of thought, closely related to the Enlightenment, which arose in England around 1650. It aimed at a rational reconstruction of Christian revealed faith as a rational and universally natural religion. [Among its more prominent exponents were Lord Herbert of Cherbury (*De veritate*, 1624), John Locke (*Reasonableness of Christianity*, 1695), and Matthew Tindal (*Christianity as Old as Creation*, 1730).—MBL] Through deism, among other factors, traditional theology was stimulated by the perspective of the history-of-religions school, in which the concept of religion received special significance. On this point, cf. Reventlow, *Authority of the Bible*.

[31.] The original Latin meaning of *religio* is "binding" or "obligation." On the history of the word *religio*, see Feil, *On the Concept of Religion*.

[32.] Lagarde, "Über das Verhältnis des deutschen Staates zu Theologie, Kirche und Religion." [Long before the rise of National Socialism, Lagarde was a virulent anti-Semite and an early proponent of a nationalist theology.—VB]

[33.] Otto Dudzus (*GS* 5:186): "Along with this radical individualization came theology's capitulation to the empirical-monistic concept of science. Arising from natural

is presupposed: unscientific science. (Not until the theory of relativity and quantum theory was this overturned.) No science could except itself from it: the study of history, philosophy, psychology, and sociology. Around the turn of the twentieth century, the error of this concept began to be noticed (Rickert, Dilthey).[34]

In theology's discussion of specific results of the natural sciences [. . .],[35] but the usual apologetics are simply insane (Overbeck!).[36] Religion as historical and piety as psychological fact are accessible to precise research. (*Eusebeia*[37] only in the [NT] pastoral letters,[38] in Luther in a good and a
147 bad sense,[39] a favorite idea of pietists, in theology since Schleiermacher.)

Theology must proceed by analysis and synthesis: the devout consciousness is taken into the system of categories.

Three roots of the concept "religion," three kinds of interest: (1) pedagogical interest; (2) interest in [religion as] a product of the intellect; (3) [interest] as in history-of-religion and psychology of religion. These three interests are often confused but [should be] kept separate.

### *§ 3 The concept of religion as a mediating concept*

Schleiermacher established the proper territory [Eigenrecht] of religion by localizing religion in the religious province[40] of the s[oul]. The object

---

science, this concept had subjugated the study of history, philosophy, psychology, sociology, and finally theology as well."

[34.] Heinrich Rickert expressly objected to the universal method of natural science, according to which the "common elements of things are identical to the essential elements of concepts" [trans. by VB]. Research in the humanities must presuppose morally justified purposes in order, when describing and explaining its objects, to distinguish between essential and nonessential characteristics (Rickert, *Limits of Concept Formation in Natural Science,* iii [see esp. 36–45—MBL]). Cf. his *Science and History* and his *Die Probleme der Geschichtsphilosophie.* Wilhelm Dilthey had criticized historiography's orientation toward the method of the natural sciences and developed a specific method for the humanities, oriented toward understanding, a so-called hermeneutics. See Dilthey, *Introduction to the Human Sciences* and his *Formation of the Historical World in the Human Sciences.*

[35.] Illegible.

[36.] Franz Overbeck, *How Christian Is Our Present-Day Theology?* esp. pt. 2, chap. 2: "Contemporary Apologetic Theology," 47–73. Cf. also his *Christentum und Kultur,* esp. 241–48.

[37.] "Piety."

[38.] Bonhoeffer is pointing out that this concept only appears in the Deutero-Pauline letters, and even there it is not of central importance.

[39.] Cf. Luther's interpretation of Psalms 5 and 22 in his lecture "Operationes in Psalmos," 1519–21 (*WA* 5:125–199 and 598–673).

[40.] Cf. Schleiermacher, *On Religion,* 17: "It [religion] springs necessarily and by itself from the interior of every better soul, it has its own province in the mind in which it

of theology [is] religious self-consciousness. Question of truth not raised; that Christianity and scholarship [Wissenschaft][41] must go together was taken for granted. Religion [is considered] the most subjective and comprehensive consciousness of human beings.—Ludwig Feuerbach, on the same basis, came to the opposite conclusion. The primal drive of the ego is the drive to live, [the] primal inhibition is death; all religion [originates] from the experience of death as inhibition, from the fear of death. In praying to God, the human being prays to the idealized form of his drive toward life. That is why there has always been only anthropology in Christianity.[42] Feuerbach thinks highly of humankind because of this 148
elevated capacity that human beings have. Hume had already attributed religion to human emotions.[43] Feuerbach was Schleiermacher's most consistent pupil, but he regarded as an illusion what for Schleiermacher was an unproved assumption.[44]

Friedrich Engels: Feuerbach and the end of classical German philosophy. Religion as dependence is a soc[ietal] expression of capitalist society, which socialism eliminates.[45] But because religion has also been a device

---

reigns sovereign, and it is worthy of moving the noblest and the most excellent by means of its innermost power and by having its innermost essence known by them."

[41.] [The German term *Wissenschaft* (or *wissenschaftlich*), used frequently in these lectures, can have variant meanings depending on context. It has a primary meaning of "science" ("scientific") or "scholarship" ("scholarly") but can also refer to an "academic knowledge" ("academic").—MBL]

[42.] On what follows, cf. Feuerbach, *Theogonie nach den Quellen des klassischen, hebräischen und christlichen Altertums*. In his last written critique of religion, Feuerbach no longer explains the origin of religion as in *The Essence of Christianity*, namely, as a psychological act of compensation, but rather the object of religious ideas has now been replaced by the power of humanity as a whole.

[43.] David Hume rejects traditional metaphysics as the philosophical grounds for religion and provides a psychological and genetic explanation for religion in "The Natural History of Religion" (in his *Principal Writings on Religion*, 306–63). From the "ordinary affections of human life" (ibid., 140), i.e., from human uncertainty about external natural events and the vicissitudes of human life, the idea of unseen powers and divinities arises as a hypostasis of sensory experiences.

[44.] For Feuerbach's critique of Schleiermacher, see his "Zur Beurteilung der Schrift 'Das Wesen des Christentums,'" 211: "My reproach to Schleiermacher is not, like that of Hegel, that he makes religion a matter of feeling, but only that he was too inhibited theologically and unable to draw the necessary conclusions of his position . . . that *objectively* God's very self is nothing other than the *essence of feeling*, if subjectively feeling is what religion mainly is. In this regard I have so little against Schleiermacher that he becomes instead an important support to me, actually the affirmation of my conclusions based on the nature of feeling" [trans. by Isabel Best].

[45.] Engels, *Ludwig Feuerbach*, 305. [See also Marx and Engels, *On Religion*, 213–68, esp. 266.]

of capitalism, socialism opposes it not only as a symptom but also as a power. Its single theological idea has thus taken on worldwide historical dimensions.

Friedrich Nietzsche took up Feuerbach's doctrine of the whole human being. [A human being is] not a transcendent being that only appears to exist but is *ens realissimum*,[46] with regard not only to thoughts but also to drives.[47]

So, Feuerbach's two questions to religion: (1) the truth of its proposi-
149 tions (illusion); (2) whether it corresponds to real life. These remain essentially unanswered by theology, which is one reason why socialism [arose]. He was right to spurn what only appear to be answers. The cause of this failure runs deep; it involves the possibility and truth of all theology. Hegel took up this issue with the most radical critique, but for him truth was the relation of spirit to itself.[48] Monistic thinking,[49] understood by Feuerbach and Kierkegaard subjectivistically, thus the same idealistic approach as in Schleiermacher.

Official theology was much too outwardly oriented, linked with the problem of religion. This should have been set aside, but the debate among worldviews was so important. Religion was kept distinct from all intellectual areas yet still regarded as together [with them].

Julius Kaftan: *Wesen der Religion*; *The Truth of the Christian Religion*. Protested by Frank, who begins with the Christian system of belief and is not interested in religion.[50] Christ cannot be made the object of natural knowledge. Only by starting from the absoluteness of Christianity can the nature of religion [be] determined. But [Frank] did not go that far. Kaftan boasted

[46.] "The most real [entity] that exists"; in scholastic theology this was reserved exclusively for God. In the ontological proof of God's existence, it was the central argument.

[47.] Nietzsche, *Human, All Too Human*, 85: "An actual human being is something altogether *necessary* (even in those so-called contradictions), but we do not always recognize this necessity."

[48.] "Truth is not only *in itself* completely identical with certainty, but it also has the shape of self-certainty, or it is in its existence in the form of self-knowledge" (Hegel, *Phenomenology of Spirit*, 485).

[49.] The concept of monism was coined by Christian Wolff, in his *Psychologia rationalis*, 24–25 (§§ 32–39). In a monistic view, all things are of one substance or can all be derived from the one unitary being. In a methodological sense, a scientific procedure that uses only one method (as opposed to several) in analyzing different objects can also be called monism.

[50.] See Frank, *System der christlichen Gewißheit*, 1:23–27. Here Frank develops the concept of theology already presented in § 1 as "scholarly recognition and presentation of Christian certainty" as firmly "distinguished from the philosophy of religion."

that such narrow definitions were becoming ever rarer.[51] Dogmatics must be supported by the history-of-religions method,[52] theology as academic knowledge must seek points of connection [Anknüpfungspunkt][53] in the realm of reality.[54] Religion should be integrated into intellect[ual] life 150
in its entirety; it is a mediating concept between church and reality. This connection must be made; otherwise the position of theology is untenable. Kaftan rejects (1) the way of psychology of religion (Schleiermacher), for lack of a criterion for truth and falsehood; (2) the way of a purely philosophical understanding of religion (Hegel, Biedermann);[55] what is proved is that which has been presupposed; (3) the way of deciding on the nature of religion based on Christianity alone, because it would easily lose its point of connection to reality, and violence would be done to the other religions. Christian religion should be linked with reality in a way that preserves, on the one hand, its superiority and, on the other, its being in the context of other intellectual areas: [this is] the way of the history-of-religions method. In every religion there is an immanent and a transcendent concern; Christianity unites the two in a particular way; [as] religion of redemption and as service to immanent orders.

But Troeltsch already raises a critique against the possibility of determining Christianity's absoluteness through the history-of-religions approach.[56] Kaftan assumes that religion is an integrating factor in human life, but then he wants to prove it. He presupposes a system of reason into which he places religion.

Could Kaftan make the concept of religion a point of connection to reality and at the same time make it a criterion for Christian religion? To do both is impossible, because the immanent would be confused with the transcendent.

---

[51.] On what follows, cf. Julius Kaftan, *Dogmatik*, chap. 1, § 2, "Die christliche Religion," 7–23, esp. 8–15.

[52.] [A reference to the "history-of-religions school," a scholarly movement that promoted the scientific study of religion, using a comparative historical method. It arose primarily in nineteenth-century German biblical studies and examined especially the way cultural factors conditioned texts and ideas.—MBL]

[53.] [In the theological debates of the time, the term *Anknüpfungspunkt* was used to mean that theology should search for certain nontheological, prereligious elements to which it could link its message. The editors thank Christiane Tietz for this insight.—VB]

[54.] Paraphrase from Kaftan, *Dogmatik*, 11.

[55.] Cf. Hegel, *System of Ethical Life* (1802–3) and *First Philosophy of Spirit* (pt. 3 of his *System of Speculative Philosophy*, 1803–4), 242–44, §§ 572–73 [see H. S. Harris's exposition in the Hegel volume, 81–85 and 180–81—MBL]; Alois Emanuel Biedermann, *Christliche Dogmatik: 1, Principieller Theil.* Chap. 1 "Das Wesen der Religion" §§ 8–82, 22–109.

[56.] Cf. Troeltsch, *Absoluteness of Christianity and the History of Religions*, 63–83.

*Troeltsch*

Represents well the theology of the period. Born 1865, [professor of philosophy] in Berlin 1915, died [1923]. Almost unlimited influence. Student
151 of Albrecht Ritschl, then [of] Eucken, James, Bergson. Consciously takes his place in critical philosophy: Windelband, Rickert.

*Theory of Religion*[57]

Between two fronts: monism, [including]: (1) belief in natural law as the ultimate authority, (2) belief in progress, evolutionism, (3) aesthetic-literary monism, pessimistic pantheism.[58] The other front: unscientific [unwissenschaftliche] theology: (1) the dogmatic method (Hengstenberg); ("Historical and Dogmatic Method in Theology," "Vernunft und Offenbarung bei Joh. Gerhard").[59] Unscientific because its starting point is removed from history and reason, its aut[hority] comes from outside;[60] (2) the historicist history-of-religion. Religion only the expression of economic conditions, the question of truth excluded from consideration. Dogmatic theology neglects the historical question, and the history-of-religions method [Religionsgeschichte] [neglects] the question of truth. So no point of connection to either reality or Christianity. Way to a synthesis sought by Kant and Schleiermacher. Psychological and historical proofs are insufficient for religion. Eucken compares intellectual life with the life of the soul.[61] Troeltsch's
152 first demand: theology must be supported by philosophy of religion; general theory of religious knowledge, critical analysis of religious consciousness. He seeks to develop Schleiermacher's program.[62]

---

[57.] Bonhoeffer's lecture on Ernst Troeltsch's theory of religion assembles a collage of central passages and quotes from important essays by Troeltsch published in vol. 2 of his collected works. Where specific connections to Troeltsch's writings could be reconstructed, they are given in the editorial notes that follow.

[58.] For this threefold characterization of monism, see Troeltsch, "Aus der religiösen Bewegung der Gegenwart," 34–37. The term "pessimistic pantheism" refers to Drews, *Christ Myth*, 33.

[59.] Troeltsch, "Historical and Dogmatic Method in Theology" and *Vernunft und Offenbarung bei Johann Gerhard und Melanchthon*.

[60.] Troeltsch, "Historical and Dogmatic Method in Theology," 20: [The dogmatic method] "starts from a firm point of origin completely beyond the relativity of historical scholarship. . . . Its essence is that it possesses an authority that, by definition, is separate from the total context of history, not analogous to other events, and therefore not subject to historical criticism and the uncertainty attaching to its results."

[61.] On the comparison of "intellectual life" and the "life of the soul" in Rudolf Eucken, see Troeltsch, "Aus der religiösen Bewegung der Gegenwart," 30–31.

[62.] For the following academically systematic grounding of theology in the philosophy of religion and philosophy of history, see Troeltsch, "Half a Century of Theology," esp. 76–81.

Religion needs proof, from the epistemological perspective, that it is a necessary element in the nexus of reason. A religious a priori[63] must be found; then religion's validity is proved. The modern spirit of refusing any assumptions must be satisfied. Religion is given its place in the modern spirit. The religion that fits in most simply is the highest. Perspective of the philosophy of history on the treatment of the religions, prospect of a future religion where the modern spirit and theology are united, a humanist Christianity free of dogmatism, religion of fulfillment of the personality.[64]

Troeltsch [has been] condemned by other students of Ritschl because of his proximity to philosophy.[65] The grounding of religion must be free from metaphysics, but the goal [is] the connection of theology and philosophy. For Ritschl, religion [is] there where human beings fear they can no longer assert their personalities over against nature.[66] This is not far from Kaftan's psychological basis, nor from Troeltsch. Here, too, religion [is] to be understood from the world. Troeltsch no longer allows any separation 153
of theology and philosophy. Theology [is a] special branch of the study of religion, which is a special branch of philosophy.[67]

*The Philosophy of the Neo-Kantians*

Rudolf Eucken; Hermann Cohen and Paul Natorp (Marburg).

Philosophy asks, unencumbered: How does religion fit into the finished philosophical system? Here we see much more clearly than from the point of view of theology.

Eucken (d. 1926 in Jena), 1905, *The Truth of Religion*.[68] His ideas were already outdated. But [he had] great influence in his time. His interest: not to allow himself to be carried away by positivism, but rather to have

---

[63.] See Troeltsch, "On the Question of the Religious a priori."

[64.] Cf. Troeltsch, "Aus der religiösen Bewegung der Gegenwart," 32.

[65.] On the dispute of Ritschl's students with Ernst Troeltsch, see esp. Kaftan, *Truth of the Christian Religion*; Herrmann's review of Troeltsch's *Die Absolutheit des Christentums und die Religionsgeschichte* and of his *Die Bedeutung der Geschichtlichkeit Jesu für den Glauben*, both in *Theologische Literaturzeitung*.

[66.] Cf. Ritschl, *A Critical History of the Christian Doctrine of Justification and Reconciliation*, 199: "In every religion, what is sought, with the help of the superhuman spiritual power reverenced by man, is a solution to the contradiction in which man finds himself, as both a part of the world of nature and as a spiritual personality claiming to dominate nature. . . . In this juncture, religion springs up as faith in superhuman spiritual powers, by whose help the power man possesses of himself is in some way supplemented, and elevated into a unity of its own kind which is a match for the pressure of the natural world."

[67.] For a more precise definition of the relations among theology, the study of religion, and (religious) philosophy, see Troeltsch, "Religion and the Science of Religion," esp. 89–94.

[68.] On the following, see Eucken, *Truth of Religion*, 72–186.

an idealistic philosophy of life [Lebensphilosophie] with the philosophy of religion as foundation. Clear development: he is very sensitive to the contrast between subject and object, between the principle of nature and that of spirit.[69] The life of the soul belongs to the first,[70] so in human beings soul stands in opposition to spirit. As opposed [to] Klages,[71] [the issue here is] the dominance of the spirit. Individual spirit cannot resolve the contradiction. Is the mind's pride perhaps an illusion? Intuition must empower a human being to become aware of a common life of the spirit.[72] Only where the subjective individual spirit finds its place in a common life of spirit can it stand over against its own nature. The consciousness of the coherence of cultural activities [Kulturarbeit] of the spirit is the first step of int[ellectual] recognition. But then, facing new resistance from powers
154 of nature, to assert nevertheless the priority of the life of the spirit[73] is the universal religion.[74] Cultural[75] activity [is] the function of God, at first [as] an impersonal concept of God.

---

[69.] [Eucken was one of the most influential figures in promoting spiritual philosophy in the early twentieth century and was widely read both in Germany and in the English-speaking world. Rejecting speculative philosophy in favor of a more holistic view, he nonetheless appealed to a sharp idealist contrast between nature and spirit, in which the natural, necessary in itself but meaningless and impersonal, has significance only in becoming spiritual in relation to a universal Spirit. Religion is pervasive in exhibiting spirit within but beyond nature, and Christianity is the highest manifestation of absolute spiritual religion. See Macquarrie, *Twentieth-Century Religious Thought*, 58–63.—MBL]

[70.] [I.e., the principle of nature.—VB]

[71.] See Klages, *Der Geist als Widersacher der Seele.*

[72.] On the synthesizing function of religion for the life of the spirit, which is splintered within itself and consequently turns to "characteristic religion," see Eucken, *Truth of Religion*, 284–96 and 364–409.

[73.] On the grounds provided by religion for the independence of the life of the spirit, see Eucken, *Hauptprobleme der Religionsphilosophie der Gegenwart*, 1–33.

[74.] Otto Dudzus's reconstruction (*GS* 5:190–91): "Rudolf Eucken, who died in 1926 in Jena, was, when he published *The Truth of Religion* in 1901, already basically outdated in his thinking. But in his time he was very influential. His accomplishment was not to be carried away by the dominant positivism, but to offer an opposing idealistic philosophy of life on the basis of a philosophy of religion. His proposal has the advantage of a clear structure. He is very sensitive to the contrast between subject and object, between the principle of nature and that of spirit. To the first belongs the whole broad realm of psychological life. Thus in human beings themselves the soul stands in opposition to the spirit. However, individual spirit cannot resolve the contradiction. Is the pride of the intellect, its claim to superiority, perhaps an illusion? By the power of intuition, the individual person must become aware of a common life of the spirit. Only when the subjective individual spirit finds its place in the common life of the spirit can it stand over against its own nature. Thus the awareness of the coherence of the cultural activities of the spirit is the first level of intellectual recognition (or 'recognition of God'?)."

[75.] [There is no period in *DBW* between "religion" and "cultural," but the syntax would seem to require it.—MBL]

From there on, new depths of reality. The life of the spirit is in turmoil within itself, the different disciplines in conflict with one another. That Eucken sees this clearly makes him stand out within idealistic philosophy. Religion must ultimately be, in its deepest roots, more than the basis for culture. Change from universal to characteristic religion. Human beings touch God personally because the personal God who is above culture touches them. What is meant here is Christianity. Its center [is] the free personality.

[If] religion [is] seen as the consummation [Vollendung] of the life of the spirit, [then] theistic religion alone [is] capable of completing the picture of the universe; otherwise a duality [remains]. Thus religion claims leadership of the whole of intellectual life. But [there is] such a close connection with cultural activities that these are the only path to religion. Religion is ultimately the means of asserting oneself over against nature. But Eucken sees that this still does not say anything about the truth of religion. It is the revelation of the life of the spirit, [. . .][76] proves the truth of religion by the truth of culture. The concept of culture [is] both starting point
and goal. Through this reversal, Eucken's intention to establish the tran- 155
scendence of religion therefore fails.

Natorp shows what becomes of theology when it allows itself to be taken over by Kantian thinking.

"Religion within the limits of humanity," impression made on their students by Cohen and Natorp [was] enormous![77] Cohen: Religion [is] identical with ethics; *Die jüdischen Schriften*, 1925: especially fine.

Natorp: instead of Kant's "pure reason," humanity.[78] (Elimination of the transcendental thing-in-itself.) Concept of the *humanum* [is] the ultimate form of unity for all content. The thing-in-itself[79] [has] become the immanent infinite task,[80] no longer transcendental boundary-concept

[76.] Illegible. Dudzus (*GS* 5:191) adds: "But he does not pursue the idea of revelation any further."

[77.] The student transcription has "enormous on."

[78.] Paul Natorp adopted the title of Immanuel Kant's text *Religion within the Limits of Reason Alone* in modified form. In the paragraph that follows, Bonhoeffer gives a very abbreviated summary, with interpretive comments, of Natorp's *Die Religion innerhalb der Grenzen der Humanität*, chap. 3: "Religion," esp. 35–39.

[79.] On Immanuel Kant's "thing-in-itself" [*Ding an sich*], cf. Kant, *Critique of Pure Reason* (in *Cambridge Edition of the Works of Immanuel Kant*), 161–62, 170–71, 371–77, 427–30, and 548–50.

[80.] According to Paul Natorp, the finite subject's approach to the infinite object in science, morality, and art is only attainable through collective humankind (Natorp, *Die Religion innerhalb der Grenzen der Humanität*, 46–52). Cf. also Hermann Cohen's interpretation of the "thing-in-itself" as a task (Cohen, *Kants Theorie der Erfahrung*, 519–23).

[Grenzkonzept],[81] but rather the infinite task of the epistemic, moral, and esthetic process. Religion cannot go beyond this humanity. What can exist besides pure knowing, willing, and feeling, and the synthesizing act of consciousness? The subject produces its object; therefore the object cannot go beyond these categories. The question is, therefore, how religion arises within consciousness. But it is distinct from all other products of consciousness, namely, because of its object; its object is intended to go beyond human limits. But a transcendental object is self-contradictory. Thinking and willing always remain within human limits, but religion seeks to go beyond them, so it [is] located in indeterminate feeling; it is the original unity of subjectivity, here containing the infinity of the task, even though still unformed. Thus the claim to transcendence [is] only the self's con-
156 fused claim to have produced the world itself. Religion attends the overall work of culture and humanity as the awareness of the infinity of the task. Religion's objects cannot be any other than the objects of culture. Religion, the subject, takes the place of God. The line extending from Schleiermacher is especially plain here: what he calls the "feeling for the infinite" is for Natorp "infinite feeling."[82]

Theology as an academic discipline [is here] thrown out altogether; Schleiermacher must ultimately take the credit for this, notwithstanding the fact that it was he who wanted to make theology capable of academic study.

G. Simmel, *Die Religion*: religious phenomena, anthropological view [is one] among others; none has a claim to absolute validity.[83] The dogmatic works of R. Seeberg,[84] Stange,[85] and Biedermann[86] begin with such a

[81.] [This means a concept that names intellectual boundaries; i.e., reason cannot grasp the thing-in-itself. The editors thank Christiane Tietz for this explanation.—VB]

[82.] Natorp, *Die Religion innerhalb der Grenzen der Humanität*, 38: "Not simply feeling in itself, but rather *feeling for the infinite* is supposed to be religion according to Schleiermacher. Though feeling has no object in the true sense, infinity could not be the object for a finite consciousness, both understood in the true sense. Actually it is much more the *infinity of feeling* that one seeks to express in saying that the infinite is the object of a feeling" [trans. by Isabel Best].

[83.] See Georg Simmel, *Die Religion*, 2nd ed., 1912, 53.

[84.] Seeberg, *Christliche Dogmatik*. For his basis in the philosophy of religion, cf. esp. vol. 1, bk. 1: "Religionsphilosophische und erkenntnistheoretische Grundlegung der christlichen Dogmatik (Apologetik und Methodologie)" (Foundations of Christian dogmatics in philosopy of religion and epistemology [apologetics and methodology]), 1–296 (§§ 1–13).

[85.] See Stange, *Dogmatik*, vol. 1, *Einleitung in die Dogmatik* (no second volume published).

[86.] See Biedermann, *Christliche Dogmatik: 1, principieller Theil*, §§ 8–147, 22–158.

philosophy of religion; this is especially clear in the case of K. Stange, who closely follows Kant.[87] Religion alone has an answer to the question of whether my experience can grasp reality in its entirety, thus continuation and completion of all experience. This is the transcendental necessity of religion.[88] *Christentum und moderne Weltanschauung*, 1913; *Religion als Erfahrung*, 1907, 2nd ed., 1919. 157

Reinhold Seeberg does not go significantly further than this; [he adds] only voluntarism.[89]

William James also belongs to this group: *Will to Believe, The Varieties of Religious Experience* (Wobbermin).[90]

Pragmatism thinks through every problem from the viewpoint of a living human being; therefore the problems of German idealism are not problems! Everything depends on what is "useful." Life [is] the criterion for truth; only that which affects it (occurs) is true. Religion [is] in the first place a psychological phenomenon; the claim to have a grasp of higher

---

[87.] See Stange, *Dogmatik*, vol. 1, esp. chap. 1, "Die Theologie als Wissenschaft," 1–45. The assumptions from philosophy of religion that enter into the constitution of the concept of theology as a "positive, critical science" of Christianity concern in particular the concepts of religion and of experience.

[88.] Stange does not follow Kant's explanation of religion in the narrower sense, according to which the idea of God is established as a postulate of practical reason; he merely takes up Kant's intention to define religion as an essential factor in the context of the life of the human spirit, though making use of Kant's concept of experience. See Stange, *Christentum und moderne Weltanschauung*, 31–41, and *Die Religion als Erfahrung*, 23–36. For his concept of experience, broader than Kant's, as the basis for proving the transcendental necessity of religion, see Stange, *Christentum und moderne Weltanschauung*, 66–89, and *Die Religion als Erfahrung*, 37–48.

[89.] A theory is designated as voluntarism if it gives primacy to the will over intellect or reason. Either all that has being, in a metaphysical sense, is derived from a creating Will, or the will is considered, under epistemology or anthropology, to be the primary principle as opposed to the other intellectual and psychological capacities. Both forms of voluntarism are found in Reinhold Seeberg's thought; see his *Ewiges Leben?* esp. 18–24, and *Christliche Dogmatik*, 1:195–222; for his exposition of the doctrines of the Trinity and divine attributes as aspects of the divine will, *Christliche Dogmatik*, 1:366–95 and 395–434.

[90.] William James, *Varieties of Religious Experience*. Translated into German by Georg Wobbermin in 1914. Wobbermin, however, freely reformulated the original, especially the last chapters, abridged many passages, and omitted James's afterword, stating that the latter "advocates a metaphysical position (that of a religious-metaphysical pluralism) which I must, from my own position, completely reject, and which furthermore has no direct connection to the rest of the book" (xiii) [trans. by Isabel Best]. In Bonhoeffer's first report on his studies [at Union Theological Seminary in 1930–31—VB] to the Church Federation Office, he said that he had read almost the complete works of William James (*DBWE* 10:310). Cf. Bonhoeffer's discussion of James, *DBWE* 10:310–12, and his short report on James, "The Varieties of Religious Experience," *DBWE* 10:438–40.

158 realities.[91] Feeling of the presence of the supersensible inspires human beings in every sphere, and to this extent it is true. Here, too, there is similarity to Schleiermacher. Religion [takes its] place among the necessities of life; whether transcendental or pragmatic, it remains anthropology (Feuerbach!).

[This] contradicts the entire positions of Cremer,[92] M. Kähler,[93] Schlatter (*Die philosophische Arbeit seit Cartesius*, 1906).

Open contradiction: Reischle and W. Herrmann.[94]

Reischle: the concept of religion may be derived only from religion that is personally acknowledged, from Christianity.[95] "Whoever knows this religion, knows them all" (Harnack),[96] not: "Whoever knows one religion, knows none" (Max Müller).[97]

---

[91.] Charles Sanders Peirce is considered the founder of pragmatism, the most influential philosophical trend in early twentieth-century America. His demand that the meaning of concepts be empirically provable was supposed to make possible successful philosophical communication, free of basic metaphysical presuppositions. Peirce's fundamental idea of developing concepts, the relevance of which could be tested, was interpreted by William James in the sense of an empirically relative concept of truth: only those concepts and facts whose usefulness, that is, their function in the practical life of the subject, could be proved, could claim to be true or valid. This applies in the same way to all religious concepts.

[92.] See Cremer, "Dogmatische Prinzipienlehre," and *Reply to Harnack*.

[93.] See Kähler, *Die Wissenschaft der christlichen Lehre*, vol. 3.

[94.] [See below, Bonhoeffer's sharp contrast of Herrmann's approach compared to Reischle. The "contradiction" here refers to Herrmann's counter-insistence on revelation and immediacy, which may have influenced Barth. See ed. note 99.—MBL]

[95.] See Reischle, *Die Frage nach dem Wesen der Religion*, esp. chap. 3, 37–60, "Induktiv gewonnener Allgemeinbegriff oder Normbegriff?" (Inductively achieved general concept or normative concept?), and chap. 4, 60–76, "Die Gewinnung und Bearbeitung des Normbegriffs der Religion" (Recovery and treatment of the normative concept of religion). According to Reischle, deducing a "normative concept" of religion from whatever one acknowledges personally as the highest religion is only making the specific characteristic of humanistic understanding concrete as a presupposition for any analysis in the academic study of religion (*Religionswissenschaft*), which, in contrast to knowledge in the natural sciences, can only understand its object by virtue of subjective empathy, i.e., in accordance with its own subjectivity.

[96.] Harnack, "Die Aufgabe der theologischen Fakultäten und die allgemeine Religionsgeschichte," 168: "Anyone who does not know this religion [i.e., Christianity], knows no religion, and anyone who knows [Christianity] including its history, knows all [religions]" [trans. by Isabel Best].

[97.] In the context of his thesis of comparative language studies as a foundation for comparative religious studies, Max Müller writes: "When the students of Comparative Philology boldly adapted Goethe's paradox, '*He who knows one language, knows none*,' people were startled at first; but they soon began to feel the truth which was hidden beneath the paradox. . . . The same applies to religion. *He who knows one, knows none*" (*Introduction to the Science of Religion*, 15–16). This part of the lecture notes is followed by a half-empty

No tracing religion back to psychology and cultural studies any more than to the unity of consciousness (Schleiermacher). The object of religion [is] not affected here [i.e., in these propositions]. The feeling of dependence [is] not religion itself, [but] only one side of it. The Neo-Kantians and Troeltsch are rejected because they make religion too subjective. 159

How different are the matters that are important to Herrmann? God, reality, revelation, and the communication between the Christian and God are the central questions.[98] Apologetics are, for him, [the] greatest danger. By nature, faith has no defenses, [so] philosophy of religion should not [be] its weapon. "A God who has been proved is of the world, and a god of the world [is] an idol."[99] Religion does not belong among psychological facts.[100] But he does provide a concept of religion[101] as a mediating concept. Religion [is] the capacity to see "the actions of God in events."[102] This concerns reality and ways of viewing it; [this] is experience. This is the central statement of his theology. Religion can be recognized only by the person who experiences it. But in making the way to religion plausible through moral demands—here Kant comes through in Herrmann: the creating human being is self-contradictory, [thus] lacks true life in the midst of real life.[103] The solution lies only in the religious experience of reality. 160

---

page, before the beginning of the next paragraph. Possibly something additional was to be inserted here. Yet the text that follows shows no sign of a gap.

[98.] See Herrmann, *Communion of the Christian with God* and *Der Begriff der Offenbarung*.

[99.] See Herrmann, "Gottes Offenbarung an uns," 79. This quote also appears in Karl Barth's essay "The Principles of Dogmatics according to Wilhelm Herrmann," in Barth, *Theology and Church*, 238–71: "A proved God is world, and a God of the world is an idol" (243); its style of argument is followed by Bonhoeffer.

[100.] Barth points out that Herrmann in 1908 "flatly rejected the possibility of a psychology of religion 'because religion does not belong to psychic facts'" (*Theology and Church*, 244n3).

[101.] The following observations on Herrmann's concept of religion are mostly based on his *Systematic Theology*, especially pt. 1, "Religion," chap. 2: "The Intellectual Apprehension of Religion" (20–29), and chap. 3: "The Foundation of the Science of Religion in the Historical Fact of Religion" (30–31), esp. section 11: "The Way to Religion" (33–34).

[102.] See Hermann, *Systematic Theology*, 20: "This general idea of religion, which is obvious to every religiously minded man without any profound investigation, runs as follows: To every religiously minded man religion means seeing the working of a God in the events of life."

[103.] Ibid., 33–34: "We are continually possessed by the idea that we enjoy an independent life. At the same time the fact forces itself inexorably upon us in ever new forms that we have no life that is really such. . . . It may still be possible for us, out of our own individual and private experience, to find our way to a real life for ourselves. This is a question that must arise in the mind of everyone who finds it intolerable to live a life devoid of reality. And here, for the cultured man of to-day, lies the way to religion."

Instead of the way to religion, Herrmann can also speak of the way to God. Whether this way does lead to God, again, is up to God alone. A fault line runs through Herrmann's concept of religion. He cannot reconcile certain pairs of assertions, [on one hand,] general validity, moral will, experience, on the other, denunciation of religion as dogma, philosophy, etc., and yet: the rule of God, grace, revelation. Experience [is] indescribable for him. If this path too were cut off, only the way from God to humankind would remain.

Though Herrmann too succumbed to confusion, he certainly advanced further than the others. He believed that because he knew about revelation, in speaking of religion he must also be speaking of revelation. In Herrmann the fissure [is] still shrouded by the concept of religion, but the fissure was there.

*§ 4 Epistemology and religion*

Troeltsch:[104] Philosophy is epistemology (Kant). How is objective recognition possible? The thinking self [is] the ultimate authority on all knowledge. The questions of truth and of reality coincide essentially. Reality is being [Sein] in the unity of the thinking self, being heard by reason. There is no naively real outward reality. Also influence from James: feeling of presence [of the supersensible]:[105] [it is] characteristic of all religion to have a psychological moment where one must start in order to push forward to
161 the transcendental.[106] Psychology [is the] gateway to epistemology.[107] Possibility through epistemology to consider how psychological reality is reconcilable with God. How is the religious experience of the supersensible possible? Psychology does not go beyond the empirical. For a Kantian, the supersensible is only the sphere of the intelligible. But this [can] never be proved empirically. Troeltsch attempted several corrections to the Kantian approach but then reversed them.[108] An empirical experience of a tran-

[104.] In the following discussion, Bonhoeffer refers largely to Troeltsch, *Psychologie und Erkenntnistheorie in der Religionswissenschaft.*

[105.] Cf. Dudzus, *GS* 5:195.

[106.] See Troeltsch, *Psychologie und Erkenntnistheorie in der Religionswissenschaft,* 16: "In keeping . . . to the most intense experiences, he [James] defines as the characteristic of religious states the sensing of a presence of the 'divine.'. . . He describes these experiences of presence and clarifies them by comparing them to visionary and hallucinatory imaginings of the abstract" [trans. by Isabel Best].

[107.] Ibid., 34: "Thus psychological analysis is actually required for a proper grasp of all these laws [of epistemology]. Psychology is the gateway to epistemology" [trans. by Isabel Best].

[108.] On Troeltsch's four points, intended to correct the Kantian approach to the philosophy of religion, see Troeltsch, *Psychologie und Erkenntnistheorie in der Religionswis-*

scendental object is impossible. So he is gradually pushed to consider the question of the truth of the religious act; indeed, it is here that, according to Kant, reality is contained. Troeltsch abandons James and yields to transcendentalism. [The question of the truth of a religious act can] only be answered by proving the connection between religion and the entirety of reason, with its peculiar claim to the truth. Doctrine of the religious a priori, that is, knowledge, is attributed to a unity of reason, which is necessary for experience to be possible. A priori is a rational concept that recognizes the principle of reason as the ground of all knowledge. Thus religion is not [a] product of consciousness. The rational a priori needs to be complemented by an irrational principle, which psychic reality demands, but the two cannot be forced to become one. Thus the claim of religion cannot be satisfied by Kant's epistemology.

Four stages in the philosophy of religion: (1) psychology; (2) epistemol- 162
ogy (religious a priori); only that which has proved its validity in the first sphere survives into the second, third, and fourth; (3) consideration of historical religions, question of the perfect, absolute religion; (4) metaphysics of religion: place of the highest knowledge of God in the view of the world; balance between religious and philosophical knowledge. This is the philosophy of religion in its true sense.[109]

The second stage supports Troeltsch's system, but he thought initially of the first stage as doing so. The value of his work [consists in] his wrestling with his difficulties so clearly that it is easier for us to recognize his errors.

### *Rudolf Otto*

[His thinking] too [begins] with Kant, [but] with correctives. Religious knowledge [is] a priori only when it also retains awareness of the irrational: (1) not produced by reason, (2) not accessible to it. He claims to find

---

*senschaft*, 24–50. Troeltsch sees his theory of the "actualized," i.e., the factual religious a priori combining rational and irrational moments, as an entirely productive continuation of Kant's basic intention to find a synthesis between empiricism and rationalism. However, Troeltsch modifies it by taking renewed account of the "irrationality of psychological actuality" and thus understands his theory also as "breaking out of Kantian rationalism, which is still far too strict" (50–51) [trans. by Isabel Best].

[109.] The four stages mentioned come from Troeltsch, "Wesen der Religion und der Religionswissenschaft," esp. 487–98. However, the four points do not refer to the philosophy of religion but rather denote the structure of the modern study of religion conceived as a phenomenological investigation of the nature of religion. The philosophy of religion in its real sense is here only the fourth stage, as "philosophical critique and inclusion of the concept of God in the whole of knowledge in principle" (496).

this in Fries:[110] All knowledge (cognition) ends in [a] judgment based on evidence; confidence that reason itself is speaking; this is what Fries calls faith. Knowledge [Wissen], on the other hand, arises from experience. The categories also work without intuition[111] (contrary to Kant), so that the ideas are acknowledged as knowledge of the absolute being of the soul,
163 freedom, and godhead. The third distinctive form of knowledge is presentiment [Ahndung],[112] which brings us very close to ideas. [It is a] faculty in addition to knowing and believing. It does not require rational proof but also [presupposes] the a priori activity of reason.

Otto brings to this (1) religious presentiment as a priori; (2) assertion of reality; (3) irrationality of presentiment.[113] But any a priori is the ultimate imaginable unity; this must come into conflict with irrationality. Such is the conclusion from direct observations of the psychology of religion.

In all religions there is that which cannot be expressed rationally: the numinous. The object of religion [is] truly outside the human person. The only faculty the person has is presentiment, which is simply a priori. This [is] built into the schema of Kantian transcendental philosophy.[114] There are irresolvable contradictions here. Can one imagine an irrational a priori? Either a religion of reason is not transcendent, or presentiment [exists]

---

[110.] For Rudolf Otto's debate with Jakob Friedrich Fries, see Otto, *Philosophy of Religion*. For the epistemological foundation of Fries's philosophy of religion gained from his study of Kant, see Fries's main critical work on knowledge: *Neue oder anthropologische Kritik der Vernunft*. For his systematic differentiation of knowing, believing, presentiment as distinctive forms of knowledge, see Fries, *Knowledge, Belief, and Aesthetic Sense*.

[111.] [The German *ohne Anschauung* refers to Kant's concept of *Anschauung*, which is one of the two philosophical elements of recognition for Kant; "without intuition" is the standard translation. The editors thank Christiane Tietz and Clifford Green.—VB]

[112.] [*Ahndung* is an old philosophical term; Fries believed that in *Ahndung* the person becomes aware of an aesthetic-religious harmony of everything; Kant uses the term as well. Here it has been translated as "presentiment," with the meaning that there is a sense of the future. The editors thank Christiane Tietz.—VB]

[113.] On Otto's dependence on Fries's exposition, see Fries, *Knowledge, Belief, and Aesthetic Sense*, 151–57.

[114.] These are the basic ideas from Otto's main work on the theory of religion, *The Idea of the Holy*. The "holy" as the religiously experienced characteristic of the divine is in principle, according to Otto, "the rational but also the non-rational [as] *a priori* elements" (136), yet essentially irrational. Otto calls this irrationality of the holy, which is only ascertainable through religious feeling, the "numinous" (5–7). Religious feeling itself is thereby considered to be made possible only by "the numinous . . . felt as objective and outside the self" (11). [Otto understands the reception of this external numinal reality through both "direct" (e.g., *viva vox*) and "indirect" (e.g., artistic representation) means (60–71).—MBL] This capacity, posited in religious feeling as a priori, "of genuinely cognizing and recognizing the holy in its appearances" (144), Otto follows Schleiermacher in calling "divination" (cf. 145–50).

but is no longer a priori to the unity of reason. Transcendental thinking cannot recognize anything transcendent. The Kantian tradition wrestles with the sensitive analysis of reality found in religions.

Schaeder[115] and Ihmels[116] are also among those whose tendency is to produce a situation of equilibrium.[117] This will only be upset where one speaks of God's own reality and claim. In Troeltsch and others [one can] already [see] sheet lightning. 164

*§ 5 The essence of Christianity*

Harnack,[118] *What Is Christianity?*[119] 1900, one hundred years after the *Speeches on Religion.*[120] The way this is formulated already shows that certain theological assumptions have been made. What is sought is a historical religion and its meaning for today, using the methods for the study of history in general. It asks about the relation between historical religion and personal piety, which includes the question of the absoluteness of Christianity.

First: history and faith. To speak of the essence [Wesen] is to distinguish between essence and appearance, which are separate but belong together; appearance is relative, essence is absolute, timeless. Essence can be found only in the relativity of historical appearances, but history is only the transitional stage to essential truths. The meanings incarnate in events are truth for us. We must therefore be able to express Christianity so that it simply stands there as timeless truth. This could be as (1) dogmatic doctrine; (2) categorical imperative; (3) an eternal institution.

How can I discover the essence? Three ways: (1) that of dogmatic thinking: starting with dogma, I seek the historical sources of the dogma and find the essence there, so I know beforehand what this essence must be, [because] I am approaching it with a certain dogma; (2) in reason, human 165

[115.] See Erich Schaeder, *Religion und Vernunft*, esp. sec. 1: "Die Vernunftnotwendigkeit der Religion (Das religiöse Apriori)," 7–52.

[116.] See Ludwig Ihmels, *Die Selbständigkeit der Dogmatik* and *Die christliche Wahrheitsgewißheit*, in the latter esp. chap. 4, "Die christliche Wahrheitsgewißheit und die natürliche Wahrheitskenntnis," 302–31.

[117.] Bonhoeffer is referring here again, in summary, to the many attempts by theologians to reconcile the numinous, i.e., the object of their knowledge that cannot be rationally defined, with the terminology and methods of their scholarship.

[118.] On Bonhoeffer's relationship with Harnack, see Kaltenborn, *Adolf von Harnack*; Staats, "Adolf von Harnack."

[119.] [The German title, *Das Wesen des Christentums*, although published in English as "What Is Christianity?" means "the essence of Christianity" and this term "essence" (*Wesen*) is key in the following discussion.—MBL]

[120.] Schleiermacher, *On Religion*.

beings have the criterion to distinguish [between] truth and appearance. It [reason] ascertains truths out of the randomness of history as reason discerns the essentials; even here, history cannot make corrections to the result. Catholic, Orthodox, and rationalistic thinking [are] therefore unhistorical.

(3) The path of Harnack and the liberals.[121]

"What does 'essence of Christianity' mean?"[122] Troeltsch developed the philosophical premises. Attempt to reconcile history and faith. First, one must purely be open to history. But the phrase "purely historical" presupposes an entire worldview.[123] It calls for an overview of all phenomena connected with Christianity, and also the ability to abstract the essentials from the religious material as a whole. Thus here there are already individual moments. The transition from the empirical-inductive method to the philosophy of religion[124] is abstraction and interpretation. The standard [for it] is criticism [that remains] immanent, thus purely historical, but is a task that also presupposes a religious-ethical personality.[125] The historical essence is revealed in the origins. But the development of history
166 [is] to be included also. Thus "essence" [is] not only [a] critical but [also a] historical developmental concept.[126] (*RGG* article "Prinzip").[127] Prin-

[121.] [A reference to the theological school known as "liberalism."—VB]

[122.] Troeltsch, "What Does 'Essence of Christianity' Mean?"

[123.] Ibid., 133–34: "'Purely historical' entails a whole world-view. . . . If, however, the definition of the essence is a purely historical matter it is only so in the sense that it follows the general principles of critical history and applies the unavoidable process of abstraction with concerted energy to Christianity as a whole."

[124.] Ibid., 134: "The definition of the essence grows out of the method and spirit of empirical-inductive historical writing but is nevertheless a higher order task. It lies at a point of transition from empirical-inductive history to philosophy of history." Troeltsch's basic criticism of Harnack is his failure to account for this difference. [See Drescher, *Ernst Troeltsch*, 169–76.—MBL]

[125.] Ibid., 137–45: The conception of the essence is *"at the same time a criticism of the manifestations"* and this criticism "is what is commonly called an immanent criticism. To this extent it is in fact conceived purely historically; for the historical is measured by the historical, the individual formation is measured against the spirit of the whole conceived intuitively and imaginatively" (141–42). "Admittedly it is a task which demands for its fulfilment important scientific and spiritual resources, a personality at one and the same time trained in the exactness of history and disciplined in religion and ethics" (142).

[126.] Ibid., 145–56. The organic connection between historical origin and further historical development makes the concept of "essence" more precisely "a concept which includes from the start both flexibility and richness; *it must be a developing spiritual principle*" (151).

[127.] Troeltsch, articles on "Prinzip, religiöses," in *Religion in Geschichte und Gegenwart*, vol. 4, and in the 2nd ed., vol. 4. [This has not yet appeared in *Religion Past and Present*, the English edition of *Religion in Geschichte und Gegenwart*.—MBL] To the extent that

ciple: bringing the psychological-historical together with the eternal. The first breaking through of this principle means revelation, which, however, never ends. We see this principle differently from Luther. Jesus was the first to see it.

Thus history should not have external dogmatic or rationalistic categories applied to it; history [is] to be understood only on the basis of history. The decision about the essence of Christianity therefore depends on the present form of the continuum of Christianity; but this [is] not the ultimate form: there is also an ideal concept.[128] The conception of Christianity therefore depends on one's ideal concept as an individual. Definition of essence = forming of essence. To understand history is to make a personal decision through one's historical act.[129] In this way the relativity of all historical judgment is acknowledged. Harnack's attempt [is] thus only 167
one attempt among others to give a form to the essence, but he has the same claim to be right as Luther, for example. The objective definition of essence on the basis of history is recognized as impossible. For Troeltsch, this dilemma [can be] resolved only by resorting to force: we have the right to interpret according to our theology; we can judge history.[130] In this way Troeltsch again arrives at the error of rationalism. [He has] placed a

"the use of the expression 'principle'" means "application of the historical-psychological method to religion," it gives rise to "the new concept of revelation, which allows revelation to be recognized in the fundamental breaking through of the unity of the mind's power, or of principle" (*Religion in Geschichte und Gegenwart*, 2nd ed., 1500–1501) [trans. by Isabel Best].

[128.] Cf. Troeltsch, "What Does 'Essence of Christianity' Mean?" 158: "The future development will have to be counted in with the developing essence, and since the future development is controlled by our insight into how it ought to be according to the essence and driving force of the Christian idea, *the essence changes quite automatically from being an abstracted concept to being an ideal concept.*"

[129.] The connection to be made, within the concept of essence as an ideal concept, between the objectively fixed historical tradition and the subjective positive evaluation of Christianity, takes place according to Troeltsch only by means of a "creative act" (ibid., 160): "Only the courage of an act combines the past and the future, by so emphasizing the historically grasped essence of a cultural complex for the present, that the future arises out of the essence in a manner demanded by the present and yet at the same time exhausting the depth of the historical impulse" (161). In this way Troeltsch arrives at the programmatic statement: "To define the essence is to shape it afresh. . . . The definition of the essence for a given time is the new historical formulation of Christianity for that time" (162).

[130.] Dudzus (*GS* 5:199) interprets this as follows: "This dilemma [can be] resolved only by resorting to force, such as that employed by Troeltsch in claiming the right to interpret history, and to judge it as well, according to his own theology" [trans. by Isabel Best].

considerable accent on the position of the subject within history. He discovers no objective access.

New example of this: Harnack's *What Is Christianity?*

In his *History of Dogma*:[131] history of the assimilation of the gospel with the Greek spirit; because the pure gospel is proclaimed at the Reformation, the history of dogmatics ends then; there is no Protestant history of dogma. Harnack was a historian; thus his assumption that Christian faith is based on history does not come from the history-of-religions (teacher Albrecht Ritschl!).[132] He keeps his distance from any speculation. Christianity must have the same methods applied to it as any other historical fact. He wants to find the kernel; the ephemeral wrappings must be stripped away and the timeless truths uncovered.[133] In the New Testament, two layers: (1) the proclamation by the original Christian community, behind it (2) Jesus's
168 own preaching. One must get through to this point. Here, too, the husk must be distinguished from the kernel. What proves to be timeless is that which has proved to be generally valid to this day. Essence: a devout Israelite who lives by doing God's will.[134] His preaching:[135] (1) The message of the coming of the kingdom, whose timeless meaning is independent of all eschatological fantasies; it concerns God and the soul,[136] but that is

[131.] Harnack, *History of Dogma*, 7 vols. in 4.

[132.] Bonhoeffer is referring to the fact that Harnack distinguished himself from the history-of-religions school, which considered itself to be influenced by his theology, but at the same time turned against Albrecht Ritschl; cf. ed. note 157.

[133.] Cf. Harnack, *What Is Christianity?* esp. the introductory remarks on the methodological principles of his investigation: 1–18 [the introductory lecture—MBL]. Of the methodological starting point in answering the question of the essence of Christianity, he says: "It is solely in its historical sense that we shall try to answer this question here; that is to say, we shall employ the methods of historical science, and the experience of life gained by studying the actual course of history" (6). The metaphor of kernel and husk that runs through his entire study indicates the difference between the enduring, timeless essence and the changing historical forms in which it appears (cf. 10–15).

[134.] Dudzus (*GS* 5:199) interprets this as follows: "The essence that emerges from the New Testament: Jesus is the devout Israelite who lives by doing the will of God."

[135.] The three points that follow paraphrase and explain the three subsections of section 1 ("The Gospel," 10–77), part i ("The Leading Features of Jesus' Message," 19–52) of Harnack's *What Is Christianity?*: (a) The kingdom of God and its coming (52–62); (b) God the Father and the infinite value of the human soul (63–70); (c) The higher righteousness and the commandment of love (70–78).

[136.] Harnack, *What Is Christianity?* 56: "The kingdom of God comes by coming to the individual, by entering into his soul and laying hold of it." It concerns only "God and the soul, the soul and its God." With this formulation, Harnack emphasizes that the dawning of God's rule takes place purely within, as that which is radically new in Jesus's preaching as opposed to contemporary apocalyptic and eschatological ideas.

still in the sphere of the ideal. (2) Preaching about God the Father and the infinite worth of the human soul. Essentially an admonition, which again is only realized in the ideal of humankind. (3) The better righteousness and the commandment of love. The gospel can be comprehended as an ethical message. Rather than religion and cult, Jesus wants religion and morality; the common root [is] humility; that we can achieve.[137]

Intentionally, no mention of the person of Jesus Christ; [he is seen] only as an example. "The Gospel, as Jesus proclaimed it, has to do with the Father only and not with the Son."[138] Jesus did not seek any other faith in his own person than that which is included in the keeping of the commandments.[139] 169

In his second main section, [Harnack speaks] of the gospel in history.[140] He intentionally excludes the apostolic doctrine about reconciliation, etc. Sorting out and resolution not [to come] until the Reformation. Theology should increasingly reveal the timeless kernel and keep pruning away further restrictions. In him, i.e., Luther personally, there is still too much [talk] about the person of Christ.[141]

Harnack has great inner warmth and true striving for the truth. In his lifetime the book [was] very much reviled.[142] Few have been as open to serious contradiction as Harnack himself.

Three reservations: (1) Harnack ends with [an] ethical maxim only, the radicalism of Jesus's preaching [is] crimped into the mild idea of the communion between God and the soul; the nobility of the human soul [arises]

---

[137.] Ibid., 73: "In Jesus' view, this humility, which is the love of God of which we are capable . . . is an abiding disposition towards the good, and that out of which everything that is good springs and grows."

[138.] Ibid., 144. With this widely contested statement, Harnack distances himself from dogmatic Christology, which in his view misrepresents Jesus's witness about himself. "The sentence 'I am the Son of God' was not inserted in the Gospel by Jesus himself, and to put that sentence there side by side with the others is to make an addition to the Gospel" (145–46).

[139.] The first main point in Jesus's witness regarding himself is, according to Harnack, that "he desired no other belief in his person and no other attachment to it than is contained in the keeping of his [God's] commandments" (ibid., 125).

[140.] Ibid., sec. 2, "The Gospel in History" (152–301), for the following esp. part i: "The Christian Religion in the Apostolic Age" (152–89), and part v: "The Christian Religion in Protestantism" (268–301).

[141.] Dudzus (*GS* 5:200) adds: "Even Luther still speaks too much of the person of Christ."

[142.] For the fierce debate on Harnack's *What Is Christianity?* see the bibliography in Karl H. Neufeld's *Adolf Harnacks Konflikt mit der Kirche*, 207–16.

from humility. The definition of the essence here [is] really forming of the essence; religion adapts itself too closely to the Christian humanism[143] of the time.

(2) [It is] not comprehensible why a moral admonition is called a gospel [Euangelion];[144] [there is] no joy there, but rather law and ideal. But the law is abolished by grace. In this respect Jesus didn't produce anything new that goes beyond Judaism ([Harnack's] book [was] therefore very much welcomed by Jews, could serve as a meeting ground for Jews and Chris-
170 tians).[145] This nomism[146] could also be of use to Catholicism. One finds God on the way to religion and piety; religion [is] the highest body of law, so that the highest human ideal may be realized. This thinking [based on] the human and its possibilities [is also found] in Jewish and neo-Kantian thinking. Ethical and rational thinking [are] ultimately identical.[147] The laws of reason can be carried out; humankind can realize its ideal. Ethics can always be made part of a rational system; only faith cannot be made part of any ethic. Thus Harnack can rightfully be taken up by Judaism.

(3) Christianity [is] seen as doctrine. This doctrine can be communicated without absolutely requiring the presence of God.

---

[143.] For Bonhoeffer's criticism of the late nineteenth-century bourgeois idea of the world, which he labels "humanism," see his 1928 lecture "Jesus Christ and the Essence of Christianity": Humanism is "born of cultural confidence, it believes in the divine in every human being, in the unlimited potential of the human spirit in the general sense, and in a progressive history moving toward God" (*DBWE* 10:355). According to Bonhoeffer, this is "the Greek spirit, the most severe enemy of Christianity ever" (ibid.).

[144.] "The good news."

[145.] On the Jewish reception of Harnack's *What Is Christianity?* which led to a debate within Judaism about the "essence of Judaism," see Uriel Tal, "Theologische Debatte um das Wesen des Judentums." [Cf. Tal, *Christians and Jews in Germany*, 203–18. This work is a translation from the Hebrew monograph, distinct from the German text cited above.—MBL]

[146.] Nomism, from the Greek νόμος (law), indicates here the defining influence of legal concepts on worship, statements of faith, and ethics.

[147.] The idealized understanding of history favored by Hermann Cohen, in which religion is based on ethics, uses an exact methodology like that of natural science and a criterion for truth independent of historical facts. As the natural sciences constitute the natural world by means of logical and mathematical concepts, "so, too, the idealistic understanding of history methodically seeks out analogous ethical concepts for all material conditions in the economy, to show that these, with all the evils they produce, are the roots, and that all realities in the culture come from these sources"; the criterion for truth here is contained in moral ideas (Cohen, *Zur jüdischen Religionsphilosophie und ihrer Geschichte*, 198). [Cohen was a Jewish philosopher within the Marburg school of neo-Kantianism, renowned widely for his erudition and wisdom. For the context here, see Macquarrie, *Twentieth-Century Religious Thought*, 77–83.—MBL]

Cremer, 1901 counter-lecture series with the same title;[148] Reinhold Seeberg, *Grundwahrheiten der christlichen Religion,*[149] 1902; Walther, *Wesen des Christentums,* 1902;[150] Johannes Lepsius, *Adolf Harnacks Wesen des Christentums.* Criticism especially of setting aside the person of Jesus; Lepsius particularly criticizes nomism.

R. Seeberg seeks to be modern and positive.[151] He is a historian of 171
dogma; Harnack was more [interested] in [the] connection with intellectual history, Seeberg in the internal theological aspects. Long before Holl, Seeberg had the same insight about Luther. He intends to be consciously Lutheran. Dogmatics in two volumes, 1924–1925. Religion [is] not to be explained on the basis of human reason but may be understood only in connection with revelation.[152] But certain conditions for it [exist] in the human spirit. If religion were something unreasonable, it would not exist. This connection is human receptiveness and activity. Absolute receptiveness = faith, absolute activity = love.[153] In Christ, God subjugates the human

[148.] Cremer, *Das Wesen des Christentums,* published in English [in 1903] as *A Reply to Harnack on the Essence of Christianity.*

[149.] Seeberg, *Fundamental Truths of the Christian Religion.*

[150.] Probably refers to Wilhelm Walther, *Adolf Harnacks Wesen des Christentums für die christliche Gemeinde geprüft* (1901). Other articles by authors of the same name, which also refer to the debate of that time about Harnack's *What Is Christianity?* and thus could also have been the one Bonhoeffer had in mind are Friedrich Walther, "Harnacks 'Wesen des Christentums' in seinen Grundsätzen beleuchtet," and Johannes Walther, "Das Wesen des Christentums."

[151.] Reinhold Seeberg drew up a program for a "modern and positive" theology, intended, on one hand, to honor German idealism while, on the other, seeing revelation not only as a stimulus for theological reflection but also as a means to a new relationship between God and humankind.

[152.] Seeberg, *Christliche Dogmatik,* 1:7: "If, however, the precondition of every religion knowledge is a divine revelation, then if there is also religious knowledge outside Christianity, a certain revelation in all religions must be assumed. . . . The denotation 'natural knowledge of God' is not to be commended at all, for what it means should be inherently immanent knowledge for the human spirit."

[153.] Ibid., 1:103–4: "Just as the general logical a priori thinking becomes effective synthetically . . . the religious a priori, too, is effective synthetically to the extent that it introduces the effect of the absolute spirit to the willing and thinking of the created spirit. . . . It proves itself with this in all immediate religious acts, that is, above all in faith and in love." "This threefold determination of interior life can now be summarized in the following concepts. It is *faith* as the taking in of God, who reveals himself to the soul and moves it; it is *love* as the devotion of human beings toward God that this brings about" (ibid., 2:8).

will.[154] Seeberg owes a good deal to the voluntarism of Duns Scotus.[155]
172 But [there is] also an apologetic tendency that causes changes in his interpretation of Luther. He finds that all this is meaningful only when faith proves to correspond to a need of the human spirit. Reasonable religion [is] therefore religion for everyone. In this way the absoluteness [of Christianity is] proved.[156]

*§ 6 The absoluteness of Christianity*

One of the most seductive questions asked of theology. It is never a question but always already an answer. The issue of missions cannot be settled by discussion but only in response to being sent.

This question [was] first posed by the history-of-religions school.[157] [It includes among others] Eichhorn, de Lagarde, Gunkel, Wrede, Bousset, Heitmüller, Troeltsch. Gunkel [considers] Christianity a syncretistic religion;[158] Wrede, *Das Messiasgeheimnis.* The bad thing was that a theology was made out of this work. Troeltsch was the first to give stature to the cause.[159] [It was] a goal of the history-of-religions to determine dogmatically that Christianity has the highest validity for our culture; question of

[154.] Ibid., 2:319: "This kingdom of God [as the product of the redemptive effect of Jesus Christ] is not only to be valued as the fulfilled and complete greatness, however, as it will be eventually after the conclusion of all history. In our context it also comes under consideration as the *humanity that is evolving toward submission under the lordship of God,* through manifold contradictions, temptations, and imperfections."

[155.] The Franciscan John Duns Scotus developed voluntarism, beginning with Augustine, as the doctrine of primacy of the will over the intellect. On voluntarism in general and that of Seeberg in particular, see ed. note 89, as well as Seeberg's *Die Theologie des Johannes Duns Scotus,* esp. 86–96 (chap. 1, I.4, "Der Willensprimat") and 152–79 (chap. 2, I.2, "Das Wesen Gottes").

[156.] Cf. Dudzus (*GS* 5:201): "Christianity is the religion that is most in accordance with this point, therefore the religion for everyone. Thus its absoluteness is considered to be proved."

[157.] The phrase "history-of-religions school" was coined in 1904 by Alfred Jeremias for polemical purposes. Ernst Troeltsch is considered the systematic theologian of this school of thought. The history-of-religions school regards itself as influenced by the theology of Adolf von Harnack and Julius Wellhausen; Albrecht Ritschl was their theological opposite. Religion was understood by the history-of-religions school as the expression of the intellectual life of peoples, taking into consideration the varied influence of the individual religions. This then also brought up the question of the independence and absoluteness of Christianity. [See ed. note 52.—MBL]

[158.] "Our thesis is: that Christianity, which was born of syncretic Judaism, has strong syncretic features" (Gunkel, *Religio-historical Interpretation of the New Testament,* 420). "Our conclusion: Christianity [as exhibited in John and Paul] is a syncretic religion" (455).

[159.] See ed. note 56.

the absoluteness of Christianity. The issue [was to be] decided by application of the historical, history-of-religions method: the basic similarity of all historical manifestations. Within history, no qualitative differences; doc- 173
trine of the history-of-religions principle.[160]

For scholarship there is therefore no absolute status for Christianity;[161] thus all false apologetics are overthrown. Harnack: Since [Christianity is] not a positive religion, therefore [it is] the religion;[162] [for] Niebergall, it is the religion by being linked with the absolutely ethical;[163] [for] Stange, transcendentally derived;[164] Seeberg: a need of the spirit.[165] Troeltsch's No takes courage; apologetics are always a product of fear. But [there were]
nevertheless two positive statements: (1) For our Western civilization, 174
[Christianity is] proved to be the absolute religion. (2) Isn't naive absoluteness enough for the faithful?[166]—namely, to know about God; but this path of the believer need not be the path for all eternity.

---

[160.] Possibly Bonhoeffer believed that in Troeltsch's thought the history-of-religions method contradicts the concern for research guided by and based on a dogmatic statement. On the history-of-religions comparative proof of the "absoluteness" of Christianity in the sense of its "highest validity" being confined to a specific cultural context and a specific moment in history, see Troeltsch, *Absoluteness of Christianity*, 107–16. Troeltsch uses the term "highest validity" in place of the traditional term "absoluteness" (ibid., 117–18). It combines the value judgment of the religious subject with the analytical principles of historical thinking: "This judgment issues from a joining together of absolute decision in the present with an interpretation of the developmental process that affirms historical relativity" (ibid.).

[161.] The reason for this is the constitutive significance of the value judgment made by the religious subject, for this value judgment about the highest validity "is a choice that depends on religious conviction, not scientific demonstration" (ibid., 112).

[162.] Cf. Harnack, "Die Aufgabe der theologischen Fakultäten," 172: "We would like the theological faculties to pursue their research on *Christian* religion, since Christianity in its pure form is not simply *one* religion among others but rather religion per se."

[163.] See Friedrich Niebergall, *Welches ist die beste Religion?* 63: "Since Christianity is so thoroughly *ethical*, it is superior to all other religions for anyone who understands the value of goodness for the long life of a community and for individuals to find true life."

[164.] See Carl Stange, *Christentum und moderne Weltanschauung*, 66–89, and *Die Religion als Erfahrung*, 37–48.

[165.] Dudzus (*GS* 5:202) adds: "for Seeberg finally, because it best satisfies the need of the spirit." Seeberg, *Christliche Dogmatik* [see ed. note 152], 1:190: "The proof that Christianity is the absolute religion is produced. . . . The two principles out of which all religion comes forth, that the human spirit is capable and in need of the revelation of absolute spirit and that the human spirit submits to the revelation of absolute spirit and is liberated through it, come in Christianity to pure exposition."

[166.] "Naive absoluteness" is Troeltsch's term for the self-evident, immediate feeling of absoluteness that devout followers have toward their own religion, without any need for a historical religious comparison as it [the feeling of absoluteness—VB] manifests itself in the times of the origins of every religion. See Troeltsch, *Absoluteness of Christianity*,

Inauthentic absoluteness [is the] product of later dogmatics; there was none of it in Jesus.[167] Apologetics first arose among his disciples. Thus Troeltsch wants to destroy absoluteness that is not genuine and uncover genuine Christianity again. The historical method as such decides the issue without needing any of the content of Christianity. The object is adapted to the method. (Kantian tradition.)

Troeltsch opposed by the supernaturalists.[168] His conception (predominated) in the widest circles of educated people.

The history-of-religions question went further: syncretistic or something new? The first concept became very widespread. Only in 1925 [did] Karl Holl, in *Urchristentum und Religionsgeschichte,* [raise] a sharp protest. Historical work forces Holl to see in Christianity something decisively new. All more-recent religions [are about] God and the sacred, but the theme in Christianity [is] God and the sinner. Jesus is the one who proclaims this new religion, but Holl leaves the cross and the resurrection to the history-
175 of-religion. Thus he comes through empirical observation to perceive some-

---

131–37. [Troeltsch wants to retain an understanding of Christianity as a historical phenomenon, thus relative, and its own claim of absolute, unique revelation. In this way, he arrives at the concept of "relative absoluteness." (See Drescher, *Ernst Troeltsch,* 162–63.) For Troeltsch, "absoluteness" is a characteristic of naive thinking. Experiential evidence shatters such naïveté and provides for a reinterpretation of reality, a transformation to scientific thinking and more reliable conceptualization. However, for Troeltsch, the "no" to which Bonhoeffer refers, i.e., a critique of naive thinking in its assumption of supreme and absolute value, is a qualified one. "What is true of scientific thought everywhere else is true of it in the area of religion as well: It transforms one's initial understanding, but it does not thereby invalidate the objective reality to which this immediate understanding refers. . . . Mature wisdom of thought signifies that reality as naïvely perceived is not denied but viewed in a higher context and . . . a scientifically informed restoration of the naïve outlook, now raised to a higher level, is to the same degree more beneficial and significant for life as a whole" (*Absoluteness of Christianity,* 134–36).—MBL]

[167.] "Artificial, apologetic absoluteness," according to Troeltsch, was reshaped by the natural self-confidence of naive absoluteness into a "lifting up of miraculous events and relations as the foundation for a theological theory of the uniqueness of Christianity" (*Absoluteness of Christianity,* 138–50, here 149). Within artificial absoluteness, Troeltsch distinguishes further between "supernatural," "rational," and "evolutionary" apologetics [ibid., 151–58—MBL].

[168.] Supernaturalism is a line of thought within Protestant theology in the late eighteenth and early nineteenth centuries that sought to uphold the Christian revelation, over against naturalism and rationalism, as a source of insight that could not be traced back to reason. Its chief representatives are Gottlob Christian Storr, Johann Christoph Friedrich Steudel, and Franz Volkmar Reinhard.

thing new in Christianity, even though he doesn't find his way out of the liberal view of Jesus.[169]

Two things overlooked by the history-of-religions school: (1) The Christian as an individual [is] an abstraction, so Troeltsch's naive absolutism cannot stand. (2) Absoluteness is [grounded] not in a religious experience but rather in the word of God, in its identity. Troeltsch did not have to preach; what would a history-of-religions sermon have to look like, as a message?

### *§ 7 The biblical Christ*

Is the historical method the only means of access? This question [is] born of the skepticism regarding the nineteenth-century image of Jesus. History-of-religions studies again saw the ultimate in the person of Jesus, not in his teachings, etc. But this [did] not deter the actual alienation from Jesus's person. [Jesus as] teacher was countered by [Jesus as] eschatological and apocalyptic prophet, but that would only make him more alien to us than before. Albert Schweitzer above all.[170] Wrede, 1901, *The Messianic Secret*; Schweitzer, *The Mystery of the Kingdom of God: The Secret of Jesus' Messiahship and Passion*: erosion of the liberal research to that point, messianic awareness [is] only congregational theology, we are unable to reach the historical Jesus. The picture of the historical Jesus [is] thus suddenly changed. Arthur Drews: Jesus [did] not actually live but [is] only the product of the community of faith.[171] If Jesus never lived, Christianity would indeed be superflu- 176
ous. *The Christ Myth*;[172] Pastor Kalthoff in Bremen, first president of the Monist Federation:[173] Jesus as an invention by social-revolutionary minds

[169.] Winterhager: "[For] *Holl* only the justification of the sinner [is] essential, without the christological background, without the cross and resurrection. He gives up the latter as syncretism of religious history. Thus Holl remains within liberalism (Ritschl)."

[170.] Winterhager: "Skepticism regarding the picture of Jesus's life gained from history (Troeltsch, Harnack) and about distancing from the person of Christ through emphasis on Christ's teachings. The humane teacher is now countered by the eschatological Christ, the apocalyptic prophet. Albert Schweitzer, *The Quest of the Historical Jesus*, 1910." [The *DBW* text cites two German editions from 1906 and 1913. English translation in 1910 and 1968.—MBL]

[171.] Arthur Drews, under the influence of theological radicalism, disputed the historical existence of Jesus, which was, according to his interpretation, only "a product of the religious 'social soul' and was made by Paul, with the required amount of reinterpretation and reconstruction, the chief interest of those communities founded by him" (Drews, *Christ Myth*, 286).

[172.] Winterhager: "Arthur Drews (a follower of Eduard von Hartmann) concludes: Christ only a product of congregational theology; *The Christ Myth*, 1909."

[173.] Albert Kalthoff and Ernst Haeckel founded the German Monist Federation (Deutscher Monistenbund) in 1906. In 1904, Haeckel's "Theses for Organization of the

in the Roman Empire. Drews's works [are] superficial, but the question had been clearly posed, especially for dogmatists, among others. To what extent does faith depend on the results of historical scholarship? However, without historical documentation it wouldn't be possible either.

For Schweitzer [however] history has been rendered superfluous, the relation to Christ [is] mystical.[174]

W. Herrmann: Ritschl emphasized the importance of the historical Jesus.[175] The church-community brings Jesus into the present day; only through the value judgment of the church-community does Jesus become the Christ.[176] Herrmann picks up here: an individual person must be struck by the value of the person of Jesus, i.e., by his inner life; all the his-
177 torical data are not part of the gospel. Everyone who truly confronts the value of Jesus is compelled to believe [in him]; this direct pathway into the life of Jesus [is] independent of all historical scholarship.[177] No one has stood up for [the] freedom of religion from history as [Herrmann] did, but the measure of the moral value of Jesus's person [is as valid] as our own. History can bring out only what is fundamentally already in human beings. The believer has standards for judging the value of this.

---

Monist Federation" called for a uniform worldview and religion based on insights from the natural sciences, which was to uplift souls through art and science, and polemicized against all unscientific explanations of the world.

[174.] "Mythical" changed to "mystical"; cf. Winterhager: "Albert Schweitzer replaces history with mysticism."

[175.] See Herrmann, "Christlich-protestantische Dogmatik," 611–12: "When *Ritschl* takes the revelation, the gospel, the Holy Scriptures as such as the starting point for dogmatics, he always sees all of them uniformly summed up in the 'historical person of Christ.'" [The sentence in the student notes is incomplete; it reads simply: "Ritschl stressed the importance. . . ."—MBL]

[176.] Winterhager: "Herrmann and Kähler had both learned from Ritschl to emphasize the importance of historicity in revelation and thus of the church-community (to this day). Certainly Ritschl had a strange understanding of the relation between Christ and the church-community. It is only through the value judgment of the church-community that Jesus becomes the Christ." For Ritschl's reasons for the special nature (*Besonderheit*) of religious knowledge, which he had been seeking to make more precise since the 2nd edition of his major work on dogmatics by recourse to the philosophical doctrine of value judgment, see Ritschl, *Christian Doctrine of Justification and Reconciliation*, 181–93. For his application of the doctrine of value judgment to Christology, see 385–484 ["Christology: Person and Work"], esp. 399–417 ["Divinity of Christ as Theological Problem"], e.g., 400: "For the thought of Christ's Godhead is never other than the expression of that unique acknowledgment and appreciation which the Christian community yields to its Founder."

[177.] On the independence of the power of Jesus's person, as experienced through faith, from historical scholarship, see Herrmann, *Die Gewißheit des Glaubens*, esp. 59–60.

Herrmann tried (1) to make religion independent of historical research, and also of epistemology; (2) to use a concept of history opposed to the static, self-contained, authoritative doctrinal edifice. Past and present [are] interdependent, held together by experience. This recalls Wilhelm Dilthey's hermeneutical theory, picked up from Holl (Luther's art of interpretation).[178] The question is whether this philosophy of history can be applied to theology.

We can no longer go back before Herrmann, but we must go beyond him.

Dogmatics already had its answer ready in 1892, long before Wrede and Schweitzer: M. Kähler: *The So-Called Historical Jesus and the Historical Biblical Christ.* Greifswald school: Lütgert,[179] Schaeder,[180] Bornhäuser.[181] [Kähler] b. 1835, pastor, 1867 professor at the Univ. of Halle, 1879 full professor, d. 1912.

Clear opposition to the research on the life of Jesus. [According to Kähler,] it uses a dogmatic picture and brings this into history, behaving as if it were purely historical. It conceals the living Christ. Whatever happens in historical research, it takes place at a level that has given up the 178
church. Faith must have its own access to history. [Kähler] agrees with Herrmann in pressing for a place where it is free to make the rules.[182] Only his solution [is] different; for Kähler, faith is not allowed to shape history in an arbitrary, subjective way; this is a danger especially in the Erlangen [school].[183] It is not [the] received doctrine that is decisive, but rather

[178.] Holl, "Luthers Bedeutung für den Fortschritt der Auslegungskunst." [Cf. Bonhoeffer's paper on the historical and pneumatological interpretation of Scripture in Seeberg's seminar on systematic theology in the summer of 1925: *DBWE* 9:285–300, esp. 290–91, where Bonhoeffer discusses Holl's interpretation of Luther's hermeneutics.—MBL]

[179.] See Lütgert, "Die Lehre Jesu" and "Die Glaubwürdigkeit des Christusbildes der Evangelien."

[180.] See Schaeder, "Die Einzigartigkeit Jesu und sein Ziel" and *Theozentrische Theologie.*

[181.] For Bornhäuser's programmatic detachment from the research on the life of Jesus, see Bornhäuser, *Das Wirken des Christus,* 1–11.

[182.] According to Martin Kähler, the study of history is an auxiliary study to [that of] theology, which obliges it to deal with the Scriptures and "biblical material from particular points of view." For "theological procedure [that] requires that the revelation is grasped by faith," however, this is not a valid procedure (Kähler, *Die Wissenschaft der christlichen Lehre,* 1:34–35).

[183.] The Erlangen school was the most important theological trend within nineteenth-century confessional theology. It was rooted in the Awakening movement (*Erweckungsbewegung*), but at the same time was strongly influenced by German idealism and romanticism. The Erlangen school sought to develop the dogmatic contents

faith takes place through encounter, then and now. Faith can only depend on the Christ of history, who is not the historical Jesus; but then this is the biblical Christ. This Christ has his place in history, but we believe in him as the one who is exalted. We cannot go back further than what the Bible says. The Christ of the Bible is the one who is preached and believed. This is the real historical [geschichtliche] Christ.[184] The disciples' faith [is] the effect of Christ in history; in faith they write the Bible and preach.[185] Now we no longer need to go back to the Jesus of history [Historie]; faith has been set free from history.[186] This preserves the objectivity of history and yet overcomes the static state, because human subjectivity is brought in through the emphasis on faith. The living Lord is the whole Christ and the believer the whole human being.[187]

179 Does pushing aside the historical [historische] concern take care of everything? It lets us escape the challenge of historical knowledge; we have to go through it, not bypass it.

Kähler's audience almost disappeared within his lifetime.

Hermann Schultz (d. 1903): *Die Lehre von der Gottheit Christi*, saw, at the same time as Kähler, the problem of faith and history; for him as well, preaching [is] the solution to the problem, but the Ritschlean idea remains that it is first [the] church-community through whom Christ is made Christ.[188]

---

of Lutheran theology, beginning with the devout subject and his or her experience of rebirth. [The Awakening movement refers to an eighteenth-century revival within Lutheranism in pietistic reaction against a dominating rationalism and toward more emotional, practical, and traditional religious experience.—MBL]

[184.] Paraphrased from Kähler, *So-Called Historical Jesus*, 65–66.

[185.] "But what is the decisive influence that Jesus had upon posterity? According to the Bible and church history it consisted in nothing else but the faith of his disciples" (ibid., 63).

[186.] [Bonhoeffer refers here to the distinction evident in the German title of Kähler's book, *Der sogenannte historische Jesus und der geschichtliche, biblische Christus*, which is not immediately apparent in the English title translation, contrasting "historical" and "historic." The German terms *Historie* and *Geschichte* offer a more complex distinction between factual history and contextual, existential history. Kähler's work played an important role in the continuing debate over the "Jesus of history" and the "Christ of faith."—MBL]

[187.] Winterhager: "Kähler still reproaches Herrmann with a subjective framing of history. Our faith depends not on the Jesus of history but on the historical Christ, the Christ of the Bible. The real historical Christ is the one who is preached. The Christ who is preached is the Christ in whom we believe—today—just as in those days. The Bible is the witness of the resurrected, present, living Lord. In the place of Herrmann's experience, Kähler puts faith."

[188.] Cf. Schultz, *Die Lehre von der Gottheit Christi*, 1–21. For his derivation of Christ's divinity, following Ritschl, from seeing Christ's work of salvation in the church-community, see 470–549.

[Kähler is] not primarily interested in having a point of connection in reality, but rather builds [his] structure in his own way, which [doesn't] depend on fitting [into] the system of the sciences. The problem of faith and history would be the theological counterpoint to his entire theology. Kähler becomes the theologian of justification.

*§ 8 Justification and sanctification*

The issue of the Reformation had faded away by the turn of the century. Even Kähler and Cremer were not able to get this bell ringing sufficiently to awaken anyone from sleep.

[The] doctrine of justification [is] dir[ectly] connected with Christology. For Luther, Christ [is] *exemplum*[189] or *donum*.[190] In the first case [*exemplum*] Jesus is a divine teacher whom we are to imitate; if he is the ultimate 180 lawgiver, then the understanding of justification becomes impossible. The doctrine of justification is about the end of the law, of ethics. But is the end [tantamount to] abolition or fulfillment? How it is understood is essential for the shaping [of ethics], but first comes something fundamentally alien to all ethics: God comes face-to-face with the ethical human being, destroying and lifting up. For a teacher of morality, there can no longer be mercy, except perhaps leniency, *benignitas*,[191] "letting up." This is an intolerable softening of the concept of God. God's commandments [are] either totally serious or not at all, and God's love is the same. The God of liberal theology [is] a sentimental God. To Troeltsch's question, How do I find my soul? the Bible gives no answer. The Reformation knew it was answering only the question, How can I have a merciful God?[192] Harnack does not refer

[189.] "Example" in the sense of "model."

[190.] "Gift" (of God). Cf. Paul Drews's exposition of Christ as *donum seu sacramentum et exemplum*, to which Bonhoeffer refers in his seminar paper "Luther's Views of the Holy Spirit according to the Disputationen of 1535–1545 edited by Drews" (*DBWE* 9:325–70; see p. 338, ed. note 54). [Bonhoeffer wrote this paper for Holl's seminar "Luther and the Holy Spirit" in the winter semester of 1925–26, based on Paul Drews's edition of Luther's disputations at the University of Wittenberg.—MBL]

[191.] "Good-naturedness," "goodwill."

[192.] This core question of Reformation theology is referenced in Luther's fundamental statements about the Reformation as his own turning point; cf., however, his *Predigten über die Taufe* of 1534 (*WA* 37, 627–72, esp. 661), in which Luther, looking back on his time as a monk at Erfurt, says: "For I myself was a monk for fifteen years; as to what I had experienced before, I industriously read all their books and did everything I could, yet I could never comfort myself with my baptism, but instead always thought: O when will you finally become pious and do enough that you receive a merciful God? And through such thoughts I was driven to the monastery." Otto Scheel, in his biography of Luther, which was very well known in Bonhoeffer's time, described Luther's entering the cloister and his time in the Augustinian monastery at Erfurt, which was marked by his

to justification in any way. In Wrede's *Paulus*, 1904, the doctrine of justification is not the main point. Paul can be fully understood without it; it is a doctrine of struggle against Judaism.[193] There is no great significance in the opposition between justification by works and by faith. But is there
181 a religion without works? Isn't Judaism only a characteristic form of what religion is in general? According to Wrede, justification is not to be considered as a psychological process; it is nothing other than Christ's historical act of redemption.[194] Justification of humankind only through the death of Christ: [here we have a] view of the essence of justification that is very worthy of consideration, but assessment of it presumes that Christianity is an ethical religion.

Cremer and Kähler counter this with sharp polemics. Here Christ is not the one who reveals but rather the revelation. What happens on the cross is total justice, which is total love. The incarnation is the judgment on humankind, which at the same time is grounded in forgiveness. How can we appropriate this? Here is where the doctrine of justification comes in. We have all died with Christ; this is the judgment imposed on the world by God. In being raised from the dead, God is again judging us; thus the cross is grace at the same time. Therefore human beings, being judged and pardoned [begnadigt], are righteous and can now stand before God. Acknowledging this judgment is faith.

This is essentially what Cremer says: the saving judgment of God in Christ [is] the most essential opposition to liberalism. *Die paulinische Rechtfertigungslehre im Zusammenhang der geschichtlichen Voraussetzungen*; *Gethsemane*; *Biblisch-theologisches Wörterbuch*. During the liberal period, Cremer's writings and his students were strongly disputed.

---

inner conflict with the Catholic understanding of justification by works and by understanding God primarily as a judge, programmatically as a "struggle for a merciful God" (cf. Scheel, *Martin Luther*, 1:250–61 and 2:231–45).

[193.] Wrede, *Paul*, 84: "The Pauline world of thought stands in unmistakable contrast to Judaism. But this antagonism governs no more than a definite circle of ideas. Paul's actual doctrine of redemption is not among them; it is a complete whole in itself."

[194.] Ibid., 113–15: "An objective redemption is indeed not unknown to the dogmatic . . . exposition today, but in their doctrine of salvation they are always thinking of what happens in the individual self. They ask how the process which imparts the benefit of Christianity goes on and must necessarily go on in the individual soul. . . . The doctrine of salvation is therefore in great part a doctrine of human piety and its normal origin or religious psychology. This whole chapter is absent from the Pauline teaching. The reason: in his doctrine, he is not thinking of the individual at all but of the race, of humanity as a whole. . . . All the leading ideas of his theology [of salvation] bear this historical stamp. . . . Christ stands as the turning point between an old and a new age."

Kähler's work goes even further. He was the first who built an entire theology on the doctrine of justification: *Die Wissenschaft der christlichen Lehre*.[195]

Three ways of thinking: (1) Christianity [is one] religion like other reli- 182
gions, that is, human beings are determined by religion and morality; but these are judged on the basis of the experience of justification. This is what Kähler calls Christian apologetics; in the end, only one religion remains. (2) From the object of belief in justification, Protestant dogmatics. (3) From putting it into practice: theological ethics.[196]

In the second part comes the decisive discussion. Everything is related to justification. The difference from the Erlangen school[197] is that justification is similar to an experience of rebirth; in being reborn, I keep reorienting myself to my recognition of the truth, its extent and certainty. But according to Kähler, faith is oriented only to objective facts. For him, the act of justification is distinct from psychological experience. Faith is not a property or a quality; instead, it is an act; one has it only by holding on to it. Justification begins not as an effect on the inner person, but rather from outside the person, as the beginning of his or her renewal. According to Cremer, justification is a synthetic, forensic judgment.[198] Growth in faith [does] not [mean] growing sanctification; rather, sanctification exists in the death of the human being.

Lütgert accordingly distinguishes between the judgment of faith and that of experience. The only ground for believing in my own righteousness is the cross.[199]

---

[195.] Winterhager: "*Die Wissenschaft der christlichen Lehre*; this work is dedicated to the preacher Heinrich Hoffmann in Halle (originally a pietist)."

[196.] Winterhager: "First way of thinking: Christian apologetics based on the presuppositions of the doctrine of justification—Second way of thinking: Protestant dogmatics—Third way of thinking: putting belief in justification into practice: theological ethics."

[197.] This is where Martin Kähler differs from the Erlangen school, which derived justification, along with all other dogmatic content, from the experience of rebirth.

[198.] Winterhager: "In the second way of thinking, belief in justification must be distinguished from that which the Erlangen school calls the 'experience of rebirth,' which derives all dogmatic laws from human beings themselves. Belief in justification is oriented away from myself and from all theology of immanence, toward the facts of God." Cf. Cremer, *Die paulinische Rechtfertigungslehre*, 329–49.

[199.] Cf. Lütgert, "Die Lehre von der Rechtfertigung," 50–70. Justification is "to be protected from being misunderstood as a subjective experience. Justification is, instead, an objective action of God, therefore not an object of experience, but rather one of faith. The reason for this faith in my own righteousness is nothing less than the cross of Christ" (63–64).

183 This is especially directed against the concept of community that came from Oxford.[200] This is the third front, besides those of Troeltschian subjectivity and the theology of Erlangen, opposed by Cremer and Kähler.

(Fleisch, *Die moderne Gemeinschaftsbewegung in Deutschland*; minutes of the Eisenach conferences (Lepsius);[201] Jellinghaus, *Das völlige, gegenwärtige Heil durch Christum*).

Circa 1875 from America and Oxford: Pecell Smith;[202] three branches in Germany: (1) Gnadau conference (Count Pückler, moderate);[203] (2) brusquely antichurch, [anti]-theological, [anti]-cultural; Blanckenburg Alliance.[204] (3) Eisenach conferences (1902 onward),[205] moderate and scholarly, education of theologians.

1905 new upsurge [of the Blankenburg Alliance,] led by Modersohn.
184 Doctrine of development: comm[unity] of the particularly saintly.[206] In

[200.] This probably refers not to the religious renewal movement of 1833–45 that originated in Oxford, the so-called Oxford movement, but rather to the New Oxford Movement founded by Robert Pearsall Smith, which staged its "days of blessing" in Oxford, beginning in 1874. The "communities" under Smith's influence sought to be Christians in the strict sense and join in following the example of the first Christian communities, to strengthen one another in faith and to serve one another and others in love. They developed the idea of sanctification by faith, healing through prayer, and revived the early Christian gifts of the spirit (speaking in tongues).

[201.] Lepsius, *Berichte der Verhandlungen der Eisenacher Konferenzen.*

[202.] Robert Pearsall Smith, a Philadelphia Quaker businessman who became an influential lay leader and preacher in the holiness movement of the 1870s and 1880s, both in the United States and in England, including Oxford.

[203.] The Gnadau Pentecostal Conference was constituted in 1888 in Gnadau, near Magdeburg. This organizational unifying of the communal movement in Germany gave rise in 1894 to the German Committee for Cultivating Protestant Communities.

[204.] The Blankenburger Allianz; within the communal movement, the Blankenburg Alliance Conference, which was unrelated to or alienated from the church and met after 1886 in Blankenburg in Thuringia, pursued relations with similarly minded English groups. Its leader was Ernst Modersohn.

[205.] Founded by Johannes Lepsius, Samuel Keller, and Theodor Jellinghaus, the Eisenach Conference, known as the Eisenach Federation from 1905 onward, was one section of the communal movement (*Gemeinschaftsbewegung*) that sought to preserve the connection between that movement and "devout theology and church." In 1910, a serious crisis developed with the established church when the Eisenach Federation gave its support to the Pentecostal movement.

[206.] See Modersohn, *Men of Revival in Germany.* Modersohn, as leader of the Blankenburg Alliance, which considered itself a part of the communal movement that was close to the church, complained about Adventist and New Apostolic preachers who "preached people out"(10). Besides new pietistic ideas such as "serious self-examination" (80) and life before conversion as "a big shame" (87), Modersohn also proposed that there are elect persons whom God uses as instruments "to teach and bless us" (9).

1907 [there was] uproar in Kassel[207] over assemblies out of all human control, speaking in tongues and ecstatic speeches. The Pentecostal movement separated [from the Blankenburg Alliance]; catastrophe was averted.

The goal was holiness based on faith, coming from pietism and Methodism,[208] led by Jellinghaus, Stockmeier,[209] and Lepsius. Main themes: cross of Christ; necessity of conversion. Theology of blood [is] very prominent, and the idea of judgment. Conversion must take place suddenly, or at least be a very clear act. There is only one conversion; thereafter everything counts as growth, etc. Every person will always have sins but can reach a state in which no more sins are committed.[210] Pastor Paul (Pentecostal) preached a state of being perfectly without sin.[211] The Oxford Group movement still [exists] today, is especially strong in America.[212]

*Karl Holl*

("Was hat die Rechtfertigungslehre dem modernen Menschen zu sagen?" Vol. 3 of [Holl's] *Gesammelte Aufsätze zur Kirchengeschichte.*) He sees the themes of theology in justification. God is [both] completely just and completely merciful. [Holl] does not consider this paradox[213] resolved in Ritschl's 185
and Cremer's thinking, because there God [only] declares righteous; an

[207.] Kassel, Großalmerode, and Wildungen were "Pentecostalist" centers; see Mühlhausen, "Von der schwärmerischen Bewegung in Kurhessen."

[208.] [The holiness movement, largely influenced by the theology of John Wesley, was centered on sanctification as cleansing from a sinful nature through faith and the gift of the Holy Spirit, often ecstatically in a revivalist setting, striving for a heart converted to purity and an ideal of Christian regeneration and perfection.—MBL]

[209.] Otto Stockmayer, pastor and Protestant theologian, leading theologian of the holiness movement. Winterhager: "Ludwig Thimme, *Kirche, Sekte und Gemeinschaft* on the conversion of Stockmeier."

[210.] Winterhager: "Conversion: sanctification in faith: a person can get so far as to commit no further sins. This is distinct from having sins (John)" [perhaps a reference to 1 John 3:9—MBL].

[211.] Jonathan Paul, Protestant pastor, a free evangelist after 1899 and leader of the Pentecostal movement.

[212.] [The Oxford Group movement, to be distinguished from the Oxford Movement within nineteenth-century High Church Anglicanism, was founded by Frank Buchman. Buchman was a Lutheran pastor from Philadelphia who stimulated an evangelistic and social reform movement in Oxford in the early 1920s, influenced by Anglican missionary bishops. He and his followers traveled widely in the United States, Canada, South Africa, and Europe, advocating the spiritual transformation of society through "moral rearmament." After 1938, it became known as Moral Rearmament and then, still later, the Caux Movement. Cf. *DBWE* 6:123, ed. note 93, and *DBWE* 8:430, ed. note 33.—MBL]

[213.] Holl, "Was hat die Rechtfertigungslehre dem modernen Menschen zu sagen?" 566: "The concept of God to which the doctrine of justification leads contains a paradox. It places the idea of a righteous, relentlessly demanding God next to the other idea, that

arbitrary act. In God's eyes human beings must already be just, [they are] made holy not in their inner world, but rather eschatologically. The doctrines of justification and sanctification are considered together. Justification [is an] analytical judgment.

The reason for justification [is] not Christ but rather the First Commandment, which is confirmed within my conscience.[214] The final authority for certainty [is] one's conscience; thus [Holl] describes Lutheran ethics as the ethics of conscience. (Refuted by Gogarten and H. M. Müller.)[215]

*§ 9 The problem of ethics and culture*

Ripening of the process of secularization in the culture (medieval city life, Renaissance, Enlightenment, humanism).[216] Modern humanism: naturalistic concept of evolution, less aesthetic in its nature, more rational.[217] Every area of life seeks a way to connect [with this process] within the secular sphere. The rules of action [arise] from the laws immanent in the mat-
186 ter [at hand]: autonomous laws.[218] Objective conduct would then amount ethically to autonomy.[219] Assumption that the things that are present have

God is full of amazing kindness. The one should be thought of as distinctly and completely as the other, without any attempt at an inner reconciliation between them. But this paradox is simply the nature of Christian belief in God."

[214.] Winterhager: "For Cremer, justification means forgiveness of sin; Holl says: [one is] not arbitrarily declared just. Whoever is justified by God has already been made holy eschatologically (sculptor's stone: the work is done). Justification [is] no longer a synthetic but rather an analytical judgment. Holl emphasizes the First Commandment and conscience more than the cross of Christ."

[215.] Gogarten, *Von Glauben und Offenbarung*; Hans Michael Müller, *Erfahrung und Glaube bei Luther.*

[216.] [The German here is *Humanität*, which would mean "humaneness." Because Dudzus clearly indicates this as "humanism" in his notes (cf. ed. note 217), it has been translated here as "humanism."—VB]

[217.] Dudzus (*GS* 5:210) adds: "The twentieth century brought us the ripening of the process of secularization of the culture. This process began with medieval city life and broadened through the Renaissance, humanism and the Enlightenment. Modern humanism is no longer of such an aesthetic nature as the earlier form, instead more rational. It receives its strongest impetus from the naturalistic concept of evolution."

[218.] There had been a controversy in theological ethics since the mid-nineteenth century as to whether, within theonomy, the worldly orders could be allowed their own autonomy (*Eigengesetzlichkeit*). However, the word was not coined until around the turn of the century, and it is disputed whether this came from the debate, in the theory of science, about the claim to objectivity of the method of natural science, and the term it used for its laws, or whether Karl Holl or Max Weber coined the word (see Graf, "Gesetz," 118).

[219.] Winterhager: "The new rules of action are borrowed from the needs immanent in the matter [at hand]; autonomy of action, objectivity, i.e., tied to functions."

the right to be there and are good. [They are] thought of as willed by God; their creatureliness displays God's commands in creation. If existence is good, then acting on the basis of this thing must be good.[220]

In principle, human beings are in a position to allow things in their creatureliness to act, without doing them any harm; we only have to conform to the immanent laws. This is the level of purely autonomous culture. Christian ethics then only means to be convinced of the morality that is the effect of the things themselves. [The] Reformation is said to have opened up the secular sphere, to have made culture possible. Christianity was seen in its cultural optimism and its humanism.

F. Overbeck, *Die Christlichkeit der Theologie.*[221] Here the attempt to connect Christianity with culture is denounced as the greatest betrayal. Overbeck stands on the ground of culture, but he saw very clearly the boundary between the Greek and the Christian mind, which had been blurred by Harnack.[222]

¶Nietzsche rejected Christianity entirely, as the most disastrous inhibition of autonomous culture. For him, compassion is basically and principally unnatural in human beings, and he considered it the principle of Christian ethics.[223] It turns decadence into a principle. However, since Christianity can never bring itself to total asceticism, it has become the ideal of ordinary
people. Evil is made common, [for] in asceticism a person must idolize a 187

[220.] Winterhager: "From the orders of creation [*Schöpfungsordnungen*], laws based on creation [are] derived." [See Bonhoeffer's more general treatment of creation and commandment in the outline for a lecture (given January 19, 1932): "Theses: The Discernible Nature of the Order of Creation" (2/8). This theme was a key contention for Bonhoeffer in 1932, in his ethical thinking as well as in his ecumenical discussions. His critique of "orders of creation" emerges again in the summer seminar (1932) topic: "Is There a Christian Ethic?" (see 2/10) and in two ecumenical papers in relation to the Youth Peace Conference at Ciernohorské Kúpele (July 20–30, 1932): "On the Theological Foundation of the Work of the World Alliance" (2/14) and its outline of theses (2/15).—MBL]

[221.] [*Über die Christlichkeit unserer heutigen Theologie: Streit- und Friedensschrift.*—MBL]

[222.] Cf. Bonhoeffer's characterization of the late nineteenth-century bourgeois worldview, described as "humanism" and as an expression of the "Greek spirit" (*DBWE* 10:355) in his 1928 lecture "Jesus Christ and the Essence of Christianity" (*DBWE* 10:342–59). [See also p. 204, ed. note 143.—MBL]

[223.] Nietzsche, *Antichrist*, aphorism 7: "Christianity is called the religion of *pity*. Pity stands opposed to the tonic emotions which heighten our vitality: it has a depressing effect. We are deprived of strength when we feel pity. That loss of strength which suffering as such inflicts on life is still further increased and multiplied by pity. Pity makes suffering contagious" (*Portable Nietzsche*, 572–73).

part of the self, the weak part, and deny the strong side.[224] But everything good is the transformation of something new. Thus Christianity misjudges humankind and the world and is the deadly enemy of culture.[225]

Two different ways for theology to respond to this: (1) most emphatic rejection; (2) taking it seriously; much of it could also be said by Christianity, for example, the Overman [Übermensch] theory [is] identified with Christians (for example, by Friedrich Rittelmeyer; Martin's "doctrine of the new human person").[226] In any case [Christians] don't want to accept that Christianity is hostile to culture.[227] It is significant that both responses take for granted the synthesis [of Christianity and culture].

The great social decisions of the time forced people to reconsider. They saw that an economy operating by autonomous laws had produced terrible consequences, for the autonomous law of the economy is basically always the self-will of a social class.[228] In some way, socialism was recognized. But
188 it was (1) connected with the struggle against religion; (2) in revolution against the form of the state government. Both [i.e., religion and form of government] had to be defended by the church. It could appeal to property owners to be charitable, but the conditions remained the same. Hence the Inner Mission,[229] an attempt to combat the demands of autonomous law,

[224.] Ibid., aphorism 18: "The Christian conception of God—God as god of the sick, God as spider . . .—is one of the most corrupt conceptions of the divine ever attained on earth. . . . God—the formula for every slander against 'this world' [*Diesseits*], for every lie about the 'beyond' [*Jenseits*]! God—the deification of nothingness, the will to nothingness pronounced holy!" (*Portable Nietzsche*, 585–86).

[225.] Ibid., aphorism 6: "Life itself is to my mind the instinct for growth, for durability, for an accumulation of forces, for *power*: where the will to power is lacking there is decline. It is my contention that all the supreme values of mankind *lack* this will—that the values which are symptomatic of decline, *nihilistic* values, are lording it under the holiest names" (*Portable Nietzsche*, 572).

[226.] Cf. Rittelmeyer, *Friedrich Nietzsche und die Religion*, esp. lecture 4: "Nietzsches bleibende Bedeutung" (75–97); Martin, *Das Evangelium vom neuen Menschen*.

[227.] For Bonhoeffer's understanding of culture and Christianity, see his two lectures at the Barcelona congregation, "Jesus Christ and the Essence of Christianity" (1928; *DBWE* 10, 2/2) and "Basic Questions of a Christian Ethic" (1929; *DBWE* 10, 2/3).

[228.] See Tillich, *Religious Situation*, 110–11: "The fateful result of this whole situation is that men, particularly the masses, are impoverished spiritually for the sake of their service to the machine, that the mechanical production of the human mass takes place. . . . The mechanical mass and its instinctive movements are the terrible, destructive by-products of the demonic element in the capitalist spirit. . . . Spirit in the service of a rational management of things and an irresponsible spirit—these are the two consequences of the fact that capitalist society has sundered the reference of the spirit to the eternal" (110–11).

[229.] [The central office for the Protestant social ministries that arose during the late nineteenth century.—VB]

but [it] never [fights] on the front lines, only as the ambulance service. No one looked into the causes behind these victims. These operations on the symptoms even concealed the disease-causing agents. No connection with reality [was] achieved.

A. Stöcker[230] was the first to look deeper into these matters. Though loyal to the monarchy, he knew how to separate the concerns of socialism from the struggle against the state and religion. He understood the idea of rationalization [Durchrationalisieren].[231] Same meaning as public-spiritedness. From this stance [he] struggled fiercely against every kind of liberalism. [He] tried to give socialism a Christian ethical foundation, but for a monarchist [this was] a hopeless task from the beginning.

Fr. Naumann was the more modern [of the two]. He gave up the old attempt at synthesis;[232] *Briefe über Religion*, 1903 and 1907.[233] Being a Christian is obviously something other than what we all are. On the other hand, [with him we find] a challenge to complete obedience to the Sermon on the Mount. Naumann fails in his attempt to make these two views coalesce.[234]

---

[230.] For the following discussion, see Stoecker, "Sozialdemokratisch, Sozialistisch und Christlich-sozial," and "Christlich-konservative Ziele für die Gegenwart." The concept of "rationalization" (*Durchrationalisieren*) refers here to the government support and organization that Stoecker promoted, particularly the forms of social organization such as protections for workers and social welfare legislation. [However, see also the following editorial note.—VB]

[231.] [While the student notes here read *Durchrationalisieren*, it is very likely that the reference is to Max Weber's theory of "rationalization." Stoecker and Weber were both involved in the Protestant Social Congress (which Stoecker founded), and Stoecker was influenced in some of his writings by Weber's thought. "Rationalization" simply referred to the historical movement that had culminated in the rational mastery of social problems and the development of social/political solutions.—VB]

[232.] Under the leadership of Friedrich Naumann, the "young" people in the Christian social welfare movement detached themselves from the conservatives, who remained under Adolf Stoecker's leadership. In 1896, Naumann founded the National Social Welfare Society, which worked for a socially conscious and democratic reorganization of government and the economy and sought to win over workers for the state, the nation, and the "social welfare empire."

[233.] Refers to the 6th edition of this work (1917), which contained the afterword, "Nach 13 Jahren."

[234.] See Naumann, *Briefe über Religion*, 57–58, 62, 74. In these passages Naumann emphasizes the impossibility of consistently christianizing all of life, especially the difference between Jesus's ethic of love and the principles of capitalist business. "A theoretically pure Christian is not possible in this world" (74). Cf. also Bonhoeffer's 1929 observations on this problem in "Basic Questions of a Christian Ethic" (*DBWE* 10:374–75). Winterhager: "Church social agencies provide service to the victims of the way society is set up; but society itself [is] considered inviolable, so there is no combating the roots

189 This means that Christian ethics consciously capitulates to the autonomous law of the world, while seeing that this law is demonic. The path to God leads through the idols. Here[235] we also find Ibsen, Strindberg, and the Impressionists.

Naumann's thought goes as far as the total yawning gap, but he does not draw the final conclusion; he insists again on synthesis. Christians can live as Christians in this world if they submit to their fate of being under two masters. But how can we really lead a personal life that is not built on our working life? There is no longer any point at which one could be a Christian, not even in our most personal lives. This is what Naumann could not admit, nor Troeltsch either, in "Grundprobleme der christlichen Ethik."[236] In former times, the structures that were present [were] sanctioned as willed by God; now [there are] new forms, and thus new solution[s] to the ethical problem: uncoupling the immanent purposes of culture from those beyond this world; the one is not reducible to the other. Morality consists of many contradictory purposes, and the balance among them remains a problem.[237] [There remains the] deep insight that any
190 preemptive solution is wrong. But if the decisive issue is that moral purposes are standardized through action, then obviously morality as such is no longer self-contradictory; it is decided by one act in favor of a single solution. Cultural life should also be worship and as such should transfigure the world.[238]

---

of the evil. Naumann was the first to see how demonic the fallen creation is; Stoecker is too deeply rooted in bourgeois society." Dudzus (*GS* 5:212): "In attempting to translate it into a socially concerned life, Naumann fails."

[235.] I.e., among those who have recognized this problem.

[236.] [Troeltsch, "Grundprobleme der Ethik."—MBL]

[237.] Winterhager: "Troeltsch ('Grundprobleme der Ethik,' 1901) comes to conclusions similar to those of Naumann. Ethics is a matter of compromises (among the many divisions of morality's aims). Thus only decisions based on autonomous law (with regard to the possibility of carrying them out) [can be made], and no Christian decisions (based on obedience overall)." Troeltsch, in "Grundprobleme der Ethik," 658, defines the "many divisions" among the purposes of morality more closely as the "polarity of religious and human morality" that is inherent in human nature. For any Christian ethics, this would imply that moral purposes now have to be "standardized" under the dominance of Christian morality's highest goal. Because human moral goals are irreducibly defined as ends in themselves, Christian ethics necessarily takes the form of a compromise. However, Troeltsch does not draw the conclusion from this state of affairs that only decisions from autonomous law and no Christian ethical decisions exist, as formulated in Winterhager's notes. Instead, it is precisely Christian ethics that Troeltsch regards as the morally highest form of mediation between immanent and transcendent ethical goals.

[238.] Dudzus (*GS* 5:213) interprets as follows: "But if he says he has found unity among moral purposes in the actions of an ethical person, then morality as such is obviously not self-contradictory. Thus, through the medium of the person who acts, he can

We must reject this solution. Both Christian ethics and humane ethics exist; it is a matter of compromise. There is a great deal of truth here; only we draw another consequence from it: for can we really no longer be Christians if there is a clear distinction between Christian and humane purposes? Where does the humane aim end and the Christian aim begin? I would have reserved for myself the decision as to when I could take a Christian action and when a worldly action, where it seems possible to me to carry out such. Since one is a Christian only when totally obedient, it becomes impossible to speak of a human person being a Christian at all. Troeltsch and Naumann did not draw this conclusion because they both still saw morality as the highest human quality. The only possible solution would have been a new understanding of Christianity. Modern cultural ethics suppresses Christian ethics completely.

Wilhelm Herrmann[239] made a different attempt to save the situation, by asserting Kant's unconditional obligation in a purely formal way. The Sermon on the Mount [understood not] based on its content, but as an unconditional obligation. Autonomous ethics [is] thus released and made subordinate to Christian ethics. But what is the difference between being committed to Christ and being committed to the moral law of reason? This reestablishes the synthesis with culture; [the] result [is] the same as that of 191
Naumann and Troeltsch, only they see more of the reality.[240]

The "ethics" of the time proceed with greatly simplified schemes and also solve ethical problems right away, without allowing their weight to have an impact. (Seeberg,[241] Schlatter,[242] etc.) naive, hasty solution; the ultimate reason for it [is] not knowing what to do with the problem of autonomy and with the heteronomy of Christianity. Question of the relationship between the orders of creation and of redemption. But this question cannot [be] resolved if understood ethically. The essential function of Christianity is to represent the bond holding together the cultural heritage of the age.

---

declare cultural life to be worship of God and assign this worship the task of transfiguring the world."

[239.] On the following, see Herrmann's *Ethik*, esp. 44–52 (§11 "Das sittliche Gesetz") and 153–70 (§ 24 "Das sittliche Gesetz nach der Auslegung Jesu Christi"), also his *Die sittliche Weisungen Jesu*.

[240.] Winterhager: "Wilhelm Herrmann proposes a formal ethic, very closely related to Kant. Does not know what to do with the autonomy of culture or with the relationship between the orders of creation and redemption. People feared the breaking up of their cultural heritage. People considered it the task of Christianity to be the bond holding together the cultural heritage of their time."

[241.] Seeberg, *System der Ethik im Grundriss dargestellt*.

[242.] Schlatter, *Die christliche Ethik*.

Connection to the culture of personality by Harnack and Troeltsch. Under their influence and that of Nietzsche is Johannes Müller:[243] the modern ideal of the personality should be christianized.[244] To become [fully] human is the goal of humankind and can be realized by those who look to the cross of Christ. In the end, Jesus is only the deepening and the
192 justification of the modern ideal.[245] But the Christian idea of the person is something totally different from the modern [idea of] personality. Lhotzky's work [follows] a similar line.[246]

No synthesis can be reached by appealing either to socialism or to the culture of personality.

(Last chapter of Troeltsch's *Social Teaching.*)[247] The masses of the proletariat speak quite a different language from that of the Nazarene bringing them the gospel under sunny skies. But he must be there, only where and how? Here the question of Troeltsch and Naumann disintegrates. But they get the credit for asking it in the way they did. [They represent] the pinnacle and the turning point of theology at the turn of the century.

*§ 10 The turning point*

In all three areas (the problems of knowledge, history, and ethics), there was the issue of balance with culture. In all three [there is] the same structure; culture should not be confronted with a claim that is unsustainable.[248]

[243.] Müller, *Das Urgeheimnis*, 98–99: "The elementary action of God . . . the unconditional, unceasing, unshakable and irrepressible life force . . . that governs everything that has being, is the divine will to life. We experience it in the two strongest drives that human beings know, the drive to self-preservation and the sex drive, one preserving the individual and the other the race."

[244.] Such statements could not be found in direct form in Müller's work. Bonhoeffer must mean here the high value that individual self-assertion had for Müller, even in the religious domain. Cf. Müller's *Hemmungen des Lebens*, 38: "On the other hand, your severe physical suffering is not a hindrance, from the moment when you are willing to accept it and bear it heroically. Receive it from the hand of God, and regard yourself as having been blessed with a heavy task."

[245.] Ibid., 24–25: "It is my most sacred duty to wrestle with the powers of darkness and give proof of the greatest heroism to which a human being can be called. For it is this development of the power to overcome in one's personal life from which the redemption of the world will arise. Christ carried the sin of the world because he was able to do so."

[246.] Lhotzky, *Religion oder Reich Gottes.*

[247.] Troeltsch, *Social Teaching of the Christian Churches.* In what follows, Bonhoeffer is referring not to the last chapter (chap. 3) [i.e., the entire second volume of the English translation constitutes chap. 3, dealing with Protestantism—MBL] but to the conclusion of the treatise [titled "Developments in Christian Social Doctrine since the Eighteenth Century"—MBL] (991–1013).

[248.] Dudzus (*GS* 5:215) adds: "In the last decades of the nineteenth century, theology was concerned to stay in balance with culture in all important areas; epistemology,

In the first decade [there were] more and more [thinkers] whose attempts to fit things together broke apart. It began with the tragic philosophies of Dilthey, Troeltsch, Simmel; there was no sense of anything beyond the historical.[249] Resistance to metaphysics [is characteristic], most of 193
all in Max Weber's case.[250] Incredible objectivity, that is all theology can learn from him. Max Scheler: the realm of values and the realm of being fall apart so thoroughly that nothing remains [for the realm of being] but a system of bestial humanity[251] (*Man's Place in Nature*).[252]

The attempt at objectivity is also part of the development at the turn of the century, but without revolutionary power. Ethos of restrained objectivity that classifies things but also [has] an inkling that the autonomous culture is breaking down. Still seen as a unity in the 1890s, the culture itself began to show cracks. But it was more exploding than breaking down, each area standing out against the other. Countless separate units emerged side by side. In the process, the church received its last gift of grace from the culture: its independence. For Dibelius, the church [is] definitely a gift from the culture; it values its connection to the culture like every other area.[253] The church's program is no different from the programs of the turn of the century. It would be completely wrong [to assert] that the church's specific 194

the problem of history, and ethics. One took care not to expect more of culture and society than they could bear."

[249.] Winterhager: "Religious epistemology with the help of the Kantian system. In the face of this epistemology, Christianity had to prove itself socially acceptable. [This means] justification before a forum that was not competent in theology. Historical-liberal theology makes Christianity dependent on a contemporary religious need."

[250.] Weber, "Science as a Vocation": "All scientific work presupposes that the rules of logic and method are valid; these are the general foundations of our orientation in the world," and "redemption from the rationalism and intellectualism of science is the fundamental presupposition of living in union with the divine" (142–43).

[251.] For the refutation of Scheler's view, see Bonhoeffer's inaugural lecture, "The Anthropological Question in Contemporary Philosophy and Theology," *DBWE* 10, 2/7. [See also the discussion of Scheler in *Act and Being* (*DBWE* 2:64–67).—MBL]

[252.] Winterhager: "Max Scheler: the realm of being raised up into the realm of values.—In *Man's Place in Nature*, he arrives, by way of Plato and Thomas Aquinas, at the stance of Dilthey's tragic philosophy."

[253.] Dibelius, *Das Jahrhundert der Kirche*, 223–24: "A Protestant church needs a confession of faith. But it also needs a clear and definite cultural program. It is supposed to preach the gospel—but a gospel intended to be effective in the life of the world. . . . He [Luther] gave his advice on married life as well as on political and economic life. And behind all of this stood a simple but clear and definite cultural program founded on the gospel!" Winterhager: "Many organizations acquire their independence from the breakup of cultural unity. Such a gift of grace is also received by the church. Its structure is like the structure of other cultural institutions of our time; it [the church] teaches us to stay connected with the culture; here there was no turning point."

nature was being given expression today,[254] that the church leadership [represented] a church perhaps parallel to Barthian theology! The church today does not see itself as fundamentally different from what it was thirty years ago; there [has been] no turning point here.

During the world war the process had to go through its catastrophe, through the crisis of culture itself. To see the power of fate amid the ruins could mean the turning point; being uprooted from the world of harmonious finitude into God's transcendence could be the turning point. But here[255] [we are] talking about another turning point. Critical theology is not to be explained by the breakdown of war; that is the most foolish impertinence and ignorance! We refuse to give in to the amateurish spirit that turns up its nose, we protest!

Even before the war there were flickering signs of the turning point, and during the war: Overbeck, Kutter, Blumhardt.[256] The war only completed the bankruptcy of the culture. Barth too [was] among those for whom the experience of the war was decisive. Hopefully this will be true of every theologian. However, Barth's message does not come from [that experience], nor from the cultural problems, but rather from a new reading of the Bible, a new way of seeing humankind from God's perspective,[257] from the most positive and the most negative, from God's own word spoken in God's revelation.[258] With the cross as starting point, he fundamentally surmounts the question of the relation of religion and culture, which is still at the basis of Tillich's work, for example.[259] The issue is that of God and humankind;
195 culture merely takes its place on the side of humankind and of religion. To the extent that Barth no longer wants to confuse religion with God, this

[254.] I.e., after the state church had been dissolved. [The Weimar Constitution of 1919 established the principle of separation of church and state. In the prior arrangement, the Protestant *Landeskirchen* held the established status of state churches, with close official recognition and administrative privilege.—MBL]

[255.] I.e., in dialectical theology.

[256.] Refers to Christoph Blumhardt the younger (1842–1919).

[257.] [Barth would write of that time: "What expressions we used—in part taken over and in part newly invented!—above all, the famous 'wholly other' breaking in upon us 'perpendicularly from above,' the not less famous 'infinite qualitative distinction' between God and man, the vacuum, the mathematical point, and the tangent in which alone they must meet" (*Humanity of God*, 42).—MBL]

[258.] See Barth, *Church Dogmatics*, I/1, 117: "The decisive content of these statements, the positive thing they state and the evident negations by which this is surrounded, the relation in which the statements are true, is their relation to *revelation*. But revelation is simply the freedom of God's grace."

[259.] Cf. also Bonhoeffer's 1930 inaugural lecture, "The Anthropological Question in Contemporary Philosophy and Theology" (*DBWE* 10, 2/7, esp. 397–98).

indicates that the turning point has been reached; it is not psychosis resulting from war but rather listening to God's word.

Barth [comes] not from the trenches but rather from the pulpit of a Swiss village church. This means everything for his understanding. The struggle here is no less decisive than that of the war; it is a fight between God and the devil; the pulpit is the strangest place in the world. Barth's theology comes from preaching; this is his only concern. But what does it mean to preach rightly? It means to speak the very word of God.[260] Where does this terrible "as if" come from?[261] But it should come to the speaking of God. I am to speak, yet it is not I, but God—I have to confess that I am not capable of it.[262] Thus I can do nothing but speak about God, in the knowledge that it is God who must speak; I can only wait and pray for this.[263]

Talking about God is a different thing from speaking from God.[264] 196
[These are] two different spheres. Our preaching may be boring, or may not be; what happens in church is what has to happen there; otherwise nothing happens in church. It is God who must speak on Sundays at ten

---

[260.] Barth, *Die christliche Dogmatik*, 38: "So the church believes in that it dares in the sermon to preach presence, event, deed. . . . But just this: *God's* presence, event of *his* acting, *his* deed. . . . His self-proclamation is not only first on the plan, rather also last."

[261.] Ibid., 92: "But how we arrive at the point where we count on it [the reality of the word of God] as we would a necessary precondition, not merely as a logical postulate, not merely as a Vaihinger-style 'as if,' but rather as a reality that is the measure and norm of the given reality of Christian speech, which therefore is the essential subject of Christian dogmatics" [Barth is referring to the philosopher Hans Vaihinger and his work *The Philosophy of "As-If."*—VB]

[262.] Bonhoeffer emphasizes more strongly than Barth the problems in the epistemology around speaking of God. The relation between speaking of God as such and God as the object of speech, which only God makes possible, Bonhoeffer always sees from the viewpoint of the speaker (on this problem, cf. also Bonhoeffer's introductory remarks on "God" in §11 of this course, p. 229.

[263.] Winterhager: "Overbeck, Kutter prepared for the bankruptcy of the so-called highest cultural values; the turning point came after the war. A new view of humankind's proportions; this view appears strange at first, because [it is a view] in light of the Bible. Karl Barth's message finds its footing under the long-abandoned sign of the cross. God (completely revealed in Christ) and humankind, not religion and culture. Religion [is] no longer confused with God. Listening to God's word, not psychosis resulting from war. Barth comes not from the trenches but from the pulpit of a little Swiss village church. Barth's theology comes from preaching. The contradiction [lies in the fact] that it is God's word that should be preached, although only the word of a human being can be preached. The turning point comes from the pulpit. The word has a concrete content, God's action in and through Christ, that makes it different from talking about the transcendent. Secularity means that the creation is in need of redemption."

[264.] [This is a key distinction in Bonhoeffer's understanding of preaching, a difference in the source from which the preached word comes, i.e., not a human word *about* God but the word *from* God through the act of preaching.—MBL]

o'clock if anything is to happen at all, [no matter] whether the sermon is stupid or wise. My words [are] like the spokes of a wheel; the hole in the middle stays empty. Where God comes, human beings know that terrifying things happen. It is so easy for our words to cover up God's word. Troeltsch and others saw that, but it didn't disturb them: there was no other way [in their view, only speech about God is possible].

We can also speak of "humankind" in another sense, as for instance Tillich did. New life in nature, community, rediscovery of transcendence, etc.[265] But there are very different ways of speaking of transcendence. A great deal of mischief [has been] done with this word as found in Barth. What does he mean by it? [It is about] the humiliation of the human being who is supposed to speak the word of God but only talks about God. Human beings do not have God at their disposal. But the word [is] bound to the past act [Tun] of God (of Christ).[266] For Tillich and the youth movement, transcendence means broadening one's perspectives;[267] for Barth, stand-
197 ing in the decision, the God who is to come in contrast to the God who is there. God [is] not far away and not near, but rather is the One who is to come.

So this turning point is not a general historical event but rather something eminently taking place in theology. There is really a desire again to "speak rightly of God."

---

[265.] See Tillich, "The Protestant Message and the Man of Today," in *Protestant Era*, 202–3: "Protestantism must witness to the 'New Being' through which alone it is able to say its word in power, and it must do this without making this witness again the basis of a wrong security. The New Being, which for Christian faith is manifest in Jesus as the Christ, is effective in the life of the individual personality as well as in the life of the community, and it is not even excluded from nature. . . . Protestantism can be open for everything, religious and secular, past and future, individual and social. All these differences are transcended through the power of the New Being, which works in all of them, breaking through their exclusiveness and separation."

[266.] Barth, *Church Dogmatics*, I/1:118: "Precisely in view of revelation, or on the basis of it, one may thus say of proclamation and the Bible that they *are* God's Word, that they continually *become* God's Word" by subordinating themselves; under the revelation, the act of divine freedom, which is the ground and the limit of the Bible and the church's preaching. [See also *DBWE* 2:90.—VB]

[267.] According to Bonhoeffer, neither overcoming the monadic idea of the bourgeois personality within the masses nor creating a community based on shared experiences is adequate as the foundation of the church, "which is simultaneously a historical community and one established by God" (*Sanctorum Communio, DBWE* 1:126; see also 280–81).

*§ 11 God*

Barth would protest that this [is] not the way[268] to introduce a theology. He would say that, for him, this is only a marginal comment with the aim of speaking only of God. Nevertheless, we do not misunderstand Barth if we spell the word "God" in a new way, if we remove it from edifying speech, because it is not at all self-evident. One acts as if one is sure of all that and goes on to peripheral matters. But one can never assume a God of mercy and judgment; one can only reach out toward such a God![269] Whoever talks in that way is not speaking of God, as much as he may say he is. If God stands behind someone, that person now has other concerns.[270] But God is not only the One who did come but also the One who comes again and again, and is only wholly the First through also being the Last. Who knows that God is merciful, if he or she does not know it now! Who knows that God judges, if not [the person] whose sin has just been forgiven today! God's truth [is] never general truth but rather always new truth.[271]

The meaning [of this] for human religious life: There can be no point in human life when we can speak of God as our possession. Barth opposes religion in the name of God. (Line: from OT—Luther—Kierkegaard.) A 198
struggle against religion that exists to cater to humankind. There is no such thing as spiritual recovery by religion, but only becoming ill through God. [Religion is] always [in] danger of thinking it has God, knows about God, even humbly and modestly. Religion then becomes one area among others, possibly as the basis, but still only one among others. With this as the starting point, the central issue becomes that of religion and culture. God is then not allowed to speak in God's own voice. That God also judges

[268.] According to Barth, a theology cannot begin by defining the concept "God" because that would mean taking up God like any other object, and not as the all-embracing, self-defining unity of definition and being-defined.

[269.] [The German here has a play on words (*nicht davon ausgehen, sondern nur dahin [gehen]*), i.e., that one cannot assume (or use as one's point of departure) God's mercy, but go toward it.—VB]

[270.] [The German phrase here is *im Rücken stehen,* that is, to stand behind someone's back to support him or her. Bonhoeffer used this metaphor in *Act and Being* in his critique about defining God as the subject of one's existence and theological thinking rather than as "the creator and lord of both" (*DBWE* 2:125).—MBL]

[271.] Winterhager: "[Talk about God has] been released from the matter-of-factness of our vocabulary. Who knows that God is merciful, except one who has experienced it today? God's truth is not [a] general, ever-present, always ready to be applied truth, but rather a living truth that is always to come. [It is] in a struggle against human religion to the extent that it allows the human spiritual heritage to be grasped firmly, to the extent that it allows the harmony of humankind. Religion is in reality only the imprint of the seal (image from K. Barth)."

religion, and passes over pious actions, is an attack on the whole person.[272] The issue of God is ever and again [one] that is open for human beings. The space that is open to God remains open to the end of time. The future is still to be awaited. Humankind is still oriented to God and to the word of God.

These [are] all conclusions to be drawn from the freedom of God. They say the decisive word: God remains Lord. [This is] the epitome of an act ex nihilo,[273] [a] predestination and rejection that can no longer be accounted for: eternal beginning, not something that continues.[274] God is always the One who is to come; that is God's transcendence. One can only have God by expecting God. Instead of beginning with religion, theology should begin by speaking from the word of God.

It appears that this idea of God arose from philosophical speculation. This God cannot be arrived at by any kind of thinking; this would be another way of accounting for God.[275] God must be the One who says, "I am the absolute beginning." We know about God only when God is the One who speaks. This is not a concept of revelation postulated after the fact; only from the revelation itself do we know God as the absolute beginning
199 of self-revelation in Jesus Christ, in a generally understandable way. This word is really God's as such, wholly free, but at the same time shrouded in the garment of history, in humanity. God is indeed something entirely different from humankind, but when God speaks, the speech is veiled; my hearing is shrouded by religion. Faith is not something supernatural but rather [takes place] in the forms of the physical, but [it is] only faith to the extent that God judges and has mercy upon it. To the question of why, there is only [this answer]: Look upon and listen to the Word, Christ, preaching. We would know nothing about God if God did not come in this way. That God comes in such a way is the mystery of God. Every attempt to account for this would mean that God is not absolutely free after all. There can no longer be any general accounting given by religion, unless we are trying to

[272.] Winterhager: "God continually judges human actions (especially religious actions) and, beyond this, ever and again acknowledges the whole person."

[273.] God's creating "out of nothing" is the central concept of the Christian doctrine of creation.

[274.] In the name of God's absolute freedom, Bonhoeffer opposes the idea of the *conservatio* (God's "sustaining" the world) as *creatio continua* ("constant creation" of the world).

[275.] Bonhoeffer dealt more thoroughly with the difference between philosophical knowledge of God and that of Barthian theology in his 1930 inaugural lecture, "The Anthropological Question in Contemporary Philosophy and Theology" (*DBWE* 10, 2/7, esp. 399–402).

go back behind God. We should begin with God's own beginning set for us. Nobody knows that in advance; we must each receive it as told to us; God's word [is] the absolute *petitio principii.*[276] *Deus dixit*[277]—to accept this is the beginning of all genuine theological thinking, to allow space for the freedom of the living God.

*§ 12 The Word of God and Theology*[278]

Theology may not, at any price, be confused with the philosophy of religion or with the doctrine of faith [Glaubenslehre].[279] In the philosophy of religion, reasons must be given for that which theology takes as its object, because this means giving evidence for the truth. But the object of theology [may] only be the *logos theou,*[280] the act of God, which is its own reason for being. Human beings cannot go back behind this beginning. Theology no longer has to ground its truth outside itself in another discipline, but must proceed from its own basis, its own presuppositions. [Is theology] a positive science, which accepts its object[281] like biology? To a certain degree 200
this is true. But the objects of study for the other branches of knowledge can be accounted for by general considerations that precede them, and mathematical axioms could be false. In theology, however, truth itself is the object; [it has] no foundation in general knowledge; it begins with a proof of God established by the word of God, which is its own proof,[282] but this

[276.] Literally, "assuming the initial point," colloquially "begging the question," i.e., assuming at the beginning of a discussion the thing that has to be proved. Scholarly arguments use this to indicate a faulty process of proof in which that which is to be proved is already included in the premise. Barth and Bonhoeffer turn this to positive use, for if God has no relation to anything outside, that is, if God represents all of reality, then theology can only move within this circle (cf. Barth, *Die christliche Dogmatik,* 106–7).

[277.] "God has spoken." [*Deus dixit* is the formula through which Barth explores revelation in his dogmatics.—MBL]

[278.] See the collection of Karl Barth's essays with this title including the title essay "Das Wort Gottes als Aufgabe der Theologie," translated as "The Word of God and the Task of the Ministry" and published in Barth, *The Word of God and the Word of Man,* 183–217.

[279.] [See Barth, *Word of God,* 186–98, for the context etc. for the context and framing critique, which Barth and those influenced by him, including Bonhoeffer, regarded as descriptive of most nineteenth-century Protestant theology in Germany from Schleiermacher onward.—MBL]

[280.] "Word of God."

[281.] ["Object" here in the sense of subject matter.—MBL]

[282.] Dudzus (*GS* 5:220) interprets as follows: "Only that the objects studied by other branches of knowledge can be attributed to, and therefore accounted for, by general considerations that precede them. In theology, however, the object is the truth itself. The truth does not precede the object as a basis in general knowledge. It begins with a 'proof of God' established by the word of God, which is its own proof."

is a real proof for the truth, a *petitio principii*[283] that cannot be abolished. It begins with an act of recognition. The only possibilities are rejection or acknowledgment, and neither can be accounted for. So also in theology, in the beginning is faith. This does not mean that a theologian must be a believer; we cannot distinguish between converted and unconverted theologians. The *logos theou* demands to be believed; only where one still believes at all does theology make any sense.

Theology: as a doctrine of faith [Glaubenslehre]? "God and faith belong together" (Luther).[284] So theology is to be traced in the consciousness of a believer? (E. Schaeder, *Das Geistproblem*, 1920). The subject that speaks in the word of God is always God, [but this is] not to be turned into thinking of God as an object.[285] We can believe the word of God, but only in such a way as to leave God fully as subject. It is not possible to go backward from faith to God. The doctrine of faith [Glaubenslehre] always makes God an object.

There is another immanent critique to be directed at the theology of consciousness of faith [Glaubensbewußtsein]. I am always looking for
201 something that I already know beforehand. Isn't this examination of consciousness a deceptive maneuver, putting on an act in the marketplace of knowledge? When philosophy sees through this performance, there is bound to be laughter. It is better to admit openly that we are defenseless (contrary to Schaeder[286] and also Althaus).[287] Only when our essential

[283.] See ed. note 276.

[284.] Martin Luther, "Der große Katechismus. Der erste Teil: Die Zehn Gebote Gottes," 1529 (*WA* 30/1:123–238, 133).

[285.] Dudzus (*GS* 5:220) interprets as follows: "In this process, God is never to be transformed into an object."

[286.] Bonhoeffer is referring to Schaeder, *Das Geistproblem der Theologie*. For Schaeder, the starting point for the recognition of divine spirit and the reality of God is the human experience of faith (ibid., 52–55), in which "our starting from a finite consciousness is completely accounted for by the fact that God or the Spirit of God is never, and in no context, at our mercy as an object of study without this being God's will. We can only reach God in such a way as God reaches us, that is, because of God's self-revelation to us, which takes place, at least in its final form, in our consciousness, in order to be considered a revelation" (62–63).

[287.] Here Bonhoeffer is referring to Paul Althaus's doctrine of the "original revelation" (in his *Grundriss der Dogmatik*, 1:8–47), which deals critically with the abstract concept of God and the Christ-centered concept of revelation of dialectical theology (cf. also his "Theologie und Geschichte"). The "original revelation" as God's self-demonstration in humankind's experience of itself, in nature and history, in human consciousness of truth and in theoretical and practical reason, satisfies a condition, one that differs from a natural theology, for general recognition of salvation history's revelation of God in Christ.

weakness is ruthlessly uncovered are we pointing to the power of the word of God, like the boy David against the Goliaths of the other academic disciplines.

Only when God as subject consents to become the object of theology can any theology be done. God is entirely free to decide whether to be known and to be sought by us. Thus no philosophy of religion can be the starting point; true theology begins with *veni creator spiritus*[288] (Anselm, Kierkegaard). To know is to acknowledge, to think [is to] reflect [Nachdenken].[289] Seeking and finding God means being sought and found by God. 202
Theology begins with the *petitio principii.*[290]

How does theology account for this unique state of affairs? The only appropriate form of speech [for theology is] dialectical speech. The word of God exists only in shrouded form, appears to have become an object like Jesus Christ, the Holy Scriptures, and preaching. The historicity [Geschichtlichkeit] of God's word is its objectivity. The divinity of God's word is its nonobjectivity. From God's viewpoint, of course, the word is one; from ours, we always see it in this double character. I speak of God's revelation, though I ought to say that this is not revelation; I say Jesus and must say Christ, and vice versa, etc. Dialectics aims to defend the freedom of God and the mystery of pre[destination]. We may speak of God never along one line only but [always and only] in thesis and antithesis.[291] But even this invention [of dialectics is] not a way of capturing God after all. Genuine dialectics places thesis and antithesis over against each other, but the truth [remains] somewhere beyond, in the unintuitable middle. God is still free and above even dialectics.

[Is] Barth's theology one among the many that come and go? Barth does not insist that God be defined by his theology; on the contrary, he insists

[288.] "Come, Creator Spirit" ("Komm Schöpfer des Geistes"), the Pentecost hymn attributed to Hrabanus Maurus, although there is some debate about his authorship. See the conditions for communion with God: "'In the mind's eye' one persistently prays: come creator spirit! And doesn't turn that into an indicative or perfect tense, precisely because one recognizes nothing but the indicative and perfect in *God.* But never, ever in one*self*!" [The *DBW* edition cites Barth, *Kirchliche Dogmatik* I/1:208, as the source for this quotation, which does not appear there; it is unclear where it does appear.—VB] Cf. also the collection of sermons by Barth and by Eduard Thurneysen, *Come Holy Spirit!* Moreover, Adolf von Harnack's tombstone bears the inscription *veni creator spiritus* (Zahn-Harnack, *Adolf von Harnack,* 566).

[289.] [*Nachdenken,* here translated as "reflect," is to "think after" what has been given in revelation. It suggests the image of a mirror that only reflects an object after it has been put before the mirror.—MBL]

[290.] See ed. note 276.

[291.] [I.e., in thesis and antithesis, the two elements of the dialectical method.—VB]

much more that God is free of such definition. Barth makes use of the philosophical language of neo-Kantianism; he knows that all terminology acts as a lens.[292] The concept is never the thing itself. Thus he is not a neo-Kantian but a theologian. So [for him it is] essential to speak adequately of nonobjectivity. P. Natorp: *Praktische Philosophie*, 1925, related to Barth in his use of terminology, and to some extent in content. The nonobjective is the absolute origin and culmination. Thus God is Not-God, since God as a concept [has] often already become an object once again.[293] Atheism
203 from religion [appears to be] the end of neo-Kantianism. Perhaps Barth, in his *Epistle to the Romans*,[294] did not always see the danger of this proximity. But he begins with the concrete revelation; where Natorp and Tillich[295] say Not-God, he has to say Jesus Christ.

The object of theology [is] the word of God [as it appears] indirectly in the form of Christian speech in the church. The task of theology [is] the effort to speak rightly of God. Thus theology is completely the servant of the church. *Habitus practicus*[296]—most decidedly the enemy of all apolo-

[292.] Cf. ed. note 302.

[293.] See Natorp, *Vorlesungen über praktische Theologie*, 534–35: "Theo-*logy*, however, is a very questionable concept. God is not the topic of any sort of -ology. . . . If philosophy has something to say about God, then only if it says that, and why, it has nothing to say about God. The case is rather that even in making the latter statement, it is only saying something about itself, and especially here, only about its own limits, and that in no sense, positive or negative, does it have anything to do with God. So from beginning to end it is nothing more than teaching about categories."

[294.] As far as can be determined from Bonhoeffer's style in these lectures, he was using the 2nd edition of Karl Barth's *Epistle to the Romans*, published in 1922.

[295.] See Tillich, "Critical and Positive Paradox"; also Barth's reply, "The Paradoxical Nature of the 'Positive Paradox': Answers and Questions to Paul Tillich"; and Tillich's reply, "Answer to Karl Barth." Tillich's fundamental criticism of the dialectical theology of "crisis" concerns its "positive" and therefore undialectical "root" (Tillich, "Critical and Positive Paradox," 139). For a "proclamation of crisis" (135) presupposes recourse to a "unity of judgment and grace" (135) that is already given; this is seen by Barth and Gogarten as positively present in the historical event of the revelation of Christ, through which, according to Tillich, its own presupposition that "the imperceptible, non-objective character of faith" is broken (140). In this way the "theology of the critical paradox" becomes the "theology of the positive paradox" (141). Within the context of modern spiritual circumstances, this—according to Tillich: unavoidable and fundamental—"positive paradox" of theology can no longer be directly and completely identified with the traditional names of God and Jesus Christ: "For example, it is impossible for the one who is aware of this situation to speak of God as if this word could directly convey to him its essential richness. Therefore we must speak of the *unconditioned*" (Tillich, "Answer to Karl Barth," 156).

[296.] Literally, "habit gained through practice." [Bonhoeffer also understood *habitus* in terms of the metaphysical meaning it has in Catholic theology—as a metaphysical,

getics. Theology begins in the middle, without introduction. Brunner's thinking [is characterized] more and more by the will to explain himself: eristic.[297] [According to] Gogarten and Bultmann, Barth has his philosophy and has contaminated his theology,[298] not having [a] clear foundation 204
in philosophy; terminology must be clarified beforehand.[299] Of necessity Barth rejects this; he knows about his philosophy, but this is his way of being a human being, and as such he hears God's word. The quality of theology cannot depend on good philosophical terminology, which [is] a piece of pietistic perfectionism in the conception of academic work. Thus philosophy is only a technical aid. The mark of good theology [is] that it provokes good philosophers until their blood boils ([cf.] Luther's disputation).[300]

### *§ 13 Preaching*

What should we preach? This question has no clear answer, [for] if it did, it would be in our hands again. It is not the statement of something as being true but rather refers to something which is becoming true, has already become true. It is the proclamation of the spoken, and ever to be spoken anew, word in Christ.[301] The way to God for human beings has been

permanent quality. See his 1932 lecture on "Theological Anthropology" (*DBWE* 12, 2/2), particularly the section on "Christian Character," where he writes: "The *habitus* of Christian character distinguishes itself from that of individuality in that it is gained through practice." Cf. also his 1944 letter to Bethge, *DBWE* 8:312.—VB]

[297.] "Eristic" was the heading under which Emil Brunner presented his anthropological and ethically based approach to theology, which he developed in his 1929 programmatic essay, "Die andere Aufgabe der Theologie." Besides presenting the context for individual statements of faith, theology has a second, apologetic, and polemical task. As eristic, it must assert the biblical call to conversion over against humankind's nonreligious self-understanding (ibid., 260–61).

[298.] See Bultmann, "Karl Barth's *Epistle to the Romans* in Its Second Edition," 113: "What Barth says of the contrast of world and God is also largely applicable to the contrast of nature and intellectual life (culture). . . . It is not possible to do justice to the problem of culture by regarding it, as Barth does, simply as a product of nature. . . . The concept of world and man in the light of the dialectic opposition of No and Yes threatens to break down into transcendental philosophy."

[299.] Gogarten, "Karl Barths Dogmatik," 61: "The most striking thing [about Barth's dogmatics] is the lack of a foundation in the philosophy of religion." Gogarten criticizes Barth in general for his failure to clarify theological concepts, particularly the "theologically inadequate concept of 'human beings who find themselves in opposition to God and to themselves'" (ibid., 71; cf. 75, 77–78, and 80).

[300.] Martin Luther, *Disputatio de homine*, 1536 (*WA* 39/I:175–77); "Disputation concerning Man," *LW* 34:137–44. In forty theses, Luther debates the philosophical (theses 1–19) as opposed to the theological definition of the human being (theses 20–40).

[301.] Winterhager: "Not the statement of something as being true, but rather a reference to something that is becoming true. To speak of God's coming because God in

205 diverted once and for all by God's way toward humankind;[302] here is no Christian way to God either.[303] But our faith can always also be regarded as religion. This is how the word of God is veiled in that which is human. We can be free of this ambiguity only in the act of believing. God's way is judgment and mercy together as one. The word means quintessentially falling, [it is] impossible to pull oneself back. In the depth of his being he nevertheless discovers the divine spark. Against it comes, through the cross, the radical No of God, the word telling the person, you don't have any possibility to reach God.[304] As human beings, we must not make a work out of having heard this, or out of humility; this is the most dangerous form of arrogance to which church Christians are subject. Nietzsche saw through this; his critique of glorying in one's servitude[305] [is] often really a Christian critique.[306]

---

Christ has already come. Preaching only what has become true in Christ and what is the word of God, the truth of which is now renewed again and again through the Holy Spirit."

[302.] See Barth, "The Problem of Ethics Today," 181: "This is the reason that they [Paul and Luther] preached the forgiveness of sins as the fundamental answer to the ethical question. But note that forgiveness always takes the *way from God to man* and never otherwise. And note also that there is no other way to this way, but that the way itself is the way to this way. *I* am the way! *Our* ways lead elsewhere."

[303.] Winterhager: "There is only one way from God to humankind through Christ. This way is judgment and mercy and signifies the end of all human ways. The way to God for human beings is always the way of justification based on works."

[304.] [In other words, the divine spark is an illusion.—MBL]

[305.] This concept cannot be documented in the work of Nietzsche. Bonhoeffer is referring to his critique of decadence. See Nietzsche, *Antichrist*, aphorism 24: "Decadence is only a *means* for the type of man who demands power in Judaism and Christianity. . . : this type of man has a life interest in mankind *sick* and in so twisting the concepts of good and evil, true and false, as to imperil life and slander the world" (*Portable Nietzsche*, 593–94). [On the concept of servitude, see Nietzsche's critique of slave morality in *Toward a Genealogy of Morals*, e.g., the selection in *Portable Nietzsche*, 451–54.—MBL] In his 1929 lecture in Barcelona, "Basic Questions of a Christian Ethic," Bonhoeffer takes up the critique of Nietzsche and states that the "Overman [Übermensch] is not, as he imagined, the opposite of the Christian; without realizing it, Nietzsche imbued the Overman with many of the features of the free Christian" (*DBWE* 10:366–67). Cf. Gal. 5:1: "For freedom Christ has set us free. Stand firm, therefore, and do not submit again to the yoke of slavery."

[306.] Winterhager: "Kierkegaard's remark that the Pharisee and the tax collector have exchanged roles in the church of today; humility has become arrogance. Nietzsche's attacks on Christians' glorying in their servitude." Dudzus (*GS* 5:223) includes Winterhager's text and interprets as follows: "Here the most dangerous reversal is lurking. Kierkegaard points out that Pharisee and tax collector have exchanged roles in the church of today. Tax collectors have learned thoroughly to boast of their humility, but this arrogance is the more unbearable because it is perverse and false. Nietzsche, with

When a human being says Yes to the radical No, God's righteousness [Gerechtigkeit] is restored. God has taken back God's rights [Recht] and has received *satisfactio*.[307] Thus human beings receive their righteousness from God alone and are open to God; there are no issues remaining between them and God. In this relationship of obedience, God affirms human beings. People do not become worthy of mercy through total denial of themselves. Since Christ, the Yes is no longer grounded in the No, but the No is grounded in the Yes. We hear the Yes only in the No, but only because the Yes is there do we hear the No. 206

This is the essential difference from Tillich. It is at the boundaries of our existence that [according to Tillich], we experience the radical No; if we accept this boundary situation we find ourselves affirmed. In recognizing that we are sinners, in essence we already have the recognition of mercy.[308] This identification (Holl) must be broken; it means preemption, by our own power, of God's act of grace.[309] [God] is completely free, even above and beyond the recognition of sin.

When the No turns to a Yes, that is of course an act of God in complete
freedom and is not based on the No. It is God who must overcome God's 207
own No and become angry at God's own anger (Luther);[310] [this is] the reason for the cross. Christology is by nature bound up with the doctrine

his acid critique of many church Christians' glorying in their servitude, has done us a necessary and often truly Christian service."

[307.] "Satisfaction." [Technical term central to Anselm's doctrine of atonement (*Cur deus homo*, in 1098) according to which God's anger and justice is atoned for, or satisfied, by the gracious offering of the God-man in the sacrifice of the cross.—MBL]

[308.] This assertion not documented in Tillich's work. Bonhoeffer is presumably taking issue here with the concept of redemption, unspecific in a Christian sense, as the recognition of the "new Being." For Tillich, "Protestantism must witness to the 'New Being' through which alone it is able to say its word in power. . . . The New Being, which for Christian faith is manifest in Jesus as the Christ, is effective in the life of the individual personality as well as in the life of the community, and it is not even excluded from nature" ("The Protestant Message and the Man of Today," in *Protestant Era*, 204).

[309.] See Holl, *Die Rechtfertigungslehre im Lichte der Geschichte des Protestantismus*, 8: "This attitude of Luther's was already revolutionary with regard to the prevailing view. Something primal in him rises up against the Catholic view of basic religious concepts. . . . *For him, consciousness of guilt and communion with God*, which in the lives of Catholics can run parallel to each other, *are simply mutually exclusive*. . . . From the gospel he has learned to understand that it is God who makes it safe for human beings to stand in God's presence, a stance for which they would struggle in vain by their own power alone. For the forgiveness of sins that God gives is intended by God to establish an *enduring, firm* communion."

[310.] What Luther says about God's anger must be understood within the dialectic of *opus alienum* (alien work) [this means that it is done by God but differs from God's "proper work" of love; the editors thank Clifford Green and Christiane Tietz for this

of justification. In Christ, God gets serious with human beings about our dependence on *iustitia aliena*.[311] The human being still remains totally *peccator*,[312] and righteousness of the human being [is] quintessentially imputed.[313] Even faith is not a divinely determined human capacity but rather the expression of the most profound human passivity;[314] [it is] to be understood not as a psychic phenomenon but rather as the determination of human beings in their existence, which by itself is *mere passive*.[315] Here religious states and experiences are no longer taken into consideration; it is still *iustitia aliena*, even with regard to our Christianity.[316]

If justification is understood as receiving a share in a divine power, a Catholic tendency is introduced; [it can] not be thought of together with
208 psychological justification (Holl,[317] R. Seeberg).[318] Here again we

observation—MBL] and *opus proprium* (proper work), or of the law and the gospel; the wrath of God is *opus alienum* to God, since it is caused by human sin (Lectures on Genesis 1535–45, *WA* 42,356; *LW* 2:132–34 on Gen. 9:1, 2), since sin, by offending against the First Commandment, is an attack on God's divinity and thus provokes God's wrath, which is grounded in God's zeal for his divinity. ["There are reliable and excellent proofs that God no longer hates man but is kindly disposed toward him. . . . His compassion is more abundant because it is a part of God's nature, since wrath is truly God's alien work, in which He engages contrary to His nature, because He is forced into it by the wickedness of man" (*LW* 2:134).—MBL]. Through Christ's atoning death, the believer in Christ is no longer subject to the wrath of God (*WA* 28,117: sermon on John 17:6). Through faith, the "anger of God's discipline" is turned into the "anger of God's grace" (*WA* 3,69: Commentary on Psalm 6, *LW* 10:78–92); see also Luther's Lectures on Romans, 1515–16, Glosses (*WA* 56,196, *LW* 25:179; reference to Rom. 2:8). God's wrath as the "alien work" of God is understood in juxtaposition to God's love as God's proper work. Cf. also Althaus, *Theology of Martin Luther*, 169–78, esp. 169–73.

[311.] "Alien righteousness" [sometimes: "external righteousness"—MBL].

[312.] ["Sinner."]

[313.] ["Imputed" righteousness is not a quality that is possessed or something a person achieves, but is a juridical judgment passed upon him or her.—MBL]

[314.] ["Passivity" here means not inactivity but rather that one is the recipient, not the creator of grace.—MBL]

[315.] Latin *mere passive*, "purely suffering."

[316.] Winterhager: "God's No also negates every human No. But since Christ, the No is no longer the basis for the Yes. *No longer a logical dialectic, which deduces the Yes, but a real dialectic that hears the Yes in the No.* In knowledge of sin, one has the knowledge of grace. Human beings are dependent on *iustitia aliena (externa)*. We remain *peccator* [sinner]; there is no *gratia infusa* [infused grace], and no *habitus infusus* [received habit] is formed."

[317.] Holl, "Was hat die Rechtfertigungslehre dem modernen Menschen zu sagen?" 565–66: "Human beings cannot relinquish the desire to be personalities that have validity in God's eyes, because only then would they be free and live forever. Yet precisely there we feel repulsed and under the judgment of God, for even our innermost part, our best is sinful. There is no other way out of this dilemma than that to which the doctrine of justification points. It establishes a sovereign intervention by God."

encounter a *iustitia interna.*[319] Human beings exist only in being face-to-face with the crucified one. Where judgment is seen as having begun, even in part, I no longer see myself as the absolute *peccator.* Then Christ, through what he has done for me, has made himself superfluous; this is why, for Holl, the doctrines of justification and Christology are no longer the main focus.

Both these things are given fundamental significance by Barth. Preaching can be preaching only when it is preaching of Christ and his righteousness. Christ is completely present in history, but [this then] is qualified prehistory;[320] its qualification as such remains invisible. A historian sees only the Jewish rabbi, but he is seen as something [more] at the point where history is revealed as prehistory, that is at the same time a God event. Jesus on the cross is the *kyrios* [Lord]; in him the church-community sees the sentence of death and of judgment meted out to all flesh. Through the res- 209
urrection, God's righteousness in Christ [becomes] our righteousness. The Holy Spirit [is] not a dynamic principle through which this act of Christ is appropriated. For then the cross is made superfluous. The Holy Spirit allows human beings to believe and to hear that the righteousness of humankind lies entirely in Christ.

All that we say must remain Advent speech. Like the OT, the NT also [has the character of] promise; Christ alone [is] the world of Christmas. The human attitude is to be captivated by the future. This future [is] in every case Christ himself, as the absolute One who is outside us. The gospel [has an] essentially eschatological character.

---

[318.] Seeberg, *Dogmatik,* 1:138: "In this however the twofold experience, that we are a new creation in Christ and that through him we can also be certain of forgiveness for our evil, the confidence or hope arises that in future also, God will *give* us a new will and *forgive* us the old one." Winterhager: "[An] existential human passivity is required, but not a psychological passivity.—The Reformation calls it *mere passive* [pure suffering]. Christology and the doctrine of reconciliation become the focus."

[319.] An "inner righteousness," i.e., one that human beings can attain by their own powers.

[320.] Barth, *Die Christliche Dogmatik,* 230: "We characterize the Word becoming flesh, the revelation of God in Jesus Christ, as 'prehistorical event.' . . . *Revelation is prehistory.*" Cf. ibid., 233: "It is clear that 'prehistory' understood in this sense is not an academic historical term, but rather a theological, a dogmatic one"; and 239: "That revelation is more than eternal history is illustrated by the fact that it is a point in temporal history. That it is also more than temporal history is illustrated by the fact that it is not bound by the irreversible progression of temporal events, that the rest of history closes the circle around it as the center, even when distinguished as before and after. And this is the positive relationship of all history to prehistory: it can behave like the periphery to the center, like prophesy to fulfillment, like Advent to Christmas."

Between the first and the second edition, [Barth] made essential changes in his eschatology:[321] [in the 1st ed.], the visible coming of God into this world; [in the] second edition: only coming from time to time.[322]

210 *The problem of ethics, of obedience*

A human being remains totally *peccator* [sinner]; the works of the justified are never holy. The kingdom of God [is] not for us to build. Only when God says that God is pleased with this work, then it is a good work. The conscience is not the judge of what is good. To do well means to act at God's good pleasure.[323] In faith we are called to obedience, but in obeying we

[321.] The 1st ed. refers to *Die christliche Dogmatik*, the 2nd ed. to *Church Dogmatics* I/1 as a revision of the former. However, we have here a misinterpretation or a very abridged rendering of Karl Barth's argument, for even in *Die christliche Dogmatik* Barth has in mind the twofold character of revelation as historical and prehistorical fact, and this is retained in *Church Dogmatics*. In the latter, however, history and prehistory are weighed differently. See *Die christliche Dogmatik*, 46: "The word of God in its first original form or address, in which it was spoken in prehistory, immediately and exclusively within history but on the boundary of history, is God's word." See also *Church Dogmatics* I/1:117: "According to all that has been said revelation is originally and directly what the Bible and church proclamation are derivatively and indirectly, i.e., *God's Word*. We have said of church proclamation that it must continually become God's Word. . . . The reference of this 'continually,' of course, is not to human experience. . . . The reference is to the freedom of God's grace. . . . But this cannot be said about revelation. When we speak about revelation we are confronted by the divine act itself." See also *Church Dogmatics* I/1:118: "One may thus say of proclamation and the Bible that they *are* God's Word, that they continually *become* God's Word." [It should be noted here that Andreas Pangritz has shown that this source reference is very probably wrong; he argues convincingly that the text to which Bonhoeffer refers is the 1st and 2nd ed. of Barth's commentary on Romans; see Pangritz, "Vom 'sichtbaren Kommen Gottes auf diese Welt.'"—MBL]

[322.] Winterhager: "Christ has been [here] and will come again. The New Testament too was only a harbinger (an *Advent* one) and a promise. In the Christmas world there is only Christ. To preach a sermon is to come from the future, to be captivated by that which is coming upon us from the future. [Church] activities (missions, etc.) often preempt the future, which belongs to God alone. A human being is not half *iustus*, half *peccator*, but rather entirely both. This threatens morality. We have to speak of humans being godless even in their greatest accomplishments, and of their being close to God, even the godless. [According to information from the Karl-Barth Archiv provided by Christiane Tietz, the reference here is to Barth's text "Verheißung, Zeit-Erfüllung" in which Barth contrasts the bourgeois Christmas tradition with what Christmas really means; Christ alone is the Christmas world, not some special place created to celebrate Christmas.—MBL]

[323.] Cf. Barth, *Ethics*, 79: "The same misunderstanding obtains where *conscience* is made the court which man must obey or not obey in moral decision. Conscience is the totality of our self-consciousness inasmuch as it can be the recipient and published of the command that comes to us."

are always in need of forgiveness. Obedience [is] thus our sacrifice to God, and God remains fully free to accept it or reject it.

Naumann: Human beings first serve themselves as human beings, and then [beyond that] are Christians.[324] Barth: [the human being] is first of all a human being, and not a Christian at all. But because [he experiences] forgiveness of sins, that is what makes [him] a Christian. Does this mean morality is threatened? Yes, it must be, to the extent that it is a morality that does not think it needs to put itself at the mercy of God.[325] God says of godless persons whatever God wills. But those who know that they are dependent on the Christ who is to come bow in obedience, as if pointing out their own weakness in the faith, so that in their weakness Christ may give his power its full sway.

### *§ 14 Where do we stand?* 211

The clichés about Barth have been consciously avoided. This is a theology that seeks to understand completely the *sola fide*[326] and therefore speaks from [the viewpoint] of predestination, and therefore dialectically. There are questions to be asked of this approach. In all of recent literature no one is seriously the equal of Barth.

(1) To understand the *sola fide* requires the concept of God's radical freedom. Barth's term "from time to time [je und je]"[327] (does justice to this concept). Only this is an adequate way to speak of grace. By nature God

[324.] The sentence "Human beings first serve themselves as human beings" probably refers to Naumann's view that one must first assure the continuation of one's own existence as the condition for putting the Christian ethos into practice. "In short, I know that all of us need, in order to go on living, to have as the basis of our existence a grasp of nature's requirements for the struggle for life, and that only on this basis do we have the freedom to put into practice the higher morality of the gospel, to the extent that this basis makes it at all possible" (Naumann, *Briefe über Religion*, 75).

[325.] In his lectures, Bonhoeffer seems to have been guided less by Karl Barth's lectures on ethics, in which the pragmatic issues of life are secondary to the debate with philosophy and liberal theology, than by the 2nd ed. of Barth's *Epistle to the Romans* (1922), 430: "In point of fact, it is grace alone that is competent to provide men with a truly ethical disturbance; and if grace is to perform this function, it must be treated as covering the whole field of human life, and must be permitted to make that absolute assault upon men without which ethics are completely meaningless." [See ed. note 294.—MBL]

[326.] "Through faith alone."

[327.] See *Church Dogmatics* I/1:117; cf. above ed. note 321. [By translating "je und je" with "continually," the English edition of *Church Dogmatics* loses the eventful character of the German; a better rendering would be "ever and again" or "from time to time." —MBL]

is understood as act [Akt], without predicates of being, because otherwise [we would be conceiving of God] as an object.[328] On the other hand, the Lutheran: [It is] God's freedom and honor to have completely bound himself to the word. Not freedom from, but rather freedom for.[329]

Everyone in the church-community may forgive the sins of another. It is God who has promised that I may speak for God to others; from that the church-community lives in freely given continuity, which is the very presence of Christ, but not directly as an object, rather only through faith. [According to this] concept of the church, [the church] is not only the community of sinners and pardoned persons who hear the word, but rather the presence of Christ himself.[330] Preaching and sacrament [are] not only promises but rather partake themselves, with their word, in the world of Christmas, on the authority of the church-community and not depending on the need of the individual preacher. The church-community is the world
212 of Christmas. The most important change for Christology: helpless wavering between old substantive concepts and new dynamic concepts. Neither [alone is] adequate.

The pure interpretation of the act does not do justice to New Testament thinking and that of Luther. (Here) again the confessional issue [becomes clear]. A situation of which today's Lutherans must be ashamed; [they stand for a theology] that no longer perceives the boundary between itself

[328.] Winterhager: "Barth's works speak of God who is to come, of *iustitia aliena* and of predestination, because [the meaning of] *sola fide, sola gratia* [by grace alone] is taken completely seriously. This requires a concept of God constituted by freedom: God comes from time to time [*je und je*]. God understood as act, since by nature God cannot be described with predicates of being." ["Act" (*Akt*) for Barth is a technical term different from ordinary English connotations like "action," "acting," etc. For an introduction to Barth's "actualism," see George Hunsinger, *How to Read Karl Barth*, 107–9, 226–28, 271–72; for Bonhoeffer's appropriation of, and debate with, Barth on this point, see his *Act and Being* (*DBWE* 2).—MBL]

[329.] [See a basis for this concept in *Act and Being*, in Bonhoeffer's understanding of the character of revelation as the foundation of theological thought, i.e., the freedom of God manifest in the word as covenant with humanity, "free not from human beings but for them" (*DBWE* 3:90–91). This concept is found also in Bonhoeffer's lectures: "Creation and Sin: A Theological Exposition of Genesis 1–3" at the University of Berlin in the winter semester of 1932–33 (*DBWE* 3:67) and in his 1941 reflections on William Paton's book, *The Church and the New Order* (*DBWE* 16, 532).—MBL]

[330.] Winterhager: "But God has promised to be in the church-community—in the freely given continuity of the revelation of Christ, and that we may speak for God to our neighbor (in the church-community). Christ existing as church-community (preaching and sacrament)." For the formulation "Christ existing as church-community," see *Sanctorum Communio* (*DBWE* 1:198, ed. note 218).

and Catholicism. Barth saw and recovered the Reformed boundary with Catholicism.[331]

(2) Clarification of the relation between philosophy and theology. We recognize the difference in their object. Is theology to be integrated into the system of fields of knowledge, and [if so,] where? As a positive academic discipline [Wissenschaft], should it be subordinate to philosophy, or should it again become the primary discipline?[332] Should it be detached [from universities and be taught] in church academies?

The relation between church and state plays a role here.

(3) The problem of ethics. Barth's conception of it as demonstration[333] excludes any concrete teaching and any teaching of ethics based on principles.[334] How is Christian ethics as an academic discipline possible? How 213
shall I preach the law? The statement of forgiveness is the foundation of the Ten Commandments. The dogmatic statement retains its primary importance. Preaching of the gospel and of the law are not coordinated. To preach Christ concretely means also that one always preaches within

[331.] Dudzus (*GS* 5:226) interprets as follows: "The pure interpretation of the act does not do justice to New Testament thinking and that of Luther. Here the confessional issue comes up anew, for Barth's actualism in the concept of God and revelation carries on a Reformed tradition. Lutherans of today should be ashamed that they don't know how to define the Lutheran understanding of revelation by differentiating it both from Catholic substance thinking and from Reformed actualism."

[332.] [In the Middle Ages, especially after the thirteenth century, theology claimed to be *prima scientia,* popularly translated as the "queen of the sciences," e.g., in Thomas Aquinas's *Summa Theologiae,* 1a.1.2 and 1a.1.5.—MBL]

[333.] Barth, *Epistle to the Romans,* 2nd ed., 1922 (see above ed. note 294), 474: "'*Vengeance is mine, I will recompense! saith the Lord.*' Me—I. In order to demonstrate this—*if thine enemy hunger, feed him! If he thirst, give him to drink!* These actions demonstrate that precisely in the enemy the coming Kingdom of God Himself and of God only has been recognized. . . . We must not, therefore, make of the 'love of the enemy' that is here required of us a visible human action which is in itself ethical. We are here in the presence of the ethical paradox of the One in the other." For Barth's reasons for seeing ethics as a demonstration, see *Epistle to the Romans,* 432–33 and 492–502.

[334.] Ibid., 429–30. Cf. Barth's lectures on ethics in the winter semester of 1928–29 in Münster, of which Bonhoeffer had a set of notes (cf. 1/6, letter to Erwin Sutz). According to Barth, ethics, like law and custom, is legitimized only in relation to its true foundation, as that which "deals with us in the name and by the commission of God" (Barth, *Ethics,* 369). [Barth is speaking here about the authenticity of the teacher who must understand this commission and the "hidden" work of God in helping the student learn what is better in moral education, i.e., "better than what I previously knew and wanted" (369).—MBL] See also *Ethics,* 36: "God, however, is the Lord who in the church and theology as well as his whole creation can be served only by those who are appropriated without being able to boast of having appropriated to themselves what is worth boasting about."

a concrete situation. What [is] the scholarly basis on which ethics is to be constructed? Where [is] the principle of concretion of the general call to obedience?[335]

Our messages from the church have so little power because they sit in the middle, between general principles and concrete situations. The trouble with the church[336] [is] also the trouble with theological faculties, but this trouble is so little noticed.[337]

Luther was able to write *On the Bondage of the Will*[338] and his piece on usury[339] at the same time. Why can't we do that anymore?

*Who will show us Luther!*[340]

214 **4. Thesis Fragment about M. Heidegger and E. Grisebach**[1]

Heidegger[2] and Grisebach[3] in common:

There is an access to reality that precedes conceptual knowledge [Erkennen]. Reality [is] not constituted first through conceptualization [durch den Begriff].

The reality that already exists [das Vorgegebensein] characterizes the finiteness of existence.

---

[335.] Winterhager: "The problem in preaching is that of Christ's concrete relation to the situation under the law. How do I find the way to making it concrete? How can I preach the law from the pulpit? Where do I find the principle for making it concrete?"

[336.] See Barth, "Die Not der Evangelischen Kirche." For Barth, the trouble with the church is that, through the theological dispute with Catholicism and through meeting the demands of its practice in worship and sacrament, it forgets to bring out the gospel in all its power (ibid., 113).

[337.] Dudzus (*GS* 5:227) interprets as follows: "It is only that as a rule they are blind."

[338.] Martin Luther, *De servo arbitrio*, 1525 (*WA* 18:600–780); *LW* 33:3–295; cf. Bonhoeffer's commentary on this piece in his seminar paper, presumably for Reinhold Niebuhr, "The Character and Ethical Consequences of Religious Determinism" (*DBWE* 10:440–44). [This paper, titled "Charakter und ethische Konsequenzen des religiösen Determinismus," was written in German for Niebuhr's first semester course on "Religion and Ethics" (1930).—MBL]

[339.] Luther, "Großer Sermon von dem Wucher," 1520 (*WA* 6:36–60; "Long Sermon on Usury," *LW* 45:273–308).

[340.] Winterhager: "Theology as church scholarship? How much is theology possible within the system of academic disciplines?—Who will show us Luther?" [By this final question Bonhoeffer was asking: how do we pursue theology simultaneously as dogmatics and practical ethics?—MBL]

[1.] *NL*, A 31,1; handwritten draft. Previously published in *GS* 3:160–61. As Eberhard Bethge concluded from the paper being used, these theses are presumably connected with the seminar "The Idea of Philosophy and Protestant Theology in the Twentieth Cen-

Problem: How is the reality that already exists to be interpreted?

1. For Heidegger, through [the] understanding of being [Seinsverständnis] of the being-in-the-world [Dasein],[4] in the sense that the reality that already exists is again and again taken up [aufgehoben] into the existing reality of the understanding intellect.

2. For Grisebach, through a particular sphere of experience, which is to be understood as the human manner of existence, through "existing in the present," through "experience" of the present.[5] How is it possible that thought comes to grasp the manner of existence as existing in the present, since thought, after all, is essentially remembering, and remembered experience of the present is not the present. Therefore, it remains impossible for philosophy to speak of the "manner of existence in the present" [Existenzweise in Gegenwart], that is, in no way does it approach that which already exists.

In Heidegger, that which already exists is absorbed into the understanding being-in-the-world and deprived of its nature as already existing. In Grisebach, that which already exists remains inaccessible. This means, however, that philosophy can never attain the desired understanding of human existence as finite existence. Philosophy claims the infinity of human beings and of itself.

For the relationship between philosophy and theology, this means that 215
philosophy precedes theology in both cases (Heidegger and Grisebach).

(1) Theology agrees to this insofar as
  (a) it makes use of philosophical terminology and thereby places itself under the claim of the omnipotence of the concept;
  (b) in this respect it is actually a positive science subordinated to philosophy, even as a systematic one;
  (c) philosophy can do nothing other than to view it as such.

tury," which Bonhoeffer offered in the winter semester of 1931–32. No student notes or transcriptions of the seminar were preserved. [For standard English translations of some core concepts in Heidegger's works, the "Genealogical Glossary of Heidegger's Basic Terms, 1915–1927," in Kisiel, *Genesis of Heidegger's Being and Time* (490–511), has been consulted.—VB] .

[2.] On Bonhoeffer's critique of Heidegger, see *DBWE* 10:394–402 and *DBWE* 2: 96–99.

[3.] Bonhoeffer drew upon Grisebach several times in *Sanctorum Communio* and *Act and Being* (see *DBWE* 1:43–52 and notations, pp. 82–85; *DBWE* 2:86–87 and 111–12). On Bonhoeffer's critique of Grisebach, see *DBWE* 10:397–99 and 402–3.

[4.] Cf. Heidegger, *Being and Time*, § 9.

[5.] Cf. Grisebach, *Gegenwart*, especially chap. 12: "Vom Gestern, Heute und Morgen" (Of yesterday, today, and tomorrow).

(2) Theology disagrees with this insofar as
(a) it knows of its subordinate character [Knechtsgestalt], which corresponds to the subordination of the church below the institution of culture and the subordination of Jesus Christ below the[6] religious heroes;[7]
(b) it recognizes its contrast to the concept "to gaze" [Begriff–Schauen];[8]
(c) it knows of the eschatological possibility of a *philosophia Christiana*.[9]

### 5. Lecture: The Right to Self-Assertion[1]

The Right to Self-Assertion[2]

No working person today can escape the observation that he is replaceable,
216 that, indeed, behind him stand many who are only waiting, either to convince him of his dispensability during his very lifetime, or are just as eagerly ready to assure him of an immediate honor in his memory in the newspaper when things get serious. We are infinitely unimportant not only in terms of the overall picture of working humanity, but even from the particular place where we happen to find ourselves: It is extremely unimportant, whether I am studying or not; names are trivial and boring. Numbers say more and

[6.] Uncertain reading.
[7.] Uncertain reading. Cf. *GS* 3:161.
[8.] Cf. 2 Cor. 5:7 ["for we walk by faith, not by sight." Cf. also *DBWE* 2:60–61.—VB]
[9.] "Christian philosophy."

[1.] *NL*, A 32,1(1); handwritten outline. Partially reproduced in *GS* 3:258–69. This public lecture was held at the Technical College (Charlottenburg-Berlin) on Thursday, February 4, 1932. In addition to Bonhoeffer's lecture, the lecture series at the Technical College included two other evenings. On Thursday, January 23, the general secretary of the German Christian Student Organization, Hanns Lilje, spoke on the theme "Technology—the Human Being—God." On Thursday, February 18, Arnold F. Stolzenburg, whom Bonhoeffer knew from their work together in the systematic theology department, and who was named extraordinary professor [i.e., without an official appointment—VB] at Berlin University in 1927, spoke on "Christianity and the Occult." The lectures had been initiated by Bonhoeffer as student chaplain at the Technical College, together with the chapter of the German Christian Student Organization in Charlottenburg. [The German Christian Student Organization was not associated with the pro-Nazi German Christian movement; it was the German branch of the ecumenical World Student Christian Federation.—VB]

[2.] On the question of self-assertion and self-denial as a foundational issue in Bonhoeffer's Christian ethics, see *DBWE* 6:239–45. [In this section of his *Ethics*, the first ver-

are more appropriate. And what city dweller does not know this impression of empty, futile importance at 7:30 in the morning, in the streets, on the trains, as thousands hurry to their work, to their livelihood, a condemned, patient, replaceable mass. It conveys something endlessly desolate and boring, yet exciting and outrageous at the same time. And we belong in the midst of the superfluous ones, and even our own situation has at the same time something very boring and very shocking for us. Partly out of boredom, partly out of indignation, we then decide in some way to put an end to the feeling of our being superfluous, be it through fired-up work performance, be it by getting married and bringing new beings into superfluous human existence and making them dependent on us, be it by forgetting our own pointlessness and now simply allowing ourselves to take it easy and enjoy ourselves in a vegetative existence [dahinvegetieren]. These are, indeed, three very different behavior patterns, but no one likes to be superfluous and one becomes inventive in making excuses.[3]

Every day you read new statistics in the newspapers that have only one purpose, namely, to show that there are too many people out there. Between 35 and 50 percent of all the pupils at the secondary schools, around 50 percent of university students, and 60 percent of the students at the technical colleges will not find a position. In the job market[4] basically everything hinges on one question: Who buys people? People become like goods, which are devalued by the massive scale. There are too many examples of
this kind. This devalues the individual and the species. One can deceive 217
oneself about this state of affairs and dream, if one happens not to be personally affected, but one cannot deny the situation. In any case, this situation offers a major opportunity, namely, to submerge, easily and always excusably, to fit into an environment where one feels comfortable and where

---

sion of the section "History and Good," Bonhoeffer returns to the theme of self-assertion as historical-social responsibility within a context of the Sermon on the Mount, a renewed theological context that had preoccupied him as early as 1931 and continued through his Finkenwalde teaching. He raises a critique of false realism on the basis of a presumed dichotomy between historical-political action and Christian action, in which self-assertion is set over against self-surrender. But this is based on a pseudo-realist abstraction negated by actual historical limits and, more importantly, overruled by the Christian understanding of love and self-denial in the "concrete worldly action" of God become human in the reality of Jesus Christ. See *DBWE* 6:240–41.—MBL]

[3.] "One becomes inventive in making excuses" replaces "each one seeks his own excuses."

[4.] In February 1932, unemployment reached its highest point, with 6,128,000 persons unemployed [over 30 percent of the German workforce—VB]. This was a recurring issue for Bonhoeffer in 1932. See the German editor's afterword to this volume, p. 477, and the editors' introduction to this volume, p. 2.

one actually also probably belongs. And the weak person and the frivolous person will not let this opportunity pass by. To all others, this state of affairs poses the one question of life: How do you come to do something that a thousand others could and would want to do just as well and even better? How do you come to earn money, where two thousand others have nothing? What right have you to enjoy status and honor, where thousands like you live from the bread of charity? What right do you have to assert yourself in the struggle for human existence, in full awareness that you are thereby ruining, destroying, and leaving the lives of others prey to meaninglessness? Stand up for your rights! Or surrender them! We are here today to discuss this problem.

We also know, however, that today the question of the right to self-assertion is not only posed to the individual with particular urgency but rather that it signifies the question of existence [Daseinsfrage] of almost all large communities. The trade professions are waging a desperate battle for their right to exist; the fragmentation of society into classes has driven these groups into increasingly sharp confrontations against one another. The bourgeoisie [Bürgertum][5] is threatened in the most dangerous way and is fighting to preserve the bourgeois spirit and its rights. The proletariat believes that it will be able to shape its own rights only on the ruins of the middle class.[6] However, even the basic forms of human communal life are questioned and called upon to preserve their rights. Marriage and family are experiencing a violent crisis. Has the institution of marriage, as it has been conducted for hundreds of years, a right to make a stand against the attempts at dissolution? Or has it not proved sufficiently that it leads to human catastrophes, that it has become an outdated, lifeless form? And the same questions would then be leveled at the institution of the family.
218 The new form of the childless marriage and, for instance, the ever stronger removal of children from the family and pulling them into school and clubs makes this question clear. Or let us consider the struggle for existence of two institutions, once looked upon as most powerful cultural factors: the university and the church. The university is supposed to become

[5.] [The terms "bourgeoisie" and "proletariat" convey the broader cultural and political nuance of Bonhoeffer's reference here to the concerns of the propertied and the working classes.—MBL]

[6.] See *DBWE* 6:117–18. [In the section "Heritage and Decay" of his *Ethics*, Bonhoeffer discusses the relation of liberation, human rights, and social need in the historical context of the French Revolution and the contemporary context of an upheaval between the middle and the working classes.—MBL]

the vocational school, and the church of the people [Volkskirche][7] the private religious association. What right does the university have to assert itself? What right does the church have to fight for its existence in defiance of all attacks and slander as being an outdated, ever reactionary, obsolete institution? It is rare in history to see that without exception all the previous orders of human life are being questioned, dragged into an existential struggle so that they are confronted with the alternative of justifying their right to exist or else surrendering it. And now we cannot stop here, for even the greatest[8] and highest[9] forms of human social life, the nations themselves, are not untouched; they are particularly addressed by the question:[10] What right to existence [Daseinsrecht] do you have? Do you have any right as an old nation to face the striving young nation, to deny its rise? Do you have a right, as a young, strong nation [Volk], to take over the old one with violence, to push it out?[11] Do you have any right to extend your boundaries, if your fellow citizens are suffocating in these narrow confines? Do

[7.] [The *Volkskirche* (literally, the "peoples' church") refers to the majority churches—the German Evangelical Church and the Roman Catholic Church, to which the great majority of German citizens belonged—in contrast to the much smaller and diverse minority churches; the term is still used in this sense today. It does not mean an established "state church," nor was it originally an expression of nationalism. Nonetheless, with the rise of the German Christian movement and Nazi rhetoric about the centrality of the *Volksgemeinschaft*, the word certainly began to acquire nationalistic connotations. It is clear from several documents in this volume (cf. esp. 2/11 and 2/14) that Bonhoeffer's attention was on the rising tide of a *völkisch*, nationalistic movement within the church, especially among young people. See *DBWE* 1:18, esp. ed. note 48, and Borg, "Volkskirche, 'Christian State,' and the Weimar Republic."—MBL]

[8.] "Greatest" replaces "old."

[9.] "Highest" replaces "most secure."

[10.] "Question" replaces "challenge."

[11.] Many nationalistically minded theologians perceived the displacement of an older nation by a younger nation as a "historical order of creation." On Bonhoeffer's earlier sharing of this opinion, see *DBWE* 10:371–74 and 10:371, ed. note 32. [In his lecture "Basic Questions of a Christian Ethic," delivered to his German congregation in Barcelona on February 8, 1929, Bonhoeffer reflects briefly on God as the Lord of history, a holy will governing the course of history, yet with a concomitant call to peoples "to create their own history." This earlier view, however, is Bonhoeffer at his most nationalistic, justified on theological grounds. It is not found in this present text or in his later writing. The obvious reference here, against "pushing people out," is to the German political discussion at that time about enhanced German territory, "space" (*Lebensraum*), already a part of the Nazi expansionist rhetoric in the early 1930s. It is clear that Bonhoeffer in early 1932 had completely rejected a basis for such political action in an "order of creation," as reflected, for example, in his discussions within the Working Group of Theologians and Economists and the controversy with Pastor Friedrich Peter. See 2/8 and the editors' introduction to this volume.—MBL]

you have a right to destroy the thriving culture of the neighboring land for the sake of your own? You, people, preserve your right or give it up. [. . .][12] It is possible here to dismiss all this and say: These are all questions not of rights but simply of historical development, of the division of power, of might. This possibility exists, but it is not a moral possibility, and it has never
219 been a German possibility so far. We want to note this as well.

Our purpose this evening is to trace all these questions back to one question and thereby answer it. The right to self-assertion is the single question, whose multifaceted contemporary meaning we have only illustrated up to this point.

Humanity has given essentially two answers to this fundamental question [Urfrage] of all life. One emerged in the distant, fertile, sunny, form- and idea-rich world of India, in which the body is easily provided with good things and thus the soul is left free for surrender and self-deepening. The world in which the active, productive hand of work need only open itself in order richly to receive its fruits engenders a great tranquillity in the heart, and the soul breathes the life that surrounds it in its abundance, penetrating the experience of life in the midst of this great abundance, uniting itself with it, probing and pondering its rhythm[13] and its depths, which are basically the depths of the soul itself, and the expanses of the Indian soul are the expanses of all living things. In this way the submerging soul recognizes itself again in all that lives, as if in thousands of mirrors; out of every form of nature it hears the quiet[14] answer: *tat tvam asi*,[15] this is you, you yourself. And the eternal awe of the sanctity of all life comes over the soul. It aches if nature suffers from violence; it is torn apart when living things are injured. You should not kill, for life is the soul, and life is you yourself; you should not do violence to any living thing; you should resist and reject anything in you that stimulates you to get your way with violence; you should

[12.] Here there are four illegible letters with periods, probably an abbreviation for "And that is today."

[13.] Deleted: "vessels and."

[14.] Uncertain reading.

[15.] Chandogya Upanishad, VI.12.3, in Mahadevan, *Principal Upanishads*, 462. [The full refrain is "That which is the subtle essence, this whole world has for its self. That is the true. That is the self. You are that [*tat tvam asi*]." This is the teaching of the great sage Uddalaka to his son, Svetaketu, teaching him that his true self or essence is identical with the whole of existence. The editor is indebted to the Sanskrit scholar John J. Holder for this clarification.—MBL] The sentence was often cited by the philosopher Arthur Schopenhauer (see, for example, Schopenhauer's *World as Will and Representation*, 1:220, 355, 374, and 2:600).

tame the thirst of your passions, your hatred and your love, if they drag you to assert yourself and hurt other life. Learn to suffer, learn to go by, learn
to die, all this is better than to assert oneself and to violate and live. Only 220
in this way will your soul, which indeed is the soul of the Universe [das All], be uninjured and holy. Through love and suffering, we enter the Universe [das All] and overcome it.

In order to understand this idea, it is necessary for us to be clear that at the beginning there is the sentence: *tat tvam asi.* Everything is you. You are alone. You are also responsible solely to yourself, live for you yourself and your soul, for you are the whole. It is the powerful act of Gandhi[16] to extend this teaching of life, which is directed toward the individual, now toward a people in a national question and now, too, to place the community under the commandment: You should not destroy any life; suffering is better than living with violence. If it then happens that at a gathering, thousands of Gandhi's followers, who are to be dispersed by the government police, attempt to carry out their will without force in passive resistance till the white machine guns are pointed at them, and hundreds are mowed down there,[17] then this is the great expression and solution that the question of the right to self-assertion still finds today in India.[18]

The other big solution is that of European-American civilization, the solution of wars and factories; already, the first look[19] at Western history teaches us that this has been a history of wars. The history of India is to this day a history of suffering. And that war in European history had a very different intellectual [geistig][20] structure and significance than, for instance, war between two wild tribes, could, in my opinion, be proved by the writing of history. It is, so to say, the forerunner of the machine in its intellectual meaning. But this means, of course, that it[21] was truly to be overcome in the era[22] of the machine. But be that as it may, the machine and the war

[16.] On Bonhoeffer's interest in India and the plans to visit Mahatma Gandhi, see 1/14, *GS* 2:181–82, and *DB-ER,* 406–9.

[17.] [The reference is to the Jallianwallah Bagh massacre in the Punjab city of Amritsar on April 13, 1919, in which a contingent of British soldiers killed and wounded over 1,500 unarmed men, women, and children attending a protest rally that Gandhi had initiated but was prevented from attending.—MBL]

[18.] "Still finds today" replaces "has found."

[19.] "Already, the first look" replaces "that is, the resolution in action."

[20.] [The term *geistig,* used here and in the following sentences, can be translated as "intellectual" or "spiritual" and has nuances of both. This context seems to prefer "intellectual."—MBL]

[21.] [I.e., war.—VB]

[22.] Uncertain reading.

are the two forms of the Western solution to our problem.[23] And we must seek to grasp its intellectual [geistig] meaning, in order to understand the problem.

221 One might now think that this is the quintessential animalistic, instinctive solution, whereas the Indian solution is the essentially humane one. But this is superficial. In both cases the human being steps outside the connection to nature and is something utterly different from an animal.[24] The animal lives only through adapting itself to the laws of nature; the human being stands facing nature, ruling and conquering it. In the Oriental world this happens when the human being is able to suffer for the[25] soul's sake; in the West, the human being is able to master nature, fight against it, force it to his service. This position of human mastery over nature is the fundamental theme of European-American history. The human being in India, too, is deeper and stronger than nature, because he understands it and, knowing it, suffers for it and from it. But the human being is deeper and stronger than nature, because he is its enemy and conqueror. The human being has this as an innate priority over all that lives. For that reason, a European also cannot love nature without taking note of its demonic powers, which threaten him, and in the deep delight that the fear of nature and the struggle against it gives him, the human being loves it. The human path to nature is a broken one. It[26] refuses him everything; for that reason he must extract it from it against its will; for the sake of this struggle he loves it. The individual human being receives everything from nature and loves it for that; his life is not a struggle against it but rather a receiving from it.

The European must struggle against nature to receive the right to life, but not only against nature, but also against other human beings. His life means in the most essential sense "killing." This has never been so horrifyingly clear as in the last decade and a half.[27] And yet we all stand in this life; we have all apparently already decided to affirm this fate, whether consciously or not. In any case, the decision has been made, and now the task is to understand what we have thereby done.

Not only the attitude toward nature is something else for the European
222 but also the attitude toward history and toward other human beings; and

[23.] Cf. *DBWE* 6:120–22. [At this point in the *Ethics*, Bonhoeffer reflects upon the inherently unstable interrelation of nationalism, technology, and mass movements. —MBL]

[24.] Deleted: "he stands as it were over against nature and overcomes it."

[25.] "The" replaces "his."

[26.] [I.e., nature.—VB]

[27.] Bonhoeffer is referring here to the First World War and the events in Russia during and after the Russian Revolution.

only from this starting point can we completely understand the European-American resolution of the question. Right to self-assertion is right to life. Life, however, is not primarily something that we give ourselves but something that is given to us, something that we suffer. Through our birth, our life is determined primarily passively. And it is now a characteristic of mature European thought to acknowledge this passive event as a bond. Life means being bound through history and that means to other human beings. I grow up in a world that I do not give myself but which determines me and to which I acknowledge my bond. Thus life means being connected backward and forward, to have claims made on me from outside, from the other human beings in my surroundings; it means to be responsible. Here we have in principle the possibility of the great individualists to curse this being bound through birth and life as horrible destiny, as Jeremiah cursed the day of his birth[28] and as Nietzsche's Zarathustra did in a similar fashion.[29] This means tearing oneself out of history and society, and for that reason it ultimately means nothing other than the proclamation of the right to the great human possibility, which testifies most deeply to the human being's freedom from nature, superiority over the animal, the right to a free death, the right to suicide. Here the individual becomes outraged against his destiny and defies it to the end. The human being is free over nature and history if he is free unto death. The right to self-assertion becomes here the right to a free death. That is one possibility. And it is the unmistakable truth that the human being only becomes human, first truly asserts himself, when he is free unto death. But this truth will also be heard and absorbed there where the human being seizes his historical bonds in responsibility, where he understands himself not as master over his own life, but where he understands his life as responsibility toward his fellow human beings.[30] 223
He lives here not alone but fundamentally through and for the others with whom he is associated in responsibility.[31] Only out of responsibility does life take its right to self-assertion, not because it belongs to me, but rather because it belongs to society, to others, to the fellow human being. Here the possibility of free death is dismissed on principle, but the deeper truth that it contains is taken up in the much more unfathomable depth of a different thought, and out of these hidden dark depths that life of responsibility wells

[28.] See Jer. 20:14–18.

[29.] Bonhoeffer is referring to the repeated expressions of disgust and weariness about human existence in Nietzsche's *Thus Spoke Zarathustra*, 307.

[30.] Deleted: "and where he sees that only as such is life present."

[31.] [This concept will become a central feature of Bonhoeffer's ethical theology, e.g., in his *Ethics* (*DBWE* 6:259).—MBL] up: the human being is free[32]only in death; right to self-assertion means right to death, freedom unto death, now, however, not to the free death of self-destruction, but rather to the freedom to sacrifice.[33] This is the consummation of the thought[34] of life as responsibility, as being bound to history and society, that this life has right only through sacrifice. There is right to life only through the ability to die for the other, in responsibility. Living means killing. For that reason, however, life itself must be open to death, now, however, not for the glorification of personality but as sacrifice for a brother. Only where the individual is able to understand and assess his life from the perspective of death does he win the answer to the question of his right to life, of the right to self-assertion.[35]

But already through saying this, we expand our view. We are not only individuals, but we are also placed within life-communities. It is precisely here that our burning interest lies today. Our marriage, our church, Germany are called before the forum of responsibility. And now what counts is to see these communities in the light of that which gives an individual's life the right to self-assertion—in the light of responsibility for the other and of the ability to die. And what we say in the following holds true for each community that acts responsibly, whether it be a community of blood, of work, of a factory, or of a commune. Every community, even the great community
224 of the people, lives not only for itself but for the others, lives in responsibility for the brother, for the people to whom one is bound in brotherhood [Brudervolk].[36] There is absolutely no isolated life for the people [das Volk]. It is bound through its birth onward to the community and through its life to the peoples in brotherhood. Admittedly, even for the people, there is that demonic possibility to tear itself out of the historical context, the

[32.] "Free" replaces "human."

[33.] [Cf. Bonhoeffer's poem many years later: "Stations on the Way to Freedom," written as a gift for Eberhard Bethge from Tegel prison in the context of the events of July 20, 1944 (*DBWE* 8:512–14).—MBL]

[34.] Deleted: "knowledge."

[35.] [Bonhoeffer returns extensively in the second version of the section on "History and Good" in his *Ethics* to the interconnection of freedom and responsibility within an analysis of the "structure of responsible action" and as "mutually corresponding concepts. . . . Responsibility presupposes freedom . . . just as freedom can exist only in the exercise of responsibility. Responsibility is human freedom that exists only by being bound to God and neighbor" (*DBWE* 6:283).—MBL]

[36.] [Bonhoeffer is extending here the concept of personal brotherhood to corporate or communal brotherhood (*Brudervolk*), particularly for national communities that are tied together through historical circumstances, such as Germany and France. The context is his critique of an ascending movement of exclusionist and assertive nationalism in Germany at this time.—MBL]

attempt of absolute being-alone and being-for-itself, the denial of responsibility, which in turn draws its strength from the possibility[37] of the free death of the entire people. And the danger of this action hangs above the community as it does above the individual life. This means that a people has a right, there where life is unbearable for it, to curse its birth and to bring itself to an end with an honorable death, but in turn here, too, this thought must[38] be taken up and led into the depths of the responsible life.[39] It is true that a people only lives, which means [it] may destroy life, if it is free unto death; only in the light, only out of the power of death does the community live. But when a people responsibly affirms its bond to history, its bond to its brothers, to other people in brotherhood [Brudervolk] that may at the same time be its deadly enemy, then it no longer has the freedom to a free death, but rather lives solely from the freedom for sacrificial death for its brothers. It may live only because it is ready to die for the brother. War and machine as a means to the self-assertion of the community demand sacrifice of individuals, but they have their sole right from the readiness of the community for sacrificial death for others, even for the enemy brother; never may they become a means for egoism and self-idolization, and where they lower themselves to this, it is time to protest. War originates from the era when the European thought that only by killing the other could one create living space [Lebensraum] for oneself. The machine directs this fight primarily not against the human being but against nature. That is the reason why its means are more ruthless. That is why it leads to catastrophe, where the machine is placed in the deliberate service of destroying human
life. The machine has[40] made war impossible, not just according to its idea 225
of subjugating nature to human beings and thus letting them live, but also according to its [i.e., the machine's] reality. But this only incidentally.

Peoples, too, can and should sacrifice themselves. And in this way the view broadens and encompasses the entire earth, humanity. And now today[41] our Western thought is universal; the concept of humankind is a Western concept. It governs[42] our entire thinking. But we reach it in no other way but by the historical path through the individual and the community; here, however, as a historical final concept, it has its inextricable meaning. The life and sacrifice of the individual is for the brother, for the

[37.] "Possibility" replaces "power."

[38.] Deleted: "that is the heroic deed."

[39.] Cf. *DBWE* 6:246–98.

[40.] Deleted: "the death."

[41.] Abbreviated in original ("U.d.i.h.," presumably *Und das ist heute*).

[42.] Uncertain reading.

community that embraces him; the life and sacrifice of the community is for other peoples in brotherhood [Brudervolk], for the brotherly community that embraces it, and so it grows into the understanding that life, responsibility, and sacrifice finally belong to the unity of the human race, to a human being as such who alone can live through the sacrifice.[43] Humankind lives through the sacrifice that the individuals and the communities bring to it. But why should we hold back the last question, which is indeed unavoidable? Does humanity itself no longer need the sacrifice, the openness toward death, because humanity is what finally, unconditionally, only demands sacrifices but does not sacrifice itself? Does it have its right simply through itself, through its very existence [Dasein]? Or must even it fight against this, through the readiness unto death?

And now today:[44] Why should we not simply at this decisive point take the step forward that has become necessary through what has just been said? Even humanity, even the human being as such, who is nothing as a human being, hence even humanity, according to our thinking, is responsible for its right to life, and it exercises this responsibility only where it sees
226 that it too only lives from being able to die, from death, from sacrifice. It lives from the sacrifice that it now brings simultaneously to itself and to the brothers in the one who has made them all brothers[45] and in whose spirit and life they are all one. The end of human beings, of humanity, is the readiness for this deed, for sacrifice for the fellow human being, and that is offered to the Spirit, who lives out of himself and creates life.

And now, here in the background of this Western conception, Christianity emerges on the horizon and in it the figure of Jesus of Nazareth, the Son of Man, who is called the Son of God, the Christ. He fulfills the sacrifice of humanity, out of which alone humanity can live, and now, since the act of Golgotha, humanity lives entirely out of that act, which the Son of Man offered for the brothers to the Father. He also really lived, but his faithful[46] see his life in the shadow or in the light of the act of Golgotha, his death for the brother[s]. Because he was free to die, therefore he could live, because he died as sacrifice for the brotherhood of the world, therefore his life was plainly life in service to the most holy brotherhood. For that reason the Gospels proclaim that all should take up their cross and follow

---

[43.] "Who alone can live through the sacrifice" replaces "who [raises] the question about the right to life."

[44.] Abbreviated in original ("U.d.i.h.," presumably *Und das ist heute*).

[45.] "Who turns everybody to brothers" replaces "who stands beyond them."

[46.] "His faithful" replaces "Christianity."

him;[47] his death sanctifies his life, his death and our death sanctify our life, and only when we become free to sacrifice for the holiest brotherhood of humanity, for whom the prophet from Nazareth, the Christ, died, only so do we become free for life.

## 6. Essay: Pastoral Care for Protestant Students at the Technical College[1]

Pastoral Care for Protestant Students at the Technical College

The average student today is alienated from the church. Everyone knows
this. The reasons too are known, the real ones and those that are bandied 227
about; even the church knows them. In fact, the church now is reflecting on this phenomenon more seriously than one might think. How successfully is the second question, and that does not depend on the church alone. In any case, the present situation is that groups with the most diverse worldviews have once again drawn attention to what is happening in the church. What the church needs now, however, is nothing less than observers and nothing more than coworkers. And for this reason it is appealing to students as strongly as it can. Whoever looks at these things seriously cannot avoid the fact that the shape of the future church and the shape of the future German are essentially interconnected. Yet the church demands that even students take a position and become engaged, not for the sake of something else but rather because the church is the church.

But the church ultimately is taking seriously not itself but rather that task that was given it from the very beginning. The church believes in all seriousness, in a time of the deepest ideological division, that it can and may stand there where ideologies reach their end and something new and ultimate begins. The church will proudly preserve that which it has and not market it like false goods, perhaps under deceptive names. For the church knows that nothing is greater than to be there where people really want the church to be, to help with all the resources that it has. This is what the church is telling the student body when it assigns a student chaplain to work with them.

Today whoever still believes that he can live life alone is living in an illusion. Things have become too difficult to do so. No one knows that better,

---

[47.] Cf. Mark 8:34. [See also Matt. 16:24; Luke 9:23.—MBL]

[1.] Published in *Die technische Hochschule: Akademische Zeitschrift der Technischen Hochschule Charlottenburg* 10 no. 9 (February 1932): 200–201. Previously published in *GS* 6:215–16. See *NL*, A 32,6.

perhaps, than today's Protestant pastor. The student also knows this in a special way. And this realization connects them. Where people are questioning together, why shouldn't they struggle together for an answer?

Pastor Lic. Dietrich Bonhoeffer, Lecturer at Berlin University, Berlin-Grunewald, Wangenheimstrasse 14.

Office Hours: Tuesday and Wednesday, 1:00–2:00 p.m., at the Student House, Baracks 15, Room 17. Friday, 6:00–7:00 p.m., in the residence. Telephone: Pfalzburg 2616.

228 Events will be posted on the bulletin board of the Protestant Student Ministry at the Technical College. A series of lectures is planned for the months of January and February.[2]

### 7. Draft for a Catechism: As You Believe, So You Receive[1]

As You Believe, So You Receive[2]
Attempt at a Lutheran Catechism
by
Dietrich Bonhoeffer and Franz Hildebrandt

Preface

This catechism is for students in a confirmation class and yet is intended not only for them. It serves their distinctive concerns, as it attempts to formu-

[2.] See 2/5, ed. note 1.

[1.] *Monatschrift für Pastoraltheologie* 28 (1932): 167–72. Previously published in *GS* 3:248–57. Cf. *NL*, A 32,2a); typewritten copy with handwritten corrections by Franz Hildebrandt. The Hildebrandt papers include two carbon copies of the draft catechism with minor corrections in both Hildebrandt's and Bonhoeffer's handwriting. Regarding Bonhoeffer's work on the catechism, see also p. 96. [The German title, "Glaubst du, so hast du," translates literally "If you believe, you will have it."—VB]

[2.] This title picks up a formulation from Luther, which Franz Hildebrandt had previously cited in his dissertation; see Hildebrandt, *EST*, 27. With this he wanted to emphasize in the discussion concerning the Lord's Supper that for Luther there is no true perception of reality [keine Objectivität] apart from faith [i.e., in this context faith is a way of perceiving—VB]. Cf. Martin Luther, *The Freedom of a Christian*, 1520 (*WA* 7:24, 12–17; *LW* 31:348): "The promises of God . . . declare the glory of God, saying, 'If you wish to fulfill the law and not covet, as the law demands, come, believe in Christ in whom grace, righteousness, peace, liberty, and all things are promised you. If you believe, you shall have all things; if you do not believe, you shall lack all things.' That which is impossible for you to accomplish by trying to fulfill all the works of the law—many and useless as they all are—you will accomplish quickly and easily through faith. God our Father

late[3] what the Lutheran faith is saying today. Questions and answers are posed for carefully focused reading.[4] Additional material and interpretations remain reserved for the lesson time.

What is the gospel? 229

This is the message of God's salvation that has appeared to us in Jesus Christ and has been conveyed to us through his Spirit. This is the message of the kingdom of God that is contested in the world and intended for God's righteous. This is the message of God's will, which speaks today and decides over life and death.

Who is *Evangelisch*?[5]

Whoever rejoices in God's grace, professes the name of Christ, and invokes the Holy Spirit. Whoever is ready for God's rule, does not fear outside power, and knows that all will be fulfilled ultimately. Whoever hears God's word preached, loves his church-community, and lives from forgiveness.

The Protestant faith confesses that God has given himself fully and completely to us, with all that God is and has (Luther),[6] in these words:

"I believe in God, that he is my creator, in Jesus Christ, that he is my Lord, in the Holy Spirit, that he is my sanctifier. God has created me and given me life, soul, body, and all goods; Christ has brought me into his lordship through his body; and the Holy Spirit sanctifies me through his Word and the sacraments, which are in the church, and will sanctify us wholly on

---

has made all things depend on faith so that whoever has faith will have everything, and whoever does not have faith will have nothing." Cf. also Luther, Sermon of April 27, 1522 (*WA* 10/3:92, 13–14). [In this sermon at Borna, Luther claims: "So he [Christ] comes to us in the gospel. Indeed, it is much better that he does come through the gospel, because if he comes right now simply through the door, you would not know him, . . . [But if] you have faith, so you have [him]; if you don't have faith, then you don't have [him]."—MBL]

[3.] In the carbon copies (see ed. note 1) it reads: "It attempts to formulate; . . ." The text printed in the *Monatsschrift für Pastoraltheologie* includes Hildebrandt's corrections.

[4.] Insertion by Bonhoeffer in the carbon copy: "and challenges the confirmands to independent reflection. The confirmand today needs someone to expect something from him."

[5.] [We have chosen to use the German word *Evangelisch* here because of its nuances for this Lutheran catechism. Throughout most of *DBWE*, it is usually translated as "Protestant," referring to the Protestant Church of Germany, which encompasses Lutheran, Reformed, and United traditions. Yet the meaning in this case is clearly those who follow the gospel as taught by the Lutheran Reformation (the German word for "gospel" is *Evangelium*). The editors thank Hans Pfeifer and Clifford Green for their insights.—VB]

[6.] Cf. Martin Luther, "Confession concerning Christ's Supper," 1528 (*WA* 26:505, 38–39; *LW* 37:366): "These are the three persons and one God, who has given himself to us wholly and completely, with all that he is and has."

the last day. [. . .] This is the Christian faith: to know what you must do and what has been given to you" (Luther, *WA* 30/1:94;[7] *LW* 51:169).

*Of the true God*

Where does my knowledge of God come from?

From your baptism, because before you even asked, God had spoken to you. From your church, for as you sought God, you were already part of the church-community. From the Bible, for your church lives from the power of its preaching.

Why is God present in this way?

God alone is the Lord. God can speak of himself wherever he wishes. It is, however, in God's loving-kindness that he encounters us in earthly form, and that we can know where he is to be found. That is the revelation in Christ and in his church.

Is this the only God?

In every other case, you pray to the god of your wishes. There is only one God who comes to you himself, so that you can no longer elude him. His word alone calls the whole world into life, and you as well as his own.

*On faith*

How can I be certain of this?

Through faith alone, which has grasped the good news with both hands. No other way is given to us, for if we were able to see God, we would be in eternal life. Therefore, it is faith that dares to put our trust in God.

Where do we find the proof for this?

A god who could be proved by us would be an idol. The Lord in whom we trust binds us so firmly to himself that we become free of superstition and the desire for proof through miracles. The one to whom God has given the gift of faith in turn presents faith back to God, no matter what happens to that person.

---

[7.] See lines 14–22 (Catechetical Sermon of December 10, 1528). [*WA* 30/1:94 (Latin text): "I believe in God, because God is my creator, in Jesus Christ, because he is my Lord, in the Holy Spirit, because he is my sanctifier. God has created and given to me life, spirit, body, and every good thing, Christ *has brought me into his community* through his body, and the Holy Spirit has sanctified me through word and sacrament, which are in the church, and will sanctify us perfectly at the last day. This doctrine is different from that of the theologians who teach that we ought to act in such a way that we will be acceptable to God. Therefore, faith gives that which you need. This, then, is the Christian faith: to know what you are to do and what has been given to you." Italicized text in German in original.—MBL] Already in his dissertation Hildebrandt had cited the confession and commented: "A formulation of the confession of faith, in which attention to dogmatic and liturgical matters cannot be emphasized urgently enough" (*EST*, 99n364).

Is God really concerned about me?

Whoever acts all too piously[8] in contrast is thinking not of what is divine but rather of what is human. Because that is the glory of God, that God comes down to us in Christ in order that we might be raised in the Spirit to God. He is the trinitarian God.

*Since God belongs to us and we to God, we proclaim faith in the Father: I believe in God, who is my creator.*

May we call God our Father?

This is the only name that discloses the mystery of God to us. God cannot 231
forget what God has created. How should we forget that we are his children!

Doesn't the creation story contradict science?

To engage in scientific research and to have faith are two different things. Science has its own full and distinctive authority. Every child knows that the earth did not come about simply in six days. Yet not everyone knows that God creates the world through his Spirit and human beings according to God's own image.

Why don't we see this image in anyone?

It sounds really strange to us. The demonic spirits of the world, such as money, power, desires, rob us of God's light, so that we have to die. God's orders have been destroyed. Through our disbelief, we have abused our freedom, using it against God, and this has made us slaves to our false idols.

How can a righteous God allow so much injustice?

The catastrophes of nature and of humankind render our wisdom silent. Where God's gracious will is concealed entirely from us, our will certainly cannot judge God. Nonetheless, we know that to those who love God all things work out for the best.[9]

What, then, am I to pursue in the world?

You should do what your occupation has given you to do. God has called each of us to a particular work in a particular time. This is God's law. And we owe God our obedience, until God summons us.

Is there no unrighteousness in our occupation?

Admittedly, everyone today who earns his living is taking bread from another. Work becomes a curse[10] whenever our power over things reverses

[8.] In both carbon copies, "all too piously" replaces "out of religiosity."

[9.] Cf. Rom. 8:28.

[10.] Cf. Gen. 3:17.

itself into the power of things over us. Whoever knows this becomes humble and asks that God[11] make him joyful once more in his work.

How may a Christian own property?

Certainly, he would often be happier without it. He knows the power and deceptiveness of money, but at the same time he wants to care for the other person. So he should possess all that he has as though he did not have these things.[12]

Is the instinct for self-preservation in fact a sin?

232 Nature and the unnatural are completely interwoven in it. As Christians, we believe that our body belongs to God. But wherever the drives of hunger and sex break away from their origins, they blindly go astray.

Are there no rules for our physical life?

Deliberately to destroy one's health is to harm one's soul and God's possession [Eigentum].[13] To fulfill the communion [Gemeinschaft] between body and soul, God has given us marriage. Whoever has been given eyes open to the miracle of each birth will shy away from laying hands on another's life and will ask God to forgive him when he sins by being arrogant and falling away from God.

But doesn't one have to destroy life in war?

For that very reason the church knows nothing of the sanctity of war. For in war, the struggle for existence [Dasein] is fought with dehumanized means. The church that prays the Lord's Prayer calls to God only for the cause of peace.

But isn't that unpatriotic?

God has arranged it so that all races of humanity of the earth come from *one* blood (Acts 17:26). Therefore, a defiant ethnic pride [ein völkisches Trotzen] in flesh and blood is a sin against the Holy Spirit. Zeal that only blindly asserts itself is brought under control by the state. God has established the state for the service of God, so that we might serve God as Christians.

How then should the Christian behave politically?

As much as the Christian would like to remain distant from political struggle, nonetheless, even here the commandment of love urges the Christian to stand up for his neighbor. His faith and love must know whether the dictates of the state may lead him against his conscience. In every such deci-

[11.] In Bonhoeffer's carbon copy (see ed. note 1), there is a handwritten addition that is then crossed out: "protect [him] in the face of such need and."

[12.] Cf. 1 Cor. 7:29–30.

[13.] In both carbon copies, "property" (*Eigentum*) replaces "order" (*Ordnung*).

sion, he experiences the irreconcilable conflict between the peace of Christ and the hate of the world.[14]

Have Christians no other solution? 233

We recognize that we are wrong in thought and deed. For this reason, the whole world restlessly hopes for the appearance of the Savior and the justice of God. We pray to God that we be not judged but rather that God would make us truly ready for his work.

*That God enters into our life and we into God's, we proclaim our faith in the Son: I believe in Jesus Christ, that He is my Lord.*

Did Jesus actually live?

Whoever knows the Bible and the Gentile testimonies about Jesus sees the proof of his life through its variety and contradictions. The Jews themselves have never contested that. The statements such as in Matt. 11:19; 21:31; Mark 10:18; 15:34; Luke 14:26, and images as in Matt. 15:21ff.; Mark 10:13ff.; 14:32ff.; Luke 7:36ff.; 15:1ff. could not have been invented. All attempts to dismiss his church by denying Jesus fail before the experience of his inescapable presence.

How does Jesus of Nazareth help me today?

To know about Jesus does not yet mean to believe in him. Merely considering him to be true is, of course, lifeless. Faith depends not on lifeless letters but rather on the living Lord who stands commandingly before us, above all doubt about the Bible and its stories.

Why is actually Jesus the Lord?

He is the answer to every human question. He is the salvation in all the sufferings of the world. He is the victory over all our sins. In him, you have God himself in his power and the human being in complete powerlessness.

How can a human being be God?

[14.] In the carbon copies (see ed. note 1) the whole section originally read as follows: "The command of the state could attempt to lead us against our conscience. Whether we then obey the state or not, our faith and love must discern. We stand, as long as we live, within the struggle between Christ and the world." There is a handwritten addition from Bonhoeffer in the carbon copy as follows: "[illegible] one learns that one is able to do nothing out of one's own strength. He would like to keep his conscience pure of political strife, but the law of love pressures him to do God's will even here in his personal decisions. Wherever he attempts to reconcile his Christian duty with politics, he learns that he can do nothing from his own power." The final version of the paragraph published in the *Monatsschrift für Pastoraltheologie* follows the corrections of Hildebrandt.

In no other way than that God miraculously humiliates himself in order to share everything with us. The human Jesus, born of his mother, Mary, through temptation and suffering until death on the cross, is the miracle
234 and word of God. He himself says this, and on this authority he acts. "This is the person to whom you should point and say: Here is God" (Luther).[15]

Why do so few acknowledge this?

Even if Jesus were today still performing miracles, we would remain unconverted. We want a prouder God than the one who became our brother in the manger and on the cross. This God, however, willingly became veiled in sin and death for our sake, so that solely by faith we might see that which remains incomprehensible to the rest of the world.

Why did Jesus have to go to the cross?

This remains God's secret. We can say only this about it: What takes place here is not human heroism. Here is God's own action. The Holy One enters into a world alienated from God in order to bring the sinners home. He has to suffer being forsaken by God and death just as we do. It is his very own sacrifice for us that judges and overcomes our sins and opens for us the door to our Father's house.

Has evil thereby really been driven from the world?

Christ is risen. He has taken away Satan's power. Yet nobody sees that, and there is still a battle in the world between Christ and the Antichrist. Only within his church-community does he appear as the conqueror, as the head to its members. He makes the church to be his body and through it to reveal his life.

---

[15.] It is unlikely that this is a literal citation from Luther. In his dissertation Franz Hildebrandt cited it this way: "I point to human beings and say: this is God" (Hildebrandt, *EST*, 82). According to the evidence there, this "citation" was combined from two Luther passages: from the "Confession concerning Christ's Supper," 1528 (*WA* 26:440, 34–35; *LW* 37:297: "I point to the man Christ and say, 'This is God's Son,' or, 'This man is God's Son'. . ."); and from "The Babylonian Captivity of the Church," 1520 (*WA* 6:511, 37–38; *LW* 36:35: "Both natures are simply there in their entirety, and it is truly said: 'This man is God; this God is man'" [*Sed integra utraque natura vere dicitur: Hic homo est deus, hic deus est homo*]). ["Thus, what is true in regard to Christ is also true in regard to the sacrament. In order for the divine nature to dwell in him bodily [Col. 2:9], it is not necessary for the human nature to be transubstantiated and the divine nature contained under the accidents of the human nature. Both natures are simply there in their entirety, and it is truly said: 'This man is God; this God is man'" (*LW* 36:35, 2–8).—MBL] In the 1528 treatise on Christ's supper, Luther arrived at numerous similar formulations using synecdoche [derived from a Greek term for a figure of speech or image capable of simultaneous understandings, e.g., part of something that also refers to the whole or the whole referring only to a part, where one substitutes for the other, much as in a metaphor. Luther frequently used such substitutionary expressions.—MBL].

Does the church, then, act according to the will of Christ?

The church knows today more than ever how little it obeys the Sermon
on the Mount. Yet the greater the discord in the world becomes, the more
Christ wants to have proclaimed the peace of God that reigns in his king-
dom. The church still continues daily in prayer for the return of its divine 235
Lord, and he lays his hand upon it, until he leads the church to its fulfill-
ment.

*That God exalts us and we him, we proclaim by our faith in the Holy Spirit: I believe in the Holy Spirit, who is my sanctifier.*

Who is the Holy Spirit?

The Holy Spirit is no spirit of this world but rather the Spirit of God and Christ, who is present in the church. Without this Spirit, we would know nothing of Christ, just as we would know nothing of God without Christ. In the Spirit divinity perfects itself on earth, since[16] "were you to have no church, then you would not be God" (Luther).[17]

Is God to be found only in the Christian church?

The spirit of hope has spoken in every people and in every age. Yet the Holy Spirit is the Spirit of fulfillment, by which every other spirit is judged. Where apart from Christ humanity's religion is determined by fear or delusion, the Holy Spirit leads Christianity to grace and truth.

Why, then, are there so many churches?

We really should be *one* church. Due to our inexplicable disunion, we insist on a new community of all Christians. To have such a new community is never possible for us as human beings other than in expectation and in a faith that is faithful to God's church.

Where is the true church?

The true church is where preaching stands and falls with the pure gospel of a gracious God over against all human self-righteousness. It is where the sacraments depend on the word of Christ without any element of magic. It is where the community of the Spirit exists in service and not in domination.

---

[16.] "Since" is added in handwriting in both carbon copies (see ed. note 1).

[17.] The German translated here adapts Luther's Latin in his "Dictata super Psalterium" (1515–16; *WA* 3:578, 29): "Nullam Ecclesiam haberes, tunc vere non esses deus," "You would have no Church and then truly you would not be God" (*First Lectures on the Psalms II, LW* 11:63). [In Luther's lecture he addresses Christ and says there would be no church if everyone made the church in his own image, with the result that Christ would have no church and would not be God. Bonhoeffer and Hildebrandt adapt these words to refer to the Holy Spirit.—Clifford Green]

Do I need the church?

Were you to know what the church is and why it needs you, you would not ask such a question, but rather you would rejoice. The good news would leave you no peace as long as you could have it. You would seek the com-
236 munity where one exists for the other in prayer, tells him all and forgives him all, and the promise that here one may become "a Christ to the other person" (Luther).[18]

Will one become a different person through the church?

Here, God awakens you out of sleep into sober awareness, out of narrowness into breadth, out of servitude into freedom. Here, you surrender yourself daily and become in your discipleship of Christ [Gefolgschaft Christi] lord of all things.[19] This is faith and the new life. But as long as the church is in the world, no one can decide whom God has chosen for eternity.

Who is chosen?

At the beginning and the end of every life there stands the mystery of the divine Spirit, who pardons and repudiates whomever he chooses and allows every question and every law to fall silent. In the midst of history stands the cross of Christ who died for us all. To him we flee and pray that he might make us certain of his grace until all the world gives God alone the glory.

What do we know of eternal life?

Whether we want it or not—as truly as God lives—our life has come under God's judgment and has been sustained by God's hand. Not flesh and blood, but rather spirit, soul, and body are to rise up from the dead. We know not when the hour will come, but the church looks forward with all creation to a new earth and a new heaven.

*This is the Christian faith: to know what you must do and what has been given to you.*[20]

---

[18.] Cf. Luther, "The Freedom of a Christian," 1520 (*WA* 7:35, 34–35; *LW* 31:367): "I will therefore give myself as a Christ to my neighbor, just as Christ offered himself to me." In *Sanctorum Communio*, referring to Luther and Holl, Bonhoeffer had formulated it this way: "We are God through the love that makes us charitable toward our neighbor" (*DBWE* 1:178 and ed. note 160; cf. Martin Luther, "Kirchenpostille," 1522 (*WA* 10.I/1:100, 18–20), and "Dictata super Psalterium," 1513–16 (*WA* 4:280, 2–5; *LW* 11:412) ["In the same way, every Christian is obligated to admit that he is supreme, because through the faith of Christ that dwells within him, he has become God, as a son of God and infinite, and so because now God dwells within him"—MBL]; Holl, *What Did Luther Understand by Religion?* 100. See also 2/9, p. 318: "I have Christ in my brother; in Christ I am directed toward my brother."

[19.] [Allusion to Luther's "Freedom of a Christian"; see ed. note 18.—Clifford Green]

[20.] Martin Luther, "Ten Sermons on the Catechism" (*WA* 30.I:94, 21–22; *LW* 51:169).

*Confirmation*
You should thank God that your church has the gospel. You should ask God that your faith remain loyal to God. You should vow to God that you dare to live your life according to God's word.

*The Lord's Supper* 237
You have the first Lord's Supper, which Christ himself gives you. You have in this holy Lord's Supper the daily bread of the church-community and consolation for all sadness. You have the eternal Lord's Supper in the blessedness of the kingdom of the Father.

### 8. Theses: The Discernible Nature of the Order of Creation[1]

The Discernible Nature of the Order of Creation

1. In fallen creation, we must speak of order of preservation rather than order of creation.[2]

---

[1.] Archiv des Diakonischen Werkes, Berlin, KSB 410; handwritten outline; at the upper left is a handwritten entry: "AG," apparently from the recipient Reinhold Krause (see the accompanying letter, 1/36). The abbreviation "AG" stands for Arbeitsgemeinschaft von Theologen und Nationalökonomen (Working Group of Theologians and Economists), which was part of the Church Social Federation (Kirchlich-sozialen Bundes). Regarding Bonhoeffer's participation in this working group and its relationship to the theses on the discernment of the order of creation, see 1/18, ed. note 2, and 1/36, ed. note 2. Cf. also 1/18, 1/33, and 1/49. The theses were discovered shortly before publication of the German *DBW* volume by Günter Brakelmann in the Archiv des Diakonischen Werkes after it acquired the Church Social Federation records. [At the request of Reinhold Krause, Bonhoeffer was invited to give a lecture for the Working Group of Theologians and Economists, originally scheduled for December 14, 1931, but this proved impossible for Bonhoeffer (see 1/18). He presented the lecture on January 19, 1932, on "the discernible nature of the order of creation," followed by such an intense discussion that a decision was made to continue the topic at the group's next meeting on February 9 (see 1/28 and 1/33). The document at hand is the outline of theses based on the January lecture that Bonhoeffer subsequently sent to Krause on February 17 (see 1/36), presumably influenced by the group's extended discussion on February 9 and intended for its continuing debate. These theses became a part of Bonhoeffer's critique of the views of Pastor Friedrich Peter, a member of the working group who presented an opposing paper to the group on March 1 titled "The People and the State." Bonhoeffer strenuously objected to Peter's fusion of grace, the created order, and historical destiny, clearly reflective of Peter's participation in the German Christian movement. See 1/49 and the editors' introduction, p. 16.—MBL]

[2.] With respect to Bonhoeffer's central concern in the early 1930s to replace the concept of "order of creation," a concept misused to offer theological legitimacy to *völkish* thought, with the concept of "order of preservation," see especially 2/10 and 2/13. See also Strohm, *Theologische Ethik*, 36–39.

2. The concept of order of preservation differs from that of order of creation in that historical orders as such do not possess ontological validity [keine Daseins- oder Soseinswertigkeit] in an absolute sense but are only preserved by God for the sake of their openness toward the gospel, for the hope of new creation.

3. We recognize an order as God's order of preservation if the gospel
238 can still be heard in it. We must loudly protest against an order in which the gospel can no longer be heard, even if it were to be among the oldest orders in human history.

4. The commandment of the creator is hidden from us under the form of the law of God's wrath. We cannot point to it by saying look, it is here or there. Rather, we only have it each time that we plead for forgiveness of our sins.

# C. Texts from University Lectures

## Summer Semester 1932

### 9. Lecture Course: The Nature of the Church (Student Notes)[1] 239

(Introduction)[2]

I. The Place of the Church
   (a) The Church in the World
   (b) The Church in Christendom
   (c) The Church in Dogmatic Theology

[1.] *NL*, B 2,1; handwritten lecture notes by Hanns Rüppell, 88 pages. In addition to the notebook with the lecture notes, there are eight additional pages with Rüppell's notes that refer to the lectures. The table of contents from that is published here preceding the lecture notes. According to Rüppell's notes, beginning on April 20, 1932, Bonhoeffer lectured every Wednesday and Saturday for a total of twenty hours. Wolf-Dieter Zimmermann's forty-two-page handwritten notes have also been preserved (*NL*, B 2,2) and are not as strongly formulated. This text has been consulted and is cited in the footnotes identified by the abbreviation "WDZ" where it deviates from Rüppell's notes or where Rüppell's notes have large gaps or omissions that lead to contradictory or confusing statements. Furthermore, this second set of notes is included at several places in order to establish more reliably Bonhoeffer's authorship of important or characteristic theological expressions. Where the drift of the argument or the syntax in Rüppell's notes is incorrect, the probable omissions of the notetaker are marked by [. . .] without commentary. Despite some of the shortcomings of the notes, the fundamental ideas in Bonhoeffer's lectures have nevertheless been secured. After the Second World War, both Rüppell and Zimmermann reported that Bonhoeffer's lectures had fascinated them and the other listeners (cf. Otto Dudzus's preface to his compilation of the notes in *GS* 5:227–28, and the entire text of the compiled notes in *GS* 5:228–75). The lecture includes many of Bonhoeffer's statements from his 1927 dissertation, "Sanctorum Communio"; regarding this entire essay, see *DBWE* 1. [For the title of his lecture course, Bonhoeffer possibly had in

II. The Form of the Church
  Preliminary Comment about (the concept) "Form"
  (A) Adam and Christ
  (B) Church and Christ: The Present Christ [. . .] of the Church as the Body of Christ
    (1) Christ's Vicarious Representative Action[3] as the Founding of the Church
      (a) Ethical Concept of Vicarious Representative Action
      (b) Christ's Vicarious Representative Action
        1. Incarnation
        2. Christ enters into the community of the people [Volksgemeinschaft] and fulfills the Law vicariously
        3. Christ dies on the Cross
        4. Christ is risen
    (2) Jesus Christ and the Founding of the Church
    (3) Fundamental Structure of the Church in and through Christ
      (a) Structure of Unity: Christ Existing as Church-Community[4]

---

mind Harnack's famous lectures on "The Essence [Wesen] of Christianity," translated as *What Is Christianity?* If so, Bonhoeffer chose to emphasize the church rather than a generic concept such as Christianity.—Clifford Green]

[2.] The lecture contents are included in Rüppell's notes on two separate pages. Nonessential deviations from the actual text are indicated by brackets around remarks added by the German editors. In the actual lecture course, Bonhoeffer presented a lengthy introduction about the contemporary question of the church before proceeding to part I, "The Place of the Church." This introduction is not listed in the table of contents. [As indicated here, where the text of the student notes was incomplete or unclear the German *DBW* editor added or revised text, indicated here by brackets; brackets are also used here for the insertion of original German words where those are significant. Parentheses in the text are from the original student text. In the footnotes, bracketed additions from *DBWE* editors are initialed; other bracketed insertions in the notes are by the German *DBW* editor.—VB]

[3.] [*Stellvertretung*, a central concept in Bonhoeffer's Christology and ethics, is translated throughout *DBWE* as "vicarious representative action" (cf. *DBWE* 1:120, ed. note 17). The basic idea is one who stands in the place of and acts for the sake of others, whether collectively or individually. God's becoming human in Jesus Christ is the paradigmatic instance of *Stellvertretung*.—CG]

[4.] [This is the standard *DBWE* translation of *Gemeinde*. It is Bonhoeffer's preferred word to describe the church as a theological entity, and it emphasizes its communal character. *Christus als Gemeinde existierend*, Christ existing as church-community, is the axiom of Bonhoeffer's ecclesiology. For discussion of *Gemeinde* and related terms in Bonhoeffer's ecclesiology, see *DBWE* 1:14–17. Contexts where *Gemeinde* simply means congregation are usually obvious.—CG]

(b) Structure of Lordship in the Church: Christ as the Lord of the Church-Community

(c) Christ, the Brother

(C) The Acting Church-Community: The Acting Christ 240

I. The Holy Spirit and Christ

II. The Church and Religious Community

III. Proclamation and the Church: The Word—the Assembly of the Congregation—the Office of Preacher—Confession of Faith [Bekenntnis]

Theology, Dogma, Council

IV. The Priesthood of All Believers—(the) Being-for-One-Another [Füreinander] Is Constituted by the Being-with-One-Another [Miteinander] in the Church-Community!

(1) The Neighbor's Readiness to Make Every Sacrifice

(2) Intercession

(3) Forgiveness of sins

(D) The Worldliness of the Church[5]

The Renunciation of Purity (Excommunication)!

(E) The Christianity[6] of the Church

Actualization in the world as visible church and believed church

(F) The Boundaries of the Church

Bonhoeffer: The Nature of the Church
Summer Semester 1932—Berlin—Wednesday and Saturday
9–10:00 a.m.

April 20 [1932]

[Introduction]

*Do we need the church*? This is the question asked by lukewarm, skeptical individuals from [the] historical tradition of liberalism, from the history- 241
of-religion,[7] or from [the] bourgeoisie. Others who have been inspired by mysticism: the same question. Another group from the church spectrum: the church is necessary; great *official authority* of the church, *the ideology*

[5.] Bonhoeffer merged sections D and E into one section by the final version of his lecture course.

[6.] [*Christlichkeit* (literally "Christianness").—VB]

[7.] This should be the "history-of-religions school" (see p. 206, ed. note 157).

*of leadership* [Führertum],[8] community is necessary (emphatically so).[9] Models of the Anglo-Saxon nature of the church, the ecumenical forms! (In the Anglo-Saxon model: church action is encouraged! Misuse of the word, of speech.)[10] Among us in Germany, the general direction of Dibelius's[11] conception: the most powerful intrusion of Anglo-Saxon influence into Germany.[12] [. . .] Cultural encounters between Anglo-Saxons and Germany.

The demand for the ideology of leadership [through] the youth movement [and] National Socialism. The leader in the church, who dares to give orders. We need strong direction in the church; that is why we need [the ideology of leadership in the] church.[13] *Community* is necessary: the youth movement is behind this; in [the] postwar years community was the basis of
242 all life.[14] Theological working communities.[15] Outside the church, one found fulfillment of the meaning of life in [the] community.[16] Religious community [is] a special group. Because of this one needs church.

---

[8.] [The ideology of *Führertum* began to have popular appeal during the 1920s, particularly among youth, and was already a central precept of Nazi ideology and rhetoric by the early 1930s. See also Bonhoeffer's 1933 radio address "The Führer and the Individual in the Younger Generation" (*DBWE* 12, 2/9, esp. 274–75), in which he draws a clear distinction between *Führung* and *Führertum*. See also ed. note 13 below.—VB]

[9.] See, for example, E. Stange, *Volkskirche als Organismus*; Thimme, *Im Kampf um die Kirche*; and Heim, "Das Führerproblem."

[10.] Within the context of his ecumenical activities, Bonhoeffer often criticized the practical church activism of Anglo-Saxon participants, who did not appear willing or able to ground their work theologically and ecclesiastically. (See pp. 356–57, 369–70, and 385.)

[11.] See Otto Dibelius's *Das Jahrhundert der Kirche* (1927), which was already in its 5th edition by 1928. Dibelius expressed the new self-consciousness of the church in the Weimar Republic after the crisis of 1918 and emphasized the opportunities of the new situation for the church in a secular state but in his argumentation remained entirely on the church-practical level. For a discussion of Dibelius's famous book, see his *Nachspiel* and Barth, "Quousque tandem . . . ?"

[12.] Cf. WDZ: "American ways of life flowing back toward Europe since the first separation [i.e., the emigration of the so-called left wing of the Reformation to America]."

[13.] On the youth movement phenomenon at the end of the 1920s, see the contemporary judgment from the ecclesiastical and theological point of view in Stählin's article "Jugendbewegung: I. Geschichte und Bedeutung," 506–12. On Bonhoeffer's critique of the National Socialist ideology of the Führer, see his "The Führer and the Individual," *DBWE* 12, 2/9.

[14.] See, for example, Heim, "Das Führerproblem."

[15.] See Stählin, "Jugendbewegung: I. Geschichte und Bedeutung," 511–12.

[16.] One of the most significant of these was the Ecclesiastical Society in Württemberg, founded in 1930. [The Württemberg Society became particularly important during the Nazi era as the voice of the radical Confessing Church there; see Barnett, *For the Soul of the People*, esp. 211, 222, and 224.—VB]

This demand [for an ideology of leadership and community in the church] arises out of the *secular* realm.[17] Authority, community in the state. [A] "Führer"[18] [is] not named in [the] Bible; there are apostles, etc.[19] In [the] Reformation [there is the] preacher [and the] teacher, insofar as he serves properly,[20] not insofar as he leads properly. Transposed now into the ecclesiastical realm having moved first out of the secular realm.[21]

[There has] always been a "call for the church." Today the source of [the call] openly in the secular realm. Community arising from romantic life-forms, kenotic.[22] The concept of community in communism [and] in National Socialism.[23] Church demand for community in secular form. Yearning arises out of events in the secular sphere. Here the church is the means for other purposes! Community, authority, a Führer are demanded directly. Church [is] only secondary.

Skepticism: "We need the church"? Doubt about [the] word "need." [Is] the *need* decisive, where God is simply there as Lord, where he wants us, where we are here for him? *"Do I need God?"* is senseless. We are bound to him. The word and revelation of God even in the church, where he so speaks to human beings. "I need" for my own purposes always! But not in this case. Question about [the] usefulness of the church is senseless.[24]
God has spoken and has revealed himself to us in the church. "The Church 243
of Christ" as the revelation of God! We believe this because we believe in Christ. *What is the church as the revelation of God!?* That is our question! "Do I need a Christian God?" This is a question one cannot ask because then "God" is not. *"One does not need the church!"* [. . . particularly not] as church with its human servants, its errors. In this context, the deep need of the

[17.] Sentence reversed. WDZ: "All these values are taken from *the secular sphere*."

[18.] [We have retained the German word here because it was already a loaded term in Germany, even before the National Socialists came to power. The "ideology of the Führer" was attractive to German youth throughout the 1920s. See Bonhoeffer's early reflections on this in *DBWE* 12, 2/8 and 2/9.—VB]

[19.] WDZ cites Paul's letters to the Corinthians and the Ephesians. Bonhoeffer probably was referring to 1 Cor. 12:28 ("apostles, prophets and teachers") as well as to Eph. 4:11 ("apostles, prophets, evangelists, pastors and teachers").

[20.] This must mean "teaches." Cf. WDZ: "Reformation: to teach correctly, not to lead correctly; teacher-student does not mean leader-follower."

[21.] The youth movement—despite all its religiosity—initially developed at a distance from and in opposition to the churches. (See Stahlin, "Jugendbewegung: I. Geschichte und Bedeutung," 512–13).

[22.] The word "kenotic" here should probably be "erotic"; cf. WDZ: "community" [the overcoming of individualism as a foundation; erotic; surrender. [. . .]"

[23.] WDZ: "The new community in Bolshevist theory and National Socialism."

[24.] WDZ: "I cannot ask whether I need God; therefore I cannot ask whether I need the church."

church [is] visible.[25] [. . .] The church doesn't bind us [anymore]. [. . .] The church is (the) *place where God speaks, where God is!!!*

April 23 [1932]

One cannot bypass God.[26] "Do I need?" is a question that simply may not be asked in theology.[27] He [God] is simply here! No postulates of thought![28] Theology is related to the God-given realities given to us that [are] not bound to us.

*What is the church as the revelation of God? What is the claim* of the church!? The Catholic concept of church seems not to include thoughts of claims on the church (the church is a being!)[29] Barth: seemingly speaks only of claims and sees therein the essential nature of the church. (The church is an *actus.*)[30] One must speak of the being and act of the church together.

---

[25.] WDZ: "The need of the church. With the contemporary church God has become poor."

[26.] WDZ: "The church is the place where God speaks. He who passes by the church passes by God. One can [. . . one illegible word] not do so, however. One can only go against God."

[27.] WDZ: "The 'religious need' (R. Seeberg). The presupposition of theology, redemption, grace, the church is there *for me.*" Seeberg maintained the view that the Christian religion is to be grounded not on the basis of reason but with respect to revelation. There the prerequisites in the human spirit must also be taken into account (see Seeberg, *Grundriss der Dogmatik,* 5–6). For Seeberg, the superiority of the Christian religion manifested itself in the fact that it did the best for human spiritual need. Bonhoeffer also disagreed with Seeberg on other points (see his 1930 letter to Rößler, *DBWE* 10:205, as well as pp. 204 and 239 in this volume).

[28.] WDZ: "Theology has nothing to do with the postulates of our spirit, rather with realities! Sin and redemption *exist.*"

[29.] WDZ: "Catholicism has church as essence without claim." Cf. *DBWE* 2:104–5. On Bonhoeffer's critical discussion of the Catholic concept of church, see *DBWE* 1:125, 256–57, 260–61, and 187–88. For the literature cited by Bonhoeffer in his critique of Catholicism, see *DBWE* 1:125–26, ed. note 11.

[30.] WDZ: "Barth speaks only of claim without speaking of essence or being." During the 1920s, Barth developed his concept of church within the determination of the relationship between God and the human being, which was characterized by a newly promulgated claim of God to the individual human being (see, for example, Barth, *Die christliche Dogmatik,* 295). Cf. also Bonhoeffer's discussion with the "actualism" of the early Barth and his attempt to overcome the opposition between act and being in his 1930 dissertation (*DBWE* 2:82–87). [For Barth the church is not "being," e.g., qua institution, but rather "event," as an act of God speaking and the believer responding to God's word. This event character is Barth's "actualism." See Hunsinger, *How to Read Karl Barth.*—CG]

Disposition 244
I. Locating the church as the place of God in the world! Locality has both being and claim at the same time.[31] *God* is, as far as we can think of God, *in one place.* In [the] church, in [the word], as "God for us."[32] "God without a place" is an expression of modern religiosity (stemming from mysticism—Angelus Silesius—and from rationalism).[33]

II *The Form of the Church*: (a) Adam and Christ; (b) The present Christ [in] the church as the body of Christ; (c) the acting congregation, the acting Christ; (d) worldliness of the church; (e) Christianity of the church; (f) boundaries of the church! (can be seen through [the] concept of the world and predestination and the kingdom of God).

[Literature]
(Systematic, not historical lecture)[34]

Holl in: Luther;[35] Kattenbusch: *Der evangelische Kirchengedanke im Anschluß an Luther*;[36] C. L. Schmidt: Kirche des Urchristentums;[37] Löhe: 245
*Three Books concerning the Church* (Congregation); Kliefoth: *Acht Bücher von der Kirche* (office).

The present: Karl Barth, [in] *Zwischen den Zeiten* 1927: Begriff der Kirche;[38] 1930: Quousque tandem;[39] and Barth 1931: The crisis [Not] of the Evangelical Church, in *Zwischen den Zeiten*.[40] Dibelius's reply: *Verant-*

[31.] WDZ: "Being without a place [*Ortlosigkeit*] is simultaneously being and claim. In place [*Ort*] someone is facing us." The expression "without a place" may have appeared in another connection, since the sentence is so meaningless and Ruppell's notes here retain the more suitable concept of having a place (*Örtlichkeit*).

[32.] WDZ: "So far as God is for us, he is in one place; to what extent God is God for himself, and is the absolute, we do not know."

[33.] WDZ: "Rationalism and mysticism created the concept of God's having no place (Angelus Silesius)." Angelus Silesius's mystical concept of God had at its center the idea that God can have no being outside the soul itself. On this basis, we find the portrayal of a fusion with God in various images.

[34.] WDZ: "The development of the history of dogma in the Christian church is set forth in the RGG [the multivolume *Religion in Geschichte und Gegenwart*—VB]." See Hohlwein, "Kirche."

[35.] In WDZ the reference is to Holl's "Die Entstehung von Luthers Kirchenbegriff," in his *Gesammelte Aufsätze*, 1:288–325.

[36.] Kattenbusch, *Der evangelische Kirchengedanke* (1930).

[37.] K. L. Schmidt, "Die Kirche des Urchristentums" (1927).

[38.] Barth, "Der Begriff der Kirche" (1927).

[39.] Barth, "Quousque tandem . . . ?" (1930).

[40.] Barth, "Die Not der Evangelischen Kirche" (1931).

*wortung der Kirche*[41] [. . .]; Dibelius's *Das Jahrhundert der Kirche*, 1927;[42] Berneuchenerbuch[43] (symbolic interpretation);[44] Erik Peterson (converted to Catholicism), *Was ist Theologie*;[45] *Die Kirche*, 1921;[46] Adam, 1926: The Spirit of Catholicism;[47] Georg Schulz: Sinn der Kirche, 1927.[48]

I. The Place of the Church

(a) in the World
Today's theology is the theology of understanding, not of the solution. That is decisive. Here also [that is, in the doctrine of the church] the question of understanding.[49] [. . .] Churches and castles towered over the Middle Ages; today note New York (Trinity Church!).[50]

246 1. Our church is without a place
[The] desire of our church to be everywhere results in its being nowhere. That which is tangible becomes unassailable![51] The church is never and nowhere itself anymore.[52] Existence without a place is the existence of Cain, of the refugee.[53] Therefore despised! Misfortune: [The] church did not wish to isolate itself, wanted to fit in. Only since then has [the] church remained behind. The attitude of the world [toward the church] is deter-

[41.] Dibelius, *Die Verantwortung der Kirche* (see above p. 272, ed. note 11).

[42.] See p. 272, ed. note 11.

[43.] *Das Berneuchener Buch: Von Anspruch des Evangeliums auf die Kirche der Reformation* (1926). Ludwig Heitmann, Karl Bernhard Ritter, and Wilhelm Stählin were primarily responsible for its final form.

[44.] In a similar fashion, Bonhoeffer's friend Franz Hildebrandt had already emphasized the central role of symbols in the *Berneuchener Buch* to convey divine and human reality—in a critical fashion. See Hildebrandt, *EST*, 68.

[45.] Peterson, *Was ist Theologie?* (1925).

[46.] Peterson, *Die Kirche* (1929).

[47.] Adam, *Das Wesen des Katholizismus*, 2nd ed., 1925. [Because this exists in English translation, the English title is given in the text.—VB]

[48.] Schulz, *Vom Sinn der Kirche* (1925).

[49.] WDZ: "Theology of understanding and of seeing anew. Barth introduced new insights" [cf. above pp. 224–44].

[50.] Trinity Church Wall Street, at the southern tip of Manhattan, stands in the shadow of countless skyscrapers.

[51.] [There is a wordplay here in the German; Bonhoeffer is contrasting *greifbar* (tangible) with *unangreifbar* (unassailable). The editors thank Christiane Tietz for this observation.—VB]

[52.] WDZ: "The flight from itself; disguise. Nowhere is the church itself. The church became utterly of the world; the world did not become the church."

[53.] Cf. Gen. 4:12–16.

mined essentially by the fact that the church has no place. [The] sects that [are] tied to a place are often to be taken much more seriously.[54] Because the church has become without a place, the church has only favored and no longer *actual* places.

April 27 [1932]

(2. The church has only favored places in the world)[55]
[The] church is hated because it [accidentally][56] prefers certain places [. . .] although it doesn't know that it is placeless.[57] Favored places [are] still available where traditional ties still [exist]. The *bourgeoisie* is the favored place [of the church], until it finds its own place again. Anxious conservatism and place-bound conservatism; our church does not belong to the first sort of conservatism. The transformation of our church by *bourgeois standards.*[58] (Tillich: *The Religious Situation*).[59] Ecclesiastical action con- 247
cerns itself mostly [only] with [the] *petite bourgeoisie*; it cannot incorporate intellectuals, capitalists, and workers. (The needs of the *petite bourgeoisie* are those mostly mentioned; [the] needs of the enemies of the church [are missing.])[60] [The] horizon shrinks!

[The] church has lost its *real* place and has become acculturated [verweltlicht].[61] Dibelius: the church [has] become independent and occupies

[54.] WDZ: "One takes sects seriously today because they *stand* in a specific place. An object can be described only when it occupies a specific place. Here [. . . one illegible word] nothing else can stand. [This is true] also of the concept of God; everywhere and nowhere. The church cannot bear the sense of loneliness where it stands."

[55.] This is the way WDZ retains the heading.

[56.] [*Zufällig*; this could also be translated as "the church happens to . . ." The reader is reminded that this and all additions in brackets have been inserted by the German editor.—VB]

[57.] WDZ: "The church doesn't know its own place anymore. It no longer feels comfortable anywhere. 'This is it!'—An expression about a place; [there is a] gradual difference in its ability to adjust. [It is] no longer the standard for *the* place. The church is hated for the sake of its preferred place; or the less preferred place."

[58.] The criticism of the bourgeois transformation of the church can be found in Bonhoeffer's 1927 dissertation; see esp. *DBWE* 1:271–74.

[59.] See Tillich's criticism of the bourgeois transformation of the Protestant churches in the nineteenth century in *The Religious Situation*, 191–219.

[60.] WDZ: "Worship services are aimed at only the *petite bourgeoisie.* (One knows only the needs of the *petite bourgeoisie,* and only these are supported; the needs of economic leaders, the needs of the intellectuals, atheists, revolutionaries [are missing]."

[61.] WDZ: "The church becomes radically acculturated; [it] puts down roots in worldly ceremonies. A bourgeois institution. Claim to [a] specific place."

its own place.[62] But this place since 1918, is *not* its *own place*![63] Autonomous culture has been shaken off. Now that the church [has] supposedly become autonomous, it has made itself harmonious with culture, and it seeks new cultural forms; therefore it has become the slave of culture.[64] Church—place of today is privileged place! (built into [the] contemporary culture); the church is without a place.

(3) What is the proper place of the church?
[This] cannot be stated concretely. [It is the] place of the present Christ in the world. It is God's own will that chooses his place. [That is] the *place of God*
248 *himself*; therefore it can never be [a] place assumed by a human being.[65] It must be qualified through God's gracious presence. God must reveal himself to it.[66] The place that could be the proper place as such cannot be the locus of the church. The church cannot appeal to the particular place. The church is really and truly without a place! No human being can dispose over this; even the church cannot.[67]

[The] place of God in the world is not the same as [the] place of the church. How can [the] church make the historical place a real place? It must be conscious of the fact that it can never create the place itself. The church cannot do this, but *it should know that God can do this deed.* The church

[62.] Dibelius advocated the view that the Protestant church stood "at the beginning of its century." (See Dibelius, *Das Jahrhundert der Kirche*, 197, and elsewhere.) He came to this optimistic estimation not least because of the new situation of a relatively free church within the secular (*religionslos*) state after 1919. Against this background, Dibelius defined the church's irreplaceable achievements as the setting of moral standards for culture and the life of the state (ibid., 223–32) and pointed to the limited possibilities for the state to preserve the highest values and a complete development of the people (232–41). See also ed. note 11.

[63.] In the August 11, 1919, Weimar Republic constitution, the concept of a state church was, on the one hand, rejected; on the other, however, Articles 137 and 138 gave the churches extensive rights and the status of public legal corporations (see H. Hildebrandt, *Die deutsche Verfassungen*, 102).

[64.] WDZ: "The place is not its own proper place but rather [the] place given to it by autonomous culture as a gift of grace. The church is harmoniously integrated into the cultural whole. And therefore never its own proper place? Connection to other forms of culture is bondage to the autonomous culture."

[65.] WDZ: "Therefore the place of God; for this reason not one that can be indicated or captured by a human being."

[66.] [I.e., to the place.—VB] WDZ: "A place that is qualified by God's free will; God acknowledges this place."

[67.] WDZ: "The church is now robbed of every place that this could be (not the state church, not the bourgeoisie). Basically the church is without place. For no human being can determine its place, only God."

is aware of its own lack of a particular place, [therefore] that there is no favored place for it before God chooses the place for it. The church's characteristic place is there where it waits *for God to give it [its] characteristic place* ([namely] to be the place of God himself). God has no place; the church must know this. It is then that it has escaped from the human odyssey of being without a place.[68] *There where no human place can establish the church, there is [the]* place *of the church*; namely, there where God is alone with his congregation! Yet the church is always in the midst of culture. The same "Yes" and the same "No" of all human places, the absolute center of the church! There where God allows the church to find its own place, is the place of the church! Then the church [will be] loved or hated only because of its own cause (the gospel).[69] The church's proper place is [the] "*critical center of the world.*" From that point [there are] no longer any favored places. [The] *crisis is God himself,* not the pastor; the church is the critical center.[70]
Where [one] is completely without a place, where [one is on] the periphery, 249
there is [the] critical center of the world (*Galilee* in the Roman Empire or *Wittenberg*).[71]

April 30 [1932]—no lecture held.[72]

---

[68.] WDZ: "[It is] reliant upon God alone. There are no favored places any longer. [It is] the church awaiting the word of God, to be God's place in the world. It can never find its place alone. The church that knows this has the promise of God. Therefore, the human lack of place will not happen. [The church is] the place where God must come, the place of waiting filled with promise.

[69.] WDZ: "Hated for Christ's sake."

[70.] WDZ: "That is its meaning: [to be] the critical center, where all is judged [*wo alles gerichtet wird*]. The church must be there where God speaks. No one knows where this center is. But God makes it visible and everyone must pass by it. The church can only witness to the center of the world, which God alone creates. It must attempt to give God room."

[71.] WDZ: "Catholic: Where the sacraments are performed, there is the church. Protestant: [. . .] what is done, [happens] from above. There are no favored places from God's point of view; all are under the same light. God is the critical middle, determined only by God; there is no obvious place for this."

[72.] [Bonhoeffer was a participant in the theological conference of the Provisional Bureau for Ecumenical Youth Work, April 29–30 in Berlin, and wrote the primary report of its proceedings. See 2/13.—MBL]

May 4 [1932]

(b) The Place of the Church in Christendom

On what has the hatred for the church [been founded]? [It is] not hatred against the Christian people.[73] *The church on the periphery*: where [the] life of the individual stands at its high points or turning points (baptism, confirmation, marriage, death), there are the high points of the ecclesiastical activities of Christianity. There is the church.[74] *Nature* and celebration belong together, so one thinks; the church is merely the bond. *Ecclesiastical celebration of nature!* The church is the exception from the everyday. Celebration is (1) only, to *interrupt* everyday activities, [and yet] always [with] an eye to [the] everyday; celebration as the boundary of the everyday. (2) In the midst of celebration everyday thoughts are to be suppressed. The church should *distract*, deepen, and ennoble.[75] A worship service is an ecclesiastical celebration. [And yet] under [the] rule of the everyday the church still stands.[76] The church feels comfortable as the *place of celebration*.[77] A cinema:[78] doesn't a cinema serve this purpose better (than the church)?[79] The sphere of profanity. *Profanity can be celebrated better in a cinema.*[80]

250 *The contemporary church is only "celebratory" Christianity.*[81] The Christianity of everyday life is not in [the] church. The church is on *the periphery of life*, not in the center![82] The church would like to step into the center. But [it is] abandoned on Sundays. Therefore, *hate* for the church exists

[73.] WDZ: "The church and Christianity [are] not identical."

[74.] WDZ: "Where life stands before that which is unique (primarily [has] nothing to do with Christianity), there are high points of life and [of] what is Christian: confirmation, marriage, birth, baptism, death."

[75.] WDZ: "Everyday thoughts should not be touched upon, deflected, raised up, deepened in celebrations: that is the church's position today."

[76.] WDZ: "Sunday worship is a church celebration. [The] church service stands under the law of the everyday. What the everyday person wants, that's what it [the church] does."

[77.] WDZ: "There the church feels indispensable."

[78.] WDZ: "The church [is] emptier—the cinema fuller."

[79.] WDZ: "Exceptional interruption of the everyday. [The] cinema serves this need better than the church."

[80.] WDZ: "The sphere of profanity is better in the cinema (tragic, criminal, comic). The church [is] actually not profane. [It oozes] tact, when one goes to the cinema to celebrate."

[81.] WDZ: "The church encompasses only [the] celebrating Christianity."

[82.] WDZ: "[The] church acts as though it stood in the center."

[. . .] church's place on the periphery! From lack of criticism,[83] the church speaks about central matters [from] the periphery.[84]

What is *the proper place of the church in Christianity,* [the] church of Christ? God's reality must not be seen as [a] kind of exception, also *not as a holiday in an ethical or religious sense!* Therefore, the celebratory character of the church.[85] God is not [an] aspect of reality! [The] *entire reality, including the everyday,* must be seen! Even [the] Christian religion can have the character of an exception, but God cannot. One does not celebrate with thoughts [alone] of God. God penetrates the entire everyday reality and must be felt in everything![86] *The* absolute exception is the church as the word of God for all of Christianity. Where the word breaks in, there is the church, is *the center of Christianity*; there the church as *a whole* is Christianity, insofar as it hears God's word over *all* reality. *The church* [Kirche] *is the church-community* [Gemeinde], *is there where the word is believed and obeyed; there is the center!*[87] The church is the center of the world and is the church-community of God.[88] It is not true that the church-community can refer to itself as the center (Rome!),[89] rather insofar as it points to God, who occupies the center.[90]

Christianity is not removed from the world.[91] [It] is in the everydayness 251
of the world. Therefore, the word must stand in [the] sphere of the everyday. [The church is] not an "exceptional light" outside the profane realm, not a separation of church and the world.[92]

[83.] This must mean "self-criticism."

[84.] WDZ: "In an unsuitable way, judgmental words about the center of life come from the periphery. The church is the ennobled profane; it has no right to make judgments."

[85.] WDZ: "Therefore the worship service [as] an exception in [the] church. This is only *one* aspect of reality. The *whole* reality and everyday reality [is] in the church; it [i.e., the whole reality] will be seen as it comes to stand under the judgment of God."

[86.] WDZ: "His judgment and word penetrate the whole of everyday life in the center. That is *the* exception from *the* center of reality; as the word of humanity; all-powerful as the word of God over all of Christianity. The church is [the] center of Christianity."

[87.] WDZ: "Only God creates the center."

[88.] WDZ: "Where God calls out Christians, there is [the] church."

[89.] See p. 274, ed. note 29.

[90.] WDZ: "The church-community of God is [the] center of the world. It does not point to itself; rather it points to the Lord, who occupies the center."

[91.] WDZ: "Christianity still belongs entirely to the world."

[92.] WDZ: "No distancing! The world [is] seen as a whole: [as] the reality of God."

(c) The Place of the Church in Dogmatic Theology

Theology is a function of the church.[93] How is a scholarly understanding of the church about its nature [possible]?[94] *Augustine*: "church" writings;[95] with him [the] problem of the church is solved for the Catholic Church. [It was first treated again] in 1489 [by] Cardinal Torquemada in [his] *Summa de ecclesia*.[96] For one thousand years, [one did not] see this problem. Only the primacy [of the pope] is problematic; [beginning with] Hus and Wycliffe we have ecclesiastical literature again.[97] In [the era of
252 the] Reformation the article "De ecclesia"[98] [was] worked out by Bellarmine.[99] *Scholasticism* needed no treatise [about it]:[100] [it was] naturally a self-evident presupposition. There would be no theology if [the] Catholic Church did not exist. In scholastic dogmatics *the concept of the church stands*

[93.] See p. 284, ed. note 107, and p. 285, ed. note 117. The formulation oriented toward Barth, "theology as function of the church," can already be found in Bonhoeffer in his 1929–30 postdoctoral dissertation. Cf. *DBWE* 2:130.

[94.] In reply to the question Bonhoeffer at first gave a historical survey. [See also Brown, *Augustine of Hippo*, 212–32.—MBL]

[95.] Augustine developed his concept of the church in discussion with the North African Donatists, who had separated themselves from the Catholic Church because they regarded sacraments performed by those who had committed mortal sin as ineffective. Augustine's most important work on his concept of the church is the principal work, completed in 426, titled *The City of God*. See also Flasch, *Augustin*, 155–72 and 384–88.

[96.] Cardinal Juan de Torquemada composed his *Summa de ecclesia contra impugnatores potestatis summi pontificis* around 1450. At the Council of Basel, he defended the leadership demands of Pope Eugene IV against the attacks by the conciliar circles.

[97.] [Instead of "ecclesiastical" the word should be "ecclesiological."—CG] In his writings "De ecclesia" and "De potestate papae," John Wycliffe turned primarily against the power of the papacy in the church. In his recognition of the immediate access of the faithful to the grace of God, he came close to Luther's formulation of the priesthood of all believers. Johannes Hus's understanding of the church in his tract about the church depends partly on Wycliffe's tract (cf. *Magistri Ioannis Hus tractatus de ecclesia*, edited by S. H. Thomson). On the understanding of the church by Wycliffe and Hus, see also M. A. Schmidt, "Dogma und Lehre im Abendland," 1:728–34 and 743–47.

[98.] "About the church."

[99.] Cardinal Robert Bellarmine, a theologian who excelled in controversy, developed his ecclesiology in the debate with the Reformation critique of the Roman church. Accordingly, large sections of his expositions about the church defend the pope's claim to primacy as well as his "temporal" or worldly power that extends beyond the spiritual. Cf. Bellarmine, "Disputationes de controversiis christianae fidei adversus huius temporibus haereticos" (1586–93), in *Opera omnia*, 1:451ff.; 2; and 3:1–322. Cf. also Galeota, "Bellarmini, Roberto." WDZ: "In the dispute with (the) Reformation, Bellarmine founded the Catholic definition."

[100.] Cf. Hohlwein, "Die Kirche," 798: "*Scholasticism* has, as a whole, hardly ever touched upon the article, *de ecclesia* [about the church]."

*outside the problematic brackets!*[101] [. . .] Articles [are] mere pieces of theology. Augustine thought of the church as the presupposition of all articles of dogmatics.[102]

May 7 [1932][103]

The church in the world cannot declare favored places as its own proper place. People consider [the] place of celebrations as the place of the church; it is, however, the most easily expendable for any person. The right place for the church is available only for those who are in the church. [. . .] [The] state cannot give the church its proper place.

The essential problem: why does Catholic *Scholasticism* leave [a] lacuna where [an] article "de ecclesia" [should be included]? Historical explanation! But [similarly] a substantive explanation is necessary. The significance of the church is made clear where the church is the presupposition of all theology. [An] isolated theology cannot build [a] private opinion about God, Christ, and [the] Holy Spirit, because previously the genuine testimony (has occurred) inside the church; therefore one can [not] put 253
the church inside the brackets. [But this does] not leave a lacuna [there]! [It is] a sign of uncertainty when one finally again refers to "Articulus de ecclesia."[104] The church is the presupposition. Treatment of the concept of

[101.] For example, in the monumental *Summa Theologiae* by Thomas Aquinas, there is no section about the doctrine of the church. [Here and in the following passages Bonhoeffer uses the image of "brackets" that enclose the entire content of dogmatics. Because the self-revelation of God confessed in the faith of the church is the presupposition of all theology, the church stands "outside" the brackets, as the presupposition that qualifies everything "inside" the brackets. In other words, one cannot treat the church as just one article within dogmatics, as if one could talk about Trinity, creation, reconciliation, and redemption apart from the church. The fact that the church is not "inside the brackets" of the system of dogmatics does not mean dogmatics has a lacuna—the church as the presupposition of all theology means it pervades the whole.—CG]

[102.] See p. 282, ed. note 95.

[103.] The following section at the beginning of the new lecture hour presents a postscript to "(b) The Place of the Church in Christendom" and interrupts the train of thought within the paragraph "(c) The Place of the Church in Dogmatic Theology."

[104.] "Article of faith about the church." Bonhoeffer's thought is more clearly expressed in Zimmermann's notes: "Why does Catholic dogmatics have this lacuna of the article 'de ecclesia'? (This cannot be) explained historically. In the church everything that can be said in theology about the individual topics of dogma takes place daily. It is already there in praxis. Therefore, the concept of the church can be the presupposition. True happening in the church; this is what dogmatics should speak about. Real self-testimony in the church. When one later wants to fill in this lacuna (concept of church), one's own uncertainty becomes evident. That which is out of the question becomes worthy of discussion."

the church becomes more and more isolated. Protestant theology became more independent [and] could when necessary be understood even without the church.[105] *Schleiermacher* brings back [the] connection between the church and theology[106] (as Barth does today in a different way).[107] In him,[108] there is a new valuation of the church. [. . .] The central thought is the "church." [. . .] His "church" is the voluntary union of pious Christians. Thereby [the] church is traced back to the piety of the individual. The church is not the ultimate presupposition. Individual religiosity is the presupposition of everything.[109]

254 *Ritschl*:[110] Ideas about the congregation![111] He too doesn't see the church as presupposition of everything.[112] Insight into [the] Catholic, Scholastic theology, therefore, is missing here as well. For the Scholastics,

[105.] WDZ: "*Protestant* dogmatics has always had an article on the church. The more development, the more powerful is the concept of the church within the brackets. Protestant theology, therefore, appears more independent; no tie to the church. Theology can be understood from within itself."

[106.] Schleiermacher defined the relationship of theology to the church as functional: "Christian theology, accordingly, is that assemblage of scientific knowledge and practical instruction without the possession and application of which a united leadership of the Christian church, i.e., a government of the church in the fullest sense, is not possible" (Schleiermacher, *Brief Outline of Theology*, 20).

[107.] In 1932 the first volume of Barth's monumental *Church Dogmatics* appeared. He changed the title from the original *Die christliche Dogmatik im Entwurf* (1927) to *Church Dogmatics*. On the one hand, he wanted to set a good example in light of giving up the superficial use of the great word "Christian" that he had fought against. On the other hand, he explicitly pointed out that "dogmatics is not a free science. It is bound to the sphere of the church, where alone it is possible and meaningful" (Barth, *Church Dogmatics*, I/1:xiii).

[108.] The reference is to Schleiermacher.

[109.] Cf. Schleiermacher, *Christian Faith*, § 115: "The Christian church takes shape through the coming together of regenerate individuals to form a system of mutual interaction and cooperation." On Bonhoeffer's dispute with Schleiermacher, see *DBWE* 1:158–61, esp. Bonhoeffer's note 18 on p. 159. Bonhoeffer's criticism of Schleiermacher's individualism follows that of Ritschl (cf. *Critical History of the Christian Doctrine*, 1:485–87).

[110.] WDZ: "Ritschl pursues this point."

[111.] Albrecht Ritschl gave the idea of the congregation a central position in his three-volume work published in 1870–74, *The Christian Doctrine of Justification and Reconciliation*. According to Ritschl, the divine intention of justification is directed not immediately to the individual but rather to the congregation. The individual can be forgiven only within the congregation. Compare Ritschl's understanding of the church in vol. 3, *The Positive Development of the Doctrine*, 284–90 and 452–72.

[112.] Already in *Sanctorum Communio*, Bonhoeffer had criticized Ritschl's individualism in his doctrine of sin. See *DBWE* 1:113–14.

to speak of God is to no longer have God at one's disposal. Theological expression is not isolated but rather stands within the church.[113]

We Protestants approach Catholic dogma with the wrong premise: we look at it as an isolated factor. [Its] emphasis is [the] daily witness of God in the church. [The] Catholics carry dogma lightly. We have lost [this] knowledge. Theology must emerge from [the] *isolation* from *what happens in the church*; otherwise [theology] is a lost outpost. Until today *Protestant theology has been in isolation,* [so it has become] a heavy, earnest matter. Catholic theology [by contrast] is a "cheerful matter."[114]

*Barth* experienced the burden of dogmatic theology. He seeks relief from this burden, therefore [sets something] before the brackets as the presupposition.[115] Theology is related to the *"preaching" church*![116] [Theology] is the church's function.[117] Church as legally constituted, orga- 255
nized church is not the premise for theology.[118] [Thus understood,] it is not the ultimate presupposition. Barth seeks the power *that constitutes the Church,* i.e., *predestination.* [So finally] predestination is the presupposition that stands before the brackets of theology! Predestination exists; [it] appears daily in the proclamation; therefore, one can speak daily about God [and the] Holy Spirit. *[A] theological statement [stands] in connection with [the] daily event of predestination!* There [is] exoneration! [The] cramp of theology is dissolved here. Barth doesn't execute these ideas; [rather] he merely opens a way for them. Theology should nevertheless express [the] burden and in every sentence point to the fact that predestination [stands] behind everything. Now Barth burdens everything once more

[113.] WDZ: *"The church is the presupposition for theology!* This was done by the Catholic Scholastics. That's why one did not understand Scholastic theology. Every false word is judged by the living God. No longer control over God; no isolation. *This is true for the entire Catholic dogma."*

[114.] WDZ: "In Catholicism, dogma weighs lightly because it is not isolated; rather it is seen in God's daily self-witness. Dogma [is] the reflection of real events. Visible sacramental church! [There one has] the advantage of a knowledge over us: theology must be relieved of its isolation; otherwise it remains a lost outpost. Our theology [is] isolated until now, [in] contrast [to] Catholicism. For this reason, Catholic theology is more cheerful."

[115.] WDZ: "[The] church encompasses all of theology."

[116.] Cf. Barth, "Menschenwort und Gotteswort in der christliche Predigt," 134ff., esp.137.

[117.] Cf. Barth, *Christliche Dogmatik*, 422; cf. also his "Die Theologie und der heutige Mensch," 375, and *Church Dogmatics*, I/1:3. See also above p. 282, ed. note 93.

[118.] WDZ: "Church [is] not legally constituted and institutionally organized as in Catholicism."

*with the reservation of predestination* (dialectical procedure)![119] The concept of predestination gained through the concept of the church is the presupposition, yet [the] burden remains.[120] Dogmatic theology treats the church as an element of doctrine but is [nevertheless also] in the entirety of its statements conditional on the church!! That is the difficult problem. The church is *presupposition for and object of dogmatics at the same time.* Two possibilities:[121] (1) What [is] meant here by "object" [Gegenstand] and presupposition [Voraussetzung] must be explained. *Dialectics!* This tense relationship must be expressed thus: where one speaks of the spirit and [of] God as "object," one must always say that this is [also] a presuppo-
256 sition! One cannot speak simultaneously about object and presupposition. [From this arises] the difficulty of the dialectical language.

May 11 [1932]

The Catholic sacramental church [stands] before all theology. Barth: the concept of predestination gained through the church [stands] before all theology. [The] *problem* for the Protestant situation: *church is presupposition and at the same time object of theology.*

*Two possibilities:*

1. *Dialectical theology*: in every doctrinal element of dogmatics one must point out [the] ultimate presupposition of that doctrinal element[122] (e.g., [. . .] church is Protestant; [. . .] not church as an objective thing).

---

[119.] WDZ: "Barth begins this; in addition he always summons us not to be satisfied with using it as a presupposition. [This] is [a] dialectical procedure."

[120.] WDZ: "*Has Barth guaranteed the Protestant concern?* Theology: the church as doctrine. Does theology exist only with respect to the church? Yes! Only with regard to this place can the church speak about revelation. The church is simultaneously presupposition and subject matter or object [*Gegenstand*], a doctrine of dogmatics. [It must] express in each individual doctrine of dogmatics that this is a presupposition, a given. [It is] not really an object [*gegenständlich*]."

[121.] The second possibility will be developed only after the new explication of the first possibility at the beginning of the next hour (see p. 287).

[122.] WDZ: "The objective word is the presupposition that one can speak dogmatically, [that] is the dialectic. A dogmatic concept is handled objectively. Then one can say that it is really a presupposition. A presupposition is that which is self-grounding and self-authenticating. Basically I cannot grasp this. [The] object must also be treated as a presupposition. Objective pronouncements about presupposition!—The suggested solution is dialectic. An objective statement is inadequate for every subject, for the real objective content is behind as presupposition."

*Critique:*

(a) Does a scholarly possibility of a reference exist? No. Does the presupposition [remain] a complete presupposition? [A] reference is always only [possible] to an object. [There is] no possibility for a scholarly reference from the object to the presupposition.[123]

(b) [The] necessity of such a reference from the object to the presupposition must be doubted. This is an impossible and unnecessary attempt on the part of dialectical theology!! [Its] value [lies] in [the] posing of the problem![124]

2nd attempt:[125] The church as presupposition, as the place of revelation. Theology is not metaphysics when it serves the church concretely in the sermon.[126] *The empirically concrete church* is presupposed by theology. [. . .][127] Although, according to Barth, predestination is the ultimate presupposition.[128] 257

Critique: The presupposition of theology can only be the empirical church. The presupposition and boundary of theology is the empirical church. Theology is [the] boundary of the word of forgiveness and grace. *The first presupposition is predestination, which is the boundary of the church*; from this (emerges a) *theology* of the empirical church, which *is limited* by *the empirical church.*[129] Is this [a] Catholic concept of church?? No. For there church is eschatological [. . .][130] Here the church is already realized for

[123.] WDZ: "Reference from the object to the presupposition possible? Not in a scholarly or scientific sense. Even the reference to [the] presupposition is objective. Therefore, this no longer [involves an] absolute presupposition."

[124.] WDZ: "[The] necessity of such a reference [does] not exist. It [is reasonable] for one to serve the presupposition, but not continuous reference back to it if one is really subordinate to it. This presupposition will always reveal itself without emphasis. If one, however, is not subordinate to the presupposition, then every reference to it is useless."

[125.] WDZ: "*2nd Solution.*"

[126.] WDZ: "Theology should serve the church in concrete obedience. Then one does not do metaphysics in the church! [There is a] deficiency of theology vis-à-vis the church; a judgment of the God who is revealed in the church."

[127.] Here there is about a half line of empty space, suggesting that the note taker apparently could not follow Bonhoeffer's train of thought for a moment.

[128.] Cf. WDZ: "[Is the] church founded upon predestination? Presupposition [is] the *empirical* church! Theology is the function of the empirical church-community, not the eternal congregation of God. The presupposition [is] the empirical church with its struggle, dogma, [and] councils."

[129.] WDZ: "Empirical theology has its limit in the empirical church."

[130.] In his dissertation, Bonhoeffer accused Catholicism of a religious misunderstanding of the church, since the church was mistaken for the kingdom of God and the historicity of humankind and of the church was "objectified and deified" (*DBWE* 1:125).

us; Bonhoeffer is speaking of Protestant theology; it [i.e., the church] has eschatological boundaries. Theology must allow the church itself to assign [its] place.

*The Concept of the Church in the Theological System*[131]

Where in dogmatics should we talk about the church? [. . .] Picture of dogmatics. [. . .] Theology as monad.[132] [The] method of theology must be descriptive, not deductive. *Synthetic* theological method: proceeding
258 from the cause;[133] Georg Calixtus brings [the] *analytical* method (*finis*[134] → *subiectum*[135] → *media*[136] (church), coming from the future).[137]

[The] starting point in theology [begins] with contemporary knowledge. God's giving himself in revelation. Dogmatics must *begin with the church as [the] place of revelation.*[138]

Protestant theology [however] proceeds from the individual.[139] The concept of church as presupposition points to the fact that the *community* is *primum*[140] (church [Kirche] as church-community [Gemeinde]).[141] The

---

[131.] Crossed out: "[. . . one illegible line]."

[132.] WDZ: "When one speaks about a dogmatic article, then the concept of God, Christ, sin, [and] the church belong [to it]. These concepts also include all else within themselves. Dogmatics is Leibniz's picture of monads. The totality of the others is mirrored in one."

[133.] The synthetic arrangement of the material of dogma moves from the origins to the effects, and thus moves from the development of the concept of God forward to the process of salvation.

[134.] "Goal."

[135.] "One who is affected."

[136.] "Means or medium."

[137.] After the Reformation had confined itself to the treatment of individual theological loci as a counterpoint to the Scholastic systems, early Protestant orthodoxy returned to the construction of theological systems. In keeping with the general scholarly method of the time, the analytical method of the practical discipline was employed. The old Scholastic disposition was accordingly changed, so that one began with the goal of salvation and then showed the means of salvation offered to sinners to reach the eternal goal and the presuppositions of the process of salvation. Before the 1619 *Epitome theologiae* of Georg Calixtus, Reformed philosopher Bartholomäus Keckermann and Lutheran Balthasar Mentzer had already employed the analytical method in their depiction of theology.

[138.] WDZ: "God as cause, God as end—God as the one who is given, gives himself in Christ. The other remains totally beyond our knowledge. Neither the past nor the future is given to us. In theology one must begin with the revelation now given to us, the church."

[139.] WDZ: "Source of error: individualistic thinking. One began with the pious individuals, etc."

[140.] "First."

[141.] WDZ: "The primary given is the congregation!"

significance of the concept of church for theological prolegomena![142] The basic error of our Protestant theology heretofore has been [the] individualization. Luther wanted to preserve the original church-community of Christ (not only teaching activity; that is secondary).[143] [For Luther] disentanglement from the church is burdensome;[144] pain because of the
lost theological community. [. . .] Thus [a] Lutheranism developed that had 259
broken away from the communal idea of the church![145]

May 25 [1932]

*Isolation of theology* from the church-community! Even individual points of theological doctrine become isolated (e.g., justification). [The] knowledge of God in [the] church-community becomes the knowledge of God by the individual; *Troeltsch: the individual is the subject of knowledge of God.* He finds this in the religious a priori.[146] Dialectical theology: there is no systematic knowledge of God a priori, but rather always and ever knowledge as God speaks to the individual (*revelation* [means]: God brings knowledge, not an a priori)![147] The character of revelation of that which is to be known. That which should be known is subjectivized in Barth, no communication with the other, who can only know of God ever and again.

The starting point for Barth and Troeltsch is still the same: *the individual's* knowledge of God! Yet, knowledge of God has as its primary subject the

[142.] WDZ: "The significance of the concept of church in theological epistemology. Theological thought only in relation to [the] community."

[143.] WDZ: "Immediately after Luther, there was a disintegration of the idea of the church-community. Luther: the battle for the early Christian church-community." Bonhoeffer determines this following up on his teacher Karl Holl's works on Luther's understanding of the church (cf. esp. Holl, "Die Entstehung von Luthers Kirchenbegriff").

[144.] Cf. the preceding note and its related sentence in the text.

[145.] WDZ: "In *original* community with the Catholic Church [and] yet torn apart. This pain over the lost community was itself lost; only struggles over doctrine followed. The hardening of propositions, because they did not grow out of the idea of the church-community. Protestantism [became] the protest against [the] church."

[146.] For Bonhoeffer's argument with Troeltsch's understanding of a religious a priori, see above pp. 187–89 and 196–97.

[147.] See Barth, *Die christliche Dogmatik*, 61: "One will not trace his [namely, the preacher's] knowledge of God . . . back to an original or an acquired suitability of the human subject to such knowledge (neither to a religious organ or a priori nor to a religious experience!), rather we must understand it as a qualification of one's incapacity, as *docta ignorantia* [learned lack of knowledge], as obedient and promising (and thus seizing its object, because seized by him) not-knowing." Cf. also *Die christliche Dogmatik*, 52–58 and 301–5, as well as p. 274, ed. note 28).

*church-community* (Luther).[148] The church knows, my testimony is unburdened [entlastet].[149] The objective statement, which takes place within
260 the realm of the church-community. [. . .] I [am unburdened] as a member of the church-community. The church-community knows the truth (of the knowledge of God); it is no longer a matter of my personal faith. [The] church-community believes always, because God has given himself to it. The church-community does not protect my testimony; it judges my testimony; therefore my theology is unburdened.[150] [The] congregation, which has authority, is [a] function above me. The church-community is the subject of knowledge! Therefore I too [can] be objective. The challenge of a nonexistential knowledge.[151] [The] *foundation is the knowledge of the church-community! Ecclesial epistemology*, not a transcendental philosophy.[152] The church as presupposition of all theology.

The question about the place of the church must first be redirected toward the other issue: the place of dogmatic theology in the church. The empirical church is the presupposition for theology. However, the church also remains the object of dogmatic theology. As such, it is to be treated as the first topic of dogmatics. The recognition of the church (church-community) as presupposition of theology means overcoming false Protestant subjectivism, not only for theological prolegomena but also for every individual point of doctrine. It's a matter of the discovery of a new ecclesial way of thinking and knowledge (ecclesial epistemology).

In all that has been said about the place of the church, the peculiar difficulty is to identify this place. The reason for this is that the church has empirical places [favored places]; however, as an empirical church of God, the church can only have the place that God chooses for it and to that extent as the place of God in the world is itself the presupposition of all possible places (in the world, [in] Christianity, [and in] dogmatic theology).

---

[148.] Bonhoeffer here and elsewhere in his lectures (see pp. 319–21) refers to Luther's 1519 sermon on "The Sacrament of the Holy and True Body of Christ," *LW* 35:45–67. There Luther had developed the idea that Christians are a part of the church as the body of Christ. Here he emphasizes that the individual, precisely in his temptation, was dependent on his incorporation into the body of Christ through the Lord's Supper, to gather strength and support of the body of Christ; see *LW* 35:53–55.

[149.] WDZ: "[The] church knows about God's truth. Therefore my acknowledgment and statement [is] unburdened; not in my conscience but rather objectively."

[150.] WDZ: "What I say does not need to be protected by [the] congregation; [it] can also be judged. Therefore my statement is objectively unburdened."

[151.] "Knowledge" replaces "thought."

[152.] WDZ: "Congregation [is] subject of knowledge. Thus I [am] personally lifted above the reservations. Not transcendental philosophy or existentially; *church* thought!"

[Part] II: The Form [Gestalt] of the Church 261

(A) Adam-Christ
(B) The Church and Christ
(C) [The] Acting Church-Community
(D) [The] Worldliness of the Church
(E) [The] Christianity [Christlichkeit] of the Church

Preliminary Comment about "Form"
Form means unity, multiplicity within the finite boundary. Form is never only finite; form is infinite because it transcends the sum of all boundaries.[153] Synthetic forms are inauthentic (e.g., synthetic precious stones).[154] The human will tries to create wholeness [for a certain] *goal*.[155] Beauty [for example] is a goal. Communities can be similar to genuine ones; they become inauthentic when they are created for a purpose. Genuine forms, [these are] the forms that precede all the human deeds and desires and are existentially related solely to God,[156] forms as reconciliation, redemption, [or] creation.[157]

We see and think in forms (a priori conceptual perception in forms)![158] How broadly do we think in genuine and inauthentic forms (question of philosophy, also question of theology)? The primal state [Urständlichkeit] of thinking is thinking in forms.[159] The inauthentic forms of our thinking are in opposition to the genuine forms. Those force the genuine forms

---

[153.] WDZ: "Finite is the sum of finite unities. This boundary crossed: [a] whole [is] infinite."

[154.] WDZ: "*Inauthentic forms* are synthetic. [They can] be taken apart at any time."

[155.] WDZ: "The human will tries to create particular wholenesses for [a] purpose; these are forms with purpose."

[156.] WDZ: "Existing not in and of itself or through the human being, [rather] existing through God, coming out of his freedom."

[157.] [In the background of this paragraph are ideas about a typology of social forms that was worked out in *Sanctorum Communio*; see *DBWE* 1:86–94.—CG]

[158.] WDZ: "We see and think in forms. Being and consciousness in the world is a priori consciousness of our reason. We see and think forms. Human being: Table. Categories [reference to Aristotle's Table of Categories, the first section of his *Organon*, the collection of his logical treatises—CG]. To clear up the last visible forms is epistemology. Do the forms that we see resemble the genuine forms? The genuine forms alone [are] the forms of revelation."

[159.] [In *Sanctorum Communio*, the terms *Urstand* and *Urständlichkeit* refer to the contrast between the primal created state and the fallen state; see *DBWE* 1, esp. chaps. 3 and 4. The contrast between Adam and Christ is the contrast between the fallen state and the redeemed state. But *Urstand* can also mean a "primal" state in other contexts, as here, philosophically. The editors thank Clifford Green for this reference.—VB]

back into their primal state and do not grasp them as form in the being of God.[160]

262 May 28 [1932]

The form[-]unity established by God is genuine form, and indeed this can be in the form of creation, redemption, or forgiveness. Our thinking is fulfilled in the form of human logos. Our thinking is blind to the forms of revelation.

The church as the form of revelation of God should be portrayed. But: With our thinking we will always portray [only] the inauthentic form of the church![161]

The church as a genuine form is *unity*, basically the unity of God! The form reveals itself under the presupposition of unity. Differentiation: the church over against a religious community (arisen from individual converging wills!) [is necessary]. The church is the *primary unity*. Those who do not start with unity confuse the church with a religious community.[162] Unity is not [the] ideal of a world church; it is not "unity [Einigkeit] of the church" (Roman, ecumenical, Anglicanism). Only faith in [the] unity of God in Christ [is possible]. "Wholeness" is to be understood not as the state of not being broken, [but rather] as the wholeness of the revelations of God. The church is not just any *form of revelation* of God, but rather the *entire* form of revelation of God. The *believed form of the church* is the genuine form. It can only be believed; [it] is *never visible*.[163]

---

[160.] WDZ: "Primal state [*Urständlichkeit*] of thinking. The forms of God are in opposition to this. Our forms wish to destroy them. Our thought forces every form into [the] human logos. The ur-form preceded human logos. [We] can therefore not grasp [the] divine revelation: [it] lies earlier."

[161.] WDZ: "Authentic form of the church as the form of the revelation of God. Our means [are] inadequate. We always represent forms that are not authentic."

[162.] WDZ: "The form comes from God a priori; [against this] false form of logos. The church is primarily unity, wholeness [stemming from God]. It is the unity of God himself, the one whole. The form discloses itself under the *presupposition* of unity and wholeness. The church [as] inauthentic, synthetic form is [the] *religious community* (conceived out of converging wills; Schleiermacher)." On Schleiermacher's understanding of the church, see p. 284, ed. note 109.

[163.] WDZ: "Dogmatic unity [does not mean] the unity of the church (ecumenical!). Only unity of God in his form of revelation, which has to be believed. Wholeness is not lack of brokenness, wholeness of the revelation of God (where it exists, it is whole, because God is always wholly God). The church is [the] *whole* form of revelation of God. The whole form of the church is believed form."

(A) Adam and Christ[164] 263

The church is the newly created humanity through Christ, the new people, the second humanity.[165] [It] is a collective form! On the ground of the humanity-in-Adam [Adamsmenschheit]! There is only *humanity-in-Adam and the church!* The first already overcome by the second, yet [they are] always struggling [against each other].[166] "Humanity" [is] not [a] biological concept, rather derived from revelation. It encompasses [the entire] history of the world; not until the end of the world can there be something entirely new.[167] Everything is *a struggle between humanity-in-Adam and the church!* Faith and unbelief is [the] issue of humanity as old and new.

The relationship between these collective forms: Adam is the rebel against [the] Creator, destroyer of the community of God [Gottesgemeinschaft]. He sees the other human being as object of his own desire, not as one given to him for community, as the creature of God.[168]

(1) [The] human being has thrown off the reign of God! His own *master*! (2) The community of God is torn asunder! [The] human being wants to be *alone*![169]

Paradise is torn asunder; therefore a kingdom arises where [the] human being is [his] own master and is alone; this is the world of Adam. The human being cannot come out of [the] isolation; his voice remains without an echo. Adam is a human being; he is simultaneously *individual* and *species*.[170] The category of individual means that the human being stands over against God entirely as individual. There the human is wholly species. Where the highest deed of the individual [is] done, [it is] also a deed of the

[164.] On the following, see *DBWE* 1:107–18.

[165.] WDZ: "Humanity that is seen by God through Christ; excluding the humanity-in-Adam and yet still also including."

[166.] WDZ: "There is only humanity-in-Adam or in [the] church. [The] one [is] overcome by the other and [yet] the battle [still continues]."

[167.] WDZ: "Disobedience [versus] obedience vis-à-vis the Creator. This is how salvation history emerges. Its [i.e., salvation history's—VB] end brings something entirely new: intensification of history."

[168.] WDZ: "Adam and Eve [are] separated by the snake." (Cf. Gen. 3:1–13.)

[169.] WDZ: "The community of God as well as the God-created human community [is] torn apart."

[170.] [In *Sanctorum Communio* and *Act and Being*, Bonhoeffer had worked out the idea of *Kollektivperson*, "collective person," a figure who represents and personifies a certain mode of existence of both individuals and communities—in the cases of Adam and Christ, representatives of the old sinful humanity and of the new humanity inaugurated by Christ. Foreign as such vocabulary is to an individualistic and atomistic anthropology, Bonhoeffer holds that it does justice to the biblical narrative as well as giving a realistic description of human affairs.—CG]

264 entire species.[171] *Sin is sin of the individual and of humanity* at the same time. Therefore, *all humanity falls together in Adam.* In Adam all humanity sins.[172] Addressed by God, [the] human being is simultaneously wholly individual and wholly the human species.[173] Where this [is] understood, Adam's sin is understood.

Who is Adam? *The one who committed the first sin.* Actually there [is] no difference: every sin is the first sin, a tearing asunder of community with God. [Also] *every* sin that follows is the first sin. *Every human* then is *Adam*! We are guilty of the sins of humanity. Adam is "one" human; he is all of humanity in one. Adam is the person who personifies the whole [Gesamtperson].[174] Every individual human must recognize himself as humanity's Adam and allow himself to be judged.[175] ". . . is entirely my burden."[176] *Not the community of sinners*; everyone is an individual as sinner, everyone is Adam alone [Allein-Adam].[177] In the humanity-in-Adam, all forms of community are formed, even *the religious community.*[178] Here humanity-in-Adam is not overcome. Form of Adam! Every individual is this whole Adam. With every new

[171.] WDZ: "An animal is an example of a genus. By contrast the human being is entirely an individual. Therefore he is absolutely the whole human being. As the one standing over against God, the human being is wholly himself as human being and species. Where [the] animal is entirely without individuality, it is entirely animal (picture of the genus)."

[172.] WDZ: "Not procreation as the transfer of sin." With this Bonhoeffer draws a line between himself and the doctrinal form of original sin developed by Augustine and before him similarly by Tertullian. According to this, sin is something passed on by the act of procreation. (Cf. also *DBWE* 1:107–11, ed. note 11.)

[173.] WDZ: "When God addresses him, each human being is wholly individual and wholly human (theological)."

[174.] [Bonhoeffer's use of the term *Gesamtperson,* literally "person of the whole," recalls the fifteenth-century English morality play *Everyman,* in which the title character is understood as the representative human being. *Gesamtperson* and *Kollektivperson* (see ed. note 170 above) are interchangeable and are key terms in the argument of *Sanctorum Communio,* on which these lectures draw heavily; see, for example *DBWE* 1:77–79.—CG]

[175.] WDZ: "Thereby the burden is not placed upon one 'collective' person [*Gesamtperson*]. *Every* human being must allow *himself* to be recognized and judged as this collective person."

[176.] See Paul Gerhardt, "O Haupt voll Blut und Wunden" (*Evangelisches Kirchengesangbuch,* 63, verse 4; [the English translation is "O Sacred Head, Now Wounded," *Lutheran Hymnal,* 172—VB]. Verse 4, translated here directly from the German, reads: "Now O Lord, what you have patiently borne is my burden; I bear the guilt myself for what you have borne. Behold me, here I stand a poor thing who has earned your wrath; give me, O my redeemer, the aspect of your grace."

[177.] WDZ: "Everyone is and remains alone. [There is] no community of sinners, [much more] hate for one another."

[178.] WDZ: "Religious community is comprised of human beings who try to fool themselves about being alone and about hate."

human being Adam starts anew.[179] [The] new humanity is created on the *cross of Christ.*[180] The cross is the *dividing line between old and new humanity.* 265
[There] humanity-in-Adam is overcome! Insofar as [the] human being recognizes sin and the "no" of the cross, he is set straight.[181]

[In the] resurrection of Christ, the Yes of God [is] spoken to the human being.[182] The cross and resurrection of the human Jesus and of the Christ: Christ is fully human, individual and species in one.[183] Golgotha is at the same time the act of the individual and the species. The new, whole humanity is set in Christ. Christ as new humanity, as church; the church is with Christ on the cross and resurrected with him. *Only one* is Christ; only one has broken through the humanity-in-Adam![184] New humanity,

June 1 [1932]

since Christ's merit belongs to humanity itself. The new humanity knows itself to be holy, just, because God knows it as holy, just. [The] humanity of Christ understands itself only through Christ! He is the Lord! Not Adam! [The] Christian too is Adam, but overcome through Christ. [The] church has its own foundation and object in Christ. Christ is the unifying principle of the church.[185] The church as the unity set in Christ is the true form of revelation!

---

[179.] WDZ: "The one Adam [is] torn and every individual gets torn anew every day. Every human being [is a] *new* beginning of humanity."

[180.] WDZ: "The rebellious will of the human being must be humbled. [. . .] The cross of Christ."

[181.] WDZ: "Analogy to Adam. Second Adam overcomes [the] humanity. God-human takes the judgment of God as Adam upon himself; he takes the divine wrath upon himself even unto being forsaken by God on the cross (cf. Matt. 27:46); fulfilling the law positively. [It is the] action of a human being who is individual and entire species. He acts as humanity in accordance with the righteousness of God. [The] human being should acknowledge this. Obedience toward God occurs on the cross of Christ."

[182.] WDZ: "The resurrection is [the] Yes of God over all humanity as over his *obedient* creature; a second, complete beginning with humanity. God vs. God; [. . .] free grace [. . .]; [it is a] judgment of God upon himself."

[183.] WDZ: "Christ is fully human. Thus he conquers all humanity. He is an individual and wholly species. [. . .] New humanity. [. . .] The handling of humanity *kat' exochen* [par excellence]."

[184.] WDZ: "Only one is Christ. Only one has done God's will [. . .] the Son of God. *This may not be historicized or psychologized.* [. . .] The individual as the one who sins. Only when he has become entirely individual [in sin] will he become wholly a human being."

[185.] WDZ: "New humanity at one point: Christ. He is [the] unifying principle of the church."

266 B. Church and Christ

(1) Christ's Vicarious Representative Action[186] as the Founding of the Church

One stands for all; Christ is the vicarious representative of humanity.[187] Adam [stands] not in [the] place of the other but rather in his own. Christ stands in [the] place of humanity!

(a) Ethical Concept of Vicarious Representative Action

[. . .][188] For example, soldiers in a war, [the] friend [in Schiller's ballad] "[Die]Bürgschaft."[189] Possessions, body, [and] honor are goods that the one gives away for the other. The sphere of existence and the ethically independent person [is here]. I can allow myself to be given goods with the feeling that I am worthy of them. The other person cannot ever stand in my place before the ethical command. He must then always degrade me.[190] That person cannot stand where there [is] suffering and judgment.[191] The other can never take "punishment" as such upon himself for me without degrading me, but only the consequence of the punishment.[192] Punishment can only be taken on vicariously when one also accepts the evil of the other person.[193] First of all, [it is a] negation of my person as an ethical being when the other person takes my responsibility. Second, [it is an] illu-

[186.] ["*Stellvertretung*," which appears already in *Sanctorum Communio* as a central christological and anthropological concept, is translated in *DBWE* as "vicarious representative action." Its basic meaning is to step into the place of another person or community and to act on their behalf, to do on behalf of others what they could not, or do not, do for themselves; hence its vicariousness. It has a strong corporate reference, as here, where Bonhoeffer refers to Christ acting on behalf of all humanity, and the ethical concept of a soldier acting on behalf of fellow citizens; another example he gives is of a biblical prophet who repents on behalf of his people.—CG]

[187.] WDZ: "One for all those for whom God's judgment is fulfilled; vicarious representative action."

[188.] WDZ: "One should take on the destiny of another; men in war."

[189.] "The Hostage." See Schiller, *Complete Works*, 1:163–67.

[190.] WDZ: "A boundary through worldly goods; otherwise the other person will be humiliated."

[191.] WDZ: "I must be worthy for the other who is giving me the goods. He can stand where I am supposed to stand with these things of value. He cannot, however, take over my responsibility as a vicarious representative without humiliating me."

[192.] WDZ: "He cannot take my guilt and punishment upon himself. He cannot be judged in my place. He can take only [the] consequences of the punishment upon him, not the punishment itself."

[193.] WDZ: "If he takes [the] punishment in my place, he puts himself into the evil I did. To accept [the] responsibility of another is not possible in [the] *ethical sphere*."

sion that another person [can] step in as vicarious representative[194] in the place of my ethical personality. The sacrifice of goods must be accepted, for 267
the sake of the ethical side of the person. *In cases where the sphere of the person is not involved, a vicarious representative sacrifice can be made*; not, however, where the sphere of the person [is] touched.[195] [The ethical] is built upon humanity-in-Adam.[196] The attempt to have a community is illusory[197]—only Adam torn asunder is there.[198]

(b) Christ's Vicarious Representative Action

[This is] not an ethical concept of vicarious representation. *Vicarious personal sacrifice*, not a vicarious sacrifice of goods! *His suffering is a vicarious representative act for the new humanity.*

*[Four Steps:]*[199]

1. *Incarnation*: God becomes human. In order to destroy humans, God becomes human.[200] Here [the] human being is judged in [his] ethical self-responsibility.[201] Action on his person, which with others of the whole humanity [is] taken up by Christ.[202]

2. *Christ enters the community of Israel: he fulfills the law as vicarious representative.*[203] Israel should live from the law in community. Transgression produces isolation of the individual. Justified wrath of the law;[204] Christ takes
this upon himself [and] fulfills it. Not as individual but as new humanity, 268

[194.] "As representative" replaces "in the other's place."

[195.] WDZ: "There where [the] boundaries of the sacrifice of goods are crossed, there is a negation [of the personal sphere]; the personal sphere may in ethics not be touched."

[196.] WDZ: "*The ethical is built upon [the] humanity-in-Adam.*"

[197.] WDZ: "The attempt to transcend one's being alone. As long as the community [. . .] is constituted, creating the community is illusory."

[198.] WDZ: "Everyone remains [in the realm] of sacrifice of goods, when one stands up for another with his life. Each person is bound by sin. In his deed against God, everyone becomes isolated. As a person he remains alone. There is no community in Adam."

[199.] Thus in WDZ.

[200.] WDZ: "Invasion of the *independent* personal sphere of human beings, in order to destroy the human being."

[201.] WDZ: "Now [the] human being is judged in his ethical responsibility."

[202.] WDZ: "It is not an isolated person who is dealt with but rather one who is taken up into Christ."

[203.] WDZ: "Christ steps entirely into [the] community of Israel and puts himself into the law."

[204.] WDZ: "The community of God. Transgression. Now the power of wrath in the place of constituting law, since it was broken. [The] human being has failed to obey God's law. [As a consequence] every individual is isolated."

[he] is the vicarious representative [actor] for the church. [He] is the one who acts [as the new] humanity.[205]

3. *Christ dies on the cross* and takes [the] wrath of God upon himself to the end. [His] sacrifice is *vicarious representative personal sacrifice*![206] In Christ [the] human being must suffer the death of his ethical conscience. Vicarious representative action is this; [it] is the negation of ethical independence. In the ethical sphere this was impossible. [. . .] As true punishment for true sin![207] Christ steps into the place where the human being was a sinner. He becomes "the greatest robber and sinner" (Luther).[208] With this our independent standing before God is made impossible. [We are] judged in him and with him on the cross. Christ is risen!

June 4 [1932]

The breakthrough of humanity-in-Adam by Christ! Independent stance before God is impossible for us all. We are judged with Christ on the cross. Christ did the will of God in that he suffers his will. Doing the will [of God], of the good is only to be suffered![209] *Vicarious representative "suffering" of the will of God!* "Suffering" [is] deepened here. Suffering does not only [mean] death and poverty. Being strong in God can also only be endured against all fleshly lust.[210] Our suffering is both negated and overcome [aufgehoben] in Christ's suffering. The vicarious representative action of Christ is also the vicarious representation of suffering for humankind. Yet all suffer in Christ.
269 [211] There [the] humanity-in-Adam in the church is affected: [the] disunity

[205.] WDZ: "Vicariously acting for his church [a human being alone cannot fulfill the law of the people]."

[206.] WDZ: "Not [only] the sacrifice of a possession."

[207.] WDZ: "Since the wrath earned by humanity has been taken and the punishment been carried [by Christ], [it is] *real* punishment for real sin."

[208.] Cf. Luther, "Tischreden aus Johannes Aurifabers Sammlung" (*WA.Tr* 6:74, 30–40); cf. also Sermon of April 19, 1538 (*WA* 46:289, 18); Sermon of June 4, 1523 (*WA* 11:125, 2); Sermon of July 2, 1528 (*WA* 27:233, 26); Sermon of March 20, 1529 (?) (*WA* 28:389, 3).

[209.] WDZ: "Only in this way can one do the will of God. God's Son alone accomplishes it. He wishes to endure the good."

[210.] WDZ: "Representative suffering of the will of God. Not [only] the will, which leads us into suffering, but also that which allows us to be strong and healthy must be suffered. Also the will works against all lust [fleshly asceticism, martyrdom]. Thus Christ as the suffering one is the fulfiller of the law."

[211.] WDZ: "The church is founded on Christ's suffering; all suffer together in Christ."

is overcome where one suffers on its behalf. "If one member is honored, all rejoice together with it!"[212]

4. *Christ is risen.* Humanity is justified in Christ. [The] righteousness of a human being is judged on the cross. Righteousness can never be done. Christ does, suffers righteousness. The dead body becomes the resurrected body, so too the *corpus Adae*[213] becomes *the corpus Christi.*[214] The resurrection community is the church!

*Vicarious representative action* thus means that (1) Jesus did what no other could do; he is the *Lord.* (2) He did it in such a way that the whole new humanity acts and suffers with him.[215] Thus is Christ the *brother*! In the ethical sphere there is not the Lord and the brother (isolation and lack of brotherhood). Christ is Lord of the church-community. *Community under the lordship of Christ* and at the same time characterized by *brotherhood.* (3) *Christ existing as church-community.*[216] These are the three fundamental conditions for the church. Paradoxical state of contradiction. Yet these three orders are not possible without one another.[217] Church-community as subject, being-with-one-another is the church-community in Christ; Christ as the church-community is the most intimate in-one-another [Ineinander]!

[(2) Jesus Christ and the Founding of the Church]

Problem: *Jesus Christ and the founding of the church* (to point 2) [One can raise] the objection: [the] church is the religious community founded by Christ; [it was] founded already before the cross and resurrection. Therefore, the church is not to be understood from the point of view of the cross and resurrection.

Cf. Matt. 16:18; 18:17:[218] Jesus wanted a messianic community, [at first] all Israel. Later he wanted [a] representative, [the] remnant of Israel, which

[212.] Cf. 1 Cor. 12:26.

[213.] "Body of Adam." [Here in the sense of humanity-in-Adam (*Adamsmenschheit*). —CG]

[214.] WDZ: "All righteousness comes from Christ. He makes [the] human being good before God; [that is the] new creation of the human being. Christ stands before God for him."

[215.] WDZ: "He did this so that in his suffering all humanity suffers with him."

[216.] WDZ: "Only in Christ does the church exist; therefore, unity." [Bonhoeffer here quotes the ecclesiological axiom of *Sanctorum Communio*, "Christus als Gemeinde existierend"; cf. *DBWE* 1:121 and throughout.—CG]

[217.] WDZ: "Fundamental ordering of the formation of the church."

[218.] The reference is probably to Matt. 18:17–20.

inherits the kingdom.[219] This follows out of the messianic self-conscious-
270 ness of Jesus. The messianic community. [Yet] first [it] must be broken up and must be under the promise of unification in the new Lord's Supper (meaning of the act of the Lord's Supper) [. . . ];[220] Good Friday: the messianic community is really broken apart. There is no community beneath the cross, only individuals, as Jesus dies. The community is torn apart. Humanity-in-Adam is victorious; every person bears alone the guilt of the entire world.[221]

Under the cross Adam triumphs![222] Every single person is guilty of this. Here Adam understands himself as the one he is. [The cross is] the end of God for the community [and] is the end of the community [itself].[223] [The] *resurrection now [means]*:[224] from the broken *corpus Adam* emerges the *corpus Christi*. [The church-community is] indeed a broken church-community [but] a church-community in which the cross is seen from the perspective of Easter. The church-community gathers around the center. The light [of the resurrection] cannot be seen without the cross. *Paradoxical form of a church-community of the cross!*[225] The church-community is founded precisely through God's act (through the cross). Under the cross alone there is no church-community. [Even] here in the community of the resurrection it is not yet church. [The] community of the resurrection still lives with Christ until the day of the Ascension. After that Christ lives in the church-community. The church is decisively determined through the vicarious suffering and action of Christ.

[219.] WDZ: "then a host of disciples. Community should gather under his leadership as the remnant of Israel."

[220.] WDZ: "This circle [is] sealed and confirmed in the Last Supper. With this action the church-community cannot be preserved; it must be torn apart under the promise of a new Lord's Supper in the kingdom of God."

[221.] WDZ: "Jesus dies on the cross alone. [The] messianic congregation is broken. The disciples are scattered as individuals. The church that Jesus has established [is] broken up the following day. Each carries [the] guilt of the entire world alone."

[222.] WDZ: "Under the cross Adam triumphs and there first finds himself wholly himself."

[223.] WDZ: "[The] cross is the end of the presence of God for the community, the end of the community itself."

[224.] WDZ: "In [the] resurrection the promise becomes alive again. [The] community is reawakened in him [Christ]. Through [the] cross there is a broken church-community. It is what it is through death and resurrection of its Lord."

[225.] WDZ: "Church-community of the cross; the end because there everyone is an individual. The community will be reestablished through the cross, following Easter."

June 15 [1932]

As Christ [is] crucified, the community collapses, but through [the] resurrection, [the] church [Kirche] becomes the church-community [Gemeinde] 271
it could not be during his [life]time. Jesus did not wish to found the church during his lifetime, but the church is newly created as the community of the resurrection.[226]

*Christ is not the founder* of a new religion and religious community. He is the Redeemer, *the foundation* of the church, *not the founder.* The religious community that [Jesus] Christ founded is [not] our contemporary church! Death and resurrection now constitute the church after the outpouring of the Spirit. [The] apostles (especially Paul) are the founders. As such a one, who he is, Christ is the new humanity. Christ is simultaneously the foundation and beginner and fulfiller of the church. In his historicity and divinity, Christ is the beginner and the fulfiller of the church.[227]

(3) Fundamental Structure of the Church in and through Christ

(a) Structure of Unity: Christ Existing as Church-Community

The church-community is Christ; *Christ is the church-community.*[228] How is the church structured through the vicarious representative action of Christ? [The] form of revelation as person [or the word of God][229] is Christ and Spirit; as work [Werk] [it] is the creation. [The] church itself is the present Christ! [The] presence of God on earth is Christ; [the] presence of Christ on earth is the church. [. . .] *Person is the church, is the form of the presence of the Second Person of the Trinity.* The church-community is Christ; Christ stands 272
where the church-community stands before God.[230] [It] has conceded its

---

[226.] WDZ: "Are baptism and the Lord's Supper sacraments that Jesus put in place? Is baptism [. . .] the religious community founded during Christ's lifetime? It is broken before his death."

[227.] WDZ: "*Temporally* speaking, the community of the disciples runs through the life, death, and resurrection of Christ. Only through the Holy Spirit is there a real church."

[228.] Cf. WDZ: "Hegel: the Holy Spirit existing as congregation." Bonhoeffer, in his 1927 dissertation, refers to the version of Hegel's philosophy of religion edited by Marheineke (cf. *DBWE* 1:198). There it reads: "God existing as community" (Hegel, *Lectures on the Philosophy of Religion*, 3:331). In opposition Lasson writes in his edition of Hegel's lectures on philosophy of religion: "The community itself is existing Spirit, Spirit in its existence, God existing as community" (Hegel, *Christian Religion*, 256).

[229.] As in WDZ.

[230.] WDZ: "The for, in, and through Christ can only be understood when one sees the church as primary. Christ is the church-community; the church-community is

existence to him as the vicarious representative! 1 Cor. 12:12; 6:15; 1:13: *To be in Christ is to be in the church.* ([Cf.] Kattenbusch in [the] Harnack Festschrift, 1921;[231] Traugott Schmitt, σῶμα;[232] Bousset, co-community;[233] Deißmann, Zu Jesus Christus.)[234]

1 Cor. 1:30; 3:16; 6:15; 2 Cor. 6:16; 13:5; Col. 2:17; 3:16; Gal. 3:28; Eph. 1:23; 4:24; 5:30; Rom. 6:13; 13:14;

For Paul [the church-community] [in the sense] of the idea of identity is the body of Christ (body is not to be separated from the person! [It represents the] person).[235] Christ [as] the head is [first of all a] second idea; first [church-community as] body and person [of Christ only afterward:] Christ is the Lord, is head. Originally, where the body is, there is the person of Christ! Christ existing as church-community is not visible, rather [only] to be believed.

To put on the new Adam is to put on Christ, to put on the new church-community![236] *Christ also stands over against the church-community.* In the Catholic conception there is no one standing over against the church. Different identification; it may not be absolutely set in our tradition.[237]
273 [For] Christ has ascended, eschatological! [. . .] The law[238] (Gal. 4:8;[239] 1 Thess. 4 [and] 5;[240] Phil. 3:20; 1 Cor. 15:23!)! Christ is there [the] Lord of the church-community.

---

Christ; only through his existence [does it] exist; the Christ acting on the cross and in the resurrection."

[231.] Kattenbusch, "Der Quellort der Kirchenidee" (1921).

[232.] [*Soma*, or "body."—VB] Traugott Schmidt, *Der Leib Christi*; cf. esp. Kattenbusch, "Der Quellort der Kirchenidee," 143–46.

[233.] In *Sanctorum Communio* (*DBWE* 1), Bonhoeffer had remarked that Bousset in his interpretation of 2 Cor. 5:17 demonstrated the identity of "in Christ" to "in the church-community" (*DBWE* 1:140, Bonhoeffer's note 8). Cf. Bousset, *Der zweite Brief an die Korinther* (on 2 Cor. 5:17). Like Bousset, Kattenbusch also argues for the identity of "in Christ" and "in the church-community," whereas Schmidt was more reserved on this question. For Bonhoeffer's evaluation of the cited literature, see *DBWE* 1:140, Bonhoeffer's note 8.

[234.] Deißmann, *Die neutestamentliche Formel "in Christo Jesu" untersucht*; see esp. vi.

[235.] WDZ: "Where [the] body is, there also is the person. If Christ is the head, then that is an entirely different idea."

[236.] WDZ: "Not pietistic rebirth; as visible church not necessarily Christ."

[237.] WDZ: "In Catholicism the one over against us falls away. The church is no part of the world; [. . .] Identity. In our tradition [by contrast] there is never absolute identification."

[238.] WDZ: "We await him as judge."

[239.] This must be Eph. 4:8.

[240.] 1 Thess. 4:15–18; 5:1–4.

(b) The Structure of Lordship[241] in the Church: Christ as the Lord of the Church-Community

Christ is our Lord, because he justifies.[242] He is the one who has been exalted (Ascension!). He stands before God as the intercessor for the church-community! The church-community not seen without Christ by God! Christ in the front of the church-community. The Father must act with the church-community through the Son.[243] *Intercessio Christi!*[244] Christ as Lord [is] the perpetual intercessor! Through him we have God's grace! The church-community is oriented toward its Lord![245] Judgment and righteousness only through Christ. The church-community can never be sure of itself[.] (Catholicism has daily offering in the Mass, but it rests in the hand of the priest;[246] [that] subordinates the idea of the Lord to the idea of identity. [. . .] unified structure of the church-community; [. . .] Christ as the brother.[)]

(c) Community Structure: Christ Is the Brother

[He is this] to the individual, never to the church-community. Christ *stands there as vicarious representative where my brother should stand.*[247] He, my brother, cannot really be my brother. He does not transcend the sphere of 274
goods; he never [enters] the sphere of the person. He cannot see my person (he sees me as "It" not as "You"). Christ is there where [the] brother should stand! For *Christ is my brother; our brother is Christ.*[248] The other as human

[241.] [In *Sanctorum Communio* Bonhoeffer argues that the church, understood from revelation, has a unique sociological structure, combining aspects of community (*Gemeinschaft*), society (*Gesellschaft*), and authority or rule (*Herrschaft*). He then interprets theologically each of these terms taken from the systematic sociology of his time, thus transforming their normal meaning. Hence, Christ's lordship (*Herrschaft*) leads to the statement that "God's love, in ruling, serves" (*DBWE* 1:63; see also 60).—CG]

[242.] WDZ: "Christ judges our sin upon the cross and gives us grace."

[243.] WDZ: "God cannot see [the] church-community without Christ. He must act through Christ. Christ takes with him those whom he has chosen."

[244.] "Intercession of Christ." Cf. WDZ: "Until [the] hour of the Last Judgment, there must be faith alone in the intercession of Christ before God."

[245.] WDZ: "The church-community cannot point to itself; [it] expects everything from the Lord. Judgment and righteousness."

[246.] Bonhoeffer relies upon the Reformers' criticism of the contemporary Catholic understanding of the Lord's Supper (according to which the priest repeats the sacrifice of Christ on the cross in order to make it take effect for the communicants).

[247.] WDZ: "Christ becomes fully human; so he is the brother. He stands opposite us like a brother."

[248.] WDZ: "Where another challenges or gives himself as a whole person, there Christ is also. The other one becomes Christ to me; [. . .] identity. He is not the absolute

being will never truly become physically a Christ; the brother is *never* Christ; (it is) not (to be understood) as an absolute! Matt. 25: I was hungry.[249]

June 18 [1932]

I[250] *The church of today is the presence of Christ on earth.*
II (a) This presence is to be understood as follows, that the church-community is Christ. The bodily characteristic of the church-community.

(b) *Christ as Lord* of the church-community; (c) *Christ is the brother.* Catholicism remains at II (a) [. . .] A priest remains Lord as Christ![251] [The] word "You belong to me because I belong to you" makes the other a brother. God pronounces the identical statement![252] Vicarious representative action makes Christ our brother.[253] The brotherhood established through Christ is built upon [the] law of vicarious representative action!

The character of the church as a unity! Community character is equally original. [It is] not possible to have one thought without the other: "Brother" [is] never absolute, always Lord at the same time. *[An] absolute judgment about identity is never* possible; that would lead to Catholicism. I can never stand before God for myself;[254] [. . .] *iustitia aliena*;[255] through vicarious
275 representative action *imputativa iustitia*[256] [. . .] Four directions of structure: identity, community, individual.[257]

---

Christ, but rather for me, as in Matt. 25:35" (cf. Luther, "Von der Freiheit eines Christenmenschen," 1520 (*WA* 7:35, 34). [This citation of "The Freedom of a Christian" is in the dedication of the essay to Muhlphordt, most of which is omitted from the *LW* translation.—CG] See also 2/7, ed. note 18.

[249.] Cf. Matt. 25:35 and 42.

[250.] The following sections I, II, a, b, and c are missing in WDZ; this is simply a schematized repetition of the previous material.

[251.] In his dissertation, Bonhoeffer criticized the Catholic conception of divine character of the church as an institution, which is constructed through its office (*Amt*). (See *DBWE* 1:256.) For Bonhoeffer's criticism of the Catholic conception of church, see also above p. 274, ed. note 29, and p. 287, ed. note 130.

[252.] WDZ: "God says this and the neighbor tells it to me."

[253.] WDZ: "Only in the Christian church-community does he become brother; vicarious representation is constitutive for brother."

[254.] WDZ: "I can never stand before God for myself; rather this is only possible through Christ's church-community, [through the] brother."

[255.] "Alien righteousness"; cf. WDZ: "*Iustitia aliena*; [is] pronounced to me.

[256.] "Imputed righteousness."

[257.] In the following summary Bonhoeffer includes four concepts: "authority," "unity," "community," and "individuality" through which the structure of the church-community is characterized.

[Summary][258]

Guiding principle: "The church is grounded in and through Christ, who as vicarious representative actor is simultaneously individual and humankind." The vicarious representative action of Christ means the deed by which he puts himself in our place where we must stand before God. Vicarious representative action in the ethical sense is the sacrifice of goods; in the deed of Christ it is the sacrifice of a person. As the vicarious representative actor, Christ acts as the new humanity, and the new church is grounded in him. The church is not the foundation of Jesus Christ during his lifetime; rather it is founded in the reality of his vicarious representative action as God-human; the following characteristics of the form of the church emerge from the concept of vicarious representative action: (1) Christ is himself the church-community; (2) Christ is [the] Lord of the church-community; (3) Christ is [the] brother in the church-community.

Thereby the church-community is structurally determined by concepts of authority, unity, community, individuality. Every one of these concepts is to be interpreted solely through the concept of vicarious representative action. The reality and the law of vicariousness are constitutive for the church of Christ!

(C) The Acting Church-Community

I. The Holy Spirit and Christ

The Holy Spirit *actualized*[259] that which has been realized[260] through Christ.[261] [The] church was actually there with [the] resurrection: [it] is actualized on Pentecost: the occurrence of judgment and grace! Through 276
the spirit we know the I and You and We of God (that is already included in Christ!).[262] [The] deed of the Spirit is proclamation and the appropria-

[258.] Bonhoeffer dictated the following paragraph, which is literally the same in WDZ.

[259.] WDZ: "The church as deed of the third article; is the second article removed through the third? The Holy Spirit actualizes that which has happened through Christ." [Bonhoeffer in *Sanctorum Communio* (*DBWE* 1) argues that the church is an ontological reality in Christ that is socially and historically actualized by the Holy Spirit.—CG]

[260.] "Realized" replaces "has happened."

[261.] For the difference between "realization" and "actualization," see *DBWE* 1:143–44.

[262.] "The church was really created but first actualized through [the] Holy Spirit. That which has occurred is brought to Christians. Pentecost [is] not completion of the realization; it is nothing new. It involves the appropriation through human beings in history. Through the Holy Spirit we know about the I, You, and We of God; all of that

tion of the deed of Christ! [The] Spirit is the proclaiming Spirit; therefore the Spirit is word.[263] Only the Holy Spirit assures us of the presence of Christ.

The church realized as Christ is actualized through the Spirit! The church may not be individualized through the fact that [the] Spirit drives [the] individuals and therefore the church-community together! [The] concept of *individualism* [is] still enriched in Schleiermacher![264] The church [is] not [the] community of individual pious people.[265] The church regarded in that way is [something] secondary, not the form of divine revelation. Primarily it would then be the piety of individuals. In that case one would then also have to appeal for a willing of churchliness [Kirchlichkeit].

The main thing would be the knowledge of Christ [whereby one is] necessarily led into the church. This leads to [the] socialistic phrase: the church is a *private matter*![266] Schleiermacher forged [the] weapons for this![267] Psychological and historical view of the leadership of the church![268] Church, however, is *the church that is already actually established in Christ*!! The
277 church is there through [the] act of God, and has not been made by human beings![269] Actualizing and acting congregation! Church is not something derived, not something secondary! It is there where it is seen as religious community.

---

is already in Christ and his events; all this is made understandable to us [on Pentecost —VB]."

[263.] WDZ: "Not the representation, rather *Christus praesens* through the Holy Spirit; not a substitute, [much more] the Holy Spirit is the interpreter of the present Christ, but exactly present only in the interpretation."

[264.] WDZ: "*The danger of individualism*; Schleiermacher enriches this through social reference."

[265.] For Bonhoeffer's criticism of Schleiermacher's understanding of the church, see p. 284, ed. note 109, and p. 292, ed. note 162.

[266.] In WDZ: "Religion is a private matter." At the beginning of the Weimar Republic, the view of religion as a private matter, the separation of church and state, as well the secular school were the church policy principles not only of the Independent Social Democratic Party but also of the Social Democratic Party and other groups.

[267.] In the article referenced by Bonhoeffer, "Kirche: III. Dogmengeschichte," Hans Hohlwein comments that in Schleiermacher the Enlightenment concept of association has not been overcome (801). [On the church as association (*Verein*), see *DBWE* 1:252–57.—CG]

[268.] This should be "formation of the church"; cf. WDZ: "The process of formation of the church [here is] viewed historically and psychologically. The theological process [is] forgotten."

[269.] "Human beings" replaces "God." WDZ: "The church is there. Individuals are in the church because God has called them through Christ from eternity."

II. Church and Religious Community
*Church* [is not to be understood] *as a religious community*![270] Church is [a] reality of faith. [An] ideal of experience, rather than [of] reality, [that] is religious community.[271]

June 22 [1932]

Religious community is always something secondary, [even when the] concept of community is derived from [the] concept of religion, for religion must be there [first].[272] Three attempts to derive community from religion: (1) purely conceptual [derivation]; (2) psychological derivation; (3) derivation through philosophy of history.

Regarding (1)[273] *Max Scheler*:[274] hierarchy of values with a priori intrinsic laws [Wesensgesetzen]. The higher the value the less divisible [it is].[275] The Holy is the highest. [The] concept of the religious community should be derived from *the value of the Holy*! The entire value of the Holy becomes the basis of the community. But[276] [this is based on] the concept of possibility. Each one enjoys the value alone; this is the only possible community.[277] [This attempt is] *thoroughly individualistic* [and] purely *formalis-* 278
*tic*, since there is no distinction made from the diabolical. The same thing is possible in the diabolical.[278]

[270.] WDZ: "Today one means ecclesial community [*kirchliche Gemeinschaft*] everywhere." Cf. Cordes, *Der Gemeinschaftsbegriff*, and Bonhoeffer's discussion of the work in this volume, 2/20.

[271.] WDZ: "Where the church is, [there] is the reality of faith. The ideal of experience, [this] is community."

[272.] WDZ: "The church [as] the church established by Christ is actualized by the Holy Spirit. The whole church is there in Christ. Individuals are first affected by the Holy Spirit. They come together, yet they belong together already through Christ."

[273.] The following passage corresponds extensively to statements in *Sanctorum Communio*. See *DBWE* 1:127–30.

[274.] See Scheler, *Formalism in Ethics*, 93–96, 546–49, and 554–57.

[275.] [This is actually a quotation from Scheler, *Formalism in Ethics*, 93; cf. *DBWE* 1:128, ed. note 17.—VB]

[276.] Deleted: "not."

[277.] WDZ: "Each person enjoys the value for himself alone. Each as individual [is] connected to the value. No true community; only possibility."

[278.] WDZ: "Where [is the] boundary of that which occurs with the value of the holy or with the value of the true, or the beautiful? Why not there as well?"

*Heinrich Scholz*:[279] [The] concrete form of religion is proof [. . .]![280] [The] religion of revelation is [an] example [of this]. Religion belongs first of all to the things that the human spirit ponders. Religion, second, is a religion of revelation. [There] is [the necessity of] *education* [in religion]; this is possible only through community![281]

[Critique:] Neither [a] general value of the holy nor [the] concept of the religion of revelation contains religious community. Religious community cannot be derived from religion conceptually.[282]

Regarding (2) psychological: religious community [arises] through the human drive to communicate, evangelize, etc., to human beings. Yet that [is nonetheless] not a specific religious community. This need to communicate is a sign of every community.[283] Piety [is] also possible individualistically. Mutual communication is not [a basis for a] religious community, for this has a purpose while the former is merely being sociable.[284] The goal or purpose that is external to a society [Gesellschaft] is in a community [Gemeinschaft] constitutive—the goal of being together is an end in itself. Every purpose of a community [is] intrinsic to itself.[285]

279 Regarding (3) religion is [a] highest achievement of human culture! Religious community [here is] understood as the crown of cultural com-

[279.] Cf. Scholz, *Religionsphilosophie*, 115ff. and 292ff. Scholz refers to religion, on the one hand, as a determination of the feeling of life but, on the other hand, seeks to establish it on the concept of revelation.

[280.] The following passage corresponds extensively to statements in *Sanctorum Communio*. Cf. *DBWE* 1:30.

[281.] WDZ: "Only community hands down correctly."

[282.] WDZ: "How does tradition occur through community? Is it different in the field of religion? Is the phenomenon of community not the same? For the one who has religion isn't it necessary to be in a community? [Bonhoeffer here is summarizing the arguments of others.—VB] Community is necessary only because of education, for handing down. [A] religion of revelation does not include the concept of community. In religion the possibility of religious mysticism must always be conceded."

[283.] WDZ: "[This is] not specifically religious. Every experience pushes itself outward. [. . .] [There] are phenomena that do not have that desire, [for example,] Buddhism."

[284.] Uncertain reading.

[285.] The meaning of Bonhoeffer's point is obscure in the German manuscript. Bonhoeffer takes Ferdinand Tönnies's distinction between society (*Gesellschaft*) and community (*Gemeinschaft*) and directs it against the attempt to psychologically derive community from religion. The sociologist Tönnies had differentiated between a community in which togetherness itself was the desired purpose and a society that was constituted for a purpose outside itself (cf. Tönnies, *Community and Society*, §1 and §19). According to this, as Bonhoeffer inferred, the drive for communication was not the basis of a community but only of a society, since the purpose lies in a third external goal, namely, communication. Cf. also *DBWE* 1:86–96. [See also *DBWE* 1:329.—CG]

munity. [Derived from the] concept of culture! (Lohmeyer: concept of religious community!)[286]

Against this: [the] concept of church-community cannot be derived from [the] concept of religion. Religious community is individualistic. Religious community is atomistic. Religious community is [the] *form of community of* humanity-in-Adam*;* [it is a] final attempt on the part of humankind to save itself from being alone, saving itself selfishly.

[There are] proposals for improving [a] new community life in the church: the youth movement, the ecumenical movement, and others.[287] [But] church can only be believed, this [is] possible only through faith in Christ. For the most part, this church of faith is not seen; rather [only] the religious community is seen! The church *cannot be experienced.*[288] Walking in faith, not in seeing.[289] The church proclaims in every word, [. . .] grounded in baptism. Without wishing to or willing to, [the] human being is incorporated into the church. This cannot be understood from the standpoint of the concept of religious community.[290] *The understanding of the difference between church and religious community is decided with baptism.* [The] word of God alone constitutes the church; this can only be believed. Baptism is only a form of the word of God. The church is experienced there where it becomes clear that only the one Lord makes all human beings 280
equal. Genuine community of human beings in the church and the community of the Lord's Supper. As paradoxical unity, which God has established, that encompasses militarists, pacifists, and the like! Thus no religious community is the church. With religious experiences, we remain in humanity-in-Adam![291]

[286.] Lohmeyer, *Von Begriff der religiösen Gemeinschaft.*

[287.] WDZ: "The believed church is not meant there. Foundation [is rather] pious experience."

[288.] WDZ: "The church is the vicarious representative action of Christ and the Holy Spirit making this intelligible. We see only the works, not the persons who are in God."

[289.] Cf. 2 Cor. 5:7.

[290.] WDZ: "Here [. . .] is self-confession! [Baptism is] a completed whole act of God with the human being, who does not yet want or know. Only [the] church can baptize."

[291.] WDZ: "Religious retreats, hikes, [and] convents do not create a church; [rather] the church is experienced there where one knows that there is no longer a community between you and me; [where] one knows that one has the same Lord; where employer and employee go together to the Lord's Supper. We are not one here, yet we are one in Christ. In [the] large city the church is the most available to experience. God establishes the church. [The] poverty of faith cannot be replaced by rich experiences."

III. Proclamation and the Church

[(1) The Word][292]

[The] church is constituted through [the] word of God in Christ's redemptive act.[293] The word, and nothing else, is constitutive! [The] church is always already there. What [comes] from Christ comes out of the church and is directed toward the church. Because [there is] the word, there is the church; because there is the church, there is the word. [The] word exists *only* in the church! "Outside the church there is no salvation;"[294] that is Protestant! The church is always already included when we talk about the word. [The] holy community speaks to the church-community in the word.[295] [The] Protestant concept of the congregation [is] built upon [the] church because [it] is built upon [the] word.

June 25 [1932]

[The] church is constituted by the word of Christ. [The] concept of the *church-community* is included in the concept of the *word.* Christ is the new humanity itself. In the center stands [the] church-community. [The] word
281 comes out of the church-community; *church as word and as church-community.* [The] word of justification is [the] word from the church-community for the church-community.[296] "Word and congregation belong together."[297] Church-community is there where the word is proclaimed, and [it] is absolutely *visible church-community.* [In] contrast [to this], [faith] is invisible.

[292.] [This and the following subtitles for each division were added by the German *DBW* editor.—VB]

[293.] WDZ: "[The] church is newly actualized through [the] sermon."

[294.] Bonhoeffer takes the well-known phrase by Cyprian of Carthage, "Salus extra ecclesiam non est" (Outside the church there is no salvation). [In 1936, Bonhoeffer paraphrased this statement during the heated debates in the Confessing Church about legalization: "Whoever consciously parts with the Confessing Church in Germany parts from salvation." See *DBW* 14, 2/19, p. 676.—VB]

[295.] See *DBWE* 1:227: "Preaching is a divinely ordained activity *of the church-community for the church-community.*" See also WDZ: "In the word of God the church-community speaks because Christ speaks."

[296.] WDZ: "*Iustitia aliena* [alien righteousness] in word and [in the] church-community. Troeltsch." Troeltsch had criticized Luther and Lutheranism because of its individualistic striving for "salvation by justification" (see Troeltsch, *Social Teaching of the Christian Churches*, 2:467–77, 494–503, and elsewhere). Bonhoeffer, referring to Karl Holl's essay "Die Entstehung von Luthers Kirchenbegriff" (see pp. 328–29), had disagreed with this because of the insoluble connection between justification and church-community, particularly where it is developed in Luther's early sermons (see pp. 318–20 and 316).

[297.] The source of this quotation cannot be established. Cf. Luther, "On the Councils and the Church," 1539: "For God's word cannot be without God's people; and conversely, God's people cannot be without God's word" (*WA* 50:629, 34–35; *LW* 41:150).

[The] faith of the church-community is invisible; [yet] as church community [it is] visible.[298]

[(2) The Assembly][299]
Where [the] word is, there must also be the *assembly* around this word. *[The] word of God is primarily in the assembly for worship!* To keep the word is to adhere to the assembly! For the Christian this is self-evident. The Spirit is received within the church-community.[300] [The] Catholic Church preserves the assembly.[301] Reformation: [did not preach] freedom of the individual far away from the assembly. Luther is not to be understood individualistically.[302] [The] *experience* of the church [is something] for pious individuals.

I belong to Christ, to the assembly. Where [the] word is, there am I primarily. I belong in the assembly. I cannot ask: "What do I get out of this?" (as: "What do I get from my mother?").[303] I belong to her! Why was 282
this so in early Christianity? Why is this no longer so today?[304] In ancient days something happened in the assembly: God's revelation [was] present there.[305] I hear God's word entirely and really: one can barely think this now. Then one would say: [from] there I take my existence; there God gives it to me again and again. [Reasons for the change:] "Our pride?" Or [is the] gospel no longer proclaimed rightly? Or has "God" taken away [his] promise? The illness of the church-community: is it unto death?[306]

---

[298.] WDZ: "[The] difference between [the] church-community and those who attend occasionally is invisible. God alone sees the truly faithful."

[299.] Cf. for the following *DBWE* 1:226–31.

[300.] WDZ: "In [the] assembly wonders of speech, spirit, and forgiveness occur (cf. Acts 2)."

[301.] WDZ: "In Catholicism a duty is made of this. There is first a falling off, but [the] meaning of the assembly [is] preserved."

[302.] WDZ: "Luther wants free independence of worship life, not individualistic freedom."

[303.] WDZ: "Isolated piety [asks]: *Why do I join the congregation, etc.?* An individualistic explanation. A false basic beginning. Unhappiness of the congregation: clever excitements. No plausible reasons for going to the assembly. [This is an] unchristian question. [Rather, the following is true]: the miracle and *the* act of God that the congregation is given to us."

[304.] WDZ: "Every inhibition [is] set aside among sects and political gatherings. In these gatherings things are possible that are no longer possible in Christianity."

[305.] WDZ:" In [the] assembly something really happened; God and his will are perceived. Revelation occurred there."

[306.] Reference to Kierkegaard, *Sickness unto Death.*

[(3) The Office of Preacher][307]

[The] word [is] given to the church-community through God: the word from the cross is proclaimed through [the] sermon. Who should preach? Who may preach? The unbeliever? [The] sermon is the office of the church-community of Christ. Even the unbeliever can preach and proclaim the word. [The] charisma of the office is [the] charisma of the church-community. Proclamation must occur rightly.[308] Who can do this? He who has learned these things and studied them. People who have studied [the] word are pastors. [The] church-community remains the bearer of the sermon. [The] preacher has received [the] commission to carry out the office from the church-community.[309] Priesthood of all believers.

283 The office is never the permanent property of the pastor. The pastor has [the] *promise* of the office.[310] This promise does not become invalid [even] when the pastor himself does not have faith. [The] promise depends on the correct preaching of the pastor, not on faith. The word is there (even when I cannot believe it)! Therefore I preach. [. . .] He should speak the word correctly.[311] Then he has the promise. Preaching leads away from one's own faith.[312] [The] recognition of faith must be distinguished from the recognition of preaching: The message on the basis of the commission.

[(4) The Confession of Faith (Bekenntnis)][313]

The assembly and the office of preacher belong to the church-community.[314] It must confirm that it lives through the word alone. It does this in the confession of faith. There is no worship without confession of faith. The

[307.] On the following passage, cf. *DBWE* 1:231–36.

[308.] WDZ: "Correct proclamation; corresponding to [the] Bible and Reformation interpretation. One must learn this."

[309.] WDZ: "The pastor is not the bearer of the office; the church-community is. He becomes [. . .] the officeholder. [The] office belongs to every member of the church-community. It remains the office of the church-community."

[310.] WDZ: "He also has the promise that as long as he holds [the] office, his work is not in vain."

[311.] "Correctly" replaces "law."

[312.] WDZ: "He should only speak the word correctly, which then includes the promise. [It is] completely directed to the church-community away from his own faith."

[313.] [The standard translation for both *Bekenntnis* and *Beichte* (see p. 317 below) is "confession," but the two German terms refer to different things. *Bekenntnis* means a confession that articulates and affirms the articles of faith (the Augsburg Confession, the Barmen Confession, etc.) held by the entire community; *Beichte* is the personal confession of one's sins. To make the distinction clear to the reader, *Bekenntnis* is translated here as "confession of faith" and *Beichte* as "confession of sin."—VB]

[314.] WDZ: "Preaching exists so that confession of faith happens; because confession of faith happens, preaching exists."

church-community must confess or deny.[315] We cannot remain neutral.[316] One can leave the confession of faith [. . .] be—this is the constitution of the church-community.[317] The confession of faith is [the] only genuine constitution, in the confession the church-community separates itself from the world. The confession of faith must be *completely true.* [It is] the answer to the true word of God. Confession of faith concerns immediate presence. [. . .][318] "I recognize your *truth* and I confess it!" The confession must contain what the truth proclaims. *Against the Apostles' Creed Bonhoeffer* [offers the objection]: questions of liberalism (and Harnack) [are] still open; [that] is not a finished matter.[319] Confession of faith concerns our true stance
before God! Confession is not uncertain; [it] is one's confession to truth. 284
It should be universal confession of all of Christianity.[320] Yet we do have a different confession.

June 29 [1932]

*Truthfulness of the confession*: The *word* itself must be true! Not just what it means! "Descended into hell," "born of a virgin."[321] *The clarity of the word* must be for the sake of the church-community. Often the creedal confession is [a] deterring element![322] The word must be true and clear, also in consideration for those who do not yet believe. No general truth should be laid down in a confession of faith. Specific recognition of truth in the confessio must be retained in the confession. Heim and Schmitz [want] discussion

[315.] WDZ: "This cannot remain undecided. Aesthetic inhibitions say nothing."

[316.] WDZ: "The difference: church-community—public."

[317.] WDZ: "Confession is [a] constitution that it gives to itself."

[318.] WDZ: "It is not prayed but rather confessed. 'God, I acknowledge and confess your truth.'"

[319.] The first dispute about the Apostles' Creed broke out after 1871 due to remarks made by liberal theologians of the Protestant Association. The second so-called dispute about the Apostles' Creed arose after 1890 in Württemberg and Prussia concerning the question of eliminating the pastors' commitment to the Apostles' Creed and its use in the worship service. In 1892, Adolf von Harnack had published an article in *Christliche Welt* about questions from his students relating to this discussion of the Apostles' Creed. He maintained that a historically educated Christian must necessarily disagree with some points in the Apostles' Creed (cf. also Harnack, *Das apostolische Glaubensbekenntnis*). The dispute often flared up again later.

[320.] WDZ:" The unification with all of Christianity. The Bible, Lord's Prayer, baptism in common."

[321.] These statements in the Apostles' Creed had already been criticized by Harnack (see ed. note 319 above).

[322.] WDZ: "The creedal confession is [a] deterrent for those who do not yet believe in a worship service."

[about this]![323] "κύριος Χριστός"[324] they recommend for all![325] Everyone, however, means something else by these words. Among us [this means]: "by grace alone!" The Protestant confession must [. . .] this side of . . .[326]

We can no longer confess our faith as the first Christians did! Now only
285 as Protestants or Catholics. *[The] Apostles' Creed is not adequate for the Protestant Confessio.* The ordination of the pastor on the basis of the Apostles' Creed is not tenable!! [The] new liturgy puts other possibilities beside the Apostles' Creed.[327] This does not remove the offense. The question of the confession is not yet resolved! Confessionalism [Bekennertum] and confession are different: confessionalism uses confession as a means of propaganda against the godless. Confession of faith belongs in the Christian assembly of the faithful. Nowhere else is confession of faith sustainable (for example, confession is not sustainable in [the] "confessional hours").[328] *The first confession of the Christian church-community before the world is the deed!*[329]

[323.] See Heim, "Tolstoj und Jesus"; also Schmitz, "Jesus der Herr."

[324.] "Christ the Lord."

[325.] The following preface is added to the contributions by Heim and Schmitz on behalf of the German Christian Student Organization: "Jesus the Lord. Our circles put this confession into the movement of the *Volkskirche* [cf. 2/5, ed. note 2—VB] these days, from which we hope for a new revival of the worn-down life of our people. Jesus the Lord—that is the motto with which we enter into the recent spiritual battle in Germany and experience the unifying power of God's revelation, beyond all politics and economics." [This is a reference to a preface to the published lectures from the 1919 German Student Christian Conference, *Jesus der Herr*, edited by Karl Heim and including a contribution by Otto Schmitz, p. 5.—MBL]

[326.] This phrase remains incomplete in Ruppell's notes. Cf. WDZ: "The early Christian confession is not sufficient. [The] split lies there and cannot be bridged. No ordination on the basis of this Apostles' Creed. One can subject oneself to this only out of love for the church-community. [. . .] General synods for this purpose [namely, the decision about the use of the Apostles' Creed]."

[327.] The Prussian general synod decided in 1925 to begin preliminary work for the publication of a new liturgy. A draft was submitted in 1931 as the result of the work on revisions of the old 1895 "Liturgy for the Protestant Regional Church." This draft was allowed to be used publicly but was never approved as a final liturgy. The draft is characterized by a stronger orientation to the church year and drew inspiration from the "older liturgical movement." (See Niebergall's article, "Agende," 2:69–70.)

[328.] The so-called confessional hours newly taken up at the time were supposed to be a preparation for the struggle with the opponents of the Christian faith.

[329.] WDZ: "The deed interprets itself. When the deed [becomes] power, then the world will also demand the verbal confession. Only then can the deed be consecrated within the worship service."

(Confession belongs as *arcanum*[330] within the worship service.)[331] Then after the deed the church-community needs the verbal confession of faith. The confession is not to be screamed loudly in a propagandistic manner; it must be preserved as the sacred possession of the church-community. The deed alone is our confession before the world.

In summary: That of which we have spoken is an uninterrupted series: word, assembly, office of preacher, confession of faith. Always a *vertical line*! [From God to human beings and] from human beings to God. The church-community as a unity: "I (as the "I" of the assembly) believe"! *Unified* structure and structure of *identity* (with Christ) and structure of *lordship* (of Christ) at the same time. The church-community[332] is itself the Lord;
he [. . .] confesses the congregation.[333] Then there is the *horizontal line* 286
of the church-community *as the structure of community*. The Spirit actualizes the church-community only where there is correct preaching. The gospel is correctly proclaimed in the Protestant church (not true for the Catholic Church);[334] [the] rightness of the proclamation is characteristic of the confession. How can the *"recte docere"*[335] of the pastor be *secured*?

[(5) Theology]

That is the *task of theology*! Theology must come to the aid of the pastor. No Protestant sermon, no Protestant confession of faith without theology. Theology is absolutely necessary. The church's first duty after liturgy [außerkultisch] is theology. A correct sermon doesn't come from living, correct religiosity alone! Arrogance toward theology is unjustified.[336]

---

[330.] "Arcane" or "concealed."

[331.] Bonhoeffer is referring to the early church's "arcane discipline" (*disciplina arcani*) [which understood certain "hidden" aspects of the church's liturgical life that expressed mysteries of faith revealed in Christ—VB]. In the early church between the second and fifth centuries, baptism and the celebration of Holy Communion were kept strictly hidden. [In earlier *DBWE* volumes, Bonhoeffer's German term *Arkandisziplin* is translated as "discipline of the secret." Because this is somewhat misleading, it is translated here as "arcane discipline"; it is a concept to which Bonhoeffer refers throughout his theology, particularly in his book *Discipleship* (*DBWE* 4).—VB]

[332.] This should be "Christ."

[333.] WDZ: "The church-community as the structure of unity: 'I believe.' The individual [is] not meant here. One in Christ and Christ as Lord. The church-community is the presence of Christ. It hears and confesses, because Christ is Lord."

[334.] WDZ: "The pastor *must preach correctly*. Only then (is there) actualization. Therefore a difference from Catholicism."

[335.] "Right teaching."

[336.] Deleted: "not."

[(6) Dogma]
*Dogma* is the formed shape of theology, is not personal confession of faith.[337] No theologian creates dogma; only the *entire church* as theologically responsible creates dogma.

[(7) The Council]
The "council" alone creates dogma,[338] as an aid to preaching and the confession!

The church-community alone can protest against the council.[339] The concept of "heresy" is a component of the concept of "council"! Today there are "ecumenical assemblies," but they have no heresies.[340] Today [there are] no longer any true councils! Because our[341] theology for the past two
287 hundred years [is] disorganized and because [. . .] the crisis [affects] the church momentarily as the preaching church! Alongside the sermon and the assembly, theology and council appear with dogma!

[(8) Summary][342]
The church of the word is as such the church-community! Assembly, the office of preacher, and confession create [a] necessary connection and are necessarily established in the church as proclamation of the word of Christ. Not a single one of these three can be understood apart from the word. Every attempt at an individualistic rationale must fail! The *correct* proclamation of the word requires *theology* as the first extra-ecclesial function next to the church, the assembly of the church (council), which makes decisions about theology (heresy), and the *dogma* created by the council. This trinity is intended to serve the first trinity. The first shall rule and should allow itself to be served!

---

[337.] WDZ: "When theology becomes dogma, then the task [is] fulfilled."

[338.] WDZ: "A council is a theological assembly."

[339.] WDZ: "The proclamation of the living Christ himself in the church-community is [the] boundary against [the] council."

[340.] WDZ: "Heresies don't exist there. [. . .] The heresy of the church constitution!"

[341.] "Our" replaces "the."

[342.] The following section is almost verbatim in the notes by WDZ and was probably dictated by Bonhoeffer.

July 2 (1932)

IV. The Priesthood of All Believers[343]

Luther's concept has been individualized today.[344] It [is] false [to make a] right of the individual [out of this] and thereby conclude that the priest, the assembly (private religiosity) [as well as the] church and priesthood, [or the] worship service, are superfluous.[345] That is contrary to Luther's thinking!![346] Individual confession of sin [Beichte] is not superfluous; 288
it is necessary.[347] [A] priest stands for everyone before God.[348] [The] decisive function of the priest must belong *to all*; therefore the office can belong to only one. Everyone needs the other as priest. Everyone [is] dependent on the other! Through this the members of the church-community are closely bound to one another.[349] [. . .] Permanent proclamation. [. . .] *communio sanctorum*.[350] The congregation [Gemeinde] is primarily

[343.] On the following section, cf. *DBWE* 1:165–92.

[344.] See pp. 319–22.

[345.] WDZ: "The individual [stands] without priestly mediator immediately before God. [That is] the right of the individual. The superfluousness of the priest. The right to private religiosity. Worship service without church and priest."

[346.] On Luther's concept of the priesthood of all believers, see, for example, "A Treatise on the New Testament, That Is, the Holy Mass," 1520 (*WA* 6:370, 12ff.; *LW* 35:101); "To the Christian Nobility of the German Nation," 1520 (*WA* 6:407, 10ff.; *LW* 44:127–28); "On the Freedom of a Christian," 1520 (*WA* 7:27, 17ff.). [The latter citation from the dedication is not translated in *LW* 31.—CG] Bonhoeffer's teacher Karl Holl had already pointed out that Luther's concept of a priesthood of all believers not only refers to the relationship of the individual to God but also is to be understood in relation to a new founding of the church office [i.e., the ministry—VB] in the entire church-community. (See Holl, "Die Entstehung von Luthers Kirchenbegriff," 273–74n5.) On Bonhoeffer's incorporation of this idea, see *DBWE* 1:236.

[347.] Luther emphasized the necessity of personal confession for the Christian. His criticism of the medieval practice of personal confession directed itself primarily against compulsory confession and the dogmatization of certain doctrines about the effectiveness of penance. (See, for example, the summary of the sermon on Reminiscere Sunday, 1522, on private confession: *LW* 51:97–100, esp. 98.)

[348.] WDZ: "[The] priest [has a] decisive function. This function cannot remain in the hands of one; rather [this] function belongs to everyone; therefore it can be given to one."

[349.] WDZ: "The priest does not isolate but rather binds the church-community closely to one another."

[350.] "Communion of saints."

community [Gemeinschaft].[351] The horizontal line![352] Christ is the brother as human being, who stands in the church-community of Christ. [The body is a] multiplicity of members.

[. . .] The relationship of the horizontal line to the vertical line.[353] The Christian basis for individualization. Originally, not every single person can have God alone; that is individualizing; rather, originally there is a church-community of brother with brother, without a detour through God. I have Christ in my brother; in Christ I am directed toward my brother. No individualizing of the church!

289 Actualization [occurs] through the proclaiming Spirit.[354] Proclamation is the constitutive element for pastoral care as it is for the church. [Proclamation also occurs] in the solitude of the liturgical dialogue between brother and brother. Christ is in the center where [the] brother speaks.[355] (That is [the] central event for the Christian church-community.) That is *love!* This love is not a deed that the human being does from his own power. God alone tears the human being out of hell, through his deed upon the

[351.] [Here Bonhoeffer emphasizes the communal character of the congregation as an end in itself. In *Sanctorum Communio* (*DBWE* 1), he argues that the church also had other sociological characteristics: like a society (*Gesellschaft*), it has a purpose, namely, mission, and like an association under authority (*Herrschaftsverband*), it is under the lordship of Christ.—CG]

[352.] WDZ: "For the horizontal [. . .] expression of the *community* that was founded in the deed of Christ."

[353.] WDZ: "Troeltsch [and] Harnack [to the contrary believe]: The individual [stands in direct relation to] God and only [after that] in community with [the] brother." On Bonhoeffer's criticism of Troeltsch's individualism, see pp. 209 and 311 above and *DBWE* 1:177, Bonhoeffer's note 39 (with the citation from Troeltsch's *Social Teachings*, 56); for criticism of Harnack's famous book first published in 1900, *What Is Christianity?* see above in Bonhoeffer's lectures on the history of systematic theology (2/3, pp. 199–205). Bonhoeffer objected that in their interpretation of Christianity both were striving for a closer connection with a "culture of personality": cf. 2/3, p. 224. Moreover, the relationship of the individual to God in the church should not be separated from or subordinate to the relationship to the brother. Cf. WDZ: "[Here] is the original primary community of brother with brother. These two are objectively identical in the church-community. In the brother I encounter Christ and in Christ I hear the brother for the first time. The horizontal and the vertical lines [are] inseparable from each other."

[354.] WDZ: "Actualization of the church realized in Christ (vicarious representative action) through [the] Holy Spirit."

[355.] WDZ:" Christ should be in the center [. . .] speaks as brother to brother. Christ the brother is proclaimed as brother. [The "central event" is a reference to preaching. —CG]

cross. The love of God on the cross of Golgotha. *The love of God in Golgotha* steps between brother and brother, poured into hearts by the Holy Spirit.[356] There is only one love of God, which the human being receives through faith. Love can be received only through faith in the love of God. *Love is faithful behavior toward the other!* Faith is the believing relationship to God! *Faith and love* structure the church along [the] horizontal line.[357] *Unity of faith! Community of love!*

Concept of the *community of love*: not the activated side of the concept of the church. Love of the one to the other brother is *the reception of the love of God.* Action in love is always passive: reception from God.

(1) The structural being-with-each-other[358] of members!
(2) The structural being-for-each-other[359] of the members[360]
[The] church-community is the overcoming of loneliness, not as togetherness! Where one member [is], there is the entire body of Christ. The church-community has *one* life; it is impossible to think of its members as separated. Where the church-community is, there Christ [is] always also; (Ps. 139 [presence of Christ!]):[361] as forgiving or judging. [The] structure [is] therefore that of being-with-one-another. Not primarily the reality of consciousness.[362] The church-community leads *one* life. [The] need of the other must be such that I feel it as mine. (Luther's sermon on the sacraments, 1519, W. A. II 750ff.;[363] sermon on the Holy Body and dying 290

[356.] WDZ: "The action of the one upon the other: [that] is the tearing away from hell; that is love."

[357.] WDZ: "Vertical and horizontal. The separate functions of one *reality*; community but both together. Faith is unity; love is community."

[358.] [Cf. *DBWE* 1:178. The editors thank Christiane Tietz for this reference.—VB]

[359.] [Ibid.—VB] [Here appropriated from his first book is found the recurrent key concept of "being-free-for" the other, which remains formative in Bonhoeffer's thinking through to *Letters and Papers from Prison*.—CG]

[360.] The second header here was mentioned by Bonhoeffer in conjunction with the first; however, it introduces the section below that begins on p. 322.

[361.] Bonhoeffer understands the omnipresence of God described in Ps. 139 as that of Christ.

[362.] [Bonhoeffer is saying that it is not primarily a question of being conscious (of the situation of the other); cf. *DBWE* 1:181. The editors thank Christiane Tietz for this reference.—VB]

[363.] Luther, "The Blessed Sacrament of the Holy and True Body of Christ and the Brotherhoods," 1519 (*WA* 2:742–58, esp. 750ff.; *LW* 35:49–73, esp. 61ff.).

[Clemen];[364] sermon on baptism;[365] *Tesseradecas consolatoria pro laborantibus*, W. A. VI, 130ff.).[366]

You must allow your heart to feel the infirmity that your brothers experience as [if it were] your own![367] The strength of the other is my strength. My temptation is borne by the faithful church-community.[368] My dying [is] not alone. Christ and the church-community suffer and die with us.[369] W. A. vol. 17 p. 100[370] (book 10, vol. 3 p. 308).[371]

---

[364.] See the previous note. The sermon was reprinted in vol. 1 of the four-volume Luther edition of Otto Clemen, 196–212. The note taker confused the title of this sermon (cited in the preceding ed. note) with another one by Luther, "A Sermon on Preparing to Die," 1519 (*WA* 2:685–97; *LW* 42:99–115).

[365.] Luther, "The Holy and Blessed Sacrament of Baptism," 1519 (*WA* 2:727–37; *LW* 35:29–43).

[366.] Luther, "Fourteen Consolations for Those Who Labor and Are Heavy-Laden," 1520 (*WA* 6:99–134, esp. 130ff.; *LW* 42:121–66).

[367.] Luther, sermon on "The Blessed Sacrament of the Holy and True Body of Christ," 1519 (*WA* 2:750, 30–32; *LW* 35:61): "You must take to heart the infirmities and needs of others, as if they were your own. Then offer to others your strength, as if it were their own, just as Christ does for you in the sacrament."

[368.] Cf. Luther, ibid. (*WA* 2:745, 7–9; *LW* 35:54): "The immeasurable grace and mercy of God are given us in this sacrament to the end that we might put from us all misery and tribulation [*Anfechtung*] and lay it upon the community (of saints), and especially on Christ."

[369.] Cf. Luther, ibid. (*WA* 2:745,10–16; *LW* 35:54): "Then we may with joy find strength and comfort, and say, 'Though I am a sinner and have fallen, though this or that misfortune has befallen me, nevertheless I will go to the sacrament to receive a sign from God that I have on my side Christ's righteousness, life, and sufferings, with all holy angels and the blessed in heaven and all pious men on earth. If I die, I am not alone in death; if I suffer, they suffer with me. [I know that] all my misfortune is shared with Christ and the saints.'"

[370.] Luther, "Fastenpostille," 1525 (*WA* 17/2:100, 14–23): "For no one will want to fulfill God's law for the other; each must fulfill it for himself, as St. Paul says in Gal. 5 [should be Gal. 6:5]: 'For all must carry their own loads.' And 1 Cor. 5 [should be 2 Cor. 5:10]: 'For all of us must appear before the judgment seat of Christ, so that each may receive recompense in the body for what has been done, whether good or evil.' Therefore, it is said, You, you, you alone should love. Don't let someone else love for you. For although one can and should pray for the other that God be merciful and help him, no one becomes blessed thereby, unless he has fulfilled God's law for himself. Therefore, do not pray alone for someone that he remain unpunished, as the indulgence boys do, rather much more that he becomes pious and holds God's law."

[371.] Luther, "Predigt am 7 September 1522" (*WA* 10/3:308, 1–10): "And furthermore: if at the same time all angels, if God's compassion itself stood there for you, it would not help, for you must depend on it with your own faith, but it can well do this if it creates your own faith and helps you. As with Christ, as he died for us and gave his body and life, blood and flesh for us, it would still not help us, only through faith. But he can

July 6 [1932] 291

I and You are not fused together! [The] "I" before God is not abolished. The individual is perceived as [standing] within the church-community as soon as he is perceived as individual before God![372] Structural existence [Dasein] of the church-community there where the individual is!![373] [. . .]
Without always knowing about the suffering of the other. In this case the 292
church-community is Christ himself. [The] merits of the brothers, the merit of Christ, are also my merits.[374] No one has himself alone; the individual lives the church-community. Close to[375] Catholic teaching of "*thesaurus sanctorum*."[376] But the human being can never do more than he is obliged

---

help us when he steps before the Father and says, 'O Father, this I have done for humankind; give them faith that they may believe this,' in that way we are helped and his merit becomes our own, whenever we believe that his merit is our own."

According to WDZ, Bonhoeffer countered the saying about Christians being a part of the body of Christ with the seemingly contradictory thought at the beginning of Luther's sermon on Invocavit Sunday, March 9, 1522: "The summons of death comes to us all, and no one can die for another. Everyone must fight his own battle with death by himself, alone. We can shout into another's ears, but everyone must himself be prepared for the time of death, for I will not be with you then, nor you with me" (from the first of "Eight Sermons at Wittenberg," *LW* 51:70). Cf. WDZ version: "I do not die alone. Christ and [the] church-community [are] with me. The seriousness of the responsibility is not removed. 'Sermon to [the] people of Wittenberg.' Opposition! Each equally necessary and objective. Where the individual is wholly individual, the church-community steps in. [. . .] Only where [the] human being is wholly himself is he redeemed and reconciled in the church-community, WA X 3, 308; 17, 103. Where [the] human being is wholly individual, in death, his isolation [is] lifted and [is] redemption. The church-community, however, then suffers with him as well. That is the structure; [that] is not discernible. This double meaning may not be removed. Where an individual [is] wholly himself, he will be captured by Christ and by [the] church-community. And yet everyone stands for him before God because he stands before God as an individual."

[372.] WDZ: "When the individual is perceived wholly as an individual, then he will be perceived as standing in [the] church-community."

[373.] WDZ: "The church-community according to its structure is there where the individual is. [The] church-community is the community most filled with life; it baptizes and buries every day."

[374.] WDZ: "The prayer of the other helps me. Everything is in common."

[375.] Should read "to the."

[376.] "Treasury of the saints." The doctrine of the *thesaurus ecclesiae* (treasury of the church) or the *thesaurus meritorum* (treasury of merits) unfolded as part of the theory of penance during the Middle Ages. According to this, the church has been entrusted with a treasure of a "surplus of satisfactions," through the surplus merits of Christ and the saints; on the basis of these the pope or even the bishops could grant the faithful indulgence after fulfilling certain conditions.

to do. The treasure is the merit of Christ in the church-community.[377] Christ allows the one to enjoy the deed of the other. We cannot do the intercession of the other, we cannot achieve abstinence for the other, but Christ makes this action of the other great for me! The Catholic doctrine is objectification and rationalization:[378] [The] deed of the other is in and of itself effective.

[(2) The structural being-for-each-other of the members]
*[The] being-for-each-other of the church-community is established in the being-with-each-other of the church-community: (a) The readiness to give up anything or to make any sacrifice for one's neighbor! (b) Intercession! (c) Forgiveness of sins.*

Regarding (a) [the] sacrifice refers first to [the] goods of life, to all the everyday things.[379] [The] one who owns goods steps into the place of the one who owns nothing; the people of honor step into the place of those who have no honor. One's own life, one's honor is a good,[380] which the good person receives in order to serve the weak! One has honor for the common good (1 Cor. 12:7). [One] paradoxical, strange possibility consists in the following: sacrifice of community with God for the sake of one's
293 brothers, voluntary bearing of wrath (Exod. 32:32!)![381] [Such a thing] is hardly mentioned in the Bible (Rom. 9!).[382] Only these two passages concern themselves with this possibility. The paradox of love for God [is shown here]! Paul loves the community with God more than the community with human beings.[383] He fulfills the last commandment in place of the cursed [verdammten][384] beloved people. [This is not a] moment of weakness of Paul but rather [the] final fulfillment of the commandment of Christ.[385]

[377.] WDZ: "[There] is no surplus of merit of a human being. The way is only Christ in the *church-community*."

[378.] Cf. WDZ: "Catholicism: rationalization and moralizing; clarification." Cf. also *DBWE* 1:183.

[379.] WDZ: "Everyday things, possession, life, honor."

[380.] WDZ: "One's own honor [is] not the ultimate reality of life, [is] not identical with one's own existence."

[381.] WDZ: "The greatest sacrifice of brotherly love is [the] sacrifice of community with God. This is the voluntary bearing of wrath in the place of one's brothers."

[382.] See Rom. 9:1–3.

[383.] WDZ: "In order to bring his brothers peace with God he is ready to be damned."

[384.] [This may be a misreading (it contradicts Rom. 11:1ff., where Paul states that God has not rejected his people), but it is impossible to determine what Bonhoeffer would have said here. See, however, the comment in the following note.—VB]

[385.] WDZ: "Paul [practices] obedience to the commandment of giving oneself fully for the other. Because he allows himself to be accursed, he remains in the *deepest* communion with the will of God; a final obedience." [Here *verbannen lässt* has been translated

[The] imitation of Christ [is] almost tried here.[386] This leads as a biblically inspired act almost to insanity. This must be fulfilled over and over again; [it is] not a foregone conclusion! [. . .] It is like a possibility at the margin of human existence, close to blasphemy![387] [The] promise of the resurrection [is valid] here also.

Regarding (b) Intercession. The church-community leads *one* life. My prayer belongs to the church-community; the church-community prays in the prayer of the individual.[388] (Chomjakoff: "Einheit der Kirche," Collection: *Östliches Christentum* by Hans Ehrenberg).[389] The power of inter- 294
cession! If there [is] still any doubt about this, then [behind it stands a] self-righteousness of the human being (he doesn't want to be given anything). I really stand in the place of the other. Not particularly a gift of empathy (empathy for the other one's suffering), rather vicarious acting by one for the other.

July 9 [1932]

Intercession [is] vicarious representative action. [. . .] Not primarily a gift of empathy; otherwise there is no prayer for the other. Intercession is not limited psychologically. [The] boundaries are where the boundaries of the

---

as "accursed," as in Rom 9:3, which has the same Greek word that the Luther Bible translates as *verbannt.* Since WDZ uses both *verdammt* and *verbannen,* it is unclear which word Bonhoeffer actually used, since he refers to Romans 9 and that usually means the entire passage Rom. 9–11.—CG]

[386.] WDZ: "This is the imitation of Christ himself. What Paul strives for is what Christ did on Golgotha. This act of Christ's should be fulfilled again and again; yet this is not a foregone conclusion, whereas [to give] honor, etc., is a foregone conclusion."

[387.] WDZ: "Paul stands at the edge of the abyss of the eternal downfall and blasphemy. Over all this the resurrection shines brightly. 'The curse of the godless is more pleasing to God than the hallelujahs of his pious worshippers' (Luther), referring to this marginal possibility." Cf. Luther, *Lectures on Romans,* 1515–16 (*WA* 56:401, 12–14; *LW* 25, 390): "Cum tales blasphemie, quia sunt violenter a diabolo hominibus invictis extorte, aliquando gratiores sonent in aure dei quam ipsum Alleluja vel quecunque laudis iubilatio" [For such blasphemies shall once sound more pleasant in God's ear than even the Hallelujahs or any other hymn of praise, because they have been forced out by the devil against the will of the people]. Bonhoeffer had already introduced this passage in his postdoctoral dissertation, *Act and Being* (see *DBWE* 2:160, Bonhoeffer note 31, and *DB-ER,* 176; cf. also 1/6 above, ed. note 5).

[388.] WDZ: "The individual *cannot* pray for himself. Intercession is vicarious representative action. I move into the place of the other; prayer arises from his temptation [*Anfechtung*]. The other person is not a state of affairs, not a prayer for change. I must wish to stand in his place and be tempted by his sins."

[389.] See Chomjakow, "Die Einheit der Kirche," 21–22.

church-community are. [There is the] possibility of incorporation! For the one who is hated by God, there is no prayer, for the devil.[390] But one may believe the love of God against God's own word. Here there is not something that can be psychologically experienced. [The] intercession [is] grounded in the recognition that the church-community carries the guilt of the individual, that each person is guilty of Christ's death. In this way, each person can become Christ for the other, even when he does not know him. [Compare the reference to] the "sins of the unknown sailor" [in prayer spoken in worship service]: "One guilt, that is my guilt." In this way the brotherhood of vicarious representation for all happens. There only intercessory prayer is possible.[391] [The] individual finds the gift of the church-community through intercession. It is based only in the congregation. [. . .] Vicarious endurance for the other. Thus [the individual is] led into the church-community more and more through intercession.[392]

295 [Regarding] (c) [It is a] marvel of the church-community that one person cannot only sacrifice himself, but rather also that one person has the *authority to forgive sins* through Christ. In the Old Testament this is still impossible: Ps. 49![393] [The] law and [the] gift of the community[394] became the possession of Christ! The congregation acts as *Christus praesens*,[395] what Jesus once did. The form of Christ multiplied a thousandfold. Either this is the worst kind of profanity. Or else it is the coming of the living God himself. [It is a] miracle of God that the human being is redeemed by the other. The daily bloodless repetition of the sacrifice! This one deed is ever and again actualized through the church-community. The Catholic interpretation: this attempt reaches back behind the revelation of God in Christ![396]

[390.] WDZ: "[The] boundaries of intercessory prayer [lie] where [the] boundaries of the church-community are. Even intercession for all humankind [cf. 1 Tim. 2:1–2] draws them into the church-community. For the one who is hated by God [i.e., the devil—VB], I should not intercede."

[391.] WDZ: "The impossibility of intercession [of the individual is] based on the fact that the church-community bears the guilt."

[392.] WDZ: "No one knows what intercession will yield him. Each receives [the] gift of the church-community with gratitude. Apart from [the] church-community, it is magic. Within the church-community, even Pauline intercession is understandable. To renounce for the other person vicariously is only possible within the church-community and leads more deeply into the church-community."

[393.] Cf. Ps. 49:8–9.

[394.] [Cf. *DBWE* 1:17.—VB]

[395.] "Christ present."

[396.] It is difficult to tell from the wording in the notes whether this passage contains a Catholic criticism of the position mentioned before or whether a Catholic doctrine of sacrifice is being described.

[. . .] Speculation. Matt. 18:18. John 20:23: What you have loosed on earth, shall also be loosed in heaven.[397] How is this to be understood?? Luther: [as] members of the church-community, we are all Peter.[398] This word has been spoken to us all. God has put his entire power into the church-community. In the church-community the divide between the kingdom of God and the kingdom of the world is consummated.

It is not we who carry the word with our faith; rather, the church-community carries the word and carries us as well.[399] The first and second word is given to us: from the gospel [and] office follows: preaching of reconciliation is the first word.[400] [The second point, the] proclamation of the wrath of God is unbearable for us; [. . .] the binding transcends the power of responsibility.[401] In both promises [lies] God's word: in fact our responsibility [rests on][402] both words. The love and wrath of God is also God's 296
will and stands under [the] heavy weight of responsibility. The forgiveness of sins within the church-community is only possible through [the] preaching of the gospel. The preaching of the gospel [becomes] judgment when it is not believed.[403] This is spoken not only in the assembly but also in the confession of sin, where the congregation confesses itself as sinful and pronounces forgiveness.

[There is confession of sin only] in connection with the sacrament![404] [The] proclamation of the word in the sermon [is] not to be understood by itself; in the sacrament something new enters in: here the pastor [is] bound.[405] The promise of God stands over the sacraments. Here the pastor

[397.] [The citation in the text is from Matt. 18:18. John 20:23 in the NRSV reads: "If you forgive the sins of any, they are forgiven them."—VB]

[398.] Cf. Luther, "Eine kurze Form des Vaterunsers," 1520 (*WA* 7:219, 17–25; *LW* 44); cf. also Luther, "Ein Sermon von dem Sakrament der Buße," 1519 (*WA* 2:716, 25–35; *LW* 35); Luther, "De instituendis ministries Ecclesiae," 1523 (*WA* 12:183, 30–34; *LW* 40).

[399.] WDZ: "We do not carry the word with our faith, but rather the church-community carries us when we dare to speak the word."

[400.] Inserted by Rüppell: "The following is sentimental:"

[401.] WDZ: "The one is exactly as difficult as the other and involves the same responsibility. Otherwise it is sentimentality. A prophet is a prophet through his proclamation of wrath. This too must be dared in [the] Christian church-community."

[402.] This must read "in."

[403.] "The love of God becomes judgment of the human being when he does not believe, hear, follow."

[404.] WDZ: "*Confession of sin* only in connection with [the] Lord's Supper. [The] church-community confesses itself as completely sinful and pronounces forgiveness in Christ."

[405.] WDZ: "The pastor [is] bound to words and actions. This action has the promise of God. [The] pastor is free from his personal words; Christ present [*Christus praesens*] acts."

is free from his own word. There [is] not less certainty in the sermon; the sermon is borne by the sacrament.[406] He, the pastor, may administer the sacrament.

[A] church without sacrament loses the sermon and the confession of sin! In confession of sin consecration[407] occurs. Here the word of God is spoken; here [is the] occurrence of the Last Judgment.[408] Here punishment and absolution take place! Whoever goes to confession, [performs] not [an] act of personal trust but rather [a] *confession of truth*; [only], however, where the other is seen as a brother. In the confession of sin, we cannot avoid speaking simply out loud! The act of confession of sin was until now like a loud scream for everyone, the birth of a new world. Here, however, is now the answer of God through the brother, which ends all torture.
297 Because [the] word of God's truth takes place through the brother, therefore authorization. [The] word of God follows the untrue word of human beings. [Personal confession of sin is not] the possibility of κάθαρσις,[409] but rather a self-positioning toward the truth![410] [This is] different from the psychoanalytic hour. "[The] doctor is the father confessor today!"[411] Confession of sin is misunderstood. The self-expression in one's own interest is only a degree of talking about oneself that people of all time have done. This has nothing to do with confession of sin. The purpose of the confession of sin is for the one who confesses to receive God's truth. It is the occurrence of God's truth! That is [the] center of the church-community. There is no longer a church-community where there is no confession of sin.

---

[406.] WDZ: "The sermon is borne by [the] reality of the sacrament. Because the pastor administers the sacrament, he can preach. [It is] nonsense when [a] vicar preaches [but is not permitted to administer the sacrament]. A sermon without a sacrament loses its fruit." [A vicar was a theological student who had passed his or her first exams and was in a period of training in a congregation before taking the ordination exams.—VB]

[407.] Should probably read "concretion"; cf. the version repeated in the following quotation from WDZ.

[408.] WDZ: "Individual confession of sin: what is said authoritatively in [the] church-community carries authority for the individual. Becoming concrete for the individual. Between the two, the event of the Last Judgment takes place. [Here will be] judged and acquitted."

[409.] "Cleansing." [The Greek word is literally "catharsis."—CG]

[410.] The conjecture emerges from Zimmermann's notes, which is truer to the general point; see WDZ: "Not a method of cleansing, but rather a setting of the self *of both* toward the truth. Interest in one's own complicated nature, [that] is [the] everyday human being."

[411.] [A familiar aphorism of the nineteenth-century French author Jules Barbey d'Aureville from his novel *Les Diaboliques*, translated into German as *Das Glück im Verbrechen* in 1900.—CG]

Luther fights against compulsory confession in order to remove the routine observance of confession of sin.[412]

July 20 (1932)

Hearing confession belongs to the pastoral office [Amt]. Hearing confession is a commission of the church-community; [it] exists only among brothers.[413] To take the sins of the brother upon oneself because one knows that Christ bears one's sins. The constant flooding back of sinful deeds upon Christ. Confession of sin is founded on the reality of the vicarious representative action of Christ. Even private confession [has been] frequently eliminated after [the] Reformation![414] Thereby a living fountain for the church-community has died off (Löhe: *Drei Bücher von der Kirche*).[415] [The] reason [for this lies] solely in the process of increasing individualism in Protestantism. The church, however, is [the] present Christ. One does not believe this any longer.[416] We must once more learn to see and believe properly in the 298
church-community and the church. We do not believe that the truth is spoken in the church.[417] We must learn again what confession of sin is.

Isn't this abstract? Is there not priestly action and beside it the vicarious representative action of the brother? "Christ is the *donum*[418] and the

[412.] Cf. *DBWE* 1:165–92.

[413.] WDZ: "To hear confession is [an] office, [a] commission, that the church-community has. Hearing confession is only among brothers; pastor only as brother! A brother does that which can occur as the last possibility in a church-community. He takes the sins that he forgives upon himself. This is borne by the church-community (= Christ). Christ carries his sin, and therefore he can carry the sins of others. Christ present in the church-community."

[414.] WDZ: "[If the] private confession is eliminated, with that the living core of the church-community [is] destroyed. It cannot simply be revived, [since it] is not an isolated phenomenon but rather a process of individualization of Protestantism."

[415.] Cf. Löhe, *Three Books concerning the Church*, 192–95.

[416.] WDZ: "One does not believe that the brother can speak Christ's words with full authority."

[417.] WDZ: "When we do not believe, the truth does not become urgent for us. Confession of sin. Dostoyevsky." Bonhoeffer refers to the novel *Crime and Punishment* by the Russian novelist Fyodor Dostoyevsky. The prostitute Sonja reads the story of the resurrection of Lazarus from chapter 11 of the Gospel of John to the murderer Raskolnikov. He can only come to faith in the resurrection, however, after he has experienced the love of Sonja on the path through confession and punishment, where he understands himself as coming from death to life, as one who had killed himself through the murder.

[418.] "Gift."

*exemplum*!"[419] This is also true for Christians in the church-community. It must be a gift for the brother, a priestly act of absolute validity. But [the] human being also stands before the brother as a human example. The concept of the tradition, of history, [plays a role here]: One must "come clean" to the brother. One must accept advice from the other! [From this follows] a twofold picture of the pastoral care of the Protestant church: (1) ministerial pastoral care based on vicarious representative action; (2) counseling pastoral care! Both are near each other here!

(D) and (E) Worldliness and Christianity [Christlichkeit] of the Church

[. . .] Our church is here. [It is] not an ideal; otherwise we would still be in Advent. Christ is present in his church today. [That is] no ideal but rather reality. [The] worldliness of the church is real, not only illusion [Schein]. [The] church is wholly world![420] Furthermore, where [the] church [has]
299 become homeless, this must be so.[421] [The] church has become quite worldly for our benefit.[422] It denies itself everything except Christ's word. The church existing in the world knows that it must renounce everything else.[423]

The church is in the world:[424] it does not wish to give a picture of the church-community of saints; renunciation of [the] ideal of purity. As such, as something becomes worldly, it is not pure from the beginning onward; even the early Christian church-community is not pure. ([To believe this would be a] confusion with [a] religious experience as ideal)![425] [There are] perfectionistic sects up to today ("communities").[426] Everywhere [this

[419.] "Example." The formula of "Christ as gift and example" was used frequently by Luther (see, for example, Drews, *Disputationen Dr. Martin Luthers in den Jahren 1535–1545*, 392).

[420.] WDZ: "[The] church has become world like Christ. It is heretical to take it only as an illusory church. The church is wholly world; it [is] in all weakness and [all] suffering subordinate to the world."

[421.] WDZ: "The church, like Jesus, can become homeless."

[422.] [Here, as distinct from above where Bonhoeffer spoke of the church as acculturated and secularized, the sense is as in WDZ like incarnation or kenosis (cf. Phil. 2).—CG]

[423.] WDZ: "Genuine worldliness [tends] to renounce everything else except for Christ and [the] forgiveness of sins. In view of this, it can deny itself everything else."

[424.] [This paragraph repeats the argument of *Sanctorum Communio* (*DBWE* 1:222).—CG]

[425.] WDZ: *"[The] church [is] from its very beginning not pure."*

[426.] [Here the word *Gemeinschaften* (communities) is used with the meaning of "sect" as in the church-sect typology of Weber and Troeltsch.—CG]

is] an attempt to usurp the kingdom of God;[427] it should be exposed.[428] One wishes to see [the] kingdom in the saintliness of human beings. As [the] church that has become worldly, it may not let itself succumb to this temptation because it knows that it faces justification and the Last Judgment.[429] It cannot uproot [the] weeds.[430] The church cannot be pure before God and [the] world. Everyone baptized belongs to the church.[431] *Renunciation of purity*, a return to solidarity with the sinful world! The church as a wholly worldly church; courageous confession to worldliness;[432] in this way [the] church is free from the world! The church no longer shrinks
from [the] sanctuaries [Heiligtümern][433] of the world.[434] It is then free 300
among [the] "pariahs" and the "aristocracy." [Its] place [is] not only among the poor; it will not disdain the wealthy, the pious, or the aristocrats. Both groups are "world." The church will be unbeholden to both sides.[435] [The] faith has conquered the world for the pariah and the rich. Renunciation of purity alone makes the church free!

[But also the] boundaries of worldliness must be taken seriously; the church must concern itself about purity![436] *The wish to be pure* [. . .] must be in the world at the same time: discipline, purity of doctrine, and [. . .] the individual [. . .] pastors may not be moralists, clericalists [Pfaffen],

[427.] See Matt. 11:12.

[428.] WDZ: "From the mysticism of the Greeks to Tolstoy, [the] attempt [has been undertaken] to usurp [the] kingdom of God." In Greece a speculative mysticism developed from the Orphic mysteries and the Dionysian cult, which promised the freeing of the earthly elements from the bodily world and rising up to the world-soul and from this to the spirit. In many ways, particularly via Hellenistic Judaism and Neoplatonism, Greek mysticism has influenced Christianity. The Russian poet Leo Tolstoy championed an absolute obedience to the sayings of the Sermon on the Mount as an alternative to the Christianity of the church of his time.

[429.] WDZ: "[The] church may not justify itself to itself and to the world in this way. It cannot anticipate God's Last Judgment. 'You shall not judge' [see Matt. 7:1]."

[430.] See Matt. 13:24–30 and 36–43.

[431.] WDZ: "Every baptized person belongs to the church, however the *opera* [works] look."

[432.] WDZ: "It knows better what the world is. Solidarity with the world embraces the world more deeply."

[433.] [Literally, "the things that are sacred."—VB]

[434.] WDZ: "It is among the godless and the pious, among all. All are world. The church may not remove itself from any sphere in order to remain pure. Faith has overcome the world entirely."

[435.] The German *DBW* editor has slightly revised this sentence.

[436.] WDZ: "The boundaries of worldliness; within these boundaries [the church] concerns itself about its own purity."

demagogues. No politics in the worship service,[437] no outward celebration.[438] The church will reject letting oneself go, deliberate worldliness. The Protestants [. . .] not vain bondage. [The] church will wish to be most sharply conscious of its purity.

[There is a] justification for *excommunication* as the last step, in cases where the church-community itself is at risk. [But there are also] concrete limits to this act. Today it is to be decided according to each particular case. [. . .] Also, the sphere in which excommunication is pronounced remains open. (1) The church may execute the ban only for the sake of the church-community. (2) The ban can be pronounced only "in order to save a soul";[439] "Sancta" is the predicate of the believed church. [As the impure we are] *sancta ecclesia*[440] concretely today.

July 23 [1932]

*Realization* [Verwirklichung][441] *[occurs] in the world as visible church*! Therefore, [it is the] *una ecclesia,*[442] the believed church. There is a disunity, not only in form but in the truth as well! The church will not want to reach [an]
301 illusory unity. Sincere, bona fide faith [is] not to be confused with the truth of the content of faith (ecumenical danger: [the] question of heresy is no longer noted). Heresy of doctrine is to be combated sharply! [The] church must deny itself the act of portraying the unity of truth. Division is to be carried as cross; believing that God [has] called it as *una sancta.*[443]

[The] *visible unity* of the church is demanded for the sake of the church and the world. *Catholic*:[444] [this is a] predicate of the church that concerns its worldliness. Even the Protestant church raises the complete *claim* to be the catholic church, *not in* [the sense of a] *world power,* but rather *in the proclamation of the worldwide word of Christ*! As a whole it remains invisible, yet [it is] visible within given boundaries. [The] church [exists] *in regno crucis.*[445] (Against this the Catholic Church [says]: *in regno gloriae.*)[446] To take world-

[437.] WDZ: "The worship service [may] not [become] politics or sweetness."
[438.] WDZ: "Such a posture does not overcome the world."
[439.] See 1 Cor. 5:5.
[440.] "The holy church."
[441.] ["Realization" in the sense of becoming reality.—VB]
[442.] "The *one* church."
[443.] "The one holy."
[444.] "The universal."
[445.] "In the kingdom of the cross."
[446.] "In the kingdom of glory." [This sentence is standard Lutheran polemic asserting a *theologia crucis* against an imputed Roman Catholic *theologia gloriae.*—CG]

liness seriously on the basis of taking the divinity of the church seriously is the Christianity [Christlichkeit] of the church.

[(F)] The Boundaries of the Church

[The] church as the revelation of God in the world is [a] whole. But [there are] boundaries, because [the] church is in the world where people do not know of God's revelation in the church. Here, from within, one can speak of the boundaries. [The] boundaries of the church [are] given in the concept of *predestination* [or] the *kingdom of god,* respectively, and of the *state.* The first one is [the] boundary toward the new world; the other is [the] boundary toward the old world. [The] church is built on the *doctrine of the cross of Christ* (Reformed churches build on *predestination*).[447] [The] knowledge of God in Christ is [the] only revelation. The church-community that believes
in this is the church! [There is a] danger when one seeks another word 302
behind the one word of God! But the church must be able to proclaim this one word with authority. [The] concept of predestination may not [desire to] say more than what is said in the cross.

[The] church is not the *kingdom of God*; [it] does not even know those who belong to the kingdom. It may not [even] know this for the sake of its worldliness. It knows about the will of God, that God has mercy for all. God alone must give faith. The church must see the cross and also the brothers in need. [It remains a] mystery. [It is] mysterious that God [wishes to] help all[448] and yet gives only these human beings faith. [We are left only] with astonished sighing and hoping for the church as we bow beneath the mystery of God. It knows: there is salvation in no other![449] But it also knows: God is greater. He wants to help all human beings. That is why [there is] mission. But it uses the Lord's word against the Lord. It hopes that God can do great mysterious things with the other. Prayer about this [is necessary]; [this] touches on the mystery of God himself, which will one day be revealed, but now the church lets the mystery remain! [The] word of Christ and the promise (grace and judgment) given to it,[450] [that is the] *boundary* of the church! It knows that God is free and that God can withdraw his word from the church![451] The church must bear the mystery when God

[447.] Calvin, in bk. 3, chaps. 21–24 of his *Institutes of the Christian Religion* (1559), develops the doctrine of double predestination. According to this, membership in the church depends on the eternal decision of election through God, just as does being damned. Election to the church corresponds to the election of Israel.

[448.] See 1 Tim. 2:4.

[449.] See Acts 4:12.

[450.] [The church.—VB]

[451.] The German editor has substituted "from the church" for "from it."

says No upon it. [The] church awaits the visible revelation, the new world of God. It knows of the fulfillment. It knows that one day it will be in the visible sacrament of God, in the new creation. [Then the] subjugation of the world [will] have occurred. [. . .] God is the master and the servant in his church-community [. . .] in the new world.

Finally, boundaries in the *state.*[452] God's word has power also over the state. [Through this the] state is [set] as a critical warning [for the church], that God has not given the judging sword of power to the church. Its sword is [the] word and [the] prayer. Thereby it serves the state. When it is threat-
303 ened by the state, it fights against the state. It will not try to govern the state. [The] goal is the proclamation of the lordship of Christ over the whole world in faith and [in the] word. The church and the state [are] side by side. The church [may] not become the state; the state [is recognized] as an autonomous worldly power. [. . .] A call to a completely responsible, true action, each according to its own office. Obedience to [the] state exists only when [the] state does not threaten the word. [The] battle about the boundary must then be fought out![453] The decision will be difficult in the development of our future state:[454] [The] office of the state is neither Christian nor godless; the office must be carried out in a responsible and objective[455] way. [The] existence as church depends on whether its criticism can come from listening to the gospel alone. Criticism of the state [is] demanded where [it] threatens [the] word. The church can come [through] difficulties only when it sees to it that it stands or falls with the word of *Christus praesens* as its Lord alone.

End July 23, 1932

[452.] [The German editor suggests reading: "The church, finally, finds its boundary in the state." This can be misunderstood if "finally" is taken to mean the "ultimate"' or as the last and final boundary. Bonhoeffer clearly states that the eschatological boundary of God's kingdom is the fulfillment of the new world over against the old world, that is, the truly final or ultimate boundary. The natural reading of the student notes is that *zuletzt* (finally) means the final point of the lectures. Hence the translation: "Finally, boundaries in the *state.*"—CG]

[453.] [That is, the battle must be fought when the state threatens the church's free preaching of the word.—CG]

[454.] Bonhoeffer made this assessment about the future relationship of state and church three days after the dismissal of the Prussian government by Reich Chancellor von Papen and one week before the decisive Reichstag elections of July 31, 1932, in which the National Socialist party won 37.2 percent of the vote, making it the strongest faction in the Reichstag.

[455.] [The German is *sachlich*, which here means according to the state's proper purposes.—CG]

## 10. Seminar: Is There a Christian Ethic?[1]

## 10.1 Excerpts from Student Notes[2]

Is There a Christian Ethic?

First of all, [the question is] negated on the basis of its absolute character.[3] [According to this] philosophical ethics [has] the same root [as Christian 304
ethics]. Second, [the question is negated on the basis of the concept of an] autonomy [of distinct spheres of life]. [As, for example, in] Naumann[4]

---

[1.] Of Bonhoeffer's seminar "Is There a Christian Ethic?" held in the 1932 summer semester, there remains only a single, short set of notes (10/1) with many omissions—aside from the "Fragment of a Transcript" that follows it (10/2). There are lengthy passages where Bonhoeffer's train of thought can no longer be reconstructed dependably; thus only part of the notes is published here, and only to a limited degree can the text be considered as authentic evidence of Bonhoeffer's thought (cf. Otto Dudzus's preface to his attempted reconstruction of the seminar, *GS* 5:275–77, and to the entire text itself, *GS* 5:277–300). The fragmentary character of the text often makes it impossible to reconstruct parts of the text—or to put into proper order a precise text, on the basis of literature mentioned by Bonhoeffer, his comments, or the interpretation, and perhaps misunderstanding, of student notes. The basic ideas of the seminar are, however, clearly evident in the introduction, which contains a definition of the problem and presents the seminar plan, as well as in the final section. These sections have been outlined in the following text. The extensive footnotes provide information about the intended process of the seminar, to the extent that Bonhoeffer actually followed the seminar plan that he had designed. Another reason for publishing sections of the notes is that they contain the basic outlines of Bonhoeffer's early concepts of ethics, and with that important foundations for the later *Ethics* drafts are evident. The seminar reflections that have been preserved only as fragments are to be understood in connection with two texts that appeared almost at the same time: Bonhoeffer's April 1932 report on a theological conference of the Provisional Bureau (2/13) and the July 1932 lecture "On the Theological Foundation of the Work of the World Alliance" (2/14). The similarity of content at numerous points, as for example on the question of the church's authority in the proclamation of the concrete commandment and the rejection of the concept of the order of creation in favor of speaking of "the Order of Preservation toward Christ" (*auf Christus hin*), makes a parallel illumination of the three texts possible. [*DBWE* 3 translates this as preservation "for" Christ; cf. *DBWE* 3:140, esp. ed. note 3. The editors thank Clifford Green for this reference.—VB] The student notes do not indicate how the scheduled [lecture] hours were divided up. According to a date in the notes, the presentation of part I (see the anticipated seminar plan, p. 336), which consisted primarily of a discussion and criticism of ethical literature, lasted beyond the first half of the semester. The notes for this are even more fragmentary than those in part II, where the rudiments of a new ethic from the gospel were sketched. This ends with part II, section B, of the given outline (see p. 336). There are no longer any notes for section C, which is mentioned in the outline (see 2/10.2, ed. note 46).

[2.] *NL*, B 3,1; handwritten seminar notes from Wolf-Dieter Zimmermann, 22 pages.

[3.] The reference is to a conception of Christian ethics that claims universal validity.

[4.] Since the turn of the century, Friedrich Naumann had emphasized the alien character of the Sermon on the Mount in modern culture. It was impossible to base one's

305 and Troeltsch.[5] Christian ethics [here has only] a partial character. [An] expansion through cultural ethics [is then necessary] ([because of the] inherent autonomy of existing structures, for example, capitalism). One knows the "should" [and] thus God's will (Kant: a priori).[6] One also knows the "should" from the secular sphere.

Third, [the question is negated on theological grounds:] Do we know about the "should"? Do we know the will of God as an imperative? Can one know this? [Does it then apply to] church [and] world equally?

[Compare Karl] Barth: [The] will of God is granted, giving, indicative [and] totally independent from human action (predestination).[7] How [then is there to be a] connection to human action? [The] will of God is self-creative, active.

[Regarding clarifying formulation of the questions:]
*Who* [is the subject of ethical action]?

I. Is there [a] personal knowledge of [the] imperative will of God? (personal)

---

entire life on the foundations of Christian ethics. State and politics, but also economic and professional life, had withdrawn themselves from this. Here, according to Naumann's conception, laws other than the love of neighbor apply, even though Christian love penetrates world culture at least in rudimentary ways in the form of personal Christian conviction (see Naumann, *Briefe über Religion*). On Bonhoeffer's dispute with Naumann, see also pp. 221–23. [See also *DBWE* 6:58 and 237–38, ed. note 74.—CG]

[5.] In view of the fact that the synthesis of Christianity and culture was crumbling, Troeltsch attempted to detach immanent cultural intentions from transcendent (überweltlichen) ends. He did, however, see a unity of moral aims in the action of ethical subjects, on the basis of which cultural life can be understood as worship (see Troeltsch, "Grundprobleme der Ethik"). On Bonhoeffer's dispute with Troeltsch's understanding of the relationship of Christian ethics and culture, see p. 223.

[6.] Kant's ethics were determined through the fundamental principle that the moral demand issues generally and apodictically ("a priori"). This categorical imperative is to be followed without consideration of conflicting motives and inclinations or chances of success. Since the imperative as categorical cannot be dependent on a presupposed purpose, its contents are the universality of the form of the will itself. Further, Kant defines the content of the good as purely formal, as the will in opposition to all inclinations. For Kant, "all moral concepts have their seat and origin entirely a priori in reason" (Kant, *Foundations for a Metaphysics of Morals*, 32).

[7.] In his essay "The Problem of Ethics Today," Barth had pointed to the doctrine of double eternal predestination as the last word in the attempt to determine the relationship of the sinfulness of humanity and God's grace, which alone makes the doing of good possible. (See "Problem of Ethics Today," 168–69.)

II. Is there the promise being proclaimed [verkündigende Zusage][8] of the imperative will of God to others? 306

III. [Is there a] scholarly knowledge concerning [the] will of God? (Universal valid form; standardization)—Piper.[9]

*Whence* [does one know the content of ethical action]?

I. [Is there a] knowledge of principles? [from the] Sermon on the Mount; [or through] a hearing shaped by conscience?

II. What are the sources from God that are imperative? [Possible answers:] Conscience; order of creation; the written and handed-down Law (Moses;[10] Sermon on the Mount); natural-dynamically conceived sanctification (R. Seeberg: alteration of *habitus* through attaining faith);[11] hearing the commandment in the concrete situation.

---

[8.] [*Zusage* means "promise" or "commitment" but linguistically means "to speak to" (*zu-sagen*). Particularly here where Bonhoeffer is describing the nature of the church's proclamation, it also has the nuance of being authoritative: it is a promise being proclaimed.—VB]

[9.] Bonhoeffer had probably asked about the possibility of a generally valid formulation of the will of God and thereby referred to Otto Piper, *Die Grundlagen der evangelischen Ethik*, vol. 1 (1928), vol. 2 (1930). Piper, following the philosopher Max Scheler, had developed a system of values in theological ethics (cf. Piper, *Die Grundlagen*, 2:3–269). At the same time, he emphasized to his critics that there is no possibility of an a priori rationale for ethical values. The ethical capacity of reason is in itself purely formal and can emerge as a system of ethical values only through the establishment of a particular value as a concrete absolute. "We now allow only those values to count that are based on revelation, because only here is there a complete correspondence between the values and the goal of events in personal life as it is in the world. This system of values is reasonable [. . .] but cannot be proved" (cf. Piper, *Die Grundlagen*, 2:iv). The second theme mentioned here by Bonhoeffer refers to Piper's attempt at a "norming" (*Normierung*) of the ethical demand through theological ethics (cf. Piper, *Die Grundlagen*, 2:236ff.). According to Piper's conception, the norms of theological ethics do not appear to the one who proclaims in the form of a command or counsel but rather represent the systematic description of the value concepts, which are the basis of the church's proclamation (cf. Piper, *Die Grundlagen*, 2:249ff.).

[10.] The Decalogue in Exod. 20:1–17 and Deut. 5:6–21.

[11.] Cf. Seeberg, *Christliche Dogmatik*, 2:509–10, and Seeberg, *Ethik*, § 40. According to Seeberg's thought, the decision for faith lays the foundation for "a new direction of life." The succession, one upon another, of acts of love growing out of faith creates "a habituation of religious and moral life." On Bonhoeffer's criticism of Seeberg, see also 2/3, pp. 238–39. [*Habitus* is a term in Catholic doctrine that describes permanent qualities or characteristics that exist in distinction from *dispositio*, which is transitory.—VB]

*What* is the content of ethical action?

307 [Possible answers:] I know about a formal "ought"[12] (conscience); the restoration of creation; the law; direction of love.

Is there [any] source that justifies an absolute claim?

Organization

*Part I:* The gospel as the end of ethics (end of law)[13]

[A.] Barth: "The Problem of Ethics Today."[14] Millennialism.[15] Epistle to the Romans XIII; XIV[16] (chapter on ethics); "Doctrine of the Holy Spirit," 1929 (Supplement to *Zwischen den Zeiten*).[17]

[B.] Althaus: "*Grundriss der Ethik*"

[C.] Gogarten: "Ethik des Gewissens oder Ethik der Gnade," 1923 (points against Hirsch;[18] Holl).[19] "Ächtung gegen Autorität."[20]

---

[12.] See p. 334, ed. note 6.

[13.] See ed. note 1. Bonhoeffer essentially held to the plan named in what follows. Except for the second text mentioned by Gogarten ("Wider die Ächtung der Autorität") there are comments in the notes on all the works listed in the lecture plan.

[14.] Barth, "Problem of Ethics Today."

[15.] In the essay discussed by Bonhoeffer, Barth described the prospect of a thousand-year empire as a prospect that only seemed very remote. "For many of our contemporaries—and I confess that I belong with them—this conception [i.e., of the millennium—MBL] has taken the definite form of the socialistic ideal" ("Problem of Ethics Today," 157). Furthermore, "without nationalistic millennialism [chiliasmus], and even if only the smallest portion," it would not be possible to have ethics at all (158). Behind this stands the interest, in all eschatology, not to disregard earthly history and to take most seriously the question of what needs to be done. [Although the phrase "thousand-year Reich" clearly brings to mind the Nazi rhetoric of the 1930s, Barth's 1923 essay referred to the biblical idea of the one-thousand-year period mentioned in Rev. 20.—VB]

[16.] Barth, *Epistle to the Romans.* Barth's explanations of the exhortatory chapters of the Epistle to the Romans include his first extensive remarks about the questions of ethics as part of his new theological departure.

[17.] Barth, *Holy Ghost and the Christian Life.* [The German edition, *Der heilige Geist und das christliche Leben,* was published in 1930.—VB]

[18.] Gogarten described Emanuel Hirsch's concept of ethics as an ethic based on the law ["law" here in the theological sense—VB]. Law without gospel and an ethic so grounded would be in immediate relationship to the eternal, to God. Against Hirsch's view, Gogarten put forward a plan of ethics that rests on law in light of the gospel. Ethics here could no longer exist in immediate relationship to God, for the relationship between God and the human being lies as a positive act entirely in God's forgiveness of sins, not, however, in fulfilling works of law (see Gogarten, "Ethik des Gewissens," 20). Moreover, Gogarten often criticized Hirsch's high estimation of conscience as the place and voice of revelation (see esp. Gogarten, "Ethik des Gewissens," 16). According to

*Part II:* The new ethics *on the basis of the gospel*[21] 308

A. Personal knowledge of the imperative will of God[22] (conscience; creation; law).[23]

B. [The] promise being proclaimed in the sermon.[24]

C. [The] possibility of a theological ethic.[25]

---

Gogarten, conscience in the relationship between God and the human being belongs unequivocally on the side of sinful and errant humans. "This, however, signifies the transformation of the autonomous, self-sufficient conscience, secure in its unconditional freedom, into the conscience that is comforted and places itself under the revelation and its grace" (ibid.).

[19.] Gogarten turned against Holl's understanding of Luther's faith as a religion of conscience (see Holl, *What Did Luther Understand by Religion?* 32–86, and Gogarten, "Ethik des Gewissens," esp. 11–12 and 20–22; see also Bonhoeffer's assessment of a christological deficiency in Holl in 2/3, pp. 208–9.

[20.] Gogarten, *Wider die Ächtung der Autorität.*

[21.] In conducting the seminar, Bonhoeffer set out a transition from part I to part II or an introduction to the last three basic possibilities [listed as A, B, C above—MBL], in order to conjoin law and gospel (two pages of student notes about this have been preserved). In the first definition of the relationship, law provides the context in which the gospel is inserted as new law. As a second possibility of a definition of the relationship of law and gospel, Albrecht Ritschl's reflections on this are outlined (see Ritschl, *Critical History of the Christian Doctrine*, chap. 3, § 28, and *Christian Doctrine of Justification and Reconciliation*, chap. 2, § 21). Bonhoeffer emphasizes here that law remains nevertheless as the relevant context, even when its particular demands are replaced by a faith that is understood as a basic moral position. The third possibility [C], which was discussed in greatest detail, presented the thought of the group around Karl Barth and its so-called dialectical theology. These views are characterized by Bonhoeffer to the effect that it is not a category of law that stands at the beginning but rather revelation. There is no continuum between the human being and God, not even law or acts of the law through human beings. The considerations conclude with a programmatic expression, which Bonhoeffer formulates in correspondence with "dialectical theology": "Ethics [is] not to be grounded in a self-contained human realm. [Is there an] ethics of revelation? Then the gulf [would] again [be] bridged, as an act of God himself. In Christ (forgiveness) the boundary is crossed. [The] beginning of Christian ethics is [the] forgiveness of sins."

[22.] According to the student notes, Bonhoeffer began to treat this section on Saturday, July 2, 1932.

[23.] The actual course of the seminar—not reprinted in what follows—deviated from the original plan as it is set forth here: In section A, Bonhoeffer first treated quite generally the problem of an imperative will of God and the question of a distinction between law and commandment, then moved on to attempt to ground a Christian ethic in creation, and finally to additional elements that emerge out of conscience and law.

[24.] See the following section, II.B.

[25.] See 2/10.2. There is no record of this in Zimmermann's notes. A fragment is included in the typewritten notes by Jürgen Winterhager (see p. 340, ed. note 46).

309 [Part II: B. The promise being proclaimed of the imperative will of God in the sermon][26]

*Church—Assurance*[27] *[The] preaching office [has the task of] proclaiming forgiveness and* preaching [the] law and judgment. Both [are] revelation of the will of God.

Advice is not authoritative promise.[28]

[Note the following:]

(1) Revelation in the word [is] clear in the word [of] forgiveness; not [however] in the word of the law.

(2) Gospel [is] also doctrine, [but] the commandment never comes from doctrine.

(3) Authority of the brother [in advice and commandment].

In his sermons, Luther [offered] advice and [proclaimed] commandments.

[. . .] *Doctrine* [. . .] *Commandment.* Luther teaches [the] Ten Commandments. [He] leads them back to faith.[29] [. . .] *donum*[30] [and] *exemplum*[31] [in Christology].[32] Teaching is [. . .] a priestly act; thus, it cannot be doctrine. Dogmatic teaching—the gospel. [The] essence of preaching is [the] promise. [. . .] Preaching: actualization through the Holy Spirit. The word that is not heard is judgment! Preaching [is] not the presentation of content. *Preaching is direct promise to Christians.* "Your sins are forgiven." The intention of preaching is [the] promise. I know that whoever is baptized and who hears is saved. [It is] clearer in the sacrament that there exists a stronger promise. If one takes the promise away, then one does not preach God. God does not wish to make human beings doubtful (question of pre destination *in* the church; [. . .] not the kingdom of God.

[26.] The incomplete and in large measure barely understandable notes for part I and part II, section A are not reproduced (see the preliminary remarks of the German *DBW* editor, p. 333, ed. note 1).

[27.] To that which follows, compare pp. 361–62.

[28.] In the later manuscripts for his *Ethics*, Bonhoeffer explained precisely the distinction between the church speaking by the authority of the word of God from speaking "on the authority of responsible counsel by Christian experts" (*DBWE* 6:361).

[29.] See, for example, Luther, "Von den guten Werken," 1520 (*WA* 6:196–276); "Treatise on Good Works" (*LW* 44:15–114).

[30.] "Gift."

[31.] "Example."

[32.] See pp. 327–28.

The promise of the gospel. [. . .] to the one who does not believe, it [the gospel] becomes [. . .].[33] The most important[34] commandment is faith in Christ, who has died for you! Concrete explanation of what this means is [. . .] to love. I must do this until it is believed. Thereby one must enter into [the] most concrete situation. To what extent [is] promise in a concrete situation possible? Somehow I have to move from doctrine to promise! How do I enter into the situation of the other (for example, choice)? Where the church does not know [the answer], it must be silent.[35] Where is the boundary of being concrete? (Faith in the face of godlessness is already [something] concrete!) 310

*The main goal: promise*; preaching [must] face the situation of faith or not listening. [One] must make [the] expression so concrete that the listener himself has to decide. So, the church can place individuals before [the] decision. [The] pastor as the voice of the church should speak concretely of the will of God! How far does concretion go? [. . .] Doctrine—promise.

[. . .] Concrete promise in the sacrament. [. . .] Commandment: "You shall love." Forgiveness of sins through [the] sacrament that places one before faith or judgment.[36] [. . .] One must believe the word. [. . .] Everyone can do this through personal confession [Beichte].

[. . .] no doctrine, but promise! [. . .] In [the] sermon it should proceed[37] in this way. How [does one come to] making the commandment concrete? He [namely, the preacher] must proceed in this way! Yet he cannot actually do this. [The] faith in Christ [must run] the risk of concreteness (even to the point of mistakes).[38] For this the congregation supports me.

[The] sacrament of the commandment is concrete reality.[39]

[The] prophets and *apostle* [. . .] *church*. There is prophecy and immediacy of the word. The church as the congregation of saints stands above the prophets. [The] prophets have called in concreteness.

Every pastor speaks differently about the will of God in the concrete case. But always with the demand of truth. [When this is not possible, then] 311

[33.] Perhaps "to judgment."

[34.] Illegible.

[35.] Cf. p. 358.

[36.] This incorporates the Lutheran tradition according to which participation in the Lord's Supper by nonbelievers renders divine judgment.

[37.] This must be "happen."

[38.] Cf. pp. 359–62.

[39.] Cf. pp. 361–62.

silence (despairing) [is appropriate]![40] Can we utter [the] commandment without announcing the gospel?

Because the gospel is concrete, [the] commandment must be concrete.[41] [. . .] The nonbeliever must first hear the claim in [the] commandment and follow his unbelief.

[The] commandment [becomes] concrete through the one who proclaims it.[42]

[The] word (gospel) [becomes] concrete through those who hear it.[43]

Interpretation, what it means to believe in Jesus Christ: "As you believe, so you receive."[44] [The] organized church *must* maintain itself for [the] *communio sanctorum*.[45]

### 10.2 Fragment of Student Notes[46]

The faithful attitude: to count on God [is the presupposition of the possibility of a theological ethic].

A principle of action is not thereby provided. It is not the case that on the basis of one's attitude of faith a principle is given that is always applicable. The principle in itself [is] false. The possibility of a judgment that our
312 actions are good lies solely in CHRIST.[47] The six possibilities of certainty must lose their [validity] continuity here:

---

[40.] Cf. 358.

[41.] In a portion of part II, section A, that was not reproduced, the handwritten notes contain a formulation that is relevant here: "[The] gospel becomes concrete through [the] sacrament; [the] commandment [becomes concrete] through reality. [The] word spoken without the sacrament [this "word" refers to the commandment—CG] needs concretion (commandment!)" (see pp. 360–62).

[42.] Cf. pp. 359–60.

[43.] Ibid.

[44.] See Luther, "Von der Freiheit eines Christenmenschen," 1520 (*WA* 7:24, 13); "The Freedom of a Christian," *LW* 31:348–49. Bonhoeffer had attempted such an interpretation in conjunction with Franz Hildebrandt's conceptual attempt at a Lutheran catechism with the same title (see 2/7). [See also *DB-ER*, 186–88.—VB]

[45.] "Communion of saints."

[46.] *NL*, B 3,2; fragment of a typewritten transcript by Jürgen Winterhager, 1 page. In a handwritten notation on the page is the date: July 20, 1932. However, the contents here do not match the handwritten notes by Zimmerman that are dated July 20, 1932. This material may have been treated at the last meeting of the seminar, which is evidently missing from Zimmerman's notes. According to the seminar plan, Bonhoeffer was to have lectured on this material under the heading: "C. The possibility of a theological ethics." Within his version of the lecture contents, Winterhager presented a summary of sections A and B from the second half of the seminar (see p. 337].

[47.] In the unpublished material from part II, section A, the handwritten notes indicate a literal formulation from Bonhoeffer as a quote: "'[Christ is] the deed that is oriented to the completion of creation.' The [i.e., another] point of identity is missing here."

1. Orders of Creation.

It is not possible to say: In the orders of creation, an action is a good action because the orders are fallen orders.

2. Conscience.

[The] conscience is the place in which God is heard, but [it] is not God's voice. [The] conscience [is] dependent on sociological conditions, etc.[48]

3. The Christian principle of love.

4. The situation.

5. Belief in the forgiveness of sins.

6. The Sermon on the Mount[49] (as law).

It is commanded that our actions be determined by the Christ who is always drawing near but who is not at all within our power. For the one who always comes anew, however, a continuum is no longer open. The thought of the continuum is constructed on the basis of objective realities that are self-contained (as "given by God"). These realities are, however, part of a fallen creation. Their God-givenness and their fallen state—creation and sin—both are [indissolubly] bound up with each other.

We may act within the orders only to the degree that they are open for Christ. The orders that continue for us are therefore only *orders of preservation* directed toward Christ.[50] [They are] orders that are not closed within themselves but rather that point beyond themselves to Christ; no longer orders that are very valuable or worthy in themselves but rather fragile orders, which are only sanctified by their being directed toward Christ.

Even the order of the biblical commandment: love your neighbor as 313
yourself, is an order that can be broken through. The authority of the Bible is not a demonstrable thing but rather is determined through the decision of an individual or of a church-community *in faith.*

The present Christ is the place from which our action is always determined anew.

---

[48.] [Cf. *DBWE* 1:108: "Conscience can just as well be the ultimate prop of human self-justification as the site where Christ strikes home at one through the law." The editors thank Clifford Green for this reference.—VB]

[49.] In part II, section A, Bonhoeffer also discussed the Sermon on the Mount. Zimmermann's notes record the following: "[The] Sermon on the Mount is [a] gift [that shows] how a commandment of faith could appear. [It is] the consequence of concretely hearing a commandment. The Why is always the same, but [there is always] another How."

[50.] Cf. 2/8 and 2/13.

# D. Texts from Ecumenical Work

## July–October 1932

### 11. Report on the Youth Conference of the World Alliance in Epsom[1] 314

Ecumenical Youth Work
English-French Youth Conference of the World Alliance for Promoting International Friendship through the Churches

On April 4, the International Youth Committee of the World Alliance met under the chairmanship of the bishop of Ripon.[2] The three youth secretaries[3] gave reports about their work, among which the report of the French[4] representative was particularly noteworthy, since he expressed the greatest hopes for the prospects of the World Alliance's work among French youth. Nowhere do the possibilities for contact seem as difficult to find as presently in Germany.[5]

---

[1.] *Die Eiche* 20 (1932): 260. Previously published in *GS* 1:119–20. Cf. *NL*, A 34,3 (a): handwritten draft; and *NL*, A 34,3 (b): typewritten copy. See also Bonhoeffer's talk on "a very superfluous conference" in a letter to Erwin Sutz, 1/59, p. 120.

[2.] See 2/1, ed. note 13.

[3.] Bonhoeffer, Pierre Toureille, F. W. Thomas Craske (see also 2/1, ed. note 16).

[4.] Pastor Pierre Toureille.

[5.] The protocol of the session (Minutes of the Meeting, London 1932, cited in *GS* 1:118) reports on Bonhoeffer's comments during the session of the International Youth Committee: "Herr Bonhoeffer said that the results of the Cambridge Conference [see 2/1] were few in Germany, owing to opposition to the work of the World Alliance on the part of nationalist theological professors [see 2/1, ed. note 2]. The YMCA would not be sending any delegates to international conferences this year. A Central Organisation for Youth of all religions had been formed, which cooperated in finding delegates for conferences [see 2/2]. Dr. Stählin was President, and Herr Bonhoeffer Secretary. They were producing a list of names of young people who were willing to come to international

315 From April 5 to 8, the regional youth conference prepared by the French and English youth secretaries met in Epsom. The undersigned was invited as the German international youth secretary and welcomed in the friendliest way. The three main themes were as follows: Is Christianity practicable in state life, in social life, in industrial life?[6] There was lively discussion about this in the groups, although at the beginning the discussion involved merely an exchange of information. As soon as the discussion moved beyond this point, it became clear that people were stuck at the threshold of the main question, because no clarity could be found on what "Christianity" today really is. The wish emerged quickly that agreement should be reached first on this point. And it became apparent that on the English side the immediate connection of Christianity to practical questions was always more strongly expressed than by the young French representatives. However, everyone agreed on a fundamentally positive answer to the central question. The differences were primarily on where to put the emphasis. Yet, from a German perspective, the theological positions of the young French and English delegates at this regional meeting were not so far from each other and not so close to the German point of view as we seemed to feel when we were still in Cambridge.[7]

It is always dangerous—and this became evident here, too, quite powerfully—to arrive at certain "results" through so-called group findings,[8] which usually do not even exist but have to be forced. This is particularly the case when the discussion of such far-reaching problems lasts only two to three hours; such a thing should not even be allowed. Here one touches on the second danger that also became very apparent at this conference. It is more than questionable whether one should approach such far-reaching problems without the most intensive common preparation (through cor-
316 respondence or basic principles, commonly read literature). Usually time runs out before one arrives at the point that is most interesting. And the conversations very much run the risk of being frittered away. This deplorable state of affairs must be confronted most decisively, especially in youth conferences. We should not become so accustomed to the beautiful feeling of international friendship that we lose the time for serious work. Only through such work—this was in any case the judgment of the German youth

---

conferences [see 2/2, p. 174]." [This passage from the minutes is in the original, unaltered English.—MBL]

[6.] [Bonhoeffer wrote these themes in English.—MBL]

[7.] See 2/1, pp. 168–69.

[8.] ["Group findings" in English.]

delegation in Cambridge—is the expense of an international conference justified.

It goes without saying that the English hosts, as they have always known how to do, gave the entire group the sense of fellowship in the friendliest possible way.

Dietrich Bonhoeffer

## 12. Preliminary Report on a Conference of the Provisional Bureau[1]

Theological Conference
of the Provisional Bureau for Ecumenical Youth Work

The *Provisional Bureau for Ecumenical Youth Work*, with the very kind support of the Church Federation Office, issued an invitation to a theological conference on April 29–30.[2] Today those working with youth who want to create an audience for ecumenical ways of thinking know better than anyone else that we lack a proper theological foundation for this work. So it is understandable that it is precisely the work of the Provisional Bureau for Ecumenical Youth Work to introduce itself by way of such a theological conference. The two fundamental questions of ecumenical work were examined directly. General Superintendent Dr. Zoellner spoke about "the Church and the Churches";[3] Professor Stählin spoke about "the Church and the Peoples."[4] The ensuing discussions led us directly to the most basic presuppositions of ecumenical thought and there, understandably, 317
things became bogged down. No one could fail to notice that we are in a state of deep helplessness, particularly in facing the most decisive questions. It was a natural desire of all the participants to continue the discussion in the fall. A detailed report about the lectures and discussions follows later.[5]

Dietrich Bonhoeffer

---

[1.] *Die Eiche* 20 (1932): 260–61. Previously published in *GS* 1:121–32. Cf. *NL*, 34,3 (a): handwritten outline; also *NL*, A 34,3 (b): typewritten copy. See also 2/13.

[2.] See 2/2, pp. 175–76.

[3.] "Die una sancta ecclesia und die Einzelkirchen."

[4.] "Die Einheit der christlichen Kirche und die Völker."

[5.] See 2/13.

## 13. Primary Report on the Conference of the Provisional Bureau[1]

Report on the Theological Conference of the Provisional Bureau for Ecumenical Youth Work
April 29–30, 1932, in Berlin

Under the chairmanship of *Dr. Stählin*, the first session of the theological conference of the Provisional Bureau for Ecumenical Youth Work took place on April 29, commencing at 4:00 in the afternoon. The theses from General Superintendent Dr. Zoellner's lecture have been reprinted on pp. 328–29 of this journal.[2]

After some introductory remarks about the difficulty of revitalizing the word "church" and about the indispensability of the word itself, *Dr. Stählin* summarized the fundamental thoughts of his lecture in five questions, which he posed for *Dr. Zoellner*.

1. Should we speak seriously about "church" or should we empty the concept of "church" religiously by applying this expression only to its institutional forms, in contrast to the true Christian *communio*[3] (church-community or kingdom of God)? Ecumenical work is meaningful and possible only when we take seriously the "churches" as a manifestation of the "church."

318 2. Is the origin of the church to be judged as a Pauline or post-Pauline fall from grace on the part of Christianity,[4] or does its beginning already lie in the community of disciples gathered by Jesus, in which case some of the parables about the kingdom of God may be simultaneously interpreted as descriptions of the church? Ecumenical work is only possible when it is also possible to justify, through the gospel itself, that Jesus's call to discipleship simultaneously means a call into the church.

3. May the church be understood sociologically as an association [Zusammenschluß], a communal experience of Christian individuals, or is this something established originally,[5] in which all concrete manifestations of

[1.] *Die Eiche* 20 (1932): 361–65. Previously published in *GS* 1:121–32. Cf. *NL* A 34,4 (3): typewritten manuscript prepared for the publisher. Bonhoeffer wrote the report at the end of June 1932, after he had requested that the participants send him a written summary of their notes on the discussion (see 1/67). On the entire matter, see Glenthøj, *Zu Dietrich Bonhoeffers Eintritt.*

[2.] This must refer to pp. 328–32 in *Die Eiche* 20 (1932). See 2/12, ed. note 3.

[3.] "Community."

[4.] [This may be a reference to a theory developed in association with Adolf von Harnack's thought, in which institutionalization is at the expense of a more genuine individualized, ethical appropriation of gospel values.—MBL]

[5.] [The reference is to the church as an establishment of God.—MBL]

the church (though not always chronological) have essentially been preordained? If the church is to be understood as an association, then it has been left up to our decisions and our considered purposes whether we want to pursue such an association in a particular instance. If the church, the one church, is inherently preordained, then ecumenical work is the unavoidable duty of every Christian church.

4. Is the church a place where Christ is "preached" without something special occurring in this place, or does this church testimony mean that in this witness Christ himself becomes present and powerful (the church as the body of Christ, as ongoing incarnation)?[6] Pulpits can stand next to one another without any connection, but the meaning and obligation of ecumenical work emerge from the concept of the body of Christ.

5. Does the eschatological character of the church mean that only one promise is entrusted to it, so that all churches on earth would stand only in the not-yet, or does the "interim nature" [Vorläufigkeit] of all earthly church realities mean, simultaneously yet above them all, an actual beginning, a material event toward an end (growth emerging from the head)? Only from this faith, where the church deals with the actual being, life, and work of Christ in the world, can ecumenical work emerge.

*Dr. Zoellner* replied to the questions in the same sense that *Dr. Stählin* used in the concluding sentences to his five questions. Then the discussion focused increasingly on the concluding reflections of Dr. Zoellner's lecture, 319
about the relation of the particular church to the *Una Sancta*.[7]

*Pastor Peter*:[8] That the congregations (the churches) distinguish and limit their membership both formally and in a natural manner is not so

[6.] [The very question reflects a powerful and prevalent christological-ecclesiological movement, reflected in Protestant and Catholic theological voices from the nineteenth and twentieth centuries, e.g., Johann Adam Möhler, Matthias Joseph Scheeben, and Eric Lincoln Mascall. See the editors' introduction to this volume, p. 21.—MBL]

[7.] "The one holy church." In the 1920s, the attempts at unification among Christians of different confessions received new impetus through the formation of the Una Sancta movement. The Protestant discussion partners generally came from ecumenical circles, the High Church movement, the Berneuchen movement, and the Brotherhood of St. Michael. [The Berneuchen movement emerged out of the German youth movement in the 1920s as a group of liturgically "High Church" Protestant Christians, originally in Pomerania, who were focused on a spirituality of Bible reading, daily prayer, and an intense commitment to the Eucharist as a basis for Christian unity. It spawned a separate Brotherhood of St. Michael, principally in Switzerland. Later Bonhoeffer was quite critical of the Berneuchen and Oxford Group movements as "reactionaries, backward looking," seeking "religious renewal" in a way that completely misunderstood the problem. (See Bonhoeffer's letter of June 8, 1944, to Bethge from prison, *DBWE* 8:430).—MBL]

[8.] Friedrich Peter.

much the consequence of a second fall into sin as it is more an expression of obedience to God, who requires in such communities the affirmation and preservation of God's diversified orders of creation in the interim time until the second coming.[9]

There will always be a gulf between the Una Sancta[10] and the individual churches, wherever it is thought that faith, hope, and love must be organized. There have been many failed attempts in this direction in church history. We must guard against the view that any ecclesiastical organizational effort would be closest to the true church when it is universal in the geographical sense. We are hardly in the position to judge whether the congregations that, under earthly conditions, are divided until the second coming of Christ have "form and beauty"[11] or not, since they obviously lack the harmony that humans so love. We must also refrain from judging the organizational division of congregations, namely, where this is contingent upon ethnicity [das Volkhafte],[12] to be a consequence of being entangled in wickedness. The concepts of destiny and guilt are insufficient to provide an explanation of the actual facts here. At the same time, it is necessary to speak of divine necessities in this world.

*Professor Dr. Adolf Deißmann* emphasized that he had learned much about
320 church problems from his participation in the ecumenical movement, especially through personal contact with foreign churches in the east and the west. Because of this he believes it would be a central task of our German corporate churches to find their way back to the church as body [Korpuskirche].

In the era of its origins, which we know primarily through Paul, the Christian church was above all a church as body. Though it was held together through very loose forms of association, it had the self-awareness of being the "*soma Christi*."[13] This ecclesial consciousness, only comprehensible as a collective expression of an apostolic mysticism centered in

[9.] Bonhoeffer did not insert the following passage, sent by Peter upon request in a manuscript written after the meeting: "on [thesis] 3: 'The hidden church is no abstract idea, but [is] the spirit, bound to and emanating from the manifestation of Christ, which creates for itself the body [i.e., the church].'"

[10.] See ed. note 7.

[11.] [The German wording here, "*Gestalt und Schöne*," is from Isa. 53:2; the NRSV text reads: "He had no form or majesty that we should look at him, nothing in his appearance that we should desire him."—VB]

[12.] [Friedrich Peter's comment here clearly reflects his nationalistic convictions. —VB]

[13.] "Body of Christ."

Christ,[14] was never lost by the ancient church. With the emergence of the early Catholic Church [altkatholischen], too, the corporate consciousness was strengthened by the richest unfolding in the forms of legal organization, yet the consciousness of the mystical body remained the driving force of the church—so much so that for Catholic ecclesiology everything that we call "church law" and value in a secular way [weltlich] has become a holy "canonical" law on the basis of conceptions of the body. This is also true after the split from the Eastern Church as well as within the Western Catholic Church until today. Further, it gives its soul and weight to the worship in these churches, which in the end intends always to be the self-manifestation of the living Christ. The uniqueness of the Mass and the sacraments is to be understood solely from this perspective.

In the Reformation churches, consciousness of the body has not been entirely abandoned. The creed of the Una Sancta movement[15] is certainly recited as if it were self-evident. But the consciousness of the body in the Protestant churches, because of their territorial dispersion [Atomisierung], is often suppressed behind their consciousness of themselves as corporations; in this connection their canon law has become heavily secularized. Our Protestant task within the ecumenical movement is that we, even though "members" [Mitglieder] of secularly organized churches as corporations, must awaken in ourselves and in others the consciousness that we are "limbs" [Glieder] in the body of Christ. This means, therefore, that within the authentic Protestant concentration on the New Testament, 321
the original Christian thinking about the body and being members of the body is to be grasped in its original character and to be preserved in its continuity. The corporate churches can remain constituted as membership churches, if they have the soul of the church as body, when, in other words, the statistical fact of individual membership is enlivened through the dynamic consciousness of being a "member" of the body. This push toward the church as body must be the ethos of our collaborative work, particularly with the Lausanne movement.[16]

---

[14.] On this thesis, see also Deißmann, *Paulus*.

[15.] See ed. note 7.

[16.] Since 1920, the Faith and Order movement had been preparing the world conferences for Faith and Order, held in Lausanne in 1927 and in Edinburgh in 1937. Besides the World Alliance for Promoting International Friendship through the Churches, founded in Constance in 1914, and the Movement for Practical Christianity (Life and Work), founded in 1919 in Oud Wassenaar to prepare for the "General Conference of the Church of Christ for Practical Christianity" in 1925 in Stockholm, it [the Lausanne "Faith and Order" movement—VB] was the third important group within the ecumenical movement.

The church as body in this specified sense is not identical with a nebulous *ecclesia invisibilis.*[17] Rather, it is the productive and effective church of Christ within this age, a visible and evident church.

In the theses on the relationship of the Una Sancta[18] to the particular churches, *Lecturer Bonhoeffer* raised the objection about whether the question of truth has not been unfairly abridged here. The concept of heresy has been lost in the ecumenical movement.[19] Dr. Zoellner proceeds from the presupposition of a basic truth given uniformly to the churches, which is then simply expressed in diversified ways by all the churches. But on this very point the sharpness should not be blurred through psychologizing and historicizing. The intrinsically disturbing problem of ecumenical work—as it is perceived by the younger generation at any rate—is not the relationship of organism and organization but rather that of truth and untruth in the proclamation of the various churches. The dogmatic differences between the various Protestant churches that participate in the ecumenical movement are more substantial than those originally between Protestantism and
322 Catholicism. From where, however, is the right of church fellowship derived, where there are two fundamentally different "ideas of truth," of which only one can be true and the other is heretical? *Pastor Lilje* supported these ideas in reference to Luther. *Dr. Zoellner* emphasized his thought that most of the contradictions are merely a reflection of the different languages, as for example the doctrine of justification in Paul and the same concept in James, only expressed in different languages. *Dr. Stählin* opposed Dr. Zoellner's view and believes that the self-evident habituation to the existence of different Christian churches (to which we Germans are additionally tempted, through the territorial divisions of the church) must be resisted; then the looking above and beyond, and if necessary even the debate, that is, the struggle for the correct understanding of the one truth, will become a required form of the confession of the unity of the church. We have lost our aversion to the concept "catholic." It is unjustified to remove arbitrarily the word "universal" in the Apostles' Creed. Only as a member of a universal Christian church does the existence of an individual Christian church have meaning and justification. In the debate with which we have been charged, surely we have the special task to assert the genuine churches (Lutheranism) that were defined in the German Reformation. But we must ask with equal seriousness if the polemical requirements of the Reformation period

[17.] "The invisible church."

[18.] See ed. note 7.

[19.] [This and the following sentences are a paraphrase of what Bonhoeffer said and thus express his views.—VB]

have not isolated German Protestantism in a dangerous way and if today we do not need to overcome errant developments in our church (heresies in the constitutional understanding of the church).[20] On the other hand, it may be necessary to win back the perceptions and powers that our churches have lost to a large extent. Examples of this would be the significance of sacramental reality not turned toward consciousness, the significance of priestly vicarious representative action [Stellvertretung] and the service 323
of the saints for the existence of the church, the ascending ordered steps of spiritual life, and the mature and authentic spiritual leadership that emerges from this. Dr. Stählin noted that Bonhoeffer is arguing on the basis of an anthropological consciousness, an argument that depends on that which lies behind what has become conscious. In rebuttal, *Lecturer Bonhoeffer* replied that one has to take an expression of the truth at its word and may not retreat from it or pretend that one unconsciously "means" the same thing if at the same time it is not expressed in clear and fitting words.

The session ended at 8:45 p.m.

On April 30, at ten o'clock, the second session under the chairmanship of Superintendent Diestel began. The lecture "The Unity of the Christian Church and the People" was delivered by Professor Dr. W. *Stählin* (Münster). The basic principles are printed on pp. 332–33 of this issue.[21]

In the discussion, Dr. *Bonhoeffer* opposed the entire draft by *Stählin* on the basis of the underlying concept of the order of creation[22] and his use of it in the discussion of the foregoing problem. It is not possible to lift out certain given elements in the world as orders of creation apart from others and to ground a Christian moral [sittlich] way of acting upon that. On the contrary, this is possible only if conceived from the perspective of revelation in Christ, which is not the case here. Stählin's distinction between the separation of the peoples and the diversity of the peoples,[23] of which only the

---

[20.] In 1530, Article 7 of the Augsburg Confession named correct preaching and administration of the sacraments as sufficient signs of the church (*Book of Concord*, 174ff.), in order to avoid a split between the Protestant churches and the Roman Catholic Church. In large sectors of later Lutheranism, the conclusion was drawn that the external order of the church, in particular its constitution, is not to be determined by the confession of faith but rather could be conformed to the respective realities of its age.

[21.] *Die Eiche* 20 (1932); cf. 2/12, ed. note 4.

[22.] See pp. 267–68, 341, 362–63, and 370.

[23.] [What follows is a highly significant discussion. It illustrates that by April 1932 German Protestants were debating the elements of the *völkisch* theology that were central for the German Christian (*Deutsche Christen*) movement that subsequently sought to nazify the church. In May 1932, only weeks after this ecumenical meeting, the German Christian movement published its "Ten Guidelines" (see Bergen, *Twisted Cross*, 23–24), which professed "a faith in Christ appropriate to our race (*artgemäß*), as we see in him

second belongs to the doctrine of creation, does not work out. Where does the language belong that establishes this separation as diversity (cf. Gen. 11)?[24] Following exactly from this presupposition, however, that is, from the order of creation, strife between nations is justified (theses 3[25] and
324 5).[26] In the draft itself, however, these difficulties are already mentioned. In thesis 2,[27] the talk is about the "given realities" of differences due to fate instead of differences based in the creation. The concept of destiny, if it indeed has any place in theology, presupposes the fall. Realities due to fate and those due to the creation are for this reason entirely different. A related difficulty also lies in thesis 6, number 4.[28] When the problem of

---

the German Lutheran spirit and heroic devotion" (cf. Gauger, *Chronik der Kirchenwirren,* 1:67). One of the central elements in this debate was the distinction between fixed "orders of creation," which provided a theological foundation for drawing permanent and racialized distinctions between different peoples and ethnic groups, and "orders of preservation," which viewed such distinctions as transitory in anticipation of the redemption of the world. Here and elsewhere Bonhoeffer strongly takes the latter view, opposing the "orders of creation," which even in 1932 were clearly identified with more-nationalistic theologians such as Emanuel Hirsch. (Cf. Bonhoeffer's comment on this in his 1933 essay, "The Church and the Jewish Question," *DBWE* 12:362, esp. ed. note 6.) It should be noted that Stählin did not become a member of the German Christians, but Pastor Friedrich Peter, who is cited here throughout, was already a member of the Nazi Party in 1929 and became a leading German Christian. See also thesis 6 below, as well as 2/16, ed. note 11; *DBWE* 3:11–12; and Ericksen, *Theologians under Hitler,* 98–104. See also the editors' introduction to this volume, pp. 3, 16.—VB]

[24.] See Gen. 11:1–9.

[25.] "The unity of the Christian church as the people of God called out from the nations does not annul either the diversity of peoples or the problem of strife that emerges from this in the world, as it is" (Stählin, "Die Einheit der christlichen Kirche und die Völker," 333).

[26.] "So long as the peoples threaten or hurt one another in their necessary space to live [*Lebensraum*] and in the unfolding of their self-determination, then the struggle for the life and freedom of a particular people belongs to the duties to which we are bound in our temporal situation. Belonging to the Christian church does not suspend these obligations but only points us to them even more appropriately as the temporal sphere in which we have to preserve obedience and faith" (ibid.).

[27.] "The deepening knowledge about the fateful differences between peoples and the task of struggle grounded therein is strengthened in the opposition against the intellectual underestimation of such fateful realities in general, as well as against the anti-Christian ideal of equality as applied to the peoples of the world" (ibid., 332).

[28.] Thesis 6: "In this situation, we deny the unity of the church when we set faith as the driving force in the service of national [*völkish*] self-preservation; when we refuse to experience in the message of Christ and his kingdom also the boundary and judgment on every people's will to live [*völkische Lebenswill*]; when we sever the nationally defined churches from the unity of the entire Christian church; when we identify our struggle for our own people with the struggle for the things of God and Christ" (ibid., 333). [Again, this language and thinking illustrates the racialized theological language that was

conflict originates in obedience to the specific order of creation of God, why shouldn't a person then understand his fight as a fight for the cause of God? One can only doubt this where the certainty of knowledge about the order of creation is shaken. Bonhoeffer is of the view that one must exclude the concept of the order of creation from the discussion of this subject. It is a dangerous and treacherous foundation. Rather, in place of the order of creation, one should introduce the concept of the "order of preservation"[29] of God. The difference would be that, from the perspective of the concept of the order of creation, certain orders, that is, given realities that are seen as worthy and original in themselves, will be considered "very good" on the basis of being such orders. Whereas with the concept of the order of preservation, it would be understood that every given reality is a reality maintained solely from God in grace und wrath, in view of the revelation in Christ. Every order under the preservation of God would then be aligned with Christ and only preserved on his behalf. An order is seen as an order of preservation of God only as long as it is open to the proclamation 325
of the gospel. Wherever an order, even though it appears to be most fundamental, such as marriage, nation, and so on, is fundamentally closed to this proclamation, it must be surrendered. Instead of proceeding from the order of creation, the solution to the overall ethical problem and to the ecumenical problem as well must be sought exclusively from the revelation of God given in Christ. Finally, thesis 10,[30] with its eschatological viewpoint, demonstrates that it is precisely here that creation, as that which is "very good" and in no need of improvement, is not taken very seriously. As something in need of redemption, creation is always fallen creation. As creation in itself, however, it is very good and needs no redemption.

This was followed by an extensive fundamental discussion about the applicability of the concept of the order of creation. *Pastor Peter* said that an order of creation is not an epistemological matter but rather simply a given reality. One must under all circumstances hold fast to the concept of the order of creation. *Pastor Lilje* disputed the possibility of identifying the orders of creation with concrete realities. *Dr. Knak* stated that the experiences of the mission to Africa show that the people [das Volk] can

already in use in German Protestant circles in 1932 and was being debated at this meeting. See also Bonhoeffer's earlier reflections on the substantial nature and consequences of this issue in the theses of his January 1932 presentation before the Working Group of Theologians and Economists (2/8) and his lecture at the Technical College in Berlin in February, "The Right to Self-Assertion" (2/5).—MBL]

[29.] See 2/8, pp. 267–68, and 2/14, pp. 363–64.

[30.] The article printed in *Die Eiche* offers only nine theses by Stählin.

be designated not as an order of creation, for example, but rather as a product of history.[31] *Dr. Stählin* opposed the thinking that orders of creation are perceived only on the basis of Christ. There are also convictions about creation outside Christianity. Through Christ, faith in creation is eschatologically defined. There is a diversification in what God has established. If, with the concept of the order of preservation, there is the possibility of abandoning an existing order for the sake of Christ, then it is debatable that we have the possibility to determine when this moment has come. On the contrary, this approach would lead very easily into certain weak, pacifist ideas, which seem unchristian.

*Pastor Peter* spoke to thesis 6:[32] it is dubious whether the sentence: "we
326 deny the unity of the church when we set faith as the driving force in the service of ethnic national [völkisch] self- preservation," can be sustained, if otherwise the political configuration and the arena of responsibility for the natural foundation of existence are not to be excluded generally from the life of faith. What is withdrawn from the realm of the church does not necessarily need to be withdrawn from the realm of faith. The realm of faith reaches at least beyond the empirical form of the faith community. Therefore, some things that the community does not recognize as its charge may still be the charge of a personality called by God in Christ.[33] Here, too, it is questionable whether one may speak of a nationally defined church, or whether it is not the case that national determination is a matter that affects the individual human being, since in baptism God has set him within two orders, the order of creation and the order of salvation.

To thesis 7,3:[34] this raises the question of whether we can validly maintain any longer the "protest against the sinful shattering of the world," to the degree that we, too, after such a deep experience of war and its after-

---

[31.] [The issue of *völkisch* theology was the source of an early clash between Bonhoeffer and Peter within the discussions of the Working Group of Theologians and Economists in January 1932 (2/8). This critique of nationalist theology and the "orders of creation" that were part of the theology of Pastor Peter (who was both a German Christian and a member of the Nazi Party) would be an ongoing issue in Bonhoeffer's ecumenical writing (see 2/15). Knak and Lilje were instrumental in this discussion as well.—MBL]

[32.] See ed. note 28.

[33.] [Given Peter's Nazism and his theological presuppositions, this is likely a direct reference to Adolf Hitler.—VB]

[34.] "Conversely, we confess the unity of the Christian church, [. . .] by preserving Christian fellowship with the Christians of other peoples, even where we are enmeshed in the struggle between our peoples; the decisive expression of this is through the community of prayer and the sacraments" (Stählin, "Die Einheit der christlichen Kirche und die Völker," 333).

math, are now once more considering going to war or at least reckon with its possibility through maintaining defense-ready troops and an army. If this protest creates doubt about the justification of the military spirit, it must, however, be clear to us that we cannot arrive at a sense of responsibility regarding conscientious objection that is prescribed by the gospel. At least not to such a sense of responsibility that would extend to a statesman charged by the state and its people to make clear decisions for the whole in the hour of danger.

*Lecturer Bonhoeffer* considered it virtually essential to risk these decisions, in contrast to the reservations that Stählin expressed about responsible thought, if the moment were to come when the maintenance of the pres- 327
ent order must be broken because it is no longer open to the revelation in Christ.[35] And this act of decision is distinctly different from weakness.[36]

The meeting had to be adjourned around 1:45 p.m., yet only after it was unanimously proposed that a continuation of the discussion take place at a meeting in the fall.

---

[35.] See 2/14, pp. 363–64.

[36.] In Bonhoeffer's draft for the published report (*NL*, A 34,4[3]), there is an insertion at this point that was not included in the printed version: "Dr. Heckel believes that the differences between Stählin and Bonhoeffer are typical for the contemporary theological situation. But they are equally clearly expressed in the problems of Germans living abroad." Bonhoeffer had requested the reports, i.e., the contributed talks, in printed form from the speakers. In a letter of June 23, 1932, to Schreiber, a member of the High Church Council, Bonhoeffer reported that the talk by Theodor Heckel was still missing. Schreiber passed on the question to Heckel, who then replied with this note: "My part must remain missing because I do not put any value on it, and I no longer know precisely what was said" (Glenthøj, *Zu Dietrich Bonhoeffers Eintritt*, 25; cf. also 1/74.2). [This exchange set the stage for the subsequent strong differences between Bonhoeffer and Heckel. Heckel, who in February 1934 was appointed bishop and director of the German Evangelical Church Foreign Office in Berlin, became the spokesman for the church policies of Church Chancellery president Friedrich Werner, who was a Nazi Party member and active German Christian. While Heckel himself was never a German Christian or party member, his statements at ecumenical meetings and his oversight of German foreign congregations (including the ones that Bonhoeffer served in London from 1933 to 1935) consistently represented the official church and government positions. In fact, Heckel denounced Bonhoeffer following the latter's return from London as an "enemy of the state" (*Staatsfeind*). See esp. the correspondence between Heckel and the London congregations in *DBWE* 13, 1/28, 1/38, 1/45, 1/82, and related material in that volume.—VB]

## 14. Lecture in Ciernohorské Kúpele: On the Theological Foundation of the Work of the World Alliance[1]

### On the Theological Foundation of the Work of the World Alliance[2]

There is still no theology of the ecumenical movement. Whenever the church of Christ in its history has come to a new understanding of its nature, it has brought forth a new theology commensurate with this self-
328 understanding. A change in the church's self-understanding [Selbstverständnis] proves itself to be genuine when it brings forth a theology. For in theology the church arrives at agreement about its own nature [Selbstverständigung], rooted in its understandings of the revelation of God in Christ. This agreement about its own nature begins necessarily wherever there is a new course in the church's self-understanding. If the ecumenical movement emerges from a new self-understanding of the church, it must and will bring forth a theology. If it does not succeed in this, it is a sign that the church is nothing but a new church organization in keeping with the times and for a certain purpose. One requires no theology of such an organization but rather merely specific concrete action in a concrete task. There is also no theology in the street ministry [Mitternachtsmission].[3] It is, however, very important to see that depending on the circumstances the ecumenical movement is something completely different.

It would be false if one were to say that it would be the work of Lausanne[4] to produce the theology of the ecumenical movement. It is more important here to ask: what was the basis for the collaborative theological work at Lausanne? Is it in itself an expression of a new ecclesial self-understanding, or is it ultimately an organization for the purpose of improving

[1.] *Die Eiche* 20 (1932): 334–44. Previously published in *GS* 1:140–58. Bonhoeffer delivered the lecture on behalf of ailing Superintendent Max Diestel on July 26, 1932, at the International Youth Peace Conference hosted by the Czechoslovakian church. The conference was held in Ciernohoské Kúpele on July 20–30, 1932. (See *DB-ER*, 246–48, and in this volume p. 383.) The lecture incorporates numerous reflections on theology and ethics that Bonhoeffer had developed in his 1932 summer seminar, "Is There a Christian Ethic?" (see 2/10). See also the summary theses for this lecture (2/15) as well as the introductory remarks in Ciernohorské Kúpele (2/16).

[2.] Original footnote: "Lecture delivered at the Youth Conference in Ciernohorské Kúpele, Czechoslovakia, July 26, 1932."

[3.] [Literally "midnight mission," this was the church's ministry to the homeless, prostitutes, etc.—VB]

[4.] See 2/13, ed. note 16. [The ecumenical Faith and Order movement was founded in Lausanne, Switzerland, in 1927; here and elsewhere in this essay "Lausanne" is a shorthand reference to that movement.—VB]

mutual understanding among divergent theological languages? Depending on the answer to this question, one may know what one may or may not expect from Lausanne. Undoubtedly, ecumenical work is inseparable from practice. The consequence has been that a large group of old practitioners, right up to today, view the work of theology with a certain disregard. "Praise God that we don't need to do theology here, that here we are finally free from such crippling problems and can focus on Christian action"—or so they say. But it is this very attitude that is destructive and demands our fullest protest, because it has led to the touchy consequence that ecumenical work was at the mercy of fluctuations in the political atmosphere. Because the ecumenical movement has no theology, the ecumenical concept, for 329
example, has currently become powerless and meaningless through the political wave of nationalism among the youth.[5] And it is no different in other countries. We lack a theological anchorage against which the waves from left and right would batter in vain. Our helplessness is at present profound, and the confusion of concepts knows no bounds. Whoever is involved in ecumenical work must allow himself to be chided as unpatriotic and untruthful,[6] and every attempt to counter this is easily shouted down.

¶Why is all this the case? Only because we have failed in a timely way to work out clear theological lines along which ecumenical work should move. This is not to speak about the practical work that the church has achieved. We have every reason to have gratitude and respect for these achievements. But what is it then that at recent international youth conferences broke through so forcefully, again and again?[7] What is it that gave these conferences so little of a "practical" character? What is it that revolted against the usual form of agreement by resolution? It is the recognition of a deep sense of perplexity about the very questions that should be the *foundation* of our gatherings. What is this Christianity that we always hear so much about? Is it essentially the content of the Sermon on the Mount,[8] or is it the message of reconciliation in the cross and resurrection of our Lord? What significance does the Sermon on the Mount have for our action? What meaning is there in the message from the cross? What relationship do the forms of our modern lives have to the Christian proclamation? What do the state, the economy, and our social life have to do with being Christian? It cannot be

[5.] See 2/2, part III.

[6.] Regarding these charges, see 2/1, ed. note 2.

[7.] Conference of the International World Youth Alliance, August 29–31, 1931, in Cambridge; the French-British regional conference, April 5–8, 1932, in Epsom, England; and the German-French regional conference, July 12–14, 1932, at the Westerburg, Germany.

[8.] See 2/10.2, ed. note 49.

denied that all of us must confess our ignorance here, but it is equally undeniable that we should recognize this ignorance as guilt. We really *should* know more about this. We have failed to think with clarity and decisiveness,
330 and we have failed to take a stand. And now we only notice in the middle of the lake that the ice upon which we stand is cracking.

The consequence of all this for us, however, is this: this issue that has been clearly recognized should not be covered up again at any price. Nothing good can come of pretending to act before the world and oneself as though one knew the truth, when in reality one did not know the truth. For this truth is too serious, and it would be a betrayal of the truth if the church hid behind resolutions and pious, so-called Christian principles, when it is called to look the truth in the face and above all to admit for once its guilt and its ignorance. Such resolutions cannot be either complete or unambiguous if the entirely serious nature of the complete Christian truth, as the church knows it or admits not to know it, does not stand behind it. Qualified silence[9] would perhaps be more appropriate for the church today than speech that is possibly very unqualified. That means a protest against every form of church [Kirchentum] that does not honor the question of the truth above all. The next thing we must demand is that this question be asked anew in utter seriousness. The concern of the youth who are actively engaged in ecumenical work is this: how does our ecumenical work, in particular that of the World Alliance, appear as we reflect on the truth of the gospel? And we believe that we cannot come closer to these questions other than through wholly serious and rigorous renewed theological work on the biblical and Reformation foundations of our ecumenical understandings of the church, without regard to consequences or success. We demand a responsible theology of the ecumenical movement for the sake of truthfulness and the certainty of our cause.

That which now follows, then, is to be understood as an attempt to outline clearly some of the basic theological questions that particularly relate to the work of our World Alliance and to situate them theologically. It is absolutely a matter of questions that are posed from within and not from
331 the outside, from the disinterested position of the observer. But those who nonetheless hold these questions as questions "from the outside" should be told that these very questions are posed *today* from within.

The work of our World Alliance—consciously or unconsciously—is grounded in a very distinct conception of church. The church as the one church-community of the Lord Jesus Christ, who is the Lord of the world, has the task of speaking his word to the entire world. The range of the one

[9.] See also *GS* 5:340 (1933).

church of Christ is the entire world. There are local boundaries for the proclamation of each individual church, but the *one* church has no boundaries around it. The churches of the World Alliance have joined together in order to express their claim, or rather the claim of our Lord, on the entire world. They understand the task of the church as that of making the claim of Christ audible to the entire world. This includes the rejection of the idea that there are God-willed characteristics of life that are removed from the lordship of Christ,[10] that do not need to hear this word. It is not a holy, sacred district of the world that belongs to Christ but rather the entire world.

Now one must first ask the question: *under which authority does the church speak, when it proclaims this claim of Christ on the world?* Under the only authority in which the church is in a position to speak, in the authority of the Christ who is present and living in it. The church is the presence of Christ on earth; the church is *Christus praesens*.[11] This alone gives its word authority. The word of the church is the word of the present Christ; it is gospel and commandment. It is not one thing alone, and it can be understood as the one only when it is also understood as the other. The church would revert back to the synagogue[12] if its proclamation were only command; it would be a falling away of the church into Enthusiasm[13] if it were to deny the command of God for the sake of the gospel.

As the word out of the authority of the present Christ, the word of the church today must be considered as the valid, binding word. I can be spo-
ken to with full authority only when a word from the deepest knowledge 332
of my humanity hits me in my full reality, here and now. Every other word is powerlessness [Ohnmacht]. The word of the church to the world must therefore touch it out of the deepest knowledge of the world in its complete present if it wishes to be authoritative. The church must here and now be able to speak the word of God, of authority, out of its own knowledge in the most concrete way,[14] or it says something entirely different, something human, a word of powerlessness. The church therefore can proclaim not principles that are always true but rather only commandments that are true

[10.] See p. 331.

[11.] "Christ present"; see pp. 242, 277–78, and 301–2.

[12.] Before 1933 Bonhoeffer used the term "synagogue" as a metaphor for legalism (cf. *GS* 5:329). [While there is no record of an explicit repudiation of this after 1933, it doesn't appear in his writings after that date.—VB]

[13.] [The reference is to the Enthusiast (*Schwärmer*) wing of the Reformation; the Enthusiasts emphasized the experience of the Holy Spirit as authoritative for Christian life.—VB]

[14.] See pp. 167 and 339 as well as *GS* 5:338–39.

today. For that which is "always" true is precisely not true "today": God is for us "always" *God* precisely "*today*."

How can the gospel and the commandment be proclaimed by the church in authority, but this means in its most complete concretion? This is an extremely difficult and significant problem. Is the church able to proclaim the commandments of God with the same certainty with which it proclaims the gospel? Can the church say that we need a socialist economy, or: do not go to war, in the same way that it can say: "Your sins are forgiven"? Apparently the gospel and the commandments are proclaimed with authority only where they are wholly concretely proclaimed. Otherwise it remains on the level of general knowledge, in what is human, in the powerlessness, in the lie. Where does the principle of the concrete lie in the gospel, and where does it lie in the commandments? This is how the problem must be solved. *The gospel becomes concrete in its listeners; the commandment becomes concrete through those who proclaim it.* The sentence: "Your sins are forgiven" as it is spoken in the gospel, in a sermon, or during the Lord's Supper, is spoken to the congregation in such a manner that it encounters the listeners in a completely concrete way. Over against this, the commandment needs concretion in content through the one who proclaims it; the commandment: "Love thy neighbor" is as such so general that it requires the strongest concretion if I am to hear what it means for me here and today.
333 And only as such a concrete word to me is it God's word. He who proclaims the word must therefore be aware that he must include the respective situation within the form of the commandment,[15] so that the commandment is relevant to the real situation. The church must in the event of a decision about war not only be able to say: There should be no war; but there are also necessary wars, and then leave it to each individual to apply this principle—rather, the church should be able to say concretely: fight this war, or do not fight this war. Or so far as a social question is concerned: it should not be the church's last word to say: it is wrong that one person has a surplus of material things when another person goes hungry, but property is willed by God and may not be touched; and then leave the application of this in turn to the individual. Rather, when the church really has a commandment of God, it must proclaim this in the most concrete form out of the fullest knowledge of the matter and call others to obedience. A commandment must be concrete or it is not a commandment. God's commandment demands something absolutely particular now from us. And the church must proclaim this to the church-community.

[15.] See p. 338.

Now, however, there arises a tremendous difficulty. If the church must know the situation in detail before it can command, that is, if the validity of its commandment depends on its detailed knowledge of the matter—for example, about war, disarmament, minorities, social questions—there is always the danger that the church in its commandment will nonetheless overlook this or that objective point of view or underestimate it, and therefore the church will be made completely uncertain in its commandment. Therefore, the commanding church's understanding of the subject matter is, on the one hand, the precondition of a real commandment and, on the other hand, makes every one of its commandments uncertain, again and again, because it is dependent on the complete knowledge of reality. Fundamentally, there are two ways to face this insoluble dilemma: first, avoidance and withdrawal to the level of principle. This is the path that the churches have almost always taken. Or, however: the difficulty is faced directly, and then all dangers are faced defiantly, namely, *either* a conscious 334
and qualified silence of ignorance, *or* the commandment is dared in every conceivable concretion, exclusivity, and radicalism. The church thus dares to say, for instance: do not wage this war; be socialists today, this commandment as *God's* commandment out of the clear recognition that it is possible therewith to take the name of God in vain, that the church is in error and is sinful, but it may speak it in faith in the word of the forgiveness of sins that holds true for the church as well. Thus, however, the proclamation of the commandment is founded in the proclamation of the forgiveness of sins. The church cannot command unless it itself stands in the belief in the forgiveness of sins and without directing all those whom it commands to emphasize this proclamation of the forgiveness of sins. The proclamation of the commandment experiences the assurance of its validity through the proclamation of the forgiveness of sins. Does this proclamation of forgiveness of sins, too, require another protection of its validity? The assurance of the validity of the proclamation of the forgiveness of sins is the sacrament. Here is the universal statement: "Your sins are forgiven," bound to water, wine, and bread; here it comes to its own peculiar concretion, which is understood by the believing listeners as the concrete here and now of the word of God. What the sacrament is for the proclamation of the gospel, the knowledge of concrete reality is for the proclamation of the commandment. *Reality is the sacrament of the commandment.*[16] Just as the sacraments of baptism and the Lord's Supper are the only forms of the first reality of creation in this aeon, and just as they are sacraments for the sake of their creative

[16.] See pp. 339 and 340, ed. note 41.

origins, so is the "ethical sacrament" of reality to be characterized as sacrament only so far as this reality itself is completely grounded in its relation to the reality of creation. As the fallen world and fallen reality continue to exist only through their relationship to the created world and the created reality, so the commandment is based on the forgiveness of sins.

The church proclaims the gospel and the commandment with authority.
335 As far as the task that the World Alliance has set for itself is concerned, our concern is the question of the telling of a certain divine command to the world. We have seen that the commandment can only be told on the basis of faith in the forgiveness of sins. But it must be told as long as the world is not the church.

Whence does the church know what God's commandment is for this hour? For apparently this is not self-evident. "We do not know what to do," 2 Chron. 20:12.[17] "Do not hide your commandments from me," Ps. 119:19.[18] The knowledge of the commandment of God is an act of the revelation of God. Where does the church hear this revelation? *The first answer* could be: the *biblical law,* the *Sermon on the Mount* is the absolute norm for our actions.[19] We must simply take the Sermon on the Mount seriously and realize it. That is our obedience toward the divine commandment. Over against this, it must be said: even the Sermon on the Mount may not become a literal law for us. In its commandments it is the illustration of that which God's commandment can be, but not exactly what it is today and especially for us. No one can hear this except we ourselves, and God himself must say it to us. The commandment is not there once and for all; rather it must be always given anew. Thus alone are we free from the law that stands between us and God, and thus do we listen to God alone.[20]

The *second answer* finds the commandment of God in the *order of creation.*[21] Because if there were certain orders of creation, one should not struggle against them but accept them humbly. One can then argue as follows: because the peoples are created differently, therefore each one is duty bound to preserve and develop its individuality. This would be obedience to the creator. And when this obedience leads one into battle and into
336 war, this also can be understood as part of the order of creation. Here

[17.] In *Die Eiche,* this is erroneously referred to as 2 Kings 20:12. Bonhoeffer referred to this passage in 2 Chronicles often during 1932–33 in various contexts (see the May 8, 1932, sermon on 2 Chron. 20:12 (3/8) and *GS* 5:340.)

[18.] Cf. *GS* 5:340.

[19.] See p. 341.

[20.] On Bonhoeffer's distinction between commandment and law, see also p. 337, ed. note 23.

[21.] See pp. 267–68, 341, and 351–54.

too, therefore, the commandment of God is conceived as something that is there for all time and is always a given and can be found in certain orders. A special danger lies in this argument, and because it is the one that is utilized the most in the present age,[22] we must pay special attention to it. The danger of this argument is basically that everything can be justified on its basis. One need only portray something that exists as willed and created by God and then everything that exists is justified for eternity: the strife among the peoples of humanity, national struggle, war, class distinctions, the exploitation of the weak by the strong, economic competition as a matter of life and death. Nothing is easier than portraying and sanctioning that all this is intended by God simply because it exists. The mistake, however, lies in this: that in the solution of this seemingly so simple equation we overlook the great unknown that makes this solution impossible. That the world has fallen and that sin now rules and that the creation and sin are so intertwined that no human eye can see them as separate, that every human order is the order of the fallen world and not of creation, all that is not seen in its seriousness. The possibility of addressing some things as such as orders of creation and hearing God's will in them *immediately* no longer exists. The so-called orders of creation per se are no longer revelations of God's commandment; they are hidden and invisible. Through this, the concept of the order of creation as fundamental for the knowledge of the commandment of God is waived. Therefore, neither biblical law as such nor the so-called order of creation is the divine commandment for us that we accept today.

*The commandment cannot come from anywhere except that place where the promise and fulfillment come from, namely, from Christ.* From Christ alone we must know what we should do. Not, however, from him as the preaching prophet of the Sermon on the Mount, but rather from him who gives us life and forgiveness, as the one who has fulfilled God's commandments for us, as 337
the one who brings and promises the new world. Only there where the law is fulfilled, where the new world of God's order exists, can we hear the commandment. With this, we are wholly directed toward Christ. Through this, however, we understand the entire world order of the fallen creation as directed only toward Christ through the new creation. That which was formerly dark and hidden in our sight comes into a new light. Not that we now know all at once through Christ which given things we should regard as the order of creation and which not, but rather that we know that *all* worldly orders exist only because they are directed toward Christ; they *all* stand

[22.] See 2/13.

alone under God's preservation as long as they are still open for Christ; they are *orders of preservation*,[23] not orders of creation. They receive their value completely from the outside, from Christ, from the new creation. Their value does not rest in themselves; yet this means they should not be looked upon as orders of creation, which are "very good" in and of themselves; rather they are God's orders of preservation, which have continued existence only as long as they remain open for the revelation in Christ. The preservation is the act of God with the fallen world through which he guarantees the possibilities of a new creation. The orders of preservation are forms of purposeful formation against sin in the direction of the gospel. *Every order*—be it the oldest and holiest—*can be broken*—and must be, when it is locked within itself, hardened, and when it no longer permits the proclamation of the revelation. From this point, the church of Christ must judge the orders of the world. And from this point, the church of Christ must hear the commandment of God. In the historical change of the orders of the world, it must keep its eyes on this alone: which orders are most likely to stop this radical decline of the world in death and sin and will thereby be in a position to hold open the way for the gospel. Only from Christ, not out of any established law, nor out of any eternal order, does the church hear the commandment, and it hears this in the orders of preservation. The
338 commandment from Christ is therefore also the absolute critical and radical commandment that is not limited by anything else—not by any so-called order of creation. It can demand the most radical destruction precisely for the purpose of the *one* construction. The venture and decision of the church for or against an order of preservation would be an impossibility if it did not occur in faith in the God who in Christ also forgives the church's sins. But it is in this faith that things must be ventured and decided.

The churches bound together in the World Alliance believe that they recognize a very specific order as that commanded us by God today. The order of *international peace* is God's commandment for us today.[24] Through this, a completely concrete understanding of God's will for our time is expressed. The understanding should now be analyzed and interpreted on the basis of what we have said so far. What can the church say about international peace as God's commandment? That is the question. First of all: like everyone who speaks God's commandment, it may be suspected of being Enthusiastic and of proclaiming dreams, that is, of speaking out of the flesh and not out of the spirit. It also cannot "qualify" its word as God's commandment by anything, except through a continued, monotone, sober pointing to this

[23.] See pp. 267–68 and 353.

[24.] See p. 436.

commandment. It will try in vain to refute the irritation of pacifist humanitarianism, where the commandment of peace itself has not already been understood as God's commandment. The church must know this and must renounce every attempt at a justification of the commandment of God. It conveys the commandment but nothing more.

To date, under the overpowering influence of Anglo-Saxon theological thought in the World Alliance, the freedom meant here has been understood as a reality of the gospel, let us simply say, as a piece of the kingdom of God on earth. From this standpoint the ideal of peace is made absolute, that is, now no longer understood only as a form with a purpose [Zweckgestaltung] and an order of preservation, but rather as a final order of fulfillment that has value in itself, as an order from the world beyond, breaking into the fallen world. External freedom is as such a "very good" situation. 339
With this it is a divine order of creation and the kingdom of God and as such is to be preserved unconditionally. This perception, however, must be rejected as Enthusiastic[25] and therefore not Protestant. International peace is not a reality of the gospel, not a piece of the kingdom of God, but rather a commandment of the wrathful God, an order of the preservation of the world toward Christ. International peace is therefore also not an absolutely ideal condition but rather an order that is aimed at something else and that is not valuable in and of itself. Naturally, the establishment of such an order of preservation can have absolute urgency, although never for its own sake, but rather for the sake of its goal, namely, for the sake of the hearing of revelation. The broken character of the order of peace is expressed in the fact that the peace demanded by God has two boundaries: first, the truth; second, justice [Recht].[26] A community of peace can exist only when it does not rest on *a lie* or on *injustice*. Wherever a community of peace endangers or suffocates truth and justice, the community of peace must be broken and the battle must be declared. If the battle from both sides is really about truth and justice, then the community of peace, even when externally broken, will be realized more deeply and strongly in the battle for this very cause. If, however, it should become clear that one of the combatants is fighting only for his own personal goals, that is, should even this form of the community of peace be broken, then the reality exposed here is the final and only enduring basis of any community of peace: the forgiveness of sins. The sole reason that Christians have a community of peace is because the one wishes to forgive the sins of the other. Even where the order of external peace in truth and justice remains secure,

[25.] [See 2/14, ed. note 13.—VB]

[26.] See p. 381.

forgiveness of sins remains the only basis for all peace. It is therefore also the last foundation upon which all ecumenical work rests, particularly where the brokenness seems hopeless.

340 In Anglo-Saxon thinking, truth and justice remain subordinate to the ideal of peace. Indeed, the present peace is the very proof that truth and justice are secure; precisely because the order of peace is a reality of the gospel and of the kingdom of God, truth and justice can never be against it. It has become clear, however, that this very perception is illusory. Neither the external order of peace nor of the peace struggling for the same cause, but only the peace of God who creates the forgiveness of sins is the reality of the gospel in which truth and justice are preserved together. Neither a static concept of peace (Anglo-Saxon) nor a static concept of truth (the Hirsch-Althaus explanation!)[27] grasps the evangelical idea of peace in its vivid relationship to the concept of truth and justice.

*Struggle* as possible action with respect to Christ becomes understandable if the order of external peace is not timelessly valid but can be disrupted at any moment, precisely because the complete violation of truth and justice would threaten to make hearing about revelation in Christ impossible. Struggle is not an order of creation, but it can be an order of preservation for the future of Christ, toward the new creation. Should the situation arise, the struggle can protect the openness for the revelation in Christ better than external peace, in that it breaks the hardened, self-enclosed order.

Today, however, there is a widespread and extremely dangerous error that says that in the *justification of struggle* there is already the justification for war, that this contains the *fundamental Yes to war*. The right to wage war can be derived from the right to struggle no more than the right to inflict torture can be derived from the necessity of legal process in human society.[28] Whoever has read seriously in the history of the concept of war in Luther[29]
341 through Fichte[30] and Bismarck[31] up to the present knows that the word has remained but that the subject has become absolutely and incomparably different. Our contemporary war does not fall under the concept of battle because it means the certain self-destruction of both warring sides. For

---

[27.] See p. 165, ed. note 2.

[28.] See p. 380.

[29.] For Luther's position on war, see "Ob Kriegsleute im seligen Stände sein können," 1526 (*WA* 19:623–62).

[30.] After 1806, Fichte placed himself in the service of the uprising against Napoleon. In his 1807–8 essays, "Der Patriotismus und sein Gegenteil" and "Reden an die deutsche Nation," he tried to promote the creation of a German national consciousness and called for a general armament of all citizens.

[31.] Cf. Engelberg, *Bismarck*, 451–56.

that reason today it is utterly impossible to characterize it as an order of preservation toward revelation, simply because it is absolutely destructive. The power of destruction reaches the inner life as well as the external life of human beings.[32] Today's war destroys soul and body. Because there is no way for us to understand war as God's order of preservation and therefore as God's commandment, and because war needs to be idealized and idolatrized in order to live, today's war, the next war, must be *condemned* by the church. We do not express any judgment against past deeds, even in the last war—that is not our right—"thou shalt not judge"[33]—but we must face the next war with all the power of resistance, rejection, condemnation. Not out of the Enthusiast establishment of a commandment—for example, the fifth[34] above the others—but rather out of the obedience to God's commandment that affects us today, that there should be no more war because it robs us of the view toward revelation. We should not balk here at using the word "pacifism." Just as certainly as we submit the ultimate *pacem facere*[35] to God, we too must *pacem facere* to overcome war. Certainly this will not lead to an eradication of strife as such from the world. But we are concerned here with a very specific means of struggle forbidden today by God. Understood in this way, the protest of the World Alliance could be a genuine listening to God's present commandment.

God's will is directed not only at the new creation of humanity but toward
the new creation of the conditions as well. It is not right that only the will 342
could be good.[36] Conditions can also be good; the creation of God was as such "very good." Even in the fallen world conditions can be good but never through themselves, rather always only in view of the action of God himself, in view of the creating anew. We cannot reconstitute creation, but we should create such conditions under God's commandment—and on this rests the entire weight of God's commandments—that are good in reference to that which the God who commands today will do someday himself, in reference to the new creation through Christ. Conditions are only good "in reference to" something else. But as such they are good. And as such the peace that overcomes war is "good."

---

[32.] [Bonhoeffer is referring to Luther's distinction between the two parts of the human being, the inner (i.e., the soul or the relation to God) and the outer (the relation to the world and oneself through the body). The editors thank Christiane Tietz for this note.—VB]

[33.] See Matt. 7:1

[34.] See Exod. 20:13.

[35.] "To create peace."

[36.] This was Kant's thesis in his writings on practical philosophy and metaphysics of morals.

The World Alliance now believes that it can ensure this peace by working for "understanding." We ask: how is such *understanding* conceivable and achievable *in Christian terms*? The original and undoubtedly still leading Anglo-Saxon viewpoint of the World Alliance is understanding through getting to know one another. As indispensable as this first step certainly is, it is by far not the only and most important one. Socialism has been able to establish itself on an international basis not because the German worker knew the French and the American worker but rather because they have a great, common ideal. This means that Christians too will first learn to think transnationally when they have a great, common proclamation. More than anything else at the present time, we need a great unifying proclamation in the ecumenical movement. We do not wish to fool ourselves: we do not yet have this proclamation. The language of the ecumenical movement is—despite everything—weak. This proclamation will exist only in connection with a theology. And thus here at the conclusion, we are led back to our first concern. In the large and genuine sense, mutual understanding exists only through proclamation and theology that is fully in the present. There is an infinitely great danger that at the international conferences we
343 become good friends and find good fellowship[37]—and otherwise nothing. But "pagans and tax collectors do this also."[38] Our concern is something else, a new knowledge and a new will. And any conference not aiming for this goal with complete seriousness is a lost and gossipy time. And everyone who has visited these international conferences with this goal in mind knows that this costs hard work and difficult struggles. But that is why such conferences exist.

To conclude, there are two short questions: To whom does the church speak? And who is this church that speaks in this way?

The church that convenes in the World Alliance speaks to Christianity so that it may hear its word as God's commandment as it emerges from the forgiveness of sins. It also, however, speaks to the world so that it might change the conditions. The world cannot hear the true voice of the church, nor can the state; the voice of the church cannot be its authority, but the state

[37.] "Good fellowship" in English in the original.

[38.] See Matt. 5:46–47. [NRSV: "Do not even the tax collectors do the same?"—VB]

finds in the church a critical boundary of its possibilities and must therefore regard the church as a critic of its actions.[39]

Who is this church? The church of the gospel, the church that proclaims the gospel in accordance with the truth. And here a dreadful crisis [Not] breaks open. It is the question of the truth that threatens to destroy all that has been said up to now. The churches that are members of the World Alliance do not have a common recognition of truth but are instead most deeply torn asunder on this very point. When they say Christ or gospel, each of them means something very different. At present this is our most pressing problem in ecumenical work. We can speak only as the church that proclaims the truth of the gospel. But the truth is torn asunder. And that makes our word powerless, even mendacious. But even more terrible than this is the fact that we ignore this lightheartedly. One must not play with the truth, or it will destroy us. We play perilously close to the abyss. If only our eyes would open on this point. But admittedly, this does not remedy the reality of the disunity of the one true church that alone is empowered
to speak. And I do not now wish to conclude with an emphatic claim that 344
thinks it can remove this difficulty from the world. I do not know the solution for this problem. I would only like to give this bit of advice, namely, there where the church knows the guilt of its ruptured knowledge of the truth, and where it thinks that it nevertheless must speak under God's commandment, the forgiveness of sins for the humble is established and promised. Naturally, this piece of advice can be not the human *solution* to our crisis but only an expression of the expectation of the entire church for *salvation.* The last information that can be given here is that the church in its crisis must remain humble and must live on the basis of forgiveness alone.

[39.] [This passage is strikingly similar to Bonhoeffer's subsequent analysis of the different possibilities for the church's relationship to state authority, including the possibility of church opposition. See, for example, his 1933 essay "The Church and the Jewish Question" (*DBWE* 12, 2/13, esp. 362–66.—VB]

## 15. Theses for the Lecture in Ciernohorské Kúpele[1]

Framework for a Lecture in Czechoslovakia:
Toward a Theological Foundation for the Work
of the World Alliance, July 26, 1932
*Eiche* 1932/4[2]

(1) There is no theology of the ecumenical movement. If the ecumenical movement is a new form of ecclesial self-understanding, then it must bring forth a new theology. If it does not do this, it reveals itself as a purely utilitarian organization. The[3] ecumenical idea[4] becomes dependent[5] on political fluctuations of economic conditions (nationalism, internationalism)[6] if it does not rest on the foundation of its own theology. In many
345 countries today this is painfully evident. The disregard for theology by the "practitioners" must come to an end. The strongest concern of the last international youth conference of the World Alliance[7] was to pose the basic questions of theology anew and acknowledge with ruthless openness that on the decisive questions we are at a loss. This reality should not be covered up by "resolutions." What follows is intended to consider several fundamental theological questions of the work of the World Alliance.

(2) The church of Jesus Christ, who is the Lord of the entire world, has been given the task of speaking the word of Christ to the entire world. The territory of the church of Christ is the entire world.

(3) By which authority does the church speak? Because the church is *Christus praesens*,[8] it therefore proclaims the gospel and the commandment in the authority of Christ. But because it is Christ *praesens*, the gospel and the commandment must engage the concrete contemporary situation.

---

[1.] *NL*, A 34,6; handwritten draft. Previously published in *GS* 1:159–61. In the margin Eberhard Bethge has written "Theses" with reference to the word "framework" (*Gerüst*). The theses were distributed to the participants in the youth peace conference in Ciernohorské Kúpele (see *DB-ER*, 247). In his study "Die Tschechoslowakische Kirche und die regionale Jugendfriedenskonferenz," Adolf Mádr reproduced a version of the theses that does not take into account the deletions [which are indicated in notes below—VB] in Bonhoeffer's draft.

[2.] See 2/14. [First published in the ecumenical newsletter *Die Eiche* (1932), no. 4. —VB]

[3.] Deleted: "the powerlessness of."

[4.] Deleted: "among the youth."

[5.] Deleted: "and is presently so powerless."

[6.] Deleted: "and its chances." [Notes 5 and 6 in this translation occur in reverse order from that in *DBW* 11.—MBL]

[7.] See 2/14, ed. note 7.

[8.] "Christ present."

Otherwise it would not be the word of Christ *praesens*. It can do this insofar as the proclamation of the gospel becomes concrete in the sacrament that is received only by the faithful and through the fact that the proclamation of the commandment becomes concrete through the deepest realization of reality through those who proclaim it. The church should not establish principles; rather, it should command concretely. But every one of its commandments is grounded solely in the church's faith in the forgiveness of sins.

(4) How does the church know the commandment of God for this hour? Neither biblical law nor any other established orders of creation are sources of such knowledge. Both would be legalism. Only from Christ, from whom the gospel comes, do we even know the commandment. From Christ we must recognize that the entire world is a fallen world, that we no longer know its original orders. The only still-existing ones are the orders of preservation directed toward Christ, and whenever we have to judge that an order is no longer open for Christ, then this order must be broken. There are no orders that are holy in and of themselves. An order is "good" only when it is open for Christ and for the new creation. The decision of the church for or against such an order must be dared in faith. Nothing else 346
protects the church.

(5) The churches that have joined together in the World Alliance intend to discern an order that is clearly commanded by God for us today: the order of international peace. What can the church proclaim about peace? Peace is understood in Anglo-Saxon theology as a realization of the gospel, as a dimension of the kingdom of God on earth. Thus peace becomes an *absolute ideal*. This conception must be rejected; even peace is only an order of preservation that can be destroyed.[9] Peace has its boundary in truth and justice. Where truth and justice are violated there can be no peace. With the disruption of external peace, the community of peace, which rests on the common struggle for truth and ultimately for Christians rests solely on the forgiveness of sins, is not destroyed. In the fallen world, there is a right to struggle. This does not mean that there is a right to war. Just as the use of torture cannot be justified by the necessity of legal process, so too one cannot derive the right to war out of the necessity of struggle.[10] War as a *means* of struggle is an action forbidden us today by God, because it represents the external and internal[11] destruction of human beings and thus robs us of the gaze toward Christ.

[9.] Deleted: "and must."

[10.] [Here and elsewhere in this essay, there are parallel passages to 2/14.—VB]

[11.] "External and internal" are later additions made in the margins.

(6) The World Alliance works for peace in that it works for "understanding." Understanding in the Christian sense, however, does not only mean to get to know and treasure one another and become good friends. Just as socialism has succeeded in positioning itself on an international level through its message, so too the church can lay the transnational basis for understanding in a comprehensive way only through a thoroughly contemporary Christian proclamation and theology.

(7) To whom do the churches of the World Alliance speak? To Christianity, that it might hear the commandment of God. To the world, to the state, that it might change these conditions and be attentive to the critical word of the church.

347 (8) Who is the church that can speak in this way? Only the church that proclaims the pure truth of the gospel. This truth is fragmented, however, and the World Alliance churches do not have a *single* truth. That is the deepest crisis of the ecumenical situation. This crisis[12] must never be covered up. But there where the church recognizes its guilt regarding the truth and where God's commandment calls the church to speak, the church must dare to speak, solely in faith in the forgiveness of its sin.

### 16. Excerpt from Welcoming Address in Ciernohorské Kúpele (Transcription)[1]

[. . .] A characteristic feature of the work of the World Alliance in Germany is the fact that the German regional churches are not official members. The World Alliance works as a free association of persons and circles that are conscious of the ecumenical task of contemporary Christianity for peace and friendship among all nations.[2] The work for peace encounters

[12.] Deleted: "must with complete seriousness."

[1.] Mádr, "Die Tschechoslowakische Kirche und die regionale Jugendfriedenskonferenz," 149–51. Previously published in *Mündige Welt*, 5:42–43 and *GS* 6:243–44. Mádr, a former pastor in Brno-Židenice (Czechoslovakia), attempted with several colleagues to reconstruct the chronology of the conference in this extensive documentation. Because the reconstruction was written in broken German, the version published here [and in *Mündige Welt* and *GS*—VB] was revised by Eberhard Bethge and Jørgen Glenthøj. Although the reconstruction of Bonhoeffer's remarks from Wednesday evening, July 27, 1932, contains some phrases that Bonhoeffer did not normally use (e.g., "nationalistic party of Hitler," "Nazis," "Nazism," "anti-Hitler parties," "Hitler party"), the document corresponds to the general remarks of other witnesses. Despite objections, Bonhoeffer left the conference in Ciernohorské Kúpele early in order to cast his vote against the National Socialists in the national elections in Berlin on Sunday, July 31, 1932 (cf. *Mündige Welt*, 5:42).

[2.] See 2/14, pp. 364–65.

an entire series of internal and external problems.[3] In Germany there is a widespread feeling of having been treated unjustly because of the one-sided declaration of the Versailles treaty regarding the guilt of the German 348
people for the world war.[4] Even the League of Nations does not enjoy complete trust here.[5] The sense of injustice and the national consciousness are being misused by extreme elements.[6] The ecumenical powers within and beyond the framework of the World Alliance must overcome a series of well-intentioned but theologically problematic statements that are attempting to solve the problem of the nation, the war, and similar problems.[7] The youth section of the German branch of the World Alliance organizes a series of meetings of native youth, often with foreign participation.[8] In April an important meeting of young people from France and Germany was successful, and not long before this conference there was also a conference at the Westerburg,[9] where the serious question of the responsibility of 349
Christians for the political development in Germany was discussed in complete openness. The nationalistic party of Hitler misuses the democratic

---

[3.] See 2/11, ed. note 5.

[4.] Article 231 of the Treaty of Versailles, dated June 28, 1919, declared that Germany bore sole responsibility for the First World War: "The Allied and Associated Governments affirm, and Germany accepts, the responsibility of Germany and her Allies for causing all the loss and damage to which the Allied and Associated Governments and their nationals have been subjected as a consequence of a war imposed upon them by the aggression of Germany and her Allies" (cited in Teitel, *Transitional Justice*, 122).

[5.] Germans viewed the founding of the League of Nations after the end of the First World War, in connection with the Versailles treaty, which [they viewed as] forced upon them, as going far beyond national rights. Thus the right-wing anti-Republic propaganda had an easy time of drawing a contrast between the "equalizing" thoughts of the League of Nations, which had its roots in the French Revolution, and the organic German Reich concept. This is shaped by the notion that the strongest people—meaning of course the Germans—subjugate the others and function as their guardian and ruler, without being bound by external norms of justice.

[6.] The primary reference here is to the National Socialists. Regarding the other categories of old and young nationalism at the end of the Weimar Republic, see Sontheimer, *Antidemokratisches Denken in der Weimarer Republik.*

[7.] Cf. Bonhoeffer's argument above against Wilhelm Stählin's use of the concept of "orders of creation" during the theological conference of the Provisional Bureau for Ecumenical Youth Work on April 29–30, 1932, in Berlin (2/13, pp. 351–53).

[8.] According to the *Handbook of the World Alliance*, a group of approximately thirty young people met every month in Berlin (see *Handbook of the World Alliance*, 63; see also *DB-ER*, 193–94 and 238–40).

[9.] The sentence is contradictory in itself, since the German-French regional conference at the Westerburg first took place at the beginning of July. It was planned originally for April 15–17, 1932 (see 1/47). Presumably both references refer to this one conference (see 1/42).

possibilities and is striving to establish a dictatorship. The next few days will be decisive in how far the anti-Hitler parties are capable of preventing the takeover of the government by the Nazis.[10] Nazism is also pushing itself into the church.[11] The responsible theological work, supported by the ecumenical world, faces the task of strengthening those Germans and those Christians in Germany who are fighting against Hitler. The victory of Hitler's party would have unforeseeable consequences not only for the development of the German people but also for the development of the whole world. Christians must unite in their struggle against the powers that are seducing the people with a false nationalism, promoting militarism, and threatening the world with unrest from which a war could emerge. In this sense one must value the engagement of the World Alliance positively as well as the conference presently taking place here, which the Central Committee of the Czechoslovakian church has organized. We are happy that we have come to know the hospitality of our Czechoslovakian brothers and their beautiful country. All those who are attending are aware of the common problems and difficulties of our generation. It is understandable that different viewpoints about the foundation and methods of ecumenical work on peace emerge now and then. Despite the differing assessments of the situation, and despite all the disparate points of view, the conference has been successful in reflecting common understanding and respect. The church and its youth today need this understanding and the close connections most urgently.

---

[10.] On July 31, 1932, the sixth parliamentary elections took place. The National Socialist Party (NSDAP) had received a surprising electoral percentage of 18.3 percent in the previous parliamentary election (September 14, 1930), and it was now able on July 31, 1932, to expand this percentage significantly to 37.3 percent.

[11.] After February 1932, the German Christians (*Deutsche Christen*) in Berlin were supported by Wilhelm Kube, *Gauleiter* [effectively, the governor—VB] of the Mark province and chair of the National Socialist faction in the Prussian parliament. On June 2, 1932, the German Christians made their views public for the first time with the publication of their new "Guidelines of the German Christians" (cf. Scholder, *Churches and the Third Reich*, 1:189–216). [The "Guidelines" were approved in May 1932; a subsequent, slightly revised version (The "German Christian Principles") appeared in May 1933, after the Nazis came to power and in advance of the July 1933 church elections. See also *DBWE* 12:372, ed. note 4.—VB]

## 17. Address in Gland[1] 350

Address at the International Youth Conference in Gland
on August 29, 1932

Dear Friends,

"The Church is dead," a serious German man said to me recently; "what else can you do but prepare with all your zeal, all your earnestness and pathos for its honorable funeral?" The dead one does not speak, does not defend itself—a wreath of blooming flowers, which covers up and disguises the decay, that is all. Are all the doings of our Christian church, at home and here as well, particularly insofar as they are done seriously, and flourish, anything other than the winding of flowers into funeral wreathes, anything other than the intonation of a festively solemn requiem for the dead? Are not, after all, perhaps all our conferences born out of an abysmal fear that it is actually[2] too late to repair out of desperation what is no longer reparable? Has not each of us at this conference, in all seriousness, lived through hours in which this fear simply overcame him and did not let go—namely, that it is too late, that it is all over with Christ's church,[3] and that all our actions here are only to make the farewell easier for us and to delude us about reality and thus to lead us gradually into another kind of life. I ask you upon your honor and conscience, friends: who among you are unfamiliar with the fear that everything that we undertake here as actions of the church could be too late, meaningless, even frivolous? And if one of you here wished emphatically to protest that he had never thought this, that
he had never doubted in the church, then perhaps he should ask himself 351
whether he ever really believed in the church.

Faith in the living church of Christ only breaks through where one sees most clearly the death of the church in the world, the process of an ever-new collapse, where one for this reason knows that the world, if it is honest, can say nothing other than: "the church is dead," that the world can view our actions here as nothing other than the preparation for the funeral—and where one now hears, in defiance of all that is contrary, opposed, and

[1.] *NL*, A 34,8; typewritten. Previously published in *GS* 1:162–70. Bonhoeffer gave this address on August 29, 1932, in Gland, on Lake Geneva, to an international youth conference that met August 25–31, 1932, arranged together by Life and Work and the World Alliance for Promoting International Friendship through the Churches. Originally, Bishop Ammundsen was scheduled for the Monday evening session on the theme "Spiritual Summing Up: Message of the World Alliance." On the conference in Gland, see 1/15 and 1/61.

[2.] The word appears twice in the typescript.

[3.] See pp. 451–52.

hostile, how the New Testament proclaims life to the dying man and how in the cross of Christ death and life collide, and how life swallows up death—only where one sees this does one believe in the church beneath the cross. Only with clear eyes on reality, without any illusion about our morality or our culture, can one believe. Otherwise, our faith becomes illusion. The believer can be neither a pessimist nor an optimist. Both are illusory. The believer does not see reality in a particular light but rather sees it as it is and believes against everything and beyond everything that he sees *solely in God* and God's power. He does not believe in the world, not even in a world capable of development and improvement. He does not believe in his world-improving power and his goodwill. He does not believe in humanity or in the human good that must finally triumph. He does not believe in the church in its human power, but rather the believer believes solely in God, the God who creates and does the impossible, the God who creates life out of death, the God who has called the dying church into life against and despite us and through us, the God who alone does this.

The faithless world speaks: The church is dead. Let us celebrate its funeral with speeches and conferences and resolutions, which do it every honor.

The faithless world full of pious illusion speaks: The church is not dead; it is only weak, and we will serve it with all our strength and help it rise up again. Goodwill alone does this, so let us create a new morality.

The believer speaks: The church lives in the midst of dying, solely because
352 God calls it forth out of death into life, because God does the impossible against us and through us—we all want to speak like this.

What does this have to do with our conference?

We are here not as individuals who are interested in this or that problem. We are not here as advocates of special interests. We are also here not as world reformers but rather as those who have heard a voice in the midst of all their daily activities, as those who despite all the noise and clamor hear again and again, who have been awakened out of sleep and who, still half asleep or half awake, suspect, even know that something great is astir. Perhaps we are even here as the servants of whom the Lord Jesus Christ speaks, who are on guard, peering out into the night and waiting until the Lord comes.[4] It is really night that they see, but they really wait because they

[4.] See Matt. 24:43–51 and especially Luke 12:35–40. Bonhoeffer had preached on this text on November 29, 1931 (see 3/2). [Bonhoeffer delivered his first sermon on this text as a student in Sunday school; cf. *DBWE* 9:502–9. The editors thank Hans Pfeifer for this reference.—VB]

know that the Lord is surely coming. No one knows how long these servants have to keep watch. . . . Perhaps they remain on guard even today, perhaps here among us. We are not a purely functional organization of church business but rather a distinct form of the church itself. We are the community of those who are startled by the signs of the time, who in the midst of the terrors of the night have heard a penetrating call from one whom they know: it is the Lord, but is he coming to help or to judge? The World Alliance has become the anxious church of Christ, which has become terrified and sensitive, made fearful by the anxiety of the world, and calling upon its Lord.

Indeed, in everything we say and do, it is a matter of nothing more than Christ and his honor among human beings. One should certainly not think that it is about our own business, about a particular outlook on the world, a particular theology, or even only about the honor of the church. It is about Christ and nothing else. Let Christ be Christ.

We come together in order to hear Christ! Have we heard him? I can only ask here. Each of us must answer for himself. Yet I still want to say this:
is it not precisely the sense of these meetings, that where we encounter a 353
person who appears so totally strange and incomprehensible to us in his concerns and who still claims our attention, that there we hear the voice of Christ, in the voice of the brother, and that there we do not withdraw from this voice but rather take it completely seriously, hear it, and love the other precisely in his foreign nature? This is how Christ encounters us at such conferences, in that brethren encounter one another in all openness and truthfulness and need and ask to be heard by the others. Not as the community of those who know but rather as the community of those who are looking for the words of their Lord and look everywhere to see whether they might hear it, not as the knowledgeable, but as those who are seeking; we are here as the[5] starving ones, the waiting ones, as the needy, the hopeful, and so are we bound together. We encounter Christ in the brother,[6] the German in the Englishman, the Frenchman in the German.

And should a few among us now have to say honestly: we have heard nothing, and should others perhaps just as honestly have to say: we have heard infinitely much—so let me express over against both groups a great apprehension that has forced itself upon me during the entire conference, with increasing gravity: has it not become terribly clear, again and again, in all that we have discussed with one another here, that we are no longer obedient to the Bible? We prefer our own thoughts to those of the Bible. We no

[5.] This word appears twice in the typescript.

[6.] See 2/9, pp. 317–18.

longer read the Bible seriously. We read it no longer against ourselves but only for ourselves. If this entire conference is to have had a great meaning, it would perhaps be to show us that we must read the Bible in an entirely different way by the time we meet again.

The World Alliance is the community of those who want to hear the Lord as they anxiously cry to the Lord in the world on earth, in the night, and do not flee from the world, but rather want to hear the call of Christ obediently in faith within it, and know that through this call they are responsible to the world. It is not the world-reforming dimension of activity in the church
354 that has become weary of meditating on God's word, but rather it is the church, which knows about the sinfulness of the world and of Christianity, that awaits all the best from God and wants to be obedient to this God in the world.

Why is the community of brothers in the church of Christ, as it appears in the World Alliance, afraid? Because it knows about the commandment to peace, and yet with the clear gaze given to the church, it sees a reality governed by hate, by hostility, by violence. It is as though all the powers of the earth had sworn themselves against peace; money, the economy, the drive to power, yes, even love for the fatherland—all have been pulled into the service of hate, the hatred of the peoples, the hate of compatriots toward their own compatriots.

Already the situation is terribly aflame here and there—what else are the events in the Far East[7] or in South America[8] other than the proof that all human ties are being torn asunder as nothing, that there is[9] no longer any dread of anything, where the passion of hate is nourished and breaks out?

Things are coming to a crisis more horribly than ever before—*millions of starving people*[10] whose wishes have been put off or unfulfilled, desperate people who have nothing to lose but their lives and who with their lives lose nothing—*humiliated and degraded nations*, who are not able to recover from

[7.] This refers to war between China and Japan. On February 18, 1932, Japan completed the establishment of the Manchu state as a satellite state under its protection, i.e., Manchuria, which had previously belonged to China and whose former head of state, the last Chinese emperor, had fled China. In August 1932, the League of Nations condemned the Japanese occupation of Manchuria.

[8.] In March 1932, the so-called Chaco War broke out between Bolivia and Paraguay over the area of Gran Chaco. It lasted until 1935. In the Peace Treaty of Buenos Aires on July 21, 1938, Bolivia lost most of the Chaco Forest that it had claimed.

[9.] "There is" appears twice in the typescript.

[10.] On Bonhoeffer's frequently repeated theme in 1932 of "hunger," see the German editor's afterword to this volume, p. 478.

their dishonor[11]—*political extremes against political extremes,*[12] *fanaticized against fanaticized,* false gods against false gods—and behind all this, a world bristling with weapons[13] as never before, a world that is feverishly mobilizing for war, in order to guarantee peace through armaments, a world whose false gods have become the word "security," "*sécurité*"[14]—a world without sacrifice, full of distrust and suspicion, because it still feels the terrors of the past in its bones—a humanity that trembles before its very self, a humanity that is not sure of itself and that is ready at any time to do violence unto itself—how can one close one's eyes here to the fact that the demons themselves have taken control of the world, that it is the forces of darkness that here gruesomely conspire and can burst forth at any moment—how can one think that, with a little bit of education toward international understanding and a bit of "good will,"[15] these demons can be exorcized, these forces can be banished? How could it not be blasphemous flippancy to think that the call: no more war! and a new organization—even a Christian organization—could inhibit the devil? Nothing, such organizations are nothing at all, like a house of cards blown away in a whirlwind . . . nothing, our well-meant intentions, our speeches about peace and "good will" are nothing at all, unless the Lord himself comes and casts out the demons. What are so-called international attempts at reconciliation, all these attempts to understand one another, all so-called international friendship—as necessary as they are in themselves—in light of this reality? 355

Christ must again become present among us in preaching and sacrament, just as Christ as the crucified one made peace with God and humanity. The crucified Christ is our peace.[16] Christ alone adjures the false gods and the demons. Only before the cross does the world tremble, not before us.

And now the cross places us in the midst of a world that has gone haywire. Christ is not distant from the world or in an otherworldly dimension 356
of our existence. Christ went into the deepest depths of the world; his cross

[11.] The main reference here is to Germany, where an unrestrained and intransigent nationalism spread largely due to the defeat in the First World War and the humiliation of the obligation for high reparation payments and the declaration of Germany's exclusive guilt for the war in Article 231 of the Versailles treaty (see 2/16, ed. note 4).

[12.] In the seventh parliamentary elections on the July 31, 1932, about four weeks before Bonhoeffer's address in Gland, the extreme anti–Weimar Republic parties, the National Socialist and Communist parties, together received 51.6 percent of the vote.

[13.] See 2/1.

[14.] See also Bonhoeffer's warnings at the meeting of the ecumenical council and the World Alliance in Fanø two years later (*DBWE* 13:309).

[15.] ["Good will" in English in the original.]

[16.] Cf. Eph. 2:14.

is in the midst of the world. And now this cross of Christ calls forth wrath and judgment upon the world and proclaims peace. Today there should no longer be war—the cross does not want it. One must make a distinction: in the world that has fallen away from God, struggle is inevitable, but there should be no war.[17] War in its present-day form lays waste to God's creation and obscures the view of revelation. As little as one can justify torture as a means of justice out of the necessity for justice, one can just as little justify war as a means of strife out of the necessity of strife.[18] The church forsakes obedience whenever it sanctions war. The church of Christ stands against war in favor of peace among the peoples, between nations, classes, and races.

However, the church also knows that there is no peace unless justice and truth are preserved. A peace that violates justice and truth is no peace, and the church of Christ must protest against such peace. There can be a peace that is worse than struggle. Yet it must be a struggle out of love for another, a battle that comes from the spirit, not from the flesh.

With the proclamation of peace, however, the church imparts the message of a new humanity, of the holy fellowship [Bruderschaft] in Christ. Yet this fellowship is founded on the peace that Christ on the cross has brought into the world—the community of those chosen by God, of the humble who stand beneath the cross, of the watchful, the faithful, the obedient, and the community of those to whom God desires to be merciful. That is the new fellowship. Certainly this is something quite different than an international friendship on the basis of the old world . . . brethren in the hearing of the word of the *Lord* . . . of the utterly radical, this is the great commission. It[19] is not those who are so overzealously admirable but rather—tax collectors and prostitutes will sooner enter the kingdom of heaven than these[20]—
357 the community of those who repent and carry their guilt of not hearing the commandments of God as they should, even though the kingdom of heaven is near. No visible government [Staat] of God is established in this world, not even if there were to be international understanding everywhere. Everything that the church does here is temporary, solely intended to hold the collapsing orders of the world together, in order to protect them from suddenly falling in chaos. This action of the church is essential, but the new order of society and community is not the order of the kingdom.[21]

---

[17.] See pp. 367 and 371.

[18.] See pp. 366–67 and 371.

[19.] Namely, the new fellowship of believers.

[20.] See Matt. 21:31.

[21.] [I.e., of God.—VB]

All order and all community in the world will have to die away when God creates his world anew and the Lord Christ comes again to judge the old world and establish the new. In this world, there is peace only in the struggle for truth and justice;[22] in the other, however, there will be the eternal peace of God's love. That is the new earth and the new heaven that God himself will create.[23] And because we believe that we shall at some time be there together in this kingdom, we should all love one another here in our diversity.

It was a turning point in the world's history when one night Paul was overwhelmed by a vision in which he saw the Macedonian figure, the European, who bid him: come over here and help us.[24] And Paul was ready and went. For the second time, the call goes out to us, to the church. Europe calls a second time: come and help us. Europe, the world wants to be won over a second time by Christ. Are we ready?

## 18. Initial Report on the Youth Conferences of the World Alliance[1] 358

Youth Conferences of the World Alliance

At the beginning of July, corresponding to the English-French regional conference that was reported in the last issue,[2] *the German-French regional conference at the Westerburg*[3] took place on the smallest possible scale. This conference must be described as perhaps the most successful in recent years, which is due most likely to the deliberate limit placed on the[4] number of participants. The theme, "The Unity of German-French Protestantism between Catholicism and Bolshevism," proved to be fortunate, because it generally linked theological reflection with concrete and particular questions. Well in advance, theses and reports were prepared and in part exchanged. In the evenings, the questions of German and French nationalism were discussed.[5] The intensive engagement within these small groups

[22.] See pp. 365–66 and 371.

[23.] See Isa. 65:17 and 66:22.

[24.] See Acts 16:9–10.

[1.] *Die Eiche* 20 (1932): 365–67. Previously published in *GS* 1:171–74. Cf. the cover letter to the editor of *Die Eiche*, Prof. Friedrich Siegmund-Schultze (1/73) and 2/19.

[2.] See 2/11.

[3.] On July 12–14, 1932 (see 1/35, 1/47, and 1/55) [italics in original—MBL].

[4.] In the handwritten draft, "deliberate limit placed on the" replaces "small."

[5.] See Bonhoeffer's draft program in 1/47.

was an incomparable opportunity for sharing information. But beyond that, the discussion brought to light real issues, particularly the Catholic problem.[6] It appeared that the threat of Catholicism to French and German Protestantism is perceived by each at very different points, and for that reason the assessment and analysis of Catholicism will be of a very different nature for each. For everyone involved, this led to a truly new understanding of the structure of French and German Protestantism and a new grasp of the possibilities for cooperation. Just as informative was the distinction between French and German nationalism and the realization
359 that in each case the analysis of it had to take a very different course. The problem of National Socialism naturally also stood here at the very center of concern. Again and again, we Germans must encounter the strict and uncomprehending condemnation of it at these conferences emphatically, by noting that it is the politics of other nations that has to bear the greatest degree of responsibility for National Socialism in its present form.[7] For that reason, it is appropriate not to pass judgment here irresponsibly but rather to take this matter more seriously as one's own responsibility. The continuation of this work is planned for next year. The question of the revision of the treaty[8] was set[9] as one of the main possible themes. In the meantime, the work that appears to us as so full of hope will be kept up in small circles through correspondence.

---

[6.] Deleted in the handwritten draft: "in Germany and France."

[7.] The June 28, 1919, Treaty of Versailles declared that Germany bore the sole guilt for the First World War (see 2/16, ed. note 4) and established the prolonged, albeit reduced, reparation demands of the victorious powers on Germany, as well as the rearmament politics of the Western powers that at the same time strictly limited the possibilities of German rearmament. [Bonhoeffer made similar comments in speeches about German attitudes in New York during his year there as a student; cf. *DBWE* 10, 2/9.—VB]

[8.] This primarily concerns the Versailles treaty with its strict limitation on German armaments and the final agreements over the reparations to be paid by Germany under the so-called Young Plan, which had finally been adopted by the German parliament on March 12, 1930. [The Young Plan was a proposal (prior to the Wall Street crash of 1929) of an international commission led by the American banker Owen Young to revise the German reparations required by the Treaty of Versailles. The plan significantly reduced the ruinous annual payment level but at the price of extending the payments by fifty-nine years (until 1988). This was approved by the Hague Conference in 1930. The plan evoked a furious reaction and attack from the German right-wing parties, especially from the German National Peoples Party and the National Socialists, against the Weimar Republic and its leadership, principally Gustav Stresemann. Bonhoeffer had spoken at length about these issues in his lecture on "War" during his time as a student in New York in 1930; cf. *DBWE* 10, 2/9, esp. p. 416.—MBL]

[9.] Another German-French youth conference did not take place in 1933.

For the first time, the Central Committee of the *Czechoslovakian church* had sent out invitations for a youth peace conference on July 20–30 in *Ciernohorské Kúpele.*[10] In particular, the World Alliance member groups were approached. Representatives and speakers from England, France, America, Germany, and southern European countries were present. This undertaking must be welcomed with extraordinary gratitude. The entire event was organized not strictly as a conference but more as an international retreat. Accordingly, those of us who didn't know Czech had certain language difficulties; furthermore, there was a very wide range of themes, and the discussion never really showed any coherence. Everyone knows that certain dangers are inherent in such an event. It would perhaps be useful to sepa- 360
rate conference and retreat more strictly. We experienced most gratefully the great hospitality of our Czech friends, and we fervently hope that the cooperative work will continue to be promoted.

The *International Youth Assembly*, following upon last year's Cambridge youth conference[11] of the World Alliance, took place August 24–30[12] in *Gland,*[13] this time together with the youth commission of Stockholm.[14] There were about sixty participants from Europe, America, and the Far East. The major lectures were given by the bishop of Ripon,[15] Mr. Tait,[16] B. I. T.,[17] Baron von Haan,[18] Pastor Lauga,[19] Paris, C. F. Andrews,[20]

[10.] See 2/14, ed. note 1.

[11.] See 2/1.

[12.] The departure was scheduled for August 31. As an added excursion, the participants had the opportunity to visit the League of Nations in Geneva as well as the International Labor Office.

[13.] See 1/15, 1/61, and 1/71.

[14.] See 2/13, ed. note 16. See also the report of E. A. Burroughs ("International Friendship: A Hopeful Conference") that appeared in the *Yorkshire Post* on September 27, 1932. The following information about the course of the youth conference in Gland can be found in the "Minutes of Meeting of the Youth Commission of the World Alliance for International Friendship through the Churches held in London on Monday, April 4th, 1932," WCC Archives, Geneva.

[15.] Burroughs's lecture title was "Repent Ye, for the Kingdom of Heaven Is at Hand."

[16.] Tait spoke on the topic "Unemployment."

[17.] The Bureau International du Travail, or International Labor Office.

[18.] Baron von Haan spoke on the theme "The Present Economic System, or What?"

[19.] The topic of his lecture was "Spiritual Summing Up: Message of Stockholm." See 2/13, ed. note 16.

[20.] Andrews's theme was "Religious Message."

the friend of Gandhi, who to our particular joy participated in the entire conference, Prof. André Philip, Prof. Piccard, Assessor Meyer,[21] Lic. Bonhoeffer.[22] The first day was devoted to the general theme: "The Call of
361 Christianity in the Present Crisis."[23] With a reflection on the Christian meaning of our work, this was to lay the foundation for the days to follow. As might have been expected, however, it turned out that this could not be a topic for one day; rather, the entire conference stood fundamentally beneath this topic. For each individual question (such as unemployment, the meaning of work, human and machine), all the internal conflict within our fundamental position broke out anew. It became clear that the old theological school question about the concept of the kingdom of God in Continental and Anglo-Saxon theology here has an extraordinarily relevant character even now.[24] The position on the questions of the following

[21.] Philip, Piccard, and Meyer each spoke on the theme "The Way Out of the Present Political Chaos." Meyer was said to have taken the German nationalist position on this.

[22.] Besides Zernoff and Toureille, Bonhoeffer held an opening address on the theme "The Christian Call in the Present Situation." The saying that was the theme of Bonhoeffer's unpreserved address was the biblical passage often cited by him in these years (see 3/8, esp. ed. note 1): "We do not know what to do, but our eyes are on you" (2 Chron. 20:12). His audience, including Bishop E. A. Burroughs, found this address pessimistic (according to a September 9, 1932, newspaper report on the conference for the *Yorkshire Post*). On Bonhoeffer's address on August 29, 1932, see 2/17, especially ed. note 1.

[23.] See ed. notes 14 and 22 above.

[24.] The report of one working group formulates the contrast that is important for Bonhoeffer's position within the ecumenical movement: "We found through discussion of this important point—what we mean by the Kingdom of God—that there were two distinct views of it" [statement in the original, unaltered English—MBL]. The one opinion voiced in the report assumes that the kingdom of God exists in three forms: first, in the person of Jesus, second, within the struggle between Christ and the Antichrist, in the form of the good part of the human being, and, third, in relation to a worldwide catastrophe. The second opinion in this report refers to a firmly held understanding of the kingdom of God as that which begins in the present world and develops to the extent that we would accept the spirit of Jesus and allow our personal life to be changed through him. "In so far as our lives reveal the spirit of Jesus to that extent we have already established the Kingdom" (Report of English Discussion Group, WCC Archives, Geneva) [statement in the original, unaltered English—MBL].

days: "The Economic Crisis" and "The International Crisis," about which some ten[25] correspondents from different nations spoke briefly in addition to those making presentations, was in the end achieved out of this fundamental position. This time, in addition to the acknowledgment of the enormous difficulties of the debate, another difficulty emerged quite forcefully, namely, that on all sides a much stronger obedience toward biblical 362
thinking must be demanded. Yet in view of all that, there was also a great deal here that proved to be a convincing experience for many: that the church alone can be the foundation on which the international discussion, otherwise so dubious, can be conducted openly and objectively.[26] In turn, for many it was overwhelming to listen to the other who is so different, to see and simply allow him first of all just to be as he is, and from that perspective then to rediscover themselves. Without any doubt, there was utter seriousness behind this entire effort, and there is an intense urgency not to make out of these conferences another kind of craft. One wants to go much deeper than before, admittedly without knowing how and where. For that reason, the recommendation of a resolution or an official message,[27] introduced by the Anglo-Saxons, was once again vehemently rejected. It seemed clearly symbolic of something that no one wanted. This very early work should not be burdened in such an unseemly way right at the beginning. One has to be able to wait. To learn to wait—this is probably the most decisive discovery, particularly for these large international youth meetings, which are actually much more difficult to conduct and for that reason are probably less useful at present for the cause than the regional conferences. Learn to wait: this is what we shouted in Gland in all kinds of ways to our all too action-happy friends. Learn to wait—the entire youth work of the World Alliance shouts to the older generation, who probably look at these activities of the youth with some concern and impatience. Learn to wait!

[25.] Deleted in the handwritten draft: "young."

[26.] See p. 386.

[27.] Deleted in the handwritten draft: "to the youth of the church."

363 **19. Second Report on the Youth Conferences of the World Alliance**[1]

October 29, 1932

Church, Youth,[2] Peace.
On the Youth Meetings of the World Alliance for Promoting International Friendship through the Churches[3]

From a preeminently "neutral" place over against the political resurgence, namely, from the perspective of a correctly understood Christian church, a group of young people from every social class and vocation, still small but with its gaze steadfastly on its goal, is trying to get a clear view of the political reality of the present international situation, in order to assess and evaluate it in a way that is appropriate. The World Alliance for Promoting International Friendship through the Churches, founded on August 2, 1914, in Constance, created a youth group at its international meeting in Cambridge in 1931. The group got on its own feet immediately[4] and has begun independent work.[5] In the course of one year, there have been four international meetings of church youth. In September 1931 in Cambridge, one of the meetings took place with about sixty delegates from numerous European countries and from America.[6] In March and July 1932, there was a small English-French[7] and a German-French regional gathering,[8]
364 and then on August 24–30, another large international conference took place in Gland[9] with youth from almost all European countries, as well as from the Orthodox Church, from America, and from the Far East. For the

[1.] *NL*, A 34,7 b(2); carbon copy. Previously published in *GS* 1:175–78. The first side includes the following letterhead: "Lecturer Dr. Dietrich Bonhoeffer. Protestant Student Chaplain at the Technical College Charlottenburg. Berlin-Grunewald. Wangenheimstr. 14." Cf. *NL*, A 34,7 (a); handwritten draft. Attached to the draft is a draft letter to the editors of the *Tägliche Rundschau* (see 1/90). It could not be established whether this was published in the *Tägliche Rundschau*.

[2.] Originally listed as "Youth, Church."

[3.] In the handwritten outline the subtitle "On the Youth Meetings of the World Alliance . . ." replaces "The Work on the Problem of International Peace."

[4.] In the text, the word "objectively" (*sachlich*) erroneously stands here. Cf. in the outline: "immediately" (*sogleich*). In the typed version, the words "objectively" and "immediately" are written on top of each other.

[5.] See 2/1.

[6.] See 2/1.

[7.] On April 5–8, 1932, in Epsom.

[8.] On July 12–14, 1932, at the Westerburg.

[9.] See 1/15, 1/61, and 2/17.

lectures about special questions, leading scholars and practitioners in the fields of economics and politics from various countries were brought in. C. F. Andrews, the friend of Gandhi, participated with great interest in the entire meeting. The Roman Catholic Church is keeping its distance from this work.[10]

¶The fundamental theme of all these meetings is the question about the position and contribution of the Christian churches to international peace. The enormous diversity of the views expressed here is held together by a fundamental precondition that unites all the participants, namely, that these themes can be addressed objectively, that is, neutrally and responsibly,[11] solely on the foundation of the Christian church. It is only on the foundation of the church that one can speak openly and frankly. Thus, this work that we also call the "ecumenical work of the church" is in no way a matter that can be considered partisan; rather it is a concern of alarmed young Christians who have become keen listeners. They see how the basis of international discussions breaks down again and again and recognize now that only the church, correctly understood, can be the unshakable foundation[12] for this highly difficult and ever-more dubious conversation. And for those who have worked together at these meetings, it has now become a convincing experience that this underlying recognition was correct. In the German delegation, as in the others, we have had people who are closely connected to entirely different political groups, and yet the dialogue did not fall apart.

It had to be the task of the meetings in the first year to discover the general foundation of our common work anew. The themes[13] therefore had to become widely diversified, such as "Are There Christian Principles for State, Economic, and Social Life, and Can They Be Realized?" "The Call 365
and Responsibility of Christianity in the Present Crisis," and "The Unity of

[10.] [Although there were a number of significant pioneering efforts in the later nineteenth and early twentieth centuries (e.g., Malines Conversations of 1921–25; Franciscan Friars and Sisters of the Society of the Atonement), officially Catholicism rejected ecumenism as part of the threat of modernity (Pius IX, *Syllabus of Errors*, 1864). Pope Pius XI, in his encyclical *Mortalium Animos* (1928), specifically condemned ecumenical relations with Protestantism as a modernist error, prompted by doctrinal compromise and concession to the validity of independent churches over against the sole validity and authority of the Roman Catholic Church. This policy was reversed in the "Decree on Ecumenism" (1964) at the Second Vatican Council.—MBL]

[11.] In the draft, the words "and openly" are deleted.

[12.] In the draft, "the unshakable foundation" replaces "as a church in the world."

[13.] On the respective presentations, see pp. 383–84.

German-French Protestantism and the Problem of Catholicism and Bolshevism." Then more narrowly: "The Capitalistic Economic System" and "Unemployment." But the predominance of such general questions did not signify any escape into principles out of fear of concrete questions; rather it reflected awareness of the instability of all discussion about particulars where the only possible direction of all responsible questions and talk had not become clear beforehand. It was really a serious initial effort being made by young people from all over the world to bring about a Christian sense of international work for peace. If much has been achieved at these meetings, it is first the insight into the unbelievable difficulty and urgency of this kind of attempt by the Christian churches, then an ever-more decisive and serious grasp of the viewpoint of the other and a sharper limit on one's own viewpoint, and at the same time perhaps a somewhat clearer, less murky view with fewer illusions about the actual international condition today. It was often not easy, over against an Anglo-Saxon group pleased by activities and resolutions, to come to terms with these matters in a sober manner. Yet it was voted unanimously every time, or with an overwhelming majority, not to burden this existing work at such an early stage immediately with great resolutions, but rather to recognize in full and objective modesty the provisional character of the work up to now. And in their very resistance against the attempt to mask "clairvoyance"[14] right away with another "organization of goodwill,"[15] the Germans found their closest friends in this matter in the Continental delegates, especially the French. In these encounters, this huge gap between Continental and Anglo-Saxon thinking,[16] which largely determines our contemporary world and philosophical dilemma, becomes visible in a special way before our very eyes. But it is
366 now precisely this posture of hostility toward resolutions that impedes the course of this initial work in wider circles.

Yet perhaps there are some people today who have reached the point where they can have more confidence in an incredible work in this direction than in the pleophoristic language of resolutions. This work will have to be done in a Christian way, with the complete seriousness and all the consequences that the word encompasses, so that all who come together here know the full weight of the biblical commandment of peace, which makes the work simultaneously sure, pressing, difficult, modest, and time-consuming.

---

[14.] "Clairvoyance" in English in the original; Bonhoeffer means clear-sightedness.

[15.] ["Organization of goodwill" in English in the original.—MBL]

[16.] See p. 385.

For the next year, along with the basic theme of the German-French regional conference around which a special student circle has already formed, a second theme, that of revising the treaty,[17] has been set.[18] Already this year the World Alliance has spoken about this with all the requisite clarity. The fact that we encounter one another on the foundation of the church makes an ultimate openness possible that otherwise could not be conceivable at any international conference. This should be kept in mind by all those who, presumably out of political considerations that could not possibly be gone into here, believe they must reject this work of the church.[19] Everything here depends precisely on the neutrality in partisan terms of this work of the church. Only when understood in this way will the work of the church one day be taken very seriously.

---

[17.] The Treaty of Versailles. See 2/18, ed. notes 7 and 8.

[18.] This meeting did not take place, presumably because of the rapid political developments in Germany after the National Socialists took power.

[19.] See as an example the sharp criticism by Paul Althaus and Emanuel Hirsch of the German ecumenists (2/1, ed. note 2).

# E. Short Studies

## 1932

### 20. Review of C. Cordes, *Der Gemeinschaftsbegriff*[1] 367

Review of Cord Cordes, *Der Gemeinschaftsbegriff im deutschen Katholizismus und Protestantismus der Gegenwart*[2] (Leipzig, 1931)

Several typical phenomena are selected from contemporary Catholicism and Protestantism that appear suitable for illustrating the difference between the Catholic and the Protestant concept of community. (1. traditional Catholicism, 2. the People's Association for Catholic Germany [Volksverein für das katholische Deutschland],[3] 3. R. Guardini;[4] in

[1.] *Theologische Literaturzeitung* 57 (1932): 255–56. Cf. *NL*, A 35,3. Published in *GS* 3:132–33. Cord Cordes wrote this dissertation at the suggestion of philosopher Theodor Litt.

[2.] [The concept of community in contemporary German Catholicism and Protestantism.]

[3.] The Volksverein für das katholische Deutschland (Peoples' Association for Catholic Germany) was founded in 1890 by the industrialist Franz Brandts as well as the theologian and sociopolitical theorist Franz Hitze, with the support of the politician Ludwig Windthorst. The aim of the Peoples' Association was to preserve the religiously based social ethos of the old Christian-social orientation and the organic conception of the *Volksgemeinschaft* ("the community of the people" [by the early 1930s this phrase already had an ethnic and nationalist connotation—VB]), and to improve the vocational and moral education of the working classes.

[4.] Cordes draws from the following writings of Romano Guardini: *Der Gegensatz* (1925), *The Spirit of the Liturgy* (1918), *Vom Sinn der Kirche* (1922), *Liturgische Bildung* (1923).

contrast to 1. the Theology of Crisis,[5] 2. Stange,[6] 3. Heitmann,[7] 4. Gutmann).[8] In a most concise form, a clear, generally intelligible picture of these is presented. One can hardly expect that the theology of crisis is done
368 complete justice in a work this brief. Further, the fundamental work done here by Gogarten[9] should not simply be ignored. In the second part,[10] the described types become comprehensible in terms of their confession and are worked through in terms of their novelty and particularity. For the concept of community in the People's Association [Volksverein] and in Guardini, the interest in the community characteristically appears to have priority over that of the institution, whereby *communio sanctorum*[11] is understood nontraditionally as the community among the members of the church on earth; furthermore, one sees here even more distinctly the spiritual [geistig] dimension of human sociality. In Protestantism, "the experience of war" is supposed to have brought about a decisive change.[12] For this, Althaus,[13] the theology of crisis,[14] and Heitmann's approach[15] are

[5.] This refers to the group of theologians that from the beginning of the 1920s rallied around Karl Barth, Friedrich Gogarten, and Ernst Thurneysen and emphasized the inaccessibility of God, in critical distinction from the mediating attempts of the dominant liberal and theological positions that delineated and supported mainstream convictions in Protestant churches of that period, as well as a theological foundation oriented to biblical revelation.

[6.] Cordes cites two works by Erich Stange: *Die kommende Kirche*, 3rd ed. (1925), and *Volkskirche als Organismus* (1928).

[7.] Ludwig Heitmann was among the leaders of the Berneuchen movement and was one of the principal authors of the *Berneuchener Buch*. [This was a church reform movement that began in 1922; on Bonhoeffer's criticism of it, see *DBWE* 8:430, ed. note 34. —VB]

[8.] Cordes particularly discusses Gutmann, *Gemeindeaufbau aus dem Evangelium*.

[9.] Following up on Eberhard Grisebach, Gogarten had interpreted history as an encounter between I and You and expanded the conception that the claim of God engages human beings in the claim of the other (see Gogarten, *Ich glaube an den dreieinigen Gott*). At the end of the 1920s, to an increasing degree, the claim of the peoples' community (*Volksgemeinschaft*) or the state replaced it (see Gogarten, *Wider die Ächtung der Autorität* and *Politische Ethik*).

[10.] Cf. Cordes, *Gemeinschaftsbegriff*, 41–60: section II.A.

[11.] "Communion of saints."

[12.] Cf. Cordes, *Gemeinschaftsbegriff*, 53–56.

[13.] Cordes cites Paul Althaus's work *Das Erlebnis der Kirche*, which first appeared in 1919 (*Gemeinschaftsbegriff*, 52).

[14.] Cordes discusses only two works of Karl Barth: *The Epistle to the Romans* (2nd ed., 1922) and *Die christliche Dogmatik*.

[15.] Cordes draws from Heitmann, *Vom Werden der neuen Gemeinde*.

cited. The problem of organization is seen as having received a new stimulus as well. This would certainly have been the place to assess and critique the contemporary concepts of community in terms of Luther's concept of the church.[16] That would have brought more systematic clarity about what an essential Christian community actually is, that is, "where community is spoken of today with appropriate objectivity."[17] Finally, in the third section the systematic classification into confessional dogmatics follows.[18] 369
The confessional contrast is formulated as that of a differing concept of grace. The Catholic concept of grace as supernatural is supposed to lead directly to the institutional concept, while the Protestant concept of grace, "over which no earthly authority disposes,"[19] supposedly leads to the concept of community. If one knew here how this notion of community is to be understood conceptually, then the derivation of the concept of grace would be considerably more illuminating than it is here. The lack of truly systematic clarification about the concept of community probably also concerns the fact that there is almost no reference to the systematic-theological debate about the concept of community, the reference instead being to church "movements." With respect to this, then, the title of the book certainly seems to be too broadly conceived. Interestingly, the author also exemplifies his view of confessional differences by juxtaposing Guardini and Heitmann with the People's Association and Gutmann. This study concludes with a brief overview of the confessionally determined position toward social order outside the church;[20] in its brevity and lucidity it is a welcome and nice introduction to the current problematic situation.

Berlin Dietrich Bonhoeffer

[16.] Bonhoeffer's ecclesiology was influenced to a great degree by Luther's emphasis on the idea of community in the sermons from 1519, especially in the "Sermon on the Most Esteemed Sacrament of the Sacred and Real Body of Christ and on the Brotherly Community" (*WA* 2:742–58) (see also 2/9, section IV). Cordes refers to Luther's 1519 sermon on the Lord's Supper only in a footnote (*Gemeinschaftsbegriff*, 60).

[17.] Cordes, *Gemeinschaftsbegriff*, 1.

[18.] Ibid., 61–66: section II.B.

[19.] Ibid., 63. Bonhoeffer in this citation has changed the order of the words.

[20.] See the heading "Schluß: Bedeutung der dargestellten Gemeinschaftsideen im kirchlichen Leben and für wissenschaftliche Forschung" [Conclusion: Significance of the proposed ideas on community in church life and for scholarly research] (Cordes, *Gemeinschaftsbegriff*, 67). See also 67–69.

## 21. Literary Attempt on the Theme of "Vocation"[1]

One day in the last form,[2] when the master asked him what he wanted to
370 study, he quietly answered "theology" and flushed. The word slipped out so quickly that he did not even stand up; having the teacher's gaze and that of the whole class directed at him personally and not at his always excellent work performance, and being suddenly called upon to speak out like this, gave him such conflicting feelings of vanity and humility that the interruption of ordinary class conduct seemed an appropriate expression of the consternation caused by the question and the answer. The master obviously thought so, too, for he rested his gaze on him for only a moment longer than usual and then quickly and amiably released him. He was nearly as disconcerted as his pupil.[3] "In that case you have more surprises coming," he said, speaking just as quietly.

Actually the question, "How long?" had been on his lips but, as if that would have touched on the secret of his own early study of theology, passionately begun and then quickly abandoned, and also because he felt displeased with himself at having nothing better to say to a boy whom he had known and liked for a long time, he grew embarrassed, cleared his throat, and went back to the Greek text that was the subject of the lesson.

¶The boy absorbed that brief moment deep into himself. Something extraordinary had happened,[4] and he deeply enjoyed this and, at the same time, felt ashamed. Now they all knew. Now they had to hear it, hear it in silence, now he had told them all, now the riddle of his life was to be resolved, now he stood solemnly in the presence of his God, in the presence of his class, now he was the center of attention. . . . Did he look as he had wanted to look, serious and determined? Did his looks leave a positive impression? He wondered briefly whether the part in his dark blond hair effectively emphasized the impression of his sincere conviction, and he was filled with an unusual sense of well-being at the thought, though he immediately drove it away by visualizing the greatness of his confession and his task. Nor did it escape him in this moment of complete awareness

[1.] *NL*, A 32,7 (a); handwritten draft without date or title. Based on the type of paper that is used and the handwriting, the date is around 1932. Previously published in *GS* 6:229–32. Cf. *NL*, A 32,7 (b); typewritten transcript from Eberhard Bethge. With the exception of a few revisions, the translation here is from *DB-ER*, 40–41. See also *DB-ER*, 202–7.

[2.] [The German is *Prima*, which refers to the last year in the German gymnasium school, generally the final two years.—MBL]

[3.] "Disconcerted" replaces "embarrassed."

[4.] "Something extraordinary had happened" replaces "had the feeling, he was something complete."

that his teacher had been somewhat embarrassed by him and, at the same time, had looked at him with approval.[5] The moment swelled into endless pleasure, the classroom expanded into the infinite, he stood in the center of the world as the herald and teacher of his knowledge and his ideals, now they all had to listen to him in silence, and the blessing of the Eternal[6] rested on his words[7] and on his parted dark blond head. And again he felt ashamed. For he knew about his pitiful vanity. How often he had tried to master it. But it always crept back, and now it spoiled even the pleasure of this moment. Oh, how well he knew himself at the age of seventeen, he knew all about himself and his weaknesses, and he also knew that he knew himself well, and in the turmoil of his knowledge his deep vanity again forced its way into his soul and alarmed him. 371

¶It had made a tremendous impression on him when he had read in Schiller that human beings needed only to rid themselves of a few small weaknesses to be like the gods.[8] Since then he had been on the watch. It occurred to him that there was no doubt that he would emerge as the hero from this struggle; he had just made a solemn vow to do so. Now the path that he had known he must follow,[9] since the age of fourteen, was clearly marked out for him.[10] But what if he failed, what if the struggle proved vain, what if he was not strong enough to see it through . . .

¶The words "You have more surprises coming" suddenly rang in his ears; surprises about what, what could happen, what did this voice mean? What was the meaning of the curious, mistrustful, bored, disappointed, mocking eyes of his classmates? Didn't they think him capable of it, did they not believe in the sincerity of his intentions, did they know something about him that he did not know himself?

¶Why are you all looking at me like that? Why are you embarrassed, 372
sir, what sort of incomprehensible drivel are you mumbling? Look away from me, boys, for heaven's sake, denounce me as a mendacious, conceited person, Master, who does not believe what he says, but don't keep so considerately silent, as if you understood me. Laugh aloud at me, all of you,

[5.] "And, at the same time, had looked at him with approval" replaces "had scarcely [looked at] him."

[6.] "Of the Eternal" replaces "of eternity."

[7.] "His words" replaces "him."

[8.] See, for example, Schiller's poem "Das Glück," in *Schillers Werke* 1:409–11. ["Glück" means "happiness" or "fortune." An English translation of the poem can be found in Merivale, *Minor Poems of Schiller*, 137–40.—VB]

[9.] "Now the path that he had known he must follow" replaces "now he would set it up."

[10.] "Was" replaces "must be."

make noise, noise, don't be so abominably dumb—it's intolerable. There is the throng, he stands in the midst of it and speaks, speaks, fervently, passionately, his features . . . his dark blond hair, his ideal hopes—he corrects himself—a leaden silence lies over the throng, a dreadful, silent mockery. No, it cannot be, he is not the man they take him to be, he really is in earnest. They have no right to scorn me, they are unjust to me, unjust . . . all of you . . . he prays . . . God, say yourself whether I am in earnest about you, destroy me this very moment if I am lying, or punish them all; they are my enemies, and yours, they do not believe me, I know myself I am not good. But I know it myself—and you, God, know it too. . . . I do not need the others . . . I, I . . . I shall triumph. . . . Do you see how I triumph, how they feel astonished, how they retreat, their consternation. . . .[11] I am with you. . . . I am strong. . . . God, I am with you.

¶Do you hear me? Or do you not? To whom am I speaking? To myself, to you, or to those others here? Who is it that is speaking?[12] My faith? My vanity. . . . God. . . . I want to study theology. Yes, I have said so, and they all heard it; there is no more retreat. I wish to, I wish to . . . but if . . .

And just as the commotion turns to something new, all he hears is the teacher's voice from a distance—no one else could have spoken in the meantime—: "Aren't you feeling well? You don't look well." He pulls himself together, stands up, and as usual translates the difficult Greek text without error. Somewhat confused but full of pride, the teacher looks at the boy.

373 Next morning, he had his first sleepless night behind him.[13]

### 22. Literary Attempt on the Theme of "Death"[1]

He liked thinking about death. Even in his boyhood he had enjoyed[2] imagining himself on his deathbed, surrounded by all those who loved him, speaking his last words to them. Secretly he had[3] often thought about

[11.] [In the original text, there is an additional phrase here: "How they . . . [illegible word] . . ."—MBL]

[12.] "Who is it that is speaking" replaces "what do I say."

[13.] [This final sentence was not included in *DB-ER*.—MBL]

[1.] *NL*, A 32,8; handwritten draft, without date or title. Dated around 1932 on the basis of the paper that was used and the signature. Previously published in *GS* 6:232–33. Cf. *DB-ER*, 38–39 and 204–5. [Translation here, with some revisions, from *DB-ER*. —MBL]

[2.] "he had enjoyed" replaces "he had loved it for a very long time."

[3.] "Secretly" inserted.

what[4] he would say at that moment. To him death was neither grievous nor alien. He would gladly have died young, a beautiful and pious death.[5]

¶He would have liked them all to see and understand that to a believer in God, dying was not hard but a glorious thing. In the evening, when he went to bed overtired, he sometimes thought that it was going to happen. A slight sense of dizziness often alarmed him so much that he furiously bit his tongue, to make sure that he was alive and felt pain. Then in his ignorance he cried out to God, asking to be granted a deferment. These experiences confused him to some extent. For obviously he did not want to die; he was a coward; his theatrical ideas nauseated him. And yet[6] in moments of strength, he often prayed that God might after all[7] release him, for he was ready to die; it was only his animal nature that again and again made him contemptible in his own eyes, that led him astray from himself.

¶Then one day he had a grotesque idea. He believed himself to be suffering from the only incurable illness that existed, namely, a crazy and irremediable fear of death. The thought that he would really have to die one day had such a grip on him that he faced this inevitable prospect with speechless fear. And there was no one who could free him from this[8] illness, because in reality it was no illness but the most natural and obvious 374
thing in the world, because it was the most inevitable. He saw himself going from one person to another feeling stunned, pleading and appealing for help. Doctors shook their heads and could do nothing for him. His illness was that he saw reality for what it was; it was incurable. He could tolerate the thought for only a few moments. From that day on, he buried inside himself something about which for a long time he did not speak or think again. His favorite subject for discussion and for his imagination had suddenly acquired a bitter taste. He spoke no more about fine, devout death and forgot about it.

[4.] Deleted: "that which."

[5.] [This sentence was inadvertently omitted from *DB-ER*, although it is in the German edition of the biography.—VB]

[6.] Three illegible words deleted here.

[7.] Illegible word deleted.

[8.] Illegible word deleted.

# PART 3
# Sermons and Meditations

## 1. Sermon on Psalm 63:3, Berlin, Thanksgiving Sunday, October 4, 1931 (?)[1] 377

Ps. 63:3[4]: Your steadfast love is better than life.[2]

It is two and a half thousand years ago that, far from home, consumed by suffering in body and soul, surrounded by mocking doubters and enemies of his God, the pious old Jewish man thinks back over the strange paths on which God is taking him. It is not a comfortable, peaceful contemplation, but a struggle, a struggle of near desperation[3]—about life and its meaning, about God and his faithfulness. The pillars of[4] life have begun to crumble; the hand reaching out, believing it will find a firm handhold, grasps at empty nothingness. God, where are you? God, who are you? God, who am I? My life is falling to pieces, falling into a bottomless void. God, I am afraid. Where is your loving-kindness now? But you are my God, and your steadfast love is better than my life.

This is one of those Bible passages that never lets go of anyone who has once understood it. A passage that only seems to be shining so gently, but on the inside is hard and flashes out fire,[5] a word of strong emotion, evoked when two worlds collide, the world of human beings and the world of God,[6] that is, a word from the world of the Bible and not from our world. Your steadfast love is better than life: That is the shout of joy of the suffering and abandoned, the weary and the heavy laden; the cry of longing of the sick and oppressed; the song of praise[7] of the unemployed[8] and the hungry in the cities of millions;[9] the prayer of thanks of the tax collectors and prostitutes, of the public and private sinners. But is it really? No, it

---

[1.] *NL*, A 33,1 (a); handwritten draft; notation by Eberhard Bethge: "Thanksgiving, October 4, 1931? Evening Service." Previously published in *PAM* 1:228–37. Cf. *NL*, A 33,1 (b); later typewritten transcription, with handwritten editorial changes by Eberhard Bethge; previously published in *GS* 4:17–25. [In the German Bible, this verse is Ps. 63:4.—MB]

[2.] [The Hebrew word *chesed*, translated as *Güte* in the biblical text used by Bonhoeffer and as "steadfast love" in the NRSV, is often translated as "loving-kindness." When *Güte* is translated in the form of Ps. 63:3, we have used the NRSV translation "steadfast love." Elsewhere we have consistently rendered it as "loving-kindness."—MB]

[3.] Crossed out: "refusal to do what God wants."

[4.] "Of" replaces "of his."

[5.] "Only seems to be shining so gently, but on the inside is hard and flashes out fire" replaces "A word with the gleam of a pearl and the hardness and the fire of a diamond."

[6.] Crossed out: "a word full of strong emotion."

[7.] "Of the unemployed" replaces "of the masses."

[8.] Crossed out: "and lame."

[9.] Concerning references to hunger and unemployment in the large cities that recur frequently in the years 1931–32, see the editor's afterword to the German edition, p. 477.

378 is not, at least not in our world, in our time. But it is for the strange world of the Bible, which once again startles and annoys us with all its foreignness, to the extent that we still even listen to this biblical word and our sensitivity to the reality of the Bible has not become completely dulled. Or does this passage perhaps not seem so strange to us? Do we think, perhaps, that it is actually something we can take for granted and we could actually not learn much of anything new from it? That for a Christian these things have already become second nature? Well, then, let's have a look at it to see what our psalmist is actually saying here and whether that is indeed something that is so self-evident to us.

Once, in the life of our psalmist, something crucial had happened. God himself had stepped into his life. And since then his life has been completely different. I don't mean that he suddenly became good and pious—it may be that he was even better and more pious long before. But now God himself had come to him, and just that God was always there now and he could not get away from him anymore, that was what made his life so significantly different now. It tore his life right down the middle. We so often hear and say that religion makes people happy and harmonious and calm and content. That may be right about religion.[10] For God himself, the living God, it is not true, but the very opposite. And that is how it now affects the life of our psalmist. Something within him has been ripped open. He feels divided within himself. A battle begins to rage within him and becomes more heated and terrible every day. He experiences how with each passing hour more and more of that which he had loved is torn away. He fights for it; he would like to keep it. But God, who of course is always standing there before him, wrestles it away from him and does not give it back. And now the more he loses, the harder and more greedily he tries to hold on to whatever he still has, but the tighter he holds on to these possessions, the harder God must strike at him and the greater the pain when they are torn
379 away.[11] And so it continues in breathless wrestling, God winning and the human being suffering defeat. He doesn't know where this will lead. He sees himself as lost. He doesn't know whether he hates or loves the One who broke into his life so violently and disturbed his peace.[12] He fights hard for every inch. In despair he yields to the weapons of God. And all of this would not even be so hopeless for him if these weapons were not so wonderful and unique that they strike down and yet raise up, that they wound and yet heal,

[10.] On the critical assessment of "religion" in the years 1931–32, see 2/9, pp. 307–9; 3/7, pp. 432–33; and 3/11, pp. 455–56.

[11.] "When they are torn away" replaces "when they are lost."

[12.] "Disturbed his peace" replaces "destroyed his life."

that they kill and yet bring to life. God speaks: If you want my mercy, let me triumph over you. If you want my life,[13] let me hate and destroy your evil. If you want my loving-kindness, let me take your life. And now his life is at stake. Everything has been given away; the human being has been able to keep only one thing. And he wants to hold on to it, his life. But God cannot halt the battle; he attacks this last fortification. And the battle rages for all that is left. The human being defends himself like a madman. God cannot want that. He cannot want to take the only thing I have left. God is not cruel. God is kind. And he is given the answer: If you want my loving-kindness, give me the last thing you have, your life. Choose!

We get dizzy at these heights. We feel as if someone had led us to the outer limits of the world and we were looking down into a black abyss and someone said to us: Now, jump! We feel torn on the inside: To have to choose between God's loving-kindness and our life. What is our life? Everything we see, hold, hear, taste, feel; everything around us, what we own, what we are used to, what we love. What is God's loving-kindness? Certainly everything we cannot see, cannot hold, cannot understand,[14] what we can hardly even believe; certainly something we cannot own, something completely unlikely, otherworldly, standing above and behind everything that happens and yet so close by and speaking to us so earnestly.[15] Who would want to dare to make that choice freely? God himself has won the battle, and it seems like something humanly impossible when we hear now from 380
the lips of the psalmist: God, you are my God. Your steadfast love is better than life.

Now it may be that there are some among us who have become a little angry[16] and would like to object: What kind of excited and exaggerated things are being talked about here? That is not how you are supposed to talk about God's loving-kindness. That I am in good health, that my family and I still have enough to eat and drink, that I have work and a place to live, that is God's loving-kindness to me. But I don't know or understand anything about this battle with God's loving-kindness. It is certainly good if this objection is expressed. That gives us an opportunity to delve more deeply into the matter.

Dear Congregation, it is Thanksgiving Sunday today and probably the right moment to think very hard about what the loving-kindness of God

[13.] "Life" replaces "loving-kindness [*Güte*]."

[14.] [In the German there is a wordplay between *greifen* (hold) and *begreifen* (understand).—MB]

[15.] "Earnestly" replaces "urgently."

[16.] "Have become [a little angry]" replaces "are thinking."

means for us. Untouched by the torment of worries and the unrest in these times, nature continues to work outside in the world. It produces food to nourish the peoples [of the] earth. If it holds back, millions die, and if it gives bounteously, humankind thrives. No human being has power over nature. And a human being keeps still in the presence of its might and feels small and remembers the One who does have power over nature. But we celebrate this Thanksgiving Sunday today under special circumstances and with special concerns in mind. The harvest did not bring us what we had hoped for. Every hour of rain in August and September meant hours of hunger[17] and want for children and adults in the coming winter. Sometimes that has cut into our hearts. Along with that comes one of the most terrible plagues that can affect a people and that has now spread throughout the whole world, unemployment.[18] We have to expect that in the winter seven million people in Germany will be unable to find work; that means hunger will grip fifteen to twenty million people next winter, another twelve million or more in England, twenty or more in America. About sixteen million
381 are starving now in China, and it is not much better in India. Those are the bare figures and behind them stands the most gruesome reality. Should we pass that by when we celebrate Thanksgiving Sunday in church? We must not do that, but instead [we] want to measure our Christian thought and our will against these facts and sharpen and deepen them.

When we sit down tonight at the table that has been set for us and remember God's steadfast love and kindness, we will feel strange. We will be overwhelmed by the unbelievable fact that it is we who have been given such gifts. And we will remember that there is nothing, nothing at all that has made us deserve these gifts from God more than our hungry brothers[19] in our city. Let's imagine that just at the moment when we are thanking God for his loving-kindness toward us, the doorbell rings, as it happens so often now, and someone is standing there who probably would also like to thank God for the smallest gifts but who has been denied these gifts and with his children goes to bed hungry and embittered. What becomes of our prayer of thanks at such a moment? Will we want to say that God is gracious to us and angry with him? Or that the fact that we still have something to eat proves that we have achieved an especially privileged position with God? God feeds his favorite children and lets the rejected ones go hungry? May our gracious God protect us from the terrible temptation of such thoughts and this kind of gratitude. May he lead us to the right understanding of

[17.] See the editor's afterword to the German edition, p. 477.

[18.] See the editor's afterword to the German edition, p. 477.

[19.] Crossed out: "[. . . three illegible words]."

his loving-kindness. Do we not see that the gifts of his loving-kindness will become a curse to us if we have such thoughts and act on that basis?[20] If we look at ourselves instead of looking at the incomprehensibility of God and the suffering of our neighbor and becoming completely humble and aware of the immeasurable responsibility in which God's loving-kindness places us? If we want to understand God's loving-kindness in God's gifts to us,[21] we must see them as responsibility for our brother.[22] No one should say:
God has blessed me with money and possessions, and then live now as if he 382
and his loving God were alone in the world.[23] Then the hour will come when he [must] see that he has worshipped the false god of his own happiness and selfishness. The blessing and the loving-kindness of God are not possessions but responsibility.

But with this we are on the way to a deeper understanding of what God's steadfast love and kindness are. Whoever has been placed by God in a position of responsibility sees himself placed in a position between two worlds: the world of God and the world of his neighbor. From God he hears the words: If you want my loving-kindness to stay with you, serve your neighbor, for in him God himself meets you. And he sees the physical and spiritual suffering of his neighbor, which have now become his responsibility. And now the battle we have just heard about from our psalmist plays itself out. If you want my mercy,[24] give your neighbor some of what you have. If you want my love,[25] give your soul to your neighbor. If you want my loving-kindness, risk your life for your neighbor. If you do not do all of this, then everything that up to now has been God's loving-kindness to you—what you have for your body, your soul, your life—changes to become a curse upon you. And who of us would want to say that they have done all of this? That they really understood the loving-kindness of God in their own thinking and especially in their own actions? It is already a great deal if we have understood that God's loving-kindness leads us into a battle; that it is not something we receive and then simply have and own, so that we can go on

[20.] Crossed out: "Don't we see that it is the loving-kindness of God that he gives us his gift of being responsible to him, not the gifts." [German edition does not have a question mark here.—MB]

[21.] "To understand God's loving-kindness in God's gifts to us" replaces "to receive God's gifts to us as God's loving-kindness."

[22.] "We must see them as responsibility for our brother" replaces "we must forget ourselves, worship God."

[23.] Crossed out: "Possessions in themselves are not a blessing and not the loving-kindness of God, but a responsibility."

[24.] "Mercy" replaces "love."

[25.] "Love" replaces "mercy."

living, a little happier, a little richer, but essentially unchanged. But how little passion do we show as we go into this battle and how much fear, weakness,[26] hesitancy, sadness. And how little this battle affects the root of our whole existence. And yet—we do not understand this battle at all if we do [not] see it as totally radical. Your steadfast love is better than life—that means not only better than your house, than your comfort, than your food, than your work, than your honor, your reputation, than your physical
383 or musical and intellectual pleasures, than your wife and your children, it means even more than that. It is better than what you have left after you have lost all of that: than your life. Who among us has had even once the experience of God's loving-kindness bringing us into a conflict concerning the physical aspect of our life? Much less concerning our work, much less concerning our honor, much less concerning our family? Who today still lets himself be led by God into such conflicts and who still sees God's loving-kindness in such conflicts? And, finally, who sees at all that God's loving-kindness cannot be understood unless the conflict goes even deeper and attacks our life and reaches beyond it?

Let's take an example.[27] There are two human beings who love each other, and one asks the other: "Tell me how great your love for me is, how much my love is worth to you." And the other answers: "For your love I would give up all my possessions." "Is that all?" "For your love [I] would give up all of my joy and [my] happiness." "Is that all?"[28] "For your love I would sacrifice [my] reputation and my honor." "Is that the last?" "For your love I would leave my brothers, family, and friends. Oh, if I only have you . . . For your love I would give everything, everything, everything." "Even the very last thing that you still have? Will you give that up for my love?" "You mean, would I give up my life for your love? What an impossible contradiction. How can I enjoy your love without my life? Don't require that of me—and yet, your love is more, your love is better than my life."

Who would hesitate to look up in awe at the greatness and strength of such words? Who would not be proud that human beings are capable of such words? But is there a Christian who would not have to recoil in shock[29] in his innermost being when he makes the great comparison we are thinking about just now?[30] How is it that human passion can do so

[26.] "Weakness" replaces "how weak."

[27.] Crossed out: "from our life"; had originally replaced "from daily life."

[28.] "All" replaces "the last thing."

[29.] "Would not have to recoil in shock" replaces "would not with great astonishment."

[30.] "We are thinking about just now" replaces "with what is most important to him." Crossed out following this: "human passion can do unbelievably much."

unbelievably much in the battle for the beloved human being, but when it is 384
a question of God's love, where something completely different is at stake, we fail so totally? Look how that lover is happily willing to put his happiness, his honor, his life at risk for the one he loves, how he is constantly thinking of something new that he can sacrifice for his love, [how] no price seems [to him] too high to pay to have that other human being's love. And then look at how meager our thoughts and actions for God's love are in comparison, when we think that with a couple of coins in the offering, with a somewhat pleasant expression and a peace-loving attitude we have done enough for God's love. Why is it so dead and barren for us and so full of life for those others? Why does our fire die out right at the beginning but burns for them in full blaze? Is that Christian life? Is that the life of Jesus Christ that has been portrayed to us? O God, because we don't know you anymore, because we do not seek you anymore, because we no longer know what madness it is to live and not to think of you, you who stand at the beginning and the end of our life and hold judgment over us in eternity! Because we no longer look at God's love in the life of Jesus Christ and let ourselves be shaken up by it into new life. Because we are so attached to ourselves and want to be completely self-reliant, because we cannot believe that it is God alone who can truly support and carry us and give our life eternal meaning, even if it appears smashed to pieces. But that means because we have sinned against the honor and love due only to God, because we have become guilty before him. God gives us responsibility, and we fail in it because we are more attached to ourselves and believe more in ourselves than in God. God asks us how much his love is worth to us, and we answer him: certainly less than our own. In doing this we banish God's loving-kindness from our life.

But now the greatest miracle known to the world happens. Where we have fallen away from God, where we have become dead and unreceptive to God in our guilt, that is where God's loving-kindness follows us and reveals itself to us anew as the eternal promise of God in Jesus Christ, beyond all guilt and beyond all life. Only one who in the depths of the darkness of
guilt, of disloyalty, of enmity toward God has felt touched by the love[31] 385
that never ends, that forgives all and points the way beyond all suffering into the eternal world of God,[32] knows truly and completely what God's loving-kindness is.

But, of course, we are not removed from life. We still have responsibility, and again and again God asks us anew: What is my love worth to you?

[31.] "By the love" replaces "by the light."

[32.] Crossed out: "only here in the suffering of guilt do we also learn why God's loving-kindness is not only more than, but better than life."

But the more deeply we recognize what God's loving-kindness is,[33] the more filled with life our answer will be. Again and again, we are led anew by God's loving-kindness to take responsibility and through our guilt[34] led to God. When will we get to the point that at least in the Christian community the world of our psalmist breaks in,[35] that in happiness and suffering, in hunger and sickness, in fear and in worry, in sadness and in deepest guilt, in times of good and in times of poor harvest, we can rejoice anew in true harvest thanksgiving: "Were they to take our house, goods, honor, child, or spouse, Though life be wrenched away, they cannot win the day. The kingdom's ours forever!"[36] God, your steadfast love is better than life. Amen.

### 2. Sermon on Luke 12:35–40, Berlin, First Sunday in Advent, November 29, 1931[1]

Luke 12:35–40: Be dressed for action and have your lamps lit; be like those who are waiting for their master to return from the wedding banquet, so that they may open the door for him as soon as he comes and knocks. Blessed are those slaves whom the master finds alert when he comes; truly I tell you, he will fasten his belt and have them sit down to eat, and he will come and serve them. If he comes during the middle of the night, or near dawn, and finds them so, blessed are those slaves.

386 But know this: if the owner of the house had known at what hour the thief was coming, he would not have let his house be broken into. You also must be ready, for the Son of Man is coming at an unexpected hour.

A blessing [Seligpreisung][2] stands at the center of our story: "Blessed are those slaves whom the master finds alert when he comes." It's like this,

[33.] "Loving-kindness [*Güte*]" replaces "love [*Liebe*]."

[34.] Crossed out: "and so he goes ahead of us on our way toward the scene that is set up before us, as we ever more willingly love God's loving-kindness itself and as we recognize ever more deeply that it is his loving-kindness alone that."

[35.] "Breaks in" replaces "comes to life."

[36.] Verse 4 from the hymn by Martin Luther "Ein feste Burg ist unser Gott," in *Evangelisches Gesangbuch*, no. 362 [English translation: "A Mighty Fortress Is Our God" in *Evangelical Lutheran Worship*, no. 504—MB].

[1.] *NL*, A 33,2 (a); handwritten draft; previously published in *PAM* 1:237–46. Cf. *NL*, A 33,2 (b); later typewritten copy with notation by Eberhard Bethge: "Advent sermon 1931?" and handwritten editorial changes by Eberhard Bethge. Previously published in *GS* 4:26–33.

[2.] [*Seligpreisung* also means "beatitude."—MB]

isn't it: If in the face of what we see of the world with our own eyes, sometimes the world of the Bible, the world of Christ, falls apart completely for us—and to whom would that not happen?—then for us today there often remains only one thing that we feel to be the great justification for all our Christian thinking and effort: the blessings that[3] Christ speaks over all humankind. We use these to give us fresh courage when nothing else holds anymore. These words cannot have been spoken into nothingness.[4] How much Christ must have loved human beings, that[5] he[6] can say such things about them![7]

But the unique thing is this: he is not speaking about a person who fights and achieves his ideal, about a wrestling, striving person; instead, he sees the person as already having been taken fully into God's peace, already completely free of conflict, sin, and death. So he sees him here already under the power of the kingdom in which the souls[8] that have triumphed are blessed. But because Jesus sees the person in this way, we stand there, when Jesus speaks his blessing, as the unblessed—outside, on the sidelines, far away. That is why we know that he is not speaking of us, at least not insofar as we are the human beings we really are today, but instead that human beings are seen here from a completely different perspective, namely, as the people they can never be by their own power, as those over whom God's eternal peace and eternal salvation have already been spread, as people who have been completely overpowered by the coming of the new heaven and the new earth, that is, as people in the perspective of God's[9] future in
which the suffering, fighting, dying God of human history reveals himself 387
as the First and the Last, to whom the victory belongs right from the beginning. And because Christ knows of this future through his mysterious eternal knowledge, that is why he gives the human being this blessing, blessed as one over whom God will come at that future time and who already today lives completely from this coming, from being overpowered by God, blessed as the one waiting, blessed as the one who is waiting and alert. Be like those who are waiting for their master. Blessed are those slaves whom the master finds alert when he comes.

---

[3.] Crossed out: "Jesus."

[4.] "These words cannot have been spoken into nothingness" replaces "This great call, which shows the human being here."

[5.] Written above, without text crossed out: "if [*wenn*]."

[6.] Crossed out: "to him."

[7.] Crossed out: "He has with this [. . . three illegible words]."

[8.] "The souls" replaces "his [. . . one illegible word]."

[9.] Crossed out: "Because even if we are confused by God's action in the present and in the past, one thing must be certain if by God we really mean God, namely, that the

We find ourselves in an age of worldviews. Seldom—maybe never—has a period in history been so filled, moved, and divided by worldviews as ours. How one dresses, what one eats, how one exercises have already become a question of worldview. And seldom has one been as committed, as doctrinaire, as intolerant in matters of worldview as today. Now, naturally, one can smile at all these phenomena and withdraw haughtily as if it were beneath one's dignity. And yet this kind of smile is not good. One shows that one has not understood what these seemingly very strange things are all about. And it is doubtless one single great theme around which all our thinking in the matter of worldview revolves. And that is the human being of the future.[10] Wherever we stand on the question of worldview, one thing has probably become clear to all of us during the most recent events in world history:[11] that we are standing now at a turning point,[12] which obviously the human being of today, as he actually is, is unable to handle. Technology and the
388 economy have become automatic powers that threaten to destroy human beings. They set themselves up on high, and their demons have become the gods of our time. Involvement in great conflicts between nations [Völker] drives nations to their downfall,[13] and yet no one seems to be powerful enough to prevent this fate. When an artist tries to give expression to what

ultimate future belongs to God, that the suffering, struggling, dying God of our human history will then reveal himself to all the world with complete certainty as the one who triumphs, the final one, as the one to whom the victory has long belonged. That is why he sees a person as the one of the future. But in this it depends not on the person's future but on the future of God."

[10.] See Friedrich Nietzsche's version of a human being of the future in his work written in 1883–85, *Thus Spoke Zarathustra.*

[11.] The war between Japan and China (see p. 165, ed. note 4) and the world economic crisis following the New York stock market crash of October 1929; Bonhoeffer may also mean the First World War.

[12.] [The German here reads "*Wende der Zeiten,*" literally, "turning point of the times."—VB]

[13.] Since 1929, nationalism and militarism had been gaining more and more ground in Germany and other countries, first recognizable in the steep rise in votes for the National Socialists in the Reichstag elections on September 14, 1930. See also the conflict between Japan and China. [This is a striking passage, given the rhetoric of the National Socialist movement in the early 1930s and its emphasis on both the destiny of the German people (*Volk*) and what Nazism viewed as the necessity and inevitability of struggles between peoples. Particularly in his book, *Mein Kampf,* Hitler stated his belief that the destinies of the nations lay in their struggle with one another and that only the dominant "master races" would triumph. There was also a great deal of rhetoric about the need for a "new" kind of human being and what that would be like. Bonhoeffer here is describing the "new human being" of this new ideology and then countering it in the following paragraph with how the ideal human being is understood from a biblical perspective.—VB]

is going on around him, shrill, unresolved harmonies in music and painting are the result.[14] And the religions, too, have been unable to take even one step beyond this situation. And in the recognition of this defeat of the human being faced by this reality, one great hope arises for a new kind of human being, for a new birth, for the human being of the future. Whether one thinks of this human being as a political person, as an ethical person, an intellectual person, a religious person, as a combative or peace-loving person, it's all basically only[15] the one great anxiety about the human being of the future. The human being should not be driven into ruin. He should hold his own. The powers of reality should not crush him underfoot and enslave him. He should remain master of the world, master of the future. And because that is what people want, that is why they are working so feverishly to shape a new human being [Neugestaltung]. For the clouds of the future are very dark, and no one knows when and how the storm will break loose.

And now it seems as if, in this attempt to create a new kind of human being, the Bible also wants to have a word to say, as if it definitely sets up its own ideal of the human being who should go out to meet the future. It
is not the political, not the ethical, not even the religious person of whom 389
the Bible speaks, but the person who is waiting and watching, the waiting person.[16] For that is obviously what our text is saying. That is the meaning of this scene that Jesus paints before our eyes: night has fallen across the countryside. But there is a house from which light shines out into the night. Several men, with their swords at their belts and lamps in their hands, are looking out of the house across the dark countryside. They seem to be waiting. They are slaves awaiting the return of their master from the wedding, who fight off sleep and keep watch in joyful excitement to be able to open the door immediately for the master when he comes. No one knows the hour when he will come. But they know that he is coming, and that is why they are alert and watchful in the night. How long did they keep watch? No one knows—it may be that they are still keeping watch today among us. And

---

[14.] See especially the work of composer Arnold Schoenberg. In it the functional harmony that had dominated classical-romantic music lost importance. The early atonal works, since 1908–9, are considered the musical equivalent of expressionist painting, in which an attempt was made to establish the sole importance of inner content rather than external, academic form. The work of art was intended not to provide aesthetic pleasure but to elicit an emotional response and allow it to be experienced.

[15.] "Ethical person, an intellectual person, a religious person, as a combative or peace-loving person, it's all basically only" replaces "the combative, the peace-loving, or the intellectual person, the person of reason, that is, all of that is basically only."

[16.] "The waiting person" replaces "for his master."

now Jesus calls these slaves blessed and says to the disciples: so be like the slaves who are waiting for their master. You be ready, too! Be people who are waiting.

Do we still need to be told that today? Wouldn't we have to say instead: if it were only a matter of waiting, then we all would be called blessed? What else is our present life other than a constant waiting for change, for improvement? If ever a generation had to learn to wait, it is ours. We wait for better political[17] conditions,[18] for a better economy.[19] We wait for a contract. We wait for work.[20] We wait for a new morality, for a new religion. We wait, but—as it is with all waiting—with trepidation. For who knows if what we are waiting for will ever happen? Will things possibly turn out com-
390 pletely different? And because we don't know, we have to be prepared for such disappointments.[21] We can't let ourselves be thrown off balance by them. We must stand firm.

But for this reason, all our waiting also includes something of resignation.[22] Our most fervent hopes, our wishes are always paralyzed already deep inside,[23] because deep inside we have to be prepared for their remaining unfulfilled. Of course, we don't want to be unreasonable. And after all, it would be unreasonable to count on something in the future as if it were already here, to expect it so strongly, to wait and to hope for it so confidently that our whole life falls apart if it then does not come. But that is why our reasonable waiting is a tortured waiting, an unhappy[24] conflict caused by trying to grab it all, wanting to have something but not wanting to give up anything for it, of imagining into the future and yet clinging to the present, looking forward eagerly to something but yet always anticipating an unsuccessful end. And we probably sense that Christ did not call this kind of waiting blessed, that such waiting is not the waiting of Advent.

[17.] Crossed out: "economic."

[18.] The last phase of the Weimar Republic, from 1929 onward, was marked by strong growth of extreme parties opposed to the republic and a loss of authority of the various governments supported by the parties of the center (see Bracher, *Die Auflösung der Weimarer Republik*).

[19.] The New York stock market crash of October 1929 and the ensuing world economic crisis hit Germany, which continued to have to pay reparations to the victorious powers of World War I, especially hard. In this situation, especially, the deflationary policy of the Brüning government could not produce rapid economic recovery.

[20.] In the years 1929 to 1932, the number of employed persons in Germany dropped from 18.4 million to 12.9 million.

[21.] "Prepared for" replaces "prepare [. . . five illegible words]."

[22.] Crossed out "[. . . four illegible words]."

[23.] Crossed out: "You must not let yourself go; you can't do everything at one time."

[24.] Crossed out: "Waiting, as long as the blessing of Christ is not spoken."

But if through all this reasonable waiting, and beyond it, there is something else in us waiting, and if this waiting reaches beyond anything that we can expect so reasonably; if there is a completely unquenchable longing that, when everything is fulfilled, does not keep still or, when everything fails, only protests the more strongly; if there is a waiting in us that is oriented toward nothing else and nothing less than that the world be helped completely, not only by this or that means, but completely, as it is; that is, if something in us is waiting for the most unthinkable itself, namely, that God himself would come to us, then Advent could begin for us. If through all this questioning, trying, feeling our way, and waiting, we in confusion suddenly realize the terrible narrowness of our existence with all its wishes; if we are suddenly afraid that we with all our being are lost and 391
left to meaninglessness and if then the cry is wrung from us: O that you would tear open the heavens and come down . . . ,[25] then perhaps we could know something about what the Bible calls "waiting." If in the long night we become anxious so that we light our lamps and look out into the night to see if the master will not want to come soon; if among us human beings once again such hopes begin to stir, when such signs and miracles come to pass,[26] then it may not be long before Jesus's words of blessing come back to human beings with power, so that we hear as from a distance the voice of him who speaks to us: Behold! I am standing at the door, knocking.[27] And blessed are the slaves whom the master finds keeping watch. And then we will really be waiting.

Of course, that is a different waiting than our usual waiting. We are, of course, waiting for something different, completely different, for God. And of course, we can't wait for God thinking to ourselves: it would be nice if God came, but if he doesn't come, I'll just have to go on living without him. We can't wait for God with such resignation, such moderation,[28] so reasonably, as if we were waiting for a pay raise. No, it is an unreasonable, immoderate waiting, if a person is really thinking of God; if he really does not want to be satisfied with what is offered to him today from a thousand different directions as a substitute for God, but rather just keeps waiting, longing, reaching out, hoping, until finally it is God himself who comes, who helps, who consoles.[29]

---

[25.] See Isa. 64:1.

[26.] See 2 Cor. 12:12.

[27.] See Rev. 3:20.

[28.] Crossed out: "so fearful."

[29.] Crossed out: "But how can one wait for God except in this unreasonable way, by giving oneself up unconditionally, making his life depend on this one thing, whether or

Then his waiting and hoping is not just a little nostalgic fantasizing, which only makes his suffering even greater; it is his life itself. Then he only wants to live because he can wait for God. Then there are no more reservations for him, as there are for the one who is waiting in a reasonable
392 way and for reasonable things. Then he steps outside himself. Or rather, he sees himself torn out of his waiting to this point, in which he only wanted himself to survive, and dragged into a strange, overpowering, wonderful process that happens completely without any action on his part and draws near[30] to the time of God, to God's future, to his coming to this earth. Then the future becomes living reality, then he will already live today in the shadow of that which is to come, not just any threatening failure or fate, but the coming of the God of justice, of love, and of peace. It is not that he can self-confidently take the path into the future to God; no, he receives the future from God. He knows that he cannot go to God, but that God must come to him, come over him in his incomprehensible mercy, if his life is not to be lost, if he is not to have waited in vain. He can do nothing but wait, wait alertly, that is, passionately, completely taken up with it, deaf to anyone who would confuse him with doubts, blind to any power that would step between him and that future of God's. He only cares about one thing: he wants to see God. He wants to hear God. [He] wants to recognize God. He wants to know God. [He] wants to serve God. Hard as it is to understand, he does not want anything else, at least nothing else as much as he wants God.

Now, of course, our living securely from one day to the next is over. God could suddenly come in and speak his true word about our life. We can protect ourselves from other people, from fate, but no one can protect himself from the living God. Fame ends. Palaces and crowns fall. A person stands before his Creator and Judge, who has come to him overnight. Did God find him sleeping or keeping watch alertly? That is the question here.[31] It's no use referring to one's office or rank, one's reasonableness or prudence. All hope is gone—then, finally, all eyes are directed to God, waiting and
393 putting all hope in his hands. But that is why the blessing of the waiting and watching slave is the death sentence for all confident, secure living, for

---

not the waiting is fulfilled. To anyone who waits in a reasonable way and for reasonable things, it must seem to be madness for someone to really be waiting for God, to the exclusion of all else, with such tenacity."

[30.] Crossed out: "Tears away from him."

[31.] "That is the question here" replaces "[. . . three illegible words]."

all desperate attempts to keep one's life safe,[32] for all fears of the future because it threatens the secure life, for all rushing around and trying desperately to make one's life secure, for all-too-much caution. The waiting person expects everything, everything from God. He expects God himself and makes room for him; he wants nothing for himself, everything for God. Only the one who is waiting is open, ready. Only he can enter from Advent into Christmas. Blessed are those who are waiting.

We can't help asking: Who today can manage to wait this way, to live into the future as if it were the present, to live from God as if he were more certain than my own life? No one other than the one who knows that the God who is coming has already come long before, that the same God who entered into the midst of history invisibly, silently, in Jesus Christ, is the First and will be the Last. God has come. This alone is why we can wait for him to come again and again, and for him one day to come for the last time, no longer clothed in the mantle of history, of suffering and of death, but visible to all the world as Judge and Redeemer at the end of time. God has come; that is why we are waiting. But because his first coming remains a mystery to the world, and because only the one to whom God himself has revealed this mystery can see him, it is possible for that person to comprehend the mystery of his coming again.[33] No one possesses God in such a way that he no longer must be waiting completely for him. And yet no one can wait for *God* unless he knows that God has long been waiting for him.

But with this we come back to our starting point. It is not a new ideal of the human being of the future that Jesus sets before our eyes for us to make into reality; instead, it is the person of God himself of whom Jesus is speaking when he calls the one who is waiting and watching blessed. But a person of God becomes that person not by his own power but through
grace alone, through God's incomprehensible mercy, only through waiting. 394
Or not by waiting—since the person can only wait because God is coming. No one can tell by looking at a person if he is one of those blessed ones who are waiting. For no one can tell by looking at another person whether God is coming to him. This is why those among us who seriously want to be Christians ask at this hour: God, come into our waiting. God, we are waiting for your salvation, your judgment, for your love and your peace. Jesus speaks to us: Behold! I am standing at the door knocking. And we say: Yes, come, Lord Jesus. Amen.

[32.] Crossed out: "try to take it into one's own hands."

[33.] Crossed out: "in the future."

### 3. Devotions on Luke 4:3–4, Berlin, Technical College, February 4, 1932 (?)[1]

Luke 4:3–4: The devil said to him, "If you are the Son of God, command this stone to become a loaf of bread." Jesus answered him, "It is written, 'One does not live by bread alone, but by every word of God.'"[2]

There are basically only two questions that really concern people: the question of God and the question of bread. And these two questions are jealous of each other. Neither one wants to shut out the other completely, but each of them wants to be in first place. The question of God does not say that people should [not] ask the question about bread at all. And the question about bread doesn't say that, after it is taken care of, a person couldn't also ask about God. Why shouldn't he? And the latter attitude is supported by all reasonable thinking, all life wisdom[3] and knowledge of human nature, all experience and intelligence. Satisfy people's hunger, give them bread, and then speak to them about God, and they will hear you. Yes, they will make a god of you yourself, because you have given them food. All of our thinking
395 about social issues today runs just that way. You have to change the conditions in which people live. You have to give them enough bread and enough space, and only then can you expect that they will hear when you talk about God. It is said that it is brutality on the part of the church if it does not see that today its first task must be caring for physical suffering and need; if it thinks that today it should just speak again and again primarily about God and let the question of bread come second. We have all been so strongly infected by these ideas that we can hardly free ourselves from them. And what we intend with this is only, after all, not to let our talk of God become an empty phrase. We don't want to be unloving, and we think we are being unloving wherever we speak [to] hungry people about God instead of giving them bread.

In the beginning, even before the beginning of his active work, Jesus is tempted by the devil. That is, the powers of evil, of falling away from God, approach him and, at the moment when he is just starting his ministry as

---

[1.] *NL*, A 33,16 (a); handwritten draft; notation by Eberhard Bethge: "Temptation Bread Paper 1931/32 Devotion T.C.? Thursday, February 4, 1932?" Previously published in *PAM* 1:247–49. Cf. *NL*, A 33,16 (b); later typewritten transcription with handwritten editorial changes by Eberhard Bethge and with notation by Eberhard Bethge: "Two devotions in February 1932 Technical College (?) Berlin." Previously published in *GS* 4:137–39.

[2.] [The German text but not the NRSV includes the phrase "but by every word of God."—MB]

[3.] "Life wisdom [*Lebensweisheit*]" replaces "life cleverness [*Lebensklugheit*]."

the Messiah, try to cause his downfall. Jesus is out in the desert and is fasting . . . Fasting [is] no joke . . . And now the story goes that Jesus is hungry. And now the devil comes to him: If you are God's Son, speak to the stone that it become bread. If you have the strength of a god, help yourself. Work a miracle; make the stones into bread, and your hunger will be satisfied. What do you have this power for, if you don't use it? Prove your power, if you are God's Son. See, not only you are hungry, but millions of people are hungry.[4] Their eyes are turned only to the one who gives them something to eat. They are weak. They are not able to be excited about you, about God, if you do not first give them bread. They all put their hope in a God. They all put their hope in you, in the one sent by God, that he will help them. But they first hope that he will give them bread. Then, yes then, they will give up everything; then they will run after you, follow you, will worship you, idolize you, if you are able to do what no other person is able to do, if you give them bread to eat. They are pitiful, weak people, but they are not bad; they just want first to have their hunger satisfied. Do you want to be 396
unmerciful and require of them something that no one can do? Do you want to be hard-hearted and close your ears to their pleading? Do you want to give them stones when they are begging for bread? Millions are waiting for you. You are God's Son. You can help them. You can win them all over for yourself if you perform this miracle. But if you don't, they will hate you, curse you, persecute you, because they know that you do not love them, but hate them, too. Because otherwise you would have given them bread. If you are God's Son, speak to the stone that [it] should become bread and satisfy your hunger and theirs.

In this voice of apparently pleading love, Jesus recognizes the voice of the devil. This was a shocking discovery.[5] He turns the devil away: "One does not live by bread alone, but [by every word of God]." That means here, basically:[6] God does not deceive people. God could probably make bread, but the people would worship him as the one who makes them bread and not as the one he actually is, as the God who, even in hunger, even in times of want, even in the cross and in death, is still God. It wouldn't be God's love that would deceive people about what God is. Certainly, millions would be won. But for whom? For the god of bread and happiness, not for the God who has and commands honor for his own sake, for the God in the cross and death. God shows himself through himself, but not through bread.

[4.] See the editor's afterword to the German edition, p. 477.

[5.] Crossed out: "In the face of this there is only one course, to orient oneself toward God himself."

[6.] Crossed out: "God does not lead people astray by."

### 4. Devotions on Luke 4:5–8, Berlin, Technical College, Thursday before the First Sunday in Lent, February 11, 1932 (?)[1]

Luke 4:5–8: Then the devil led him up and showed him in an instant all the
kingdoms of the world. And the devil said to him, "To you I will give their glory
397 and all this authority; for it has been given over to me, and I give it to anyone I
please. If you, then, will worship me, it will all be yours." Jesus answered him, "It
is written, 'Worship the Lord your God, and serve only him.'"

We have entered into the season of Lent, and once again we must gather all our thoughts to understand what that means. Christ on the cross—that was the message with which Paul set out. That was his God. That was the God for whom the first martyrs died. It was the God that Luther rediscovered.[2] And it is the same God whom we of today are beginning to understand in a new way, or better, by whom we of today are being taken hold of in a new way. Christ on the cross, Christ the hidden king of the hidden kingdom—that is the message of the Protestant church. Christ the revealed king of a visible[3] kingdom—that is the message of the Catholic Church. So it is important that we understand what the season of Lent is about.

The passion of Christ begins not in the week of suffering but already with the first day of his preaching. His refusal to accept the kingdom as a kingdom of this world happens not just at Golgotha but right from the beginning. And this thought should come through as we tell the story.

Jesus could have been the ruler of the world. As the Messiah the Jews had dreamed of, he could have liberated Israel and led it to glory and honor. He could have entered as the visible king of this world. A remarkable man, to whom, even before he begins his active work, dominion over the world is offered. And all the more remarkable in that he refuses the offer. So it is simply true and not meant only biblically that Jesus could have become the most glorious and powerful king of this world. People would have honored him, people would have believed him if he had then dared to say that he was the Son of God. They did even believe that of the Roman emperors. Then the world would really have become Christian. It would have had Christ as
398 its king. It would have had the one for whom they had waited so long. The
one whose power extended over the whole earth, who establishes a kingdom

[1.] *NL*, A 33,17 (a); handwritten draft; notation by Eberhard Bethge: "Thursday before the First Sunday in Lent? February 11, 1932? Lent 1932." Previously published in *PAM* 1:250–52. Cf. *NL*, A 33,17 (b); later typewritten transcription with handwritten editorial changes by Eberhard Bethge. Previously published in *GS* 4:139–41.

[2.] Cf. especially Martin Luther, "Heidelberg Disputation," *LW* 31:39–70.

[3.] "Visible" replaces "earthly."

of peace on earth. So Jesus could have had all of that. It flashes through him that now from a high mountain for an instant he has a view of all the kingdoms of the world and knows that he could be their ruler. But he also knows that for this rule he would have to pay a price that is too high for him. It would come at the cost of his obedience to the will of God. He would have to bow down before the devil, sink to his knees before him, worship him. That means he would have become a slave and [would] no longer [be] free. He would be a slave to his own desire for honor, a slave of the people who want him to be that way. But he remains the free Son of God and recognizes the devil, who is trying to enslave him. "Worship the Lord your God, and serve only him."[4]

Jesus knows what that means. It means lowliness, scorn, persecution, means not being understood, means hatred, death, cross. And he chooses this path from the beginning. It is the path of obedience and the way of freedom. For it is the path of God. And that is why it is also the path to love for human beings. Any other path, even if people liked it better, would be a path of hatred and of disrespect toward human beings. For it would not be God's path. And recognizing this, Jesus refuses the devil's offer here. Because it is the path of God through the world, from the beginning he chooses the path to the cross. And we walk with him, as individuals and also as the church. We are the church under the cross—that is, hidden from view. But even here we can do nothing else but know that our kingdom, too, is not of this world. Amen.

### 5. Sermon on Matthew 24:6–14, Berlin, Reminiscere (Memorial Day), February 21, 1932[1]

Matt. 24:6–14: And you will hear of wars and rumors of wars; see that you are not alarmed; for this must take place, but the end is not yet. For nation will
rise against nation, and kingdom against kingdom, and there will be famines and 399
earthquakes in various places: all this is but the beginning of the birth pangs.

[4.] See Deut. 6:13.

[1.] *NL*, A 33,3 (a); handwritten draft. Previously published in *PAM* 1:252–63. Cf. *NL*, A 33,3 (b); later typewritten transcription with notation by Eberhard Bethge: "Sermon on Memorial Day 1932 (February 21, 1932, Reminiscere)" and with handwritten editorial changes by Eberhard Bethge. Previously published in *GS* 4:34–44. The sermon was preached in the evening.

> Then they will hand you over to be tortured and will put you to death, and you will be hated by all nations because of my name. Then many will fall away, and they will betray one another and hate one another. And many false prophets will arise and lead many astray. And because of the increase of lawlessness, the love of many will grow cold. But the one who endures to the end will be saved. And this good news of the kingdom will be proclaimed throughout the world, as a testimony to all the nations; and then the end will come.

The church does not leave anyone alone. None of you who have come here today in mourning, no one who is really looking for consolation and not just a ceremonial memorial service should remain alone today. You can seek consolation in all kinds of different places, in solitude, in nature, in work, in social life with friends. In all those places you can *search for* consolation. But you can only *find* consolation in the knowledge of God. Whoever, in the face of that which distresses him, which is incomprehensible to him, which keeps frightening and disturbing him all over again, seeks to know the will of God and only wants to bring his suffering and his questioning obediently to a place where he can hear God himself, that person is in the right place here in the church. But *only* that person. Every other person who is interested in something else besides Christian knowledge of God and his will is in the wrong place here.

Memorial Day can be observed in very different ways. It is something different if the bereaved families, something different if the state, something different if the church is observing it. In the families on a day like this, all our thoughts may be centered on the person of the one torn from our midst by the war, and it may be that here all our love for this individual person is reawakened, and our mourning is a mourning out of love. And if in great public or state memorial celebrations, the historically great German actions and sacrifices are commemorated, our mourning may be proud mourning. Finally, if everywhere else the human being and his achievements take a central place—and truly it is important enough that today we also are
400 reminded of great human deeds—all of this, though, is something *different* from what the church of Christ has to say here. When the church observes Memorial Day [Volkstrauertag], it must have something *special* to say. It cannot be one voice in the chorus of others who loudly call out the cry of mourning for the lost sons of the nation across the land and by such cries of mourning call to new deeds and great courage. It cannot, like the ancient singers of great heroic deeds, wander about and sing the song of praise [Preislied] of battle and the death of the heroes into the listening ears of enthralled young people. The church should not expect the laurels that decorate the great singer, for it does not itself make laurel wreaths for *any*

*human being. How gladly* it would do so.[2] It is hard not to be allowed to do that.[3] On this day the church stands here so strangely without ceremony, so little proud, so little heroic. The church is like the seer of ancient times who, when all are gathered to commemorate a great deed of the nation,[4] is wholeheartedly present[5] but suffers because he sees something that the others do not see and must speak of what he sees, although no one wants to hear it. We all feel it: People don't want any disturbance here. People don't want any discord. People want everyone to participate without exception. People don't want anyone to see anything different that others do not see. And if it happens anyway, you have to try to get rid of a person like that.[6] And so it happens then that such seers are thrown out of the celebration, chased away with scorn and contempt by the very people they want to help, whom they love like nothing else in the world. But especially because they love them so much, they have become seers. The one who loves the most is the one who sees deepest, sees the greatest danger. A seer has never been popular. That is why the church will also not be popular, least of all on days like this.

Today the German people remember the years 1914–18, the time in
which millions of German men and boys showed that one can and should 401
love one's fatherland unto death. They had to show that under conditions unheard of in human history up to then. And what would be more authentic and more human than to stand in silence here in deep gratitude and to affirm with great decisiveness what they intended? There are still millions living among us who, like the others, have seen death—a special, unrecognized army of men who are marked by death, in silent communion with one another and with those who have passed over into death. For us younger ones always a new reason for seriousness, for being still and becoming humble, for the older ones a source of strength when facing death, but for us all a reminder that cannot be ignored: Do not forget, never forget, that your people [Volk], that you yourself live on land that was bought with the blood of your brothers! Mourn, German people [Volk], give thanks and hope!

---

[2.] Crossed out: "and how glad it is when others do this."

[3.] Crossed out: "[. . . four illegible words]."

[4.] "Commemorate a great deed of the nation" replaces "to celebrate the great glory of a nation."

[5.] "Wholeheartedly present" replaces "will probably also be there, will probably also be present at the gathering."

[6.] A reference to the so-called Dehn case (see p. 99, ed. note 2, and the editor's afterword to the German edition, pp. 482–83). [See also Barth's letter to Bonhoeffer about this, *DBWE* 12:103, and *DB-ER*, 177 and 235–36.—VB]

What Christian would not want to speak and feel this way? Who would not want to stand together in the gathering with all the brothers who know that they are united? Who would want to dare to sow discord here?

But—we must ask further—what Christian would not know that the church, which is built on the gospel of Christ, would have more to say here, because it sees more? Precisely because every human being as a human being must subscribe to what we just said earlier,[7] that is why the church of Christ must know how to say more[8] and say more profound things, things of more ultimate importance. The monument in the Neue Wache[9] tells everyone everything we said at first: "Do not forget and thank you"—that is what the memorial wreath says, cast from the medals of the fallen brothers. "Hope"—that is what the opening to the sky says. But no cross stands there. It is a national monument, but it is not a Christian symbol. It is not a church, in which the suffering, dying brothers are joined with those who have completed their life journey[10] in the sign of the cross. Thus it is not Christian
402 mourning that unites the people there; it is not Christian hope that arises out of this mourning; it is not Christian consolation that is preached here. And perhaps that, in its own way, is quite proper. But we, who perhaps just this morning stood at the Neue Wache before one war memorial or another and this evening came from there to the church, have a right to expect to hear in this place what Christian mourning is and what Christian consolation and Christian hope are.

Especially those among us who take things seriously are repeatedly confronted and plagued on this day by the question of where, from a Christian perspective, they should stand with regard to what happened from 1914 to 1918. We want to know how we as Christians—and not only as Germans—should see all of this. There may be some among us whose Christian conscience quakes when they think of the war and its victims and who are unsure about how they should reconcile themselves to it morally.[11] And

[7.] [See the second paragraph before this one. It ends with the exhortation: "Mourn, German people [Volk], give thanks and hope!"—MB]

[8.] "The church of Christ must know how to say more" replaces "the Christian as a special type of person something."

[9.] The plain monument for the fallen soldiers of the First World War, opposite the Staatsoper (State Opera House) on the boulevard Unter den Linden; it had been built in 1931 to a design by Heinrich Tessenow, a redesign of the Neue Wache (New Guard House), which had been built in 1816–18 by the architect and painter Karl Friedrich Schinkel.

[10.] "Those who have completed their life journey [*Vollendeten*]" replaces "[. . . one illegible word] brothers."

[11.] Crossed out: "There may be others there who are convinced of the holy enterprise of war."

who among us, after all, is not among those? Who could be so clear and sure, so completely convinced of the holy cause [Sache] of the war if he knows of the commandment of peace,[12] if he knows that God is a God of peace, that of Christ it is said: He is our peace?[13] Who would not again and again be disturbed and would have to ask himself: What do the events of 1914–18, the millions of dead German men, mean for me, for us today? How is God speaking through them to me? That means once again very simply asked: How can I bring together in my mind God, Christ, and the events of the war? Should I say it was an enterprise [Sache] of God? Or shall I succumb to despair and say: Here God's power was at an end? Here Christ was far away?

For such questions we must be very determined—and what would be more natural at the beginning of the season of Lent—first of all to look at what happened on the cross of Golgotha.[14] And now doesn't exactly the
same question come up here, only even incomparably more sharply and 403
urgently: How can I bring together in my mind the cross and God?[15]

And is not precisely here *the* answer given that stands over the whole Christian message: Christ goes through the cross, only through the cross to life, to the resurrection, to the victory? It is the wonderful theme of the Bible, so frightening for many people, that the only visible sign of God in the world is the cross. Christ is not carried away gloriously from earth to heaven but must go onto the cross. And exactly there where the cross stands, the resurrection is near. Exactly there where everyone begins to doubt God, where everyone falls into despair about God's power, there God is fully, there Christ is alive and near. Where it hangs by a thread whether one will desert the cause or remain faithful, there God is, there Christ is fully. Where the power of darkness [wants] to overpower the light of God, there God triumphs and judges the darkness. So it is now as well, when Christ thinks of the day his church-community will face. His disciples ask about the signs of his coming again after his death. This is not a one-time coming again but an eternal coming again. The end-time in the Bible is all the time and every day between the death of Christ and Judgment Day. Yes, the New Testament sees the death of Christ as so serious, so decisive.

But Christ, who knows that his path leads to the cross, knows that the path of his disciples also does not lead peacefully and safely straight into

[12.] See pp. 364–65.

[13.] See Eph. 2:14.

[14.] Crossed out: "At least we must know that the whole New Testament is written with this as a starting point."

[15.] Crossed out: "Shall I say: that is entirely God's doing."

heaven; rather, they too must pass through the darkness, through the cross. They too must[16] struggle. That is why the first sign of the nearness of Christ—strangely enough!—is that his enemies become great, that the powers of temptation, of apostasy, of unfaithfulness become strong, that his church-community is led close to the brink of doubting in God. The first sign will be that his enemies hide behind the name of Christ and only under the guise of Christianity seek to lure us away from him. Oh, the name "Christ" doesn't do it. And how easy it is in times of confusion like
404 today to fight in the name of Christ against the real Christ. But then, once the spirits are confused, the power of the world will break loose openly, unconcealed.[17] The powers that want to tear the disciples away from him, that try to show them that it is madness to go with him, that Christ has no power, only words, but that they, the powers of reality, speak the language of facts; and this language is more convincing than the language of Christ. The world gangs up on the spirit of Christ. The demons rise up. It is a rebellion against Christ. And the one great power of this uprising is called war! The others are called pestilence and famine. So war, sickness, and hunger[18] are the powers that try to take Christ's dominion away from him, and they are all led by the archenemy of Christ the living one, by death. It already seemed as if with Christ the victory had been won, as if Christ had conquered death. But now these powers scream: We are here. Here, see us and be terrified! We have power. Our power has not been taken from us. Christ has not conquered; *we* conquer. Christ is dead. But we are alive. Our names are war, sickness, hunger. Why are you letting yourselves be enthralled by this false prophet who speaks of peace and love, of God and his kingdom: here we are!

And they attack the nations and drag them in. And death goes around and reaps its harvest. It mows down millions.

And now comes the great disintegration of Christianity.[19] Its ranks are broken up and torn apart. For a terrible uncertainty and fear come over the followers of Christ. They have to realize that all these attacks are basically attacks on Christ and his word and that this word apparently has no power against them. The past war caused thousands, caused millions to doubt

[16.] Crossed out: "through the church."

[17.] "Unconcealed" replaces "suddenly."

[18.] See the editor's afterword to the German edition, p. 477.

[19.] "And now comes the great disintegration of Christianity" replaces "and now it begins to . . . in the disintegration of Christianity." Immediately following this sentence is a sentence that has been crossed out: "There arise row upon row."

Christ, and among them especially those who took his word seriously and now saw themselves so bitterly disappointed. Read wartime letters,[20] read
a collection of statements from our working-class people about the church 405
and Christianity recently published by a pastor in Berlin.[21] These things are written there so that everyone can read them. "The war has shown me that Christ is not right." "The war robbed us of our faith in God." "Since the war I know that faith [is] madness."[22] Those are clear words about war, war and the church of Christ.

It's very hypocritical to simply say here: Oh, well, they didn't have real faith anyway. Dear congregation, one has to have real faith to be able to notice so clearly that one's faith has been destroyed. And who of us would say that he has such real faith that it could not be threatened by anything at all? If a person thinks he has faith like that, he should think very hard about whether this faith has not become indifference, which cannot be aroused from its lethargy by anything. So be careful with such hypocritical criticisms. Didn't those millions also have a right to Christ, who has now been torn away from them this way? What should we say about that, we who ourselves were also dragged into these events of 1914–18, who also share responsibility for their faith having been taken from them? And seen from here, things look very different. What a self-satisfied, hard Christianity we would be if, under such circumstances, even the most loyal, those with the strongest faith, were not also struck by a nameless anxiety that Christ was being torn away from us?

If even the true people of God were not troubled to the very core and if even the frightened church of Christ, under the plague of war, did not have to cry out: "My God, why have you forsaken me?"[23] Even Christ himself
cried out like this on the cross and, according to the story told by one Gos- 406
pel writer, died with this cry. Oh, it is all too understandable that millions became unfaithful, that faced with so much hate their love grew cold.

Our situation would truly be desperate if not for the word of Christ: "When all of this comes over you, see that you are not alarmed. For this

[20.] Bonhoeffer is probably thinking of Witkop, *Kriegesbriefe deutscher Studenten*, and Witkop, *Kriegsbriefe gefallener Studenten.* [An English edition of the latter volume has been published as *German Students' War Letters.*—MB]

[21.] Piechowski, *Proletarischer Glaube.*

[22.] Piechowski had collected various statements about the de-Christianizing effect of the war under the heading "How the Proletarian Lost God during the War." (See *Proletarischer Glaube*, 154–57.) The comments that Bonhoeffer cites here are not verbatim repetition of those quoted by Piechowski but only give their general meaning.

[23.] Matt. 27:46.

must take place."[24] Jesus had to tell his disciples so often: "Do not be afraid, for I am with you."[25] "Do not be afraid, for I have called you by name."[26] Even the Old Testament said this already. "Do not be afraid," the angels call to the frightened shepherds.[27] "Do not fear, only believe," Jesus says to [the leader of the synagogue].[28] "Do not be afraid, little flock, for it is [your] Father's good pleasure to give you the kingdom."[29] "When you see this, see that you are not alarmed; for this must take place, but the end is not yet."[30] We ask: Why must this all take place? Because Christ himself must pass through and beyond death, because where Christ, where God himself really is, the darkness rises up most terribly and nails him to the cross. That is why we too must pass through this. This must all happen so that the end can come.[31]

God's way in the world leads onto the cross and through the cross to life. For this reason do not be alarmed, do not be afraid—be faithful! But what does being faithful mean here other than standing and falling with the word of Christ, with his preaching of the kingdom of peace, than knowing that despite everything Christ's words are stronger than all the powers of evil? What does faithfulness of the community of Christ mean here other than calling out into this furious raging again and again—unto exhaustion, unto humiliation, unto martyrdom—the words of Christ that there should be peace, that there should be love, that there should be blessing, and that he is our peace,[32] and that God is a God of peace? And the more they rage,
407 the more we should call out. And the more we call out, the wilder they will rage. For wherever the word of Christ is truly spoken, the world senses that it is either ruinous madness or ruinous truth, which endangers its very life.[33] Where peace is really spoken, war must rage twice as hard, for it senses that it is about to be driven out. Christ intends to be its death.

But all the more passionately, all the more loyally, the church of Christ

[24.] See Matt. 24:6. Crossed out: "but now he spreads over these words the indescribable consolation that the enemies always."

[25.] See, for example, Matt. 28:10 and 20.

[26.] See Isa. 43:1.

[27.] Luke 2:10.

[28.] Mark 5:36.

[29.] Luke 12:32.

[30.] Matt. 24:6. [The NRSV translation has been altered here to correspond to Bonhoeffer's German.—MB]

[31.] Crossed out: "Only through the cross, only through the battle against the world does God lead his kingdom to salvation."

[32.] See Eph. 2:14.

[33.] Crossed out: "It feels that there is power."

will stand by its Lord and preach this word of peace, [even] though it must pass through scorn and persecution. It knows that its Lord also had to go to the cross. But now it understands the promise that Jesus [has] for it. The war will not be the end. But rather it must take place so that the end can come. The gospel of the kingdom will be preached as a witness to all nations, and then the end will come. And here now our view broadens out; our eyes are suddenly drawn up to the Lord who directs all things, whom even the demons and the forces of hell must serve. War, sickness, and hunger must come, so that the gospel of the kingdom of peace, of love, and [of] salvation can be spoken and heard all the more keenly, all the more clearly, all the more deeply. The power of enmity and of stirring up conflict between nations must serve to cause the gospel to come to all nations and be heard by all, must serve the kingdom to which all people shall belong. War serves peace, hate serves love, the devil serves God, the cross serves life. And then, when that has been revealed, then the end will come. Then the Lord of the church will lay his hand on the church, blessing and protecting it as his faithful servant.

Memorial Day in the church! What does that mean? It means holding up the one great hope from which we all live, the preaching of the kingdom of God. It means seeing that which is past, and which we remember today, with all its terrors and all its godlessness, and yet not being afraid, but hearing the preaching of peace. It means knowing that all of that has to happen
so that the end can come, so that God remains Lord. It means that we can 408
really mourn for the dead of the world war only if we, with the same faithfulness in which they stood out there, now pass on the message of peace,[34] for the sake of which their death had to be, and preach it all the more loudly. It means looking out beyond the borders of our own nation, across the whole world, and praying that the gospel of the kingdom, which puts an end to all war, now may come over all nations and that then the end may come, that Christ may draw near.

Memorial Day in the church! That means that God in the cross is near to us. [That] means pointing to Christ on the cross, who won the victory through the cross. Memorial Day in the church, that means knowing that Christ alone wins the victory! Amen.

[34.] Crossed out: "of the kingdom."

### 6. Sermon on Genesis 32:25–32; 33:10, Berlin, Laetare Sunday, March 13, 1932[1]

Gen. 32:25[24]–32[31]; 33:10:[2] Jacob was left alone; and a man wrestled with him until daybreak. When the man saw that he did not prevail against Jacob, he struck him on the hip socket; and Jacob's hip was put out of joint as he wrestled with him. Then he said, "Let me go, for the day is breaking." But Jacob said, "I will not let you go, unless you bless me." So he said to him, "What is your name?" And he said, "Jacob." Then the man said, "You shall no longer be called Jacob, but Israel, for you have striven with God and with humans, and have prevailed." Then Jacob asked him, "Please tell me your name." But he said, "Why is it that you ask my name?" And there he blessed him. So Jacob called the place Peniel, saying, "For I have seen God face to face, and yet my life is preserved." The sun rose upon him as he passed Penuel, limping because of his hip. . . . Jacob said, "No, please; if I find favor with you, then accept my present from my hand; for truly to see your face is like seeing the face of God—since you have received me with such favor."

409 Dear confirmands![3] During the last weeks before confirmation, when I kept asking you what I should say to you in the sermon at confirmation, several times the answer came: We want a serious admonishment for our lives. And I can assure you, whoever listens well today will hear many very serious admonishments. But see here, life today gives us enough serious admon-

---

[1.] *NL*, A 33,4 (a); handwritten draft. Previously published in *PAM* 1:263–72. Cf. *NL*, A 33,4 (b); later typewritten transcription with handwritten editorial changes by Eberhard Bethge. Previously published in *GS* 4:44–50. Bonhoeffer gave the confirmation sermon on March 13, 1932, Laetare Sunday (third Sunday before Easter), in the Zionskirche (Zion Church) in Berlin-Wedding. [In the NRSV, the versification of the first passage is Gen. 32:24–31.]

[2.] At the beginning of the sermon the following words of the sermon [text] are written as notes: "Genesis 32/33 I will not let you go, unless you bless me; the sun rose upon him and he limped . . . to see your face is like seeing the face of God."

[3.] Crossed out: "The day of your confirmation is not a great day because today you are the focus of a family celebration; or because—as people say—you pass from childhood into young adulthood—that fortunately doesn't happen so suddenly; or finally not because in this week your school days end and you are to start your working lives—that is, of course, a very important and serious event, but confirmation is something even more important and more serious. And who would dare to come together today in a festive and joyous celebration, when a group of you will be leaving your parents' home, who will have to get along in life on their own—and this in our life today, where everyone knows what he can expect? But that is also not what it is all about today, at least not primarily. We are in the church, and it is only a few minutes until you are to stand up before the congregation gathered here, and now of your own free will be taken anew into the church of Christ." On Bonhoeffer's confirmation work, see pp. 73–74. [See also *DB-ER*, 226–29.—VB]

ishments, more than enough.[4] And that is why I should not[5] make your view of the future more difficult and darker than it already is. And I know many of you are already seeing a great deal of the realities of life. Today you should not be made afraid of life but be given courage. That is why today in church we will have to talk more than ever about the hope that we have and that no one can take away from you.

When I look at you today, it seems to me as if I saw a crowd of young hikers before me, who after a long hike have arrived at a great, locked gate and now knock and ask to be let in. They recognize this gate and these walls from somewhere. Somehow it seems like home to them. Open up! We want to see what it looks like in there. We want to come in! So their voices call out, and they knock on the gate. Some more courageously, a little more persistently, the others a little more softly; and among them probably some
who have just let themselves be dragged along with the others. But now they 410
are all there, and they all want to get in.

What kind of a strange gate is it? And what kind of a strange land that lies behind it? It is certainly a strange land these young hikers want to go into. It is the land of which it is said that there is peace and love and justice in it; the land where there is no more suffering and there are no more tears, because a wonderful Lord rules there. It is the land that is prophesied, the promised land, the land in which God rules.[6]

Now who gave you—we might like to ask you[7]—this great idea that there was such a thing as a land like this? And you will answer: You yourselves, you, the Christian congregation and your pastors, and last of all, the one who visits us all, Jesus Christ. We are still at a loss about what we should do. We still don't know how it will turn out. How are you going to get through this gate, and what will you think of the land behind the gate?

And now we'll take a look at the story I read to you. Look, Jacob feels exactly the way you feel today.[8] He had once fled from the land of Canaan, from the promised land, the land that God had given[9] his forefathers and him, fled from his brother's anger. Then he had spent years of his life in a foreign land. But now he is drawn back. He wants to go back to his home country. He wants to go back to the land promised by the prophets. He wants to go into the land where God is the Lord and no other. And he wants

---

[4.] Bonhoeffer is referring to the difficult economic and political situation at the end of the Weimar Republic.

[5.] "I should" replaces "it cannot be the task of the church."

[6.] Crossed out: "the land of the eternal home."

[7.] "You . . . ask you" replaces "these young hikers."

[8.] Crossed out: "He has spent years of his life in a foreign land."

[9.] "Given" replaces "promised."

to go to his brother and make peace with him. He wants to go into the land of God. Don't you want to do that, too?

And now something remarkable happens to him. Evening has come, the last evening in the foreign land. He, Jacob, knows that his brother and the promised land[10] are near; tomorrow he will be in his home country. Now it is night. And he stays alone by the river. Just a few hours, then it will be
411 morning, then he will cross over into his home country. But then he notices that suddenly he is being attacked. Someone steps into his path. He puts his arms around him; he wrestles with him; he will not let him go; he tries to force him down. Jacob should not return to the promised land. He should not find peace with his brother. A terrible, powerful force steps in his way and will not allow Jacob to enter; it wants to push him back into the night, into the foreign land. Stay there, where you are coming from. You may not come into the promised land; you are a foreigner, an unfaithful one. Stay away from here.[11] And violently[12] the great unknown one tries to push Jacob away from him into the night. But Jacob's longing for the promised land gives him unbelievable strength, and he does not allow himself to be pushed away. He does not give way. He holds the other one fast in his arms, and now, in the struggle, he recognizes who his opponent is. It is God himself who is guarding his land, who will not let any intruder in, who keeps his land holy, who wants to show this person that one can't just come in so simply and happily and merrily, but that only the holy and righteous one crosses over the borders of this land. Everyone else, every foreigner, every unfaithful one must stay away in the night of loneliness and of evil. Do you hear it, and do you understand it, too? One cannot just casually enter into the promised land. Likewise, one cannot just casually become a member of the Christian church—that is, by going to confirmation. Why not? Because God steps into the path and guards his land and keeps it holy and does not want us to enter into it unholy. Your path to the altar, too—here today and in the evening day after tomorrow, when you will go to Holy Communion—should be a path into the holy[13] land. Take care that you don't start out on that path unholy.

But[14] how should we become holy, so that we can enter into the land of God? Let us look at Jacob. The night is ending and morning is coming, and Jacob is still holding off his opponent. He still does not let himself be

[10.] Crossed out: "of the promise."
[11.] "Stay away from here" replaces "a refugee."
[12.] "And violently" replaces "but Jacob must go on farther."
[13.] "Holy" replaces "promised."
[14.] Crossed out: "But now let us hear."

sent away. He is still holding him. Then comes a last, terrible blow from the
opponent: Let me go; the day is dawning and I must leave. You stay in the 412
night! And now Jacob's passionate determination [Leidenschaft] becomes immeasurable. He dares to talk back to God, to refuse to do what he says: No, I will not let you go, unless you bless me. What else does that mean other than that Jacob dares to reach into God's heart itself: you may not go away from me. You may not leave me alone in the night. I cannot be without you. I cannot. I want to see your land and live in your land. God, you will not leave me in the night, in sin, in need.[15] You can't leave me alone. It goes against your heart. No, I will not let you go, unless you bless me. I want only one thing: to know that you are not my enemy, that you no longer reject me because of the evil things I did in the foreign land; to know that you are with me, that you are merciful to me. I will not let you go, unless you bless me.

And now he doesn't know how he should hold on to God, so that he doesn't leave him. And he asks him: Tell me your name, so that I can always call on [you], so that I know who you are. But God answers: Why do you ask me for my name? It is too wonderful for you to understand it. "And there he blessed him." So that was God's answer, in which he revealed his name, which is not an angry but a merciful name—he blessed him there. That means he did not leave him alone in the night. He did not push him back. He did not turn him away but was merciful to him. He let himself be found. He promised his faithfulness. He blessed him. That means he let him come into the promised land of God. And Jacob called the place Peniel, which means: I have seen God face-to-face, and my soul is restored.[16] And at the moment when God blessed him, the night came to an end, the dawn broke, and the sun rose for him. He had won victory over the night. And God had let it become day for him. The sun came up for him, no other sun than on every day, and it shone over a land that was not any different from any other land. But the sun came up *for him*. Now God was there, who made it light around him and inside him. The day of God's mercy had dawned, and the
night was over. Jacob was standing in the promised land, for he had found 413
God and his soul was restored.

But, of course, the signs of the night, which remind him of new nights to come, were still there. He limped because of his hip, says the Bible. That means he could not forget his past. It had cost him a great deal to enter into the promised land, to receive God's blessing. One doesn't go into God's

[15.] Crossed out: "No, I will not leave you."

[16.] [In the NRSV translation of Gen. 32:30, Jacob says: "For I have seen God face to face, and yet my life is preserved."—MB]

land without scars. Have you understood? In the night where we know that we are sinners before God, where our need becomes great and God wants to turn away from us, there one must fight for God's blessing. There we should scream out: I will not let you go, unless you bless me. And then morning is near; then the day breaks. Then God himself comes and makes it light and quiet within us, and we enter into the promised land. It doesn't look any different than on the day before, but God has been there and left his mercy and [his] blessing with us, and that is why we are in the promised land.

Now it isn't long until Jacob sees his brother coming. And now, where the day of God[17] has dawned, he sees the face of his brother not as an enemy but "like seeing the face of God."[18] He sees in his brother God himself and his love. And the brother takes[19] him in, and he is in his home country, for he has found God and his brother. Do you understand? Whoever has found God finds his brother, too. He sees his brother's face as if he were seeing God's face. And whoever does not find his brother also does not find God. It is for this reason that God himself became our brother in Christ, so that behind every brother we see him again.

And now daylight should come over you. Not so that now from tomorrow on suddenly everything will go smoothly and easily. But in a way that lets you know that God, who wants to bless you, will never leave you alone. That is the sun that came up for Jacob, which also will come up for you. God's love and mercy,[20] as you see them in Christ our brother and Lord
414 on the cross and in his resurrection. In the Christian church-community, you should find God and your brother, should find your home, should have the promised land. Here one shall be the Lord, and each shall become a Christ for the other.[21]

So you should know that in our lives all of us must again and again go into the night and through the night to the day. It is not eternally day for any mortal—indeed, we probably all[22] see more night than day; don't be deceived about that either. But no one should ever take away from you the belief that God has prepared for you, too, a day and a sun and a dawning and that God brings to us this sun who is called Christ: that God wants to let us see the promised land in which justice and peace and love rule, because

[17.] "And now, where the day of God" replaces "He is no longer the enemy, but."

[18.] See Gen. 33:10.

[19.] "And the brother takes" replaces "and now gives him [. . . three illegible words]."

[20.] "The sun . . . mercy" replaces "the promised land you are entering today, the love and the mercy of God."

[21.] See Martin Luther, "The Freedom of a Christian," 1520 (*WA* 7:35, 34; *LW* 31:367). See above p. 318, ed. note 353.

[22.] Crossed out: "at present."

Christ rules, here from a distance, but one day for eternity. Why should we be afraid? Just go in, go through! God, Christ is the Lord, the church-community our home.

I will not let you go, unless you bless me! If God is for us, who will be against us?[23]

### 7. Devotions on John 8:31–32, Berlin, Technical College, Beginning of Summer Semester 1932 (?)[1]

John 8:31–32: Then Jesus said to the Jews who had believed in him, "If you continue in my word, you are truly my disciples; and you will know the truth, and the truth will make you free."

This text is good as a beginning, because it draws our attention to an idea that we often like to forget when thinking about questions of religion but which is the central idea in religion. We have become accustomed to see- 415
ing religion as something that corresponds to a need of the human soul and satisfies this need. Something that should lead from the restlessness of existence to peace, from hectic activity into calm. Something in which we can come fully to ourselves, very far away from our daily working life. We probably say then that religion is something beautiful, something valuable, something necessary in life, and that it is the only thing that can make people most deeply happy.

But with this we forget the one most important question: whether religion is also something true, whether it is the truth. For it might be that religion is beautiful but not true, and [that] this is all a beautiful, pious illusion, but an illusion nevertheless. And the battle raging most strongly against religion started because people in the church itself often spoke as if the question of truth were the secondary question in religion. But whoever speaks that way sees religion only from the point of view of the human being and his needs and not from the point of view of God and what he demands.[2] And that is

[23.] See Rom. 8:31.

[1.] *NL*, A 33,18 (a); handwritten draft; notation by Eberhard Bethge: "Seminar at the T[echnische] U[niversität] 1932 beginning of the semester?" Previously published in *PAM* 1:271–72. Cf. *NL*, A 33,18 (b); later typewritten transcription with handwritten editorial changes by Eberhard Bethge and with handwritten notation by Eberhard Bethge: "Devotions at the beginning of the Summer Semester 1932. Technical College Berlin." Previously published in *GS* 4:142–43.

[2.] Bonhoeffer's negative assessment of religion in the devotions takes up the strict contrast of divine revelation and human religion as it was developed in the early 1920s in the group around Karl Barth, Eduard Thurneysen, and Friedrich Gogarten.

why it is important that we get one thing clear here right at the beginning and we let the New Testament tell us this, that religion is primarily interested in only one thing, namely, to be true. Truth, that is the highest value not only in science but even more and more urgently in religion, which we want to have as the foundation of our life.

But how can I recognize as truth that of which Christian proclamation speaks? And here the Bible gives a strange answer: "If you continue in my word, [you are truly my disciples; and you] will know [the truth]." Not through free research, not through disinterested thinking and searching for it, but solely through the free attempt to base one's life for once completely on the word of Christ; for once to live totally[3] with him, to live by following him, to hear him, to obey him. Only the one who has completely
416 dedicated his life in this way[4] can judge whether Christ speaks and is the truth. And Christ gives the promise: Whoever once dares to do that will know the truth. Only in living does one know the truth. Only in battle can one test weapons.

And finally: The truth will make you free! That is the gift of the truth. Whoever has the power of the truth behind him is the freest man. He fears nothing; he is bound by nothing. No prejudice, no weak giving in to deceptive hopes, but bound to one thing, to the one, to the truth that is the truth of God, which gives all truth its existence. Whoever is with the truth of God is truly free. God, make us free. Amen.

### 8. Sermon on 2 Chronicles 20:12, Berlin, Exaudi, May 8, 1932 (?)[1]

2 Chron. 20:12: We do not know what to do, but our eyes are on you.

The world rests on the firm commandment of God.[2] That is God's faithfulness to the world, that he gives permanence to his commandment. It is God's anger that he conceals his commandment from us. It is the mercy of

[3.] Crossed out: "to try."

[4.] "Only the one who has completely dedicated his life in this way" replaces "the one who has dared to do that."

[1.] *NL*, A 33,5; handwritten draft; notation by Eberhard Bethge: "Exaudi sermon 1932? May 8, 1932." Previously published in *GS* 1:133–39; *PAM* 1:273–83. Bonhoeffer held the sermon in the Dreifaltigkeitskirche (Trinity Church) in Berlin. He used 2 Chron. 20:12 several times in 1932, because in his opinion the sentence expressed, on the one hand, the feeling of not knowing what to do and, on the other hand, the necessity of the concrete commandment in Christian ethics (see above pp. 121, 362, and 384, ed. note 22). [Exaudi is the sixth Sunday after Easter.—MB]

[2.] Crossed out: "as if in iron bonds."

God that he lets us know his commandment. It is the promise of God and our hope that we one day will keep his commandment. Lord, do not conceal your commandment from us. Teach us to keep your commandment. Exaudi—hear us, Lord, and proclaim yourself to us.[3]

It was a man of action, a king of Israel, who, threatened by enemies, was
supposed to march into war, a warlike man who spoke the words of our 417
text. He had gathered his people around him to take counsel about what should be done.[4] One needs plans, programs, and determination. And he speaks to the people—and now something happens that is very strange and yet so completely biblical: His plans and programs disintegrate, they turn into prayers, his determination into deepest despair and humility, and he closes his speech, his programmatic war speech, with the words: "We do not know what to do, but our eyes are on you." Truly a great programmatic speech, isn't it? We would not be thrilled if in a crucial hour for our nation [Volk] a leading man would stand up and dare to say: We don't know what we should do. We would throw him out with scorn and contempt, with insults and ridicule. You call that a programmatic speech? We're accustomed to something different, better; we know better how one is supposed to speak on occasions like this:[5] programs and plans don't dissolve into prayers, but rather, lit by the flames of enthusiasm, they become glowing symbols and banners of our own good and just cause. Determination turns into not despairing humility but an irresistible affirmation of one's own strength and one's own courage. Indeed, just the opposite happens: prayers become programs, and requests become orders. At the end of the program, the name of God must even be mentioned.[6] God, too, is called into service to promote the program, the clever plan, one's own determination, and then, yes then the Christian programmatic speech is complete, the way we like to hear it and have heard it a thousand times already, sometimes better, sometimes worse.

And in comparison how pitiful, how poor, how disgraceful and cowardly, how little willing to take responsibility, and how lacking in feeling for the fatherland must the one appear whose whole program consists of the rec-
ognition: We do not know what to do, but our eyes are on you. How ugly, 418
how uninspiring, is this man of the Bible, and how likable, glorious, how

[3.] "Proclaim yourself to us" replaces "come among us."

[4.] Crossed out: "and he speaks to the crowd."

[5.] "One is supposed to speak on occasions like this" replaces "what something like this must look like."

[6.] See p. 454, ed. notes 7–8. On Bonhoeffer's criticism of "Christian programs," see the 1932 essay "What Is Church?" *DBWE* 12, 2/7.

inspiring is our Christian programmatic speaker. And now if we would continue straight ahead on this way, we would be on the verge of changing our text just a little bit and then preaching on the text: We know what to do, but our eyes are still on you, too. And that would be an improvement over our biblical text, just as our Christian programmatic speaker would really be an improvement over the man of the Bible.

It is just a question of how dearly this improvement was bought. For the price of truth is too expensive, too high for any improvement. And it is just this price of truth that we must be willing to pay if we want to advance from the knowledge of the man of the Bible to that of our Christian programmatic speaker. Because what the man in the Bible is speaking is true and because what the other speaks is untrue, we must not go along with this improvement. It is a step away from the truth. So it is true—that is, it is appropriate to our position as human beings in the world in relation to God—that we must say: We do not know what to do, but our eyes are on you. We could know that better than ever today, although we should always know it.[7] The great disintegration of our ideals, of our human systems of order and social structures,[8] puts the question before us anew every day: What should we do? Every day we must decide between this ideal and that ideal, be these ideals of a political or an educational nature, or be they a matter of how we live our personal lives. The programmatic claims of all ideals have been shaken at their deepest foundations. Should our children's education be individualistic or collectivistic? Is the national state or are the international entities [überstaatliche Einheiten] more desirable?[9] Should
419 the form [of] marriage stay as it was, [or] does it need a new structure? That means: How shall I educate, how shall I act as a citizen, how shall I structure my marriage? All these questions have become open questions for us because of the sharp divisions in worldview. But because we all have to decide somehow, we are constantly disturbed by the question: What should we do? We do not know what to do.

But here, too, our Christian programmatic speaker is right on the spot and is more clever than we. He wants to beat us on our home turf. He

[7.] Crossed out: "Situation of disintegration . . . but know . . . not according to human ideas but before the eyes of God? What should we do? Who . . . why, don't we know . . . because creation concealed God's will, future according to *God's* will . . . He . . . We should . . ."

[8.] Already in lectures to his congregation in Barcelona in the winter of 1928–29, Bonhoeffer had spoken of "a hitherto unprecedented revolution in morals" and "unprecedented confusion with regard to the ethical problems" (see *DBWE* 10:360–61).

[9.] Cf. Bonhoeffer's lecture on the order of international peace as a present-day commandment of God in July 1932; see p. 364.

says:[10] Look in the Bible and read what it says. It is written there very clearly: You shall love your neighbor as yourself. We know the commandment to love our neighbor (and out of love for our neighbor we are doing all this). But now the very straightforward question must be asked about this as well. I know the commandment to love my neighbor. But do we really know what that means? What does it mean to "love your neighbor"? What does that mean for the politician who has to make decisions about war and peace? What does that mean in education? In marriage? For the owner of a company? What should he do, and how does he show his love for his neighbor? By expanding his company, giving his people work, and taking it away from a hundred others? By paying a hundred generously and five hundred a bare minimum? But what does it mean for us? Does it mean that we should let children grow freely? Does it mean that we should here and there force them onto prescribed paths? And why should it mean exactly this and can't it just as well mean exactly the opposite? Yes, the text "Love your neighbor" does not have a clear meaning, does not say to us unequivocally: You should do this. But just the opposite, by placing ourselves under this commandment, we come to recognize even more deeply that God's commandment
is hidden from us; we fall all the more deeply into our perplexity, into our 420
state of not knowing. And a terrible fear comes over us, a fear of the decision that we know must be made before the eyes of God and in which we do not know what we should do. We recognize with trembling that God has hidden his commandment from us. And we know in all our not knowing that it is the wrath of God that [has] come over us. We do not know God's commandment anymore; we are in the dark. We do not know what we should do. God has concealed his commandment from us—because we have violated, broken, and blasphemed his commandment, out of which the world and we should have lived, and now it comes toward us in thousands of human laws but is not God's commandment.

And we want really to pause a moment here and stay with this.[11] It seems to us as if in the midst of a beautiful landscape with a wonderful view suddenly a cold fog rolled in, which envelopes us completely, so that we can no longer see one step ahead of us, and it makes us shiver. It is to us as if suddenly the sun became dark for us, and we are standing alone in the night

[10.] Crossed out: "The objection is made: it is weakness not to know what you should do. Naturally national state, naturally education of the children at home, naturally traditional form of marriage. But also the opposite. We know what we should do. But now the Bible itself asks: do you know that from God, or just from some very human [. . . one illegible word] and where do you get this knowledge? But still the other one has an answer ready."

[11.] Crossed out: "and show us our own situation completely."

and in the cold. We do not know what we should do. We are perplexed. And if we now all the more desperately do this or that, that just makes our perplexity all the more obvious.[12]

Now we want to go back, but our way is blocked; and we want to go forward, but the way is blocked, too. And so we live from moment to moment
421 under the curse of our deeds and the wrath of the holy God.[13] And so we hear again the news that God has created the world a second time.[14] Of course, the works of this second creation are different from those of the first—they are called the cross of Christ and resurrection. In the cross of Christ, the fallen world is brought to its end and judged, with its knowledge and its deeds. The person, every person, dies this death on the cross with Christ, whether he knows it or not. A verdict is passed on him by the judge who judges all of a person's deeds and knowledge. The whole person, along with everything he thinks he knows about God and has done for God, must die along with all Christian programs, according to the judgment of God. But Christ rose from the dead and with him the new humanity. God himself did what no human being could do. He brought the person through death to life: He proclaimed anew his commandment that would lead to life and fulfilled it himself. He speaks: I do this, I all alone and no other. Believe in the gospel. That is his new commandment, that we look at him, at how he creates life in death, resurrection in the cross.[15] We have been brought to life. We have received mercy. We are sanctified and cleansed. We are justified. We have risen with Christ, but we always only know that when we look at the cross, that is, when we know that we are dead and facing God's wrath, that we are unholy and unclean, that we do not know

[12.] Crossed out: "We do not know—because the wrath of God is upon us, the wrath of God conceals his commandment from us—*for we have violated and blasphemed his commandment, out of which the world, out of which we should live,* and now God has concealed it from us and like mockery it confronts us now out of a thousand human laws and causes destruction and is no longer God's commandment."

[13.] Crossed out: "And now in our complete not knowing we do know one thing, namely: What should we do? That is the question with which we knock on the gate to the future. We want to prepare our future for ourselves. By our good deeds, we want to conquer the future ourselves. (But we must know that:) A future will be opened to us where God himself puts his commandment into power, where through his commandment he creates anew the world that has been subjected to [God's] wrath and curse. We cannot do that. God himself must create the world in which we can know what we should do. It must be a new creation; God must reveal his commandment anew and give it to the world so that it can live."

[14.] Crossed out: "and Christ the Lord. And with this the old world at an end and the new world begun."

[15.] "How he creates life in death, resurrection in the cross" replaces "because he wants to do it, or rather because he has already done everything for us."

what we should do. In this world we *see* only the cross. We also see ourselves only as those who stand condemned under the cross, as those who do not know what they should do. But in the cross we believe in life; in sin we believe in God; in hiddenness we believe in the revealed; in the hidden commandment we believe in the revealed commandment. We do not know what to do, but our eyes are on you, on the Lord, on the risen Lord. We do not know what to do—because we stand damned under the cross, and our paths are at an end. But we look to you, you who[16] in judgment and 422
mercy, in cross and resurrection, remain God and give your commandment permanence, even if because of this the world is smashed to pieces. We look to you[17] not as those who finally know, after all, what they should do, but as those who do not know at all what they should do but who know that you forgive sins and are merciful, as those who have no firm ground under their feet anymore but are grasped and held over the abyss of the bottomless void from above by you,[18] who know that your paths and your commandment are hidden in this world under the cross, but that they shall be revealed in your kingdom.[19]

And now we go home to our work—workers, civil servants, merchants, students, pastors—back to our work in which we do not know what we should do. But now we know that our work takes place under the cross, under the judgment of Christ, that the ground on which we stand has become unstable, that we cannot stand still on that ground without sinking in. And now we must go forward and—especially if we know only that we don't know what we should do—must not put our hands in our laps and rest up until God does his part. But it is for us like it is for someone trying to walk across a sea of floating ice floes.[20] He cannot rest anywhere, cannot get a foothold too long, or he will sink into the bottomless void, the abyss. As soon as he has taken one leap, he has to think about the next and so on and so on; beneath him the abyss and before him—this he knows—land. He doesn't see it yet. But he knows it is there. Our eyes are on you, on the

[16.] "You who" replaces "You who were victorious from the cross, to whom alone the victory belongs, [you] who have opened my path."

[17.] Crossed out: "But those who right in the deepest state of not knowing know that you are merciful, and just and [. . . one illegible word, possibly "your"] commandment."

[18.] Crossed out: "But those who know that you are focused on—that is, hidden in the cross in—this world. And now it could be that some think that at the end of this sermon we really should know what we should do."

[19.] "Shall be revealed in your kingdom" replaces "in the future."

[20.] [Here Bonhoeffer is using a figure of speech that Thurneysen used in one of his early texts. This became very famous, so that congregations of the time would understand the context immediately. The editors thank Hans Pfeifer for this insight.—MB]

ground of our homeland, on the land of your firm commandment, on the kingdom of the new, revealed creation, on your glory. Let us not sink on the ice floes on which we are floating. Let it not be eternally foggy and cold around us. Show us in all the darkness of the cross the light of your resur-
423 rection, your promise, that your commandment is firm. Let us love your hidden commandment. And give us hope that we one day will keep it. We children of the world, men and women of work, of action, we come before you and pray: We do not know what to do, but our eyes are on you. Do not hide your commandment eternally from us. We know that your faithfulness is great. Exaudi—hear us, Lord.

### 9. Baptism Sermon on 1 John 4:16, Berlin, Pentecost Sunday, May 12, 1932[1]

1 John 4:16: God is love, and those who abide in love abide in God, and God abides in them.

This word is to be spoken today over this child. And not the way one might give him just any[2] other word of one's choice—as they say—to take along on his way in life, but rather with the very particular claim that this is God's word at this time over this child; that means that this word becomes real at this moment and shows itself to be true and valid.[3] God is love—from today on in the life of this child that is no longer a general word of wisdom or unwisdom for his life, but is the real, only indestructible basis on which his whole life is built. It is truth, and it is reality. That is the meaning of baptism.

It is part of the role of the church that it must say such things to people who must feel that this is either a well-meant phrase and an untruth or else something you take for granted. The expression "God is love" is completely vulnerable to this criticism.[4] It is extremely tempting to consider this a

[1.] *NL*, A 33,20 (a); handwritten draft; notation by Eberhard Bethge: "Baptism May 12, 1932, Pentecost Sunday." Previously published in *PAM* 1:280–83. Cf. *NL*, A 33,20 (b); later typewritten transcription with handwritten editorial changes by Eberhard Bethge. Previously published in *GS* 4:147–50. This was for the baptism of Bonhoeffer's nephew Thomas, born August 26, 1931, the son of Klaus and Emmi Bonhoeffer. The baptism took place at the house of Bonhoeffer's parents, Karl and Paula Bonhoeffer, on Wangenheimstrasse.

[2.] Crossed out: "also that [. . . one illegible word]."

[3.] Crossed out: "In this claim of the church to have the authority of God in the word."

[4.] Crossed out: "it is all the less a harmless misunderstanding."

well-intentioned exaggeration, a phrase for use in church celebrations, 424
and[5] in doing so fundamentally to reject it as untrue and rob it of its seriousness. But the seriousness of this word is also destroyed if one considers it to be something one can piously take for granted.[6] No, when the love of God is spoken about, we are speaking about something that simply cannot at all be taken for granted, something improbable, unbelievable. But what is completely improbable here is also true, so true that a person's whole life should be built on it.

God is love. That means that the beginning and the end of this child are safely in God's hands. But at the same time, it means that something has broken into the life of this child in the world, something that contradicts everything visible, understandable, and able to be experienced, something that sets this life on a foundation that lies beyond all human possibilities, on the foundation of God himself.[7] The laws of human life are broken through when God's love comes over a person.

For that means that the human being, who we know is vulnerable to the powers of fate, is bound to the One who is also Lord over fate. That the human being, whom we know life frightens because he does not know what the immediate future will hold, is freed of this fear because he knows the ultimate future, which is God himself. That the human being, who loves himself more than God and his brother and therefore sins in this, is still loved by God and his brother, that he is forgiven. That the human being, who we know is deeply lonely in the world, can never be lonely, because God is with him and with all his called people.

When God's love stands over a person, that means not that his life goes on any differently than that of any other person but that his life has been stripped of its last selfish inclination and has been won for God. It is not that the fate of the person is love—that is how we often misunderstand this
word—but the One who is Lord over fate is love. And these are not wishes 425
that we give the child on his way, but realities of which the church assures him on behalf of the living God. It is good that this verse starts by speaking of God's love. That takes away the danger that later, when the text speaks of a person's love, we think something very human is meant. "Those who abide in love abide in God, and God in them . . ."; what can "abide in love"

[5.] Crossed out: "which as very clearly."

[6.] Crossed out: "Just the opposite is meant."

[7.] Crossed out: "It would certainly be a [. . . one illegible word] illusion, if one thought one could see from a life that God is love."

mean, at first,[8] other than being called now to break through the laws of the world as God breaks through them?

To take the very special path that love takes, a path that is foreign and incomprehensible to the world? A path that can never lead one astray,[9] that is completely self-sufficient, has its own laws, that is always right, even if it seems so strange? A path that is interrupted a thousand times, because it is the path not of the priest who blindly passes by the man who had fallen into the hands of the robbers[10] but of the one who has eyes[11] to see and sees everywhere.[12] To abide in love means to have open eyes, to be able to see something that only a few see, namely, the outstretched, begging hands of the others who are along the way, and now not be able to do anything else but to act, to help, to do one's duty, using everything one has. That may be here or there. Most important is that, wherever it is, one can always allow oneself to be interrupted by God.

But one can only abide in love unknowingly. Just as the eye does not see itself, love does not see itself. Whoever thinks that he is abiding in love is not abiding in love, because he is seeing himself. But only in blindness toward himself does the one who abides in love walk his path with the confidence of God. He believes all things; he hopes all things; he endures all things; he forgives all things.[13] If it is really *all things* until the end, then there is
426 no disappointment, no doubt, no stopping. Then it is true that love never ends[14] but continues through from time[15] into eternity.

Whoever abides in love takes not the prescribed path of excellence in the world but his own, often incomprehensible, often foolish paths. He lacks the last bit of worldly cleverness that is called selfishness. But in these foolish, strange paths the one who has eyes to see will see some of the glow from the glory of God himself.

Only one person walked that path in the world completely. It led him to the cross. It leads us through the cross, but to the true life in God.

[8.] Crossed out: "than abiding in the love that God brings us, accepting it, learning to have an eye for him."

[9.] Crossed out: "never in vain, that is always straight, even when it seems so crooked, that always."

[10.] Crossed out: "merciless."

[11.] Crossed out: "his suffering neighbor."

[12.] See Luke 10:25–37.

[13.] See 1 Cor. 13:7.

[14.] See 1 Cor. 13:8.

[15.] "Time" replaces "world."

### 10. Sermon on Luke 16:19–31, Berlin, First Sunday after Trinity, May 29, 1932 (?)[1]

Luke 16:19–31: There was a rich man who was dressed in purple and fine linen and who feasted sumptuously every day. And at his gate lay a poor man named Lazarus, covered with sores, who longed to satisfy his hunger with what fell from the rich man's table; even the dogs would come and lick his sores. The poor man died and was carried away by the angels to be with Abraham. The rich man also died and was buried. In Hades, where he was being tormented, he looked up and saw Abraham far away with Lazarus by his side. He called out, "Father Abraham, have mercy on me, and send Lazarus to dip the tip of his finger in water and cool my tongue; for I am in agony in these flames." But Abraham said, "Child, remember that during your lifetime you received your good things, and Lazarus in like manner evil things; but now he is comforted here, and you are in agony. Besides all this, between you and us a great chasm has been fixed, so that those who might want to pass from here to you cannot do so, and no one can cross from there to us." He said, "Then, father, I beg you to send him to my father's house—for I have five brothers—that he may warn them, so that they will not
also come into this place of torment." Abraham replied, "They have Moses and 427
the prophets; they should listen to them." He said, "No, father Abraham; but if someone goes to them from the dead, they will repent." He said to him, "If they do not listen to Moses and the prophets, neither will they be convinced even if someone rises from the dead."

One cannot understand and preach the gospel concretely [handgreiflich] enough. A real evangelical sermon must be like holding a pretty red apple in front of a child or a glass of cool water in front of a thirsty person and then asking: do you want it? We should be able to talk about matters of our faith in such a way that the hands reach out for it faster than we can fill them. People should run and not be able to rest when the gospel is talked about, as long ago the sick ran to Christ to be healed when he was going around healing (but Christ, too, healed more than he converted). That is really no stock phrase. Shouldn't it really be that way wherever the good news of God is spoken of? But it just isn't that way—we all know that.

---

[1.] *NL*, A 33,6(1) (a); handwritten draft; notation by Eberhard Bethge: "same writing paper as baptism sermon for Thomas, born August 26, 1931!" (see 3/9). Previously published in *PAM* 1:284–93. Cf. *NL*, A 33,6(1) (b); later typewritten transcription with notation by Eberhard Bethge: "Sermon on the first Sunday after Trinity, May 29, 1932 (?)." Previously published in *GS* 4:50–59. Bonhoeffer had a friend send him a sermon of Karl Barth's on the same text from June 2, 1931, which had become famous but emphasized different aspects (see *NL*, A 33,6[2]).

At the same time, one shouldn't content oneself with this state of affairs. Rather, there can be basically just one thing, namely, that one repeatedly asks oneself anew why this is so. And here is one—admittedly only one—of the reasons that we[2] simply hesitate to accept that the gospel is as concrete, as close to life, as it is. We have spiritualized the gospel—that is, we have lightened it up, changed it. Take our gospel of the rich man and poor Lazarus. It has become common practice to see as the whole meaning of the story that the rich should help the poor.[3] That is, it is turned into a story illustrating a moral. But this particular story especially, if one allows oneself to be affected fully by its original meaning, is something very different from that, namely, a very concrete proclamation of the good news itself. Admittedly so concretely, so powerfully worded, that we don't even take it seriously anymore.

428 Let us imagine how a crowd of the sick, the poor, the miserable, of the poor Lazaruses gathered around Christ, and then he began to tell the story of the poor, leprous Lazarus, whom even the dogs were torturing, at the doorstep of the rich man. And when the story then took a turn with the words: "The poor man died and was carried away by the angels to be with Abraham. Lazarus received evil things in his life, but now he is comforted here,"[4] perhaps shouts of joy and hope passed through the crowd. That was the good news; that was the cool water they reached for greedily. That was the love of God itself, which spoke in this way to the poor and suffering. You outcasts, you disadvantaged, you poor and sick, you who are looked down upon shall be consoled. You have much suffering in the world, but in a short while eternal joy and eternal consolation shall come over you. Look at poor Lazarus, at how he is lying scorned before the rich man's doorstep, and then look at how he receives God's consolation with Abraham. Blessed are you, you poor, for the kingdom of God is yours. Blessed are you who are hungry[5] here below, for you shall be filled. Blessed are you who weep here, for you will laugh. Rejoice and leap for joy, for your reward is great in heaven.[6] Those are the beatitudes in Luke. Nothing is said here about the poor in spirit,[7] nothing about hunger for righteousness,[8] but blessed are you poor, you hungry, you who are weeping, as we know you in the world.

[2.] Crossed out: "do not preach the gospel concretely enough."

[3.] Crossed out: "But that is only one part of the question that is being looked at here in a very special light. Whoever does this takes away the original meaning of the story."

[4.] [Bonhoeffer quotes Luke 16:22a and then paraphrases a portion of Luke 16:25.—MB]

[5.] Crossed out: "and thirsts."

[6.] Luke 6:20–23.

[7.] See Matt. 5:3.

Blessed are you Lazaruses of all the ages, for you shall be consoled in the bosom of Abraham. Blessed [are] you[9] outcasts and outlaws, you victims of society, you men and women without work,[10] you broken down and ruined, you lonely and abandoned, rape victims and those who suffer injustice, you who suffer in body and soul;[11] blessed are you, for God's joy will come over you and be over [your] head forever. That is the gospel, the good news of the dawning of the new world, the new order, which is God's world and
God's order. The deaf hear, the blind see, the lame walk, and the gospel is 429
preached to the poor.[12]

And before we interrupt ourselves to ask questions here, let us hear the other, the terrible other side. There is the rich man, who dressed in purple and fine linen. About him it says: "The rich man also died and was buried." That already sounds very harsh. And now in hell he must suffer the torment of eternal thirst, because he was full and satisfied on earth. He has to see poor Lazarus in the bosom of Abraham and beg that Lazarus quench his thirst only for a moment. But even that can't be. "Child, remember that during your lifetime you received your good things." And behind this we hear the words: Woe to you[13] who are full now, for you will be hungry. Woe to you who are laughing now, for you will mourn and weep.[14] Woe to you who dress in purple and live happily in luxury, for you shall suffer eternal thirst.

Blessed poor, outcast, leprous Lazarus yesterday and today, for you have a God. Woe [to you] who live happily in luxury and are respected yesterday and today. That [is] the most concretely preached good news of God for the poor.

But now we must listen to quite a few shocked objections before we continue.

There are always those in our midst who know better than the New Testament itself what the New Testament may and may not say. What we have just said here is, of course, a rough interpretation of the New Testament intended for rough common people. It couldn't be about that. If something in the New Testament really sounds as rough as what we just said, you have to take it and spiritualize it. We call that "sublimating," that is, refining, elevating, spiritualizing, moralizing. It's not just simply the physically poor who are blessed and the physically rich who would be damned. But the main

[8.] See Matt. 5:6.

[9.] Crossed out: "by society."

[10.] See p. 412, ed. note 20, and the editor's afterword to the German edition, p. 477.

[11.] "Body and soul" replaces "here and there."

[12.] See Luke 7:22.

[13.] Crossed out: "rich."

[14.] Luke 6:25.

thing is always what a person's attitude is toward his poverty and toward his
430 wealth. The external aspect doesn't matter at all, but rather the attitude matters: rich in God [or] poor in God . . .[15] The most dangerous thing about this criticism is that it contains some truth, but basically it is intended only to provide us with an excuse. It is so terribly easy to back away from all so-called external conditions and focus on the attitude: rich on the outside but being poor in one's so-called attitude. It is so terribly easy to say that it is vulgar to understand the gospel as if it were about outward poverty and riches, while it really depends not on that but solely on the inner aspect. Now, I ask you, where in the story of the poor Lazarus does it say anything about his inner life? Who tells us that he was a man who within himself had the right attitude toward his poverty? Just the opposite, he may have been quite a pushy poor man, since he lay down in front of the rich man's doorstep and did not go away. Who tells us anything about the soul of the rich man? That is precisely the frightening thing about this story—there is no moralizing here at all, but simply talk of poor and rich and of the promise and the threat given to the one and the other. Here these external conditions are obviously not treated as external conditions but are taken unbelievably seriously. Why did Christ heal the sick and suffering if he didn't consider such external conditions important? Why is the kingdom of God equated with the deaf hear, the blind see?[16] . . . And where do we get the incredible presumption to spiritualize these things that Christ saw and did very concretely?

We must end this audacious, sanctimonious spiritualization of the gospel. Take it as it is, or hate it honestly!

And there was no lack of this hatred precisely because people took the gospel to be as honest as it was. The hatred comes from two different sides.

431 What does a gospel that was brought to the weaklings, the common people, the poor, and the sick have to do with us? We are men, healthy and strong. We disdain the mass of Lazaruses. We disdain the gospel of the poor.[17] It undermines our pride, our race, our strength.[18] We are rich,

[15.] One of the first proponents of this interpretation, which later became widespread, was the Greek-Egyptian theologian Clement of Alexandria (ca. 140–220), who attempted to reconcile Platonism and the Christian faith.

[16.] See Luke 7:22.

[17.] "Disdain the gospel of the poor" replaces "need their gospel, we do not need it." The philosopher Friedrich Nietzsche, widely read in the 1920s, had often formulated this criticism. See, for example, *The Anti-Christ*: "Christianity is a rebellion of everything that crawls on the ground against everything that has *height*: the evangel of the 'lowly' *makes* things lower" (*Anti-Christ, Ecce Homo*, 40)

[18.] This criticism was part of the standard repertoire of attacks used by anti-Christian National Socialists. [More specifically, this kind of rhetoric is often found in the

but with pride. That is certainly honestly said. But it is also said incredibly carelessly and at the same time so full of illusions. It is so easy to disdain the masses of Lazaruses. But if just one of these would really meet you face-to-face—the unemployed Lazarus, Lazarus the accident victim, Lazarus whose ruin you caused, your own begging child as Lazarus, the helpless and desperate mother, Lazarus who has become a criminal, the godless Lazarus—can you go up to him and say: I disdain you, Lazarus? I scoff at the good news that makes you glad? Can you really do that? And if you can't do that, why then do you first act as[19] if it were something great to be able to do that?

But also, couldn't it possibly already be a mockery in itself to console those who live in suffering and misery with the prospect of a better future in another world?[20] Doesn't it almost sound as if one is just trying to keep these unfortunates from rebelling here against their fate? As if one is calling them blessed just so they will stay quiet, as they are now, and not bother the others? Isn't it downright cynical to talk about consolation in heaven because one does not want to give consolation on earth? Is this gospel for the poor not basically the deception and dumbing down of the people? 432
Does it not show that one does not take the suffering at all seriously but hides cynically behind pious phrases? Oh, countless times it has happened that way—who would deny it—right up to our present time. And[21] millions have become estranged from the gospel for this reason! But a look at the Gospels shows us what is different here.[22] Jesus calls the poor blessed,[23] but he does heal them, too, already here. Yes, the kingdom of God is at hand, for the blind see and the lame walk.[24] He takes suffering so seriously that in a moment he must destroy it. Where Christ is, the power of the demons must be broken. That is why he heals, and that is why he says to his disciples: If you believe in me, you will do greater works than I.[25] The

---

language of the German Christian movement, which was the pro-Nazi faction within the German Protestant church.—VB]

[19.] Crossed out: "Could you do that?"

[20.] Here and in the following thoughts Bonhoeffer is referring to the Marxist critique of religion. See Marx, *Critique of Hegel's Philosophy of Right,* 131: "The abolition of religion as the *illusory* happiness of the people is a demand for their true happiness. The call to abandon illusions about their condition is the *call to abandon a condition which requires illusions.* Thus, the critique of religion is the *critique in embryo of the vale of tears* of which religion is the *halo.*"

[21.] Crossed out: "it should not be that way."

[22.] "Is different here" replaces "fails."

[23.] See Luke 6:20.

[24.] See Luke 7:22.

[25.] See John 14:12.

kingdom of God is still just beginning to appear. The acts of healing are like heat lightning, [like] flashes of lightning from the new world. But now the good news becomes all the more powerful. Blessed are you who weep, for you will laugh; blessed are you who are hungry, for you will be filled.[26] No cynical consolation, but the one great hope: the new world, the good news, the merciful God, Lazarus in the bosom of Abraham, the poor and the outcasts with God—yes, indeed, this may [sound] terribly naive and concrete. But if it were really true? If it *is* true? Is it still naive then? Is it still unspiritual then? Don't we then especially have to open our ears and hear, and hear again, about the unheard-of event that Lazarus—yesterday and today—is carried by angels to be in the bosom of Abraham? And that the well-satisfied man, the full man, who lives happily in luxury, the rich man must suffer eternal thirst?

Up until now we have spoken of these two as if they actually had nothing to do with each other. That is obviously not the case. Lazarus lies in front of the rich man's doorstep, and it is the poverty of Lazarus that makes the rich man rich, just as the wealth of the other man makes Lazarus poor. It doesn't say what the rich man nor what the poor man had done or even
433 should have done, but the only common event that affects them equally is their death. That is the unusual light in which both of these men are shown here; they both must die, and another life awaits both of them. And this fact binds them closer together than any moral law that a rich man should help a poor man. They basically already belong together in the common fate that awaits both of them. In death the rich man is no longer rich, and the poor man no longer poor. There they are one and the same. And after death something new begins, over which all the powers of the world of death can have no more control. But this is obviously what the rich man did not see, that his whole world is [a] world of death and must pass away and is subject to God, that for that reason Lazarus has something to do with him, because they both must die and will live in another world, because they are brothers in death and in judgment. He did not see that behind him and behind Lazarus[27] there stand infinities, eternities—here silent, invisible, hidden under the purple garments and the naked body of Lazarus—but that they are there and are waiting and become reality. And the conversation between the thirsting rich man and Abraham leaves no doubt about the seriousness of what is meant here by eternity.

But now, in principle, there will also be no more revelation of this eternity in the world, as the rich man requests for his brothers, other than

[26.] Luke 6:21.

[27.] Crossed out: "whole worlds."

what is given in Moses and the prophets; today we would say: given in the preaching of the church. In their world of death, they have Moses and the prophets; let them hear them. The words about God's eternal commandment[28] and about the weakness and the suffering of the human being who must die;[29] about God's mercy to the humble and his judgment of the strong;[30] the words about the cross of Christ for the salvation of the poor and lost, of the curse on the satisfied and the righteous[31]—let them hear these and remember that they all live with Lazarus in the same world of death; and if they do not hear them, they will also not hear, even if one
were to rise from the dead. Even at this most visible conquest of their world 434
of death, they will not be afraid and not become wise. They will refuse to accept it. They will not know that the Lazarus before their door is an eternal Lazarus, and they will pass by the eternity that meets them in Lazarus.

And now, the last questions: Who is Lazarus? Who is the rich man? And finally, what should the rich man do?

Who is Lazarus? You know it yourself: your poorer brother who cannot cope with life's outward or its spiritual aspects, often foolish, often impudent, often pushy, often godless, but yet endlessly needy and—whether knowing it or not—suffering, who craves the crumbs from under your table. You may think with a little self-pity that you yourself are Lazarus. God alone knows if you are. But always keep asking if you are not perhaps after all the rich man. Who is Lazarus? Always the other one, the crucified Christ himself, who meets you in the form of a thousand people you would look down upon. Yes, he is the eternal Lazarus himself.

And now we must ask again: Who is Lazarus? And here at the end, in all humility, the last possibility must [be] considered, at the limits of all human and divine possibilities: We are all Lazarus before God. The rich man, too, is Lazarus. He is the poor leper before God. And only when we know that we are all Lazarus, because we all live through the mercy of God, do we see Lazarus in our brother.

Who is the rich man? Our story does not answer this question. Certainly we are not rich. We are not full and satisfied. We do not live happily in luxury. Really not? Do you mean that seriously? Even when you meet Lazarus? Or does he not meet you? Are we really not the rich man? Another story gives us an answer to this question. The story of the rich young man, who

[28.] See Matt. 5:17–19.

[29.] See Ps. 39:5.

[30.] Crossed out: "arrogance."

[31.] See 1 Cor. 2; Luke 1:48–53; and Luke 6:20–26.

was very devout and very righteous, but was sad when he was told to leave his possessions, and went away.[32] That is the rich man. And we?

And now: What should the rich man do? The answer to this question can
435 be found in the story of the Good Samaritan.[33] In our story there is only this: The rich man should see that death is standing behind him[34] and Lazarus, and that behind Lazarus God himself, Christ is standing with the eternal good news. We should see—see poor Lazarus in his full frightening misery and behind him Christ, who invited him to his table and calls him blessed. Let us see you, poor Lazarus, let us see you, Christ, in poor Lazarus. Oh, that we might be able to see. Amen.

### 11. Sermon on Colossians 3:1–4, Berlin, Third Sunday after Trinity, June 12, 1932[1]

Col. 3:1–4: So if you have been raised with Christ, seek the things that are above, where Christ is, seated at the right hand of God. Set your mind on things that are above, not on things that are on earth, for you have died, and your life is hidden with Christ in God. When Christ who is your life is revealed, then you also will be revealed with him in glory.

Dear congregation, that is certainly an extremely off-putting way to start a conversation with a person: Since you have been raised with Christ, do this and that. We have been baptized. We have been confirmed. There were times when we felt like opening the Bible. We are interested in various religious questions. Maybe we even stand by our church with loyalty and love. And finally, after all: we live in a world that over the last one and a half to two thousand years under the name of Jesus Christ has developed as a Christian world. And nevertheless: if anyone tried to start a conversation with us by just speaking to us about the fact that we have been raised
436 with Christ, we would probably prefer not to continue to speak with him. We would see that he was moved. We would see that he was excited. We would see how intensely serious he was about what he was still going to say to us. But we would distance ourselves from this assumption that he made

[32.] See Matt. 19:16–22.

[33.] See Luke 10:25–37.

[34.] "Behind him" replaces "and him."

[1.] *NL*, A 33,7 (1); typewritten transcription by Bertha Schulze with handwritten editorial changes by Eberhard Bethge and handwritten notation by Eberhard Bethge: "Two Sermons on Colossians 3:1–4, Third Sunday after Trinity, June 12, 1932." Previously published (without the editorial changes) in *GS* 4:60–69.

and from which he would not let go at any price, from this condition that he thinks he has to set so that we are even able to hear and understand everything else he would like to share with us; yes, we would distance ourselves from this assumption and this condition that we have been raised with Christ; we would turn away astonished and unfavorably impressed. We would shake our heads about a person like that.

*Actually*, this way of addressing us should come over us like a judgment. *Actually*, this one word should break in upon us—so powerful, so sublime, so exalted—that we grow pale in fear and trembling before it: for *this* glow, this glory of being raised with Christ is really not a part of our experience, cannot be seen anywhere in our lives, try as one might and looking as carefully as possible. Instead, we turn aside, astonished and unfavorably impressed. Instead, we shake our heads. Instead, when someone speaks to us like that, it seems to us baptized and confirmed Christians as if a representative of some mysterious secret society were coming up to us with his weird secret password. We must not delude ourselves: this address, "you have been raised with Christ," goes completely and hopelessly right over the heads of us Christians. We have long since banished this form of address into the sects (and then are surprised that there still are sects). We have long since left this form of address behind as obsolete and antiquated, in order to concern ourselves with apparently more important, more useful, more interesting, even with more Christian things.

What is it supposed to mean to us that we have been raised with Christ? It is incomprehensible for us. It seems foolish to us. It is completely uninteresting to us. It seems to us completely ill-suited for the beginning of a conversation. It seems to us completely ill-suited at the start of a workday, at the beginning of the plans that we are considering, at the beginning of important decisions we have to make. It seems to us completely ill-suited in
relationships we have with one another. How should the certainty that we 437
have all been raised in Christ affect the relationship of the teacher to the pupil, the friend to the friend, the wife to the husband, and the father to the son? If we tolerate this idea at all, then only as the crowning conclusion of a brilliant lecture. If this thought has anything to say to us, then only in the hours long after work, far removed from the immediate reality of our decisions, exalted pious hours, but which we grant only a very limited right to affect the rest of our life. And how should the rest of our life be influenced anyway by this enigmatic and easily misunderstood assertion that we have been raised with Christ?

Dear friends, without noticing it and as if by chance, we have just laid out the whole crisis of our Christianity. For isn't it true that on the first superficial consideration, it must be unavoidably clear: if there was a time

when there was a Christianity where people believed things like that, where people concerned themselves with such great thoughts, when a person could meet another person, speak to him, even close a business deal, all the while with that certainty that they have both been raised in Christ—then our time, our Christianity, our faith are greatly impoverished in comparison. Then we have suffered huge losses. For we don't even come close to understanding at all what it means that we all together have been raised in Christ. We stand here before this apostolic assurance *so* poorly prepared, with *so* little idea what it is about, that out of sheer lack of another explanation we think that it must be a whimsical eccentricity of the apostle, and we could justifiably leave it to the eccentrics, the sect members. And then it is completely incomprehensible to us how this kind of certainty that we have been raised with Christ should even have an effect in our lives. When we are in need, in questions of politics or the economy, in questions of the education of our children, in questions of married life, when we are unsure of what form and toward which goals we should structure our whole life, would it occur to a single one of us, whether we are the questioners or those
438 who should give the answer, to state as the first proposition of this deliberation, in all decisiveness: All of us together have been raised in Christ? You nations over here and over there—you have been raised in Christ? You men of finance, you who manage the billions of the world, and with that the savings of the small and the smallest—you have been raised in Christ? You parents and husbands and wives, you who are one another's friends, you apartment-house residents with all your difficulties and disagreements, you employers and you employees, you who yearn to become real, strong, capable people—all of you have been raised in Christ?

Dear friends, one need do nothing more than consider something like that. One need only walk through the streets, look at the people, and ask yourself whether they accept this premise and live their lives on the basis of it, in order to see that what we call Christianity is, in human terms, hopelessly in need, that it is greatly impoverished, whether the churches are filled to overflowing as in America[2] or almost empty as in much of Germany.

Our fathers still said: "In the name of God, Amen."[3] They still lived under the illusion that with that, they had said something important. They

---

[2.] In a report about his year as a foreign student in the United States in 1930–31, Bonhoeffer had complained about the lack of theological content of most of the sermons and the lack of substance in the Christian social activism of the white churches in America (see *DBWE* 10:307–10, 312–16, and 317–19).

[3.] [On June 1, 1932, Franz von Papen was named chancellor; a devout Catholic, he reintroduced the custom of opening parliament with the invocation "In the name of

still lived under the illusion that with that, they had said something that everyone had in common, that was an obligation to them all, that bound them all together. But they probably never allowed this "In the name of God, Amen" to become too dangerous, too disturbing, too revolutionary. And why should they? This opening, this premise, could just as well mean everything as nothing. Having said these words, one could confidently draw the line and just go on, unworried and unswerving, and in the name of humankind make decisions and decrees and pass statutes, whatever one thought was good and whatever one liked. One went one's way in complete freedom, the name of God harmlessly backing one up and the earthly well-being of human beings in view. And did one even really need the name of 439
God backing one up to fight for and win the earthly well-being of humankind? Should this ancient name of God, at the same time so simple and so full of meaning, be able to contribute anything to mastering the innumerable problems that had to be solved? And the richness of what is human became all the more tempting and the ancient name of the ancient God slipped more and more into obscurity. So the name of God moved further and further away, and ever nearer came the fullness of concrete life standing on its own.

What if one could finally find the key to wisdom for all areas of life? The ideal form of the state? The smoothest exchange of goods between all nations of the earth, the crisis-proof monetary system from which all instability would have been removed? The best possible educational method, the most sophisticated hygiene and diet, the infallible cure? The deepest analysis of the mind and maybe also the best philosophy, the finest art, and certainly also the best of all forms of religiosity? Isn't it true that for a large segment of our people, salvation is expected from nothing else than from these things? And the more this longed-for salvation eludes us, the more our plans come to nothing again and again, and the more our life falls from cliff to cliff and from crisis to crisis, the more we cry out for specialists, for experts. *They* must know it. *They* must be able to do it. After all, the most exact science must be able to bring us to our goal, must bring order in our chaos. How much more trustworthy, how much more promising this scientific system is, feverishly pushing forward in all areas of our human life, than that flat, unexpressive: "In the name of God, Amen," and that antiquated, long-forgotten: "If you have been raised with Christ."

But is this world that we are rushing toward at full speed really so trustworthy and filled with promise? Will we ever really succeed in bringing

---

God, Amen." Bonhoeffer's sermon may be in part a commentary on the political events unfolding around him; see also ed. note 7.—VB]

together understanding and knowledge in such a way that they no longer constantly contradict each other, in integrating all our actions and work in
440 such a way that people are not constantly acting and working against each other on this earth? And if we should succeed at that: Where should we go with it all? Is it really so that we are reeling into endlessness, into the "Never-ending" [Unaufhörliche], as a modern poet calls it?[4] The "Never-ending," of which we could only be terrified—what awaits us seems *too* empty, *too* dark, *too* bottomless. Our future looks at us with hollow eyes. Perhaps at first we are intoxicated by this grandiose prospect; we feel drunk in this gigantic freedom, without God and without hope, without a goal and without restraint, rushing violently ahead into chaos. Even the greatest futility can be intensified into pathos and art, into life and motivation. But as soon as we stop, sober up from our intoxication, come to our senses, it becomes unbelievably empty inside us: "Do you not taste the cup of nothingness, the dark drink?"[5] And now what, what do we want now? Do we want to survive another crisis and then die, or what do we really want?[6] We are told: "I have been through too much, I cannot be without religion anymore"; and that probably means: I have already looked too deeply into this nothingness to be able to stand being in it any longer. So go back—but back to where? We read that a government issues a proclamation that a whole nation should be rescued from collapse—by the Christian worldview.[7] So we are all fleeing, [the] individuals and nations, fleeing from an incomprehensible last collapse. "In the name of God, Amen" is to be used again. Religion is to be cultivated again and a Christian worldview spread.

Oh, how poor, oh, how weak, oh, how pitiful all of that sounds. Do we think that we would really let ourselves be taken captive a second time by this "In the name of God, Amen?"[8] That we would let it really determine

[4.] See the text of Paul Hindemith's 1931 oratorio *Das Unaufhörliche*, written by Gottfried Benn, in *Gesammelte Werke in acht Bänden*, 2:492–515, especially 514–15; translation here by Anne Schmidt-Lange.

[5.] Benn, *Gesammelte Werke in acht Bänden*, 2:500; cf. 504 and 506.

[6.] [Here the German text has a period instead of a question mark.—MB]

[7.] The new government under Reich Chancellor Franz von Papen, which on June 1, 1932, replaced the Brüning cabinet, which had stepped down, carried out its attempts at a restoration of a government and society based on Christian tradition and the estates (*"christlich-ständischer" Traditionen*) with the help of slogans like this. [The hope was to reestablish a political system resembling that from the days of the kaiser. The estates (*Stände*) were the nobility, the clergy, and others from the leading ranks of society who were responsible for running the country for the good of the people.—MB]

[8.] Bonhoeffer compares the propaganda of the Papen government with the misuse of this phrase in the First World War, when Germans went into battle under this motto.

all our actions, that we, you[9] and I, rich and poor, German and French, 441
would let ourselves be bound together by this name of God? Or is there not really, hidden behind our religious tendencies, our irrepressible craving for freedom and our own will—to do in the name of God what *we* want, in the name of the Christian worldview to play off one nationality against another and stir them up to conflict with one another?

And only now does it fall like scales from our eyes; only now are we overcome by the certainty of the monstrous fact—that we are fleeing from God. Whether we dare to drink that cup of nothingness,[10] that dark drink, or we avoid it by taking refuge in religious busyness and talk, we are fleeing from that other cup that the Bible has tasted and which it proclaims to the world in a powerful voice. The cup of the wrath of God, the cup of the consuming fire of the living God.[11] Our disobedience is not that we are so little religious but that we actually would like very much to be religious, find it very edifying when someone somewhere says and writes: "In the name of God, Amen," are very much reassured when some government or other proclaims the Christian worldview. It is our disobedience, it is our fleeing, it is our calamitous downfall—that we, the more pious we are, are all the less willing to let ourselves be told that God is dangerous; that God does not allow himself to be mocked; that we human beings must die if we really want to have anything to do with the living God; that we must lose our life if we really want to gain it;[12] that we must be baptized not only with water but also with fire and [the] spirit;[13] that this "In the name of God, Amen," if it really is to have any meaning and not be just empty talk, is a majestic region that one can enter only as a completely captive slave—or not at all.

To drink this cup of God's, if one really knows what one is doing, that
is serious. And to drink that cup of nothingness, the dark drink, if one 442
really knows what one is doing, is also serious—and the eternal God with his glowing promise is infinitely closer to those who do this than they from afar could imagine.

But to stand somewhere in the middle of it all with some kind or other of harmless, naive, pious or impious talk, religious or irreligious interest, fleeing from the one who is eternally alive and fleeing from the eternally dead—that is nothingness. There is no rejoicing about this among the angels of

[9.] [Bonhoeffer uses the familiar form, *Du*.—MB]

[10.] [See p. 454, ed. note 5.—MB]

[11.] See Jer. 25:15–29.

[12.] See Matt. 10:39.

[13.] See Matt. 3:11.

heaven; these are the healthy people who do not need a physician;[14] these are the ninety-nine righteous men.[15] But because we are standing there right in the middle between the two fires, because we do not know anymore, no, for good reasons do not *want* to know what it means: You have died with Christ, you have been crucified with Christ—that is why, then, we don't know anymore what it means: you have been raised with Christ. Now it is as if we had been placed under the ban, as if we *were not allowed* to know it anymore. Now it lies over us like a punishment that we must stand before these words with blind eyes and deaf ears,[16] completely at a loss about what they should mean and what we should do with them in our life.

Could it be possible that our ears and eyes be opened again, that we again understand dusty old words and perceive that they carry life within them? Life as no science, also no religious studies can give us, but only the eternal God in his eternal Son? That in [them] we find our one and only consolation and support, whether we live or die? That we have died and our life is hidden with Christ in God?[17] That we have been raised with Christ and for that reason can set our minds "on things that are above, not on things that are on earth"?

We must stop here for today. It is better and more salutary for us to see once in all clarity how far our private and public life is removed from this understanding than to explain just like that what an easy thing it is to
443 regain this understanding. If it were an easy thing, then it would not be *this* understanding but once more a couple of pious, edifying human thoughts.

But because they are *God's* thoughts, they cannot remain hidden from us in eternity. Because it is God who in this Christ bends down to us, to draw us to him, because he has loved us always and forever, that is why all of that cannot remain for us a riddle and foolishness for all time. He himself will tear away the veil that now lies over his holy words; he himself will open our astonished eyes for that glory, for it is true that we have died with Christ but have also been raised with Christ, that our true life is that which is now and always hidden with Christ in God.

And this truth of God would take us captive, would bind and be an obligation to us, would bond us together, person to person. If we come together with some "In the name of God, Amen," then we still come in our unbroken human pride, then we never really find one another, then we never really

[14.] See Matt. 9:12.

[15.] See Luke 15:7.

[16.] See Matt. 13:11–15.

[17.] [See also the following sermon, 3/12.—VB]

meet each other, then we always talk past each other, at the conferences[18] and in our families. For it is simply impossible for us to give up our demands that seem so justifiable. But if we come together as the crucified and risen ones of Jesus Christ, as those who have lost their prideful human life in order to win it anew in Christ, as those who were sentenced to death but pardoned—then we will find one another, then we would look into one another's eyes and would recognize one another completely anew, as we are recognized by God. Then and only then could we love one another. Lord, our ruler, eternal God! Send a hunger into the land. Not a hunger for bread and a thirst for water, but [a hunger] to hear the word of the Lord.[19] Amen.

## 12. Sermon on Colossians 3:1–4, Berlin, Fourth Sunday after Trinity, June 19, 1932[1] 444

Col. 3:1–4: So if you have been raised with Christ, seek the things that are above, where Christ is, seated at the right hand of God. Set your mind on things that are above, not on things that are on earth, for you have died, and your life is hidden with Christ in God. When Christ who is your life is revealed, then you also will be revealed with him in glory.

Dear congregation, it is as if our whole life were carried, raised up, and protected in these words. Say what you will against this "Seek the things that are above." You may suspect that those who are constantly seeking things above may lose contact with the ground under their feet. "If he reaches up and raises his head to touch the stars, then his unsure feet will have no foothold, and he will be the plaything of clouds and wind."[2] But no matter how the individual feels about it, human society suspects with good reason that people with their heads in the clouds like that might be useless extra

[18.] Bonhoeffer is probably referring here to the various ecumenical conferences he attended in the years 1931–32 and some of which he had helped to prepare (see the reports in part 2).

[19.] See Amos 8:11.

[1.] *NL*, A 33,7(2); typewritten transcription by Bertha Schulze with handwritten editorial changes by Eberhard Bethge and with the notation by Eberhard Bethge: "II.) Fourth Sunday after Trinity, June 19, 1932." Previously published (without the editorial changes) in *PAM* 1:304–15; previously published (with the editorial changes) in *GS* 4:69–79. The sermon was preached in the Kaiser Wilhelm Gedächtniskirche when Bonhoeffer substituted for Pastor Gerhard Jacobi there.

[2.] This is a quotation from Goethe's poem "Grenzen der Menschheit." [The English translation here is by Vernon Watkins, "Limits of Human Nature," in Goethe, *Collected Works*, 1:83.—ASL]

mouths to feed, instead of using burning hearts and a strong arm to create order and progress here on earth; that they would dream of a better afterlife and would be unfit for the great revolutionary action that each generation must take, smashing old tablets and setting up new and better ones.

Because of sentences like this, "Set your mind on things that are above and not on things that are on the earth," Christians are stood up against the wall and shot.[3] Because of sentences like this, Christianity is accused of
445 betraying the earth.[4] Stay true to the earth; set your mind on things that are on earth.[5] For countless people that is a holy cause—and we understand their zeal. We understand the jealousy with which they want to bind the planning and work and efforts of human beings to this earth. For we are bound to this earth. It is the place where we stand and fall. An accounting is demanded for what happens on earth. And woe to us Christians if we should fail there; if [at] the end of all things, it should have to be said of the godless person: Well done, good and trustworthy slave, you have been trustworthy in a few things; I will put you in charge of many things, enter into the joy of your master;[6] because he was faithful in an earthly way in the earthly tasks that were given him, because he had invested the talents that [were] entrusted to him, while it would have to be said of us Christians: As for this worthless slave, throw him into the outer darkness,[7] because we had buried our talent in the ground—for all our setting our minds on things that are above. The Russian film *The Road to Life* probably made a shocking impression on many people.[8] There you saw how whole bands of

---

[3.] The frightening news of the persecution of Christians in Russia caused great concern among German Protestants in the 1920s.

[4.] See Nietzsche, *Thus Spoke Zarathustra*, 6: "I beseech you, my brothers, *remain faithful to the earth* and do not believe those who speak to you of extraterrestrial hopes! They are mixers of poisons whether they know it or not. They are despisers of life, dying off and self-poisoned, of whom the earth is weary: so let them fade away! Once the sacrilege against God was the greatest sacrilege, but God died, and then all the desecrators died. Now to desecrate the earth is the most terrible thing, and to esteem the bowels of the unfathomable higher than the meaning of the earth!"

[5.] See the preceding ed. note, and Nietzsche, *Thus Spoke Zarathustra*, 57: "Remain faithful to the earth, my brothers, with the power of your virtue! Let your bestowing love and your knowledge serve the meaning of the earth! Thus I beg and beseech you."

[6.] Matt. 25:21.

[7.] See Matt. 25:30.

[8.] The film [the German title was *Der Weg ins Leben*—VB] about bands of young tramps with the original title *Putyovka v zhizn* was the first sound movie of Russian director Nikolai Ekk and describes the problems of poverty and rehabilitation in post-revolutionary Russia. [This film portrayed the educational experiment of Makarenko, a Russian educational pioneer at the time. The self-controlled groups of youngsters in his

neglected, criminal boys and young men were gathered by a superior leader and through voluntary and orderly work were changed from vagabonds into human beings. And the shocking part of it was this: the building where this working group was living was a cloister church. The clergy had been driven out; worship services and prayer had come to an end. But now a new era and a great earthly goal flooded through these rooms: to lead people out 446
of earthly night and into earthly light. Set your mind on things that are on earth!

Today immensely important things will be decided by whether we Christians have strength enough to show the world that we are not dreamers and are not those who walk with their heads in the clouds, that we don't just let things come and go as they are, that our faith is really not the opium that lets us stay content in the midst of an unjust world,[9] but that we, especially because we set our minds on things that are above, only protest all the more tenaciously and resolutely on this earth. Protest with words and action, in order to lead the way forward at any price. Must it be that Christianity, which began in such a tremendously revolutionary way long ago, is now conservative for all time? That each new movement must forge a path for itself without the church, that time after time the church does not see what has actually happened until twenty years after the fact?[10] If that really is the way it must be, we should not be surprised if for our church, too, times will come again when the blood of martyrs will be required. But this blood, if we really still have the courage and honor and faithfulness to shed it, will not be as innocent and untarnished as that of the first witnesses. On our blood would lie great guilt of our own: the guilt of the worthless slave, who is thrown into the outer darkness.

And yet, however grave the danger that lies in these words—"Seek the things that are above, where Christ is seated at the right hand of God"—the

---

institution had become very famous and a widespread topic of discussion, so Bonhoeffer's congregation would have been familiar with the reference. The editors thank Hans Pfeifer for this information.—MB]

[9.] See Karl Marx, *Critique of Hegel's Philosophy of Right*, 131: "The wretchedness of *religion* is at once an *expression* of and a *protest* against real wretchedness. Religion is the sigh of the oppressed creature, the heart of a heartless world and the soul of soulless conditions. It is the *opium* of the people." The formulation of religion as the opium for the people is more likely to have originated with Heinrich Heine or the young Hegelian Bruno Bauer rather than with Marx himself (see Seeger, *Herkunft und Bedeutung des Schlagwortes: Die Religion ist Opium für das Volk*, 1935).

[10.] German Protestants in the 1920s often repeated this self-criticism about the inadequate and late response of the Protestant church to the question of social issues in the nineteenth century. They saw this as one of the main causes that led to the development of a socialist workers' movement outside the church.

447 danger that we could misunderstand it, the danger that we might become useless servants, the danger that people accuse us of betraying the earth,[11] we feel nevertheless that in these words our life is carried, raised up, and protected, that only in these words our life acquires a meaning that it would not have at all, however much we were faithful to the earth, however eager for action we were, and with however holy an urge to improve the world we would storm ahead. There may be innumerable things that are urgent and necessary, but there is only one thing that is needed: just this, that our whole life be protected by God. And just that, for which we human beings did not even dare to ask from afar, is simply assured to us: You have been raised with Christ, and your life is hidden with Christ in God.

We would really like to say all of that in a more modern, plain, and simple way, wouldn't we? The way it is preached in some churches and as it is believed by all too many Christians: Set your mind on things that are above, for your life is hidden in God. That is after all what we really would like to hear on Sunday: We bring all the fullness, the whole richness of our life along with us into church. And here the priest should do his duty, should bless and consecrate, should, over the depths and heights of our days, over suffering and joy, over sorrow and tears, over work and worries, speak the one word of salvation: that all of it is protected and hidden in God, the creator of the world. Outside in the world, of course, we are told something different. We are told that with our work and with our plans we are descending into a crisis, that with all our efforts we are only pushing ahead into the dark and boundless void. Perhaps we are told that our life is hopeless, that we must be suffocated by illness, misery, and guilt. Maybe the enticing call breaks in on the life of a happy family: Set your minds on things that are below, for the human being comes from the animals and must become an animal. And from all these frightening things in the real world, we could
448 flee into the church as into an old, familiar home. There, there everything would be bright and light: see, everything you plan and do and suffer is protected in God, the creator of the world. For that reason, set your minds on things that are above.

Haven't we all already felt that the frightening truth of the world simply swallows up this church talk? If the animal in us insists on its rights, what good does it do us to talk of the godliness of human beings? If the voice in us calls to us, "Set your mind on things that are below," what help to us is the most urgent warning, "Set your mind on things that are above"? When catastrophic demonic forces attack us and tear the rudder out of our grip,

[11.] See p. 458, ed. note 5.

so that we feel as if the fate of our world were driven by a raging hurricane, what consolation for us is the thought that all this is God's will? And if even death is reaching out for us, what good is all our talk about immortality?

Set your minds on things above, for our life is hidden in God—that may be a nice, pious, edifying sentence, but it doesn't stand up to the reality of the world. And this sentence must be contradicted by the world. It must be suspected of tempting us to betray the earth, of lulling us into a false sense of being protected in God, of robbing us of the initiative of the fighter and allowing us to be at rest in the midst of the most screaming injustice in the world.

But this sentence is not in the Bible. The apostle knows very well what he is doing when—completely without concern for our cries that it was not modern enough, that it was too hard to understand, that it was not plain and simple enough—he holds fast with all tenacity to this: Set your minds on things that are above, where Christ is seated at the right hand of God, for your life is hidden with Christ in God. And as we eagerly crowd around this with all our common sense and maybe also with a great deal of human wisdom to find out what this "hidden with Christ in God" might mean—there, like a cherub with a flaming sword,[12] stands that other word in the middle of the passage: "You have died." That is the strange part about it, that wherever there is talk of the living God, this death always comes in
between; that wherever there is talk of gaining life, this losing of life always 449
comes in between. What does that mean anyway, this dying or even this having died in the midst of life?

Here an impassable boundary is proclaimed with respect to our whole life, a barrier and boundary about which not only do we not want to know anything but about which we also, frighteningly, cannot know anything. You have died—that does not mean only something like: You all without exception are headed for death; you are captive to death at every step. But that must mean: Life has already become captive to the power of that riddle which is the essential riddle of death. That last, deepest human destiny to which our dying gives such strange witness is also the destiny of our life. There is a power that stands behind our living and our dying—and this power is really not to be compared to life, as we are always tempted to do, but rather, if one is to find something comparable to it, it is more comparable to death.

Only if one could see through God's own eyes could one view death and life along the same line in this way, that is, from the perspective of death.

[12.] See Gen. 3:24.

Because for us human beings the differences between life and death are unbelievably great—for God they fall together into one. For God a person is not more and not less, not farther away and not nearer, whether he lives or dies. But when speaking in human words and for human understanding about how it is for a human being, whether he lives or dies, whether in the eyes of God even human death is like a continued living—in that case our text admonishes us with the greatest firmness to think about just the opposite case. What if it were so that in God's eyes even our life was like death? Precisely not the triumphant "Life," which we human beings make such a big thing of, but actually and fundamentally a completely unstable, futile, hopeless, and godforsaken "Death." "You have died." The Bible still dares to think that frightening thought, for which we modern people are much too weak, that it is not "nothing" that we face there, whether we live or die, that
450 we do not simply sink into emptiness, free of all responsibility, but that we come to ruin confronted with God himself and are shattered by God, who is closer to us than our own blood, that we are confronted by the wrath of God. "You have died"—that means in the final analysis nothing other than: you are lost, godforsaken, whether you die or live. That is the frightening boundary that is proclaimed to us here. That is the message against which we rebel in our innermost being. We are glad to let ourselves be taught, we even let ourselves be taught about religious matters, but we want all of that to happen in such a way that we who speak and we who hear walk back and forth together in the beautifully decorated, cozy, warm rooms of our life. We let ourselves be preached to; we let ourselves be scolded; we let ourselves be advised and helped. But no one may lead us up to that boundary. We decided that for ourselves long ago. The boundary—that whether we live or die, we could be godforsaken people—we long ago discovered that to be an antiquated, false doctrine. We, of course, know so much better that it is just the other way around, that we, whether we live or die, actually are hidden in God; that it is only one step from us over to God; that it is as if God lives in the room next door, as Rilke occasionally hinted.[13]

Because we know that our life in the final analysis is life sheltered in God, divine life, for that reason we also know what expectations we can have of the church. Our visible life should be talked about. It should be examined down to its divine depths; it should be transfigured by divine consecration and divine blessing. But where does our knowledge of all that come from? Have the sciences brought us to the understanding that the human being's

[13.] Cf. Rainer Maria Rilke's mention of God as the "neighbor" or the "gentle neighbor(s) in need" (*Sämtliche Werke*, 3:309 and 1:309).

standing before God is not so bad? Or should that possibly be true because Goethe[14] and Hölderlin[15] were of that opinion?

"You have died," says the apostle, and he certainly knows: If it is really 451
true that our living and dying are nothing before God, then our thinking is also of no use. Then we could think a thousand times about how much nicer and simpler and more edifying it would be to have a God with whom we could not be lost—but these thousand thoughts would go astray. If it is true that we have died, we will have to let God himself tell us that we have died. For a lost way of thinking doesn't realize it is lost. Neither Paul nor we would know anything about this line of death, about this boundary, this being lost, if God himself did not tell us all this. God himself speaks to us; God himself comes to us; God himself tells us that we are lost. But when God does that, he, the one we have lost, is of course already with us; then we have already long been helped; there God scoffs at all our lostness; there God triumphs over everything that could separate us from him. There God's love has drawn us to him, and no power in the world can tear us out of his hand.

The apostle wants to tell us this incomprehensible, wonderful message. You have died—he doesn't say that to us to torture us, not to cast us into despair, but simply and only because he can say in the next breath: "And your life is hidden with Christ in God." We have not been left alone at all in our lostness; instead, there is one who has stepped across the boundary that separates us from the Creator and from true life, has broken into our territory of death, has tasted all our living and dying to its deepest depths, and has still broken through this death, broken through to the eternal Father, to eternal life, where he is seated at the right hand of God. And he has pulled up the whole world with him to life and to the light, has swallowed up death in victory, has taken our whole prison captive and brought us freedom, the glorious freedom of the children of God.

Dear friends, we don't want to give the impression that we understood
all that. That is the one event that takes place beyond the boundaries of all 452
that is human and for that reason also beyond the boundaries of our understanding. That Jesus, the great wise man of Galilee, should be the Christ who breaks through the whole line of death of human dying and living and leads us in triumph to the Father—no human being yet has understood

[14.] See, for example, the poem "Divinity" ("Das Göttliche"), in Goethe, *Selected Poetry*, 53–57, as well as the poem "Human Limitations" ("Grenzen der Menschheit") in the same volume, 49–51. See also Pfaff, "Goethe, Johann Wolfgang von."

[15.] Friedrich Hölderlin speaks often of the divine in the soul (see, for example, the poem "Diotima," in *Sämtliche Werke*, 1/1:212–15, especially 213). "Only those who were themselves divine" could believe (ibid., 250; see also the poem "Die Unsterblichkeit der Seele" (The immortality of the soul), ibid., 31–35, and Binder, "Hölderlin, Friedrich."

that. There would be a thousand objections and doubts. There would be insurmountable difficulties.

But Christ came into the world not so that we should understand him but so that we should cling to him, so that we simply let him pull us into the unbelievable event of the resurrection, so that we simply have it said to us, said to us in all its incomprehensibility: You have died—and yet you have been raised! You are in the darkness—and [yet] you are in the light. You are afraid—and yet you can be glad. Right next to each other the completely contradictory; right next to each other, just the way the two worlds, our world and the world of God, are right next to each other.

"You have died, and your life is hidden with Christ in God." That is the one glowing promise that is given to us. However our visible life may be: whether it leads us to the heights and brings a rich harvest of recognition, honor, and fame; whether it has to take a lower path through humiliation and collapses under the heavy burden of misery and guilt; whether it is heroic and noble and great or petty, foolish, and dull; whether our conscience rejoices in blissful joy or throbs in terrible self-accusation: This life should not be glorified and not be raised to the heavens by us human beings. If we tried to do this, we could only come to ruin before God. But precisely that, coming to ruin before God, does not have to happen to us—however our visible life may be—if we give it up, give it up before God, if we lose it, lose it for the sake of Christ, this whole visible life that is at the same time so elevated and so hopeless.

For close by us in that majestic hiddenness where God is all in all, where
the Son is enthroned at the right hand of the Father—there, oh wonder of
453 wonders, our true life has been prepared. Our life is hidden with Christ in
God. We ourselves are already at home in the midst of our homelessness.

Our visible life flows away like a dream and often like a curse. Dominated by demonic ideas, involved in crises, laden with misery and guilt—this life is a life that has died. It takes its all-too-familiar dark paths, but all of that is taken care of in God. As that which has come under the power of death, it is torn away from death by God; as the lost, it is saved by God.

Oh, God certainly would have the power to destroy us sinful human beings and to create new human beings. He certainly would have the power first to extinguish our life and afterward to have a completely new, redeemed life ready for us. But no, he lifts up our life, just as it is, into his majestic hiddenness; just as it is, it is glorified in his boundless glory. Our visible life, with its joys and successes, with its worries and its sorrows and its painful disobedience: holy and blameless and perfect it stands now, for the sake of Jesus Christ, in that hidden world of God before the eyes of the Almighty, today and tomorrow and in all eternity. And no tear falls in vain, and no sigh goes unheard; no pain is ignored, and no rejoicing is lost. The visible world strides brutally and heartlessly and violently past all of this. But out of grace and mercy and great kindness, God gathers our burning, blazing life; he glorifies it for the sake of Jesus Christ; he builds it up new and good in that hidden world where the line of death that separates us from God has been taken away. Our true life is hidden—but it is grounded firmly in eternity. "When Christ who is your life is revealed, then you also will be revealed with him in his glory." Amen.

## 13. Sermon on John 8:32, Berlin, Ninth Sunday after Trinity (Worship Service at the End of the Semester), July 24, 1932[1] 454

John 8:32: The truth will make you free.

July 24, 1932

That is perhaps the most revolutionary passage in the whole New Testament. That is why it is not directed to the masses but is understood only by a very few true revolutionaries.[2] That is why it is a very exclusive word. It remains a secret from the crowd, or they make a slogan out of it. And that is the most dangerous of all. For the slogan takes the edge off the revolutionary aspect completely.

Who are the members of the exclusive circle of people who are being addressed here? Are they the great political or scientific revolutionaries and their loyal followers? Are they the heroes of freedom of all the different kinds of nations? Are they the fighters for progress and knowledge? Where do we find this group, and what kind of a group is it, toward which this word is somehow directed?

Each of us has been in the following situation at some time: A group of adults is together. In the course of the conversation, a subject that is extremely personally embarrassing to some of those present cannot be avoided. A terribly awkward discussion follows, which is full of lies and fear.

[1.] *NL*, A 33,8 (a); handwritten draft. Previously published in *PAM* 1:315–24. Cf. *NL*, A 33,8 (b); later typewritten transcription with notation by Eberhard Bethge: "Worship service at the end of the semester in the Dreifaltigkeitskirche [Trinity Church], Berlin, Ninth Sunday after Trinity" and with handwritten editorial changes by Eberhard Bethge. Previously published in *GS* 4:79–88. See also the order of service for the worship service at the end of the semester that has been preserved as *NL*, A 33,8 (c).

[2.] Crossed out: "in the truest sense."

A child who happens to be there and naturally doesn't understand the situation knows something that all the others also know but are shyly keeping hidden. The child is surprised that the others don't seem to know what he knows and now says it right out loud. Shocked dismay goes around the circle—the child is surprised again. Everyone stares in dismay at the child.
455 The child laughs and is happy that he knew the right thing to say. Something irreparable has happened. All at once the talk full of lies and fear has been suddenly cut off, as if by a blow. Suddenly a harsh light falls on lies and fear. They are completely revealed. They must die away in this light, powerless and desperate. What happened is nothing but that in the form of this child, so surprised about the adults, the truth came to light. The word of the child completely revealed the untruthfulness of the adults to themselves and to one another. It was something completely revolutionary that happened here. And through whom did it happen? Through the surprised, laughing, unsuspecting child, who talked about things as they were. Only the child was free.

Another scene: At the courts of princes,[3] along with the knights, the singers and poets who were the keepers of the tradition and the lies of the court, there was a man whose clothing showed that he did not belong. He stood out. He was dressed ridiculously. He was treated like one who just didn't count.[4] He was an exceptional figure at the court. But every court needed an exception. He didn't belong, but he was indispensable. He was the fool. He was the only one who was allowed to tell the truth to everyone, and everyone had to listen to it. He actually didn't count, but one didn't want to do without him either. That's the way it is for us with the truth. But he was the only free man at the court.

And now the third scene. Anyone who understood the previous scenes correctly will not find it undignified to see the third scene sketched: I mean the man who, beaten and abused, mockingly crowned king with a crown of thorns, stands before his judge and calls himself the king of truth;[5] the one of whom Pilate asks the intelligent but hopelessly worldly question: What is truth? This question, directed to the one who said of himself: I am the truth! And now, because he is the truth, he gives Pilate back his
456 question without speaking: Who are you, Pilate, confronted with my truth? Nothing else is happening here than that the truth is crucified and that Pilate is judged by this crucified truth. It is not you who ask about the truth,

[3.] Crossed out: "at which the tradition began."

[4.] Crossed out: "He was the court fool."

[5.] Crossed out: "who said of himself, I am the truth and."

but the truth asks about you! The crucified king of truth, to whom we pray, that is the third scene we want to look at when we hear the truth spoken of in the New Testament. The child, the fool, the crucified one—a strange assortment of people, of saviors of humanity, of revolutionaries. But now we know a little more about who we should think of when we hear the word: the truth will make you free.

In human life, the truth is something foreign, something unusual, an exception. When the truth is spoken somewhere, it is as if, completely unexpectedly, something suddenly and violently breaks into our life. It is not unusual for someone to trumpet into our ears loudly that we are now going to hear the whole truth. But the truth on the agenda presented is far from being real truth. Real truth is different from that slogan-like truth because it wants something very specific to happen—namely, that it redeems a person, makes him free, that it opens the person's eyes to the fact that up to now he had lived in lies, without freedom and in fear, and [in this way] gives him back his freedom.[6] And now there is the very clear[7] sentence[8] in the Bible that people are living entirely in slavery and lies[9] and that only the truth that comes from God[10] can make a person free.

Today[11] it is not difficult to speak of freedom, and to speak of it in a way that the passions of a German are aroused and set everything in him aquiver, making him forget everything else.[12] There may be some in today's Germany who, like the captive Israelites of long ago, deeply absorbed in their 457
thoughts, dream of nothing other than of[13] freedom, who see its image in great visions and grasp for it, until they wake up and the image dissolves. Yes, indeed, it is easy today to speak of freedom in that way.

[6.] Crossed out: "But where are these people who have been made free by the truth?"

[7.] "Very" (*ganz*) replaces "fully" (*völlig*).

[8.] "Sentence" (*Satz*) replaces "statement" (*Äusserung*).

[9.] "Slavery and lies" replaces "lies."

[10.] "The truth that comes from God" replaces "of God and Christ."

[11.] Crossed out: "very popular."

[12.] Bonhoeffer is referring to the widespread view that Germany had been enslaved by the victor nations at the end of the First World War. This was a reference to the forced declaration of Germany's sole responsibility for the outbreak of the war, the requirement that Germany pay extensive reparations, and the strict limitation on the Reichswehr [the German armed forces from 1921 to 1935—MB] set in the Treaty of Versailles in 1919. By attempting to portray itself as the "young German freedom movement," National Socialism, particularly after 1929, benefitted increasingly from this public sentiment, which spread beyond nationalist right-wing circles. On the way in which National Socialism was seen as a "young German freedom movement" especially among Protestant Christians, see Nowak, *Evangelische Kirche und Weimarer Republik*, 205, 216, and 328.

[13.] "Of" replaces "moving out of the desert into."

But it is very difficult to speak of freedom[14] the way the Bible does. The *truth* will make you free, that is extremely out of date[15] in any age. Our action, our strength, our courage, our race, our morality[16]—in short, *we*, we will make ourselves free. That is understandable; that is popular. But why have this dull word "truth" in this context? The word "truth" has become unpopular. We can tell that this word has something against us. It has a sharp point. Today one can do nothing more unpopular than—where the greatest words are being spoken on religious, on political topics, on matters of worldview—to ask the question completely soberly: Is that all actually true? That is exactly what no one wants to hear. It sounds so critical, so destructive, so lacking in understanding, so cold, so violent. We all live in never-ending, insurmountable fear of the truth, even where we do not think we do, yes, even where we think we have been called to bring truth into the world. We are still afraid that someone will come who can see more deeply than we can and who looks at us questioningly and under whose gaze all our values[17] fall apart. And out of fear we speak all the more loudly, as if we knew the truth.

458 We are all afraid of the truth.[18] And this fear is basically our fear of God. God is truth and no other.[19] And we are afraid of him, afraid he will suddenly place us in the light of the truth and unmask us in our deceitfulness. The truth is a power, a force that stands over us and can destroy us at any moment. It is not the blue sky of concepts and ideas but the sword of God, the threatening bolt of lightning, which strikes in the night, destroying and illuminating. The truth is the living God himself and his word, wherever it finds its mark. In the face of this truth, a human being must die. And because a person is clever and knows this, he covers himself deeper and deeper with lies and false appearances. He does not want to see the truth, because [he] does not want to die. That is why he has to learn to lie with more and more sophistication, more deeply, more thoughtfully. Yes, that is why he has to get to the point that he entangles himself so deeply in

[14.] "Difficult [to speak] of freedom" replaces "unpopular [to speak] the biblical word."

[15.] "Out of date" replaces "unpopular."

[16.] These concepts ranked high in the thinking of religious nationalist (*religiös-völkische*) and German Christian circles. On June 6, 1932, the German Christians for the first time made their new "Guidelines of the German Christians" public (see Scholder, *German Churches and the Third Reich*, 1:207–9). [See also *DBWE* 12, p. 372, ed. note 4. —VB]

[17.] Illegible.

[18.] Crossed out: "and that proves that we are not in the truth but in a lie."

[19.] Crossed out: "and our fear of God proves that we are servants of untruth, of the lie."

lies that he himself no longer knows that he is lying but thinks his lies are the truth. And that is where the person has gotten himself. And because he has gotten to that point, he thinks everything we are saying here is exaggeration and untruth.[20]

Certainly, every honest person will admit that the political lie, the conventional, worldview-related, social lie, the self-serving lie, have a devastating power over us. Even in our imagination we can't think of what would happen if all at once all the veils and layers of lies around us[21] would fall, and we would stand there just as we truly are. We don't know to what depths of our being we would be uncovered here. We only know one thing: that then a life like the one we are leading now would be simply impossible. We can only live because we live not in the transparency of light but in the opaque darkness of night. What we are asked to do here is nothing less than imagine the Last Judgment, the last day of the world.

And yet we defend ourselves against the assertion that there is not 459
only[22] much lying going on around us and in us but we ourselves are the arch-liars. And we have to defend ourselves against this until something very unexpected happens—namely, until God himself meets us as the truth and then does himself what we cannot do—namely, confronts us with his truth. And here, of course, the question is no longer about political lying or conventional lying as such, but here it's about ourselves, about us as the arch-liars ourselves in our whole existence. Here things get really merciless. Here we as the accused are dragged before the judge against our will.[23] Here we can no longer point to this, that, or the other; we ourselves have been held fast.

And now something happens, something over which we have no power at all anymore—now the *truth happens*. It confronts[24] us in a strange form, not in beaming, unapproachable glory and glowing, heart-wringing clarity, but as the crucified truth, as the crucified Christ. And the truth speaks to us. It asks us: Who crucified me, the truth? And it answers already at the same moment: See, *you* did that; *tua culpa, tua maxima culpa*.[25] You hated God's truth about yourself. You crucified it, and you set up your own truth. You thought you knew the truth, that you possessed it, that you could make people happy with the truth. And in doing this you made yourself into God.

[20.] "Untruth" replaces "false."
[21.] "Us" replaces "human beings."
[22.] "There is not only" replaces "we should see."
[23.] Crossed out: "and we must hear the verdict."
[24.] Crossed out: "looks at us—and we recognize God himself."
[25.] "Your sin, your great sin."

You robbed God of his truth, and, far from God, it became[26] a lie. You thought you could make the truth, create it, proclaim it—but with that you presumed to be God and failed in it. You crucified the truth.

And if it seems to us that this is still talking in riddles, we hear the truth speaking even more clearly: You lived as if you were alone in the world. You found in yourself the source of truth, which is only in God. And for that reason you hated the other people, who do the same. You found in yourself
460 the center of the world,[27] and precisely this was the lie. You considered your brother[28] in the world to be the domain of your rule and did not see that all of you, you and they, live from God's truth. You wrenched yourself out of communion with God and your brother and believed you could live alone. You hated God and your brother, because they contradicted your truth. That was the lie; that is why you are a liar through and through.[29] Your wanting to be alone, your hatred is the lie. That is why *you* crucified God's truth. You thought you had become free when you wrenched yourself away and hated the truth. But you became a servant. Servant of your hatred, servant of your lie. The path to truth and to freedom is closed to you. It only leads to the cross, to death. That is what the truth says to us. Its last word over us with all our supposed truth is called death. For it is the crucified truth itself that lives and speaks to us. Who believes it? Today? Tomorrow? At the Last Judgment?

Something extremely peculiar has been shown here: Our lie is a lie against God.[30] It fights against the reality and the truth of God, against communion [and] grace, against his love. Our lie hates God's love, because it thinks it does not need it. The essence of our lie is hatred,[31] because the essence of the truth of God is grace [and] love. But this makes it clear that truth and a lie are not just something one says, but also what one does[32]—that is, that in which one lives completely. Whoever lives a lie lives in hatred. That means, though, he lives shackled to himself. He has been put in chains; he is a slave of himself. But recognizing this is the first knowledge of the truth of God, a knowledge that only God gives. Whoever recognizes that he is a slave to the lie, to fear, and to hatred has already been placed in

[26.] "And [. . .] it became" replaces "and [. . .] you on his."

[27.] Crossed out: "because you knew how to create the truth."

[28.] "Your brother" (*deine Bruder*) illegible; possibly "your brothers" (*deine Brüder*).

[29.] Crossed out: "your being alone, your hatred, which wants to be alone, which hates the brother."

[30.] Crossed out: "it is hatred toward God's word."

[31.] Crossed out: "but our hatred is pride, and our pride holds us bound."

[32.] Crossed out: "doing the untruth toward God."

the truth by God. He understands that all of what he thought was freedom was only slavery and all of what he thought was truth was a lie.

And whoever hears it is overcome by an inexpressible sigh of longing to 461
be freed from his imprisonment: Lord, make me free from myself. And now the word confronts him anew: The truth will make you free.

Not our action, our courage, our strength, our nation, our truth, but God's truth alone. Why? Because becoming *free* does not mean becoming *great* in the world, free[33] in relation to our brother, free[34] in relation to God, but [means] becoming free from oneself, from the lie that I am the only one there, that I am the center of the world, from the hatred with which I scorn God's creation,[35] free from oneself for others. But God's truth alone allows me to see the other. It turns my gaze away from being distorted and directed only toward myself[36] and sends it past me to see the other person. And in doing that, it brings love to me, the mercy of God. It destroys our lie and creates truth. It destroys hatred and creates love. God's truth is God's love, and God's love makes us free from ourselves for others. Being free means nothing else but being in love. And being in love means nothing else but being in God's truth.[37]

The human being who loves because [he] has been made free by God's truth is the most revolutionary human being on earth. He is the overturning of all values [Umsturz aller Werte];[38] he is the explosive material in human society; he is the most dangerous human being.[39] For he has recognized that human beings are, in their deepest being, untruthful. And
he is ready at any time to let the light of truth fall upon them[40]—and that 462

[33.] "Free" replaces "great."

[34.] "Free" replaces "great."

[35.] "God's creation" replaces "everything else [. . . one illegible word] and."

[36.] Bonhoeffer takes up Martin Luther's description of a person's sinful existence as being bent in upon oneself (see, for example, *WA* 56:356,5.27; 357,2; [this is Luther, *Lectures on Romans*—MB]).

[37.] Crossed out: "God's truth, God's freedom, God's love."

[38.] Bonhoeffer takes up a formula often used against Christianity by Friedrich Nietzsche. Nietzsche understood it as the expression of a "moment of humanity's highest self-examination" (*Akt höchster Selbstbesinnung der Menschheit*), *Antichrist, Ecce Homo*, 121. Nietzsche wanted to give his "gospel of the future" the title "Der Wille zur Macht: Versuch einer Umwertung aller Werte" (The will to power: An attempt at the revaluation of all values). See Nietzsche, *Nachgelassene Fragmente*, 8/2:432. [*Umwertung aller Werte* has often been translated in English as "transvaluation of all values." Bonhoeffer uses an alteration of the original Nietzschean word, an alteration that had become popular at the time and added a more forceful meaning to the original. The editors thank Hans Pfeifer for this information.—MB]

[39.] Crossed out: "but it is the inventive person."

[40.] "Them" replaces "themselves."

for the sake of love.[41] But this very disturbance that comes into the world through these people arouses the hatred of the world. And that is why the knight of truth and love is not the hero people worship and honor, who is without enemies, but is instead the one they reject, whom they want to get rid of, on whose head they put a price, whom they kill. The path that God's truth took in the world leads to the cross. From then on, we know that all truth that wants to stand up before God must go to the cross. The congregation that follows Christ must go with him [on]to the cross. For the sake of its truth and freedom, it will be hated by the world. But a people,[42] as well, cannot find truth and freedom if it does not face the judgment of the truth of God. A people, too, remains in lying and slavery until it receives its truth and freedom from God alone and wants to receive it; until it knows that truth and freedom lead to love;[43] until it knows that the path of love leads [on]to the cross. If a people today really knows that, it will be the only people that can justifiably call itself a free people, the only people that is not the slave of itself but the free servant of God's truth.[44]

All of us, each one [for] himself and we as a whole, feel the oppressive burden of our chains. God, we cry out for freedom. But, O God,[45] keep us
463 from dreaming of a false image of freedom and staying in the lie.[46] Give us the freedom that throws us fully onto you, onto your mercy.[47] Lord, make us free with your truth, which is our [Lord] Jesus Christ. Lord, we are waiting for your truth.

---

[41.] Crossed out: "He knows that the sentence: to be free from the other one [or 'other(s)'] for me is wrong and should be: to be free from myself for the other one [or 'other(s)']."

[42.] Crossed out: "that boasts of its being Christian cannot [. . .] in truth."

[43.] Crossed out: "but the path of love is not necessarily the path to."

[44.] Bonhoeffer is again (see p. 467, ed. note 12) referring to the situation of the German nation after its defeat in the First World War. These sentences must be understood as criticism of the propaganda of the right-wing nationalists, who—especially after 1929—had called the moderate revisionist policies (*Revisionspolitik*) of the different cabinets toward the Allies a "politics of appeasement" (*Erfüllungspolitik*). In July 1932 the disarmament conference of the League of Nations failed after months of negotiations, due in large measure to the obstructionist policy of Reich Chancellor Franz von Papen, who had led the government since June 1, 1932. The worship service at the end of the semester took place one week before the election of the new Reichstag on July 31, 1932, which Bonhoeffer considered decisive (cf. *DB-ER*, 237).

[45.] Crossed out: "let us [. . .] the false image of freedom."

[46.] "Staying in the lie" replaces "to fall away from you."

[47.] "Throws us fully onto you, onto your mercy" replaces "in your [. . . one illegible word]—puts [. . .] in your word."

## 14. Baptism Sermon on Ephesians 5:14, Berlin, October 1932[1]

Eph. 5:14: Sleeper, awake! Rise from the dead, and Christ will shine on you.

This first encounter of your child with the ancient church of Christ carries not only the symbolic significance of affirming the connection to the forefathers,[2] *whose own* life was somehow decisively shaped by the Christian church. It is not only the expression of the parents' wish to place their child in this life context because certain values, however weak and distorted they may be, can be found there that they would like to pass on to this child for his life.[3] More than that, this first encounter is an event that reaches far beyond all our wishes and actions, an event of a completely different order, an event originating not from human beings but from God. Tradition and values—including and especially our so-called Christian traditions and values[4]—are breaking down.[5] This child will experience this much more than we will. Only God endures in eternity.

God himself breaks down and builds up as he will, including his church.
There is no way to keep a person safe from the future, from God. The 464
ancient church and its Christianity are no protection like that for a person. For the future—also for this child and also for this church—belongs to God alone. What he gives and what he takes away, what he will give this child and what he will take away from him, is his incomprehensible will, unknowable in advance, against which we cannot protect ourselves—but also should not protect ourselves. To give oneself completely over to the will of God, to let him alone be the Lord and no other with him, no false gods of our own wishes—even if they be the most idealistic, most morally upright, most religious wishes. Let God be God; that is what the message of the church of Christ[6] is about. That God alone wants to be God for this child in eternity, that is God's mercy, which the church assures to this child today.

---

[1.] *NL*, A 33,21 (a); handwritten draft. Previously published in *PAM* 1:324–27. Cf. *NL*, A 33,21 (b); later typewritten transcription with editorial changes and a notation by Eberhard Bethge: "Sermon on the occasion of the baptism of a nephew October 1932." Previously published in *GS* 4:150–53. This was the baptism of his nephew Friedrich, son of Karl-Friedrich and Grete Bonhoeffer. It took place at the house of his parents, Karl and Paula Bonhoeffer, on Wangenheimstrasse.

[2.] Crossed out: "[. . . eight illegible words]."

[3.] "For his life" replaces "[. . . two illegible words]."

[4.] "Tradition and values—including and especially our so-called Christian traditions and values" replaces "even the highest values and traditions."

[5.] Crossed out: "[. . . ca. nine illegible words]." [There are interesting parallels to Bonhoeffer's commentary on the passing of the old traditions in the 1944 baptismal sermon for Dietrich Bethge. See *DBWE* 8, 3/145, esp. pp. 384–85 and 389–90.—VB]

[6.] "Christ" replaces "over this child."

And now the church of Christ calls out; it speaks to this child, who does not yet understand its words. But it speaks of God's eternal will to life, which reaches beyond understanding and not understanding, before which we are all like children. Sleeper, awake! Rise from the dead. It is God's word of creation itself that calls this child through the church to be awake, calls to life before God.

A person should not sleep but be awake. To be awake means to be realistic, to live not in dreams and wishes but in the bright light of reality. To be awake means to love the day and its work. It means to be without illusions, because illusions idolize the world for us and hide our view of the one God, of whom one should make no idols, and allow us to see the world in the colors of our own wishes and prejudices. To be awake means to see the world as it is before God, without passing judgment. To be awake means to be open, to be ready for the future, to look it in the eye and not be afraid. It means[7] to see the bright day of God as it is, to love his creation and his works, but also to see the suffering of creation, the misery and helplessness of the other person,[8] to hear his pleading, even where it remains unspoken; and [it means] to know about eternal guilt.

465 This being awake is something a person cannot give himself. It is not a person's sly, malicious alertness for the bad in others and the good about himself. Rather God must call a person to this being awake, just as in that painting Adam, sleeping on the freshly made earth, is summoned awake solely through the touch of God, called to life before God.[9] To be awake means to live before God. To be awake means to live before God alone, because he alone is the immortal one.[10] That is why [it] says: Rise up from the dead—that means, live. What is meant by this all-encompassing word remains completely inexpressible. But it must mean something like: Be who you are, and be that way before God. Don't let anyone put any masks on you, not the mask of one who might understand the art of living and yet behind the mask is actually dead. No mask at all! Not that of the constant striver and not that of one who is always content. Not that of one who is moral or of one who is immoral, of one who is pious or of one who is a cynic. But live! Be alive! Rise from the dead. Live before God as the one into [whom] he made you! But this word "live" cannot, of course, be a command but is the

---

[7.] Crossed out: "[. . . two illegible words]."

[8.] Crossed out: "and see his eternal guilt."

[9.] The reference is to Michelangelo's fresco in the Sistine Chapel [*The Creation of Adam*—VB] that attempts to portray the creation of the human being.

[10.] "Because he alone is the immortal one" replaces "do everything for him, for him great."

word of creation of God himself. It means: You are already living, you live through me, before me alone. And you will live. You no longer belong to the dead. You belong to eternity.

Sleeper, awake! Rise from the dead, and Christ will shine on you. Just as in that picture of the creation of Adam, in which, through the touch of God, Adam, who is sleeping on the freshly created earth, is awakened to the glory of the day, here an image comes before our eyes of a person who, at the call of a voice, rises up out of the dark earth in which he sleeps, in which he was dead, and is now flooded by the light[11] of God[12] in the world,[13] illuminated by Christ. A person who is completely in the world, strongly rooted in the earth, but now seeing this world in the light that shows him all its misery and all its hope. To be illuminated by Christ means
to see through love all the sorrow and suffering that Christ saw, into which 466
he entered completely until his death on the cross. And it means knowing in love of the last hope[14] for all suffering, which comes from the Lord of the world, who alone is no idol and will glorify[15] his works. To be illuminated by Christ means to love God above all things and your neighbor as yourself.[16] That alone can be called "living." To be called to this life is [the] grace of God in baptism.[17]

The future of this child remains in the dark, and we should not try to reveal this secret.[18] God will not let that be taken away from him. He walks with this child; he leads him, not we. And he keeps his word. Amen.

---

[11.] Crossed out: "of Adam."

[12.] Crossed out: "of Christ."

[13.] Crossed out: "of Christ."

[14.] Crossed out: "of the world and."

[15.] "Glorify" replaces "does not leave."

[16.] "Yourself" replaces "himself also."

[17.] Crossed out: "Perhaps a life like this, which is lived in this way in the grace of God, illuminated by Christ, may remain completely hidden; no one can see it in him; the light of God is no light of our world, but shines on the cross. But, after all, that doesn't matter, but."

[18.] "Secret" replaces "darkness."

Christoph Strohm

# Editor's Afterword to the German Edition

## I 467

On December 25, 1932, Bonhoeffer wrote to Helmut Rößler, a friend from university days, about a remark Bonhoeffer himself had made "a long time ago" about his personal "disinterestedness" in politics: "It now actually strikes me as frivolous. It was only meant to indicate the parameter within which I see these problems through the objective reality of the church."[1] By the end of 1932, political developments had clearly acquired greater significance for Bonhoeffer's theological work. At the same time, however, and in a fashion intimately related to these same developments, this young, twenty-five-year-old theologian was acquiring his own independent theological profile, which would remain decisive even for his later theological thinking during the 1940s.[2]

We have no indications that Bonhoeffer had developed any particular interest in political developments in Berlin, the national capital, prior to his departure for the United States in the summer of 1930. He seems instead to have been focused entirely on completing his postdoctoral thesis.[3] After returning from the United States in the summer of 1931, however, he found himself confronted in his various activities by the political and economic crisis of the waning Weimar Republic. The preserved notes and sermons from this period attest to the considerable extent to which he was distressed by the high unemployment, which had risen precipitately

[1.] *DBWE* 12:85.

[2.] See pp. 490–91.

[3.] *DB-ER*, 125–37.

since 1929, and by the fundamental problems of hunger among the population at large during 1931–32.[4] When the number of votes in favor of the National Socialists increased so abruptly during the parliamentary elections of September 14, 1930, he could only take note from afar, from his vantage point in America.[5] After returning from the United States, however, one of the primary tasks of his own ecumenical activities was to
468 deal with the nationalist and National Socialist anti-ecumenical sentiment. Moreover, the recent experiences in the New World of this twenty-five-year-old university lecturer and pastor, as well as his ongoing conversations with his brothers and brothers-in-law, had considerably enhanced his understanding of the political, economic, and social situation.[6] Bonhoeffer's lectures and sermons palpably attest to his growing awareness of the inability of both theology and the church to deal with the oppressive problems that confronted Germany during these years.[7]

## II

Allusions to national Protestantism and the populist [volkstümlich] theological sentiment of the sort one still finds in Bonhoeffer's congregational lectures in Barcelona during the winter of 1928–29 had disappeared in the face of his encounters with American Christianity and his friendship with the French pacifist Jean Lasserre.[8] His focus now shifted from the potential opposition between younger and older nations and peoples to the one, supranational, universal people of Christ.[9] At the behest of his superior, Superintendent Max Diestel, Bonhoeffer, who had both experience abroad and knowledge of foreign languages, began to participate on a variety of ecumenical committees at the very time when the harassment of German ecumenists by right-wing nationalists was reaching a momentary crescendo.[10]

---

[4.] See 2/5, pp. 246–47; 2/17, pp. 378–79; 2/18, pp. 384–85; 3/1, pp. 401, 403–5; 3/2, p. 412; 3/3, pp. 416–17; and 3/10, pp. 444–45.

[5.] Cf. *DB-ER*, 148–49.

[6.] Concerning the decisive influence that his family and the Grunewald academic community had on shaping the young Bonhoeffer, see the German editors' afterwords for *DBWE* 9 and 10.

[7.] See esp. the lectures in Ciernohorské Kúpele (2/14) and Gland (2/17) as well as the sermon from May 8, 1932, on 2 Chron. 20:12 (3/8).

[8.] See esp. *DBWE* 10, 372–74; see also H. E. Tödt, "Dietrich Bonhoeffer's Ecumenical Ethic of Peace."

[9.] See *DBWE* 10:372.

[10.] See 1/4, p. 35; 2/1, pp. 165–66; and 2/11, p. 343, ed. note 5.

At the very first ecumenical conference in which he participated—the annual conference of the World Alliance for Promoting International Friendship through the Churches, held in Cambridge, September 1–5, 1931—he was elected one of three youth secretaries of the World Alliance. A short while later, he became secretary of the ecumenical Provisional 469
Bureau, which under Wilhelm Stählin was charged with the urgent task of raising awareness among the country's youth about the situation of the hard-pressed ecumenical movement. Hence, after the autumn of 1931, Bonhoeffer was engaged in the ongoing task of dealing with National Socialism and those allied with it in the so-called young nationalism.[11] The task of critically countering Nationalist Socialist ideas as the primary enemy of the ecumenical movement in Germany was all the more urgent insofar as it was precisely among the country's youth that these ideas were spreading especially fast. Bonhoeffer's continuing contact with Western countries since his year of study in the United States solidified and strengthened his rejection of the anti-Western polemic propagated by the National Socialists and their sympathizers among the nationalist right wing.

The central focus at ecumenical conferences during 1931–32 was the position the ecumenical movement itself should take toward the growing arms race in Europe, an arms race quite in violation of the stipulations of the Treaty of Versailles. Whereas arms development in Germany was strictly regulated and limited by the treaty, England and France were bound only by what were in fact more general declarations of purpose with regard to future arms reduction. That the Western powers' activities and efforts with regard to arms reduction were anything but transparent presented particular difficulties for German ecumenical participants. How were they, the German ecumenical participants, supposed to advocate increased international understanding at home when the impression in Germany itself was that the victors of the Great War were in fact engaged in unfettered arms development and were doing so at the cost of an oppressed Germany?

Like the other German ecumenical participants, Bonhoeffer, too, admonished church representatives of the Western powers to provide more unequivocal evidence of arms-reduction efforts on the part of their countries; he also reminded them of the part played by the victor nations of the Great War in the emergence of National Socialism. Moreover, he now began to introduce his own, quite distinct opinions at conferences, countering the industrious drafting of resolutions with his own call to engage first in a reflection on the theological foundations of ecumenical work. In his 470

[11.] See Glenthøj, "Zu Dietrich Bonhoeffers Eintritt," 194–200.

understanding, the World Alliance for Promoting International Friendship through the Churches could work effectively on behalf of peace in the face of the challenges at the beginning of the 1930s only if it understood itself as a form of church, rather than as an ad hoc organization for attaining a certain goal, regardless of what that goal might be. Amid the contrasting positions of, on the one hand, a strong Anglo-Saxon group that, overestimating the human possibilities, was interested in contributing toward the actualization of the kingdom of God and, on the other hand, the German ecumenists, the majority of whom insisted on maintaining the present boundaries and differences between nations as part of the order of creation willed by God, Bonhoeffer for his part soon developed an independent position oriented toward the new theological perspective of Karl Barth.[12]

III

Apart from his ecumenical activities, as an assistant pastor in the city of Berlin Bonhoeffer was also considerably occupied with various pastoral and social welfare responsibilities within the church itself. He was responsible for delivering sermons and talks at the Technical College, taught a confirmation class in the working-class districts of Berlin-Mitte and Prenzlauer Berg, and established a youth center for the unemployed in Charlottenburg. One of the important factors influencing this unusually intensive engagement with children of the Berlin working class was the experiences he had had in New York's African American district, Harlem, during his year of study at Union Theological Seminary, experiences he considered among the most moving of his entire stay in the United States.[13] To improve his ability to guide his confirmation class in the Zion congregation in Prenzlauer Berg, which had essentially gotten out of control, he rented a room for three months at the beginning of 1932 in the district where his charges themselves lived. In the meantime, however, the intensified engagement on behalf of these boys did come at the price of his teaching activities at the
471 university.[14] Bonhoeffer was so moved by his work with the proletarian boys that after completing the stipulated period of one compulsory year in an assistant capacity, he applied—albeit unsuccessfully—for a position as pastor in the northeast section of Berlin. A short time later, on January

[12.] See section V below (pp. 484–85). One notable difference between Bonhoeffer and his theological role model was Bonhoeffer's concentrated interest in the church's concrete ethical proclamation.

[13.] Cf. *DBWE* 10:315, 318–19; also *DB-ER*, 229–30.

[14.] See Zimmermann, *I Knew Dietrich Bonhoeffer*, 65–66.

30, 1933, Hitler's acquisition of power brought Bonhoeffer's work with the youth center to an abrupt end.

Bonhoeffer's work as a student chaplain at the Technical College seems not to have been particularly successful. There was no preceding tradition on which to build, and he found it difficult even to draw attention to his devotional services and talks.[15] Here, too, just as in his ecumenical work, he had to deal with the increasing presence of National Socialist ideology. For example, in his talk "The Right to Self-Assertion" he opposed the absolutizing of such a right with regard to international relationships, as the biological and social Darwinism of the National Socialists advocated.[16]

Although Bonhoeffer did not really have his own pulpit in 1931–32, one of the focal points during these years was the sermons he delivered at Trinity Church [Dreifaltigkeitskirche], where one of his colleagues, the student chaplain Ernst Bronisch-Holtze, worked, or when he filled in for Gerhard Jacobi at the Kaiser Wilhelm Memorial Church.[17] Otto Dudzus quite correctly finds that "there is an element of brooding in them[18] up to the end of 1932. They are full of criticism and doubts concerning the church, sometimes virtually to the point of despair."[19] Although it was not until the beginning of 1933 that this tone yielded to one of firmer resolve, even in the sermons of 1931–32 one can discern the emergence of a more clearly defined theological center in Bonhoeffer's repeated references to the cross of Jesus Christ, from the perspective of which the path of discipleship to Christ appears not merely as the expression of a demand on the individual but also as an expression of promise and liberation.

The sermons preserved from this period eloquently attest to how oppres- 472
sive Bonhoeffer found the circumstances to be during the waning years of the Weimar Republic. Although he strictly avoided taking any direct position concerning political events, references to contemporary political and economic developments are unmistakable. At the beginning of 1932, when the Brüning administration, which the Bonhoeffer family and their circle of friends thought was the last chance for maintaining continuity,[20] was

---

[15.] *DB-ER*, 222–26.

[16.] See 2/5.

[17.] See Otto Dudzus's discussion in *PAM* 1:24–35.

[18.] [I.e., the sermons.—MBL]

[19.] *PAM* 1:33.

[20.] See Karl Bonhoeffer, "Lebenserinnerungen," 99. Bonhoeffer's brother-in-law Hans von Dohnanyi, who was closely associated with the German Democratic Party (after 1930, the German Staatspartei, or State Party), similarly referred to Brüning as probably the last man who could still prevent the republic from disintegrating (see Christine von Dohnanyi, "Fassung A des Berichts über die politische Tätigkeit Hans von Dohnanyis"

succeeded by that of Papen, Bonhoeffer preached in unmistakable terms against the misuse of the name of God by the new government.[21] A week before the parliamentary elections on July 31, 1932, in which many feared yet another increase in the number of votes in favor of the National Socialists, he rejected the latter's demagogic promises, summoning his listeners instead not to allow themselves to be misled by the ultimately illusory promises of some allegedly new freedom for Germany.[22]

These sermons attest in a sometimes oppressive fashion the foreboding of an uncertain future with regard to the church and of future conflicts with the state.[23] On several occasions, Bonhoeffer mentions the possibility of future martyrdom involving the church.[24] For Memorial Day in 1932, the Reminiscere Sunday on February 21, he chose an eschatological sermon text that emphasized the church's obligation to proclaim the commandment of peace over against the shouting of the world.[25] This sermon implicitly refers to the disputes surrounding statements made by the alleged pacifist Günther Dehn, concurring with the latter's admonishments for the
473 church to proclaim in a more resolute fashion the biblical commandment of peace.[26] With regard to future disputes between the church, on the one hand, and National Socialism or a state dominated by it, on the other, both Bonhoeffer and Dehn recognized the exemplary nature of the controversy already surrounding Dehn's warning against perverting the mourning for those previously killed in action into a glorification of war.[27]

## IV

What is known as the "Dehn affair" also represents the first occasion in which the young university lecturer and pastor took a position against the growing national right wing by means of his own, independent initiative.[28] Although Bonhoeffer understood his opposition against the denunciation of the "pacifist" Günther Dehn wholly as a theologically grounded position,

["prepared at the behest of von Schlabrendorf for an American office"], p. 1, in Nachlaß von Dohnanyi, Ordner 26/Nr. 12).

[21.] See the sermon of June 12, 1932, 3/11, pp. 454–55.

[22.] See the sermon of July 24, 1932, 3/13, pp. 467–68 and 472.

[23.] See 3/5, pp. 420–22, and 3/13, pp. 467–68; see also 2/9, p. 322.

[24.] See 3/5, p. 426, and 3/12, p. 439.

[25.] See 3/5.

[26.] See 3/5, pp. 420–23 and 425–27.

[27.] Cf. Dehn's afterword to the publication of documents relating to the controversy surrounding his remarks, in Dehn, *Kirche und Völkerversöhnung*, 81.

[28.] See 1/40.

the piece that he and Hans Fischer, a follower of Barth, authored in February 1932 on Dehn's behalf had unequivocal political implications as well. The reaction to the text written by Bonhoeffer and only slightly modified by Karl Barth also clearly revealed the final collapse of the group of so-called dialectical theologians around Karl Barth, Rudolf Bultmann, and Friedrich Gogarten.

Barth himself pointedly mentioned Bonhoeffer's actions in a letter to his friend Georg Merz on March 5, 1932:[29]

> I learned through Niesel that you did not want to sign the Bonhoeffer summons despite the impeccable form I gave it *ex cathedra loquens*.[30] Whatever your reasons may have been, I certainly do not hold it against you, and instead came to an understanding with Niesel to the effect that, should the familiar band of those standing on the
> left decide they in fact do want to sign it, as will probably be the case, 474
> it is probably better to sound the retreat for this entire undertaking (which, after all, is ultimately not absolutely necessary in any case). I continue to find both astonishing and, as an overall phenomenon, somewhat questionable the tenacity with which the entire—and I do mean the entire—theological community, including those associated with *Z.d.Z.*,[31] including even my closest circle of friends, including Georg Merz,—the tenacity with which at the decisive moment all these people repeatedly and ever anew tilt to the right as if it really could not be otherwise. But I have no intention of firing off many rounds in this affair. The German disposition is determined on going its own way, and I for my part am not the one called to change its path.

Even as early as his university days, Bonhoeffer had already been significantly influenced by Karl Barth's writings.[32] Moreover, he had also been in personal contact with Barth since his three-week visit in Bonn in July 1931, immediately after his return from the United States. The letters from this period eloquently attest how profoundly Barth had influenced Bonhoeffer. Even though Bonhoeffer would later establish wholly independent positions, especially in his ecclesiology and the foundations of his ethics, he

[29.] Karl Barth-Archiv, Basel.

[30.] "Speaking from the chair."

[31.] The periodical *Zwischen den Zeiten*.

[32.] See, e.g., Bonhoeffer's report on historical and pneumatological interpretation of Scripture during the 1925 summer semester (*DBWE* 9:285–300).

nonetheless felt part of this new theological direction and tried to address further the questions it had raised.[33]

## V

Despite Bonhoeffer's comprehensive ecumenical activities and his conscientious attention to his pastoral obligations in the church and in the sphere of social welfare, his true center of gravity during 1931–32 was his theological work at the university. During both the winter semester 1931–32 and the summer semester 1932, he offered a lecture course as
475 well as a seminar. His lecture course during the winter 1931–32, "The History of Twentieth-Century Systematic Theology," took a position reflecting an awareness of the new situation that followed the theological reorientation prompted by Karl Barth's circle.[34] The seminar he offered that same semester, for which we unfortunately have no notes, seems to have moved in the same direction in dealing with the relationship between philosophy and Protestant theology.

For the summer semester 1932, Bonhoeffer then offered a lecture course on ecclesiology, on the one hand, and a seminar on the basic problems of Christian ethics, on the other, thereby addressing the two main themes of his own theological work. Here, generously drawing from his own ecumenical experiences, he developed the basic outline for an ethics of the church, which at least in part would remain decisive even for his later theological thinking. Important lines of thought presented in his lecture on the nature of the church and in the seminar on ethics overlap with ideas Bonhoeffer developed in talks he gave at ecumenical conferences.[35]

Even as early as his 1927 dissertation, he had tried to provide concrete content for Karl Barth's demand that theology be founded exclusively on the revelation of the word of God. He describes the social relationships within the church itself—the church understood as the *Christus praesens*—as the concrete locus of revelation. He picked up these reflections in his lecture on the nature of the church during the 1932 summer semester and simultaneously developed more fully their christological foundations in the incarnation. God's act of becoming human in Jesus Christ characteristi-

[33.] By contrast, for example, he thought Emil Brunner's book on ethics, *The Divine Imperative*, to be inadequate and too hastily written; he had begun to read the book just after it appeared in March 1932 (see 1/59, p. 121, and *GS* 5:335–39).

[34.] Cf. *DB-ER*, 212–13.

[35.] See esp. his talk in Ciernohorské Kúpele in July 1932 (2/14) and in Gland in August 1932 (2/17).

cally determines both his ecclesiology and his entire ethical concept. It is here that Bonhoeffer found himself prompted to be more concrete in his theological-ethical pronouncements in general and to strive to incorporate the concrete reality of the world into the understanding of ethical decisions. In this context, Bonhoeffer's demand for more concreteness in the ethical proclamation of the church was not merely the expression of an element of reserve over against Barth. It was also unequivocally directed 476
against church leaders who had tried to remain neutral in the face of the destruction of the Weimar Republic by taking refuge in merely vague or general demands.

## VI

Through his concept of an ethics of the church, Bonhoeffer intended to find an alternative, on the one hand, to the ethics of the kingdom of God as advocated by the Anglo-Saxon ecumenists and, on the other, to the regnant ethics in Germany itself, the latter of which, picking up on ethnic-populist [völkisch] thinking, took the alleged orders of creation as its point of departure. Whereas in Bonhoeffer's understanding, the former viewed the order of international peace as a "piece of the kingdom of God on earth" and absolutized the ideal of peace itself, the latter tended to inflate the significance of the orders of creation without first seeking within the Christ event the standard of their very validity.[36]

The center of Bonhoeffer's understanding of ethics is an incisive ecclesiology of *Christus praesens*.[37] It is solely through the presence of the living Christ within it that the church acquires the authority to proclaim the concrete commandment. "The church is the presence of Christ present on earth; the church is *Christus praesens*."[38] Just as one can speak about Jesus Christ only in a twofold fashion, so also about the church. "It is one and the same church, its visible form and its hidden divinity. As it is one and the same Lord, the carpenter's son from Nazareth and the Son of God."[39]

---

[36.] See 2/8; 2/13, pp. 351–55 ; and 2/14, pp. 362–66.

[37.] Bonhoeffer expressly understood the World Alliance for Promoting International Friendship through the Churches, in which he himself was active as a youth secretary, as a form of church and not merely as an ad hoc organization for church action. In his understanding, this organization was "the anxious church of Christ, which has become terrified and sensitive, made fearful by the anxiety of the world" (2/17, p. 377). This understanding constitutes an extraordinary expansion of the concept of the church far beyond the boundaries of the institution of the church proper.

[38.] See 2/14, p. 359.

[39.] From his 1932 essay "What Is Church?" in *DBWE* 12, 2/7, p. 264.

477 For Bonhoeffer, the concrete demand and promise of Jesus Christ is bound wholly to the church as the present Christ. Over against Karl Barth's understanding of ethics as mere demonstration, Bonhoeffer objected that such a position, while indeed excluding any ethics of principles, also thwarts any concrete ethics.[40] Bonhoeffer countered by maintaining that concrete, contingent revelation took place and indeed continues to take place in Jesus Christ. It is here that the word of God genuinely enters into empirical history. Jesus Christ is the "counter-logos within history," which develops as a contradiction to the law of the world.[41] He is the word become flesh and thus genuinely, really present in present events.[42]

## VII

Bonhoeffer's insistence that authoritative speaking can take place only within the utmost concretion has far-reaching consequences for his understanding of theological ethics. The church cannot simply proclaim Christ's claim and demands on the world as something nonconcrete, as something based solely on principle, and thus as something timelessly universal. Nor, however, should it surrender the comprehensive perspective of the dominion of Christ over the entire world in favor of options for concrete action derived from detailed and specialized knowledge of the present situation. Instead, it is precisely the indissoluble interconnection between these two aspects from which the commandment of the church itself derives.[43] The proclamation should always be mindful to incorporate present circumstances into the hearing of the commandment such that the commandment itself enters into the real, concrete situation. In a fashion, one criterion of the truth of God's commandment is whether it summons us to obedi-
478 ence "in the most concrete form out of the fullest knowledge of the matter."[44] Bonhoeffer himself saw the "tremendous difficulty" that arises. "If the church must know the situation in detail before it can command, that

[40.] Cf. 2/3, §14, p. 243.

[41.] *DBWE* 12:302 and *GS* 3:169.

[42.] "Christ as Word of God in the sense of word spoken to us does not mean Christ as timeless truth, but rather as truth breaking into a concrete moment, as God's speaking to us" (*DBWE* 12:317). Cf. H. E. Tödt, "Dietrich Bonhoeffer's Ecumenical Ethic of Peace," 121.

[43.] "The word of the church to the world must therefore touch it out of the deepest knowledge of the world in its complete present if it wishes to be authoritative" (2/14, p. 359).

[44.] See 2/14, p. 360.

is, if the validity of its commandment depends on its detailed knowledge of the matter . . . there is always the danger that the church in its commandment will nonetheless overlook this or that objective point of view or underestimate it, and therefore the church will be made completely uncertain in its commandment."[45] This objective, informed orientation of the church in its capacity to issue commands is, on the one hand, a precondition for any real commandment and, on the other, continually renders all its commandments uncertain insofar as they always depend on a complete, informed knowledge of the attendant reality. Bonhoeffer believed that one can attempt to solve this dilemma in one of two ways, namely, "avoidance and withdrawal to the level of principle,"[46] on the one hand, and the courage to dare making a decision, on the other. One takes a risk despite all the dangers, "namely, *either* a conscious and qualified silence of ignorance, *or* the commandment is dared in every conceivable concretion, exclusivity, and radicalism."[47] The first path, one that in Bonhoeffer's opinion churches have generally taken, ultimately leads to a denial of the validity of the gospel in all spheres of life. The church can dare to proclaim a concrete commandment only if it believes in the forgiveness of sins. But it should do so with the clear understanding that despite conscientious examination and the willingness to follow in discipleship, it may still err and sin; it is, however, certainly permitted to speak that word from within its own faith in the forgiveness of sins. How, though, is the church to know what God's commandment is in the hour at hand? Bonhoeffer's response was that knowledge of that commandment is an act of present revelation.[48] In response to attempts to derive that commandment from a literal understanding of biblical laws or from alleged orders of creation, he emphasized that the 479
commandment cannot possibly come from anywhere other than "*that place where the promise and fulfillment come from, namely, from Christ.*"[49]

Bonhoeffer's explications on the Sermon on the Mount reveal how this statement is to be understood. On the one hand, the Sermon on the Mount merely illustrates that which God's commandment *can* be, not what it is for us here and now. Any proclamation of its promises and demands must assess the present state of affairs and refer the commandment to that state such that the commandment speaks to this particular situation. On the other hand, Bonhoeffer demanded simple discipleship within a disposition

[45.] Ibid., p. 361

[46.] [Ibid.—VB]

[47.] Ibid. [italics in original—MBL].

[48.] Ibid., p. 362.

[49.] Ibid., p. 363 [italics in original—MBL].

of simple faith.[50] "Faith . . . must be simple; otherwise it will bring about reflection rather than obedience; the left hand will know what the right hand is doing, and this is not discipleship, which knows nothing of good or evil."[51] "To the simple reader of the Sermon on the Mount, what it says is unmistakable."[52] The contradiction between the demand for simple faith, on the one hand, and the incorporation of concrete knowledge of the real situation at hand, on the other, can be avoided only if reflection on the concrete, present form of the commandment illustrated in the Sermon on the Mount is itself understood as part of the event of revelation of that commandment. Bonhoeffer's ethical theory can accomplish this with the help of an unambiguous understanding of the church as *Christus praesens*. In effect, the church's own efforts to determine the concrete commandment acquire the dignity of becoming part of the revelatory event, something understood, moreover, in analogy to God's revelation in the concrete human being Jesus of Nazareth. This analogy derives from the correspondence inhering within the dual nature of Christ's dominion or demand and the church's own detailed knowledge of the given situation in its proclamation of the concrete commandment, on the one hand, and Jesus Christ's dual nature as both God and human being, on the other. Just as Christian faith can speak about God only as the one who became human in Jesus of Nazareth, so also can God's claim be described not as a universal demand
480 or as a demand based on principle but rather only as the concrete commandment shaped by a consideration of the conditions and circumstances of a particular place and situation in the world in the here and now.[53] This analogy between present revelation and revelation in Jesus of Nazareth follows from the understanding of the church as the present Christ and from the assertion that the commandment can never come from anywhere except from precisely this Christ.

[50.] See "Christ and Peace" from December 1932, which was probably written only a few months later (*DBWE* 12:258–62; *GS* 5:359–40; see also *Mündige Welt*, 5:69 and *DB-ER*, 208–10).

[51.] From the 1932 lecture "Christ and Peace," in *DBWE* 12, 2/6, p. 259.

[52.] Ibid.

[53.] The influence of the particular kind of pragmatism with which Bonhoeffer became acquainted during his stay in America in 1930–31 is evident in the demand that the church is permitted to proclaim not principles that are always true but only commandments that are true today precisely because God is "for us 'always' *God* precisely '*today*'" (2/14, p. 360, italics in the original).

## VIII

Two fundamental decisions characterize the foundations of Christian ethics as sketched by Bonhoeffer in 1932. First, he picked up on his understanding of the church as the body of the present, historical Christ and as the locus of God's revelation, an understanding he had already developed in the 1927 dissertation. Although this understanding of the church does indeed betray a certain proximity to the Catholic understanding, its constitutive element is not the notion of office as represented within a hierarchy but the new community of mutual vicarious representation in the sense of the young Luther.[54]

Second, the biblical message of God having become human determines the entire course of the argument. By way of analogy, the confluence of divine and human reality in this primal event shapes every theological statement about God and the world. Just as one can speak about God only as the God who has become human in the carpenter's son Jesus of Nazareth, so also can one never speak about the church as an invisible, divine reality without the accompanying, often enough feeble, visible human reality. The commandment is similarly understood as a confluence of the comprehensive perspective of Christ's dominion over the world, on the one hand, and the requisite consideration of the "objective circumstances" attaching to 481
the present, given situation in the world, on the other. This fundamental event of God's becoming human also helped Bonhoeffer transform the opposition between reason and revelation into a paradox. The communicative event in the church between people with specialized skills—skills based on reason—from the various spheres of life can be viewed as the requisite human side of the event of revelation. One factor influencing this elevated claim on the church as the locus of the communal search for an informed position from which to make ethical decisions may well have been the intensive dialogue that Bonhoeffer as a theologian carried on with the jurists and scientists in his own family and circle of friends.[55] Not least of all, here

[54.] See also the direct reference to Luther's sermon "The Blessed Sacrament of the Holy and True Body of Christ and the Brotherhoods," 1519 (*WA* 2:742–58; *LW* 35:49–73), in Bonhoeffer's lecture on the nature of the church. (See 2/9, p. 319).

[55.] See Strohm, *Theologische Ethik im Kampf gegen den Nationalsozialismus*. To Bonhoeffer, the church seemed to be the last place where objective discussion was still possible within the escalation of political disputes at the end of the Weimar Republic (see 2/19, pp. 386–87).

Bonhoeffer recognized the necessity of including specialists in ethical decision making and in the proclamation of the commandment.

## IX

Bonhoeffer intimated at this concept of an ethics of the church as the body of Christ more than he really developed it, and many of the thoughts he expressed in 1932 find no parallel in his later work.[56] With the beginning of the Church Struggle, theological reflections on ethical theory receded at first, since Bonhoeffer's sole concern now was to speak and concretely articulate the biblical commandment in the face of the current threat. The demand on the church intensified that it now represent Christ's vicarious representative action on behalf of humankind. After repeated disappointment with the Confessing Church's failure to take an unequivocal position and after its acute crisis in 1938, Bonhoeffer revised the elements that tended toward an elite understanding of the church. After 1940, the discur-
482 sive theological focus on the proclamation of the concrete commandment, which became necessary in face of the acute political threat during the years of the Church Struggle, yielded to a renewed discussion of the fundamental questions of ethics, and in this Bonhoeffer picked up and developed further the various ideas from 1932.

Just as Bonhoeffer's ethical reflections can be traced to the beginning of the 1930s, so too his ethics fragments after 1940 have their center in an understanding of reality conceived strictly from the perspective of the incarnation.[57] At the beginning of the 1940s, the locus of God's becoming human was for Bonhoeffer no longer solely the church but the entirety of the world's reality. One can find the preconditions of this view in Bonhoeffer's early understanding of the church. In connection with his ecumenical work, he had already advocated an extraordinarily broad understanding of the church, one by no means restricted to the institutionalized church, with his demand that the World Alliance understand itself as "church." In his characterizing of the structures of the responsible life, he also picked up and developed further the notion of the confluence within Christian ethics of the perspective, on the one hand, of Christ's world dominion, and, on the other, of informed knowledge of the fundamental laws and circum-

[56.] See, for example, his articulation of an understanding of reality as a sacrament of the commandment (2/14, pp. 361–62).

[57.] See esp. *Ethics* (*DBWE* 6:224–33 and 259–69). In Bonhoeffer's understanding, reality or, expressed differently, that which is factual, is an abstraction if it is not viewed from the perspective of "the real" as determined by God's actions in the world.

stances of the concrete world.[58] Hence several important fundamental ideas of Bonhoeffer's later ethics fragments were already anticipated during 1931–32. Although the effect of the Church Struggle during 1933–34 and up until 1938 was more to deter Bonhoeffer from undertaking a more thorough explication or development of a theological ethics, his attempts after 1938 in this direction, attempts that also undoubtedly incorporated his experiences in that struggle, nonetheless also picked up directly on his reflections from the years 1931–32.

Hence the texts from the years 1931–32 assembled in the present volume document fundamental theological decisions that occupy a significant place in Bonhoeffer's work and life path. The disputes, decisions, and positions taken at the beginning of the 1930s were not merely preliminary skirmishes of the coming struggle; instead, they set a course that would have 483
considerable consequences that to a large degree remained decisive even beyond the more acute stages of the Church Struggle.

## X

The years documented in this volume are also of considerable significance for Bonhoeffer's private life. If a more profound turn in his life in the larger sense can be discerned, it took place during these years. A retrospective letter that he wrote to an acquaintance at the beginning of 1936 speaks in an excited and perhaps exaggerated fashion about this event:

> But then something different came, something that has changed and transformed my life to this very day. For the first time, I came to the Bible. That, too, is an awful thing to say. I had often preached, I had seen a great deal of the church, had spoken and written about it—and yet I was not yet a Christian, but rather in an utterly wild and uncontrolled fashion my own master. I do know that at the time I turned the cause of Jesus Christ into an advantage for myself, for my crazy vanity. I pray to God that will never happen again. Nor had I ever prayed, or had done so only very rarely. Despite this isolation, I was quite happy with myself. The Bible, especially the Sermon on the Mount, freed me from all this. Since then everything has changed. I have felt this plainly and so have other people around me. That was a great liberation. It became clear to me that the life of a servant of Jesus Christ must belong to the church, and step-by-step it became clearer to me

[58.] See *Ethics*, *DBWE* 6:257–89.

how far it must go. Then came the crisis of 1933. This strengthened me in it.[59]

From his family, Bonhoeffer acquired an assured manner of self-presentation that left an impression on others. Behind that self-assurance, however, he concealed an inner life full of great emotion and burdened by enormous tensions. What he had discovered intellectually in theology,
484 he now also tried to appropriate for himself personally as well. And this involved a turn to a more intensive study of the Bible and service in the church as an expression of attachment to and solidarity with Jesus Christ. The piety he developed here was, even amid all subsequent searching, a piety that entailed serious consequences. Bonhoeffer, however, perceived this not as a burden but as liberation from excessive self-contemplation and from disorientation. It was particularly the Sermon on the Mount, with its seemingly so unrealistic presumptions, that seized him and no longer turned loose of him; from it he drew one consequence that took his circle of acquaintances completely by surprise: "Christian pacifism, which a brief time before . . . I had still passionately opposed, suddenly appeared to me as something utterly self-evident."[60]

For a highly intellectual theologian from upper-middle-class circles to resolve in this way to follow a path of simple obedience to the precepts of the Sermon on the Mount seemed astonishing amid the nationalist wave, which even before 1933 washed through the public sphere and through broad circles within the Protestant church. But it was not least also his lofty intellectual disposition that had made Bonhoeffer lonely, a condition he perceived virtually as abandonment. This oppressive mood, however, now receded as Bonhoeffer became what may be called a virtuoso of friendship and a teacher who not only fascinated his students but also turned to them both spiritually and personally. When in 1933 the National Socialist seduction and threat coerced many people into passive conformity, Bonhoeffer had already dealt with the enormous tensions within himself such that he was now able, with both steadfastness and clarity of mind, to take the difficult path of the minority who rejected the National Socialist regime not just occasionally but fundamentally.

---

[59.] From a letter of January 27, 1936, to Elisabeth Zinn (*DBW* 14, 1/47, p. 113); see also *DB-ER*, 205.

[60.] Ibid.

# Appendices

## Appendix 1
## Chronology of *Ecumenical, Academic, and Pastoral Work: 1931–1932*

**1931** 487

| | |
|---|---|
| After June 26 (Friday) | Return to Berlin from the United States (to the Bonhoeffer home on Wangenheimstrasse 14) |
| *July* | |
| 7 (Tuesday) | Conclusion of the Paris negotiations about U.S. President Hoover's plan for an international debt moratorium |
| 10 (Friday) | Superintendent Max Diestel grants Bonhoeffer's request for leave from his church duties until October 1, 1931 |
| | Spends three weeks in Bonn (Lennéstrasse 44) |
| 11–13 (Saturday–Monday) | Visits Margarete and Karl-Friedrich Bonhoeffer in Frankfurt |
| 13 (Monday) | German banking crisis; general run on banks, which stop payments |
| 15 (Wednesday) | Evening discussion at Barth's home with monks from Maria Laach |
| | Visits Maria Laach |
| | First emergency decree regulating financial sector |
| 21–23 (Tuesday–Thursday) | Seven Powers Conference in London[1] |

[1.] [This was to address the German banking crisis; short-term credits were extended to Germany.—VB]

| | |
|---|---|
| 23 (Thursday) | Lunch with Karl Barth |
| 24 (Friday) | "Open Evening" at Karl Barth's home, organized by his students |
| 25–26 (Saturday–Sunday) | Bonhoeffer travels to Düsseldorf to visit his cousin Gertrud Wedell for the weekend |

*August*

| | |
|---|---|
| 1 (Saturday) | Bonhoeffer accepts a special position as assistant to Wilhelm Lütgert in the Department of Systematic Theology in Berlin |
| 4 (Tuesday) | Reich Chancellor Brüning's radio speech concerning the financial crisis |
| 14–27 (Friday–Thursday) | Participation at the International Holiday House at Westcliff-on-Sea and St. Leonards-on-Sea |
| 27–29 (Thursday–Saturday) | Bonhoeffer may have participated in the Seaford Conference (Westhill) |
| 29–31 (Saturday–Monday) | Conference of the Youth Commission of the International Section of the World Alliance for Promoting International Friendship through the Churches in Cambridge |

*September*

| | |
|---|---|
| 1–5 (Tuesday–Saturday) | Conference of the World Alliance for Promoting International Friendship through the Churches in Cambridge |
| 488 | Bonhoeffer elected one of three youth secretaries and appointed to the Management Committee and the International Section of the World Alliance |
| 3 (Thursday) | Stock markets reopen |
| 21 (Monday) | German stock markets close |

*October*

| | |
|---|---|
| 1 (Thursday) | Bonhoeffer begins as student chaplain at the Technical College in Berlin-Charlottenburg |
| 4 (Sunday) | Sermon on Ps. 63:3 (evening service) (?) |
| 6–10 (Tuesday–Saturday) | Third emergency decree for securing economic and financial institutions and for checking political excesses |
| 10 (Saturday) | The Reich president receives the National Socialist party leader, Adolf Hitler |

11 (Sunday) Rally of the "national opposition" (National Socialist German Workers Party [NSDAP], German National People's Party [DNVP], Stahlhelm ["Steel Helmet," League of Frontline Soldiers]) in Bad Harzburg; formation of the Harzburg Front

14 (Wednesday) Meeting of all Berlin pastors to discuss the "winter problems"

20 (Tuesday) Meeting of the Provisional Bureau for Ecumenical Youth Work

28 (Wednesday) H.-L. Henriod, secretary of the International Section of the World Alliance for Promoting International Friendship through the Churches, assigns Bonhoeffer to plan a French-German regional conference

*November* Excursions with his confirmands

2 (Monday) Semester begins; Bonhoeffer offers the lecture course "History of Twentieth-Century Systematic Theology" and the seminar "The Idea of Philosophy and Protestant Theology"

14 (Saturday) 10:00 a.m. meets with Consistory Councilor W. D. A. Coulon

5:00 p.m. meets with General Superintendent Ernst Vits in the latter's apartment, Matthäikirchstrasse 22

15 (Sunday) Bonhoeffer ordained by Ernst Vits

Appointment as city synodal vicar at the Zion Church (district III; present-day Berlin-Wedding and Prenzlauer Berg)

That evening visits Franz Hildebrandt, who on the occasion of Memorial Day preaches on the 100th anniversary of the death of G. W. F. Hegel

16 (Monday) Meeting of the Working Group of Theologians and Economists

20 (Friday) Great Britain: First decree concerning import customs 489
duties

21 (Saturday) Friedrich Wilhelm University informs Wilhelm Lütgert that Bonhoeffer can take the special position of assistant that has just come open

25 (Wednesday) Bonhoeffer becomes secretary of the Provisional Bureau for Ecumenical Youth Work

| | |
|---|---|
| 29 (Sunday) | Sermon on Luke 12:35–40, first Sunday in Advent |
| *Winter* | Unemployment reaches its highest level (over 6 million) |
| *December* | |
| 4 (Friday) | France issues decree concerning imports from countries with foreign-exchange controls<br>1:30 p.m. Bonhoeffer and his confirmands attend the funeral of Pastor M. Müller |
| 5 (Saturday) | Sermon on Luke 12:35–40 |
| 8 (Tuesday) | Fourth emergency decree for securing economic and financial institutions and for the protection of domestic peace |
| 14 (Monday) | Swiss announcement of the Swiss-German trade agreement |
| *Mid-December* | Two-day retreat with confirmands |
| 24 (Thursday) | U.S. president Hoover signs the moratorium for reparation payments and war debt |
| **1932** | |
| *January* | |
| 1 (Friday) | Bonhoeffer moves to Oderbergerstrasse 61, Berlin N 58, for three months |
| 14 (Thursday) | Bonhoeffer signs the contract for the special position as assistant at the Friedrich Wilhelm University in Berlin (the contract runs from August 8, 1931, to June 30, 1933) |
| 28 (Thursday) | Sino-Japanese War breaks out |
| 29 (Friday) | Decree by Reich Armed Forces Minister Groener concerning the incorporation of the militias into the armed forces |
| *February* | |
| 2 (Tuesday) | Opening of the international conference on disarmament in Geneva |
| 4 (Thursday) | 6:00 p.m. Bonhoeffer delivers a talk at the Technical College, "The Right to Self-Assertion" |
| 21 (Sunday) | Evening sermon on Matt. 24:6–14 |

| | |
|---|---|
| *March* | Trip with students from the winter semester 1931–32 |
| 13 (Sunday) | First primary for the Reich presidential election (Düsterberg, Hindenburg, Hitler, Thälmann)<br>Confirmation Sermon on Genesis 32:25–32 |
| 19–29 (Saturday–Tuesday) | Retreat with confirmands in Friedrichsbrunn/Eastern Harz 490 |
| *April* | |
| 2 (Saturday) | Trip to London via Amsterdam |
| 4 (Monday) | Conference of the international youth secretaries in Epsom near London<br>Meeting of the Gland Directing Group |
| 5–8 (Tuesday–Friday) | Franco-British regional conference of the World Alliance for Promoting International Friendship through the Churches in Epsom |
| 9 (Saturday) | Bonhoeffer flies from London to Amsterdam and then takes the night train to Berlin |
| 10 (Sunday) | Bonhoeffer in Berlin to participate in the main Reich presidential election (Hindenburg is reelected) |
| 11 (Monday) | Karl Barth delivers a talk in the main auditorium at Berlin University: "Theology and Mission in the Present" |
| 13 (Wednesday) | SA and SS banned by an emergency decree at the recommendation of Reich Armed Forces Minister Groener |
| 15 (Friday) ? | Devotional in the Technical College on John 8:31–32 |
| 29–30 (Friday–Saturday) | Theological conference of the Provisional Bureau for Ecumenical Youth Work at the Church Federation Office, organized by Wilhelm Stählin and Bonhoeffer |
| *May* | Construction of a hut in Biesenthal, northeast of Berlin, as a weekend retreat for students |
| 6 (Friday) | Semester begins; Bonhoeffer offers the lecture course "The Nature of the Church" and the seminar "Is There a Christian Ethic?" |
| 8 (Sunday) | Sermon on 2 Chron. 20:12 in Trinity Church |
| 12 (Thursday) | Sermon on 1 John 4:16 at the baptism of his nephew Thomas (born August 26, 1931), son of Klaus and Emmi Bonhoeffer, at Wangenheimstrasse 14<br>Reich Armed Forces Minister Groener resigns |

| | |
|---|---|
| 29 (Sunday) | Sermon on Luke 16:19–31 |
| 30 (Monday) | Brüning's cabinet falls |
| *June* | |
| 1–2 (Wednesday–Thursday) | Papen's cabinet organized |
| 4 (Saturday) | Dissolution of parliament |
| 12 (Sunday) | Sermon on Col. 3:1–4 in the Kaiser Wilhelm Memorial Church |
| 491 16 (Thursday) | Lifting of the ban on the SA and the ban on uniforms by emergency decree<br>Conference in Lausanne concerning the waiving of German reparation payments |
| 19 (Sunday) | Sermon on Col. 3:1–4 |
| 20 (Monday) | Prussian civil administration deposed; Reich Chancellor von Papen installed as Reich Commissar |
| *July* | |
| 12–14 (Tuesday–Thursday) | Franco-German regional conference in Westerburg, which Bonhoeffer organizes in his capacity as youth secretary of the International Section of the World Alliance |
| 18 (Monday) | General ban on demonstrations |
| 20 (Wednesday) | Papen assumes power in Prussia ("Prussian coup") |
| 24 (Sunday) | Sermon on John 8:32 in Trinity Church (worship service at end of semester) |
| 20–30 (Wednesday–Saturday) | International Youth Peace Conference in Ciernohorské Kúpele (Czechoslovakia) |
| 25 (Monday) | Bonhoeffer arrives in Ciernohorské Kúpele |
| 26 (Tuesday) | Bonhoeffer delivers his talk "On the Theological Foundation of the Work of the World Alliance" |
| 29 (Friday) | Bonhoeffer departs for Berlin earlier than anticipated |
| 31 (Sunday) | Parliamentary elections in Germany |
| *August* | |
| 1 (Monday) | After completing his year of church service, Bonhoeffer receives the position of assistant pastor |
| 12 (Friday) | Dissolution of parliament |

| | |
|---|---|
| 13 (Saturday) | Negotiations collapse between the Reich government and Adolf Hitler regarding the participation of the NSDAP in the government |
| 16–17 (Tuesday–Wednesday) | Bonhoeffer spends two days at the vacation home of Jean Lasserre's family in Le Tremble, near Chamonix, France |
| 19–22 (Friday–Monday) | Conference of the Management Committee of the International Section of the World Alliance for Promoting International Friendship through the Churches in Geneva |
| 23 (Tuesday) | Meeting of the Gland Directing Group in Geneva |
| 25–31 (Thursday–Wednesday) | Youth conference of the World Alliance for Promoting International Friendship through the Churches and of the Universal Christian Council for Life and Work in Gland, on Lake Geneva, Switzerland<br>Bonhoeffer chairs the German discussion group |
| 25 (Thursday) | Morning: Bonhoeffer meets with Toureille and Zernoff |
| 28 (Sunday) | Evening: Bonhoeffer delivers an address 492 |
| 29 (Monday) | German note to France concerning the armaments question |

*September*

| | |
|---|---|
| 18 (Sunday) | Official declaration of Great Britain concerning the Franco-German exchange on disarmament and equal rights |
| 25 (Sunday) | Bonhoeffer attends the conference of student chaplains in Friedrichroda |

| | |
|---|---|
| *October* | Sermon on Eph. 5:14 at the baptism of Bonhoeffer's nephew Friedrich, son of Karl-Friedrich and Grete (née Dohnanyi) Bonhoeffer |
| 23 (Sunday) | Letter to Hans Brandenburg requesting advice concerning the establishment of the "youth club" |
| 25 (Tuesday) | Supreme Court verdict on the dispute between Prussia and the German Reich |

# APPENDIX 2
# UNPUBLISHED MATERIAL FROM BONHOEFFER'S LITERARY ESTATE, 1931–1932

493 The following list of unpublished material includes document numbers as cited in the Bonhoeffer *Nachlaß* volume (these are the numbers as they appear in the Bonhoeffer microfiche collection).

*1. Letters, Documents from Bonhoeffer*

| | |
|---|---|
| A 30,1(15) | Bonhoeffer's handwritten draft of an announcement, March 1932 |
| A 28,3(11) | To Pierre Toureille, fall 1932 |

*2. Reports, Theological Writings, and Texts from the University Period*

| | |
|---|---|
| A 31(6) | Notes from Bonhoeffer's time as assistant at the Institute of Systematic Theology:<br>(a) list with presentation topics, fall 1931<br>(b) rules for use of the departmental library, fall 1931<br>(c) literature list for Professor Stolzenburg, fall 1931 |

*3. Sermons*

| | |
|---|---|
| A 33,8c | Order for the worship service at the close of the semester, ninth Sunday after Trinity, July 24, 1932 |

# Appendix 3
# Texts Published in *Gesammelte Schriften* and *DBWE* 11

| ***GS*** | ***DBWE* 11** |
|---|---|
| 1:17–18 | 1/4 |
| 1:18 | 1/5 |
| 1:18–22 | 1/6 |
| 1:22–24 | 1/11 |
| 1:24–26 | 1/27 |
| 1:26–29 | 1/39 |
| 1:30–33 | 1/59 |
| 1:33–35 | 1/72 |
| 1:35–37 | 1/89 |
| 1:60–62 | 1/14 |
| 1:113–17 | 2/1 |
| 1:119–20 | 2/11 |
| 1:121 | 2/12 |
| 1:121–32 | 2/13 |
| 1:133–39 | 3/8 |
| 1:140–58 | 2/14 |
| 1:159–61 | 2/15 |
| 1:162–70 | 2/17 |
| 1:171–74 | 2/18 |
| 1:175–78 | 2/19 |
| 3:132–33 | 2/20 |
| 3:160–61 | 2/4 |
| 3:248–57 | 2/7 |
| 3:258–69 | 2/5 |
| 4:17–25 | 3/1 |
| 4:26–33 | 3/2 |

| ***GS*** | ***DBWE* 11** | 500 |
|---|---|---|
| 4:34–44 | 3/5 | |
| 4:44–50 | 3/6 | |
| 4:50–59 | 3/10 | |
| 4:60–69 | 3/11 | |
| 4:69–79 | 3/12 | |
| 4:79–88 | 3/13 | |
| 4:137–39 | 3/3 | |
| 4:139–41 | 3/4 | |
| 4:142–43 | 3/7 | |
| 4:147–50 | 3/9 | |
| 4:150–53 | 3/14 | |
| 5:181–227 | 2/3 | |
| 5:227–75 | 2/9 | |
| 5:275–300 | 2/10 | |
| 6:203–4 | 1/3 | |
| 6:204 | 1/7 | |
| 6:204–5 | 1/40 | |
| 6:206–7 | 1/52 | |
| 6:207 | 1/79 | |
| 6:211–12 | 1/0 | |
| 6:212–13 | 1/2 | |
| 6:213–14 | 1/34 | |
| 6:215–16 | 2/6 | |
| 6:216–17 | 1/54 | |
| 6:217 | 1/92 | |
| 6:217–18 | 1/91 | |

| *GS* | ***DBWE*** **11** | *GS* | ***DBWE*** **11** |
|---|---|---|---|
| 6:221 | 1/18a | 6:238–39 | 1/35 |
| 6:222 | 1/26 | 6:239–40 | 1/47 |
| 6:223–24 | 1/48 | 6:240 | 1/56 |
| 6:225–26 | 1/86 | 6:241–42 | 1/55 |
| 6:229–32 | 2/21 | 6:243–44 | 2/16 |
| 6:232–33 | 2/22 | 6:245 | 1/61 |
| 6:235 | 1/51 | 6:246–47 | 1/68 |
| 6:237 | 1/43 | 6:247–48 | 1/71 |
| 6:238 | 1/58 | | |

# Appendix 4
# Ecumenical and German Protestant Church Organizational Charts, 1931–1932

**The German Section of the World Alliance** 501
**for Promoting International Friendship through the Churches**

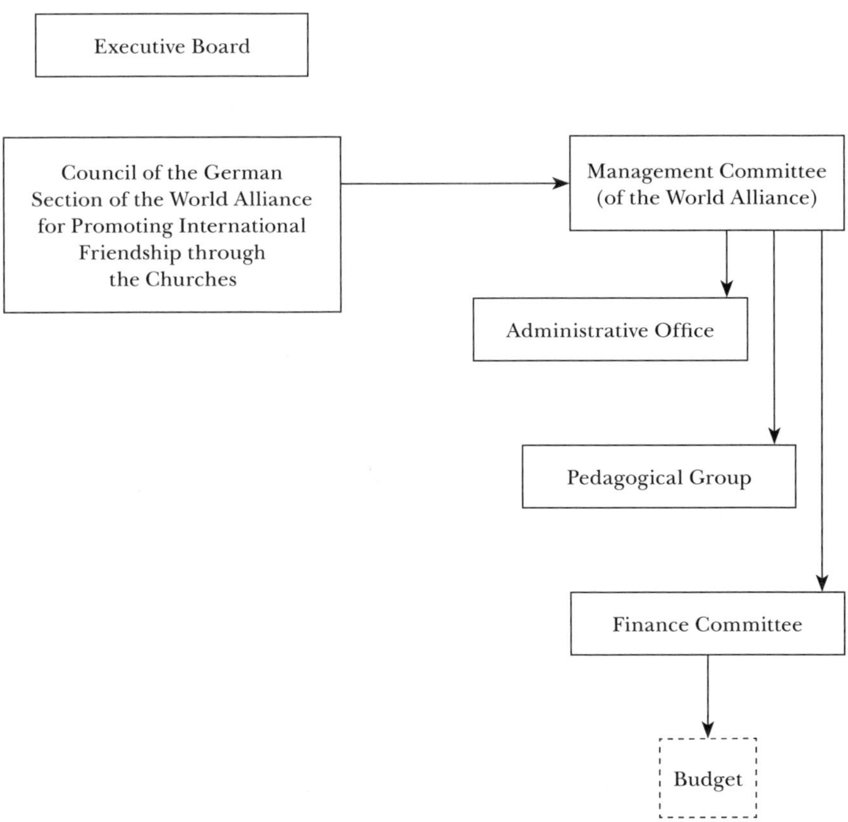

502 **The Constitution of the World Alliance for Promoting International Friendship through the Churches**

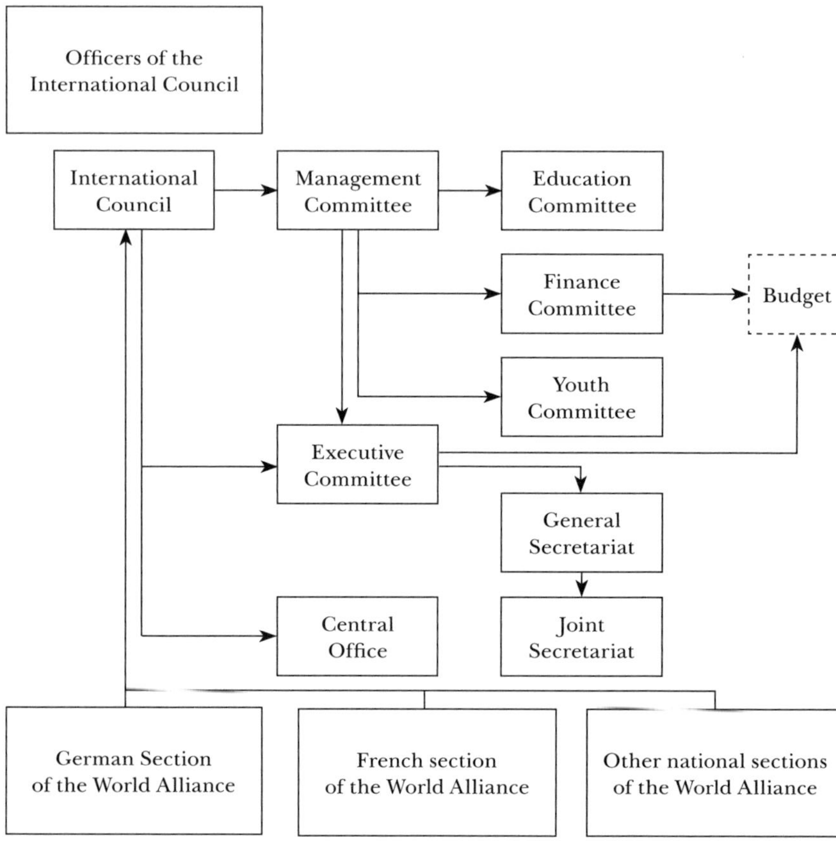


*International Council*: the highest committee of the World Alliance; it meets every three years and for politically important matters, determines the direction of the work of the World Alliance

*Management Committee*: directs the World Alliance in between meetings of the International Council; normally it convenes once a year

*Central Office*: office of the World Alliance, before 1931 in London, after 1932 in Geneva

*Executive Committee*: oversees business in between meetings

*General Secretariat*: takes care of the administrative work of the Education Committee; its members include three youth secretaries; it convenes the Joint Secretariat

*Joint Secretariat*: consists of the four international secretaries from Berlin, London, New York, and Paris

*Council of the National Sections of the World Alliance*: each section of the World Alliance sends four delegates to the International Council, with the exception of Germany, France, Great Britain, and the United States, all of which have eight delegates

## Ecumenical Institutions in Berlin in 1931 503

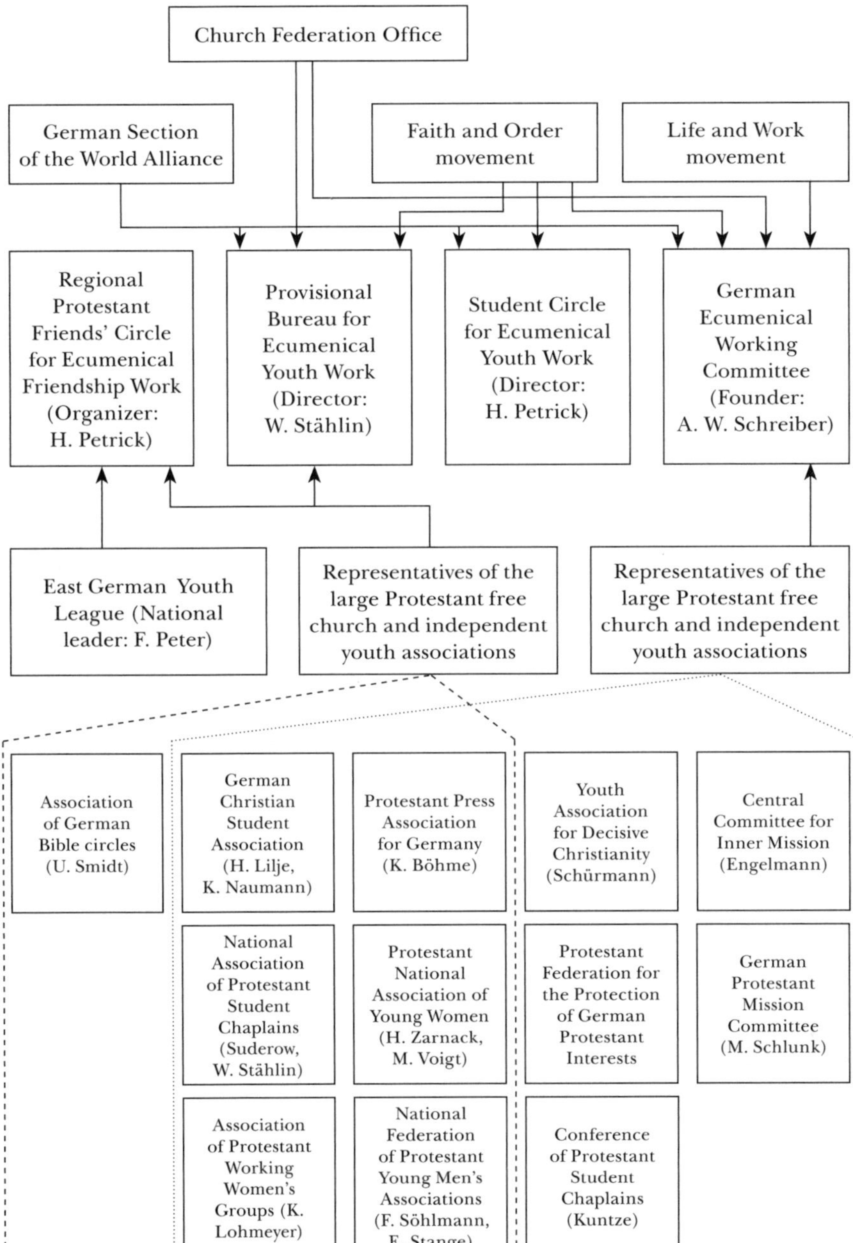

504

## The Constitution of the Protestant Church Federation, May 25, 1922

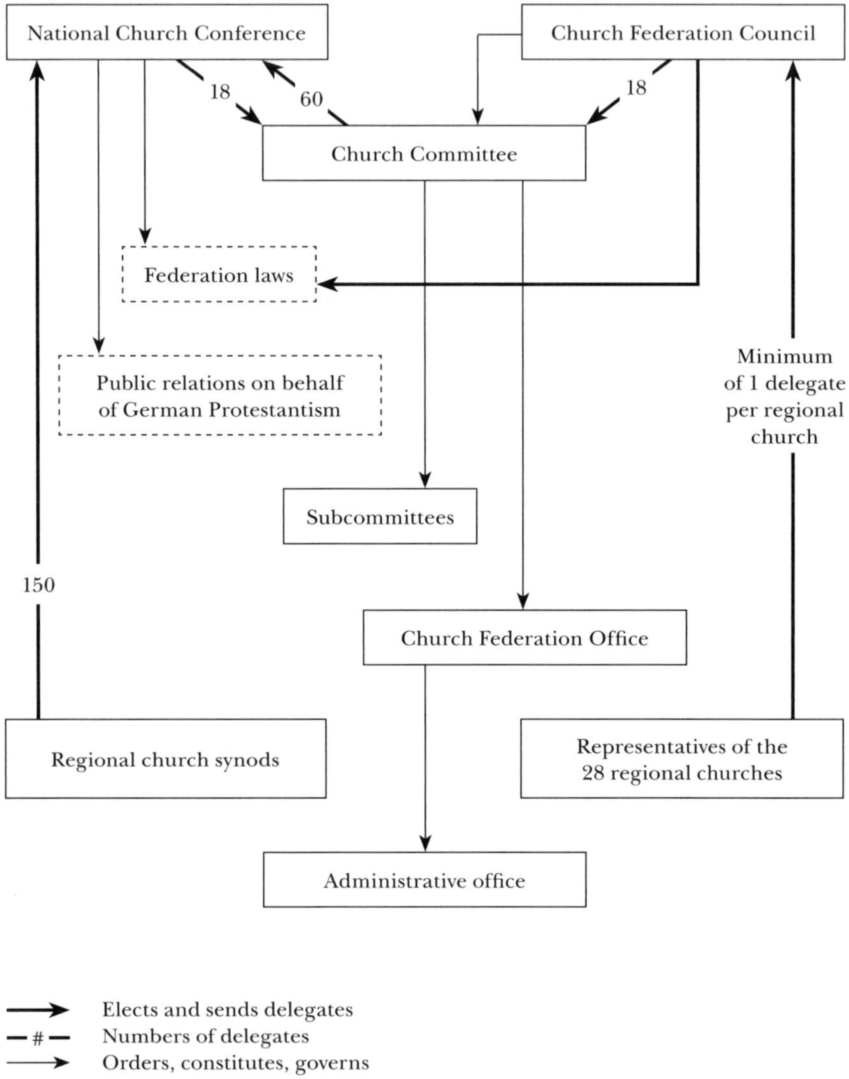


*National Church Conference*: representatives of church institutions and members; meets every three years
*Church Federation Council*: advisory body for the regional churches
*Church Committee*: managing body of the Church Federation
*Church Federation Office*: since 1924 exists as a statutory public corporation in accordance with Art. 137.5 of the constitution of the Weimar Republic

# Bibliography

Dietrich Bonhoeffer's papers and personal library, including some correspondence from others and relevant material from other archives, have been cataloged in the *Nachlaß Dietrich Bonhoeffer* volume compiled by Dietrich Meyer and Eberhard Bethge. All such citations in *DBWE* are indicated by *NL*, followed by the corresponding reference code within that published index. Not all this material is part of the actual Bonhoeffer Nachlaß in the Staatsbibliothek in Berlin; footnote citations of *NL* material from other archives also include the numbering from the respective archive. All the material listed in the Meyer and Bethge catalog, however, has been included on microfiches now located at the Staatsbibliothek in Berlin (previously at the Bundesarchiv in Koblenz) and in the Bonhoeffer Collection at Burke Library, Union Theological Seminary, New York. The designation *NL-Bibl.* in some bibliographic records indicates that a copy of the book was found in Bonhoeffer's personal library.

**1. Archival Sources and Private Collections**

Archiv des Diakonischen Werkes der EKD, Berlin (now part of the collections at the Evangelische Zentralarchiv, Berlin)
KSB 410: Bestände des Kirchlich-Sozialen Bundes CA/AC 22: Bestand Apologetische Centrale. Allgemeiner Schriftwechsel

Archives of the World Council of Churches, Geneva (WCC Archives)
World Alliance for International Friendship through the Churches
Youth Commission of the World Alliance

Archiv SEN Uppsala (Sandegren Collection, Church of Sweden *Archives)*, Uppsala, Sweden

Bundesarchiv Berlin-Lichterfelde (BA Berlin-Lichterfelde)
Nachlaß Hans und Christine von Dohnanyi

Evangelisches Zentralarchiv, Berlin (EZA)
Bestand 623: Nachlaß August Wilhelm Schreiber
Bestand 626: Nachlaß Friedrich Siegmund-Schultze
Karl Barth-Archiv, Basel
Correspondence about the Dehn case
Landeskirchliches Archiv der Evangelisch-Lutherischen Kirche in Bayern, Nuremberg (LKA Nuremberg)
Personen XVIII, Nachlaß Wilhelm Stählin Nr. 163
Paul Lehmann Collection, Special Collections, Princeton Theological Seminary Library, Princeton, New Jersey
Staatsbibliothek zu Berlin
Nachlaß Dietrich Bonhoeffer (Nachlaß 299)
Zentral- und Landesbibliothek Berlin
Nachlaß Adolf Deißmann (previously located at the Stadtbibliothek Berlin)

Private Collections (locations at the time of German *DBW* publication)
Eberhard and Renate Bethge, Wachtberg-Villiprott
Christine and Hans von Dohnanyi, Heidelberg
Franz Hildebrandt, Edinburgh
Jürgen Winterhager

**2. Literature Used by Bonhoeffer**

Adam, Karl. *Das Wesen des Katholizismus.* 1924. 3rd ed. Düsseldorf: L. Schwann, 1926. *NL-Bibl.* 6 B 1. Translated by Dom Justin McCann as *The Spirit of Catholicism.* Introduction by Robert A. Krieg. New York: Crossroad, 1997.

Althaus, Paul. *Grundriss der Dogmatik* (Outline for dogmatics). 2 vols. Erlangen: R. Merkel, 1929–32.

———. *Grundriss der Ethik* (Outline for ethics). Gütersloh: Gütersloher Verlagshaus, 1931.

Augustine, Aurelius. *Ausgewählte Schriften: Aus dem Lateinischen übersetzt* (Selected writings: Translated from the Latin). Vols. 1–11. Kempten: Kösel, 1911–25.

———. *De praedestinatione sanctorum.* Translated as *Predestinacion of saintes: Perseveraunce unto thende.* New York: Da Capo Press, 1968.

———. *Opera omnia* (Complete works). New edition, edited and corrected by Jacques-Paul Migne. 11 vols. Paris: 1841–42.

Barth, Karl. "Der Begriff der Kirche." *Zwischen den Zeiten* 5 (1927): 365–78. Translated by Louise Pettibone Smith as "The Concept of the Church" in Barth, *Theology and Church: Shorter Writings 1920–1928*, 272–85. New York: Harper & Row, 1962.

———. *Die christliche Dogmatik im Entwurf.* 1: *Die Lehre vom Worte Gottes: Prolegomena zur christlichen Dogmatik* (Christian dogmatics in outline. 1. The doctrine of the word of God: Prolegomena to Christian dogmatics). Munich: Chr. Kaiser, 1927. *NL-Bibl.* 3 B 9. Also published in *Gesamtausgabe* (Collected works), vol. 2, edited by Gerhard Sauter. Zürich: Theologischer Verlag, 1982.

———. *Fides quaerens intellectum: Anselms Beweis der Existenz Gottes im Zusammenhang seines theologischen Programms.* Series 4, vol. 3 of Forschungen zur Geschichte und Lehre des Protestantismus. Munich: Chr. Kaiser, 1931. Translated by Ian W. Robertson as *Anselm: Fides Quaerens Intellectum; Anselm's Proof of the Existence of God in the Context of His Theological Scheme.* London: SCM Press; Richmond: John Knox Press, 1960; Pittsburgh: Pickwick Press, 1985.

———. "Der heilige Geist und das christliche Leben." In Karl Barth and Heinrich Barth, *Zur Lehre vom heiligen Geist* (On the doctrine of the holy spirit). *Zwischen den Zeiten*, Beiheft Nr. 1, 39–105. Munich: Chr. Kaiser, 1930. *NL-Bibl.* 3 B 12. Translated by R. Birch Hoyle as *The Holy Ghost and the Christian Life.* 1930; London: Frederick Muller, 1938.

———. *Kirchliche Dogmatik.* Zurich: Evangelischer Verlag, 1932–67. *NL-Bibl.* 3 B 8. Translated by G. W. Bromiley as *Church Dogmatics*, edited by G. W. Bromiley and T. F. Torrance, 4 vols. Edinburgh: T & T Clark, 1956–77. Vol. 1, pt. 1: *Die Lehre vom Wort Gottes: Erster Halbband.* Translated as *The Doctrine of the Word of God.* Rev. ed. Vol. 1, pt. 2: *Die Lehre vom Wort Gottes: Prolegomena zur kirchlichen Dogmatik*; *Zweiter Halbband.* 6th ed. Zurich: Evangelischer Verlag, 1975. Translated as *The Doctrine of the Word of God: Prolegomena Part 2.*

———. "Die Not der Evangelischen Kirche" (The crisis of the Protestant church). *Zwischen den Zeiten* 9 (1931): 89–122. Revised version in Barth, *"Der Götze wackelt": Zeitkritische Aufsatze, Reden und Briefe von 1930 bis 1960* (The idol is tottering: Critical contemporary essays, addresses and letters from 1930 to 1960), edited by Karl Kupisch. 2nd ed., 33–62. Berlin: K. Vogt, 1964.

———. "Das Problem der Ethik in der Gegenwart." *Zwischen den Zeiten* 1 (1923): 30–57. Reprinted in Karl Barth, *Das Wort Gottes und die Theologie*, 125–55. Munich: Chr. Kaiser, 1924. Translated by Douglas Horten as "The Problem of Ethics Today" in *The Word of God and the Word of Man*, 136–82. New York: Harper, 1957.

———. "Quousque tandem . . . ?" *Zwischen den Zeiten* 8 (1930): 1–6. Reprinted in Barth, *"Der Götze wackelt": Zeitkritische Aufsatze, Reden und Briefe von 1930 bis 1960* (The idol is tottering: Critical contemporary essays, addresses and letters from 1930 to 1960), edited by Karl Kupisch, 2nd ed., 27–32. Berlin: K. Vogt, 1964.

———. *Der Römerbrief.* 10th printing of the new, rev. ed. of 1922. Zurich: EVZ Verlag, 1967. Translated from the 6th ed. by Edwyn C. Hoskyns as *The Epistle to the Romans.* 1933; London: Oxford University Press, 1960.

Bartmann, Bernhard. *Lehrbuch der Dogmatik* (Guide to dogmatics). 2 vols. 7th rev. ed. Freiburg im Breisgau: Herder, 1928.

Bell, George Kennedy Allen. *A Brief Sketch of the Church of England.* London: SCM Press, 1929.

*Das Berneuchener Buch: Vom Anspruch des Evangeliums auf die Kirchen der Reformation* (The Berneuchen book: The gospel's claim on the churches of the Reformation). Published by the Berneuchener Konferenz. Hamburg: Hanseatische Verlagsanstalt, 1926.

Biedermann, Alois Emanuel. *Christliche Dogmatik* (Christian dogmatics). 2nd. rev. ed. Berlin: G. Reimer, 1885.

Bousset, Wilhelm. "Der zweite Brief an die Korinther" (The Second Letter to the Corinthians). In *Die paulinischen Briefe und die Pastoralbriefe* (The Pauline letters and the pastoral letters), vol. 2 of *Die Schriften des Neuen Testaments* (The New Testament scriptures), edited by J. Weiss, W. Bousset, and W. Heitmuller, 3rd ed., 167–223. Göttingen: Vandenhoeck & Ruprecht, 1917.

*Breviarium romanum ex decreto SS. Concilii Tridentini restitutum* (Breviary according to the Tridentine rite). Published by the Roman Catholic Church. Regensburg: F. Pustet, 1898.

Brunner, Emil. *Das Gebot und die Ordnungen: Entwurf einer protestantisch-theologischen Ethik.* Tübingen: J. C. B. Mohr, 1932. *NL-Bibl.* 4, 6. Translated by Olive Wyon as *The Divine Imperative.* Philadelphia: Westminster Press, 1947.

———. *Der Mittler: Zur Besinnung über den Christusglauben.* Tübingen: J. C. B. Mohr, 1927. *NL-Bibl.* 3 B 15. Translated by Olive Wyon as *The Mediator.* New York: Macmillan, 1934.

Calvin, John. *Opera quae supersunt omnia.* Braunschweig: Schwetschke, 1863–1900.

———. *Opera selecta.* Munich: Chr. Kaiser, 1926–36.

Chomjakow, Aleksej Stephanowic. "Die Einheit der Kirche" (The unity of the church). In *Östliches Christentum* (Eastern Christianity), edited by N. Bubnoff and H. Ehrenberg, 2:1–27. Munich: C. H. Beck, 1925. *NL-Bibl. 6 C* 2.

Cohen, Hermann. *Jüdische Schriften* (Jewish writings). Edited by B. Straus. 3 vols. Berlin: C. A. Schwetschke, 1924. Partial English translation by

Eva Jospe as *Reason and Hope: Selections from the Jewish Writings of Hermann Cohen*. Cincinnati: Hebrew Union College Press, 1993.

Cordes, Cord. *Der Gemeinschaftsbegriff im deutschen Katholizismus und Protestantismus der Gegenwart* (The concept of community in contemporary German Catholicism and Protestantism). Engelsdorf-Leipzig: Eger & Siebers, 1931.

*Corpus iuris canonici* (Canon law). With commentary by Emil Friedberg and Aemilius Ludwig Richter. 2 vols. Published by the Roman Catholic Church. Leipzig: Tauchnitz, 1879–1991.

Cremer, Hermann. *Biblisch-theologisches Wörterbuch der neutestamentlichen Gräcität* (Biblical-theological dictionary of saving grace in the New Testament). 2 vols. Gotha: F. A. Perthes, 1866–68.

———. *Gethsemane: Ein Beitrag zum Verständnis der Geschichte Jesu und unserer Erlösung* (Gethsemane: A contribution to the understanding of the history of Jesus and our redemption). Gütersloh: C. Bertelsmann, 1902.

———. *Die paulinische Rechtfertigungslehre im Zusammenhänge ihrer geschichtlichen Voraussetzungen* (The Pauline teaching on justification in the context of its historical presuppositions). Gütersloh: C. Bertelsmann, 1899. *NL-Bibl.* 1 D 6.

———. *Das Wesen des Christentums* (The essence of Christendom). Gütersloh: C. Bertelsmann, 1901. *NL-Bibl.* 3 B 21. Translated from the 3rd ed. by Bernhard Pick as *A Reply to Harnack on the Essence of Christianity: Lectures Delivered in the Summer of 1901 before Students of All Faculties in the University of Greifswald.* New York: Funk & Wagnalls, 1903.

Culmann, Theodor. *Die christliche Ethik* (Christian ethics). 2 vols. Stuttgart: J. F. Steinkopf, 1864.

Deißmann, Adolf. *Die neutestamentliche Formel "in Christo Jesu" untersucht* (An examination of the New Testament phrase "in Christ Jesus"). Marburg: N. G. Elwert, 1892.

Dibelius, Otto. *Das Jahrhundert der Kirche: Geschichte, Betrachtung, Umschau und Ziele* (The century of the church: History, observation, review, and goals). 5th ed. Berlin: Furche-Verlag, 1928. *NL-Bibl.* 2 C 4 7.

———. *Die Verantwortung der Kirche: Eine Antwort an Karl Barth* (The responsibility of the church: An answer to Karl Barth). Berlin: Kranzverlag, 1931.

Drews, Arthur. *Die Christusmythe.* Jena: E. Diederichs, 1910. Translated by C. Delisle Burns as *The Christ Myth.* Amhurst, N.Y.: Prometheus Books, 1998.

Eberhard, Otto. "Grundsätzliches über die Erziehung zum ökumenischen Denken als Gegenwartsaufgabe des evangelischen Religionsunterrichts" (Fundamentals concerning educating toward ecumenical thought as a contemporary task of Protestant religious instruction). *Die evangelische Pädagogik* 6 (1931): 41–50.

Engels, Friedrich. *Ludwig Feuerbach und der Ausgang der klassischen deutschen Philosophie.* Stuttgart: Dietz, 1888. Reprinted in Karl Marx, Friedrich Engels, *Werke,* 21:259–307. Published by Institut für Marxismus-Leninismus beim ZK der SED. Berlin: J. H. W. Dietz, 1962. Translated as *Ludwig Feuerbach and the Outcome of Classical German Philosophy.* Edited by C. P. Dutt. New York: International Publishers, 1941.

Eucken, Rudolf. *Der Wahrheitsgehalt der Religion.* 3rd ed. Leipzig: Veit, 1912. Translated by W. Tudor Jones as *The Truth of Religion.* New York: G. P. Putnam's Sons, 1911.

"Die Evangelische Pädagogik" (Protestant pedagogy). *Zeitschrift der Gesellschaft für Pädagogik* 6 (1931).

*Das evangelische Westfalen* (Protestant Westphalia) 9, no. 10 (1932). Periodical published by Evangelischen Presseverband Westfalen und Lippe.

Fendt, Leonhard. *Die religiösen Kräfte des katholischen Dogmas* (The religious forces of Catholic dogma). Munich: Chr. Kaiser, 1921. *NL-Bibl.* 6 B 9.

Feuerbach, Ludwig. *Das Wesen der Religion: 30 Vorlesungen.* In Feuerbach, *Werke in 6 Bänden,* edited by E. Thies, 4:81–153. Leipzig: A. Kröner, 1923. Translated by Ralph Mannheim as *Lectures on the Essence of Religion.* New York: Harper & Row, 1967.

Fleisch, Paul. *Die moderne Gemeinschaftsbewegung in Deutschland: Ein Versuch, dieselbe nach ihren Ursprungen darzustellen und zu würdigen* (The modern communal movement in Germany: An attempt to portray and honor its origins). 3rd ed. Vol. 1: *Die Geschichte der deutschen Gemeinschaftsbewegung bis zum Auftreten des Zungenredens* (The history of the German communal movement until the manifestation of speaking in tongues). 1903; Leipzig: H. G. Wallmann, 1912.

Frank, Franz Hermann Reinhold von. *Geschichte und Kritik der neueren Theologie, insbesondere der systematischen, seit Schleiermacher: Aus dem Nachlaß des Verfassers* (History and critique of the new theology, especially systematic theology since Schleiermacher: From the author's literary estate). 1894. Edited by P. Schaarschmidt. Revised and updated by Richard H. Grützmacher. 4th ed. Leipzig: A. Deichert, 1908. *NL-Bibl.* 2 C 13.

———. *Die Theologie der Concordienformel* (The theology of the Formula of Concord). 4 vols. Erlangen: T. Blaesing, 1858–85.

Gildemeister, C. H., ed. *Johann Georg Hamann's des Magus im Norden, Leben und Schriften* (Johann George Hamann, the "magus of the north," in his life and works). 6 vols. Gotha: Perthese, 1868.

Gogarten, Friedrich. "Ethik des Gewissens oder Ethik der Gnade" (Ethics of conscience or ethics of grace). *Zwischen den Zeiten* 1 (1923):10–29.

———. *Politische Ethik: Versuch einer Grundlegung* (Political ethics: Attempt at a foundation). Jena: Diederichs, 1932. *NL-Bibl.* 4 S14.

———. *Wider die Ächtung der Autorität* (Against the proscription of authority). Jena: E. Diederichs, 1930.

Gogh, Vincent van. *The Letters of Vincent van Gogh to His Brother, 1872–1886: With a Memoir by His Sister-in-Law, J. van Gogh-Bonger.* 2 vols. Translated from the original 1914 edition in Dutch by J. van Gogh-Bonger. London: Constable; Boston: Houghton Mifflin, 1927.

Grisebach, Eberhard. *Gegenwart: Eine kritische Ethik* (The present: A critical ethic). Halle: Niemeyer, 1928.

———. *Die Grenzen des Erziehers und seine Verantwortung.* Halle: Niemeyer, 1924.

Güldenberg, Otto. "Der ökumenische Gedanke in den Lehrbüchern für den Religionsunterricht" (Ecumenical thought in the curricula for religious instruction). *Die evangelische Pädagogik* 6 (1931): 56–58.

Harnack, Adolf von. *Lehrbuch der Dogmengeschichte.* 4th newly revised and expanded ed. Vols. 1–3. Tübingen: J. C. B. Mohr, 1909–10. *NL-Bibl.* 2 C 4, 17. Translated from the 3rd German ed. by Neil Buchanan as *History of Dogma.* 4 vols. Gloucester, Mass.: Peter Smith, 1976.

———. *Das Wesen des Christentums.* Leipzig: J. C. Hinrichs, 1900. Translated by Thomas Bailey Saunders as *What Is Christianity? Sixteen Lectures Delivered in the University of Berlin during the Winter Term, 1899–1900.* New York: Harper, 1957. Reprint, with an introduction by Rudolf Bultmann, Gloucester, Mass.: Peter Smith, 1978. Cf. *NL-Bibl.* 3 B 30.

Heidegger, Martin. *Sein und Zeit.* Halle an der Saale: M. Niemeyer, 1927. Translated by Joan Stambaugh as *Being and Time: A Translation of* Sein und Zeit. Albany: State University of New York Press, 1996.

Heiler, Friedrich. *Der Katholizismus: Seine Idee und seine Erscheinung* (Catholicism: Its idea and its appearance). Munich: E. Reinhardt, 1923.

Herrmann, Wilhelm. "Christlich-protestantische Dogmatik" (Protestant-Christian dogmatics). In *Die Kultur der Gegenwart: Ihre Entwicklung und ihre Ziele* (Contemporary culture: Its development and its goal), edited by P. Hinneberg, pt. 1, sec. 4: *Die christliche Religion mit Einschluss der israelitisch-jüdischen Religion* (The Christian religion in reference to the Israelite-Jewish religion), 583–632. Berlin, 1906.

Hofmann, Johann Christian Karl von. *Der Schriftbeweis: Ein theologischer Versuch* (Evidence of Scripture: A theological attempt). 2nd rev. ed. 2 vols. Nördlingen: C. H. Beck, 1857–60. *NL-Bibl.* 3 B 44.

———. *Weissagung und Erfüllung im Alten und im Neuen Testamente* (Wisdom sayings and fulfillment in the Old and the New Testaments). 2 vols. in 1. Nördlingen : C. H. Beck, 1841–44.

Holl, Karl. "Die Entstehung von Luthers Kirchenbegriff" (1915) (The origin of Luther's concept of the church). In *Gesammelte Aufsätze zur Kirchen-*

*geschichte* (Collected essays on church history), vol. 1: *Luther,* 288–325. Tübingen: J. C. B. Mohr, 1928–32.

———. *Gesammelte Aufsätze zur Kirchengeschichte* (Collected essays on church history). 3 vols. Tübingen: J. C. B. Mohr, 1928–32.

———. "Luthers Bedeutung für den Fortschritt der Auslegungskunst" (1920) (The significance of Luther for the development of exegesis). In *Gesammelte Aufsätze zur Kirchengeschichte,* vol. 1: *Luther,* 544–82. Tübingen: J. C. B. Mohr, 1928–32.

———. *Urchristentum und Religionsgeschichte* (Early Christianity and the history of religion). Berlin: Ebering, 1924. *NL-Bibl.* 1 D 14.

———. "Was hat die Rechtfertigungslehre dem modernen Menschen zu sagen" (What the doctrine of justification has to say to modern humanity) (1907). In *Gesammelte Aufsätze zur Kirchengeschichte* (Collected essays on church history), vol. 3: *Der Westen,* 558–67.

———. "Was verstand Luther unter Religion." In *Gesammelte Aufsätze zur Kirchengeschichte,* vol. 1: *Luther,* 1–90. Translated by Fred W. Meuser and Walter R. Wietzke as *What Did Luther Understand by Religion?* Edited by James Luther Adams and Walter F. Bense. Philadelphia: Fortress Press, 1977.

Horstmeier, Marie. "Ökumenische Erziehung in höheren Schulen" (Ecumenical education in upper-level schools). *Die evangelische Pädagogik* 6 (1931): 53–56.

Hus, Johannes. *Magistri Ioannis Hus tractatus de ecclesia.* Edited by Samuel H. Thomson. Boulder: University of Colorado Press, 1956. Translated, with notes and introduction by David S. Schaff, as *The Church.* 1915; Westport, Conn.: Greenwood Press, 1974.

Husserl, Edmund. *Logische Untersuchungen.* 2 vols. in 3. 4th reprinting. Halle an der Saale: M. Niemeyer, 1928. Translated by Dermot Moran as *Logical Investigations.* New York: Routledge, 2001.

James, William. *Die religiöse Erfahrung in ihrer Mannigfaltigkeit: Materialien und Studien zu einer Psychologie und Pathologie des religiösen Lebens.* German translation by Georg Wobbermin (1907). 2nd enlarged ed., Leipzig: J. C. Hinrichs, 1914. English original: *The Varieties of Religious Experience: A Study in Human Nature.* The Gifford Lectures, Edinburgh, 1901–2. New York: Longmans, Green, 1928; reprint, New York: Simon & Schuster, 2004.

———. *The Will to Believe and Other Essays in Popular Philosophy.* New York: Longmans, Green, 1896.

Jellinghaus, Theodor. *Das völlige, gegenwärtige Heil durch Christus* (The full and present salvation through Christ). 2 vols. Berlin: Thormann & Goetsch, 1880–81.

Kaftan, Julius. *Die Wahrheit der christlichen Religion.* Basel: C. Detloff, 1888. Translated by George Ferries as *The Truth of the Christian Religion.* Edinburgh: T & T Clark, 1894.

———. *Das Wesen der christlichen Religion* (The nature of the Christian religion). 1881. 2nd ed. Basel: Gräfenhainichen, 1888.

Kähler, Martin. *Der sogenannte historische Jesus und der geschichtliche, biblische Christus: Vortrag auf der Wuppertaler Pastoralkonferenz.* Leipzig: A. Deichart, 1892. Translated by Carl E. Braaten as *The So-Called Historical Jesus and the Historical Biblical Christ.* Philadelphia: Fortress Press, 1964.

———. *Die Wissenschaft der christlichen Lehre von dem evangelischen Grundartikel aus im Abrisse dargestellt* (The science of Christian doctrine outlined from foundational Protestant principles) (1883–87). 3rd. enlarged ed. 3 vols. Leipzig: A. Deichert, 1905.

Kain, August. "Praktische Winke für die Erziehung zum ökumenischen Denken im Religionsunterricht der Volksschule" (Practical hints for educating toward ecumenical thought in religious instruction in public schools). *Die evangelische Pädagogik* 6 (1931): 50–53.

Kant, Immanuel. *Anthropologie in pragmatischer Hinsicht.* 5th ed. Leipzig: F. Meiner, 1912. Translated by Victor Lyle Dowdell as *Anthropology from a Pragmatic Point of View.* Revised and edited by Hans H. Rudnick, with an introduction by Frederick P. Van De Pitte. Carbondale: Southern Illinois University Press, 1978.

Kattenbusch, Ferdinand. *Die deutsche evangelische Theologie seit Schleiermacher: Ihre Leistungen und ihre Schäden* (German Protestant theology since Schleiermacher: Its achievements and its defects). 5th enlarged ed. of *Von Schleiermacher zu Ritschl* (1892). Giessen: A. Töpelmann, 1926.

———. *Der evangelische Kirchengedanke: Im Anschluß an Luther dargelegt* (The Protestant concept of church: As expressed with regard to Luther). 2nd rev. ed. Breslau: Evang. Zentralstelle, 1930.

———. "Der Quellort der Kirchenidee" (The source of the idea of church). In *Festgabe von Fachgenossen und Freunden. A. von Harnack zum 70. Geburtstag dargebracht* (Celebratory volume presented to Adolf von Harnack from colleagues and friends on his 70th birthday), edited by Karl Holl, 143–72. Tübingen: J. C. B. Mohr, 1921.

Kierkegaard, Søren. *Einübung im Christentum.* Vol. 9 of *Gesammelte Werke.* Jena: Diederichs, 1912. Translated from the Danish by Howard V. Hong and Edna H. Hong as *Practice in Christianity.* Princeton, N.J.: Princeton University Press, 1991.

Kliefoth, Theodor. *Acht Bücher von der Kirche* (Eight books on the church). Schwerin: Stiller, 1854.

Lagarde, Paul de. "Über das Verhältnis des deutschen Staates zu Theologie, Kirche und Religion: Ein Versuch, Nicht-Theologen zu orientieren" (On the relation of the German state to theology, church, and religion: An attempt to orient nontheologians) (1873). In *Deutsche Schriften*, edited by K. A. Fischer, vol. 1: *Schriften für das deutsche Volk*, 45–90. Munich: J. F. Lehmann, 1924; 4th ed., 1940. *NL-Bibl.* 7 P 51.

Lehmann, Paul. *Forgiveness: Decisive Issue in Protestant Thought.* With a foreword by Reinhold Niebuhr. 2nd ed. 1940; New York: Harper & Bros., 1970.

Lepsius, Johannes. *Adolf Harnacks Wesen des Christentums* (Adolf Harnack's Essence of Christianity). Reden und Abhandlungen (Lectures and essays) 2. Berlin: Reich Christi-Verlag, 1902.

———, ed. *Berichte der Verhandlungen der Eisenacher Konferenzen* (Reports of the proceedings of the Eisenach conferences). Vols. 1–3 (1902–4). Nach den stenographischen Protokollen (According to the minutes). Edited by Johannes Lepsius on behalf of the conference committee. Berlin: Deutsche Orient Mission, 1902–5. *NL-Bibl.* 69 A 194.

Lhotzky, Heinrich. *Religion oder Reich Gottes: Eine Geschichte* (Religion or the kingdom of God: A history). 2nd ed. Leipzig: J. C. Hinrichs, 1905.

Löhe, Wilhelm. *Drei Bücher von der Kirche: Den Freunden der lutherischen Kirche zur Überlegung und Besprechung dargeboten.* 6th ed. Neuendettelsau: Buchhandlung der Diakonissen-Anstalt, 1928. *NL-Bibl.* 3 B 52. Translated by Edward T. Horn as *Three Books concerning the Church.* Reading, Pa.: Pilger, 1908.

Lohmeyer, Ernst. *Vom Begriff der religiösen Gemeinschaft: Eine problemgeschichtliche Untersuchung über die Grundlagen des Urchristentums* (On the concept of religious community: A critical-historical examination about the foundations of original Christianity). Leipzig: Verlag Teubner, 1925. *NL-Bibl.* 1 D 22.

Luther, Martin. *Die ältesten ethischen disputationen Luthers* (The oldest ethical disputations of Luther). Edited by Carl Stange. Quellenschriften zur Geschichte des Protestantismus (Source documents in the history of Protestantism) 1. Leipzig: A. Deichert, 1904 .

———. *Luthers sermo de poenitentia* (Luther's sermons of penitence). Edited by Ernst Friedrich Fischer. Quellenschriften zur Geschichte des Protestantismus (Source documents in the history of Protestantism) 4. Leipzig: A. Deichert, 1906.

———. *Luthers Werke in Auswahl* (Luther's works: Selections). Edited by O. Clemen. 4 vols. Bonn: Marcus & Weber, 1912–13. *NL-Bibl.* 2 C 3, 17.

———. *Theologia Deutsch.* Quellenschriften zur Geschichte des Protestantismus (Source documents in the history of Protestantism) 7. Leipzig: A.

Deichert, 1908. Translated by Bengt R. Hoffman as *The Theologia Germanica of Martin Luther.* New York: Paulist Press, 1980.

———. *Vorlesungen über den Römerbrief, 1515–1516* (Lectures on the Letter to the Romans, 1515–1516). Edited by Johannes Ficker. 2 vols. Leipzig: Dieterich.

———. *Werke: Kritische Gesamtausgabe.* 58 vols. Weimarer Ausgabe. Weimar: H. Böhlau, 1883–. Translated as *Luther's Works,* vols. 1–30 edited by Jaroslav Pelikan, vols. 31–55 edited by Helmut Lehmann. Complete works on CD-ROM. Minneapolis: Fortress Press; St. Louis: Concordia, 2002.

———. *Die Wittenberger Artikel von 1536* (The Wittenberg articles of 1536). Edited by Georg Mentz. Quellenschriften zur Geschichte des Protestantismus (Source documents in the history of Protestantism) 2. Leipzig: A. Deichert, 1905.

Martin, Karl. *Das Evangelium vom neuen Menschen: Eine Synthese* (The gospel of a new humanity: A synthesis). Leipzig: Naumann, 1904.

*Missale Romanum ex decreto sacrosancti Concilii Tridentini restitutum* (The Roman Missal in the Tridentine rite). Published by the Roman Catholic Church. 15th ed. Regensburg, 1910.

Müller, Johannes T. *Die symbolischen Bücher der evangelisch-lutherischen Kirche, deutsch und lateinisch* (The symbolic books of the Evangelical-Lutheran Church in German and Latin). 3rd ed. Stuttgart: Liesching, 1869.

Müller, Julius. *Die christliche Lehre von der Sünde.* 6th ed. 2 vols. Breslau: Max, 1889. Translated by William Urwick as *The Christian Doctrine of Sin.* Edinburgh: T & T Clark, 1877.

Natorp, Paul. *Die Religion innerhalb der Grenzen der Humanität: Ein Kapitel zur Grundlegung der Sozialpädagogik* (Religion within the limits of humanity: A chapter on the fundamentals of social pedagogy). 2nd enlarged ed. Tübingen: J. C. B. Mohr, 1908.

———. *Vorlesungen über praktische Philosophie* (Lectures on practical philosophy). Erlangen: Verlag der Philosophischen Akademie, 1925.

Naumann, Friedrich. *Briefe über Religion—mit Nachwort "Nach 13 Jahren"* (Letters on religion—with an afterword "After 13 years"). Berlin: Georg Reimer, 1917. *NL-Bibl.* 7 B 14.

Nietzsche, Friedrich. *Zur Genealogie der Moral: Eine Streitschrift.* 3rd ed. Leipzig: C. J. Naumann, 1894. Translated and edited by Walter Kaufmann as *The Geneaology of Morals.* New York: Vintage Books, 1989.

Overbeck, Franz. *Christentum und Kultur: Gedanken und Anmerkungen zur modernen Theologie* (Christianity and culture: Thoughts and comments on modern theology). 2nd ed. Darmstadt: Wissenschaftliche Buchgesellschaft, 1963.

———. *Über die Christlichkeit unserer heutigen Theologie: Streit- und Friedensschrift.* 1873. 2nd enlarged ed. Leipzig: C. G. Naumann, 1903; reprint, Darmstadt: Wissenschaftliche Buchgesellschaft, 1963. Translated by Martin Henry as *How Christian Is Our Present-Day Theology?* Introduction by David Tracy. London: T & T Clark International, 2005.

Peterson, Erik. *Die Kirche* (The church). Munich: C. H. Beck, 1929.

———. *Was ist Theologie?* (What is theology?). Bonn: C. H. Beck, 1925.

Przywara, Erich. *Religionsphilosophie katholischer Theologie.* Munich: Oldenbourg, 1927. *NL-Bibl.* 7 B 20. Translated by Alan Coates Bouquet as *Polarity: A German Catholic's Interpretation of Religion.* London: Oxford University Press, 1935.

———. *Ringen der Gegenwart: Gesammelte Aufsätze 1922–1927* (Contemporary struggles: Collected essays, 1922–1927). Augsburg: Filser Verlag, 1929. *NL-Bibl.* 6 B 35.

Ritschl, Albrecht. *Die christliche Vollkommenheit: Ein Vortrag. Theologie und Metaphysik: Zur Verständigung und Abwehr* (Christian fulfillment: A lecture. Theology and metaphysics: Toward an understanding and rebuttal). 3rd reprint. Göttingen: Vandenhoeck & Ruprecht, 1902.

———. *Unterricht in der christlichen Religion.* 6th ed. Bonn: A. Marcus, 1903. *NL-Bibl.* 3 B 59. Translated by Philip Hefner as "Instruction in the Christian Religion," in Albrecht Ritschl, *Three Essays.* Philadelphia: Fortress Press, 1972.

Quellenschriften zur Geschichte des Protestantismus (Basic texts on the history of Protestantism). Series. Leipzig: A. Deichert, 1904–32.

Scheler, Max. *Die Stellung des Menschen im Kosmos.* Darmstadt: Reichl, 1928. *NL-Bibl.* 7 P 67. Translated by Hans Meyerhoff as *Man's Place in Nature.* Boston: Beacon Press, 1961.

Schiller, Friedrich. *The Complete Works of Friedrich Schiller.* 8 vols. New York: P. F. Collier & Son, 1902.

Schlatter, Adolf. *Die philosophische Arbeit seit Cartesius nach ihrem ethischen und religiösen Ertrag* (Philosophical work since Descartes in terms of its ethical and religious result). 1906. 2nd enlarged ed. Gütersloh: C. Bertelsmann, 1910. Cf. *NL-Bibl.* 7 A 72.

Schmidt, Karl Ludwig. "Evangelische Kirche und Völkerverständigung" (The Protestant church and the understanding among the peoples). *Theologische Blätter* 10 (1931): 178–79.

———. "Die Kirche des Urchristentums: Eine lexikographische und biblisch-theologische Studie" (The church in early Christianity: A lexicographical and biblical-theological study). In *Festgabe für Adolf Deißmann zum 60. Geburtstag, November 7, 1926* (Celebratory volume presented to

Adolf Deißmann on his 60th birthday, November 7, 1926), 258–319. Tübingen: J. C. B. Mohr, 1927.

Schmidt, Traugott. *Der Leib Christi: Eine Untersuchung zum urchristlichen Gemeindegedanken* (The body of Christ: An examination of the early Christian concept of community). Leipzig: Deichert, 1919.

Schultz, Hermann. *Die Lehre von der Gottheit Christi: Communicatio idiomatum* (The doctrine of the divinity of Christ: Idiomatic communication). Gotha: F. A. Perthes, 1881.

Schulz, Georg. *Vom Sinn der Kirche* (On the meaning of the church). Hefte der Sydower Bruderschaft 2. Gütersloh: Bertelsmann, 1926.

Schweitzer, Albert. *Das Messianitäts- und Leidensgeheimnis: Eine Skizze des Leben Jesu.* Tübingen: J. C. B. Mohr, 1901. Translated by Walter Lowrie as *The Mystery of the Kingdom of God: The Secret of Jesus' Messiahship and Passion.* New York: Macmillan, 1960.

Seeberg, Reinhold. *Christliche Dogmatik.* 2 vols. Erlangen: Deichert, 1924–25. Translated by Charles E. Hay as *Textbook of the History of Doctrine.* 2 vols. in 1. Grand Rapids: Baker Book House, 1977.

———. *Die Grundwahrheiten der christlichen Religion.* Leipzig: Deichert, 1902. Translated by George E. Thomson and Clara Wallentin as *The Fundamental Truths of the Christian Religion: Sixteen Lectures Delivered in the University of Berlin during the Winter Term of 1901–02.* London: Williams & Norgate, 1908.

Simmel, Georg. *Grundfragen der Soziologie* (*Individuum und Gesellschaft*). 1917. 2nd ed. Berlin: G. J. Göschen, 1920. *NL-Bibl.* 7 P 13. Translated by Kurt H. Wolff as "Fundamental Problems of Sociology (Individual and Society)," in *The Sociology of Georg Simmel.* 1950; New York: Free Press, 1967.

———. *Die Religion.* 2nd enlarged ed. Die Gesellschaft: Sammlung sozialpsychologischer Monographien (Society: Social-pyschological monographs) 2. 1906. Frankfurt am Main: Rütten & Loening, 1912. *NL-Bibl.* 7 P 22. Translated by Curt Rosenthal as *Sociology of Religion.* New York: Philosophical Library, 1959; reprint, New York: Arno Press, 1979.

———. *Soziologie: Untersuchungen über die Formen der Vergesellschaftung.* 1908. 3rd ed. Leipzig: Duncker & Humblot, 1923. Translated by Anthony J. Blasi, Anton K. Jacobs, and Mathew Kanjirathinka as *Sociology: Inquiries into the Construction of Social Forms.* Edited and introduced by Horst J. Helle. 2 vols. Leiden: Brill, 2009.

Spener, Philip. *Pia Desideria.* Leipzig: A. Köhler, 1841. Translated, edited, and introduced by Theodore G. Tappert as *Pia Desideria.* Philadelphia: Fortress Press, 1964.

Stählin, Wilhelm. "Die Einheit der christlichen Kirche und die Völker" (The unity of the Christian church and the peoples). *Die Eiche* 20 (1932): 332–33. *NL-Bibl.* 6 A 3.

Stange, Carl. *Christentum und moderne Weltanschauung* (Christianity and modern worldview). Leipzig: A. Deichert, 1911.

———. *Dogmatik* (Dogmatics). Vol. 1: *Einleitung in die Dogmatik* (Introduction to dogmatics). Gütersloh: Bertelsmann, 1927.

———. *Die Religion als Erfahrung* (Religion as experience). Gütersloh: Bertelsmann, 1919.

Stange, Erich. *Die Einheit der Christenheit: Ein Bibelstudium zu den Gemeindebriefen des Paulus* (The unity of Christianity: A biblical study on Paul's pastoral letters). Aus der Welt der Bibel (From the world of the Bible) 7. Berlin: Furche-Verlag, 1931. *NL-Bibl.* 1 D 30.

Stapel, Wilhelm. *Der christliche Staatsmann: Eine Theologie des Nationalismus* (The Christian statesman: A theology of nationalism). Hamburg: Hanseatische Verlagsansatalt, 1932. *NL-Bibl.* 4, 49a.

Tillich, Paul. *Religiöse Verwirklichung.* Berlin: Furche-Verlag, 1930. Translated by James Luther Adams as *The Protestant Era.* Chicago: University of Chicago Press, 1957.

———. *The Religious Situation.* Translated by H. Richard Niebuhr. New York: Meridian Books, 1956; London: Thames & Hudson. Originally published as *Die Religiöse Lage der Gegenwart* (Berlin: Ullstein, 1926). An altered version appears in Tillich, *Gesammelte Werke*, edited by R. Albrecht, vol. 10: *Die religiöse Deutung der Gegenwart: Schriften zur Zeitkritik*, 9–93. Stuttgart: Evangelisches Verlagswerk, 1968.

Troeltsch, Ernst. "Grundprobleme der Ethik: Erörtert aus Anlass von Herrmanns Ethik" (Basic problems of ethics: In response to [Wilhelm] Herrmann's ethics) (1902). In Troeltsch, *Gesammelte Schriften* (Collected writings), 2:552–672. Tübingen: J. C. B. Mohr, 1913. *NL-Bibl.* 7 A 87.

———. "Prinzip, religiöses" (Principles, religious). In *Die Religion in Geschichte und Gegenwart* (Religion past and present), 4:1842–46. Tübingen: J. C. B. Mohr, 1913; 2nd ed. (1930), 4:1499–1503.

———. "Rückblick auf ein halbes Jahrhundert der theologischen Wissenschaft" (1908). In Troeltsch, *Gesammelte Schriften* (Collected writings), 2:193–226. Tübingen: J. C. B. Mohr, 1913. *NL-Bibl.* 7 A 87. Translated by Robert Morgan and Michael Pye as "Half a Century of Theology," in *Writings on Theology and Religion*, edited by Robert Morgan and Michael Pye, 53–81. Atlanta: John Knox Press, 1977.

———. *Die Soziallehren der christlichen Kirchen und Gruppen.* Vol. 1 of *Gesammelte Schriften.* Tübingen: J. C. B. Mohr, 1912. 2nd ed., 1922. Reprint, Aalen: Scientia, 1965. Translated by Olive Wyon as *The Social Teaching of the Christian Churches.* Foreword by James Luther Adams. 2 vols. Louisville: Westminster/John Knox, 1992.

———. "Die theologische und religiöse Lage der Gegenwart" (The contemporary theological and religious situation) (1903). In Troeltsch, *Gesammelte Schriften* (Collected writings), 2:1–21. Tübingen: J. C. B. Mohr, 1913. *NL-Bibl.* 7 A 87.

———. "Über historische und dogmatische Methode in der Theologie" (1898). In Troeltsch, *Gesammelte Schriften* (Collected writings), vol. 2: *Zur religiosen Lage, Religionsphilosophie und Ethik* (On the religious situation, philosophy of religion and ethics), 729–53. Tübingen: J. C. B. Mohr, 1913. *NL-Bibl.* 7 A 87. Translated by James Luther Adams and Walter E. Bense as "Historical and Dogmatic Method in Theology," with an introduction by James Luther Adams, in *Religion in History.* Minneapolis: Fortress Press, 1991.

———. *Vernunft und Offenbarung bei Johann Gerhard und Melanchthon: Untersuchung zur Geschichte der altprotestantischen Theologie* (Reason and revelation in Johann Gerhard and Melanchthon: An examination of the history of early Protestant theology). Göttingen: E. A. Huth, 1891.

———. "Was heisst 'Wesen des Christentums'"? (1903). In Troeltsch, *Gesammelte Schriften* (Collected writings), 2:386–451. Tübingen: J. C. B. Mohr, 1913. *NL-Bibl.*7 A 87. Translated by Robert Morgan and Michael Pye as "What Does 'Essence of Christianity' Mean?" in *Writings on Theology and Religion,* edited by Robert Morgan and Michael Pye, 124–81. Atlanta: John Knox Press, 1977.

Visser 't Hooft, Willem Adolf. *The Background of the Social Gospel in America.* Haarlem, Netherlands: Tjeenk Willink, 1929. New ed., St. Louis: Bethany Press, 1962.

Walther, Friedrich. "Harnacks Wesen des Christentums in seinen Grundsätzen beleuchtet" (Harnack's "Essence of Christianity" examined in its precepts). *Monatsschrift für Stadt und Land* 58 (1901): 1251–60.

Walther, Johannes. "Das Wesen des Christentums" (The essence of Christianity). *Mitteilungen und Nachrichten für die evangelische Kirche in Russland* 57 (1901): 97–124.

Walther, Wilhelm. *Adolf Harnacks Wesen des Christentums für die christliche Gemeinde geprüft* (Harnack's "Essence of Christianity" for the Christian congregation). Leipzig: A. Deichert, 1901.

Wrede, William. *Das Messiasgeheimnis in den Evangelien: Zugleich ein Beitrag zum Verständnis des Markusevangeliums.* 1901. 2nd ed. Göttingen: Vandenhoeck & Ruprecht, 1913. Translated by J. C. G. Greig as *The Messianic Secret.* Cambridge: J. Clarke, 1971.

———. *Paulus.* Religionsgeschichtliche Volksbücher für die deutsche christliche Gegenwart, vol. 1, no. 5/6. Tübingen: J. C. B. Mohr, 1907. Translated by Edward Lummis as *Paul,* with a preface by J. Estlin Carpenter. Lexington, Ky.: American Theological Library Association, Committee on Reprinting, 1962.

Zoellner, Wilhelm. "Die Einheit der christlichen Kirche und die Völker" (The unity of the Christian church and the nations). *Die Eiche* 20 (1932): 332–33.

———. "Die una sancta ecclesia und die Einzelkirchen" (The one holy church and the individual churches). *Die Eiche* 20 (1932): 328–32. *NL*-Bibl. 6 A 3.

### 3. Literature Mentioned by Bonhoeffer's Correspondents

Bell, George Kennedy Allen, *A Brief Sketch of the Church of England.* London: SCM, 1929. Translated as "Eine kurze Darstellung der Kirche von England" in *EKKLESIA: Eine Sammlung von Selbstdarstellungen der christlichen Kirchen,* edited by F. Siegmund-Schultze, 1:9–104. Gotha, 1934.

Bonhoeffer, Dietrich. "Concerning the Christian Idea of God." *Journal of Religion* 12, no. 2 (1932): 177–85.

———. "Ökumenische Jugendarbeit: Englisch-französische Jugendkonferenz des Weltbundes für Freundschaftsarbeit der Kirchen" (Ecumenical Youth Work: The English-French youth conference of the World Alliance for Promoting International Friendship through the Churches). *Die Eiche* 20 (1932): 260–61.

———. "Theologische Konferenz der Mittelstelle für Ökumenische Jugendarbeit" (Theological conference of the Provisional Bureau for Ecumenical Youth Work). *Die Eiche* 20 (1932): 260–61.

Peter, Friedrich. *Wenn die Würfel fallen: Ein Buch von Evangelium und Politik* (When the die is cast: A book on the gospel and politics). Berlin: Verlag d. Ostdeutschen Jünglingsbundes, 1931.

Thomas à Kempis. *Imitatio Christi.* Vol. 2 of Thomas à Kempis, *Opera.* 7 vols. Edited by M. J. Pohl. Freiburg: Herder, 1904. Translated and edited by Joseph N. Tylenda as *The Imitation of Christ in Four Books.* Rev. ed. New York: Vintage Books, 1998.

### 4. Literature Consulted by the Editors

Alston, Wallace, and Michael Welker, eds. "Dietrich Bonhoeffer: Previously Unpublished Letters to Paul Lehmann." *Theology Today* 53, no. 3 (1996): 289–98. German material translated by Matthias Gockel. Also published as "Dietrich Bonhoeffer: Bisher unveröffentlichte Briefe an Paul Lehmann." *Evangelische Theologie* 56 (1996): 465–75.

Althaus, Paul. *Das Erlebnis der Kirche* (The experience of the church). 1919. 2nd ed. Leipzig: Dörffling & Franke, 1924.

———. *Staatsgedanke und Reich Gottes* (The concept of the state and the kingdom of God). 3rd enlarged ed. Schriften zur politischen Bildung (Writings for political education), 9th series: Christendom, book 1. Langensalza: H. Beyer, 1926.

———. *Die Theologie Martin Luthers.* Gütersloh: Gütersloher Verlagshaus Gerd Mohn, 1975. Translated by Robert C. Schultz as *The Theology of Martin Luther.* Philadelphia: Fortress Press, 1988.

———. "Theologie und Geschichte: Zur Auseinandersetzung mit der dialektischen Theologie" (Theology and history in the controversy with dialectical theology). *Zeitschrift für Systematische Theologie* 1 (1923): 741–86.

Althaus, Paul, and Emanuel Hirsch. "Evangelische Kirche und Völkerverständigung" (Protestant Church and the understanding among the peoples). *Theologische Blätter* 10 (1931): 177–78. Also in *Neuwerk* 13 (1931–32): 120–21.

Augustinus, Aurelius. *De Civitate Dei.* Libri XXII. In *Patrologiae cursus completus,* Series Latina 41, 13–804. Paris, 1841. Translated and edited by R. W. Dyson as *The City of God against the Pagans.* Cambridge: Cambridge University Press, 1998.

Barbey d'Aureville, Jules. *Les Diaboliques.* Paris: E. Dentu, 1874. Translated by Jean Kimber as *The She-Devils.* London: Oxford University Press, 1964.

Barnett, Victoria. *For the Soul of the People: Protestant Protest against Hitler.* New York: Oxford University Press, 1992.

Barth, Karl. "Die dogmatische Prinzipienlehre bei Wilhelm Herrmann" (Wilhelm Herrmann's doctrine of dogmatic principles). In Barth, "Die Theologie und die Kirche," *Gesammelte Vorträge* (Collected lectures), 2:240–84. Munich: Chr. Kaiser, 1928.

———. *Ethik.* Originally published in two volumes. Zürich: Theologischer Verlag, 1928 and 1973 (vol. 1); 1928–29 and 1978 (vol. 2). Translated by Geoffrey W. Bromiley as *Ethics,* edited by Dietrich Braun. New York: Seabury Press, 1981.

———. "Der Fall Dehn und die 'dialektische Theologie.'" *Neuwerk: Ein Dienst am Werdenden* (Cassel), 13, no. 6 (1932): 366–72.

———. *The Humanity of God.* Translated by Thomas Wieser and John Newton Thomas. Richmond: John Knox Press, 1960. Originally published as three monographs in the Theologische Studien series by the Evangelischer Verlag, Zollikon-Zurich: Verlag AG.

———. “Kirche und Theologie” (Church and theology). *Zwischen den Zeiten* 4 (1926): 18–40. Reprinted as “Die Theologie und die Kirche,” in *Gesammelte Vorträge* (Collected lectures), 2:302–28. Munich: Chr. Kaiser, 1928. Translated by Louise Pettibone Smith as “Church and Theology,” in Barth, *Theology and Church: Shorter Writings, 1920–1928.* New York: Harper & Row, 1962.

———. “Menschenwort und Gotteswort in der christlichen Predigt” (Word of man and word of God in Christian preaching). *Zwischen den Zeiten* 3 (1925): 119–40.

———. “Die Theologie und der heutige Mensch” (Theology and the contemporary person). *Zwischen den Zeiten* 8 (1930): 375–96.

———. *Die Theologie und die Kirche.* Gesammelte Vorträge 2. Zollikon-Zurich: Evangelische Verlag, 1928. Translated by Louise Pettibone Smith as *Theology and Church: Shorter Writings, 1920–1928.* New York: Harper & Row, 1962.

———. “Die Theologie und die Mission in der Gegenwart” (Contemporary theology and mission). *Zwischen den Zeiten* 10 (1932): 189–215.

———. “Verheißung, Zeit-Erfüllung” (Promise, fulfillment of time). *Zwischen den Zeiten* 9 (1931): 457–63. Previously published in *Münchner Neueste Nachrichten,* December 23, 1930.

———. “Von der Paradoxie des ‘positiven Paradoxes’”: Antworten und Fragen an Paul Tillich.” *Theologische Blätter* 2 (1923): 287–96. Reprinted in *Anfänge der dialektischen Theologie* (Beginnings of dialectical theology), edited by Jürgen Moltmann, 3rd ed., Theologische Bücherei 17, pt. 1, 175–89. Munich: Chr. Kaiser, 1974. Translated by Keith R. Crim as “The Paradoxical Nature of the ‘Positive Paradox’: Answers and Questions to Paul Tillich,” in *The Beginnings of Dialectic Theology,* edited by James M. Robinson, 142–54. Richmond: John Knox Press, 1968.

———. “Warum führt man den Kampf nicht, wie es sich gehört, auf der ganzen Linie?” *Frankfurter Zeitung,* February 15, 1932.

———. *Das Wort Gottes und die Theologie.* Munich: Chr. Kaiser, 1924. Translated by Douglas Horton as *The Word of God and the Word of Man.* New York: Harper & Brothers, 1957.

Barth, Karl, and Eduard Thurneysen. *Komm Schöpfer Geist! Predigten.* Munich: Chr. Kaiser, 1924. Translated by George W. Richards, Elmer G. Homrighausen, and Karl J. Ernst as *Come Holy Spirit! Sermons* (1933). Grand Rapids, Mich.: Wm. B. Eerdmans, 1978.

*Die Bekenntnisschriften der evangelisch-lutherischen Kirche.* Edited and published in the anniversary year of the Augsburg Confession, 1930. 2 vols. Göttingen: Vandenhoeck & Ruprecht, 1930. *NL-Bibl.* 2 C 31. 9th ed., 1982. Translated by Charles Arand, Eric Gritsch, Robert Kolb, William Russell,

James Schaaf, Jane Strohl, and Timothy J. Wengert as *The Book of Concord: The Confessions of the Evangelical Lutheran Church,* edited by Robert Kolb and Timothy J. Wengert. Minneapolis: Fortress Press, 2000.

Bell, George Kennedy Allen. "Eine kurze Darstellung der Kirche von England." In *EKKLESIA: Eine Sammlung von Selbstdarstellungen der christlichen Kirchen* (Ekklesia: A collection of self-portraits by Christian churches), edited by F. Siegmund-Schultze, 1:9–104. Gotha, 1934. Published in English by the author as *A Brief Sketch of the Church of England.* London: SCM, 1929.

Bellarmine, Robert. *Opera omnia* (Complete works). Edited by J. Fevre. 12 vols. Paris: Ludovicum vives, 1870–74. Reprint, Frankfurt am Main: Minerva, 1965.

Benn, Gottfried. *Gesammelte Werke in acht Bänden* (Collected works in eight volumes). Edited by D. Wellershoff. Vol. 2. With appended poems. Wiesbaden: Limes, 1968.

Bergen, Doris. *Twisted Cross: The German Christian Movement in the Third Reich.* Chapel Hill: University of North Carolina Press, 1996.

Bethge, Eberhard. *Dietrich Bonhoeffer: Theologe—Christ—Zeitgenosse; Eine Biographie.* Munich: Chr. Kaiser, 1967. Translated by Eric Mosbacher, Peter Ross, Betty Ross, Frank Clarke, and William Glen-Doepel as *Dietrich Bonhoeffer: A Biography,* under the editorship of Edwin Robertson. Revised and edited by Victoria Barnett, based on the 7th German edition. Minneapolis: Fortress Press, 2000.

Bethge, Eberhard, Renate Bethge, and Christian Gremmels, eds. *Dietrich Bonhoeffer: Sein Leben in Bildern und Texten.* Munich: Chr. Kaiser, 1989. Translated by John Bowden as *Dietrich Bonhoeffer: A Life in Pictures.* Philadelphia: Fortress Press, 1986. Translated by Brian McNeil as *Dietrich Bonhoeffer: A Life in Pictures.* 2006 centenary ed. Philadelphia: Fortress Press, 2006.

Binder, Wolfgang. "Hölderlin, Friedrich." *Theologische Realenzyklopädie* 15: 441–44.

Bizer, Ernst. "Der 'Fall Dehn'" (The Dehn case). In *Festschrift für Günther Dehn,* edited by W. Schneemelcher, 239–61. Neukirchen: Verlag der Buchhandlung des Erziehungsvereins Neukirchen, 1957.

Bonhoeffer, Dietrich. *Dietrich Bonhoeffer Werke.* Edited by Eberhard Bethge et al. 17 vols. Munich: Chr. Kaiser/Gütersloher Verlagshaus, 1986–99. Translated as *Dietrich Bonhoeffer Works.* Victoria J. Barnett, Wayne Whitson Floyd Jr., and Barbara Wojhoski, general editors. 17 vols. Minneapolis: Fortress Press, 1996–.

Vol. 1: *Sanctorum Communio: Eine dogmatische Untersuchung zur Soziologie der Kirche.* Edited by Joachim von Soosten. Munich: Chr. Kaiser, 1986. Translated by Reinhard Krauss and Nancy Lukens as *Sanctorum Communio: A*

*Theological Study of the Sociology of the Church.* Edited by Clifford J. Green. Minneapolis: Fortress Press, 1998.

Vol. 2: *Akt und Sein: Transzendentalphilosophie und Ontologie in der systematischen Theologie.* Edited by Hans-Richard Reuter. Munich: Chr. Kaiser, 1988. Translated by Martin Rumscheidt as *Act and Being: Transcendental Philosophy and Ontology in Systematic Theology.* Edited by Wayne Whitson Floyd Jr. Minneapolis: Fortress Press, 1996.

Vol. 3: *Schöpfung und Fall: Theologische Auslegung von Genesis 1–3.* Edited by Martin Rüter and Ilse Tödt. Munich: Chr. Kaiser, 1989. Translated by Douglas Stephen Bax as *Creation and Fall: A Theological Exposition of Genesis 1–3.* Edited by John W. de Gruchy. Minneapolis: Fortress Press, 1996.

Vol. 4: *Nachfolge.* Edited by Martin Kuske and Ilse Tödt. Munich: Chr. Kaiser, 1989; 2nd ed., Gütersloh: Chr. Kaiser/Gütersloher Verlagshaus, 1994. Translated by Barbara Green and Reinhard Krauss as *Discipleship.* Edited by Geffrey B. Kelly and John D. Godsey. Minneapolis: Fortress Press, 2001.

Vol. 5: *Gemeinsames Leben: Das Gebetbuch der Bibel.* Edited by Gerhard Ludwig Müller and Albrecht Schönherr. Munich: Chr. Kaiser, 1987. Translated by Daniel W. Bloesch and James H. Burtness as *Life Together* and *Prayerbook of the Bible.* Edited by Geffrey B. Kelly. Minneapolis: Fortress Press, 1996.

Vol. 6: *Ethik.* Edited by Ilse Tödt, Heinz Eduard Tödt, Ernst Feil, and Clifford Green. Munich: Chr. Kaiser, 1992; 2nd ed., Gütersloh: Chr. Kaiser/Gütersloher Verlagshaus, 1998. Translated by Reinhard Krauss and Charles West, with Douglas W. Stott, as *Ethics.* Edited by Clifford J. Green. Minneapolis: Fortress Press, 2005.

Vol. 7: *Fragmente aus Tegel.* Edited by Renate Bethge and Ilse Tödt. Gütersloh: Chr. Kaiser/Gütersloher Verlagshaus, 1994. Translated by Nancy Lukens as *Fiction from Tegel Prison.* Edited by Clifford J. Green. Minneapolis: Fortress Press, 2000.

Vol. 8: *Widerstand und Ergebung.* Edited by Christian Gremmels, Eberhard Bethge, and Renate Bethge, with Ilse Tödt. Gütersloh: Chr. Kaiser/Gütersloher Verlagshaus, 1998. Translated by Isabel Best, Lisa E. Dahill, Reinhard Kraus, and Nancy Lukens, with Barbara and Martin Rumscheidt and Douglas W. Stott, as *Letters and Papers from Prison.* Edited by John W. de Gruchy. Minneapolis: Fortress Press, 2010.

Vol. 9: *Jugend und Studium: 1918–1927.* Edited by Hans Pfeifer, with Clifford Green and Jürgen Kaltenborn. Munich: Chr. Kaiser, 1986. Translated by Mary Nebelsick, with the assistance of Douglas W. Stott, as *The Young Bonhoeffer: 1918–1927.* Edited by Paul Matheny, Clifford J. Green, and Marshall Johnson. Minneapolis: Fortress Press, 2001.

Vol. 10: *Barcelona, Berlin, Amerika: 1928–1931.* Edited by Reinhard and Hans Christoph von Hase, with Holger Roggelin and Matthias Wünsche. Munich: Chr. Kaiser, 1991; 2nd ed., Gütersloh: Chr. Kaiser/Gütersloher Verlagshaus, 2005. Translated by Douglas W. Stott as *Barcelona, Berlin, New York: 1928–1931.* Edited by Clifford J. Green. Minneapolis: Fortress Press, 2008.

Vol. 11: *Ökumene, Universität, Pfarramt: 1931–1932.* Edited by Eberhard Amelung and Christoph Strohm. Gütersloh: Chr. Kaiser/Gütersloher Verlagshaus, 1994. Translated by Anne Schmidt-Lange, with Isabel Best, Nicolas Humphrey, and Marion Pauck, with supplementary material translated by Douglas W. Stott, as *Ecumenical, Academic, and Pastoral Work: 1931–1932.* Edited by Victoria J. Barnett, Mark S. Brocker, and Michael B. Lukens. Minneapolis: Fortress Press, 2012.

Vol. 12: *Berlin: 1932–1933.* Edited by Carsten Nicolaisen and Ernst-Albert Scharffenorth. Gütersloh: Chr. Kaiser/Gütersloher Verlagshaus, 1997. Translated by Isabel Best and David Higgins, with supplementary material translated by Douglas W. Stott, as *Berlin: 1932–1933.* Edited by Larry L. Rasmussen. Minneapolis: Fortress Press, 2009.

Vol. 13: *London: 1933–1935.* Edited by Hans Goedeking, Martin Heimbucher, and Hans-Walter Schleicher. Gütersloh: Chr. Kaiser/Gütersloher Verlagshaus, 1994. Translated by Isabel Best, with supplementary material translated by Douglas W. Stott, as *London: 1933–1935.* Edited by Keith Clements. Minneapolis: Fortress Press, 2007.

Vol. 14: *Illegale Theologenausbildung: Finkenwalde 1935–1937* (Theological education at Finkenwalde: 1935–1937). Edited by Otto Dudzus and Jürgen Henkys, with Sabine Bobert-Stützel, Dirk Schulz, and Ilse Tödt. Gütersloh: Chr. Kaiser/Gütersloher Verlagshaus, 1996.

Vol. 15: *Illegale Theologenausbildung: Sammelvikariate: 1937–1940.* Edited by Dirk Schulz. Gütersloh: Chr. Kaiser/Gütersloher Verlagshaus, 1998. Translated by Victoria J. Barnett, Claudia Bergmann, Peter Frick, and Scott Moore, with supplementary material translated by Douglas W. Stott, as *Theological Education Underground: 1937–1940.* Edited by Victoria J. Barnett. Minneapolis: Fortress Press, 2011.

Vol. 16: *Konspiration und Haft: 1940–1945.* Edited by Jørgen Glenthøj, Ulrich Kabitz, and Wolf Krötke. Gütersloh: Chr. Kaiser/Gütersloher Verlagshaus, 1996. Translated by Lisa E. Dahill, with supplementary material translated by Douglas W. Stott, as *Conspiracy and Imprisonment: 1940–1945.* Edited by Mark S. Brocker. Minneapolis: Fortress Press, 2006.

Vol. 17: *Register und Ergänzungen* (Index and supplements). Edited by Herbert Anzinger and Hans Pfeifer, assisted by Waltraud Anzinger and Ilse Tödt. Gütersloh: Chr. Kaiser/Gütersloher Verlagshaus, 1999.

———. "Bericht über die theologische Konferenz der Mittelstelle für ökumenische Jugendarbeit am 29.–30. April 1932 in Berlin" (Report on the theological conference of the Provisional Bureau for Ecumenical Youth Work, held on April 29–30, 1932, in Berlin). *Die Eiche* 20 (1932): 361–65.

———. "Concerning the Christian Idea of God." *Journal of Religion* 12, no. 2 (April 1932): 177–85.

———. *Ethik.* Edited by Eberhard Bethge. 11th printing. Munich: Chr. Kaiser, 1985. Translated by Neville Horton Smith as *Ethics.* Edited by Eberhard Bethge. New York: Simon & Schuster, 1995.

———. *Gesammelte Schriften* (Collected writings). Edited by Eberhard Bethge. 6 vols. Munich: Chr. Kaiser, 1958–74. English selections edited by Edwin H. Robertson, translations by Edwin H. Robertson and John Bowden in *No Rusty Swords* (New York: Harper & Row, 1965); *The Way to Freedom* (New York: Harper & Row, 1966); and *True Patriotism* (New York: Harper & Row, 1973).

———. "Jugendkonferenzen des Weltbundes" (Youth conference of the World Alliance). *Die Eiche* 20 (1932): 365–67.

———. *Predigten—Auslegungen—Meditationen 1925–1945* (Sermons, exegeses, meditations). 2 vols. Edited by Otto Dudzus. Munich: Chr. Kaiser, 1984–85.

———. *Widerstand und Ergebung: Briefe und Aufzeichnungen aus der Haft.* Edited by Eberhard Bethge. Munich: Chr. Kaiser, 1951; expanded ed., 1970, 1985. Translated by Reginald H. Fuller as *Letters and Papers from Prison,* edited by Eberhard Bethge; translation revised by Frank Clarke et al., additional material translated by John Bowden for the enlarged edition published in London. London: SCM, 1971; New York: Macmillan, 1972; New York: Simon & Schuster, 1995.

———. "Zur theologischen Begründung der Weltbundarbeit" (On the theological foundation for the work of the World Alliance). *Die Eiche* 20 (1932): 334–44.

Bonhoeffer, Dietrich, and Franz Hildebrandt. "Glaubst du, so hast du: Versuch eines Lutherischen Katechismus von Dietrich Bonhoeffer and Franz Hildebrandt" (As you believe, so you receive: An attempt at a Lutheran catechism). *Monatsschrift für Pastoraltheologie* 28 (1932): 167–72.

Bonhoeffer, Karl. "Lebenserinnerungen" (Memoirs). In *Karl Bonhoeffer zum Hundertsten Geburtstag am 31. März 1968* (On the occasion of Karl Bonhoeffer's hundredth birthday, March 31, 1968), edited by J. Zutt et al., 8–107. Berlin: Springer, 1969.

Borg, Daniel R. "Volkskirche, 'Christian State,' and the Weimar Republic." *Church History* 35, no. 2 (1966): 186–206.

Bornhäuser, Karl. *Das Wirken des Christus durch Taten und Worte* (The effect of Christ in word and deed). 2nd ed. Gütersloh: C. Bertelsmann, 1924.

Bracher, Karl Dietrich. *Die Auflösung der Weimarer Republik: Eine Studie zum Problem des Machtverfalls in der Demokratie* (The dissolution of the Weimar Republic: A study of the problem of the decline of power in democracy). 5th ed. Reprint, Düsseldorf: Droste, 1978.

Brown, Peter. *Augustine of Hippo: A Biography.* Berkeley: University of California Press, 1970.

Brunner, Emil. "Die andere Aufgabe der Theologie" (The other task of theology). *Zwischen den Zeiten* 7 (1929): 255–76.

Buber, Martin. *Ich und Du.* Leipzig: Insel-Verlag, 1923. Translated with an introduction and prologue by Walter Kaufmann as *I and Thou.* New York: Scribner's, 1970.

Bultmann, Rudolf. "Karl Barths 'Römerbrief' in zweiter Auflage." *Christliche Welt* 36 (1922): 320–23, 330–34, 358–61, 369–73. Reprinted in *Anfänge der dialektischen Theologie,* edited by Jürgen Moltmann, Theologische Bücherei, vol. 17, no. 1., pt. 1., 119–42. Munich: Chr. Kaiser, 1977. Translated by Keith R. Crim as "Karl Barth's *Epistle to the Romans* in Its Second Edition," in *The Beginnings of Dialectic Theology,* edited by James R. Robinson, 100–120. Richmond: John Knox Press, 1968.

Burgess, John. *The East German Church and the End of Communism.* Oxford: Oxford University Press, 1997.

Burroughs, Edward Arthur. "International Friendship: A Hopeful Conference." *Yorkshire Post,* September 27, 1932.

Busch, Eberhard. *Karl Barths Lebenslauf: Nach seinen Briefen und autobiographischen Texten.* Munich: Chr. Kaiser, 1975. Translated by John Bowden as *Karl Barth: His Life from Letters and Autobiographical Texts.* Grand Rapids, Mich.: Wm. B. Eerdmans, 1994.

Calvin, Johannes. *Institutio Christianae Religionis.* In *Opera selecta,* edited by Wilhelm Niesel, 2nd ed., vols. 3–5. Munich: Chr. Kaiser, 1957–62. Translated by Ford Lewis Battles as *Calvin: Institutes of the Christian Religion.* Edited by John T. McNeill. Vols. 20 and 21 in *The Library of Christian Classics.* Philadelphia: Westminster Press, 1960.

Cohen, Herman. *Kants Theorie der Erfahrung* (Kant's theory of experience). 2nd ed. Berlin: F. Dümmler, 1885.

———. *Zur jüdischen Religionsphilosophie und ihrer Geschichte* (On Jewish philosophy of religion and its history). Jüdische Schriften 3. Berlin: Schwetschke, 1924.

Conway, John S. "Between Pacifism and Patriotism—A Protestant Dilemma: The Case of Friedrich Siegmund-Schultze." In *German against Nazism:*

*Nonconformity, Opposition, and Resistance in the Third Reich; Essays in Honour of Peter Hoffmann*, edited by Francis R. Nicosia and Lawrence D. Stokes, 87–115. New York: Berg, 1990.

Cremer, Hermann. "Dogmatische Prinzipienlehre" (Principles of dogmatics). In *Handbuch der theologischen Wissenschaften in encyclopädischer Darstellung mit besonderer Rücksicht auf die Entwicklungsgeschichte der einzelnen Disziplinen* (Handbook of the theological sciences in encyclopedic form with special attention to the developmental history of particular disciplines), edited by O. Zöckler, 3rd enlarged ed., vol. 3: *Systematische Theologie* (Systematic theology), 3:49–84. Munich: Beck, 1890.

———. *A Reply to Harnack on the Essence of Christianity.* Lectures delivered in 1901 before students of all faculties at the University of Greifswald. New York: Funk & Wagnalls, 1903. Translation of *Das Wesen des Christentums: Vorlesungen im Sommersemester 1901 vor studierenden aller fakultäten an der Universität Greifswald gehalten.* Gütersloh: C. Bertelsmann, 1901.

Dehn, Gunther, ed. *Die alte Zeit, die vorigen Jahre: Lebenserinnerungen* (The old time, the earlier years: A memoir). Munich: Chr. Kaiser, 1962.

———. *Kirche und Völkerversöhnung: Dokumente zum Halleschen Universitätskonflikt* (Church and the reconciliation of peoples: Documents on the university conflict in Halle). Berlin: Furche-Verlag, 1931.

Deißmann, Adolf. *Paulus: Eine kultur- und religionsgeschichtliche Skizze* (Paul: A cultural- and religious-historical sketch). 2nd completely rev. ed. Tübingen: J. C. B. Mohr, 1925.

DeJonge, Michael. *Bonhoeffer's Theological Formation: Berlin, Barth, und Protestant Theology.* New York: Oxford University Press, 2012.

Dibelius, Otto. *Nachspiel: Eine Aussprache mit den Freunden und Kritikern des "Jahrhunderts der Kirche"* (Postlude: An exchange between friends and critics of the "Century of the Church"). Berlin: Furche-Verlag, 1928.

———. *Was erwartet die Kirche von der jungen Theologen-Generation?* (What does the church expect from the younger generation of theologians?). Berlin: Kranzverlag, 1931.

*Dietrich Bonhoeffer: Einführung in seine Botschaft* (Introduction to his message). Wuppertal-Barmen: Presseverband der Evangelischen Kirche im Rheinland, 1956.

Dillenberger, John. *Martin Luther: Selections from His Writings.* Edited and with an introduction by John Dillenberger. Garden City, N.Y., Doubleday, 1961.

Dilthey, Wilhelm. *Der Aufbau der geschichtlichen Welt in den Geisteswissenschaften.* 1910. In Dilthey, *Geschichtliche Schriften* (Historical writings), 7:79–189. Stuttgart: B. G. Teubner, 1974. Translated and edited by Rudolf

A. Makkreel and Frithjof Rodi as *The Formation of the Historical World in the Human Sciences*. Princeton, N.J.: Princeton University Press, 2002.

———. *Einleitung in die Geisteswissenschaften: Versuch einer Grundlegung für das Studium der Gesellschaft und der Geschichte*. 1883. In Dilthey, *Geschichtliche Schriften* (Historical writings), vol. 1. Leipzig: B. G. Teubner, 1914. Translated and edited, with an introduction, by Rudolf A. Makkreel and Frithjof Rodi as *Introduction to the Human Sciences*. Princeton, N.J.: Princeton University Press, 1989.

———. *Die Entstehung der Hermeneutik* (The origins of hermeneutics) (1900). In Dilthey, *Geschichtliche Schriften* (Historical writings), 6th ed., 5:317–31. Stuttgart: B. G. Teubner, 1974.

Dostoyevsky, Fyodor Mikhaylovich. *Crime and Punishment*. Translated by Jessie Coulson. Edited by George Gibian. New York: Norton, 1975.

Drescher, Hans-Georg. *Ernst Troeltsch: His Life and Work*. Minneapolis: Fortress Press, 1993.

Drews, Paul, ed. *Disputationen Dr. Martin Luthers in den Jahren 1535–1545 an der Universität Wittenberg gehalten* (Disputations of Dr. Martin Luther held at the university of Wittenberg in the years 1535–1545). Göttingen: Vandenhoeck & Ruprecht, 1895.

Dudzus, Otto. Vorwort (Foreword). In Dietrich Bonhoeffer, *Das Wesen der Kirche* (The nature of the church), collected from notes and edited by Otto Dudzus, Kaiser Traktate 3, 7–14. Munich: Chr. Kaiser, 1971.

Ehrenberg, Hans, ed. *Credo Ecclesiam: Festgabe Wilhelm Zoellner zum 70.* (I believe in the church: Celebratory volume for Wilhelm Zoellner on his seventieth birthday). Gütersloh: Bertelsmann, 1930.

Engelberg, Ernst. *Bismarck: Urpreusse und Reichsgrunder* (Bismarck: Archetypal Prussian and founder of the empire). Berlin: Siedler, 1985.

Ericksen, Robert P. *Theologians under Hitler*. New Haven, Conn.: Yale University Press, 1985.

Eucken, Rudolf. *Hauptprobleme der Religionsphilosophie der Gegenwart* (Principal problems in contemporary philosophy of religion). 3rd ed. Berlin: Reuther & Reichard, 1909. *NL-Bibl.* 7 B 5.

*Evangelical Lutheran Worship*. Minneapolis: Augsburg Fortress, 2006.

*Evangelisches Kirchengesangbuch* (Protestant hymnal). Ausgabe für die Evangelisch-Lutherische Kirche in Bayern (edition for the Bavarian Protestant-Lutheran Church). Munich: Evangelische Presseverband für Bayern e. V., 1957.

*Evangelisches Pfarrerbuch für die Mark Brandenburg seit der Reformation* (Protestant pastoral manual for Mark Brandenburg since the Reformation). Published by Brandenburgischen Synodalverband. Edited by Otto Fischer. 3 vols. Berlin: Mittler, 1941.

Fant, Clyde E. *Bonhoeffer: Worldly Preaching.* Nashville: Thomas Nelson, 1975. (Contains "Bonhoeffer's Lectures on Preaching.")

*Federal Council Bulletin.* Monthly periodical of the Federal Council of the Churches of Christ in America. 13 (1930) and 14 (1931).

Feil, Ernst. *Religio: Die Geschichte eines neuzeitlichen Grundbegriffs vom Frühchristentum bis zur Reformation.* Forschungen zur Kirchen und Dogmengeschichte 36. Göttingen: Vandenhoeck & Ruprecht, 1986. Translated by Brian McNeil as *On the Concept of Religion.* Atlanta: Scholars Press, 1999.

———. *Die Theologie Dietrich Bonhoeffers: Hermeneutik, Christologie und Weltverständnis.* Gesellschaft und Theologie, Systematische Beiträge 6. Munich: Chr. Kaiser; Mainz: Matthias-Grünewald-Verlag, 1971. Edition abridged by author and translated by Martin Rumscheidt as *The Theology of Dietrich Bonhoeffer.* Minneapolis: Fortress Press, 1985.

Feuerbach, Ludwig. "Theogonie nach den Quellen des klassischen, hebräischen und christlichen Altertums" (Theogony according to sources of classical, Hebraic, and Christian antiquities) (1857). Excerpts in Feuerbach, *Werke in 6 Bänden,* 4:272–347. Frankfurt am Main: Suhrkamp, 1975.

———. *Das Wesen des Christentums.* 1841. Vol. 5 of Feuerbach, *Werke in 6 Bänden.* Edited by E. Thies. Frankfurt am Main: Suhrkamp, 1976. Translated by George Eliot as *The Essence of Christianity,* with an introductory essay by Karl Barth and forward by H. Richard Niebuhr. New York: Harper, 1957.

———. "Zur Beurteilung der Schrift 'Das Wesen des Christentums'" (On the critique of "The Essence of Christianity") (1842). In *Werke in 6 Bänden,* edited by E. Thies, 3:210–22. Frankfurt am Main: Suhrkamp, 1975.

Fichte, Johann Gottlieb. *Der Patriotismus und sein Gegenteil: Patriotische Dialoge, nach d. Handschrift* (Patriotism and its opposite: Patriotic dialogue, from a handwritten manuscript). Edited by H. Schulz. Leipzig: F. Meiner, 1918.

———. *Reden an die deutsche Nation.* Reprint of the 1808 ed. 5th ed. Hamburg: F. Meiner, 1978. Translated by Gregory Moore as *Addresses to the German Nation.* Cambridge: Cambridge University Press, 2008.

Fischer, K. A., ed., with Paul Fischer and Paul de Lagarde. *Schriften für das deutsche Volk.* 1924. 2nd ed. Munich: J. F. Lehmann, 1934.

Flasch, Kurt. *Augustin: Einführung in sein Denken* (Augustine: Introduction to his thinking). Stuttgart: Reclam, 1980.

Fox, Ronald Wightman. *Reinhold Niebuhr: A Biography.* New York: Pantheon Books, 1985.

Frank, Franz Hermann Reinhold von. *System der christlichen Gewissheit* (System of Christian certainty). 2 vols. Erlangen: Deichert, 1870–73. Cf. *NL-Bibl.* 3 B 25.

Frick, Peter, ed. *Bonhoeffer's Intellectual Formation: Theology and Philosophy in His Thought.* Religion in Philosophy and Theology 29. Tübingen: Mohr Siebeck, 2008.

Fries, Jakob Friedrich. *Neue oder anthropologische Kritik der Vernunft* (New or anthropological critique of reason). 1807. 2nd ed. 3 vols. Heidelberg: Christian Friedrich Winter, 1828–31. Reprinted in *Sämtliche Schriften* (Collected writings), edited by G. Konig and L. Geldsetzer, vols. 1.4–6. Aalen: Scientia Verlag, 1967.

———. *Wissen, Glaube und Ahndung.* 1805. In *Sämtliche Schriften* (Collected writings), edited by G. Konig and L. Geldsetzer, vol. 1.3. Aalen: Scientia Verlag, 1968. Translated by Kent Richter as *Knowledge, Belief, and Aesthetic Sense.* Edited with an introduction by Frederick Gregory. Cologne: Jürgen Dinter, Verlag für Philosophie, 1989.

Galeota, Gustavo. "Bellarmini, Roberto, 1542–1621." *Theologische Realenzyklopädie,* 5:525–31.

Gauger, Joachim. *Chronik der Kirchenwirren* (Chronicle of the church troubles). 3 vols. Privately published, Elberfeld, 1934–36.

Gerlach, Wolfgang. *And the Witnesses Were Silent: The Confessing Church and the Jews.* Translated and edited by Victoria J. Barnett from the German original, *Und die Zeugen Schwiegen.* Lincoln: University of Nebraska Press, 2000.

Gladen, Paulgerhard. *Geschichte der studentischen Korporationsverbände: Die schlagenden und nichtschlagenden Verbände* (History of student fraternities: The dueling and nondueling fraternities). 2 vols. Würzburg: Becker, 1985.

Glenthøj, Jørgen, ed. *Dokumente zur Bonhoeffer-Forschung 1928–1945.* See *Mündige Welt.*

———. *Zu Dietrich Bonhoeffers Eintritt in die ökumenische Arbeit: Dokumente 1931–32* (Dietrich Bonhoeffer's entry into ecumenical work: Documents 1931–32). Fredericia, Denmark: Lohse, 1974. Reprinted in *Aktiver Friede: Gedenkschrift für Friedrich Siegmund-Schultze (1885–1969)* (Active peace: Commemorative volume for Friedrich Siegmund-Schultze [1885–1969]), edited by H. Delfs, 194–200. Schriften des ökumenischen Archivs der Evangelischen Kirche in Deutschland (Documents of the ecumenical archives of the Protestant Church in Germany) 7. Soest: Westfälische Verlagsbuchhandlung Mocker & Jahn, 1972.

Goethe, Johann Wolfgang von. *Collected Works.* Vol. 1: *Selected Poems.* Translated by Michael Hamburger, David Luke, and Vernon Watkins. Princeton, N.J.: Princeton University Press, 1994.

———. *Selected Poetry.* Translated with an introduction and notes by David Luke. London: Penguin Books, 2005.

Gogarten, Friedrich. *Ich glaube an den dreieinigen Gott: Eine Untersuchung über Glauben und Geschichte* (I believe in the triune God: An examination of belief and history). Jena: Eugen Diederichs, 1926. *NL-Bibl.* 3 B 29.

———. "Karl Barths Dogmatik" (Karl Barth's dogmatics). *Theologische Rundschau,* n.s. 1 (1929): 60–78.

———. "Das Problem der Ethik und die Erziehung" (The problem of ethics and education). *Schule und Evangelium* 6 (1931–32): 225–32.

———. *Von Glauben und Offenbarung: Vier Vorträge* (On belief and revelation: Four lectures). Jena: Eugen Diederichs, 1923.

Gogh, Vincent van. *The Complete Letters of Vincent van Gogh: With Reproductions of All the Drawings in the Correspondence.* 3 vols. Boston: New York Graphic Society, 1978.

Graf, Friedrich Wilhelm. "Gesetz IV (Neuzeit) (Law IV [contemporary]). *Theologische Realenzyklopädie,* 13:90–126.

Green, Clifford J. *Bonhoeffer: A Theology of Sociality.* Grand Rapids, Mich.: Wm. B. Eerdmans, 1999.

———. "Commentary: Three Bonhoeffer Inscriptions at Union Theological Seminary Library." In *Dietrich Bonhoeffer Jahrbuch* 4:142–47. Gütersloh: Chr. Kaiser/Gütersloher Verlagshaus, 2010.

Grisebach, Eberhard. *Gegenwart: Eine kritische Ethik* (The present: A critical ethics). Halle: Niemeyer, 1928.

———. *Die Schicksalsfrage des Abendlandes: Sturmzeit, Grundlagenbesinnung, Aufbaugedanken* (The question of destiny for the West: A time of tumult, foundational reflection, and reconstructive thought). Leipzig: P. Haupt, 1942.

Grotefeld, Stefan. *Friedrich Siegmund-Schultze: Ein deutscher Ökumeniker und christlicher Pazifist* (Friedrich Siegmund-Schultze: A German ecumenist and Christian pacifist). Heidelberger Untersuchungen zu Widerstand, Judenverfolgung und Kirchenkampf im Dritten Reich 7. Gütersloh: Chr. Kaiser, 1995.

Gründer, Horst. *Walter Simons, die Ökumene und der Evangelisch-Soziale Kongress: Ein Beitrag zur Geschichte des politischen Protestantismus im 20. Jahrhundert* (Walter Simons, ecumenism and the Protestant Congress for Social Work: A contribution to the history of political Protestantism in the 20th century). Schriften des ökumenischen Archivs der Evangelischen Kirche in Deutschland 8. Soest: Westfälische Verlagsbuchhandlung Mocker & Jahn, 1974.

Guardini, Romano. *Der Gegensatz: Versuche zu einer Philosophie des Lebendig-Konkreten* (The contradiction: Attempts at a philosophy of the living concrete). Mainz: Matthias-Grünewald Verlag, 1925.

———. *Liturgische Bildung: Versuche* (Liturgical formation: Experiments). Rothenfels am Main: Verlag Deutsches Quickbornhaus, 1923.

———. *Vom Geist der Liturgie*. Freiburg im Breisgau: Herder, 1918. Translated by Ada Lane as *The Spirit of the Liturgy*, with an introduction by Joanne M. Pierce. New York: Crossroad, 1998. *NL-Bibl.* 6 B 15.

———. *Vom Sinn der Kirche: 5 Vorträge* (On the sense of the church: 5 lectures). Mainz: Matthias-Grünewald Verlag, 1922–23.

Gunkel, Hermann. *Zum religionsgeschichtlichen Verständnis des Neuen Testaments.* Göttingen: Vandenhoeck & Ruprecht, 1903. Translated by William Herbert Carruth as *The Religio-historical Interpretation of the New Testament.* Chicago: Open Court, 1903.

Gutmann, Bruno. *Gemeindeaufbau aus dem Evangelium: Grundsätzliches zu Mission und Heimatkirche* (Building the congregation on the basis of the gospel: Fundamental principles for mission and the home church). Leipzig: Verlag d. Evangelische-Lutheranische Mission, 1925.

*Handbook of the Eighth International Conference of the World Alliance for International Friendship through the Churches, Cambridge, September 1–5, 1931.* London: British Council of the World Alliance, n.d.

Harnack, Adolf von. *Das apostolische Glaubensbekenntnis: Ein geschichtlicher Bericht nebst einem Nachwort* (The apostolic confession of faith: A historical report with afterword). 1892. 27th ed. Berlin: Haack, 1896.

———. "Die Aufgabe der theologischen Fakultäten und die allgemeine Religionsgeschichte, nebst einem Nachwort" (The task of theological faculties and the general history of religion, with an afterword) (1901). In *Reden und Aufsätze,* 2nd ed., 2:159–87. Giessen: A. Topelmann, 1906. Also published in *Ausgewählte Reden und Aufsätze* (Selected speeches and essays). Edited by A. von Zahn-Harnack und A. von Harnack on the occasion of the author's one hundredth birthday. Berlin: Walter de Gruyter, 1951.

Hauschild, Wolf-Dieter. "Evangelische Kirche in Deutschland" (Protestant church in Germany). In *Theologische Realenzyklopädie,* 10:656–77.

Hegel, Georg Wilhelm Friedrich. *Phänomenologie des Geistes.* 1807. Edited by H. Glockner. Vol. 2. Stuttgart: Frommann, 1927. Translated by A. V. Miller as *Phenomenology of Spirit,* with analysis of the text and foreword by J. N. Findlay. Oxford: Clarendon Press, 1977.

———. *System der Philosophie.* Part 3: *Die Philosophie des Geistes.* Vol. 10. Edited by H. Glockner. Stuttgart: Frommann, 1929. Translated by H. S. Harris and T. M. Knox as *System of Ethical Life (1802/3) and First Philosophy of Spirit (part III of the System of Speculative Philosophy 1803/4).* Albany: State University of New York Press, 1979.

———. *Vorlesungen über die Philosophie der Religion.* Edited by Georg Lasson. Vol. 1. Leipzig: Meiner, 1925; vol. 2. in *Sämtliche Werke,* Leipzig: Meiner, 1920–30; vol. 16, edited by P. Marheineke. Berlin: Duncker & Humblot, 1832; vol. 3, Leipzig: Meiner, 1929. *NL,* 7 A 26. Translated by R. F. Brown, P. C. Hodgson, and J. M. Stewart, with the assistance of J. P. Fitzer and H. S. Harris, as *Lectures on the Philosophy of Religion.* 3 vols. Edited by Peter C. Hodgson. Berkeley: University of California Press, 1984–87. Volume 3 of the *Philosophie der Religion* was previously published as *The Christian Religion.* Edited and translated by Peter C. Hodgson. Based on the edition by Georg Lasson. Missoula, MT: Scholars Press, 1979.[1]

———. *Vorlesungen über die Philosophie der Religion: Die absolute Religion.* In *Sämtliche Werke,* vol. 14. Leipzig: F. Meiner, 1929. *NL-Bibl.* 7 A 26.

———. *Vorlesungen über die Philosophie der Religion: Die bestimmte Religion.* In *Sämtliche Werke,* edited by G. Lasson, vol. 13. Leipzig: F. Meiner, 1927. *NL-Bibl.* 7 A 26.

Heim, Karl. "Das Führerproblem in der Gegenwart und das Christentum" (The problem of the Führer in the present age and in Christianity). *Wort und Tat* (1932): 33–40.

———. "Tolstoj und Jesus." In *Jesus der Herr: Fünf Vorträge gehalten in den Teilversammlungen der 28. Allgemeinen Deutschen Studentenkonferenz* (Jesus the Lord: Five lectures for the assembly of the 28th general conference of German students), Stimmen aus der deutschen christlichen Studentenbewegung (Voices from the German Christian student movement) 2, 27–52. Berlin: Furche Verlag, 1920.

Heitmann, Ludwig. *Vom Werden der neuen Gemeinde* (On the emergence of the new congregation). Aus der Welt der Religion. Praktisch-theolo-

[1.] Bonhoeffer's quotations from the Lasson edition of the *Vorlesungen über die Philosophie der Religion* pose a peculiar problem in English translation. Lasson's edition was an editorial reconstruction combining the various preceding versions of Hegel's text; for this reason, it has been largely abandoned as a reliable source in contemporary editions of Hegel. Thus there are no contemporary English translations of vols. 1 and 2 of the *Philosophie der Religion* that follow Lasson's edition closely. English-language citations to these two volumes, therefore, refer the reader when possible to Peter Hodgson's three-volume edition, *Lectures on the Philosophy of Religion.* However, in many cases there are no exact parallels to citations from Lasson's text in Hodgson's three-volume edition; in these cases only the Lasson edition's pagination has been given in editorial notes. Lasson's edition of vol. 3 of the *Philosophie der Religion,* however, was the basis of Hodgson's earlier edition of vol. 3, *The Christian Religion.* Despite Hodgson's own subsequent misgivings about the use of Lasson's edition as a textual basis, we have used Hodgson's text when providing English-language parallel references to vol. 3 of Lasson's edition simply because *The Christian Religion* is the only modern edition of vol. 3 of *Philosophie der Religion* that substantially follows Lasson's text.

gische Reihe 4 (From the world of religion. Practical-theological series 4). Giessen: A. Töpelmann, 1925.

Helmreich, Ernst Christian. *The German Churches under Hitler: Background, Struggle, and Epilogue.* Detroit: Wayne State University Press, 1979.

Henriod, Henry-Louis. *Bericht über die Tätigkeit des Weltbundes vom März 1932 bis 30. Juni 1933* (Report on the activity of the World Alliance from March 1932 until June 30, 1933). Geneva, 1933.

———. "The Joint Oecumenical Youth Commission: How and Why It Came to Be." Geneva, 1936. Available at http://archives.oikoumene.org/query/detail.aspx?ID=42306.

———. "Nationale und übernationale kirchliche Arbeit: Die Kirche und die allgemeine Not" (National and transnational church work: The church and the general crisis). *Die Eiche* 21 (1933): 260–69.

Herrmann, Wilhelm. *Der Begriff der Offenbarung* (The concept of revelation). Vorträge der theologischen Konferenz zu Giessen (Lectures from the theological conference at Giessen) 3. Giessen: J. Ricker, 1887.

———. "Christlich-protestantische Dogmatik" (Christian-Protestant dogmatics). In *Die Kultur der Gegenwart: Ihre Entwicklung und ihre Ziele* (Contemporary culture: Its development and goals), edited by P. Hinneberg, pt. 1, sec. 4: "Die christliche Religion mit Einschluß der israelitisch-jüdischen Religion" (The Christian religion, including the Israelite-Jewish religion), 583–632. Berlin: Teubner, 1906.

———. *Dogmatik.* Gotha: L. Klotz, 1925. Translated by Nathaniel Micklem and Kenneth A. Saunders as *Systematic Theology.* New York: Macmillan, 1927. *NL- Bibl.* 3 B 35.

———. *Ethik* (Ethics). 1901. 5th rev. ed. Tübingen: J. C. B. Mohr, 1913.

———. *Die Gewißheit des Glaubens und die Freiheit der Theologie* (The certainty of faith and the freedom of theology). Freiburg: J. C. B. Mohr, 1887.

———. "Der Glaube an Gott und die Wissenschaft unserer Zeit" (Faith in God and the science of our time). *Zeitschrift für Theologie und Kirche* 15 (1905): 1–26.

———. "Gottes Offenbarung an uns" (God's revelation to us) (1908). Vorträge der Aarauer Studentenkonferenz (Lectures to the student conference at Aarau). In Herrmann, *Schriften zur Grundlegung der Theologie* (Writings on the foundations of theology), 2:150–69. Munich: Chr. Kaiser, 1967.

———. "Kants Bedeutung für das Christentum" (Kant's significance for Christianity) (1884). In Herrmann, *Schriften zur Grundlegung der Theologie* (Writings on the foundations of theology), edited by P. Fischer-Appelt, 1:104–22. Munich: Chr. Kaiser, 1966.

———. Review of Ernst Troeltsch, *Die Absolutheit des Christentums und die*

*Religionsgeschichte* (The absoluteness of Christianity and the history of religions). *Theologische Literaturzeitung* 27 (1902): 330–34.

———. Review of Ernst Troeltsch, *Die Bedeutung der Geschichtlichkeit Jesu für den Glauben* (The significance of the historicity of Jesus for faith). *Theologische Literaturzeitung* 37 (1912): 245–49.

———. *Die sittlichen Weisungen Jesu: Ihr Missbrauch und ihr richtiger Gebrauch* (The moral instructions of Jesus: Their misuse and their correct use). Göttingen: Vandenhoeck & Ruprecht, 1904.

———. *Der Verkehr des Christen mit Gott im Anschluß an Luther dargestellt.* 5th and 6th rev. eds. Stuttgart: J. Cotta, 1908. Translated and edited by Robert T. Voelkel as *The Communion of the Christian with God: Described on the Basis of Luther's Statements.* Philadelphia: Fortress Press, 1971.

Hildebrandt, Franz. *EST: Das lutherische Prinzip* (EST: The Lutheran principle). Studien zur systematischen Theologie (Studies in systematic theology) 7. Göttingen: Vandenhoeck & Ruprecht, 1931.

Hildebrandt, Horst, ed. *Die deutschen Verfassungen des 19. und 20. Jahrhunderts* (The German constitutions of the 19th and 20th centuries). 11th ed. Paderborn: Schöningh, 1979.

Hirsch, Emanuel. *Deutschlands Schicksal: Staat, Volk und Menschheit im Lichte einer ethischen Geschichtssicht* (Germany's destiny: State, people and humanity in the light of an ethical perspective of history). 3rd ed. Göttingen: Vandenhoeck & Ruprecht, 1925.

———. *Schöpfung und Sünde in der natürlich-geschichtlichen Wirklichkeit des einzelnen Menschen: Versuch einer Grundlegung christlicher Lebensweisung* (Creation and sin in the natural-historical reality of the individual person: Attempt at a foundation for Christian life instruction). Beiträge zur systematischen Theologie (Contributions to systematic theology) 1/ Tübingen: J. C. B. Mohr, 1931. *NL-Bibl.* 3 B 40.

Hohlwein, Hans. "Kirche: III. Dogmengeschichtlich" (Church: III. history of dogma). In *Die Religion in Geschichte und Gegenwart* (Religion past and present). 2nd ed. 3:792–801.

Hölderlin, Friedrich. *Sämtliche Werke* (Collected works). Stuttgart Hölderlin Ausgabe. Edited by F. Beissner. Vol. 1.1: *Gedichte bis 1800* (Poems to 1800). Stuttgart: Nachfolger, 1946.

Holl, Karl. *Gesammelte Aufsätze zur Kirchengeschichte* (Collected essays on church history). 3 vols. Tübingen: J. C. B. Mohr, 1928–32.

———. "Der Neubau der Sittlichkeit." In *Luther,* vol. 1 of *Gesammelte Aufsätze zur Kirchengeschichte,* 131–244. Tübingen: J. C. B. Mohr, 1923. Translated by Fred W. Meuser and Walter R. Wietzke as *The Reconstruction of Morality.* Edited by James Luther Adams and Walter F. Bense. Minneapolis: Augsburg, 1979.

———. *Die Rechtfertigungslehre im Lichte der Geschichte des Protestantismus* (The doctrine of justification in light of the history of Protestantism). 2nd ed. Tübingen: J. C. B. Mohr, 1922.

———. "Die Rechtfertigungslehre in Luthers Vorlesung über den Römerbrief mit besonderer Rucksicht auf die Frage der Heilsgewissheit" (The doctrine of justification in Luther's lecture on the Letter to the Romans with special consideration of the question of the certainty of salvation) (1910). In Holl, *Gesammelte Aufsätze zur Kirchengeschichte* (Collected essays on church history), 5th ed., vol. 1: *Luther*, 111–154. Tübingen: J. C. B. Mohr, 1927.

———. "Was verstand Luther unter Religion?" In *Luther*, vol. 1 of *Gesammelte Aufsätze zur Kirchengeschichte*, 1–90. Tübingen: J. C. B. Mohr, 1923. Translated by Fred W. Meuser and Walter R. Wietzke as *What Did Luther Understand by Religion?* Edited by James Luther Adams and Walter F. Bense. Philadelphia: Fortress Press, 1977.

Hume, David. "The Natural History of Religion" (1755). In *The Philosophical Works*, edited by T. H. Green and T. H. Grose, 4 vols., 2:307–63. London: Longmans, Green, 1874–75. Also published in *Principal Writings on Religion: Including Dialogues concerning Natural Religion and The Natural History of Religion*. Edited by J. C. A. Gaskin. Oxford: Oxford University Press, 1998.

Hunsinger, George. *How to Read Karl Barth: The Shape of His Theology*. New York: Oxford University Press, 1991.

Ihmels, Ludwig. *Die christliche Wahrheitsgewissheit, ihr letzter Grund und ihre Entstehung* (The Christian certainty of truth, its ultimate ground and its origin). 1901. 2nd ed. Leipzig: Deichert, 1908.

———. *Die Selbständigkeit der Dogmatik gegenüber der Religionsphilosophie* (The independence of dogmatics in relation to the philosophy of religion). Erlangen: Deichert, 1901.

Jagow, H. "Soziale Arbeit der Kirchen und ihrer freien Verbände" (Social work of the churches and their independent associations). *Kirchliches Jahrbuch* 58 (1931): 353–81.

Jaspert, Bernd. "Dietrich Bonhoeffers Vorlesung 'Die Geschichte der systematischen Theologie des 20. Jahrhunderts' in der Nachschrift W. Zellers" (Dietrich Bonhoeffer's lecture "The history of twentieth-century systematic theology," according to the notes of W. Zellers). In Jaspert, *Theologie und Geschichte: Gesammelte Aufsätze*, Europäische Hochschulschriften 23, no. 476, 2:337–63. Frankfurt am Main: Peter Lang, 1994.

Kaftan, Julius. *Dogmatik* (Dogmatics) (1897). 3rd and 4th eds. Tübingen: J. C. B. Mohr, 1901. *NL-Bibl.* 3 B 48.

———. "Die Selbständigkeit des Christenthums" (The independence of Christianity). *Zeitschrift für Theologie und Kirche* 6 (1896): 373–94.

Kähler, Martin. *Zeit und Ewigkeit (Dogmatische Zeitfragen III)* (Time and eternity [Current dogmatic questions III]). Edited by W. Kähler. 2nd enlarged ed. Leipzig: Deichert, 1913. *NL-Bibl.* 3 B 47.

Kaltenborn, Carl-Jürgen. *Adolf von Harnack als Lehrer Dietrich Bonhoeffers* (Adolf von Harnack as Dietrich Bonhoeffer's teacher). Theologische Arbeiten (Theological studies) 31. Berlin: Evangelische Verlagsanstalt, 1973.

Kant, Immanuel. *The Cambridge Edition of the Works of Immanuel Kant.* Edited by P. Guyer and A. W. Wood. Cambridge: Cambridge University Press, 1992–. *Practical Philosophy* (1996), edited and translated by M. J. Gregor with an introduction by A. W. Wood (includes new translations of *Foundations of a Metaphysics of Morals* and *Critique of Pure Reason*). *Religion and Rational Theology* (1996), edited and translated by G. Di Giovanni and A. W. Wood. Includes a translation of *Religion within the Boundaries of Mere Reason. Critique of Pure Reason* (1998), edited and translated by P. Guyer and A. W. Wood.

———. *Grundlegung zur Metaphysik der Sitten.* 1785. In *Kant's gesammelte Schriften,* sec. 1, vol. 5. Berlin: G. Reimer, 1908. Translated by Lewis White Beck as *Foundations of a Metaphysics of Morals.* With critical essays edited by Robert Paul Wolff. Indianapolis: Bobbs-Merrill, 1969.

———. *Kant's gesammelte Schriften.* Published by the Königlich Preussischen Akademie der Wissenschaften. Berlin: G. Reimer, 1903–83. Cf. *NL-Bibl.* 7 A 35.

———. *Kritik der praktischen Vernunft.* 1785. In *Kant's gesammelte Schriften,* sec. 1, vol. 4. Berlin: G. Reimer, 1903. Translated by Mary Gregor as *Critique of Practical Reason,* with an introduction by Andrews Reath. Cambridge: Cambridge University Press, 1997.

———. *Kritik der reinen Vernunft.* 2nd ed., 1787. In *Kant's gesammelte Schriften,* sec. 1, vol. 3. Berlin: G. Reimer, 1911. Translated and edited by Paul Guyer and Allen W. Wood as *Critique of Pure Reason.* Cambridge: Cambridge University Press, 1998.

———. *Die Religion innerhalb der Grenzen der blossen Vernunft* (1793). In *Kant's gesammelte Schriften,* sec. 1, vol. 6. Berlin: G. Reimer, 1908. Translated, with an introduction and notes, by Theodore M. Greene and Hoyt H. Hudson as *Religion within the Limits of Reason Alone.* With a new essay, "The Ethical Significance of Kant's Religion," by John R. Silber. New York: Harper, 1960.

Kierkegaard, Søren. *Die Krankheit zum Tode*. Vol. 8 of *Gesammelte Werke*. Jena: Diederichs, 1911. *NL-Bibl.* 7 A 43. Translated by Walter Lowrie as *The Sickness unto Death*. Princeton, N.J.: Princeton University Press, 1941.

Kimmich, Christoph M. *Germany and the League of Nations*. Chicago: University of Chicago Press, 1976.

Kisiel, Theodore. *The Genesis of Heidegger's Being and Time*. Berkeley: University of California Press, 1993.

Klages, Ludwig. *Der Geist als Widersacher der Seele* (The spirit as adversary of the soul). 3 vols. Leipzig: J. A. Barth, 1929–32.

Kodalle, Klaus-Michael. *Dietrich Bonhoeffer: Zur Kritik seiner Theologie* (Dietrich Bonhoeffer: On the critique of his theology). Gütersloh: Gütersloher Verlagshaus/Gerd Mohn, 1991.

Kolb, Robert, and Timothy J. Wengert, eds. *The Book of Concord: The Confessions of the Evangelical Lutheran Church*. Translation by Charles Arand, Eric Gritsch, Robert Kolb, William Russell, James Schaaf, Jane Strohl, and Timothy J. Wengert of *Die Bekenntnisschriften der evangelisch-lutherischen Kirche*. Minneapolis: Fortress Press, 2000.

*Das kommende Reich*. Zwei Vorträge, "Die biblische Botschaft vom Reiche Gottes" und "Dein Reich komme! Das Gebet der Gemeinde um Gottes Reich auf Erden," von Lic. Dr. Johannes Schneider und Lic. Dietrich Bonhoeffer. Privatdozenten an der Universität Berlin (Two lectures by Dr. Johannes Schneider and Dietrich Bonhoeffer, lecturers at Berlin University). Stimmen aus der deutschen christlichen Studentenbewegung 78. Berlin: Furche-Verlag, 1933. Bonhoeffer lecture translated by John D. Godsey as "Thy Kingdom Come: The Prayer of the Church for God's Kingdom on Earth." In Godsey, *Preface to Bonhoeffer: The Man and Two of His Shorter Writings*, 28–47. Philadelphia: Fortress Press, 1965.

Kupisch, Karl. "Kirchlich-sozial" (Church-social concerns). In *Die Religion in Geschichte und Gegenwart* (Religion past and present). 3rd ed. 3:1622–23.

Lederer, Stephan. *Der spanische Cardinal Johann von Torquemada, sein Leben and seine Schriften* (The Spanish cardinal Juan de Torquemada, his life and his writings). Freiburg im Breisgau: Herder, 1879.

Lehmann, Paul Louis. "A Critical Comparison on the Doctrine of Justification in the Theologies of Albrecht Ritschl and Karl Barth." ThD diss., Union Theological Seminary, New York, 1936. Published as *Forgiveness: Decisive Issue in Protestant Thought*. 1940; New York: Harper & Row, 1970.

Leibholz-Bonhoeffer, Sabine. *Vergangen, erlebt, überwunden: Schicksale der Familie Bonhoeffer*. 4th ed. Gütersloh: Gütersloher Verlagshaus Mohn,

1983. Translated as *The Bonhoeffers: Portrait of a Family*. Chicago: Covenant, 1994.

———. *Weihnachten im Hause Bonhoeffer* (Christmas at the Bonhoeffer home). 2nd ed. Gütersloh: Gütersloher Verlagshaus Gerd Mohn, 1992.

*Lexikon der Kunst: Architektur, bildende Kunst, angewandte Kunst, Industrieformgestaltung, Kunsttheorie* (Dictionary of art: Architecture, the visual arts, applied arts, industrial arts and production, and art theory). Vol. 3. Leipzig: Seemann, 1991.

Locke, John. *Reasonableness of Christianity as Delivered in the Scriptures*. Edited by John C. Higgins-Biddle. Oxford: Clarendon Press, 1999.

Lord Herbert of Cherbury. *De veritate*. Bristol: published for the University of Bristol by J. W. Arrowsmith, 1937.

Ludwig, Hartmut. "Der Pazifist und Staatsfeind soll nicht länger deutsche Theologen erziehen: Dietrich Bonhoeffer und die Berliner Theologische Fakultät" (The pacifist and enemy of the state should no longer train German theologians: Dietrich Bonhoeffer and the Berlin theological faculty). *Berliner Theologische Zeitschrift* 13 (1996): 250–66.

Lütgert, Wilhelm. "Die Glaubwürdigkeit des Christusbildes der Evangelien" (The credibility of the image of Christ in the Gospels) (1905). In Lütgert, *Gottes Sohn und Gottes Geist: Vorträge zur Christologie und zur Lehre vom Geiste Gottes* (God's Son and God's Spirit: Lectures on Christology and the doctrine of the Spirit of God), 22–32. Leipzig: Deichert, 1905.

———. "Die Lehre Jesu" (The teachings of Jesus). In *Jesus Christus für unsere Zeit: Dargestellt in Vorträgen von Haugleiter, Walther, Lütgert, Kaftan, Schaeder* (Jesus Christ for our time: Presented in lectures from Haugleiter, Walther, Lütgert, Kaftan, Schaeder), 2nd ed., 103–28. Hamburg: Schloessmann, 1907.

———. "Die Lehre von der Rechtfertigung durch den Glauben" (The doctrine of justification by faith) (1903). In Lütgert, *Gottes Sohn und Gottes Geist: Vorträge zur Christologie und zur Lehre vom Geiste Gottes* (God's Son and God's Spirit: Lectures on Christology and the doctrine of the Spirit of God), 50–70. Leipzig: Deichert, 1905.

Luther, Martin. *Disputationen Dr. Martin Luthers in den Jahren 1535–1545 an der Universität Wittenberg gehalten* (Disputations held by Dr. Martin Luther at the University of Wittenberg in the years 1535–1545). Edited by P. Drews. Göttingen: Vandenhoeck & Ruprecht, 1895. *NL-Bibl.* 2 C 3 19.

———. *First Lectures on the Psalms II*. Vol. 11 of *Luther's Works*. Edited by Hilton C. Oswald. St. Louis: Concordia, 1976.

———. *Lectures on Romans*. Newly translated and edited by Wilhelm Pauck. The Library of Christian Classics. Ichthus ed. Philadelphia: Westminster, 1961.

———. *Studienausgabe.* Edited by H.-U. Delius. Vol. 1. Berlin: Evangelische Verlagsanstalt, 1979.

*The Lutheran Hymnal.* St. Louis: Concordia, 1941.

Macquarrie, John. *Twentieth-Century Religious Thought: The Frontiers of Philosophy and Theology, 1900–1960.* New York: Harper & Row, 1963.

Mádr, Adolf. "Die Tschechoslowakische Kirche und die regionale Jugendfriedenskonferenz des Weltbundes in Ciernohorské Kúpele vom 20.–30. 7. 32 in der Tschechoslowakei mit der Teilnahme Dietrich Bonhoeffers, Manuskript mit zahlreichen Dokumenten" (The Czechoslovakian church and the World Alliance regional youth peace conference from July 20–30, 1932, with Dietrich Bonhoeffer's participation, manuscript with numerous documents). MS. Brno, 1964–65.

Maechler, Winfried. *Ein Christ in den Wirren des 20. Jahrhunderts: Stationen, Reisen, Einsichten* (A Christian in the chaos of the 20th century: Stops, travels, insights). Stuttgart: Radius Verlag, 1991.

Mahadevan, T. M. P. *Upanishads: The Selections from 108 Upanishads.* New Delhi: Arnold-Heinemann Publishers India, 1975.

Mahlmann, Theodor. "Das Axiom des Erlebnisses bei Wilhelm Herrmann" (The axiom of experience in Wilhelm Herrmann). *Neue Zeitschrift für Systematische Theologie* 4 (1962): 11–88.

Martin, Lawrence, ed. *The Treaties of Peace, 1919–1923.* Clark, N.J.: Lawbook Exchange, 2007.

Marx, Karl. "Zur Kritik der Hegelschen Rechtsphilosophie: Einleitung" (1843–44). In Karl Marx and Friedrich Engels, *Werke,* 1:378–91. Berlin: Dietz, 1958. Translated by Annette Jolin as *Critique of Hegel's Philosophy of Right.* Edited with an introduction by Joseph O'Malley. London: Cambridge University Press, 1970.

Marx, Karl, and Friedrich Engels. *On Religion.* With an introduction by Reinhold Niebuhr. New York: Schocken, 1964.

Merivale, John Herman. *The Minor Poems of Schiller.* London: W. Pickering, 1944.

Meyer, Dietrich, and Eberhard Bethge, eds. *Nachlaß Dietrich Bonhoeffer: Ein Verzeichnis; Archiv-Sammlung-Bibliothek* (Dietrich Bonhoeffer's literary estate: A bibliographical catalog; archive, collection, library). Munich: Chr. Kaiser, 1987.

*Mitteilungen der Deutschen Vereinigung des Weltbundes für Internationale Freundschaftsarbeit der Kirchen* (Reports of the German organization of the World Alliance for Promoting International Friendship through the Churches). Nos. 11 (March 1932), 12 (June 1932), and 13 (May 1933). Geneva, 1931–33.

Modersohn, Ernst. *Menschen durch die ich gesegnet wurde: Erinnerungen.* Bad Blankenburg: Harfe-Verlag, 1937. Translated as *Men of Revival in Germany.* Frankfurt am Main: Herold, n.d.

Morgan, Robert, and Michael Pye, eds. and trans. *Ernst Troeltsch: Writings on Theology and Religion.* Atlanta: John Knox Press, 1977.

Mühlhausen, Rudolf. "Von der schwärmerischen Bewegung in Kurhessen" (On the radical reform movement in Hesse). *Christliche Welt* 21 (1907): 844–46.

Müller, Friedrich Max. *Einleitung in die vergleichende Religionswissenschaft* (Introduction to comparative religious science). Strasbourg, 1874. Translated as *Introduction to the Science of Religion.* New York: Arno Press, 1978.

Müller, Hans Michael. *Erfahrung und Glaube bei Luther* (Experience and faith in Luther). Leipzig: J. C. Hinrichs, 1929.

Müller, Johannes. *Hemmungen des Lebens* (Inhibitions of life). 1907; Munich: C. H. Beck'sche Verlagshaus, 1928.

———. *Das Urgeheimnis* (The original mystery). Elmau: Verlag d. Grünen Blätter, 1930.

*Die Mündige Welt* (The world come of age). Vol. 5: *Dokumentation zur Bonhoeffer-Forschung 1928–1945* (Documents on Bonhoeffer research, 1928–1945). Edited by Jørgen Glenthøj. Munich: Chr. Kaiser, 1969.

Neufeld, Karl H. *Adolf Harnacks Konflikt mit der Kirche: Weg-Stationen zum "Wesen des Christentums"* (Adolf Harnack's conflict with the church: Stations on the way to "The Essence of Christianity"). Innsbrucker theologische Studien 4. Innsbruck: Tyrolia, 1979.

Nicosia, Francis R., and Lawrence D. Stokes, eds. *Germans against Nazism: Nonconformity, Opposition, and Resistance in the Third Reich.* New York: Berg, 1990.

Niebergall, Alfred. "Agende." In *Theologische Realenzyklopädie* 1:755–84 and 2:1–91.

Niebergall, Friedrich. *Welches ist die beste Religion?* (What is the best religion?). *Religionsgeschichtliche Volksbücher für die deutsche christliche Gegenwart* (Library of religious history for contemporary German Christianity), 5th series, no. 1. Halle an der Saale: Gebauer-Schwetschke, 1905.

Nietzsche, Friedrich. *Also sprach Zarathustra: Ein Buch für alle und keinen.* Vol. 6/1 of *Werke* (Works). Kritische Gesamtausgabe (Complete critical edition). Berlin: Walter de Gruyter, 1968. Translated by R. J. Hollingdale as *Thus Spoke Zarathustra: A Book for Everyone and No One.* London: Penguin, 1969.

———. *Der Antichrist.* In vol. 6/3 of *Werke* (Works). Kritische Gesamtausgabe (Complete critical edition). Berlin: Walter de Gruyter, 1969. Translated by Walter Kaufmann as *The Antichrist*. In *The Portable Nietzsche*, 565–656. 1954; New York: Penguin Books, 1982.

———. *The Anti-Christ, Ecce Homo, Twilight of the Idols, and Other Writings.* Edited by Aaron Ridley and Judith Norman. Cambridge: Cambridge University Press, 2005.

———. *Ecce homo*. In *Werke* (Works), vol. 6/3, Kritische Gesamtausgabe (Complete critical edition), 253–372. Berlin: Walter de Gruyter, 1969. Translated by Thomas Wayne as *Ecce homo: How One Becomes What One Is and the Antichrist: A Curse on Christianity*. New York: Algora, 2004.

———. *Jenseits von Gut und Böse: Vorspiel einer Philosophie der Zukunft—Zur Genealogie der Moral*. Vol. 6/2 of *Werke* (Works). Kritische Gesamtausgabe (Complete critical edition). Berlin: Walter de Gruyter, 1975. Translated and edited by Marion Faber as *Beyond Good and Evil: Prelude to a Philosophy of the Future*. With an introduction by Robert C. Holub. Oxford: Oxford University Press, 1998.

———. *Menschliches, allzumenschliches: Ein Buch für freie Geister*. In *Werke* (Works), vol. 4/2, Kritische Gesamtausgabe (Complete critical edition), 1–375. Berlin: Walter de Gruyter, 1967. Translated by R. J. Hollingdale as *Human, All Too Human: A Book for Free Spirits*. With an introduction by Erich Heller. Cambridge: Cambridge University Press, 1986.

———. *Nachgelassene Fragmente: Herbst 1887 bis März 1888* (Remaining fragments: Fall 1887–March 1888). In *Werke* (Works), vol. 8/2, Kritische Gesamtausgabe (Complete critical edition). Berlin; New York: Walter de Gruyter, 1970.

———. *The Portable Nietzsche*. Edited and translated by Walter Kaufmann. New York: Viking Press, 1954.

———. "Unzeitgemässe Betrachtungen." In *Werke* (Works), vol. 3A, Kritische Gesamtausgabe (Complete critical edition), 153–423. Translated by R. J. Hollingdale as *Untimely Meditations*. With an introduction by J. P. Stern. Cambridge: Cambridge University Press, 1983.

———. *Werke* (Works). Kritische Gesamtausgabe (Complete critical edition). Edited by G. Colli and M. Montinari. Pts. 5 and 6. Berlin: Walter de Gruyter, 1971.

Nold, Karl. "Zeitblick: Rückblick auf Cambridge" (Snapshot in time: Looking back at Cambridge). *Christentum and Wirklichkeit* 10 (1932): 70–73.

Nowak, Kurt. *Evangelische Kirche und Weimarer Republik: Zum politischen Weg des deutschen Protestantismus zwischen 1918 und 1932* (Evangelical Church and Weimar Republic: The political path of German Protestantism between 1918 and 1932). Göttingen: Vandenhoeck & Ruprecht, 1981.

Orlow, Dietrich. *The Nazi Party, 1919–1945: A Complete History*. Pittsburgh: University of Pittsburgh Press, 1969.

Otto, Rudolf. *Das Heilige: Über das Irrationale in der Idee des Göttlichen und sein Verhältnis zum Rationalen.* Breslau: Trewendt & Granier, 1917. *NL-Bibl.* 7 B 17. Translated by John W. Harvey as *The Idea of the Holy: An Inquiry into the Nonrational Factor in the Idea of the Divine and Its Relation to the Rational.* London: Oxford University Press, 1929.

———. *Kantisch-Fries'sche Religionsphilosophie und ihre Anwendung auf die Theologie: Zur Einleitung in die Glaubenslehre für Studenten der Theologie.* Tübingen: J. C. B. Mohr, 1909. Translated by E. B. Dicker as *The Philosophy of Religion: Based on Kant and Fries.* With a foreword by W. Tudor Jones. 1931; reprint, New York: Knaus Reprint, 1970.

Overbeck, Franz. *Christentum und Kultur: Gedanken und Anmerkungen zur modernen Kultur; Aus dem Nachlaß* (Christianity and culture: Thoughts and reflections on modern culture; From the literary estate). Edited by C. A. Bernoulli. Basel: Benno Schwabe, 1919. Reprint, Darmstadt: Wissenschaftliche Buchgesellschaft, 1963.

*Oxford Dictionary of the Christian Church.* Edited by F. L. Cross and E. A. Livingstone. 3rd ed. New York: Oxford University Press, 1997.

Pangritz, Andreas. *Karl Barth in der Theologie Dietrich Bonhoeffers: Eine notwendige Klarstellung.* West Berlin: Alektor Verlag, 1989. Translated by Barbara and Martin Rumscheidt as *Karl Barth in the Theology of Dietrich Bonhoeffer.* Grand Rapids, Mich.: Wm. B. Eerdmanns, 2000.

———. "Vom 'sichtbaren Kommen Gottes auf diese Welt': Zu Dietrich Bonhoeffers Rezeption von Karl Barths Römerbrief-Auslegung." In *Dietrich Bonhoeffer Yearbook* 3:225–30. Gütersloh: Chr. Kaiser/Gütersloher Verlagshaus, 2008.

Paton, William. *The Church and the New Order.* London: SCM Press,1941.

Pfaff, Peter. "Goethe, Johann Wolfgang von." *Theologische Realenzyklopädie* 13:552–58.

Pfeifer, Hans. "Die Bedeutung der Jugendbewegung für Dietrich Bonhoeffer" (The significance of the youth movement for Dietrich Bonhoeffer). In *Dietrich Bonhoeffer Jahrbuch/Dietrich Bonhoeffer Yearbook 2003*, 74–92. Gütersloh: Chr. Kaiser/Gütersloher Verlagshaus, 2003.

———. "Learning Faith and Ethical Commitment in the Context of Spiritual Training Groups: Consequences of Dietrich Bonhoeffer's Post-Doctoral Year in New York City, 1930/1931." In *Dietrich Bonhoeffer Yearbook* 3:251–79. Gütersloh: Gütersloher Verlagshaus, 2008.

Piechowski, Paul. *Proletarischer Glaube: Die religiöse Gedankenwelt der organisierten deutschen Arbeiterschaft nach sozialistischen und kommunistischen Selbstzeugnissen* (Proletarian belief: The religious conceptual world of organized German workers according to socialist and communist personal primary sources). 5th ed. Berlin: Furche, 1928.

Piper, Otto. *Christian Ethics*. London: Nelson, 1970.

———. *Die Grundlagen der evangelischen Ethik* (Foundations of evangelical ethics). 2 vols. Gütersloh: C. Bertelsmann, 1928, 1930.

Ploetz, Karl Julius. *Der grosse Ploetz: Auszug aus der Geschichte* (The large Ploetz edition: Excerpts from history). 3rd ed. Freiburg im Breisgau: Verlag Ploetz, 1986.

Pollmann, Klaus Erich. *Landesherrliches Regiment und soziale Frage: Der evangelische Oberkirchenrat und die sozialpolitische Bewegung der Geistlichen nach 1890* (Sovereign rule and questions of social welfare: The Protestant church council and the political social welfare movement of clergy after 1890). Veröffentlichungen der Historischen Kommission zu Berlin 44. Berlin: Walter de Gruyter, 1973.

Pugh, Jeffrey Carter. *Religionless Christianity*. London: Continuum, 2009.

Rasmussen, Larry. "Interview with Herbert Jehle." In *Dietrich Bonhoeffer Yearbook*, 2:110–21. Gütersloh: Gütersloher Verlagshaus, 2005.

Reischle, Max. *Die Frage nach dem Wesen der Religion: Grundlegung zu einer Methodologie der Religionsphilosophie* (The question of the essence of religion: Foundation for a methodology of the philosophy of religion). Freiburg im Breisgau: J. C. B. Mohr, 1889.

*Die Religion in Geschichte und Gegenwart* (Religion past and present). 5 vols. Tübingen: J. C. B. Mohr, 1909–13. 3rd newly rev. ed., 1957–65.

Reventlow, Henning Graf. *Bibelautorität und Geist der Moderne: Die Bedeutung des Bibelverständnisses für die geistesgeschichtliche und politische Entwicklung in England von der Reformation bis zur Aufklärung*. Forschungen zur Kirchen- und Dogmengeschichte 30. Göttingen: Vandenhoeck & Ruprecht, 1980. Translated as *The Authority of the Bible and the Rise of the Modern World*. Philadelphia: Fortress Press, 1985.

Rickert, Heinrich. *Die Grenzen der naturwissenschaftlichen Begriffsbildung: Eine logische Einleitung in die historischen Wissenschaften*. 1896, 1902. 2 vols. 5th expanded ed. 2 vols. Tübingen: J. C. B. Mohr, 1929. Translated by Guy Oakes as *The Limits of Concept Formation in Natural Science: A Logical Introduction to the Historical Sciences*. New York: Cambridge University Press, 1986.

———. *Kulturwissenschaft und Naturwissenschaft*. Freiburg im Breisgau: J. C. B. Mohr, 1899. Translated by George Reisman as *Science and History: A Critique of Positivist Epistemology*. Princeton, N.J.: Van Nostrand, 1962.

———. *Die Probleme der Geschichtsphilosophie: Eine Einführung* (An introduction to the problems of the philosophy of history). Heidelberg: Winter, 1905.

Rilke, Rainer Maria. *Sämtliche Werke*. Edited by E. Zinn. Vol. 1: *Gedichte: Erster Teil* (Poetry: First part). Wiesbaden: Insel-Verlag, 1955. Vol. 3: *Jugend-*

*gedichte.* Wiesbaden: Insel-Verlag, 1959. Translated with an introduction and commentary by Reginald Snell as *Letters to a Young Poet.* Mineola, N.Y.: Dover, 2002.

Ritschl, Albrecht. *Die christliche Lehre von der Rechtfertigung und Versöhnung.* 2nd rev. ed. Vols. 1 and 2 (1882), vol. 3 (1883). Bonn: A. Marcus, 1882–83. *NL-Bibl.* 3 B 58. Vol. 1 translated by John S. Black as *A Critical History of the Christian Doctrine of Justification and Reconciliation.* Edinburgh: Edmonston & Douglas, 1872. Vol. 3 translated as *The Christian Doctrine of Justification and Reconciliation: The Positive Development of the Doctrine.* Edited by H. R. Mackintosh and A. B. Macaulay. 2nd ed. 1900; Edinburgh: T & T Clark; New York: Charles Scribner's Sons, 1902. Reprint, Clifton, N.J.: Reference Book Publishers, 1966.

———. *Unterricht in die christliche Religion* (Instruction in the Christian religion). 1875. 6th ed. Bonn: A. Marcus, 1903. *NL-Bibl.* 3 B 58.

Rittelmeyer, Friedrich. *Friedrich Nietzsche und die Religion: Vier Vorträge* (Four lectures on Friedrich Nietzsche and religion). 1904. 3rd ed. Munich: Raiser, 1920.

Robinson, James M., ed. *The Beginnings of Dialectic Theology.* Richmond: John Knox Press, 1968. Partial translation by Keith R. Crim and Louis De Grazia of *Anfänge der dialektischen Theologie.* Munich: Chr. Kaiser, 1962–63.

Rohrbach, H.-C. "Studentenpfarrer" (Student chaplains). In *Die Religion in Geschichte und Gegenwart* (Religion past and present), 3rd ed., 5:425–26.

Rouse, Ruth, and Stephen Charles Neill. *A History of the Ecumenical Movement 1517–1948.* 2nd ed. Philadelphia: Westminster Press, 1967.

Sasse, Hermann. "Kirchliche Zeitlage" (Current situation of the church). *Kirchliches Jahrbuch* 59 (1932): 1–176.

———. "Die Ökumenische Bewegung" (The ecumenical movement). *Kirchliches Jahrbuch* 59 (1932): 529–53.

Schaeder, Erich. "Die Einzigartigkeit Jesu und sein Ziel" (The uniqueness of Jesus and his mission). In *Jesus Christus für unsere Zeit: Dargestellt in Vorträgen von Haugleiter, Walther, Lütgert, Kaftan, Schaeder* (Jesus Christ for our time: As portrayed in lectures by Haugleiter, Walther, Lütgert, Kaftan, Schaeder), 2nd. ed., 163–210. Hamburg: Schloessmann, 1907.

———. *Das Geistproblem der Theologie: Eine systematische Untersuchung* (A systematic examination of the spiritual problem of theology). Erlangen: Deichert, 1924.

———. *Religion und Vernunft: Die religionsphilosophische Hauptfrage der Gegenwart* (Religion and reason: The central question of contemporary philosophy of religion). Beiträge zur Forderung christlicher Theologie 21, no. 1. Gütersloh: Bertelsmann, 1917.

———. *Theozentrische Theologie: Eine Untersuchung zur dogmatischen Prinzipienlehre* (Theocentric theology: An examination of dogmatic principles of doctrine). 1909–14. 2nd ed. 2 vols. Leipzig: Deichert, 1916–28.

Scheel, Otto. *Martin Luther: Vom Katholizismus zur Reformation* (Martin Luther: From Catholicism to Reformation). 1916–17. 3rd ed. 2 vols. Tübingen: J. C. B. Mohr, 1921–30. Vol. 1: *NL-Bibl.* 2 C 32.

Scheler, Max. *Der Formalismus in der Ethik und die materiale Wertethik: Neuer Versuch der Grundlegung eines ethischen Personalismus.* Halle an der Saale: M. Niemeyer, 1921. *NL-Bibl.* 4.42. Also published as vol. 2 of *Gesammelte Werke*, 4th ed. Bern: Francke Verlag, 1954. Translated by Manfred S. Frings and Roger L. Funk as *Formalism in Ethics and Non-formal Ethics of Values: A New Attempt toward the Foundation of an Ethical Personalism.* 5th rev. ed. Evanston, Ill.: Northwestern University Press, 1973.

Schiller, Friedrich von. *Sämtliche Werke.* Stuttgart: J. C. Cotta, 1759–1805. Translated as *Schiller's Works.* Edited by J. G. Fischer, with a biographical introduction by Hjalmar H. Boyesen. 4 vols. Philadelphia: George Barrie, 1883.

Schlatter, Adolf. *Die christliche Ethik* (Christian ethics). 1914. 2nd enlarged ed: Stuttgart: Calwer Vereinsbuchhandlung, 1924. *NL-Bibl.* 4,45.

Schleiermacher, Friedrich Daniel Ernst. *Der christliche Glaube nach den Grundsätzen der evangelischen Kirche im Zusammenhänge dargestellt: Dritter Teil.* Neue unveränderte Ausgabe in vier Teilen. Bibliothek theologischer Klassiker 15: Schleiermachers Glaubenslehre III. Gotha: Friedrich Andreas Perthes, 1889. Cf. *NL-Bibl.* 3 B 64. The 2nd German ed. translated as *The Christian Faith.* Edited by H. R. Mackintosh and J. S. Stewart. Edinburgh: T & T Clark, 1928, 1989.

———. *Kurze Darstellung des theologischen Studiums zum Behuf einleitender Vorlesungen.* Edited by H. Scholz. Kritische Ausgabe. Leipzig: Deichert, 1910. Reprint, Darmstadt: Wissenschaftliche Buchgesellschaft, 1977. Translated by Terrence N. Tice as *Brief Outline of Theology as a Field of Study.* New York: Mellen Press, 1990.

———. "Über die Religion: Reden an die Gebildeten unter ihren Verächtern." In *Schriften aus der Berliner Zeit 1796–1799*, vol. 1/2 of *Kritische Gesamtausgabe*, edited by G. Meckenstock. Berlin: Walter de Gruyter, 1984. Translated and edited by Richard Crouter as *On Religion: Speeches to Its Cultured Despisers.* Cambridge: Cambridge University Press, 1996. Cf. *NL-Bibl.* 2 C 4,39.

———. "Zweites Sendschreiben über die Glaubenslehre" (Second letter concerning the doctrines of faith) (1829). In *Kritische Gesamtausgabe* (Critical complete edition), vol. 1/10: *Theologisch-dogmatische Abhandlun-*

*gen und Gelegenheitsschriften* (Theological-dogmatic essay and occasional writings), edited by H.-F. Traulsen, 337–94. Berlin: Walter de Gruyter, 1990.

Schmidt, Martin Anton. "Dogma und Lehre im Abendland, 2. Abschnitt: Die Zeit der Scholastik" (Dogma and doctrine in the West, part 2: The scholastic period). In *Handbuch der Dogmengeschichte* (Handbook of the history of dogma), edited by C. Andresen, Study ed., 1:567–754. Göttingen: Vandenhoeck & Ruprecht, 1988.

Schmitz, Otto. "Jesus der Herr: Eine Tatsache und eine Forderung" (Jesus the Lord: A fact and a challenge). In *Jesus der Herr: Fünf Vorträge gehalten in den Teilversammlungen der 28. Allgemeinen Deutschen Christlichen Studentenkonferenz* (Jesus the Lord: Five lectures given before the assembly of the 28th general German Christian student conference). Stimmen aus der deutschen christlichen Studentenbewegung 2, 53–65. Berlin: Furche-Verlag, 1920.

Schneemelcher, Wilhelm, ed. *Festschrift für Günther Dehn zum 75. Geburtstag am 18 April 1957 dargebracht von der evangelisch-theologischen Facultät der Rheinischen Friedrich Wilhelms Universität zu Bonn* (In honor of Günther Dehn on his 75th birthday, April 18, 1957, initiated by the Protestant theological faculty of the Friedrich Wilhelm University at Bonn on the Rhine). Neukirchen: Verlag der Buchhandlung der Erziehungsvereins Neukirchen, 1957.

———. "Kirchlich-sozial" (Church-social concerns). In *Die Religion in Geschichte und Gegenwart* (Religion past and present), 2nd ed., 3:1494–96.

Scholder, Klaus. *Die Kirchen und das Dritte Reich.* Vol. 1: *Vorgeschichte und Zeit der Illusionen 1918–1934.* 2nd ed. 1977; Frankfurt: Propyläen/Ullstein, 1980. Translated by John Bowden as *The Churches and the Third Reich.* Vol. 1: *Preliminary History and the Time of Illusions, 1918–1934.* London: SCM Press, 1987; Philadelphia: Fortress Press, 1988. Vol. 2: *The Year of Disillusionment: 1934, Barmen, Rome.* Philadelphia: Fortress Press, 1988.

Scholz, Heinrich. *Religionsphilosophie* (Philosophy of religion). 2nd ed. Berlin: Reuther & Reichard, 1922. *NL-Bibl.* 7 B 21.

Schopenhauer, Arthur. *Die Welt als Wille und Vorstellung.* 2nd ed. Vol. 1. Wiesbaden: Eberhard Brodhaus, 1949. Translated by E. F. J. Payne as *The World as Will and Representation.* 2 vols. New York: Dover, 1969. *NL-Bibl.* 7A 75.

Schulz, Wilfried. "Bonhoeffers Konfirmanden kamen nicht aus dem Stadtteil Wedding" (Bonhoeffer's confirmation students were not from the Wedding district). In *Dietrich Bonhoeffer Jahrbuch* 4:257–60. Gütersloh: Chr. Kaiser/Gütersloher Verlagshaus, 2010.

Schwab, Ulrich. "Günther Dehn." In *Die Religion in Geschichte und Gegenwart* (Religion past and present), 4th ed., 2:614.

Schweitzer, Albert. *Die Mystik des Apostel Paulus.* Tübingen: J. C. B. Mohr, 1930. Translated by William Montgomery as *The Mysticism of Paul the Apostle.* New York: H. Holt, 1931. *NL-Bibl.* 1 D 28.

———. *Von Reimarus zu Wrede: Eine Geschichte der Leben-Jesu Forschung.* Tübingen: J. C. B. Mohr, 1906. Translated by William Montgomery as *The Quest of the Historical Jesus: A Critical Study of Its Progress from Reimarus to Wrede.* From the 1910 ed., with an introduction by James M. Robinson. New York: Macmillan, 1968.

Seeberg, Reinhold. *Christliche Ethik* (Christian ethics). Edited by E. Seeberg. Stuttgart: W. Kohlhammer, 1936.

———. *Ewiges Leben?* (Eternal life?) Leipzig: Deichert, 1915. *NL-Bibl.* 3 B 68.

———. *Grundriss der Dogmatik* (Outline of dogmatics). Leipzig: Deichert, 1932.

———. *Lehrbuch der Dogmengeschichte.* Vol. 2: *Die Dogmenbildung der alten Kirche.* Leipzig: A. Deichert (G. Böhme), 1910. *Lehrbuch der Dogmengeschichte.* Vol. 4/2: *Die Fortbildung der reformatorischen Lehre und die gegenreformatorische Lehre.* 3rd newly rev. ed. Leipzig: A. Deichert (G. Böhme), 1920. *NL-Bibl.* 2 C 4, 44. Abridged translation by Charles E. Hay as *Textbook of the History of Doctrines.* 2 vols. in 1. Grand Rapids, Mich.: Baker Book House, 1956. (The English translation was made in 1905 from a modified version of the German 1st ed.; it does not correspond in organization and pagination to the German 3rd ed. of vols. 2 and 3 used by Bonhoeffer.)

———. *System der Ethik* (A system of ethics). 2nd rev. ed. Leipzig: A. Deichert, 1920. *NL-Bibl.* 4, 46.

———. *System der Ethik im Grundriss dargestellt* (Outline for a system of ethics). 1911. 2nd ed. Leipzig: Deichert, 1920. *NL-Bibl.* 4 46.

———. *Die Theologie des Johannes Duns Scotus: Eine dogmengeschichtliche Untersuchung* (The theology of John Duns Scotus: A dogmatic-historical examination). Studien zur Geschichte der Theologie und Kirche 5. Leipzig: Deichert, 1900. Reprint, Aalen: Scientia Verlag, 1971.

Seeger, Reinhart. *Herkunft und Bedeutung des Schlagwortes: Die Religion ist Opium für das Volk* (Origin and meaning of the slogan: Religion is opium for the people). Halle: Akademischer Verlag, 1935.

Siegmund-Schultze, Friedrich. *Die Weltkirchenkonferenz von Prag: Gesamtbericht des Kongresses für Frieden und Freundschaft, 24. bis 30. August 1928* (The World Churches Conference in Prague: General report of the Congress for Peace and Friendship, August 24–30, 1928). Berlin: Evangelische Presseverband für Deutschland, 1928.

Sifton, Elisabeth. *The Serenity Prayer: Faith and Politics in Times of Peace and War.* New York: Norton, 2003.

Sontheimer, Kurt. *Antidemokratisches Denken in der Weimarer Republik: Die politischen Ideen des deutschen Nationalismus zwischen 1918 und 1933* (Antidemocratic thinking in the Weimar Republic: The political ideas of German nationalism between 1918 and 1933). Munich: Nymphenburger Verlagshandlung, 1962.

*Sozialgeschichtliches Arbeitsbuch* (Workbook on social history). Vol. 3. Edited by D. Petzina, W. Abelshauser, and A. Faust. Munich: C. H. Bell, 1978.

Staats, Reinhart. "Adolf von Harnack im Leben Dietrich Bonhoeffers" (Adolf von Harnack in the life of Dietrich Bonhoeffer). *Theologische Zeitschrift* 37 (1981): 94–122.

Stählin, Wilhelm. "Jugendbewegung: I. Geschichte und Bedeutung" (Youth movement: I. history and significance). In *Die Religion in Geschichte und Gegenwart* (Religion past and present), 2nd ed., 3:506–12.

———. "Jugendbewegung: II. Jugendbewegung und Protestantismus" (Youth movement: II. youth movement and Protestantism). In *Die Religion in Geschichte und Gegenwart* (Religion past and present), 2nd ed., 3:512–15.

Stange, Erich. *Die kommende Kirche: Gedanken zum Werdenden innerhalb unserer deutschen evangelischen Kirche* (The coming church: Reflections on developments within our German Protestant Church). 1924. 3rd ed. Dresden: C. L. Ungelenk, 1925.

———. *Volkskirche als Organismus: Eine Fortsetzung der Aussprache über die kommende Kirche* (The church of the people as an organism: A continuation of the discussion about the coming church). Dresden: C. L. Ungelenk, 1928.

Stoecker, Adolf. "Christlich-konservative Ziele für die Gegenwart" (Christian conservative goals for the present time) (1881). In Stoecker, *Christlich-Sozial: Reden und Aufsätze* (Christian socially concerned: Speeches and essays), 2nd ed., 246–60. Berlin: Deichert, 1913.

———. "Sozialdemokratisch, Sozialistisch und Christlich-Sozial" (Social democratic, socialist, and Christian socially concerned) (1880). In Stoecker, *Christlich-Sozial: Reden und Aufsätze* (Christian socially concerned: Speeches and essays), 2nd ed., 215–32.

———. *Wach' auf evangelisches Volk! Aufsätze über Kirche und Kirchenpolitik* (Protestants, awake! Essays on the church and church politics). Berlin: Buchhandlung d. Berliner Staatmission, 1893.

Stoevesandt, Karl. "Soziale Arbeit und christliche Verantwortung" (Social work and Christian responsibility). *Zwischen den Zeiten* 4 (1926): 250–68.

Strohm, Christoph. *Theologische Ethik im Kampf gegen den Nationalsozialismus: Der Weg Dietrich Bonhoeffers mit den Juristen Hans von Dohnanyi and Gerhard Leibholz in den Widerstand* (Theological ethics in the struggle against National Socialism: Dietrich Bonhoeffer's journey with the lawyers Hans von Dohnanyi and Gerhard Leibholz in the resistance). Heidelberger Untersuchungen zu Widerstand, Judenverfolgung und Kirchenkampf im Dritten Reich 1. Munich: Chr. Kaiser, 1989.

Tal, Uriel. *Christians and Jews in Germany: Religion, Politics, and Ideology in the Second Reich, 1870–1914.* Translated from the original Hebrew by Joah Jonathan Jacobs. Jerusalem: Magnes Press, Hebrew University, 1969; Ithaca, N.Y.: Cornell University Press, 1975.

———. "Theologische Debatte um das 'Wesen des Judentums'" (Theological debate concerning "The nature of Judaism"). In *Juden im Wilhelminischen Deutschland, 1890–1914* (Jews in Wilhelmine Germany, 1890–1914), edited by W. E. Mosse in collaboration with A. Paucker, 599–632. Tübingen: J. C. B. Mohr, 1976.

Teitel, Ruti G. *Transitional Justice.* New York: Oxford University Press, 2000.

Thimme, Ludwig. *Im Kampf um die Kirche: Versuch einer Lösung der Spannungen zwischen Kirche, Theologie und Gemeinschaft.* Gotta: Ott, 1930.

———. *Sekte und Gemeinschaft als christlich-soziologisches Gebilde* (Sect and congregation as Christian-sociological structures). PhD diss., Philipps University, Marburg, December 1924. Schwerin: Friedrich Bahn, 1925.

Thomas à Kempis. *Imitatio Christi.* Vol. 2: *Thomas* à *Kempis Opera.* Edited by M. J. Pohl. 7 vols. Freiburg: Herder, 1904. Translated by William C. Creasy as *The Imitation of Christ.* Macon, Ga.: Mercer University Press, 1989.

Thomas Aquinas. *Summa Theologiae.* Cura et studio Petri Lavametto. 3 vols. Turin: Marietti, 1962–63. *Summa Theologiae,* Latin text and English translation with introduction, notes, appendices, and glossaries. Cambridge: Blackfriars; New York: McGraw-Hill, 1964–81.

Tillich, Paul. "Antwort an Karl Barth." *Theologische Blätter* 2 (1923): 296–99. Reprinted in *Anfänge der dialektischen Theologie,* edited by Jürgen Moltmann, pt. 1, Theologische Bücherei 17, no. 1, 189–93. Munich; Chr. Kaiser, 1974. Translated by Keith R. Crim as "Answer to Karl Barth," in *The Beginnings of Dialectic Theology,* edited by James R. Robinson, 155–58. Richmond: John Knox Press, 1968.

———. "Kritisches und positives Paradox: Eine Auseinandersetzung mit Karl Barth und Friedrich Gogarten." *Theologische Blätter* 2 (1923): 263–69. Reprinted in *Anfänge der dialektischen Theologie,* edited by Jürgen Moltmann, pt. 1, Theologische Bücherei 17, no. 1, 165–74. Munich:

Chr. Kaiser, 1974. Translated by Keith R. Crim as "Critical and Positive Paradox: A Discussion with Karl Barth and Friedrich Gogarten," in *The Beginnings of Dialectic Theology*, edited by James R. Robinson, 133–41. Richmond: John Knox Press, 1968.

———. *The Protestant Era*. Selected translations from the original edition, *Religiöse Verwirklichung* (Berlin: Furche, 1930), with a concluding essay by James Luther Adams. Chicago: University of Chicago Press, 1957.

Tindal, Matthew. *Christianity as Old as Creation, 1730*. Reprint of the 1730 ed. printed in London. British philosophers and theologians of the 17th and 18th centuries. New York: Garland, 1978.

Tödt, Heinz Eduard. "Dietrich Bonhoeffers ökumenische Friedensethik." In *Frieden—das unumgängliche Wagnis: Die Gegenwartsbedeutung der Friedensethik Dietrich Bonhoeffers* (Peace—the unavoidable risk: The contemporary significance of Dietrich Bonhoeffer's peace ethic), edited by Hans Pfeifer, Internationales Bonhoeffer Forum 5, 85–117. Munich: Chr. Kaiser, 1982. Translated by David Stassen as "Dietrich Bonhoeffer's Ecumenical Ethic of Peace," in H. E. Tödt, *Authentic Faith: Dietrich Bonhoeffer's Theological Ethics in Context*, 112–41. Grand Rapids, Mich.: Wm. B. Eerdmans, 2007.

Tönnies, Ferdinand. *Gemeinschaft und Gesellschaft: Abhandlung des Communismus und des Socialismus als empirische Kulturformen*. 1887. 8th ed. Leipzig: H. Buske, 1935. Reprint, Darmstadt: Wissenschaftliche Buchgesellschaft, 1979. Translated by Charles P. Loomis as *Community and Society*. New York: Harper & Row, 1963.

Torquemada, Juan de. *Summa de ecclesia contra impugnatores potestatis summi pontificis* (Summary treatise concerning the church, against those who attack the supreme authority of the papacy). Rome: Eucharius Silber, 1489.

Troeltsch, Ernst. *Die Absolutheit des Christentums und die Religionsgeschichte*. Lecture held at the meeting of the friends of *Christlicher Welt* in Mühlacker on October 3, 1901. Expanded, with a preface. Tübingen: J. C. B. Mohr, 1929. Translated from the 3rd German ed. (1929) by David Reid as *The Absoluteness of Christianity and the History of Religions*. Introduced by James Luther Adams. Richmond: John Knox Press, 1971.

———. "Aus der religiösen Bewegung der Gegenwart" (From the present religious movement) (1910). In Troeltsch, *Gesammelte Schriften* (Collected writings), 2:22–44. Tübingen: Walter de Gruyter, 1913. *NL-Bibl.* 7 A 87.

———. *Psychologie und Erkenntnistheorie in der Religionswissenschaft: Eine Untersuchung über die Bedeutung der Kantschen Religionslehre für die heutige Religionswissenschaft* (Psychology and epistemology in the study of religion: An examination of the significance of the Kantian view of religion for the study of religion today). Tübingen: J. C. B. Mohr, 1905.

———. *Religion in History.* Essays translated by James Luther Adams and Walter F. Bense. Minneapolis: Fortress Press, 1991.

———. "Religion und Kirche" (Religion and church) (1895). In Troeltsch, *Gesammelte Schriften* (Collected writings), 2:146–82. Tübingen: Walter de Gruyter, 1913. *NL-Bibl.* 7 A 87.

———. "Wesen der Religion und der Religionswissenschaft" (1909). In Troeltsch, *Gesammelte Schriften* (Collected writings), 2:452–99. Tübingen: J. C. B. Mohr, 1913. *NL-Bibl.* 7 A 87. Translated as "Religion and the Science of Religion" and edited by Robert Morgan and Michael Pye, in *Ernst Troeltsch: Writings on Theology and Religion,* 82–123. Atlanta: John Knox Press, 1977.

———. "Zur Frage des religiosen Apriori: Eine Erwiderung auf die Bemerkungen von Paul Spieg" (1909). In Troeltsch, *Gesammelte Schriften* (Collected writings), 2:754–68. *NL-Bibl.* 7 A 87. Translated by James Luther Adams and Walter E. Bense as "On the Question of the Religious a priori," in *Religion in History,* with an introduction by James Luther Adams, 33–45. Minneapolis: Fortress Press, 1991.

———. "Zur theologischen Lage" (On the theological situation). *Christliche Welt* 12 (1898): 627–31, 650–57.

Tyldesley, Michael. *No Heavenly Delusion? A Comparative Study of Three Communal Movements.* Liverpool: Liverpool University Press, 2003.

*Der Vertrag von Versailles* (The Treaty of Versailles). Der Friedensvertrag zwischen Deutschland und den Alliierten und Assoziierten Mächten nebst dem Schlussprotokoll und der Vereinbarung betr. die militarische Besetzung der Rheinlande. 2nd ed. Published by the German Foreign Office. Berlin, 1924.

Vaihinger, Hans. *Die Philosophie des als ob.* Berlin: Reuther & Reichard, 1911. Translated by C. K. Ogden as *The Philosophy of As If: A System of the Theoretical, Practical and Religious Fictions of Mankind.* London: Paul, Trench, Trubner; New York: Harcourt, Brace, 1924. Reprint, Mansfield Center, Conn.: Martino, 2009.

Visser 't Hooft, Willem A. *Die Welt war meine Gemeinde.* Munich: Piper, 1972. Published in English as *Memoirs.* London: SCM Press; Philadelphia: Westminster Press, 1973.

Weber, Max. *Die protestantische Ethik und der Geist des Kapitalismus.* In vol. 1 of his *Gesammelte Aufsätze zur Religionssoziologie.* Tübingen: J. C. B. Mohr, 1934. Translated by Talcott Parsons as *The Protestant Ethic and the Spirit of Capitalism.* New York: Charles Scribner's Sons, 1958; London: George Allen & Unwin, 1976.

———. "Wissenschaft als Beruf" (1919). In Weber, *Gesammelte Aufsätze zur Wissenschaftslehre*, edited by J. Winckelmann, 8th ed., 582–613. Tübingen: J. C. B. Mohr, 1988. Translated and edited by H. H. Gerth and C. Wright Mills as "Science as a Vocation," in *From Max Weber: Essays in Sociology*, 129–56. New York: Oxford University Press, 1958.

Wendel, Ernst Georg. *Studien zur Homiletik Dietrich Bonhoeffers: Predigt—Hermeneutik—Sprache* (Studies on the homiletics of Dietrich Bonhoeffer: Sermon—hermeneutics—language). Hermeneutische Untersuchungen zur Theologie 21. Tübingen: J. C. B. Mohr, 1985.

Witkop, Philipp, ed. *Kriegsbriefe deutscher Studenten* (German students' war letters). Gotha: F. A. Perthes, 1916; Munich: Georg Müller, 1928.

———. *Kriegsbriefe gefallener Studenten*. 5th ed. Munich: Georg Müller, 1929. Translated and arranged from the original edition by Annie F. Wedd as *German Students' War Letters*. London: Methuen, 1929. Reprint with foreword by Jay Winter. Philadelphia: University of Pennsylvania Press; Wantage, England: University Presses Marketing, 2002.

Wolf, Ernst. "Das Letzte und das Vorletzte" (The last and the next to last). In *Die Mündige Welt*, edited by R. Grunow, 4:17–32. Munich: Chr. Kaiser, 1963.

Wolff, Christian. *Psychologia rationalis* (Rational psychology) (1740). In *Gesammelte Werke* (Collected works), edited by J. Ecole et al., pt. 2, vol. 6. Reprint, Hildesheim: Olms, 1972.

The World Alliance for International Friendship through the Churches. *Annual Report*. Geneva, 1932–33, 1933–34.

———. *Handbook of the World Alliance for International Friendship through the Churches: Covering the Period from Cambridge, September 1931 to Chamby, August 1935*. Geneva: World Alliance for International Friendship through the Churches, 1936.

———. *Reports*. Geneva, 1931.

Wunder, Gerd, and Hans-Christian Brandenburg. "Die Ahnenliste Dietrich Bonhoeffers und seiner Geschwister" (The ancestry of Dietrich Bonhoeffer and his siblings). In *Festschrift zum hundertjährigen Bestehen des Herold zu Berlin* (Commemorative volume for the hundredth anniversary of the Berlin Herald). Berlin: privately published, 1969.

Wycliffe, John. *Tractatus de ecclesia* (Treatise on the church). Edited by Johann Loserth. In *Wyclif's Latin Works*, vol. 4: *De Ecclesia*, edited by George Macauley Trevelyan, 23 vols. in 36. London: Trübner, 1886. Reprint, New York: Johnson Reprint, 1966.

———. *Tractatus de potestate papae* (Treatise on the power of the papacy). Edited by Johann Loserth. In *Wyclif's Latin Works*, vol. 19: *De potestate papae*, edited by George Macauley Trevelyan, 23 vols. in 36. London: Trübner, 1907. Reprint, New York: Johnson Reprint, 1966.

Zahn-Harnack, Agnes von. *Adolf von Harnack*. 2nd ed. Berlin: W. de Gruyter, 1951. Translated by William Henry Allison and William Henry Walker as "Adolf von Harnack." Typewritten MS, Harvard Divinity School, 1941, 1949.

Zimmermann, Wolf-Dieter, ed. *Begegnungen mit Dietrich Bonhoeffer*. 4th ed. Munich: Chr. Kaiser, 1969. Translated from the 1st German ed. by Käthe Gregor Smith as *I Knew Dietrich Bonhoeffer*. Edited by Wolf-Dieter Zimmermann and Ronald Gregor Smith. London: Collins; New York: Harper & Row, 1966. London: Fontana Books, 1973.

Zimmern, Alfred Eckhard. *The League of Nations and the Rule of Law, 1918–1935*. London: Macmillan, 1936.

# Index of Scriptural References

# Index of Names

This index lists people mentioned in this volume, including authors and editors of literature cited in the notes. It provides brief profiles of the people listed and differs from the German edition by also including information about those whose work began after 1945, as well as additional information of interest to readers of the English edition. It does not include personal names that appear in book titles or only in the bibliography. When possible, dates of birth and death have been provided.

# Index of Subjects

# Editors and Translators

**Victoria J. Barnett** is staff director of church relations at the U. S. Holocaust Memorial Museum and one of the general editors of the Dietrich Bonhoeffer Works English Edition, published by Fortress Press. She has written and lectured extensively on the history of the churches during the Holocaust, and is the author of *For the Soul of the People: Protestant Protest against Hitler* (Oxford University Press, 1992) and *Bystanders: Conscience and Complicity during the Holocaust* (Greenwood Press, 1999), and the editor and translator of the new revised edition of *Dietrich Bonhoeffer: A Biography*, by Eberhard Bethge (Fortress Press, 2000) and *And the Witnesses Were Silent: The Confessing Church and the Jews*, by Wolfgang Gerlach (University of Nebraska Press, 2000). She is also the author of the essay on Bonhoeffer on the U. S. Holocaust Memorial Museum website. She is a graduate of Indiana University and Union Theological Seminary in New York.

**Isabel Best** is a freelance translator who worked for international and church organizations for twelve years in Geneva, Switzerland. She studied English literature, German, and French at Oberlin College and holds the Diploma in Translation from the Institute of Linguists, London. She was part of translation teams for *DBWE* 8, 11, 12, and 13 and also translated Ferdinand Schlingensiepen's recent biography, *Dietrich Bonhoeffer, 1906–1945* (T&T Clark/Continuum, London, 2010). She is now editing a volume of Bonhoeffer's sermons in English for Fortress Press. She and her husband, Tom Best, live in Belmont, Massachusetts.

**Mark S. Brocker** (PhD, University of Chicago Divinity School) is lead pastor of St. Andrew Lutheran Church in Beaverton, Oregon. Previously he has served congregations in Decatur and Franklin Grove, Illinois; McMinnville, Oregon; and Tacoma, Washington. From 2003 to 2005 he was a member of the Southwestern Washington Synod Council of the Evangelical Lutheran

Church in America. Currently he is on the Ecumenical Ministries of Oregon Board and serves as the chair of the Environmental Ministries Committee. He has taught courses on Bonhoeffer, theology, and ethics at the Northwest House of Theological Studies in Salem, Oregon, and at Pacific Lutheran Theological Seminary in Berkeley, California. In October 2010 he delivered the Fifth Annual Knutson Lecture at Pacific Lutheran University on the theme "No Salvation apart from the Earth." His dissertation is titled "The Community of God, Jesus Christ, and Responsibility: The Responsible Person and the Responsible Community in the Ethics of Dietrich Bonhoeffer." He was one of the founding members of the editorial board of *Dietrich Bonhoeffer Works*, English edition.

**Nicolas S. Humphrey** is an assistant professor of German and humanities at St. Norbert College, where he teaches German and general studies courses. Nick studied classical Russian ballet at the Legat School in East Sussex, UK, and continued his dance training by earning a BS degree in ballet at the Indiana University (IU) School of Music. Afterward he joined the Hartford Ballet as an apprentice and subsequently performed as guest artist with the Indiana University Ballet Theatre and the Memphis Ballet. Nick returned to IU to earn a BA in German studies and won the year-long IU scholarship to attend the Freie Universität, Berlin. He earned his MA and PhD degrees in German literature at Johns Hopkins University with a dissertation on Heinrich Heine's and Friedrich Nietzsche's use of dance as a rhetorical and symbolic device (*Sinnbild*). His current research project is a study tying his prior work on nineteenth-century German writers to Baruch Spinoza's body-mind thesis.

**Michael B. Lukens** is a professor of religious studies emeritus at St. Norbert College, where he taught the history of the Christian tradition and historical theology for nearly four decades before retiring in 2008. In addition to a doctorate from Brown University, he holds academic degrees from Johns Hopkins University; Union Theological Seminary, New York; and Princeton Theological Seminary. For many years, he maintained a research relationship with the Institut für Europäische Geschichte in Mainz, Germany. His research interests, in addition to Bonhoeffer studies, include post-Holocaust Jewish–Christian dialogue and Catholic response in the Nazi period. He lives with his wife, Barbara, near Green Bay, Wisconsin.

**Marion Hausner Pauck**, a native of New York City, studied at Friends Seminary, Barnard College, and Union Theological Seminary, New York. She served as managing editor for *Christianity and Crisis* for two years before joining the Religious Books Department of Oxford University Press, New York, where she worked for ten years. In 1964 she married the historical theologian Wilhelm Pauck, with whom she coauthored the standard biography of Paul Tillich. She now lives in Mountain View, California, where she is active in the University Lutheran Church at Stanford and works as an independent scholar. She translates in six languages, lectures on the great theologians of the twentieth century, and is working on volume 2 of the biography of Paul Tillich. She is preparing her own papers, which will be placed in the Wilhelm and Marion Pauck Manuscript Collection of the Luce Library of Princeton Theological Seminary, in Princeton, New Jersey.

**Anne Augspurger Schmidt-Lange** is a translator and researcher specializing in German-language documents. A former instructor (*Lektorin*) at the University of Göttingen, she is a graduate of Southern Methodist University and holds a master's degree from the University of Illinois. She lived in Germany for nearly ten years and has been associated for many years with congregations in Canada and the United States affiliated with the Evangelische Kirche in Deutschland (EKD) through the work of her husband, Soenke, as an overseas pastor for the EKD in metro Toronto and New York. She is a cotranslator and cotranslation editor of Hermann Guth's book *Amish Mennonites in Germany* and the author of many articles on the history and migration of Mennonite families. German-script documents from the seventeenth and eighteenth centuries are a research specialty, and some of her current projects concern documentation for the expulsion of Anabaptists from Canton Bern, Switzerland, around 1710–11. She and her husband currently live near Philadelphia, in Langhorne, Pennsylvania.

**Douglas W. Stott** is a freelance editor and translator. A graduate of Davidson College, Northwestern University, and Emory University's Candler School of Theology, he also studied in Germany at the Philipps University in Marburg and at the University of Stuttgart. His translation credits include several volumes of the *Theological Dictionary of the Old Testament* and the *Exegetical Dictionary of the New Testament*; commentaries for the Old Testament Library; *DBWE* 10, *Barcelona, Berlin, New York: 1928–1931*, and *DBWE* 14, *Theological Education at Finkenwalde: 1935–1937*; and F. W. J. Schelling's *Philosophy of Art*. He was also on the translation team of volume 1 of *Religion Past and Present*. He is currently preparing an annotated English edition of the correspondence of Caroline Schelling.

**Barbara Wojhoski** studied art history at New York University; ancient history at the Philipps University in Marburg, Germany; and anthropology at Georgia State University, and has participated in archaeological excavations of Late Woodland Period sites in the southeastern United States. Since 1995 she has been a fulltime freelance editor for academic and denominational presses and has worked on projects ranging from a dictionary of the Miami-Illinois language to contemporary fiction translated from German to theological commentaries and philosophical works.